The Columbia Companion
to Modern East Asian Literature

The Columbia Companion
to Modern East Asian Literature

GENERAL EDITOR

Joshua S. Mostow

ASSOCIATE EDITORS

Kirk A. Denton

Bruce Fulton

Sharalyn Orbaugh

COLUMBIA UNIVERSITY PRESS

NEW YORK

Columbia University Press
Publishers Since 1893
New York   Chichester, West Sussex
Copyright © 2003 Columbia University Press
All rights reserved

Library of Congress Cataloging-in-Publication Data
The Columbia Companion to modern East Asian literature / Joshua Mostow, editor.
p.   cm.
Includes bibliographical references and index
ISBN 0-231-11314-5
1. East Asian literature—20th century—Encyclopedias.
I. Title: Modern East Asian literature.   II. Mostow, Joshua.

PL493.C55 2003
895—dc21
2002035141
∞

Columbia University Press books are printed
on permanent and durable acid-free paper.
Printed in the United States of America
10 9 8 7 6 5 4 3 2 1

CONTENTS

Authors, Works, Schools

PART III   China
Kirk A. Denton, Associate Editor

Thematic Essays

Authors, Works, Schools

PART IV   Korea
Bruce Fulton, Associate Editor

Thematic Essays

Authors, Works, Schools

PART I

General Introduction

JOSHUA S. MOSTOW, GENERAL EDITOR

1

THE COLUMBIA COMPANION
TO MODERN EAST ASIAN LITERATURE

The essays in this volume are meant to serve as a guide to those exploring the modern literatures of China, Japan, and Korea. As a guide, each entry aims to give a brief biography of its chosen author or a brief outline of its topic. The essays are designed to show how each author or movement fits into the general development of the modern literature of its respective country, as well as to suggest how significant works by individual authors or in specific movements reflect the larger concerns of the author's work, the aims of the movement, or the trends of society at the time. Many of the essays present interpretations of works with which the *Companion* reader may find himself or herself agreeing or disagreeing. In either event, the aim is to suggest some critical perspectives that may deepen a reader's understanding and appreciation of a given work.

Three to four essays by the respective associate editor and other scholars precede each geographical section. These longer thematic essays are designed to provide a historical overview, as well as to discuss several themes of overarching importance in the understanding of modern East Asian literature: nationalism, the invention of a modern literary language, and the institutions that supported and constrained the development of modern literature in Asia. In addition, some of the associate editors have chosen to discuss other themes pertinent to a fundamental understanding of modern literature in their respective countries. These include gender, sexuality, and the family; the debates over "pure literature" versus the literature of social engagement; and the role of specific literary genres in the artistic landscapes that they describe.

Following the thematic essays are the individual entries: more than fifty for Japan, more than forty for China, and almost thirty for Korea. Each entry is self-contained, and entries can be read in any sequence or order. Cross-referencing, marked by an asterisk (*), is designed to suggest some possible avenues for gaining a more synoptic view of the work, author, or movement. Writers or movements mentioned in the thematic essays will often be treated in more depth in a biographical entry. Authors or works mentioned in entries on specific movements may also have more detailed entries devoted to them. Authors and topics within each geographical section are arranged chronologically as much as possible. This means that if the entries of each section are read in order, they will give a detailed narrative of the changes and developments of modern literature in that country.

The names of all authors are given in the East Asian style, surname first, given name last, except when discussing authors who publish primarily in English or used an anglicized name (e.g., Eileen Chang). In the Japan section, authors are generally referred to by their pen names; those without are referred to by their family names (e.g., Natsume Sôseki is referred to as Sôseki, but Shiga Naoya is called Shiga). In the China section, authors are also generally referred to by their pen names and not their birth names. In the Korea section, the only authors for whom pen names are used are Kim Sowŏl (born Kim Chŏngshik), Yi Sang (born Kim Haegyŏng), and Kim Tongni (born Kim Shijong), who are commonly referred to as Sowŏl, Yi Sang, and Kim, respectively. Romanization is modified Hepburn for Japanese, Pinyin for Chinese, and McCune-Reischauer for Korean.

The field of modern East Asian literature is of course a vast one, and some kind of selection was obviously necessary. The general editor and associate editors consulted widely about which authors, works, and movements were most essential to an understanding of literature in modern East Asia. We have obviously focused on authors and works whose writings are available in English translation. But in several cases we have also tried to be ahead of the curve, giving information about authors whose importance is such that we know (or are relatively certain) that translations will be forthcoming in the near future. Each entry includes a brief biography of the author or life span of the movement. It will then typically include analysis of one or two key works. It is followed by a bibliography. In general, listed critical works are limited to those in English or those specifically cited in the entry itself. Principal works in translation are also given, though space prevents these lists from being exhaustive.

The editors have also tried to represent not only what is new and recent in the literatures themselves, but also what is new in the *reading* of those literatures. In other words, we have included a great number of younger literary scholars, asking them to provide their understandings and their interpretations of works and authors both classic and contemporary. For example, works by canonical authors such as *Lu Xun or *Natsume Sôseki are being opened up to new interpretations by scholars examining them from the viewpoint of feminist criticism or queer theory. We hope that in this way the *Columbia Companion to Modern East Asian Literature* will make accessible new readings and new interpretations that are perhaps somewhat different from those found in earlier guides and histories. Thus, although for some readers the essays and entries will be introductory, we hope that even those already familiar with the works discussed will discover and be challenged by new interpretations. The *Companion* also aims to be a reference, providing important biographical and bibliographic information on modern East Asian authors and translations of their work.

In this context, there has been no way to avoid "theory" or to provide only "practical criticism." As will be clear as one makes one's way through the *Companion* as a whole, one of the crucial concerns of modern East Asian literature is precisely the definition of literature itself, and of the role of art in society. Although some readers may wish that even more space had been devoted to literary critics, we hope we have struck some sort of balance in emphasizing the importance of theory in the very definition of modern literature while at the same time fulfilling our mandate as a companion to general readers of literature in translation.

Additionally, the editors have taken the geographical rubric very seriously. Although the literatures of China, Japan, and Korea are each allotted their separate sections, we have constantly kept an eye open to those writers, works, and movements that transcend national boundaries. This includes, for example, Chinese authors who lived and wrote in Japan; Japanese authors who wrote in classical Chinese; and Korean authors who write in Japanese, whether under the colonial occupation or because they are now resident in Japan. The waves of modernization can be seen as reaching each of these countries in a staggered fashion, with eddies and backflows between them then complicating the picture further. We hope that the thematic essays and individual entries in this volume can give some sense of this dynamic interplay.

All the entries have been designed to provide the same kinds of basic information concerning their authors or movement, but the shape of each individual entry has been formed by the specific scholar writing it. Readers of the *Companion*, then, will be exposed to a wide variety of styles and concerns and will gain in this way some sense of the breadth of contemporary research on East Asian literature. And although we have attempted to include discussion of all the major genres—fiction, poetry, and theater—in each geographical section, their varying importance has inevitably been reflected in their relative emphasis.

Some readers may be disappointed that we have not been able to include certain authors, schools, or even genres. Some will disagree about the specific works chosen as representative or the space allotted to some writers or works rather than others. Such shortcomings are, alas, inevitable. Though the editors cast their nets as widely as possible and strove to be as inclusive and encyclopedic as possible, the vagaries that beset any long-term project have left their mark. The original associate editors for both China and Korea found it necessary to pass the torch after the initial stages of our work, and I am very grateful to both Kirk Denton and Bruce Fulton for taking over their responsibilities. I would especially like to thank Sharalyn Orbaugh, the associate editor for Japan, who stayed with the project through thick and thin. All the individual contributors deserve our thanks for finding time in their busy schedules to write entries that are not only informative but also often challenging. I am particularly grateful for their patience, as the project ground on for several years. I would also like to acknowledge the support of Masao Nakamura, Director of the Centre for Japanese Research, Institute of Asian Research, at the University of British Columbia. Finally, I would like to thank James Warren, executive editor for reference books of Columbia University Press, for originally suggesting this project to me and for his patience and encouragement over the years.

In East Asia, it was the vital tradition that each new dynasty or government made writing a history of its immediate predecessor one of its first priorities. I write at the end of the first full year of the twenty-first century, a fitting moment to assess the literature of what is essentially the twentieth century. And it is my hope that this *Companion* will provide an opportunity for a future editor in the latter half of this new century to compile a new *Columbia Companion to Twentieth-Century East Asian Literature,* so as to see not only what is distinctive about their own, "modern" perspective but also what was distinctive about ours.

2

MODERN LITERATURE IN EAST ASIA:

AN OVERVIEW

When speaking of, for instance, "modern Japanese literature," many critics follow the current fashion of "bracketing" each of the constitutive words of the
phrase or of putting them individually in quotation marks ("modern" "Japanese" "literature") to indicate that each element of the term is under contesta-
tion and open to debate. In other words, the meanings of the very terms *modern*,
Japanese, and *literature* are no longer taken to be self-evident, and any definition of them risks challenge from a number of quarters. To put together a "companion," then, has become a daunting task—no matter how innocuous and
even friendly the name of this genre may seem.

This state of affairs has not, of course, always been the case. Under the posi-
tivism of what is called "modernization theory," all concerned were confident
in the placement of the advent of each "modern" literature in East Asia:
*Tsubouchi Shōyō's *Essence of the Novel* (Shōsetsu shinzui) of 1886; the May
Fourth movement of 1919 for China; and 1917 in Korea, with the publication of
*Yi Kwangsu's novel *Heartlessness* (Mujŏng). In fact, it was the writers of the
day whose voices were the loudest in declaring their difference and independence from previous "old-fashioned" and "traditional" writing.

One problem is that, unlike a term such as *twentieth-century*, the word *modern* has no stable meaning. The English word comes from the Latin *modo*,
meaning "just now." As such, what the term names immediately disappears
upon its naming: "now" once uttered is already past, already "then." Regardless
of this philosophical conundrum, the term has been replaced in present-day

parlance by the word *contemporary* (as in "contemporary art"). It is in the Renaissance—in English, the late 1500s—that the term *modern* takes on the sense of "recent times" in opposition to "ancient" and "medieval." This last term means literally "middle ages," and it clearly serves simply as a buffer between the Ancients (that is, the classical culture of the Greeks and Romans) and the "rebirth" of learning with the Moderns. Nonetheless, "modern European history" is usually taken to begin with the perfection of movable type by Gutenberg in about 1450 and the voyages of exploration that culminated in Columbus's voyage of 1492. When we add to this list the effective use of gunpowder in warfare from the mid-fifteenth century, we have what some might argue were the key elements in the creation of the world as we know it, that is, the modern world: territorial expansionism, print capitalism, and the gun. Although it is undeniable that these elements were essential to the construction of the modern world, most scholars today would see the period from the Renaissance to the French and industrial revolutions as "early modern," with "modernity" proper not beginning until the advent of industrialization and with it the rise of global capitalism and imperialism, as well as the bourgeoisie; in other words, from about the end of the eighteenth century.

Asia was, of course, very much part of the early modern world. After all, Columbus had stumbled upon America in his search for an alternate route to India. China and Japan were parts of the early system of global trade initiated by the Dutch, Portuguese, English, and Spanish, with wares produced in Asia specifically for export to Europe. When Japan closed its doors to all but the most limited trade with Europe in 1615, the cultures and technologies of Asia and Europe were not all that far apart, and European travelers to Asia had often been impressed by what they saw. Korea, for example, utilized movable metal-type printing presses as early as the thirteenth century, well before Gutenburg's innovations.

Asia was confronted by a much-changed Europe in the early nineteenth century. The industrialized countries needed outlets for their products, and the international trade in tea, silk, and opium between England, India, and China meant that by the 1830s British India derived 5 to 10 percent of its total revenues from the opium trade with China (Fairbank and Reischauer 1989:273). The Opium Wars of 1839–42 amply demonstrated the military force with which the Western powers would insist on "free trade." Ten years later, in 1853, the Americans under Commodore Perry arrived in Edo Bay in a steam-powered battleship to insist on the opening of trade ports.

The inability of the Manchu Qing dynasty and samurai Tokugawa military government to resist foreign pressure rang the death knell for both. In 1867, the last shogun returned power to the imperial family, in the person of the boy-emperor Meiji, and his advisors from the western domains. This early transformation allowed Japan to jump significantly ahead of its neighbors, who soon began to feel the effects of Japanese imperialism: in 1876 the Japanese wrested unequal trade treaties from the Korean kingdom, and in 1894 Japan declared war on China, defeating its fleet in 1895 and claiming Taiwan, the Pescadores Islands, and the Kwantung Peninsula of southern Manchuria as reparations. Japanese aggression greatly stimulated Chinese and Korean nationalism, and 1911 saw the fall of the Manchu dynasty—ironically, instigated by Chinese who had lived, studied, and plotted in Japan. No such irony was afforded to Korea, however, which in 1905 became a Japanese protectorate and was annexed outright in 1910.

By the second decade of the twentieth century, then, the East Asian world order was no more. While the fates of China, Japan, and Korea would differ significantly over the course of the twentieth century, their starting points were largely the same, and this similarity is one of the reasons for certain commonalities in their modern literatures.

The first similarity is that all three countries were what has been called "diglossic," that is, operating in a more or less bilingual environment. The two languages, however, were not two modern vernacular languages—as they are, for example, in Canada with English and French. Rather, although each country had one (or more) modern spoken languages, all serious written communication was done in classical Chinese—a language that no one actually spoke. This use of written classical Chinese was linked to the major ideological foundation of all three cultures: Confucianism. Confucianism prescribed highly stratified class-based societies, with scholar-bureaucrats at the top and merchants at the bottom. Family structures were thoroughly patriarchal, and women typically had little access to education or political or economic power.

The genres of writing in Confucian cultures were also highly stratified, and their relative value or prestige was determined by their use to scholar-officials. Educated men read and wrote history and poetry—the two most canonical genres—as well as philosophy, essays, and commentaries. Vernacular fiction existed in all three cultures, but was officially despised as trivial. Writing of value was called *wen/bun/mun* (in Chinese, Japanese, and Korean, respectively) and included such diverse genres as event-based historical narratives, lyrical poems, and expository memorials to the throne or head of government.

Following the Romantic philology of Europeans (especially Germans) such as Johann Gottfried von Herder (1744–1803), the Japanese and Koreans would come to equate their modern "national literature" exclusively with their indigenous vernacular tongue. All three countries, including China, would eventually define modern literature as that written in a language closely approximating contemporary speech. Nonetheless, this process took considerable time, and in Japan, for instance, poetry written by Japanese in classical Chinese remained an important literary influence until about 1911. In fact, all the literary giants at the beginning of the modern era, such as *Mori Ōgai and *Natsume Sōseki, had been thoroughly trained in Chinese literature as boys and continued to write in classical Chinese throughout their lives. Modern Chinese writers such as *Lu

Xun and *Yu Dafu continued to write poems in the classical Chinese language even as they wrote and promoted Western-style vernacular fiction. And *Mao Zedong wrote classical poems up until his death, even during the iconoclastic fervor of the Cultural Revolution.

The resilience of Chinese verse in essentially the classical language is perhaps less surprising when we realize that change and revolution in the literary landscape typically began with verse. Most revolutionary sentiments and new political ideals were first expressed in traditional Chinese verse, whether in China, Japan, or Korea. The political and literary intersection of these three emerging nations within the genre of poetry can be seen in the Japanese Mori Kainan's (1863–1911) long poem in Chinese verse entitled "Homeward Voyage: One Hundred Rhymes" (Kishū hyaku'in, 1909). Kainan looked to the poetry of the early Qing dynasty (1644–1911) for models for his verse. His own major work was written during an ocean voyage, just as was the Chinese *Liang Qichao's "Record of Travel" (Hanman lu, 1899). But whereas Liang's voyage was from Yokohama (where he was living in political exile) to Honolulu, Kainan's recorded the return to Japan of the body of Itō Hirobumi—the elder Meiji statesman—who had been assassinated while serving as Governor-General of Korea, recently annexed by Japan. Liang's work used the expression "poetry revolution" (*shijie geming*— the latter word being what Lydia Liu has called a "return graphic loan," that is, a word that existed in classical Chinese but was used by the Japanese to translate a foreign word—in this case, "revolution"—and then reintroduced into the modern Chinese language). In 1882 several Japanese writers had issued a book of "new-form poems" (*shintai-shi*), many of which were translations from European authors, and all of which were still heavily sinified in language. Korea, too, saw "new-style poetry" (*shinch'e shi*) with the publication in 1908 of Ch'oe Namsŏn's "From the Sea to the Youth" (Hae egesŏ sonyŏn ege). Revolution in literature, then, started in all three countries with poetry.

Western culture in the nineteenth century no doubt appeared relatively monolithic: constitutional governments, the rhetoric of individualism, nationalism, and global capitalism. The Western genres of writing seemed an integral part of what made the American and European powers so irresistible. The European tradition had a very different way of classifying and valuing writing, and it had two categories that seemed incommensurable to those East Asian categories of writing: "literature" and "the novel."

It was clear that "literature" was something different from *wen/bun/mun*, or what was also referred to simply as "learning" (*xuewen/gakumon/hangmun*). This difference was clearest from the fact that at the acme of the European hierarchy of literature sat a form of vernacular fiction—the novel—while in the East Asian system the top spot was held by poetry, and fiction was relegated to the very bottom, fit only for women and the morally suspect. In other words, the hierarchies of East Asian *wen/bun/mun* and European literature were the complete inverse of each other.

Fortunately for East Asian students of this new "literature," European fiction was at this time at one of its more didactic stages. Some of the earliest novels to be translated into Japanese were Benjamin Disraeli's *Coningsby* (1844, translated as *Shun'ōden*, 1884) and Edward Bulwer-Lytton's *Ernest Maltravers* (1837, translated as *Karyū shunwa*, "A Spring Tale of Flowers and Willow," 1879) — both fictional works by well-known statesmen who were using the novel form to promote their political agendas. Such translations led to the rise of what was later called the *"political novel" (seiji shōsetsu), many with ties to the People's Rights movement. Political novels were also written in a highly sinified style, far from the Japanese vernacular, and included poems written in classical Chinese — a fact which made them very amenable to translation into Chinese, where they strongly influenced literary intellectuals such as Liang Qichao. In Japan, China, and Korea, then, the novel form was first employed primarily as a means of educating the newly formed public.

In fact, the Japanese word for "novel," *shōsetsu* (literally, "small talk" — a term adopted from the premodern Chinese vernacular genre called *xiaoshuo*) was not established until after the heyday of the so-called political novel. The term appears most significantly in Tsubouchi Shōyō's landmark *The Essence of the Novel* (Shōsetsu shinzui) of 1885–86. Shôyô called for "human emotions" to be the principle theme of the novel. This focus stood in contrast not only with the political novels of the day, but also with the writing of the late Edo period, which Shôyô saw as either frivolous or moralistic.

Although Shōyō's own strengths were in theory and translation (especially for the theater — his translations of Shakespeare remain the standards in the Japanese language), it was up to his student *Futabatei Shimei to produce what is recognized as "Japan's first modern novel," *Drifting Clouds* (Ukigumo) in 1887–89. The protagonist of the tale, Bunzō, is clearly an alienated modern, the "superfluous hero" of Russian authors such as Ivan Turgenev, who had a profound influence on Futabatei (Ryan 1965). The superfluous man also appears quite vividly in the writings of Yu Dafu, one of the founders of the romantic Creation Society, which was formed with other exiled Chinese writers in Japan in 1921.

It was around the same time as the publication of *Floating Clouds* that *Women's Education Journal* (Jogaku zasshi), which had been at the forefront of promoting both Christian humanism and women's education, took a decided literary turn, a trend that in 1893 would result in a break-away group starting the journal *Literary World* (Bungakukai), the organ of the Romantic movement in Japan.

Not until the 1890s do works of European realist fiction by Zola or Tolstoy appear in Japanese. One of the most important figures in introducing European thought, and especially German Romanticism, into Japan was Mori Ōgai, who had been sent to Germany by the Meiji government for four years to study medicine. His first work was the still-famous novella *The Dancing Girl* (Maihime) of

1890, based loosely on his own erotic experiences in Germany. Despite his success in this genre, Ōgai devoted most of his energies to criticism and translation, including the still-standard Japanese version of that harbinger of modernism, Goethe's *Faust*. In fiction he was soon overshadowed by Natsume Sōseki, who gave up a prestigious post at Tokyo Imperial University to become the staff novelist of the daily *Asahi* newspaper. The model of Sōseki as a professional writer was impressive and inspiring to the young writers of Korea and China. And as in Europe in the nineteenth century with authors such as Dickens, the serialized newspaper novel became one of the principal venues of the new fiction.

The foreign policy of China, Japan, and Korea during much of the preceding centuries had been isolationist, and even among the three neighbors themselves contact was extremely limited. This state of affairs changed dramatically with the outbreak of the Sino-Japanese War in 1894, precipitated by a struggle between the two countries for control over Korea. The effect of Japan's victory the following year was a tremendous upsurge in patriotism and cultural nationalism among victor and vanquished alike. Japanese poets such as Yosano Hiroshi and Masaoka Shiki called for traditional forms to be imbued with patriotism and martial bravery (see "The Revival of Poetry in Traditional Forms"). In China, leaders of the late Qing reform movement, such as Liang Qichao, also instituted a "poetry revolution," which resulted in poems with a decided nationalist quality.

At the same time, Japan in the 1890s saw the rise of a Romantic movement, inspired by European writers such as Byron and Shelley. Byron's influence is most clear in the writings of Kitamura Tōkoku (1868–1894), both in terms of form and in terms on the emphasis on love and the heroic individual. While the Romantic movement is often thought to have died with the demise of *Literary World* or with the advent of the Russo-Japanese War in 1904, clearly the poetry of Yosano Akiko in the journal *Morning Star* (Myōjō), as well as her translations of classical Japanese works such as *The Tale of Genji* (Genji monogatari) by the great female author Murasaki Shikibu, may be counted as part of the movement. Nonetheless, by the turn of the century this emphasis on the individual was being pursued in the form of realism and naturalism, as modeled by authors such as Zola and Tolstoy. In fact, it may not be too much of an overstatement to claim that the history of the novel in East Asia throughout the first half of the twentieth century can be told through the varying reactions to French naturalism.

European naturalism was the literary movement that was to have the most widespread influence on the course of modern East Asian literature. The term *naturalisme* was coined by Émile Zola in 1868. Zola likened the job of a novelist to that of a scientist: realistic portrayals of events and characters were designed to demonstrate the determining characteristics of heredity or race, class, and milieu, or immediate environment. These three factors had been isolated by Hippolyte Taine in his *History of English Literature*, published in French in

1864. "Taine's famous triad of forces—race, milieu, and moment—ultimately rests on the first, which he defined as 'the innate and hereditary dispositions' of the race. These dispositions are modified over time by environmental factors (the milieu), which result in a typical character or temperament. The third force, moment, is usually interpreted as age or epoch but also includes the force of past or tradition; that is, the 'momentum' or cumulative effects of the interaction between race and milieu on a given 'moment' of time. Taine's interests, however, were primarily psychological, in seeing the persistence of certain habits of mind common to the race expressed in their literature" (Brownstein 1987:439).

While Taine's approach may have been originally designed to explain the genius of the English people, transposed to Asia, it invited the use of literature to examine why the countries of the region had "failed" to modernize or had proved "inferior" to the conquering West. In other words, naturalist novels were meant to illustrate social Darwinism as propagated by such thinkers as Herbert Spencer (1820–1903). In Japan, naturalism *(shizenshugi)* combined with the previous Romantic emphasis on the self to create the *shishōsetsu*, or "autobiographical novel" (McClellan 1971), exemplified by the works of *Shimazaki Tōson and Tayama Katai (1871–1930). Writers such as these focused almost obsessively on revealing the dark and unsavory sides of their lives and personalities. In Japan the earliest example of naturalism may be the *Chikuma River Sketches* (written in 1899, but not published until 1913) by Shimazaki Tōson; its prototypical manifestation is usually taken to be *The Quilt* (Futon, 1907), by Tayama Katai. The naturalists believed that they served society by giving the unvarnished "truth," and because their own thoughts and lives were the only area where they could be sure of having access to truth, the dominant genre of the movement became the so-called *shishōsetsu*, or *"personal novel." Again, a similar approach can be seen in China with Yu Dafu, writing in the 1920s, who declared that "literature is nothing but the autobiography of the author" (although in the Chinese context this makes him a "romantic" rather than a "naturalist"). In Korea, the move to naturalism came a decade later, after the defeat of the independence movement of 1919 and in reaction to the overtly programmatic fiction of authors such as Yi Kwangsu. Writers such as Kim Tongin (1900–1951) founded their own *Creation* (Ch'angjo) journal, and portrayed the grim realities of life under Japanese occupation throughout the 1920s. (See "Realism in Early Modern Fiction.")

Naturalism was very much a male genre. In Japan, the *shishōsetsu* came to be considered the benchmark of "pure literature" *(junbungaku)*, as distinct from both Marxist-inspired proletarian literature and popular literature *(taishū bungaku)* aimed largely at women through the phenomenal growth in mass-market publications (Sakai 1987). In China popular literature gave rise to the so-called *Mandarin Ducks and Butterflies genre.

The 1920s also saw the coinage of terms for "female-style literature" *(joryū bungaku* in Japanese, *nüxing wenxue* or *funü wenxue* in Chinese) or "female-style writer" (*joryū sakka* in Japanese, *yŏryu chakka* in Korean). Although the emergence of female writers has often been seen as a distinctly modern phenomenon, recent scholarship has emphasized their roots in the early modern period. (See, for instance, "Reconsidering the Origins of Modern Chinese Women's Writing.")

Despite these similarities, by the end of the 1930s there would be a fundamental divergence of Chinese and Japanese modern literatures, defined chiefly by their differing responses to the historical successors of French naturalism, namely, realism and Marxist literature.

In China, while the May Fourth-period writers such as *Mao Dun promoted European-style naturalism and wrote novels that were influenced by it, there was also a strong reaction against naturalism, by modernists, romantics, and leftists. Instead, realism became the literary ideal that most writers shared, whatever their politics. Chinese critics generally distinguish between realism and natu ralism, with the latter being associated with a kind of pessimistic biological de terminism or superficial, photographic treatment of life, which fails to get to th heart or truth behind material reality. Naturalism in China is very different fr what happened to it in the Japanese context, where the "personal novel," c written in the first person, came to be seen as the essence of naturalism. I Chinese context, a naturalist novel, by its very nature, should be written the first person but in the objective omniscient narrator style; it should tre an individual, but society as a whole, through multiple characters from a va of social backgrounds. What is called "naturalism" in Japan would, in the C nese context, be called "romanticism."

In Japan, the rise of proletarian literature is dated to the publication of the journal *The Sower* (Tane maku hito) in 1921, though publication—banned periodically since its inception—was completely halted after the Kantō earthquake of 1923. The banner was taken up the following year by the Literary Front (Bungei Sensen), and in 1925 the Japan Proletarian Literary Front was born—the first of several such organizations.

Moving alongside the proletarian writers was another group, the *shinkankakuha*, sometimes translated as the "Neo-Impressionists" (Shea) or "neosensualism" (Prušek), but usually rendered as the "New Sensationalists." Led by the writer Yokomitsu Riichi (1898–1947) and including others such as *Kawabata Yasunari, the writing style of this group was heavily influenced by surrealism and dadaism. The self-appointed task of the group was to portray the "new sensations" of modernity, usually in the context of the cosmopolitan metropolis, with its frenetic pace and jazz rhythms—the consumer side of the newly mechanized age with its alienated factory workers. Though relations between the proletarian writers and the New Sensationalists were cordial through the mid-1920s, by 1929 the New Sensationalists had officially disbanded, but in fact they regrouped around the critic Kobayashi Hideo (1902–1983), eventually centered on

the revived journal *Literary World* and became the orthodox line of antiprole-
tarian bourgeois art (Shea 1964:195).

The late 1920s saw in Japan, China, and Korea a "debate about literature,"
but the difference in the terms of those debates is revealing. In 1927, in Japan,
*Akutagawa Ryūnosuke and *Tanizaki Jun'ichirō argued over the nature
and importance of "pure literature" *(junbungaku)*. The debate was between
Akutagawa's championing of "personal truth" of the sort promoted by the naturalists, over imaginative fiction driven by plot. (See "The Debate over Pure Literature.") Akutagawa's preference for plotless mimesis would encompass not
only the writers of "personal novels" but also most proletarian writers. But
whereas Akutagawa's touchstone was "truth," for the debate in China occurring
at almost the same time, the keyword was "revolution" *(geming)*. In 1925 Yu
Dafu and the Creation Society had announced their conversion to Marxism,
partly under the influence of literary movements in Japan. (See "The Debate
on Revolutionary Literature.") The terms of debate were precisely whether literature should be engaged in political issues or not. Interestingly, this debate
placed May Fourth writers such as Lu Xun and Mao Dun on the reactionary
side. In Korea as well 1925 saw the creation of the Korean Artist Proletarian Federation, which managed to survive under the Japanese occupation until 1935.
(See "Pure Literature versus the Literature of Engagement.") It is said that history is written by the victors, and this is no less true for literary history. The
North American perspective in literary studies is predominantly bourgeois. It
should not be surprising, then, that it is the period immediately *after* the suppression of politically engaged literature in Korea that is seen as a kind of golden
age, as writers were forced by circumstances to concentrate their energies more
on formal elements such as plot and character development, rather than a political message or action.

As Japan moved to a war footing after its 1931 invasion of Manchuria, the government carried out massive repression of all left-wing groups. Early in 1933 the
police trapped and tortured to death Kobayashi Takiji (1903–1933), author of
The Factory Ship (Kani kōsen), an event often taken to signal the end of the proletarian literature movement per se. Kobayashi's death was followed just months
later by the first official *tenkō* or "conversion" to official ideology and renunciation of Communism, made by two Communist Party leaders from jail.

In China, on the other hand, a group in Shanghai in the late 1920s and early
1930s picked up the banner of the Japanese New Sensationalists *(xin ganjue pai,*
translated as "New Sensationists" in the Chinese context) and produced some
of the first sustained modernist writing in Chinese. Yet here these writers found
themselves caught between censorship from the Nationalist government on one
hand, and criticism from Marxist writers on the other. With Japan's declaration
of war against China in 1937, the space for almost any kind of politically disen-
gaged literature disappeared. In China, both Nationalists and Communists

called for "literature for national defense" *(guofang wenxue)*. In Japan, the genre of the personal novel transformed into *jūgunki*, or "campaign accounts," often written by well-known authors sent by the Japanese government to observe the invading imperial forces. (See "Wartime Fiction.") Even poetry was enlisted in the cause. (See "The Revival of Poetry in Traditional Forms" and "Takamura Kōtarō.") In Korea, authors were forbidden for the duration of the war to publish in their own language.

Yet the very different results of the politicization of literature in China and Japan might be exemplified by the diverging trajectories of the female writers *Miyamoto Yuriko and *Ding Ling. Miyamoto devoted herself to the Japanese Communist Party. For this dedication she was repeatedly imprisoned during the war years. Although she published two novels after the end of World War II and completed her autobiographical trilogy, today only one of her short stories has been translated into English in its entirety. In contrast, Ding Ling embraced her image as a "modern girl" in 1920s Shanghai, publishing some of the first work in Chinese that portrayed female sexuality from a female perspective. Yet in the early 1930s she adopted the methods of social realist fiction. Her increased politicization resulted in her kidnapping and arrest by the Nationalist government (GMD, or Guomindang; also abbreviated KMT). Ding Ling managed to escape and make her way to the Communist headquarters in Yan'an. Her critiques of the elitism and gender disparities in Communist-controlled areas was one of the motivations for Mao's *"Yan'an Talks," where literature was placed firmly under the control of the Communist Party. Ding Ling seems to have accepted this pronouncement wholeheartedly and threw herself into literary production for the masses. With the establishment of the PRC in 1949 she enjoyed high positions in the cultural elite. Nonetheless, she was sent to the countryside for "reeducation" for twelve years—caught up in the Anti-Rightist Campaign after the short-lived *"Hundred Flowers" movement—only to be subsequently imprisoned for five more years during the Cultural Revolution. Yet even in the 1980s Ding Ling was a strong supporter of the party line and a vocal critic of bourgeois Western feminism. Ding Ling remains canonized as one of the major Chinese writers of the twentieth century, and no fewer than three book-length translations of her work have appeared in English.

The end of World War II brought profound changes to all three countries: Japan experienced atomic bombing and military occupation, China established the PRC, and Korea gained its independence, only to find itself partitioned after the Korean War. All the events are thoroughly reflected in the literatures of the period. In China, as we have seen, a doctrinaire version of socialist realism— *"revolutionary romanticism combined with revolutionary realism"—was brutally enforced. In Japan the atomic bombings gave their name to a whole genre of *"Atomic Bomb Fiction and Poetry." Male writers seemed to focus on the threat to their masculinity that both defeat in war and the American occupation represented, while women writers focused on the daily struggle of survival for their families and themselves. (See "Occupation Period Fiction.") The period also saw the rise of a kind of decadence: some writers were specifically linked to the so-called Decadent School (Burai-ha), such as *Dazai Osamu and *Sakaguchi Ango, but the general tendency—a dissipation focused on the redlight districts combined with a certain nostalgia for the sex trade of the Edo period—can be seen in writers such as Ishikawa Jun and *Nagai Kafū as well. In South Korea, the results of the Korean War led both to what is called *"The Literature of Territorial Division" as well as to identifying writers in terms of whether they "went north" (*"The *Wŏlbuk* Authors") or came south.

The 1960s were marked by the Japanese "economic miracle" and the acceptance of Japan as a part of the "West." This acceptance might be symbolized by the Tokyo Olympics of 1964 and the awarding of the Nobel Prize in literature to Kawabata Yasunari in 1968. In contrast, China became internationally isolated during the decade of the Cultural Revolution of 1966–76. Taiwan prospered in much the same way as Japan, but the strict authoritarianism of the GMD dampened literary activity. Political repression also marked Korea during this period, after far more positive initial signals: in 1960 student demonstrators precipitated Syngman Rhee's (Xi Sŭng-man) fall from power. He was replaced, however, by Major General Park Chung Hee in a military coup, which initiated a series of military juntas that lasted until 1987.

The second half of the twentieth century proved to be every bit as tumultuous in East Asia as had been the first half. China saw its international isolation end with President Richard Nixon's visit to that country in 1971. Mao's death in 1976 paved the way for economic moderates such as Deng Xiaoping. The limits of such moderation were revealed, however, in the Tiananmen Incident of 1989. This brutal repression by the government did not derail, however, the repatriation of Hong Kong in 1997. The new millennium sees the still officially socialist economy joining the World Trade Organization. In Taiwan, gradual liberalization after the death of Chiang Kai-shek in 1975 has led ultimately to the election of a Taiwanese president whose proindependence stance has exacerbated tensions with the mainland. In Korea, opposition forces finally managed to unite under Kim Dae-jung.

The second half of the twentieth century also saw five trends consistently appear in the literature of all areas of East Asia: the preponderance of women writers; the insistent exploration of sexuality and eroticism (less evident in the literature of Korea)—often of the most transgressive sort; formal experimentation in metafiction and postmodern narrative techniques such as magical realism; a general blurring of the distinction between literature and pop culture, fueled by relentless commodification and globalization; and, finally, a focusing on the diasporic experience, leading on one hand to the continued questioning of national identity, and on the other to tremendous cross-fertilization and mutation, as writers write "national" literature not only in the language of that nation but also in international vernaculars such as English.

Bibliography

Brownstein, Michael C. "From *Kokugaku* to *Kokubungaku*: Canon-Formation in the Meiji Period." *Harvard Journal of Asiatic Studies* 47, no. 2 (1987): 435–460.

Fairbank, John K., and Edwin O. Reischauer. *China: Tradition and Transformation.* Rev. ed. Boston: Houghton Mifflin, 1989.

Jelinek, Miriam. "Yokomitsu Riichi." In Jaroslav Prušek and Zbigniew Slupski, eds., *Dictionary of Oriental Literatures: East Asia.* London: George Allen and Unwin, 1974.

Kitamura Takiji. *"The Factory Ship" and "The Absentee Landlord."* Trans. Frank Motofuji. Seattle: University of Washington Press, 1973.

Liu, Lydia H. *Translingual Practice: Literature, National Culture, and Translated Modernity—China, 1900–1937.* Stanford: Stanford University Press, 1995.

McClellan, Edwin. "Tōson and the Autobiographical Novel." In Donald H. Shively, ed., *Tradition and Modernization in Japanese Culture*, 347–378. Princeton: Princeton University Press, 1971.

Prušek, Jaroslav, and Zbigniew Slupski. *Dictionary of Oriental Literatures: East Asia.* London: George Allen and Unwin, 1974.

Rowley, G. G. *Yosano Akiko and the Tale of Genji.* Ann Arbor: University of Michigan Center for Japanese Studies, 2000.

Ryan, Marleigh Grayer. *Japan's First Modern Novel: "Ukigumo" of Futabatei Shimei.* New York: Columbia University Press, 1965.

Sakai, Cécile. *Histoire de la littérature populaire Japonaise: Faits et perspectives (1900–1980).* Paris: Editions L'Harmattan, 1987.

Shea, George Tyson. *Leftwing Literature in Japan: A Brief History of the Proletarian Literary Movement.* Tokyo: Hosei University Press, 1964.

PART II

Japan

SHARALYN ORBAUGH, ASSOCIATE EDITOR

Thematic Essays

3

HISTORICAL OVERVIEW

It is a historical commonplace that Japan was completely isolated for nearly 250 years before U.S. Commodore Matthew Perry forced the shogun's government to reopen to trade, diplomatic contact, and cultural communication with the West. Although this is not fully accurate, it is undeniable that Japan's contacts with the Western world at least were remarkably restricted until Perry's successful mission in 1853. Shortly after the arrival of Perry's ships, a quick coup and brief civil war returned the country to imperial rule, ending more than five hundred years of military control. The return to imperial rule happened in 1868, the year considered to be the dividing line between modernity and premodernity in Japan. Until the death in 1912 of this emperor, whose reign-name, Meiji, meant "enlightened rule," Japan went through a period of intensive, thoroughgoing, self-conscious modernization, attempting to catch up as quickly as possible with the other nation-states of the modern world (which at the time meant exclusively the Anglo-European world). Having seen what the Western colonizing powers were doing to Qing-dynasty China, which, while large and culturally powerful, was not modernized, the leaders of the Japanese government realized clearly what was at stake. Because Japan no longer had the option of remaining "apart" in its isolation, the only choices were to join the elite group of modernized nations or to accept the abuses of unequal treaties, trade pressure, and perhaps even colonization.

As we know, Japan did achieve the elite status of full "modernity" by the end of Meiji's reign in 1912, if we define modernity in terms of cutting-edge technology, science, and medicine; an industrial (as opposed to agrarian) economy; an extensive transportation and communications infrastructure; the construction of imposing buildings for diplomatic and cultural events; and so on. All of these were, of course, hallmarks of Anglo-European modernity, as were colonial and military aggression. Japan was the first Asian nation to successfully incorporate those elements of modernity as well. The Meiji period saw two victorious wars: against China in 1894–95 and against Russia in 1904–5. From these Japan gained its first colonial possessions: Taiwan (Formosa) in 1895, and Korea in 1910, when it was formally annexed as a colony.

Several elements of modernization had been in place before the beginning of the Meiji period. The centralization of government had been accomplished with the city of Edo as the shogunal capital; the *daimyō* (feudal lords of each domain) were required to spend half their time in Edo, and their families were forced to reside there permanently. Reliable channels of communication and commerce had been thus established between the seat of central government and all the outlying regions. Urbanization, too, was well advanced in the Edo period. Besides Edo itself (which later became the city we know as Tokyo), there were numerous cities of some size and importance; in Edo, Osaka, and Kyoto in particular, urbanization was accompanied by the rise of a vibrant popular culture. Print culture—another hallmark of modernity—was at the center of pre-Meiji popular culture: woodblock print pictures and lavishly illustrated woodblock printed books were extremely popular and widely available. Lending libraries gave access to those who could not afford to purchase books. Japan also had a remarkably high literacy rate during the Edo period, even though there was no nationwide system of education. Children of *daimyō* families (usually only boys, but occasionally girls as well) were taught in special domain schools or by tutors, in a system that emphasized a traditional neo-Confucian Chinese education. But many city children and rural children of other classes had access to at least a little education at *tera koya* (private temple schools). Because of all of these factors—communication and transportation routes linking center and periphery, urban culture, print culture, and literacy—the Meiji attempts at modernization went relatively smoothly and quickly.

Japanese literature, too, underwent an intensive and self-conscious process of modernization during the Meiji period. In the first decades after the opening of the country Japanese missions were sent to the various countries of Europe and North America to conduct firsthand observations of the political and social structures of these modern nations. Besides bringing back information about education, hygiene, constitutional government, military organization, and so on, these missions also introduced to Japan information about Western philosophy, religion, and literature. With this new stimulus added to more than a thousand years of indigenous literary tradition, from the 1870s on Japan experienced a literary renaissance that may be said to have culminated—at least in terms of international recognition—a century later in 1968 with the naming of

❧

3

*Kawabata Yasunari as the winner of the Nobel Prize in literature. Since the end of World War II there has been a steady production of translations of Japanese literary works into English. Currently, writers such as *Murakami Haruki and *Shimada Masahiko publish short stories in *The New Yorker* and other major magazines, and international pop icons such as *Yoshimoto Banana sell millions of translated copies of their novels among young adults around the world.

The one-hundred-year path to a literature of international stature was not smooth, however. The introduction of the developing scientific disciplines of the nineteenth century, such as Darwinian evolution and physical anthropology, revealed that in the new "scientifically verified" hierarchies of race and gender, Japan had already been allotted an inferior status: "oriental," and "feminine" vis-à-vis the "white" nations of the Anglo-European world. (See "Nation and Nationalism," and "Gender, Family, and Sexuality.") In many areas of life the opening of the country to ideas from the primarily Judeo-Christian, Greco-Roman philosophical/religious traditions of the West raised new questions about the meaning of subjectivity, nation, and nationalism and brought about modern definitions of family, gender, sex, and sexuality. These will be addressed in the following sections.

—*Sharalyn Orbaugh*

4

THE PROBLEM OF THE MODERN SUBJECT

One of the great problems facing Meiji reformers was the recognition that the concept of modern selfhood or subjectivity—later termed *kindai jiga* (modern self) or *shutaisei* (subjectivity)—that appeared to be current in the advanced nations of the West was radically different from that in Japan. The post-Enlightenment (male) subject in England, North America, and most of Western Europe was envisioned as rational, monolithic (not changing identities according to context), and, after the eighteenth-century revolutions in France and the United States, defined by accomplishment rather than birth, repository of the highest form of state sovereignty in a secularized and democratic political system. Japan under the shogunate was, on the contrary, still structured according to the rigid neo-Confucian-based feudal system of four classes: warriors/scholars (shogun, *daimyō*, samurai), farmers, artisans, and tradespeople. Traditional Chinese neo-Confucianism had made no provision for people outside these categories, but it is crucial to note that in Japan there was a category above all these— the imperial household and the court aristocracy—and a category below, of *hinin* (literally "nonpeople," outcasts), made up of various groups such as itinerant performers and the traditional "untouchable caste" of Japan, the *burakumin*. Social status, occupation, location of domicile, and identity was, with few exceptions, fixed for life, whichever category one was born into.

From as early as 1869 and continuing through 1884, laws were enacted abolishing the feudal class system and constructing a new, drastically simplified and more "democratic" social hierarchy. The *kuge* (court aristocracy) and the highest-level *daimyō* became the *kazoku* (members of the peerage). Higher-ranking samurai became the *shizoku* (former warrior class). Lower ranking samurai, together with farmers, artisans, and tradespeople, were all combined into a single class: *heimin* (commoners). The situation of the former *hinin* (non-people) was more complicated: in 1869 they were redesignated *senmin* (the lowly). In 1871 this structure was modified, and the *senmin* were redesignated *shin-heimin* (new commoners)—a category meant to raise them to equality with all other nonpeer Japanese, but which in fact allowed for continued discrimination against them because the prefix *shin* ("new") distinguished them from all the other *heimin* (Kawauchi 1990:146). The emperor remained in a class of his own, and was, in fact, during the Meiji and subsequent prewar eras, actually raised to the status of a deity. (After 1914 an individual's class was no longer formally registered, and in 1947 the occupation government abolished the designations *shizoku* and *kazoku*. Even today, however, families are well aware of their class ancestry, and discrimination still exists against those of *hinin/burakumin* lineage; see Kawauchi 1990.)

With this Meiji-period change in legal status, commoners were allowed to take surnames for the first time and to choose their occupations and domiciles, and they were given universal access to (elementary) education. As the new conceptualization of modern subjectivity began to take hold, the slogan *risshin shusse* (advancing in the world through individual effort) became the watchword of the day.

As early as 1874 a movement to establish an elected, representative government was active: the Jiyū Minken Undō (Freedom and People's Rights Movement). This attempt to replicate the politically sovereign subjectivity of the free-born European male inspired a number of the Meiji period's most influential writers, translators, critics, and educators. Although the movement was perceived as antigovernment by Meiji rulers and was partially suppressed through censorship and restrictions on assembly, its goals were achieved at least in part when the 1890 constitution established the Imperial Diet, a bicameral legislature whose House of Representatives was elected through limited male suffrage (universal male suffrage after 1925). However, the power of the House of Representatives, though roughly equal to that of the House of Peers, was limited by the existence of several political bodies with overriding legislative powers: the cabinet, the privy council, and the emperor, among others.

GENBUN'ITCHI

It is one thing to legislate changes in the status of the subject, and another to change people's conceptualization and enactment of a new, modern kind of subjectivity. Clearly one of the most important sites through which identity is both understood and enacted is language. The Japanese attempts to create a vernacular written language that could express this new subjectivity were self-conscious and intensive from around 1880 to 1920, by which time writers and journalists were using the new language confidently.

When the Meiji government took power, the situation of the written language was one of the most fundamental problems confronting it. To put it simply, the language used in written texts bore less resemblance to the spoken Japanese of the time than Latin does to French. In contrast, the nations of Europe had for centuries moved gradually from a strict division between written language (Latin) and the various vernacular Romance or Germanic languages. By the nineteenth century, therefore, the modern nations of Europe had several centuries of language modernization behind them.

In Japan in 1868 the official written language of government remained a form of classical Chinese, bearing no relation to spoken Japanese. In addition, there were three other major written languages, each used for a specific purpose; none was close to the contemporary vernacular. For a country contemplating modernization, this situation posed several problems. In order to catch up to the technological, military, and economic superiority of Western nations it would be necessary to mobilize all of Japan's best minds and to have an educated citizenry to carry out the new systems. Although Japan was in the fortunate position of possessing a populace with an unusually high literacy rate (higher than any of its Asian neighbors, for example, and higher even than the nations of Europe), the *functional* extent of that literacy was limited by the multiple and unnecessarily complex forms of written language. Many "literate" people could read only the simplest of the four written languages, inscribed in the simplest form of orthography (Unger 1996:24–35). Moreover, literacy in Japan was achieved at a higher educational cost in terms of time and effort than in a country in which the spoken and written languages were more similar.

In attempting to implement overall modernization, as Nanette Twine explains, "language modernization ought to be one of the very first tasks tackled, since upon its successful implementation depends the greater efficiency of such other vital adjuncts of social transformation as education and communications." Nonetheless, the idea of language reform was, "at first vigorously resisted.... The notion struck at the roots of the contemporary intellectual view of writing not primarily as a servant of man but as an artistic and intellectual show-case, and as the province of the upper class" (1991:8). Despite the growing recognition that a democratization of subjectivity was crucial to modernization, many members of the Meiji government—classically educated scions of upper-class families—found it difficult to give up this elitist view of language.

The four written languages in common use ranged from *kanbun* (classical Chinese) for official documents, using only Chinese characters and based on Chinese grammar, to *wabun* (classical Japanese), using a mix of characters and *kana* (the Japanese syllabaries) and based on classical Japanese grammar and vocabulary. The others were combinations or hybrids of these two basic styles (see Twine 1991:17 for details). Whichever style was used, there was little or no punctuation supplied to aid comprehension. Moreover, there were approximately ten thousand Chinese characters in use at the beginning of the Meiji period, in contrast with the 1,945 necessary today to read a newspaper (Twine 1991:17).

Language reform was clearly necessary in three areas: replacing classical grammatical and lexical elements with a colloquial style based on the current grammar and vocabulary of the spoken language; choosing one of Japan's many spoken dialects to serve as the standard for the new written language; and reducing the number of Chinese characters in use, standardizing and simplifying their orthography, and adding a standardized system of punctuation (Twine 1991:9). Recognizing the complexity of these reformist tasks and their ideological consequences, the newly appointed minister of education, Mori Arinori, suggested the wholesale adoption of an already modernized language, English (Twine 1991:82; Gottlieb 1995:5). The suggestion was met with ridicule.

It was primarily among translators and writers of fiction that the new written language, often called *genbun'itchi* (unification of the spoken and written language) was developed. Early pioneers in the development of *genbun'itchi* include *Tsubouchi Shōyō, noted translator of Shakespeare; *Futabatei Shimei, translator of Turgenev and author of Japan's first modern novel; Wakamatsu Shizuko, the translator of *Little Lord Fauntleroy* (see "Meiji Women Writers"), among other important works; and the members of the *Ken'yūsha group. Through the efforts of these men and women the problems involved in developing a modern vernacular were slowly worked out.

Some of the aforementioned problems were readily solved through simple arbitrary decisions: the Tokyo-area Yamanote spoken dialect was chosen as the standard on which the written language should be based, and a standard system of punctuation introduced. But other issues were more complicated. Language modernization could not be separated from fundamental political, epistemological, and philosophical issues. For example, a number of the key concepts of modern Western languages simply did not exist in Japanese. Translators attempting to bring modern European texts to a Japanese audience could not solve this problem simply by introducing a new lexical item. In Japan there was no concept, and thus no word, for "century." Japanese dating systems were cyclical, based on imperial reigns. This human-centered, constantly "resettable" method of counting time was in strict contrast to the Gregorian calendar with its relentless unidirectional movement away from the center marked by Christ toward a distant end. The cultural preference to count in multiples of ten, too, differs from the Japanese historical norm. (Japan adopted the Gregorian calendar and the twenty-four-hour day in 1873.) Translators put forward several possibilities for "century" before a compound word, made up of two Chinese characters, was adopted: *seiki*.

Similarly, the word "kiss" posed problems for the early Meiji translators. The translator of Bulwer-Lytton's *Ernest Maltravers* resorted to "licking the mouth" in his attempt to render "kiss" in 1879 (Keene 1984, 1:66–67). This is not to suggest that kissing had never taken place in Japan; pornographic woodblock prints show the biting and sucking of tongues, if not full mouth-to-mouth contact. There were words to describe this. But the kissing behavior that Japanese readers found in European art and literature—with all the cultural, social, and religious baggage it carried concerning notions of gender, intimacy, and romance—was not adequately described by any existing Japanese words. Eventually *kissu*, a transliteration of the English word, became standard.

"Borrowings" in the form of transliterations were a significant feature of Japan's language modernization. Words for important concepts were adopted from various languages: part-time work, for example, became *arubaito*, after the German *Arbeit*. This willingness to introduce "loanwords" from other languages gave Japanese a useful flexibility, a way of increasing lexical items quickly and efficiently. In contrast, this practice was virtually nonexistent in Chinese, which made language modernization in China, particularly in technical and scientific areas, far more cumbersome as new words had to be created out of existing elements of language—each of which carried inescapable traditional cultural connotations.

Most important, however, the new language would have to be able to express the new, *modern* subjectivity that Meiji intellectuals wished to create, based at least partly on the individual, autonomous, apparently objective and neutral subjectivity featured in Anglo-European novels, newspapers, legal systems, and so on.

In most modern European languages it is possible to form a sentence that is apparently "neutral"—independent of its context, and independent of a specific pair of interlocutors. Newspapers, for example, make use of such sentences, as do many third-person narrators in fiction. Such a possibility was necessary for producing writing in the modern vernacular that was universally legible, and universally applicable. Literary people who had begun translating Western literatures into Japanese could see that Western-language novels were able to set up a unmarked frame around the diegetic space, which allowed for a completely transparent narrative voice—an "invisible" omniscient or semiomniscient narrator. Within that frame Western characters might use speech that marked social class or regional origin, but the frame itself was written in completely neutral language. Considering that every Japanese speech act (even today) encodes markers of hierarchical and personal relationship between speaker and hearer, how were Japanese writers to reproduce that transparent narrative frame? What sort of linguistic shape would such a sentence have in Japanese? Would readers understand it, or would they be frustrated by their inability to read the narrator's and their own "position" in the social web?

Journalists, historians, and essayists, too, realized that the similitude of objectivity that was achieved in Western languages was a useful thing—but how were they to replicate it in a language where every speech act makes its subjective point of view obvious on its linguistic surface? In Japanese it is, strictly speaking, not possible to make a declarative statement about someone else's state of mind, along the lines of "Mary is happy," for example. One can only say that Mary "looks" happy, or "seems" happy, or "is reported to be" happy. In a language so tied to the phenomenology of personal experience and interpersonal relationships, so evidently mistrustful of "omniscience," how could a linguistic stance of "objectivity" be framed?

Even more important, of course, was the *effect* of a "neutral" speech act: what would happen to the entire social structure, predicated as it was on a clearly defined web of hierarchical relationships, if those relationships were no longer *enacted*, no longer *constituted* through every speech act? The main effect of such a "neutral" language would be a social leveling of precisely the sort the early Meiji reformers were advocating. The new language would create in writing a new kind of Japanese subjectivity: the autonomous individual, equal in principal to all other autonomous individuals.

This revolutionary form of writing, *genbun'itchi*, had been developed and was in place in literature by the late 1880s, but minor struggles over the exact linguistic form of the neutral "voice" continued past the turn of the century. In fact, national debates about the writing systems—for example, the number and orthography of Chinese characters required in standard education, whether or not transliterations in the simpler syllabaries should be supplied for difficult characters, and so on—continue to the present day, revolving around the same conflicting visions of language as a tool for the elite or for the masses (Gottlieb 1995:172–201).

In the early days of the development of *genbun'itchi*, one of the major obstacles to the enactment of a truly democratic notion of the modern subject and the language with which to express it was the Meiji Constitution, promulgated in 1889, in force from 1890. This constitution and subsequent legislation (such as the Imperial Rescript on Education, 1890) repudiated many of the early Meiji reformers' progressive ideas and put in place a structure called the *kazoku kokka* (the family state), in which the emperor, who held inviolable sovereignty over his people, was envisioned as father of the nation and his subjects (including later the colonial subjects in Taiwan and Korea) as his children. This model of authority was extended to the individual Japanese household, where the father had absolute legal authority as head, and his wife and children had few legal rights. (See "Gender, Family, and Sexualities.") This reinstating of a rigid hierarchical structure of subjectivities could not easily coexist with a rhetoric of linguistic democracy. The struggles to negotiate a middle ground—which would allow for the production of an educated, literate populace so necessary to modern industrialization and militarization, but which would also maintain the elitist, hierarchical structures so necessary to the state's vision of order—continued through World War II and even beyond.

EARLY LITERARY INNOVATIONS
AND THE MODERN SUBJECT

*Futabatei Shimei is credited with having produced the first wholly successful example of the modern novel, written in *genbun'itchi*, completed in 1889. This novel, *Ukigumo* (literally "drifting cloud"), featured a protagonist who was intriguingly different from the idealized vision of the *risshin shusse*–oriented young man of the day. Bunzō, though educated and employed, cannot bring himself to replicate the self-centered ambition and drive of his colleague Noboru, nor to take action on the matter of his attraction to his female cousin, Osei. He is ineffectual and introspective, very much in contrast with those around him. His more sensitive and refined nature is depicted sympathetically by Futabatei, in contrast to Noboru's vulgar arrogance, but the author makes it clear that such qualities have little value in the Meiji man who wishes to achieve success. Futabatei's vision of the *kindai jiga*, personified by Noburu, is unattractive.

In the 1890s, *Higuchi Ichiyō, though writing in neoclassical Japanese rather than *genbun'itchi*, presents protagonists struggling with the notion of modern selfhood while still enmeshed in largely feudal social structures. Her characters—usually women, children, and men of the lower classes—may have heard of the new notions of subjectivity in the Meiji period, and may regard themselves as living in a modernized world (cf. the various modern technologies featured in "Child's Play"), but the end result of their attempts to establish an autonomous identity are thwarted by the forces of the family and class systems.

LITERARY MOVEMENTS
AND THE MODERN SUBJECT

Some writers espoused a more positive view of the possibilities of the *kindai jiga* and inaugurated literary movements or coterie groups that featured fiction devoted to depicting modern subjectivities. In 1890 *Mori Ōgai published the short story "The Dancing Girl" (Maihime), the first in a trilogy of stories heavily influenced by German Romanticism. "The Dancing Girl" was loosely based on army medical officer Ōgai's experiences in Berlin, where he had been sent by the government to study hygiene. The protagonist of the story, Ōta, falls in love with a German damsel in distress, a blonde, blue-eyed dancer. As their relationship deepens, Ōta neglects the work he had been sent to do. Just as it appears that the girl, Elise, has become pregnant with Ōta's child, his superior summons him and chides him for neglecting his responsibilities to his parents and to the Japanese government. Ōta reluctantly decides to return to Japan; leaving behind Elise, who has gone mad at the announcement of his decision.

The story bears close resemblance to the work of Goethe and other writers of the German Romantic movement, which had stressed the exploration of intense psychological states, such as madness, exoticism (including a fascination with "the Orient"), and the power of individual will. Ōgai transposed those elements to the context of the Meiji struggle over the meaning of modern subjectivity. In his story it is "the Occident" that is represented by the exotically beautiful but ultimately mad woman, and it is the "Oriental" male who chooses to abandon love and the West for the sake of national duty back in Japan. Ōgai here stakes out a particularly masculine and stalwart identity for the Japanese male subject in the international discourse of modern identity, using the familiar tropes of East versus West, male versus female, and personal fulfillment versus duty to the nation. While the Romantic movement in literature lasted only until the turn of the century, the ethnic nationalism visible in this movement—codified in the image of modern Japanese male subjectivity as strong and masculine vis-à-vis a feminized or at least emotional West, and devoted to the good of the nation—was influential until at least the end of World War II (see Doak 1994).

It was not until nearly two decades after Ōgai's "romantic trilogy" that another literary movement as influential as Romanticism would arise. The leading opposition to the Romantic movement was *shizenshugi* (Japanese naturalism), which arrived in Japan through literary translations of the work of European naturalists such as Zola and Flaubert. European naturalism had emphasized a view of the individual as constituted through a web of social networks and evolutionary forces that are beyond his or her control—the individual as a statistic. In Japan, however, naturalism was understood as emphasizing the sordid, unpleasant aspects of modern life. Naturalist writers therefore indulged in raw confessions of their own base desires and actions. Tayama Katai's 1907 *The Quilt* (Futon) is considered the first work of Japanese naturalism. The story concerns a middle-aged, married male protagonist—a thinly disguised version of Katai himself—who falls in love with a young woman boarding in his household. This love remains entirely unconsummated, but the frankness with which the protagonist's inappropriate sexual desires are expressed made it shocking to contemporary readers.

The lasting power of naturalist writing in Japanese literary circles came from its aura of truthfulness: it appeared that authors were confessing their own most secret perversions. As indicated above, the Japanese language has traditionally made little provision for the "omniscient" reporting of another person's thoughts or feelings. A story that was straightforwardly fictional, therefore, was seen by many readers as little better than a lie—entertaining perhaps, but ultimately trivial. The entertainment offered by fiction was appropriate for women, children, and the lower classes, but not a matter of high culture. In 1885 Tsubouchi Shōyō had tried to overturn this long-held prejudice, arguing that in Western literature fiction was used to express and explore the most serious and profound aspects of human life. But despite the strides made in the intervening years toward producing serious Japanese fiction capable of expressing the modern subject, the prejudice against fictionality remained. In works considered naturalist the evident "truthfulness" of an author's exploration of his own inner demons—no matter how solipsistic the result—played to this long-standing prejudice, but these works were still considered "modern" because of their evidently realistic delving into human psychology.

The later development of the *shishōsetsu* (the personal novel, also called *watakushi-shōsetsu*)—considered by many the most "Japanese" of literary forms—was an extension of this view. The *shishōsetsu*, too, focused on the personal life of its one main protagonist, whose life circumstances invariably resembled those of the author. The *shishōsetsu*'s appeal rested again on its aura of sincerity and epistemological validity.

Some late Meiji and early Taishō writers, however, were seemingly uninfluenced by imported literary schools and coteries, and were also undeterred by lingering indigenous prejudices. *Natsume Sōseki, for example, wrote obviously fictional novels that grappled with such weighty themes as the nature of the modern male intellectual subject's relation to the *kazoku kokka* state, and to modernity more generally. His fiction explored questions of individualism, egalitarianism, and the (selfish) power of the human ego.

The members of the all-female *Seitō (Bluestockings) group wrote fiction, essays, and poetry depicting the gender systems of late-Meiji and early-Taishō Japan, the place of women and the meaning of modern selfhood for women in the new social and political structures. One of the most famous, for example, was Tamura Toshiko (1884–1945), whose short works and novels explore the implications of being a woman in late Meiji Japan through metaphors and themes of the sexed body. In the case of her 1911 "Lifeblood" (Ikichi), for example, a narrative of sexual trauma implies allegorically the gendered nature of larger traumatic issues of modernity.

In the 1910s and 1920s some male writers seem to have come to terms with a subjectivity that was both Japanese and modern. The White Birch Society (Shirakabaha), whose most famous member was *Shiga Naoya, typified this confidence and comfort with its place in an implicitly international artistic world. Others, however, still struggled. Seiji Lippit argues that *Akutagawa Ryūnosuke's fascination with Japan's premodern Christians and his constant "grafting of the fragments of the past and of the foreign other onto a new context" were a literary means of exploring the hybridity of the modern subject that resulted from Japan's "primal encounter" with the West. Akutagawa's 1927 suicide seems to have been motivated at least in part by his sense that he had failed to express this complex subjectivity adequately in his writing. (See "The Debate over Pure Literature.")

In the 1920s and early 1930s Japanese socialist and proletarian writers challenged the romantic, bourgeois depictions of the modern individual in mainstream Japanese literature. Proletarian novelists such as Kobayashi Takiji (1903–1933) narrated the squalid working and living conditions of the industrial underclass in styles influenced by Russian socialist realism. Kobayashi's torture murder at the hands of the Tokkōtai (Thought Police) in 1933 was part of a larger crackdown on leftist literary sentiments through the end of World War II that virtually silenced this interrogation of modern subjectivity.

THE POSTWAR PERIOD

The "problem" involved in imagining and expressing the *kindai jiga* (modern subject) had been solved (or at least repressed) by the 1930s. But later historical circumstances also called for reevaluations of the meaning and enactment of subjectivity. The end of World War II was one such moment. Writers struggling to come to terms with the defeat, the destruction by bombing and fire of the cities, and Japan's first experience of occupation by a foreign power, produced agonized reassessments of the meaning of Japanese and human identity. For many intellectual men the immediate postwar period was a time of energetic debate over the question of Japan's war responsibility, with some leftists claiming that Japanese militarism had been caused by the failure of the Japanese people to achieve true modern individuality (Koschmann 1996:65–67). For some women writers, newly enfranchised by the 1947 constitution as full legal adults, the exploration of new subject positions within the national polity was more positive. *Hibakusha* writers (victims of the atomic bombings) are well known for their insistence on a unique understanding of modern subjectivity because of their experience. (See "Occupation-Period Fiction" and "Atomic Fiction and Poetry.")

The postwar high economic growth period of the late 1950s and 1960s—accompanied as it was by increasing public resistance to continued alliance with the United States through the U.S.-Japan Security Treaty (usually known as ANPO) and increasing concern over ecological disasters such as Minamata—fostered in the 1960s a humanist, but often somewhat existentialist, stream of fiction in the work of male writers such as *Ōe Kenzaburō, *Abe Kōbō, and Shimao Toshio. Their protagonists frequently struggle to negotiate the demands of individual conscience or desire versus duty toward a collectivity, within a context of increasing internationalization, industrialization, and urban anonymity.

Women writers of this generation, such as *Enchi Fumiko, Kōno Taeko, and Kurahashi Yumiko, often focused on literary deconstructions of the traditional prewar family system (the *ie* system), which continued to color gender relations and female subjectivity even in the postwar period. Much of their work contains graphic images of violence and explicit sexuality, supporting "transgressive" themes such as incest and murder. (See "Women Writers of the 1960s and 1970s.")

In the next generation—the first born after the war—writer *Murakami Ryū's debut novel, *Almost Transparent Blue* (Kagirinaku tōmei ni chikai burū), harks back to Akutagawa's use of grafting, fragmentation, and hybridity to express the complexity of the modern subject. For Murakami, who grew up on the edge of an American military base, it is the continued presence of the U.S. military in Japan, long after the end of the occupation, that triggers anxiety over the autonomy and legitimacy of the postwar male subject. He, too, uses graphic violence and sexuality to convey his sense of anomie.

It was in the 1960s and 1970s that some previously invisible subjectivities began to be widely recognized, winning Japan's most prestigious literary award for new authors, the Akutagawa Prize. Together with a slowly increasing number of women writers who won the award, *burakumin* (outcast) authors such as *Nakagami Kenji, and Korean-Japanese writers such as Li Kaisei began earning critical praise and public recognition during this period for their literary representations of marginalized subjectivities within Japan. (Unfortunately, relatively little of this work has yet been translated into English.)

Finally, in the 1980s and 1990s, as Japan took its place in the world as an economic superpower, some writers and performance artists attempted to depict the fragmented, decentered experience of postmodern subjectivity: *Shimada Masahiko, Murakami Haruki, Yoshimoto Banana, and *Shimizu Yoshinori, for example. It could well be argued that the previous hundred years of Japanese literary struggles with issues of subjectivity provide a particularly useful platform for considerations of what it is to be human in the transnational or even postnational context of the postmodern.

—*Sharalyn Orbaugh*

Bibliography

Doak, Kevin. *Dreams of Difference: The Japan Romantic School and the Crisis of Modernity.* Berkeley: University of California Press, 1994.

Gottlieb, Nanette. *Kanji Politics: Language Policy and Japanese Script.* London and New York: Kegan Paul International, 1995.

Kawauchi Toshihiko. *Buraku sabetsu to jinken* (Buraku Discrimination and Human Rights). Tokyo: Gendai shokan, 1990.

Keene, Donald. *Dawn to the West: Japanese Literature in the Modern Era.* 2 vols. New York: Holt, Rinehart and Winston, 1984.

Koschmann, J. Victor. *Revolution and Subjectivity in Postwar Japan.* Chicago: University of Chicago Press, 1996.

Mori Ōgai. "The Dancing Girl." Trans. Richard Bowring. In J. Thomas Rimer, ed., *Mori Ōgai: "Youth" and Other Stories,* 159–167. Honolulu: University of Hawai'i Press, 1994.

Murakami Ryū. *Almost Transparent Blue.* Trans. Nancy Andrews. Tokyo: Kodansha International, 1977.

Ryan, Marleigh Grayer. *Japan's First Modern Novel: "Ukigumo" of Futabatei Shimei.* New York: Columbia University Press, 1965.

Tayama Katai. *The Quilt and Other Stories.* Trans. Kenneth Henshall. Tokyo: University of Tokyo Press, 1981.

Tamura Toshiko. "Ikichi" (Lifeblood). In *Tamura Toshiko sakuhinshū* (Collected Works of Tamura Toshiko), 1:187–199. Tokyo: Orijin shuppan sentâ, 1987.

Twine, Nanette. *Language and the Modern State: The Reform of Written Japanese.* London: Routledge, 1991.

Unger, J. Marshall. *Literacy and Script Reform in Occupation Japan: Reading between the Lines.* New York: Oxford University Press, 1996.

5

NATION AND NATIONALISM

The concept of "nation" was one of the innovations of modernity with which Meiji leaders were confronted in 1868. Japan under the Tokugawa shogunate had been a loose and often fractious union of separate feudal domains or fiefs, each headed by a military leader called a *daimyō*, all owing allegiance to and under the power of the shogun and his government, the *bakufu*, in Edo (modern-day Tokyo). That this allegiance was at times tenuous can be seen in the fact that after 1634 all *daimyō* were required to reside half-time in Edo, and leave their families there when they returned to their home domains. Although the emperor had been at the center of government (at least nominally) from earliest recorded history until the twelfth century, after that time various military governments had held power while successive emperors lived quiet and politically powerless lives in Kyoto. By the end of the Edo period, the neo-Confucian class structure was under pressure: samurai and farmers—who were, in Confucian terms, more socially valuable than artisans and merchants—were hard pressed to pay their taxes of rice to their feudal landlords and the shogun, while merchants had capitalized on increasing urbanization to become comparatively rich. As warships from Russia, the United States, England, and other colonialist nations put increasing pressure on Japan's ports, the country was split between those who wanted to accede to their demands and open to trade, and those who wanted to "expel the barbarians" (as the patriotic saying went). When an alliance between some of the most powerful *daimyō* and the emperor's sympathizers successfully overturned the *bakufu* and restored political power to the emperor in 1868 (the Meiji Restoration), one of the first tasks of the new government was to fashion a "nation" out of these diverse and contentious materials.

In fact, many of the elements necessary to the modern nation-state were in place by the end of the Edo period: urbanization, a thriving print culture, a relatively literate populace, and channels of communication between the centers of government and all parts of the country. As an archipelago, the new nation's natural borders appeared clear. (In reality, of course, even before the military colonial expansion of late Meiji both the shogunal and the Meiji governments had pushed those "natural" borders outward, making incursions into Hokkaidō and claiming land from the non-Japanese residents. Similarly, the independent Ryukyu kingdom was dissolved in 1874, and the islands designated a Japanese prefecture, Okinawa, in 1879.)

Moreover, linguistically and culturally the people of Japan were *relatively* homogeneous. (The various dialects of the spoken language, for example, were not as diverse as those in China. And while there was a great deal of rigid social stratification, there was relatively little ethnic or cultural variation among different groups.) All of these elements made the transition to modern nationhood easier. But the new Meiji oligarchs faced the problem of creating a national *citizenry*—not bound by individual and family loyalty to a domain chieftain, who was himself bound by similar ties to the shogun, but rather a group of individuals all bound equally to the idea of Japan-as-nation by ties of nationalism/patriotism, and a sense of common identity and goals: Benedict Anderson's "imagined community." Many literary events contributed to this new concept of nationhood and citizenry, particularly the phenomenon of *translated and political novels in the mid-Meiji period. These helped to communicate Anglo-European notions of the nation-state to Japanese readers, and further helped to underscore the important potential interrelationship between literature, politics, and nationhood.

When the 1890 constitution was enacted, however, based on the Prussian and British models of constitutional monarchy, the old formation of hierarchically determined loyalties, operating simultaneously at national, local, and household levels, returned to dominance. The constitution and subsequent policy documents, such as the 1890 Imperial Rescript on Education, institutionalized the *kazoku kokka* (the family state), in which the emperor was figured as head of the national family, with absolute power and authority, and all his subjects were figured as his children. This structure was repeated at the level of the household (the *ie* system), in which the father had all authority and legal rights, and the wife/mother and children virtually none. (Male children, of course, would grow up to head their own families—either the main family if one were the eldest son, or a branch family if a younger son.) As colonies were added to the Japanese national empire—Taiwan in 1895 and Korea in 1910—the residents of those areas similarly became "children/subjects" of the emperor. Education in the Japanese language was imposed on the colonies (known as the *gaichi*, "external lands") as a way of inculcating in them a sense of commonality with the *naichi*, the Japanese main islands.

The new concepts of nationhood were explored and sometimes contested by writers. In particular those writers who had been sent abroad to study—such as *Mori Ōgai and *Natsume Sōseki—were inclined to create protagonists who struggled with the meaning of "Japaneseness" in an implicitly international context. Ōgai's "romantic trilogy" and Sōseki's essays on individualism and modernity emphasized the need for a strong stance of national literary pride vis-à-vis the already modernized Western nations (see, for example, Sōseki 1992).

Sōseki's policy of literary and cultural pride grew out of the miserable experiences he underwent while studying in Britain from 1900 to 1902. With a stipend barely sufficient for food and rent, he found his self-esteem sorely tested by the fact that he was studying English literature in its home country; he realized that English speakers would always consider his own insights second-rate. Even more difficult for Sōseki was his sense of racial inferiority:

> Everyone I see on the street is tall and good-looking. That, first of all, intimidates me, embarrasses me. Sometimes I see an unusually short man, but he is still two inches taller than I am, as I compare his height with mine as we pass each other. Then I see a dwarf coming, a man with an unpleasant complexion—and he happens to be my own reflection in the shop window. I don't know how many times I have laughed at my own ugly appearance right in front of myself. Sometimes, I even watched my reflection that laughed as I laughed. And every time that happened, I was impressed by the appropriateness of the term "yellow race" (quoted in Miyoshi 1974:56–57).

This reaction is hardly surprising when we consider that the new nineteenth-century sciences of evolution and physical anthropology taught that white Europeans were innately superior to other races. Sōseki, like other intellectual men in the Meiji period, had to come to terms with the fact that even as Japan was making remarkable strides toward modernity, it had already been allocated an inferior slot in the hierarchy of modern nations, based on race.

One important event that crystallized the thinking of many writers and intellectuals about the nation was the *junshi* (following one's samurai lord in death) of General Nogi Maresuke on the night of the funeral of the Meiji emperor, September 13, 1912. Nogi left behind a will and two death poems, all underscoring his intention to commit *junshi* out of respect for the Meiji emperor. He made three ritual cuts on his stomach, and then severed his carotid artery by throwing himself on his sword—a traditional, honorable form of suicide for samurai. At the time when Nogi performed this feudalistic act, *junshi* had been outlawed for 149 years. (Nogi's wife, Shizuko, committed suicide at the same time, but left little indication of her motives; her suicide is not considered *junshi*. See Orbaugh 1996.)

Nogi's shocking act instigated intense (and continuing) debate about the nature of Japanese modernity (Orbaugh 1996:27 n. 12). After the thoroughgoing changes of the Meiji period, Nogi's *junshi* seemed to some a repudiation of all that Japan had become. For many others, however, it catalyzed a new discourse of return to "traditional" values and beliefs, rejecting the influences of the West. The reign name of the subsequent emperor, Taishō, means "the great rectification," suggesting the opinion of many people that the mad dash to take on Western trappings needed to be rethought.

Two of Japan's most influential early literary proponents of nation, Ōgai and Sōseki, were deeply shaken by Nogi's death. From that time on, Ōgai wrote only historical fiction, based on brave deeds and famous warriors from the premodern era. In terms of both style and subject matter he rejected the notions of modern individuality that had underpinned earlier discussions of the new Japanese imperial subject. Sōseki's response to the Nogis' suicides was the novel *Kokoro* (1914), which features a protagonist who embodies the contradictions of the Meiji male intellectual. In the end he "commits *junshi* to the Meiji era," hoping to atone for behavior he now sees as too much influenced by imported ideas of ego and self-fulfillment. The ideological reverse course symbolized by the Nogis' suicides had a similarly large impact throughout the Japanese literary world.

Japan's successive victories in the Sino-Japanese (1894–95) and Russo-Japanese (1904–5) wars culminated in its participation on the winning side of World War I, occupying and patrolling Germany's colonial possessions in China and the Pacific Islands in 1914–18. This led to an invitation to become one of the founding members of the League of Nations in 1920, an event that confirmed Japan's status as a modern nation among the other powerful modern nations of the world. When the Japanese representative suggested that the founding charter contain a statement of basic racial equality, however, the other member nations refused (Dower 204). The development of a rhetoric of a unique Japanese ethnic identity—the Yamato *minzoku*, racially similar but essentially superior to other East Asians—was at least partly in response to this continuing insistence on the validity of what we now call "scientific racism" on the part of the "white" nations of Europe and North America.

The increasing militarism of the 1930s, which eventually culminated in Japan's declaration of war against China in 1937, had a directly inhibiting effect on any writer who might choose to challenge the nationalist ideology of colonialism and imperialism. The murder of proletarian writer Kobayashi Takiji in 1933 was a warning to other leftist writers to censor themselves or risk the consequences. Throughout the 1930s many socialist writers committed *tenkō* (repudiating their political beliefs) after imprisonment that sometimes included torture.

Other, more committed, writers, such as *Miyamoto Yuriko and Hirabayashi Taiko, refused to commit *tenkō* and spent most of the war years languishing in prison.

While many writers had traveled abroad in the 1920s, and had returned to put their resulting impressions of Japan's place in the world into narrative (*Nagai Kafū, Hirabayashi Taiko), the writers who traveled abroad in the 1930s and 1940s often did so at the behest of the government, for the purpose of producing propagandistic pictures of life in the colonies. (See "Wartime Literature.") Until 1945 no writings critical of the government or war effort could be published. While some writers, such as *Kawabata Yasunari and Ozaki Shirō, supported government-sponsored, patriotic literary groups, others, such as Ishikawa Jun (see "Occupation Fiction"), went silent, waiting until the war had ended to publish their work. Still others were imprisoned for their refusal to cease writing fiction that was critical of the war.

The end of the war and the beginning of the Allied occupation of Japan saw an energetic debate around issues of nation and the proper role for the national subject. The noted political philosopher Maruyama Masao argued that one of the reasons Japan had become so militaristic had to do with a lack of understanding of the difference between *minzokushugi* (an ethnically based notion of nationalism) and *kokuminshugi* (a notion of nationalism emphasizing citizenship) (Koschmann 1996:204–205). Maruyama and others on the left—such as Miyamoto Yuriko, released from prison by the occupation government—debated the best way to carry out the "democratic revolution" that they promoted for postwar Japan. Writers from many political camps wrote just as energetically about the new possibilities for Japanese nationhood in the wake of the war's destruction. But the occupation period (1945–1952) was also a time of painful exploration in fiction of the meaning of "Japaneseness" in a context of utter defeat and unconditional surrender, when Japan was no longer a sovereign nation. (Although this situation only lasted seven years, for the people living under the occupation there was no way of knowing how long it would continue.)

One group of writers had a particularly complex reaction to the defeat and occupation: *zainichi-Chōsenjin* and *zainichi-Kankokujin* (resident Koreans). Although many well-to-do Korean families had sent their sons to Japan to study or for careers during the prewar period, many more resident Koreans had been coerced through economic or harsher means during wartime to come to Japan to support the war industry (Ienaga 1985:102–112). For those Koreans forced to learn Japanese under the colonizing policy of *naisen ittai* ("Japan-Korea one body"), and for those forced into dangerous work in mines and munitions factories, the Japanese language was understandably anathema. More than one million resident Koreans accepted the occupation government's offer of repatriation to Korea within a year after the defeat. Another 500,000, however, elected to remain in Japan. Many of these were men who had been educated in Japan, and for whom the Japanese language had become an ineradicable part of their identities. Writers such as Kim Darusu (Kim Tal-su) presented an alternative model of the meaning of nation and identity during the two decades following World War II. Unfortunately, this fiction is hardly known in Japan and is considered "collaborationist" by most Korean scholars, despite its frequent criticism of the Japanese government, simply because it is written in Japanese.

Those writers who came to literary maturity after the end of the occupation in the 1950s and 60s, such as *Mishima Yukio, *Abe Kōbō, and *Ōe Kenzaburō, continued this literary exploration of Japan's place in the new, postwar international community of nations. Although Mishima advocated a return to a romanticized valorization of the samurai code and "traditional" values (in, for example, his short novel *Patriotism* [Yūkoku], based on a failed right-wing coup in 1936, and strongly reminiscent of the Nogis' suicides), Ōe launched a trend toward ideologically complex and often agonized depictions of male characters' attempts to come to terms with their national identity. Ōe also wrote many works that explore in complex terms the meaning of the emperor system in a thoroughly modernized and secularized Japan.

The 1960s also saw the beginning of a boom in writing by Japanese expatriates (nearly all women), such as *Ōba Minako, whose Akutagawa Prize-winning debut story "The Three Crabs" (Sanbiki no kani) was set in the multicultural society of an Alaskan university town. Other expatriate women, such as Mori Yōko (1940–1993), married to an Englishman, and Kometani Fumiko (b. 1930), married to an American, have added their literary views of what it means to be Japanese when immersed in a foreign culture. An even younger member of this group, Tawada Yōko (b. 1960), publishes in both Japanese and German, one of the few Japanese expatriate writers to develop a literary reputation outside Japan.

After the economic successes of the 1970s and 1980s, many Japanese writers seemed to feel that questions of national identity and the individual's relationship to the state were beside the point. Nonetheless, even *Murakami Haruki, known for his postmodern, postnational settings and characters, has written novels that reflect back on the war and its continuing influence on Japanese people's sense of identity, among them *A Wild Sheep Chase* (Hitsuji o meguru bōken) and *The Wind-Up Bird Chronicle* (Nejimakidori kuronikuru). And new generations of resident Korean writers such as Li Kaisei, Yi Yangji, and Yu Mi-Li continue to provide a viewpoint on the Japanese nation that underscores its multiplicity and fragmentation.

—*Sharalyn Orbaugh*

Bibliography

Dower, John W. *War without Mercy: Race and Power in the Pacific War*. New York: Pantheon, 1986.

Ienaga Saburō. *Sensō sekinin* (War Responsibility). Tokyo: Iwanami, 1985.

Koschmann, J. Victor. *Revolution and Subjectivity in Postwar Japan.* Chicago: University of Chicago Press, 1996.

Miyoshi, Masao. *Accomplices of Silence: The Modern Japanese Novel.* Berkeley: University of California Press, 1974.

Murakami Haruki. *A Wild Sheep Chase.* Trans. Alfred Birnbaum. New York: Plume, 1989.

——. *The Wind-Up Bird Chronicle.* Trans. Jay Rubin. London: Harville Press, 1995.

Natsume Sōseki. *Kokoro.* Trans. Edwin McClellan. Washington, D.C.: Regnery Gateway, 1957.

——. "My Individualism." Trans. Jay Rubin. In *Kokoro: A Novel and Selected Essays.* Lanham, Md.: Madison Books, 1992.

Ōba Minako. "The Three Crabs." In Yukiko Tanaka and Elizabeth Hanson, eds., *This Kind of Woman: Ten Stories by Japanese Women Writers, 1960–1976,* 87–113. Stanford: Stanford University Press, 1982.

Orbaugh, Sharalyn. "General Nogi's Wife: Representations of Women in Narratives of Japanese Modernization." In Xiaobing Tang and Stephen Snyder, eds., *In Pursuit of Contemporary East Asian Culture,* 7–31. Boulder, Colo.: Westview Press, 1996.

6

GENDER, FAMILY, AND SEXUALITIES
IN MODERN LITERATURE

As we have seen, the new Anglo-European sciences of the nineteenth century cast Japan's inhabitants as inferior to those of the "white" nations of Europe and North America, according to the evolutionary model in which "Whites" were seen as most advanced, most civilized, "Orientals" were next, and "Blacks" were at the bottom of the hierarchy. This model organized gender hierarchically as well: men were more advanced, more intelligent, more rational, and just generally more civilized than were women. It is no surprise that these two domains should be conflated: in the hierarchy of nations, Japan was seen not only as inferior but also as "feminine" vis-à-vis the more "masculine," more civilized Anglo-European world. Recognizing this view, Japanese men in the Meiji period and beyond made various efforts to remasculinize themselves, both at home and in the eyes of the world. The heavy emphasis on developing military technique and strength and the drive to colonize Asian neighbors are likely related to this issue. The unusual situation of Japan's rush to modernity after 250 years of near complete isolation, and the sudden importation of Western ideas of what counted as modern in the domains of gender roles, family, and sexuality, no doubt exacerbated these problems.

One of the most striking features of the Meiji reinvention of Japan as a modern nation was the invocation of "the traditional Japanese family system" to provide a model for the imperial state. When the *kazoku kokka* (family nation), based on the *ie seido* (family or household system) was formally established in the 1890s through legislation, educational materials, and propaganda, the emperor was made the symbolic parent of the nation, and all his subjects were told to revere him as they would a "strict father or loving mother" (Ito 2000:495; see also Ueno 1996:214). The Confucian virtue of filial piety and loyalty was thus extended beyond the immediate family up to the highest representative of the nation—this was one of the most effective tools for uniting all the regions and classes of Japan into one "imagined community." The Meiji ideologues who created and enforced the idea of the *ie seido* represented it as Japan's traditional family system, but in fact it was a modern construct. Although it was based loosely on some aspects of the family structure of the premodern samurai class (which had comprised no more than 10 percent of the population), it had never before existed as a rigid system, and it was extended in the Meiji period for the first time to people of all classes. The model of nation therefore was to be reflected in miniature in every household, with the male head of family in a position analogous to "emperor."

The *ie* stands for "the household," imagined not as a collective unit made up of specific people but as a diachronic unit based on lineage and transcending the identity of individual members, conceived primarily as the organizational building block of the nation. Within the household the husband/father held all power; his dependents were expected to defer to him and were in fact legally compelled to do so. Inheritance of the household property was strictly patrilineal: household property went to the eldest son. If the family had daughters but no sons, a man would be legally adopted into the family as husband (known as *muko yōshi*) to the eldest daughter, taking the family surname and becoming heir to the property and family headship. If the household head had no children at all he would adopt the son of a relative—often a nephew, or even his own younger brother—to become his "son" and heir. In this way the family bloodline was preserved (through the daughter in the first case, or through blood kin in the second), but, more important, the absolute rule of passing family headship from father to son was protected (Lebra 1993:129). Younger sons who established households of their own were branch families to the main family line, and owed allegiance to the main household.

In 1871 the *koseki* (household registry) system had been established, in which every individual's family affiliation was registered with the government. When a (legitimate) child was born, or a bride or an adoptive husband brought in, the family duly registered the newcomer in its *koseki* as a member of the *ie*. Although the Meiji Civil Code outlawed the taking of concubines, many men (including the Emperor Meiji) continued the practice of keeping more than one "wife," sometimes maintaining multiple residences (Lebra 1993:216). Only one of these women could be entered in the *koseki*, however. Children of concubines, or other illegitimate children, were entered in the mother's family register unless the father volunteered to bring them into his own (making them eligible to inherit, among other things). One reason given for keeping multiple "wives" was to ensure the birth of at least one male heir who would live to adulthood—something that could not be taken for granted in the nineteenth century—to continue the household lineage.

The new Meiji family-nation was marked by rigidly differentiated gender roles and a reinscription of the strict class hierarchy that early Meiji reforms had sought to dismantle. As Ken Ito explains (paraphrasing Kawashima), "an *ie* is sustained by a consciousness that includes a powerful respect for the continuity of the male line and an attendant devaluing of women in general and non-reproductive women in particular, ... the privileging of the *ie* over the individual, and the ranking of people outside the family according to the status of the *ie* to which they belong" (2000:493).

In this system women functioned as little more than items of exchange between families, place markers, or "borrowed wombs" (*karibara*) for the production of sons (Lebra 1993:224–225). Despite a competing Meiji ideology of romantic love and the nuclear family, marriage for many women before World War II, especially among the upper classes and peerage, was a matter utterly decided and controlled by others. Just as two Japanese women from noble households were given—without their consent, but also evidently without overt resistance—in arranged marriages to Prince Yong of Korea and the puppet emperor of Manchuguo, Pu-yi, to cement the alliance between Japan and its colonies, many prewar women found themselves in marriages whose primary purpose was to establish or solidify the alliance between households with common business or other interests. Even when such marriages were stable or resulted in mutual affection, the woman's position in the new household was tenuous.

In Tokutomi Roka's 1900 best-selling novel *The Nightingale* (Hototogisu), the gentle and beautiful protagonist, Namiko, beloved wife of Takeo, is "divorced" by Takeo's mother, who acts as head of the family in his absence at war, because Namiko has contracted tuberculosis and therefore will not be able to bear children to keep the family line going. That Namiko should have no say in the matter and can be summarily returned to her family, and that even Takeo, who loves her, quietly accepts his mother's decision, says a great deal about the power of the *ie* system. Although readers may have disliked the mother-in-law and sympathized with the unfortunate Namiko, they clearly understood why Takeo made no real fuss: the continuation of the *ie* was paramount (Ito 2000:526).

The Nightingale ends with a trope commonly found in Meiji and Taishō-period novels: the establishment between two men of a fictive father-son bond that transcends (or, in many cases, is predicated on) the death of the woman who originally bound them. After Namiko's death, Takeo (whose real father is dead) bonds with Namiko's father, an army general, and the two go off together talking of their military experiences. Similar examples of homosocial bonding, often including the active exclusion of females from the establishment of symbolic lineages, are ubiquitous in the male-authored fiction of the prewar period, with *Mori Ōgai, *Shimazaki Tōson, and *Natsume Sōseki (especially in *Kokoro*, 1914) providing prime examples (Orbaugh 1996:16–17).

This male-male lineage formation, excluding women, was not merely a matter of literature. Anthropologist Takie Lebra reports several cases of families who, having adopted a husband for their daughter, then divorced her and sent her away when the couple could not get along. In at least one case the parents brought in a concubine for the adopted son-in-law instead. Such seemingly illogical behavior underscores the importance of *maleness* in the maintenance of the *ie*, even when at the expense of the bloodline: "successional continuity was more important than natural kinship ... a bright adopted son was more valuable than a blood daughter" (Lebra 1993:216–217).

It is clear, however, that the patrilineal emphasis of the *ie* system engendered anxiety among men, too, which was then expressed in literature. The nervousness expressed by *Shiga Naoya's protagonist in *A Dark Night's Passing* (An'ya kōrō) over the identity of his father—Is he a legitimate son or not? Will he be properly acknowledged by his father?—is echoed in fiction by many prewar writers, including Sōseki in *Grass on the Wayside* (Michikusa).

Despite the apparent hegemony of *ie* system discourse until World War II, the Meiji period saw the birth of a competing notion of family that was also highly influential: the *katei* (the home) (Ito 2000:496–506). In contrast to the "traditional" *ie* system, the *katei* was presented by its advocates as a modern idea, inspired by the Christian ideology of monogamy and the Western ideal of romantic love more generally. The *katei* was envisioned as the Japanese version of the modern nuclear family, centered on a romantically bonded married couple and their offspring; the parents of the husband, even if he were the eldest son, had no place in this schema, in strict contrast to the multigenerational *ie* household.

Ironically, the new idea of the "couple" was promoted through woodblock prints of the emperor and empress, clothed in Western dress, appearing together at public events. In reality the emperor rarely allowed the empress to accompany him; she attended on a subsequent day. These early "photo ops" were explicitly constructed (Meech-Pekarik 1986:114). The emperor was elevated to the position of "father of the nation" in the *ie* system, but used the ideal of the *katei* as well to promote the idea of the Meiji imperium as modern.

Many men and women, however, took the idea of the *katei* more seriously. Iwamoto Yoshiharu, for example, who in 1885 inaugurated the first journal intended for the edification of women, *Women's Education Journal* (Jogaku zasshi), was a proponent of the *katei*. In this view the home was figured not in terms of a "household" persisting across generations, but as a synchronic group of people united by ties of affection. The husband/father could look to the home as a comfortable refuge from the rigors of public life, and for the children the home was a place to be nurtured and educated in the ways of society. This model, while in many ways more progressive than the *ie* system, was equally rigid in terms of the strict division of gender roles. The husband was to act in the public world, and the wife was to be the quintessential Victorian "angel in the

house," creating the warm and nurturing atmosphere that defined the
katei/home. This female role was epitomized in government propaganda by the
slogan *ryōsai kenbo*, "good wife, wise mother." Because women were prohibited
by the 1890 constitution and subsequent legislation (the Shūkai oyobi kessha hō
[Law Governing Associations and Meetings] of 1890 and the Chian keisatsu hō
[Police Security Law] of 1900) from any role in politics, the "good wife, wise
mother" ideal was promoted as the way women could serve the modernizing
nation (Nolte and Hastings 1991:154–155). The *ie* system and the notion of the
katei worked together to keep women's roles limited to the home and family.

For many women of the lower classes, however, the ideals of the *katei* were
only a distant dream, and work outside the home a necessity. As Japanese industry rapidly modernized, a mostly female workforce emerged to fill the new
factory positions. Sharon Nolte and Sally Ann Hastings report that "female
workers outnumbered males in light industry, especially in textiles, where a
work force that was 60 to 90 percent female produced 40 percent of the gross national product and 60 percent of the foreign exchange during the late nineteenth century" (1991:153). In the early years of the textile industry, young unmarried women were recruited from the urban poor and residents of nearby
areas, but after 1890, as the need for factory workers grew, young women were
recruited to the city from rural areas, sending money home to help support their
families (Molony 220). Although conditions in the factories were often substan-
dard and injurious to health, they provided a means for women to find employment in a labor market that was otherwise mostly closed to them throughout the
prewar period.

Even more unfortunate women continued to be sold to brothels either in
Japan or, as Japan's colonial holdings expanded, overseas: the *karayuki-san*.
When the Meiji government became aware that Western nations considered all
forms of prostitution immoral, it issued in 1872 the "Proclamation for the
Emancipation of Geisha and Prostitutes" (Dalby 1985:63). This proclamation
did succeed in abolishing the debts owed by geisha and prostitutes to brothel
owners, and made the management of prostitution and other entertainments of
the "water trade" the responsibility of the cities; except for these minor changes,
the trade continued (and continues) to flourish. As in earlier eras, there were
many levels of prostitutes, from the artistically skilled geisha and highest-level
courtesans to the various lower ranks of women for sale.

The figure of the geisha or prostitute has been common in Japanese literature from the Meiji period to the present day. *Higuchi Ichiyō wrote feelingly
of the women in the licensed quarters in modernizing Japan, showing that such
women and the lower-class men who worked in the quarter were deriving few
benefits from the great changes taking place in the nation. Toward the end of
Meiji and increasingly in the Taishō period, geisha and the women of the quarter came to be figured, especially by male writers, as representatives of the freedom and gaiety of the Edo period, seen as a happier time: "The 1890s were a

decade of popularity and prosperity for the geisha. Novelists like Ozaki Kōyo and Izumi Kyōka wrote stories that fixed geisha in the public mind as daring romantic heroines. Already nostalgia for the Edo period, so recently left behind, had begun to spread, and geisha, women of 'true Japanese spirit,' basked in public adulation. Some geisha became stars whose portraits were collected by adoring fans. Adolescents mooned over these beauties as, in another generation, they would idolize movie actresses. In 1898, there were close to twenty-five thousand geisha in Japan" (Dalby 1985:69).

Geisha continued to be fashion icons until the 1920s and 1930s, when Western dress became so normal a part of women's presentation that geisha were faced with the choice of making the switch to dresses and ceasing to be innovators, or retaining their kimono and Japanese hairstyles, and becoming symbolic of a more traditional life. They chose the latter, and since that time the literary depiction of geisha by male writers has been even more steeped in nostalgia for a "traditional Japanese womanhood" that no longer existed. *Nagai Kafū is well known for his depictions of geisha, as well as lower-level prostitutes working in the old-fashioned parts of the city. Prewar women writers, too—such as Okamoto Kanoko and *Hayashi Fumiko—frequently used the figure of the geisha or prostitute in their fiction, but tended to focus on the psychology and inner lives of the women rather than their symbolic value.

It comes as no surprise that much of the fiction by women in the prewar period was in explicit response to the gender and family structures imposed in the modern period. (See "Meiji Women Writers" and "*Seitō* and the Resurgence of Writing by Women.") It was not until the late 1920s, with the emergence of leftist writers such as *Miyamoto Yuriko, Hayashi Fumiko, and Hirabayashi Taiko, that women began to explore broader topics (and even these writers produced fiction indicting the family system). But by the Taishō period there had been some progress made in women's rights, despite the continuing prohibition on women's involvement in politics. The 1920s were a time of increasing democracy in Japan, as some of the strictures of the 1890 constitution were relaxed. Women had more access to birth control (illegal in the Meiji period), and the Taishō emperor was the first to have a monogamous marriage (if not entirely voluntarily; see Lebra 1993:226). A vigorous socialist and proletarian movement advocated equality between the sexes. Increasing numbers of women went to university, or at least through secondary school, swelling the number of potential writers and readers. And in the 1920s a number of magazines and journals were launched specifically to cater to these new women readers, providing more venues for women writers to be published.

It is ironic that all this progress resulted in the construction of a special category for women's writing, which has caused it to be marginalized from the 1920s to the present day. The term *joryū bungaku* (women's literature) has been applied to any work produced by someone known to be female, despite the huge diversity of such writing. Joan Ericson suggests that this bracketing off of women's literature into a separate sphere was part of a reactionary backlash against the strides toward gender equality (seen by some as gender ambiguity) made during the Taishō period (1997:23–25). Men's writing was thereafter considered *bungaku* (literature), and women's was marked as separate, and implicitly inferior. To this day most bookstores in Japan continue to shelve works by female authors in a category separate from *bungaku*, which is exclusively male.

Starting from around 1900 and increasing into the 1920s, the concepts of "childhood" and "adolescence" gained an important place in Japanese culture. Accordingly, a number of popular culture forms aimed at children—or, rather, at girls and boys separately—were developed and marketed during this period. Journals such as *Girls' Illustrated* (Shōjo gahō) and *Boys' Club* (Shōnen kurabu) supplemented public education in inculcating social lessons in entertaining ways, using stories, comics, and lavish illustrations.

The writer Yoshiya Nobuko was one of the earliest and most famous producers of *shōjo* (girls') fiction. Yoshiya was a publicly declared lesbian, and her stories feature relationships that were explicitly homosocial and implicitly homosexual, set in dreamy, romantic contexts. (This liberality of imagination regarding gender and sexuality continued as one of the hallmarks of popular culture forms for girls, even to the present day.) In contrast, boys were expected to be preparing for their eventual leadership roles in society. Therefore *shōnen* (boys') stories and comics tended in the prewar period to emphasize heroism, practicality, and adventure.

A fictional genre called *ero-guro nansensu* (erotic grotesque nonsense) also developed out of the social conditions of the 1920s and early 1930s. This was primarily a male genre that took elements from early science fiction, mystery, fantasy, and the erotic tales of the Edo period to fashion a dense and rather dark, but very popular, stream of fiction. Its proponents included Edogawa Ranpo (1894–1965; the pseudonym of Hirai Tarō, after Edgar Allan Poe), and Yumeno Kyūsaku (1889–1936). Sexual violence, perversion, and gender ambivalence were among the frequent themes of this genre.

POSTWAR GENDER AND FAMILY

The end of World War II brought enormous changes to the juridical and social structures that defined the family and gender roles. In the new constitution of 1947, imposed by the occupation government, women were given full legal rights for the first time. They were allowed to vote and to run for office. The *ie* system was quietly dismantled, although it remains influential to the present time.

For men, however, the occupation was psychologically difficult. Once again Japanese men were explicitly feminized by the Western powers; masculinity was now epitomized by General Douglas MacArthur—large, white, and English-speaking. The emperor was required to renounce his divinity and show himself out among the people. This loss of the symbolic father also contributed to the sense of loss of masculinity, explored by many male writers in *occupation fiction and thereafter.

For many women writers in the 1950s and 1960s, the residual effects of the *ie* system and the rigidly restricted roles for women remained an important literary theme. Two of *Enchi Fumiko's most famous and brilliant novels, *The Waiting Years* (Onnazaka) and *Masks* (Onnamen), were direct attacks on the slow but devastating effects on women of marriage and patrilineal culture, even when those marriages were superficially successful.

In fact, much of the writing of the 1960s engaged questions of the meaning of the family, including work by male authors Shimao Toshio, Yasuoka Shōtarō, and *Ōe Kenzaburō. These men and their cohort wrote realist, often agonized, and sometimes darkly humorous explorations of the new structures and roles within the postwar family. The women writing about family in this era—such as Kōno Taeko, Kurahashi Yumiko, and *Ōba Minako—often eschewed strict realism for more fantastic styles, and used themes of violence and aberrant sexuality to deconstruct prewar notions of family and gender. (See "Women Writers of the 1960s and 1970s.")

Writers of the 1970s and beyond, such as *Yoshimoto Banana, *Murakami Haruki, and *Shimizu Yoshinori, enshrined the postmodern "family"—usually made up of ragtag groups of troubled people, unrelated by blood or upbringing, who forge new kinds of familial bonds appropriate to the fragmented world of the 1980s and 1990s.

As we have seen, various kinds of sexualities and sexual behaviors were thematized in Japanese fiction from the beginning of the modern period: prostitution (Higuchi Ichiyō, Izumi Kyōka, Nagai Kafū, Hayashi Fumiko, *Kawabata Yasunari, Okamoto Kanoko); lesbianism (Yoshiya Nobuko, Miyamoto Yuriko, Tanizaki Jun'ichirō); male homosexuality (Inagaki Taruho); androgyny or hermaphroditism (Edogawa Ranpo, Yumeno Kyūsaku); and so on. Despite intermittent bouts of government censorship aimed at "pornographic" materials, the range of sexualities and sexual behaviors depicted in the prewar period is quite broad.

Postwar fiction depicted similar behaviors, with *Mishima Yukio, Mori Mari, and Tomioka Taeko (see "Women Writers of the 1960s and 1970s") writing about gay males; Matsuura Rieko, Murakami Haruki, and others writing about lesbians; and writers such as *Murakami Ryū featuring bisexual characters. In addition, a new focus on deviant or transgressive sex in the deconstruction of the family system in the postwar period led to the production of many stories and novels about incest, by Kurahashi Yumiko, *Kanai Mieko, Mori Mari, and Uchida Shungiku. Similarly, sadomasochism is a dominant theme of Kōno Taeko's work and of that of Murakami Ryū. Murakami also features interracial sex, especially with African Americans, as does *Yamada Eimi. And finally, issues of androgyny, hermaphroditism, or transsexuality are explored by Yoshimoto Banana, Kanai Mieko, and Hirano Keîchirō.

Perhaps because of the rigidity of the family and gender systems institution-alized during Japan's rapid modernization in the Meiji period, issues of gender, sex, and sexuality have been explored to what may be an unusual extent over the short hundred years of modern Japanese literature, providing a rich and complex picture of human interaction.

—Sharalyn Orbaugh

Bibliography

Dalby, Liza. *Geisha.* New York: Random House, 1985.

Enchi Fumiko. *Masks.* Trans. Juliet Winters Carpenter. New York: Alfred A. Knopf, 1983; Tokyo: Tuttle, 1984.

——. *The Waiting Years.* Trans. John Bester. Tokyo: Kodansha International, 1971.

Ericson, Joan E. *Be a Woman: Hayashi Fumiko and Modern Japanese Women's Literature.* Honolulu: University of Hawai'i Press, 1997.

Ito, Ken K. "The Family and the Nation in Tokutomi Roka's *Hototogisu.*" *Harvard Journal of Asiatic Studies* 60, no. 2 (2000): 489–536.

Kawashima Takeyoshi. *Ideorogî toshite no kazoku seido* (The Family System As Ideology). Tokyo: Iwanami, 1957.

Lebra, Takie Sugiyama. *Above the Clouds: Status Culture of the Modern Japanese Nobility.* Berkeley: University of California Press, 1993.

Meech-Pekarik, Julia. *The World of the Meiji Print: Impressions of a New Civilization.* New York: Weatherhill, 1986.

Molony, Barbara. "Activism among Women in the Taishō Cotton Textile Industry." In Gail Lee Bernstein, ed., *Recreating Japanese Women, 1600–1945,* 217–238. Berkeley: University of California Press, 1991.

Natsume Sōseki. *Grass on the Wayside.* Trans. Edwin McClellan. Chicago: University of Chicago Press, 1969.

——. *Kokoro.* Trans. Edwin McClellan. Washington, D.C.: Regnery Gateway, 1957.

Nolte, Sharon, and Sally Ann Hastings. "The Meiji State's Policy toward Women, 1890–1910." In Gail Lee Bernstein, ed., *Recreating Japanese Women, 1600–1945,* 151–174. Berkeley: University of California Press, 1991.

Orbaugh, Sharalyn. "General Nogi's Wife: Representations of Women in Narratives of Japanese Modernization." In Xiaobing Tang and Stephen Snyder, eds., *In Pursuit of Contemporary East Asian Culture,* 7–31. Boulder, Colo.: Westview Press, 1996.

Shiga Naoya. *A Dark Night's Passing.* Trans. Edwin McClellan. Tokyo: Kodansha International, 1976.

Tokutomi Roka. *Hototogisu* (The Nightingale). In *Kitamura Tōkoku/Tokutomi Roka shū* (Collected Works of Kitamura Tōkoku and Tokutomi Roka), 9:224–418. Tokyo: Kadokawa shoten, 1972.

Ueno Chizuko. "Modern Patriarchy and the Formation of the Japanese Nation State." In Donald Denoon et al., eds., *Multicultural Japan: Paleolithic to Postmodern,* 213–223. Cambridge: Cambridge University Press, 1996.

7

THE SOCIAL ORGANIZATION
OF MODERN JAPANESE LITERATURE

The "miracle" of Meiji Japan (1868–1912), epitomized by the slogan *"wakon yōsai"* (Japanese spirit, Western know-how), entailed the dismantling of the shogunal establishment and the aggressive pursuit of modernization based on Western models and techniques, with a strong chauvinist component. The old, stable social order was now in turmoil; achievement and ambition were the new watchwords, and acquiring a Western-style education was the sine qua non of success in a competitive social arena.

Tokyo was the political and commercial hub of the new nation and the seat of higher learning and cultural production. Young people in search of an education, a career, or mere adventure flocked to Tokyo. Achieving the ambitious goals of the Meiji enlightenment required a massive infusion of information from the West. English language study became de rigueur, and the translation of key texts was given a high priority. For Tokyo's "literary youth" who aspired to a writing career, the translation of increasingly popular Western literature served as an important apprenticeship.

As in so many aspects of Japanese life, a writer's credentials—in particular, one's academic pedigree—made a crucial difference. Much literary activity centered on the nation's elite universities—Tokyo Imperial University, Waseda, and Keiō. Each would serve as "headquarters" of a major literary faction, which published its own literary journal. And each competed for status in an emerging Tokyo-based literary establishment, the so-called *bundan*.

Many aspiring writers emerged from the ranks of Tokyo academe. The city served as the nation's literary hub, which meant that many writers would have to sever ties to family and friends in the provinces. Beginning in the 1880s, a network of Tokyo-based literary coteries developed, each promoting a certain style or stance, and each publishing a periodical that featured the work of its members. According to the eminent critic Itō Sei (1905–1969), the Meiji *bundan* served as an institutional refuge from poverty, obscurity, and uncertainty and as a source of identity and fellowship.

Another important area of *bundan* activity involved the proliferation of clubs and societies, which became an important venue for networking and socialization. For instance, there was the *Mokuyōkai*–the "Thursday Club" established by *Natsume Sōseki as a weekly "bull session" for his protégés and anyone else who cared to join in. Other groupings, such as the Ibusenkai—the "Ibsen Society"—were oriented around a more specific literary agenda.

LITERARY JOURNALISM AND THE *BUNDAN*

In a sense, then, Meiji writers constituted a marginal subculture, a loose assemblage of idealists, nonconformists, and hangers-on who stood outside the mainstream. But they were nonetheless subject to large forces that were transforming Japanese society. In particular, the rise of modern journalism would come to affect all aspects of Japanese literary production. Small coterie journals, reaching a handful of loyal readers, would come and go. But the growth of mass-circulation newspapers such as the *Asahi shinbun* and *Yomiuri shinbun* opened up a path for career advancement by introducing creative writing and literary criticism into the daily diet of an expanding national readership.

By the early twentieth century, modern literary study, and with it the very notion of "Japanese literature" itself, became established. In due course, a canon of "great works" and "major writers" emerged, and literary folk came to be identified with their respective *bundan* coterie, which would become a fixed label. At the same time, writers across the *bundan* spectrum began establishing relationships with important literary editors and publishers. Indeed, some of the most influential *bundan* figures were writers who held key editorships and dispensed patronage to newcomers requiring an imprimatur in order to get into print.

Among the early leaders of the *bundan* was *Tsubouchi Shōyō, a noted writer and critic who in 1887 assumed the editorship of the *Yomiuri* newspaper. His editorial role was taken over by Ozaki Kōyō, who in the 1890s reigned as a sort of *bundan* godfather. As head of the *Ken'yūsha (Society of the Inkstone), the dominant coterie in the 1890s, Kōyō oversaw a veritable workshop of literary protégés. His influence was so pervasive, and the trademark sentimental fiction of his Ken'yūsha scriveners so widespread, that Kōyō's premature death in 1903 was spoken of by critics as having freed the *bundan* from a form of institutional tyranny.

Class and family origins played a key role in the sociology of modern Japanese literature and its assorted movements. The dominant late-Meiji movement, *shizenshugi* (naturalism), which promoted a literature of artless confessionalism, drew its adherents largely from the middle and lower ranks of provincial society. Having experienced privation and alienation as struggling writers in the big city, naturalist writers such as Tayama Katai (1872–1930) and *Shimazaki Tōson essentially capitalized on notions of urban angst and ineffectuality by making it the subject of their writing. On the other hand, the Shirakabaha (White Birch Group) drew from the ranks of the social elite. Centering on *Shiga Naoya, Mushanokōji Saneatsu (1885–1976), and Arishima Takeo (1878–1923), this group promoted a broadly humanistic literature that sought to downplay the naturalist preoccupation with tedious accounts of domestic discord, money problems, and sexual repression.

A number of writers expressed open contempt for the petty factionalism and journalistic commercialism of the *bundan*. Not surprisingly, their number included some who were independently wealthy and others—for instance, the eminent author *Mori Ōgai, a ranking official in the military bureaucracy—who could afford to remain aloof from the rough and tumble of *bundan* life. It bears noting that the hierarchical nature of the *bundan*, and the invisibility of all but its most prominent figures, closely parallels the situation of the "common writer" in Victorian London. In both cases, an army of literary hacks worked in the trenches as proofreaders, reporters, and piece-rate scribblers.

THE EARLY TWENTIETH CENTURY

With the spread of the national dailies and the emergence of large publishing houses—most notably Hakubunkan and Shun'yōdō—beginning in the 1890s, Japan's print media gradually standardized literary publishing and mobilized writers as a professional guild, subject to the rules of the marketplace. By the turn of the century, the major publishers had embarked upon the mass marketing of literature in the form of monthly periodicals that enjoyed a wide circulation and an expanded readership that targeted women and young people.

With the late Meiji, the major dailies had literary editors and staff writers, and they featured *shinbun shōsetsu*—novels that appeared in daily serialization, reaching a vast audience. In effect, literature became a national pastime. And as with much Victorian fiction, it was standard practice for Japanese novels to be serialized before book publication. Hence, writers were obliged to work within the limits of the serial installment—the fixed number of columns of print that would appear every day.

A turning point in the social history of modern Japanese literature was the hiring, in 1907, of Natsume Sōseki as staff fiction writer for the *Asahi* newspaper. The fact that such a prominent writer and intellectual would relinquish a prestigious lectureship at the Imperial University to write novels for newspaper readers did much to popularize fiction writing, while at the same time serving to elevate the rather marginal status of writers.

By the end of the Meiji, literary modernism had taken hold in the *bundan*. The subsequent period—the Taishō—witnessed the dramatic rise of popular culture and mass media. And in due course, the Taishō *bundan* became marked by a split between writers of so-called *junbungaku* (pure literature), who disdained the rising tide of *taishū bungaku* (mass-oriented literature), and writers who catered to the marketplace.

By this time, the mainstream literary journals had developed standardized formats and practices. Serialization was the rule for longer works. There was a set pattern for contents and layout. Of special note is the prominence of the "writer feature"—personal accounts provided by the *bundan* elite. Literary editors would actively solicit such narratives, which would flesh out the several hundred pages of the numerous monthly journals. Name writers thus emerged as media celebrities of a sort, and they were obliged to respond to a rising demand for the intimate glimpse and the private revelation. Indeed, the autobiographical cast of so much Japanese literary writing owes a good deal to such journalistic underpinnings. A genre of *bundan* memoir and reminiscence—writers writing about writers, reflecting on their youth, musing on the passing scene—has continued to attract a large readership.

An easily overlooked aspect of Japanese literary life in the latter half of the nineteenth and early twentieth centuries—an inheritance, in a sense, of the authoritarian rule of the shoguns—concerns state censorship. As of the 1880s, a series of laws and regulations took aim at the media, with the express purpose of eliminating anything "injurious to public morals" (Rubin 1984). A censorial apparatus was put in place that systematically thwarted the emergence of strong social advocacy and protest on the part of the *bundan*, which remained in the shadow of the Japanese censors until Japan's surrender in August 1945. The curiously apolitical quality of much prewar literature reflects the passive stance of writers reluctant to challenge the authorities.

Yet whereas the early decades of the twentieth century witnessed little overtly political literature, the 1920s was a time of exuberant and politically radical literary experimentation. Riding a wave of economic prosperity in the wake of World War I, Japanese turned to entertainment and leisure as never before. In the literary realm, this translated into a dramatic expansion of the market for popular literature and cheap books. A burgeoning youth readership was being served by a host of periodicals, and writers such as Ogawa Mimei (1882–1961) and Miyazawa Kenji (1896–1933) dedicated themselves to fostering the new genre of *dōwa bungaku* (children's literature).

Together with other arenas of popular culture—Hollywood movies, radio, jazz clubs, baseball—literature increasingly took on the trappings of commercial entertainment. And writers who had heretofore struggled to make a living were now earning a comfortable living and enjoying a measure of social prestige. The key figure here is Kikuchi Kan (1888–1948), a "middlebrow" writer who turned to literary journalism. In 1923, the year of the great earthquake that leveled Tokyo, he founded *Spring and Autumn Literature* (Bungei shunjū), a mainstream literary magazine that achieved enormous popularity. Kikuchi would contribute greatly to the professionalization of Japanese writers. In 1935, he instituted Japan's first—and most prestigious—literary award, the Akutagawa Prize. This and other major awards—the Naoki Prize and Noma Prize, for instance—remain a tangible index of the manner in which literary success is recognized in modern Japan.

In the same sense that the profession of writing gradually took on respectability and a degree of financial security, the role of women in the *bundan*, which was negligible during much of the Meiji, began to expand during the Taishō. (See "Meiji Women Writers.") The appearance of *Seitō (Blue Stocking), Japan's first literary journal run entirely by women, was a landmark, and its firebrand editor, Hiratsuka Raichō, became a leader of the burgeoning feminist movement.

Cultural modernism and liberalism were the rage during the "democratic" 1920s in Japan, and a host of avant-garde movements flourished. What is more, the political radicalism that emerged in the wake of World War I began making inroads in Japan as well, and the notoriously fickle censors relented. The activity centered on young writers of the so-called proletarian literary movement, who banded together in their own *bundan*-like network of factions and wrote earnestly of the oppressed masses and the evils of capitalism. As with the naturalist school, which had engendered staunch opposition, the activism of the proletarian crowd, who cared little for decadent literary "art," inspired a backlash on the part of writers wanting to reaffirm an aesthetic basis for literature.

But with the 1930s, Japanese society came under the sway of a militarist regime that systematically eliminated left-wing activity and cultural progressivism as it prepared the nation for war. Politically subversive writing was banned, and members of the proletarian movement were purged. On pain of imprisonment and physical torture, most writers and intellectuals were successfully coerced into renouncing their leftist political stance and officially "converting" *(tenkō)* to the nationalist agenda. With Japan's entry into war with China in 1937, many writers were pressed into military service as correspondents and propagandists. All were expected at least nominally to demonstrate acquiescence with the prevailing order. What is more, given the paper shortages and the escalating wartime austerities, creative writing essentially ground to a halt. But writers such as *Nagai Kafū and *Tanizaki Jun'ichirō did indeed continue to write, awaiting such time as their work could see the light of day.

POSTWAR JAPAN

The end of World War II marked a transition of mind-numbing proportions for Japan. The empire was in ruin, its major cities leveled by relentless bombing, and its people were subject to widespread privation and dislocation. Yet the defeat meant the end of centuries of authoritarian rule and, thanks to the architects of the Allied occupation (1945–52), the establishment of a new order. For writers, who had effectively been silenced for a decade, the promulgation of an American-style constitution, which extended unprecedented freedoms and civil liberties to the Japanese people, signaled the end of the prewar literary establishment.

In short, literature was reborn, and writers and intellectuals were free to express themselves without fear of sanction or reprisal. They wrote of the war and of the postwar chaos. Marxism resurfaced, and those who had agreed to renounce their political beliefs through *tenkō* were dishonored. Individualism reigned. A group of dissolute, renegade writers known as the *buraiha* (wastrel) faction, centering on *Dazai Osamu and Sakaguchi Ango (1906–1955), expressed the aimlessness and "identity crisis" of a nation set adrift.

The postwar literary scene was thriving. Publishers were back in business, periodicals flourished, and cultural activity enjoyed a renaissance. But the old *bundan* network, rendered obsolete by the new economic and social order, fell apart by the 1950s. A writing career no longer required the old guildlike structures.

Japan's astounding economic recovery in the 1950s and 1960s corresponded with a golden age of literature, with Tanizaki, *Kawabata Yasunari, and the controversial *Mishima Yukio leading the way. These and other novelists acquired a reputation outside of Japan, thanks to the work of translators and scholars who had learned Japanese in connection with World War II. This new "international" profile for Japanese literature was part of a larger cultural redefinition from the postwar vantage point.

In the meantime, the nation began to enjoy the fruits of prosperity. A consumer culture took shape in the 1960s, with the mass media and popular culture as chief purveyors. The *shūkanshi* (weekly magazine) became a major venue for literary publishing. Aspiring writers angled for the prestigious literary awards, which would attract the publishers. In short, modern market forces were shaping literary careers.

In 1968, with the awarding of the Nobel Prize to Kawabata, Japanese literature may be said to have truly arrived on the world scene. Likewise, his death in 1972, which followed by two years the astounding ritual suicide of Mishima, signaled the end of Japanese literary traditionalism. By the 1970s Japan had emerged as a global economic power, and its increasingly affluent youth had only dim memories of the war and of cultural traditionalism. Pop culture was in the ascendant, with television leading the way. Bookstore sales were heaviest in the lightweight fare—the ubiquitous *manga* (comic books), the potboiler, the sci-fi novel. "Serious" authors, the "pure literature" types who remained indifferent to the rising tide of commercialism, continued to ply their wares, but theirs was a marginal endeavor. Perhaps the most salutary development of postwar literature in Japan has been the rising prominence of gifted women writers. (See "Women Writers of the 1960s and 1970s.")

THE CONTEMPORARY SCENE

Literature in contemporary Japan has come under the sway of forces that affect all developed nations: ever-expanding media conglomerates, the electronic media, the marketing of entertainment and amusement, and the changing nature of "literacy" itself. Statistically speaking, the Japanese rank among the world's most avid readers. But a large bulk of the nation's reading diet consists of comics, "lifestyle" magazines, and sporting news. A new generation of writers born in the postwar period—*Murakami Haruki, *Yamada Eimi, and *Yoshimoto Banana, among others—enjoy upscale careers and celebrity status very different from the world of the prewar *bundan*. The literary scene is an exciting place, and a number of minority voices—including a variety of foreigners and those from socially marginal groups—are being heard. The stature of Japan's "serious" literature was much enhanced in 1994, when *Ōe Kenzaburō became the nation's second Nobel laureate, but Ōe himself has expressed concern over the fate of such literature.

—*Marvin Marcus*

Bibliography

Fowler, Edward. *The Rhetoric of Confession: Shishōsetsu in Early Twentieth-Century Japanese Fiction*. Berkeley: University of California Press, 1988.

Keene, Donald. *Dawn to the West: Japanese Literature in the Modern Era*. 2 vols. New York: Holt, Rinehart and Winston, 1984.

Marcus, Marvin. "The Writer Speaks: Late-Meiji Reflections on Literature and Life." In Thomas Hare, Robert Borgen, and Sharalyn Orbaugh, eds., *The Distant Isle*, 231–279. Ann Arbor: University of Michigan Press, 1996.

Powell, Irena. *Writers and Society in Modern Japan*. Tokyo: Kodansha International, 1983.

Rubin, Jay. *Injurious to Public Morals: Writers and the Meiji State*. Seattle: University of Washington Press, 1984.

Tayama Katai. *Literary Life in Tokyo, 1885–1915*. Trans. Kenneth G. Henshall. Leiden: Brill, 1987.

Authors, Works, Schools

8

TRANSLATED AND POLITICAL NOVELS
OF THE MEIJI PERIOD

Scholars often forget the existence of numerous works that dominated the literary scene in the first two decades of the Meiji period. The usual historical narrative emphasizes *Tsubouchi Shōyō's influential essay *The Essence of the Novel* (Shōsetsu shinzui, 1885–86), allegedly marking the beginning of modern Japanese literature, all the while devaluing the vast majority of texts that preceded it. The translated and political novels of Meiji have remained in the periphery of literary history for this reason.

Translations of Western works were abundant in the early years of Meiji. Works of political philosophy were considered the top priority, but a number of literary works were imported and translated by the second decade of Meiji. In 1878, a translation of Jules Verne's *Around the World in Eighty Days* (1873) was published. Among the first literary works to be translated, this novel satisfied people's curiosity about unknown lands, knowledge of which was fostered by nonfiction such as Fukuzawa Yukichi's *Conditions of the West* (Seiyō jijō, 1866).

Translated texts of Western fiction in the early-Meiji period were often in close dialogue with the political trends of the time. For example, Benjamin Disraeli's *Coningsby*, published as *Bush Warblers in Spring* (Shun'ōden) in 1884, had a large impact upon the literary and political spheres of the time. Alexandre Dumas's works, such as *Six Years Later, or Taking the Bastille* and *The Memoirs of a Physician*, both of which are based on the French Revolution, were also translated in the second decade of Meiji. Shakespeare's *Julius Caesar* was translated by Shōyō in 1884. A number of works by Victor Hugo were also in circulation, especially after Itagaki Taisuke's (1836–1919) famous meeting with the writer during his trip to France in 1882. A well-known advocate of the Freedom and People's Rights Movement, Itagaki questioned Hugo about effective ways to spread political awareness among the "uncivilized" people of Japan. In answer, Hugo told Itagaki to have them read novels such as his own.

None of these works, however, had as strong an impact on the Japanese literary scene as Oda Jun'ichirō's (1851–1919) *Romantic Stories of Blossoms* (Karyū shunwa), an abridged translation of Edward Bulwer-Lytton's *Ernest Maltravers* and its sequel *Alice*. Written in a highly sinified language, *Romantic Stories of Blossoms* was published in 1879 and was characterized in the preface as "the representative European love story." The story revolves around the personal development of Maltravers, who in the end gains professional and romantic success. The representation of such a success story—inextricably connected with the consummation of love—attracted students who dreamed of *risshin shusse* (achievement and advancement) in the modernizing world.

The main incentive behind the translation of these works was the intellectuals' engagement with the political sphere; it is no coincidence that many of the works selected were written by political figures such as Disraeli and Bulwer-Lytton. It is not until the 1890s that we see the appearance of translations of texts we now categorize as nineteenth-century realist fiction, works that allegedly had tremendous influence on modern Japanese literature. We find an increasing number of works by French writers, such as Gustave Flaubert and Émile Zola, and those of Russian writers, such as Leo Tolstoy and Fyodor Dostoyevsky, in the later years of the Meiji.

Early works of translation clearly engaged with the emergence of *seiji shōsetsu* or "political novels" in Meiji Japan. *Romantic Stories of Blossoms* is arguably the origin of political novels that enjoyed great popularity among the intellectuals of the time. Written by advocates of the Freedom and People's Rights Movement, they thematize the political issues at hand, such as the founding of the parliament, establishment of political parties, and foreign relations. Political novels were later criticized by Tokutomi Sohō (1863–1957), a famous social critic and the chief editor of *Citizens' Friend* (Kokumin no tomo), a major literary journal that began circulation in 1887. In his essay "On the Recently Popular Political Novels" (Kinrai ryūkō no seiji shōsetsu o hyōsu) he criticizes political novels for being too "convenient," highlighting the fact that they typically feature a wealthy, beautiful woman who supports her activist lover both mentally and financially. As he rightly points out, political novels typically end with the male activists' success in politics and in love, a formula clearly drawn from *Romantic Stories of Blossoms*.

The literary movement closely followed the political climate. An 1880 work that is usually regarded as the first Meiji political novel, Toda Kindō's (1850–1890) *Storms in the Sea of Passions: Tales of People's Rights* (Minken engi—jōkai haran) is an allegorical novel that thematizes the founding of the parliament, the raison d'être of the Freedom and People's Rights movement. Yano Ryūkei's (1850–1931) *Inspiring Instances of Statesmanship* (Keikoku bidan, 1883) features issues surrounding the establishment of political parties. The subject of *jōyaku kaisei* (the renegotiations of unequal treaties) is taken up in Tōkai Sanshi's (1852–1922) *Chance Meetings with Beautiful Women* (Kajin no kigū, 1885–97), the most popular of all the political novels; its twelve-year serialization is evidence of its bestseller status.

Suehiro Tetchō's (1849–1896) *Plum Blossom in Snow* (Setchūbai, 1886) and its sequel *Song Thrushes among the Flowers* (Kakan'ō, 1887–89) must also be mentioned. Unlike *Inspiring Instances of Statesmanship* and *Chance Meetings with Beautiful Women* that set the story in foreign lands, *Plum Blossom in Snow* and *Song Thrushes among the Flowers* are based in Japan, featuring the contemporary lives of the political activists of the nation.

Although political novels continued to be written long after the publication of Tsubouchi Shōyō's *The Essence of the Novel*, the historical narrative turns away from them and begins to focus on "less politically engaged" works that were "influenced" by nineteenth-century realist fiction, suggesting that these constitute "modern literature." As the history of translated works and the popularity of political novels show, literature and politics were inseparable in the early years of Meiji. With *The Essence of the Novel*, a text that designates the *shōsetsu* (novel) to be an art form rather than a political medium, the division between politics and literature was instituted. As a result, virtually none of the works discussed in this section has been translated, and they are largely ignored in English-language literary criticism, despite their importance in the history of modern Japanese literature.

—*Atsuko Ueda*

Bibliography

Keene, Donald. *Dawn to the West: Japanese Literature in the Modern Era.* 2 vols. New York: Holt, Rinehart and Winston, 1984.

Kimura Ki. "Kaidai" (Commentary). In *Meiji hon'yaku bungakushū* (The Translated Literature of the Meiji Period), vol. 7 of *Meiji bungaku zenshū* (Complete Literary Works of the Meiji Period). Tokyo: Chikuma, 1972.

Mertz, John Pierre. "Meiji Political Novels and the Origins of Literary Modernity." Ph.D. diss., Cornell University, 1993.

Tsubouchi Shōyō. *The Essence of the Novel.* Trans. Nanette Twine. *Occasional Papers* 11. Department of Japanese, University of Queensland, 1981.

Yanagida Izumi. *Meiji bungaku kenkyū* (Studies in Meiji Literature), vols. 8–10, *Seiji shōsetsu kenkyū* (Political Novels). Tokyo: Shunjūsha, 1967–68.

Yano Ryūkei. *Inspiring Instances of Statesmanship.* Appendix to John Pierre Mertz, "Meiji Political Novels and the Origins of Literary Modernity." Ph.D. diss., Cornell University, 1993.

9

TSUBOUCHI SHŌYŌ AND FUTABATEI SHIMEI

In spite of the varying reactions to *The Essence of the Novel* (Shōsetsu shinzui, 1885–86) by Tsubouchi Shōyō (1859–1935), literary historians generally agree that it is the first work that called for the production of the modern novel. It is considered the manifesto of modern Japanese literature, and Shōyō the founder of that institution. Defining the *shōsetsu* (novel) as a work of art, it marks the beginning of modern literature, and its originary status is now rarely questioned.

In fact, however, there is a significant gap in modern Japanese literary history. By virtue of its reputation as the origin of modern Japanese literature, everything that preceded *The Essence of the Novel* is too often designated as the "premodern." The emergence of this seminal text is valorized to such an extent that *The Essence of the Novel* seems to have been produced in a vacuum. This work did not grow out of a vacuum; it is very much a product of its own historical moment, shaped by the chaotic contingencies of Japan's age of modernization.

Shōyō's endeavor is often narrated in terms of "Western influence," arguing that he urged his peers to emulate the "superior" literary practices of the West while discarding the "inferior" literature of Japan such as *gesaku* fiction (commonly translated as "frivolous" or playful writings, referring to a genre that proliferated in the Edo and early Meiji periods). This type of narrative is still dominant among most literary scholars; in fact, *The Essence of the Novel* is still known for its criticism of *gesaku*, most notably of Takizawa Bakin's (1767–1848) works. Yet this characterization is too simplistic when we turn our attention to the chaotic space of production of *The Essence of the Novel*.

The chaos is clearly inscribed in the central entity taken up in the text, namely the *shōsetsu*. Although the term *shōsetsu* is now a standard translation of the word "novel" (or "novels"), the relationship between the two terms was by no means a given at the historical time in which Shōyō wrote. Despite the fact that numerous Western texts were translated in the early years of Meiji, it was not until the second decade (1878–88) that novels began to be translated. (See "Translated and Political Novels.") The basic configuration of the Western novel was far from clear to Shōyō and to his contemporaries. We must not be misled by the translation of the title of Shōyō's work into uncritically equating *shōsetsu* and the novel. Shōyō creates and configures a new literary form, the *shōsetsu*, in the textual realm of his essay.

As a theoretical work, *The Essence of the Novel* discusses a variety of topics, ranging from themes and types of *shōsetsu* to the technical aspects of writing *shōsetsu*, such as the styles of language to employ, and how to configure a protagonist. The most famous section is entitled "The Main Theme of *Shōsetsu*" (Shōsetsu no shugan), which is often considered to be Shōyō's most notable contribution to the development of modern Japanese literature. In it, he claims that *shōsetsu* should thematize human emotions, focusing on the inner struggle of humanity. In fact, in comparison with this section, the other sections of *The Essence of the Novel* are devalued, often dismissed as a reflection of Shōyō's not-yet-modernized sensibility. The *kindai jiga* (modern selfhood), the most notable canonical theme of subsequent works of modern Japanese fiction, thus finds its origin retrospectively in *The Essence of the Novel*.

Shōyō attempted to actualize his theory in an experimental fictional work entitled *Characters of Modern Students* (Tōsei shosei katagi, 1885). Yet he himself later reflected that the work was a failure, and the overwhelming majority of critics follow his evaluation. Readers did not have to wait too long, however, for the appearance of the "true" novel, for Shōyō's disciple, Hasegawa Tatsunosuke (1864–1909)—better known by his pen name, Futabatei Shimei—began to publish *Drifting Clouds* (Ukigumo) in 1887. Published initially under Shōyō's name because he was the more famous of the two, *Drifting Clouds* marks a significant moment in the history of modern Japanese literature; it is even now considered Japan's first modern novel.

The narrative content of *Drifting Clouds* is relatively easy to summarize: the protagonist Utsumi Bunzō, a failed public servant, struggles internally with his love for his cousin Osei, continually trying to deduce her feelings for him. He is in torment when she appears to take a liking to his former colleague Noboru, a shrewd and practical man who has the social skills necessary for success in the *risshin shusse* (achievement-oriented) world of Meiji Japan, social skills that Bunzō lacks. The story remains unresolved, not only because the work is incomplete but also because of Bunzō's complete inability to make an active move to change his miserable state of affairs.

From this summary it may be hard to fathom the reasons behind *Drifting Clouds'* status in the history of modern Japanese literature. The novel's reputation rests on two important characteristics. First, its protagonist, Bunzō, is the quintessential antihero, an intellectual whose interiority is the main object of the story. Bunzō in many ways actualizes Shōyō's claim that the *shōsetsu* should feature internal human sufferings. Second, its narrative is written in **genbun'itchi*—commonly translated as "the unification of spoken and written languages"—the "modern language" of the new nation. Recent critical works such as those of Karatani Kōjin and Komori Yōichi have questioned the characterization of *Drifting Clouds* as the first and most successful example of the modern novel. Nonetheless, the emphasis on the protagonist's interiority as well as a story centering on the love relationship between Bunzō and his cousin Osei had a considerable impact on the literary scene.

Drifting Clouds had an important impact on Shōyō as well, who, after reading Futabatei's work, decided to forgo writing novels altogether. Although he is most known in literary history for *The Essence of the Novel*, he wrote several novels after *Characters of Modern Students*, including *Mirrors of Marriage* (Imotose kagami, 1886) and *The Wife* (Saikun, 1889), in an effort to overcome the failure of his first experiment. After his encounter with Futabatei's work, however, Shōyō, in retrospect, claimed that *Drifting Clouds* was the kind of novel he had aspired to write; he thereupon changed his career to that of literary critic, dramatist, and translator (known especially for his translations of Shakespeare's plays, which are still the standard). Though he had devalued drama considerably in his *Essence of the Novel*, Shōyō later devoted considerable effort in the reform of Japanese drama.

Futabatei Shimei's *Drifting Clouds* came out in several installments, often with long lapses in between. Struggling to produce a new narrative form, Futabatei's endeavor with his first work by no means went smoothly. He experimented with his writing to produce a satisfying language with which to write a modern narrative. He turned to Russian in his experiments; he was sufficiently well versed in the language to write his first draft in Russian and then translate his own narrative back into Japanese. The longest lapse in publication of *Drifting Clouds* was between parts II and III (1888–89), during which time he published two famous translations of Turgenev's works, namely "The Rendezvous" (Aibiki, 1850) and "Three Meetings" (Meguriai, 1851). In order to produce a modern narrative form in *Drifting Clouds*, he sought to emulate the narrating subjects of these two works.

Like many of his contemporaries, Futabatei was also a theorist, as is evident from his famous essay "Comprehensive Theory of the *Shōsetsu*" (Shōsetsu sōron, 1886), which analyzed techniques of portrayal that were drawn from Russian theorists, most notably Vissarion Belinsky. His ideas were actualized in many ways in *Drifting Clouds*, though he ended its publication in 1889 precisely because his own writing disillusioned him. It was not until 1906 that he wrote another fictional work of his own, *The Image* (Sono omokage), which was followed by *Mediocrity* (Heibon) in 1907. These two works fared well in the *naturalist trend that dominated the literary scene of the day, to the extent that they are now considered works of naturalist fiction.

Both Shōyō and Futabatei were writers who negotiated the turmoil of modernization in their search for new narrative configurations. In many ways their careers as translators played a significant role in their linguistic experiments. For them, in writing a *shōsetsu* the issue was not only *what* to write but also *how* to write. They lived in an era when the Japanese language was visibly heterogeneous and dispersed. (See "The Problem of the Modern Subject.") The phrase "Western influence," too often used to characterize their efforts to produce a modern *shōsetsu*, does not do justice to the complexity of their endeavors and the chaotic literary era within which they lived.

—Atsuko Ueda

Bibliography

Futabatei Shimei. *Mediocrity*. Trans. Glenn W. Shaw. Tokyo: Hokuseidō, 1927.

Karatani Kōjin. *Origins of Modern Japanese Literature*. Trans. Brett de Bary. Durham, N.C.: Duke University Press, 1993.

Komori Yōichi. *Buntai toshite no monogatari* (Monogatari As Literary Style). Tokyo: Chikuma, 1998.

Ryan, Marleigh Grayer. *Japan's First Modern Novel: "Ukigumo" of Futabatei Shimei*. New York: Columbia University Press, 1967.

Tsubouchi Shōyō. "The Essence of the Novel." Trans. Nanette Twine. *Occasional Papers 11*. Department of Japanese, University of Queensland, 1981.

10

THE KEN'YŪSHA, OZAKI KŌYŌ, AND YAMADA BIMYŌ

Ken'yūsha (Friends of the Inkstone) was a literary group formed in February 1885 by Ozaki Kōyō (1867–1903), Yamada Bimyō (1868–1910), Ishibashi Shian (1867–1927), and Maruoka Kyūka (1865–1927). They were later joined by Kawakami Bizan (1869–1908), Iwaya Sazanami (1870–1933), Emi Sui'in (1869–1934), Hirotsu Ryūrō (1861–1928), Ōhashi Otowa (1869–1901), and others. In May 1885 Ken'yūsha members began the first literary journal in modern Japan, *Rubbish Heap Library* (Garakuta bunko). The contents of the journal were diverse, ranging across fiction, poetry, and essay. The tone, playful and detached, reflected the ideals of the writer of *gesaku* (playful or comic writings), a literary form especially prominent in the eighteenth and nineteenth centuries.

Rubbish Heap Library began as a journal circulated for amusement and diversion among Ken'yūsha members, each of whom contributed to it. In May 1888 the journal was put on the market, at which point it began to exert considerable influence on the literary world. In March 1889 the title was shortened to *Library* (Bunko) and it continued under this name until publication ceased in October of that year. The demise of the journal, however, signified the beginning, not the end, of Ken'yūsha authority, for in the 1890s the group shifted to other venues for the publication of their fiction as their interests broadened and diverged under the impact of new intellectual currents, such as the vernacular writing movement (**genbun'itchi undō*) and *Tsubouchi Shōyō's treatise *The Essence of the Novel* (Shōsetsu shinzui, 1885–86).

Yamada Bimyō, for example, was a pioneer in the vernacular-writing movement. He achieved recognition in the late 1880s with some vernacular stories set in medieval Japan, then left the Ken'yūsha to edit the journal *Flower of the Capital* (Miyako no hana), an avant-garde publication that devoted much of its space to vernacular fiction. Iwaya Sazanami was a pioneer in the movement to create children's literature in Japan. His *Kogane Maru* (1891), a vendetta tale set in the world of animals, is widely considered the first children's story in the country. Hirotsu Ryūrō pursued the underside of Meiji society. He wrote such works as "Love Suicide at Imado" (Imado shinjū, 1896), set in the pleasure quarters of Tokyo, and "Rain" (Ame, 1902), a powerful and moving story of poverty. The heart of the Ken'yūsha was Ozaki Kōyō, arguably the most influential literary figure in Japan in the 1890s. Kōyō attained fame with *Two Nuns: A Confession of Love* (Ninin bikuni irozange, 1889), a medieval tale in which two nuns discover they were once both in love with the same man, and he secured his position with his works in the early 1890s. Kōyō contributed enormously to the nuanced depiction of psychological drama in the novel in his *Much Passion, Much Grief* (Tajō takon, 1896), in which a bereaved widower falls in love with his best friend's wife. He also created a masterful vernacular style for the work. Kōyō followed this with the explosively popular *The Gold Demon* (Konjiki yasha, 1897–1903), a melodramatic novel whose drama turns on the conflict between money and love. It is the story of Hazama Kan'ichi, who becomes coldhearted and turns to the profession of money lending after his cousin Miya rejects him. Miya marries instead the wealthy Tomiyama Tadatsugu but later comes to regret her choice and attempts to regain Kan'ichi's affections, but he refuses her overtures. Kōyō died before completing the novel, but *The Gold Demon* was still one of the biggest successes of the Meiji period. It was dismissed as "mere" popular fiction by many writers and critics in the first half of the twentieth century, a pejorative label that has stuck to the work, and to Kōyō's oeuvre as a whole, to this day. These critics also viewed the style—Kōyō had returned to the classical language—as a step backward.

Ken'yūsha was the most powerful literary force in the decade of the 1890s, with its only serious competitor being the group gathered around *Mori Ōgai's literary-critical journals. Ken'yūsha dominance can largely be attributed to its hold on a great number of important publishing vehicles. In 1894 Ken'yūsha member Ōhashi Otowa married into the family of one of the largest publishers of the day, Hakubunkan, and thereafter he played a large role in determining who got published. In addition, Kōyō's *Two Nuns* was published in 1889 as the first volume of the series "New Authors, One Hundred Works" (Shinchō hyakushu), devoted to new and notable writers, and the success of the novel paved the way for Ken'yūsha dominance of that important series. Kōyō's success also won for him the editorship of the arts column of the *Yomiuri*, the newspaper that invented the serialized novel in Japan. This became the vehicle by which Kōyō published the vast majority of his fiction, and the success of his serialized novels made Kōyō the first modern Japanese writer to become a truly national figure, an author who could speak to the hearts and minds of an entire country.

Kōyō's death in 1903 was a serious blow to the Ken'yūsha, but the group had already been losing cohesion owing to the sheer diversity of interests among its members. In addition, beginning around 1900 Ken'yūsha hegemony was being challenged by the literary movement that would displace it: *Japanese naturalism. Nonetheless, it is significant that several of the most prominent authors of the early twentieth century—including a few naturalists—began as apprentices and associates of Ken'yūsha writers. Izumi Kyōka (1873–1939) and Tokuda Shūsei (1871–1943), although writers of very different kinds of fiction, both began as apprentices of Ozaki Kōyō. *Nagai Kafū was associated with both Iwaya Sazanami and Hirotsu Ryūrō. In the beginning of his career Tayama Katai (1871–1930) was a great admirer of Kōyō's fiction and was associated with Emi Sui'in and Hakubunkan. Thus, although Ken'yūsha dominance is largely confined to the 1890s, the influence of individual members of the group was felt well into the twentieth century.

—*Timothy J. Van Compernolle*

Bibliography

Fukuda Kiyoto. *Ken'yūsha no bungaku undō* (The Ken'yūsha Literary Movement), 2d ed. Tokyo: Hakubunkan shinsho, 1985.

Ikari Akira. *Ken'yūsha no bungaku* (The Literature of the Ken'yūsha). Tokyo: Hanawa, 1961.

Kornicki, Peter. *The Reform of Fiction in Meiji Japan.* London: Ithaca Press, 1982.

Morita, James. "Garakuta Bunko." *Monumenta Nipponica* 24, no. 3 (1969): 219–233.

Ozaki Kōyō. *The Gold Demon.* Trans. A. Lloyd and M. Lloyd. Tokyo: Seibundō, 1917.

Tsubouchi Shōyō. "The Essence of the Novel." Trans. Nanette Twine. *Occasional Papers 11.* Department of Japanese, University of Queensland, 1981.

11

MEIJI WOMEN WRITERS

The Meiji Restoration of 1868 inspired a variety of social, political, and religious reforms. Eager to lead the country into the fold of "civilized nations," progressive-minded politicians and intellectuals encouraged modifications in language, literature, music, theater, dress, national governance, and education. Women, too, were among the targets of reform. Captivated by popular Western rhetoric, reformers believed that the status of a nation's women was the measure of that nation's civilization. Though progress was afoot in Japan on many levels, Japanese women, or so these men were convinced, were far from modern. In order to address this wrong, new reforms were encouraged. Women would be required to change their costumes, their cosmetics, their speech, and the way they arranged their hair, and some were even encouraged to learn the latest trends in ballroom dancing, all in an attempt to modernize. In 1871 five little girls were sent to the United States on a mission to study American womanhood. The following year a nationwide educational ordinance was passed making four years of schooling mandatory for all children. In journals and magazines writers began arguing for equality in marriage and the elimination of prostitution and concubinage—all to the further improvement of women's rights. Women began to assume a more prominent role outside the home—in volunteer organizations, on political platforms, and in a limited number of professions. By the late 1880s, women had begun to enter the writing arena.

Prose fiction by women writers in the modern period is generally acknowledged to have begun with Miyake Kaho (née Tanabe, 1868–1944) and her 1888 novella *Warbler in the Grove* (Yabu no uguisu). Once Kaho opened the gates, works by women trickled out yearly: eleven in 1889, thirteen in 1891, and finally, in a relative deluge of activity, twenty-four in 1895. Numerous journals and periodicals provided outlets for these works. *Women's Education Journal* (Jogaku zasshi), founded in 1885, was important not only as a forum for women's writing but also for providing the encouragement and impetus to many aspiring authors. *The Maiden* (Iratsume) was inaugurated in 1887 with the exclusive intention of promoting women's literary endeavors. Mainstream newspapers such as *Yomiuri* offered women an opportunity to publish their works. And in 1895 *Literary Club* (Bungei kurabu)—an important literary journal—published the first special issue devoted exclusively to women's writing. Although the issue would be followed by a sequel in 1897, this first era of "women writers" in the modern age drew to a close in 1896 with the deaths of three of its most prominent members: Wakamatsu Shizuko (b. 1864), Tazawa Inafune (b. 1874), and *Higuchi Ichiyō (b. 1872).

Women writers in the Meiji era were known as *keishū sakka*, a Chinese-derived term denoting women of significant talent and breeding. Generally daughters of affluent and privileged families, these *keishū sakka*—or *lady* writers—had received an above-average education. They were conversant with Western ideas and were eager to participate in the modernizing efforts of their male counterparts. In her *Warbler in the Grove*, Miyake Kaho introduces readers to two of these newly fashioned women. Namiko and Hamako, both products of the Meiji reforms, wear their imported Western gowns with grace and assurance, their conversations richly garnished with English. While Kaho's women encounter the West in their exclusive boarding school, Kimura Akebono (1872–1890) treated readers to the vision of the Japanese woman conquering the West on foreign soil. In her delightfully imaginative *A Mirror for Womanhood* (Fujo no kagami, 1889) she writes of a young Japanese woman who travels to England and the United States, where she attends college, impressing all with her beauty and brilliance. When she returns to Japan, she opens a silk factory for women workers—complete with a nursery and daycare center.

A number of the women who wrote during this period found their way to literature via the political lecture circuits, having earlier made a name for themselves as participants in the Freedom and People's Rights movement. (See "Translated and Political Novels of the Meiji Period.") When women were banned from the lecture stage in 1890, they turned their energies to writing. Their works reflect their political agenda. For example, *The Noble Flower of the Valley* (Sankan no meika, 1889) by Nakajima Shōen (formerly Kishida Toshiko, 1863–1901) is described as the first "political novel" by a woman. Loosely based on her own experience, the novel depicts a woman who abandons her political activities in order to marry. Initially depressed by what she sees as her lack of commitment to the fight for women's rights, she is heartened when several of her disciples visit her and inform her that they are busily campaigning in her stead. Shimizu Shikin (1868–1933), a former colleague of Shōen's on the lecture circuit, also recounting experiences in her own life, published "The Broken Ring" (Koware yubiwa) in 1891. Describing a woman who opts for a divorce rather than to submit to the unhappiness of a traditional marriage, Shikin takes Kaho's outwardly westernized woman and liberates her spirit.

Few women of this age possessed Shōen and Shikin's political zeal or Akebono's imaginative vision. Most were hesitant to peer beyond the confines of their own experience. Those who did often met criticism. For example, when Kitada Usurai (1876–1900) wrote of the Yoshiwara licensed quarter in her 1895 piece "Wretched Sights" (Asamashi no sugata), she was harshly rebuked by critics who felt she had overstepped her bounds as a *lady* writer. Most women writers of this age, therefore, trained their sights on the traditional marriage system and limited themselves to marriage plots. Stories of this variety invariably describe a young woman's (reluctant) preparation for marriage; her disappointment in the marital union or else her disappointment in her inability to marry the man of her choice or to marry at all; her unfair treatment at the hands of her in-laws; and her suicide (or at the very least self-sacrifice) as the result of any or all of these scenarios. Kitada Usurai, before offending critics with her study of prostitutes, had made her debut with "The Widowed Three" (Sannin yamome, 1892), which charts the fates of three young people whose lives are destroyed by a capricious family system that values only loyalty and finds no room for individual love. In "One Thousand Demons" (Oni zenbiki, 1895) she describes a woman who is tortured by her in-laws while her husband is away. Upon fleeing to her natal home, her own mother berates her so harshly that she finds little alternative but to drown herself in a well. Marriage was no more promising for Higuchi Ichiyō's heroines. Oseki in "The Thirteenth Night" (Jūsan'ya, 1895) escapes to her parents' home when she finds her marital situation intolerable. Reminded by her father of the hardships a divorce would cause her son and her brother, she returns to her marriage, vowing to will herself into a living death in order to survive the indignities. Not all women dwelt on unhappiness in the marital union. The few who wrote of companionate marriages, however, also introduced love triangles into the plot. Both Miyake Kaho's "The Bush Clover and the Chinese Bellflower" (Hagi kikyō, 1895) and Otsuka Kusuoko's (1875–1910) "Passing Autumn" (Kure yuku aki, 1895) depict women who marry the men of their dreams only to discover that their best friends had been in love with the same man. Successful love demands a price.

With the exception of Shikin's wife, who proudly elects divorce over a lifetime in a loveless marriage, for most fictional heroines the resistance of marriage does not guarantee happiness. In "White Rose" (Shirobara, 1895), Tazawa Inafune writes passionately of a young woman who fights back, struggling to retain her integrity under the patriarchal system. Intelligent, idealistic, and morally courageous, the heroine resists the marriage her father has arranged for her with the ne'er-do-well scion of a wealthy family. Learning of her refusal, the spurned groom tricks her into traveling with him to a seaside resort where he drugs her with chloroform and rapes her. Upon regaining consciousness, the woman throws herself in the sea. Because the penalties were severe for those who ignored contemporary social values in their quest for personal fulfillment, the fiction by women in this era is necessarily dark and morbid.

Perhaps in a bid to escape the limits of their own vision, a number of Meiji women elected to translate. The aforementioned Nakajima Shōen translated and adapted Bulwer-Lytton's *Eugene Aram* in 1887. Koganei Kimiko (1871–1956) was well known for her renditions of German and English works into gracefully classical Japanese. But none achieved the recognition that Wakamatsu Shizuko received for her many translations from English. Shizuko is most remembered for her translation of Frances Hodgson Burnett's *Little Lord Fauntleroy*, which was serialized from 1890 to 1892 in *Women's Education Journal*. Shizuko's translation is noteworthy not only for introducing readers to children's literature but also for forging a path to *genbun'itchi*, or a modern literary vernacular.

The first era of women writers in modern Japan began with enthusiastic vigor in 1888 but ended less than one decade later. Two factors contributed to this premature silence: death and marriage. A significant number of Meiji women writers died young—Tazawa Inafune at twenty-three, Higuchi Ichiyō at twenty-four, Kitada Usurai at twenty-five, and Wakamatsu Shizuko at thirty-two. Those who were not silenced by death found that it was inordinately difficult to continue writing after marriage. Turn-of-the-century Japan was in between two significant wars and had grown decidedly conservative. Writing—with its publicity and demands of self-involvement—was no longer an occupation women could pursue while acceding to the demands of marriage. And not marrying was hardly an option for respectable women at the time.

The first era of women writers in modern Japan was marked therefore by high hopes and equally high contradictions. Women writers were held to rigid moral standards that precluded a wide range of expression. As a result, they were criticized as unrealistic and unimaginative. Women were encouraged to write—but only as long as they conformed to literary standards deemed "ladylike." Expected to sacrifice their art for marriage, they were criticized for the shallowness of their commitment to writing when they did and despised for their selfishness when they did not. Although writing by women would never completely vanish, it would not be until the second decade of the twentieth century that women would once again earn critical recognition for their literary efforts.

—*Rebecca Copeland*

Bibliography

Copeland, Rebecca. *Lost Leaves: Women Writers of Meiji Japan*. Honolulu: University of Hawai'i Press, 2000.

Higuchi Ichiyō. "The Thirteenth Night." In Robert L. Danly, ed., *In the Shade of Spring Leaves: The Life and Writings of Higuchi Ichiyō, A Woman of Letters in Meiji Japan.* New Haven: Yale University Press, 1981.

Kimura Akebono. "A Mirror for Womanhood." *The Magazine* 3:5.

Meiji joryū bungakushū (Collection of Meiji Women's Literature), Part 1. *Meiji bungaku zenshū* (Complete Literary Works of the Meiji Period). Tokyo: Chikuma, 1966.

Shioda Ryōhei. *Shintei Meiji joryū sakkaron* (A Study of Meiji Women Writers: Revised Edition). Tokyo: Bunsendō, 1983.

Wada Shigejirō. *Meiji zenki joryū sakuhinron—Higuchi Ichiyō to sono zengo* (Early Meiji Women Writers: Higuchi Ichiyō and Her Contemporaries). Tokyo: Ōfūsha, 1989.

12

MORI ŌGAI

The literary career of Mori Ōgai (1862–1922), whose life spans the declining years of Japan's feudal epoch and its emergence as a world power, in effect recapitulates the extraordinary course of the nation's cultural modernization. Rising above the hurly-burly of the literary scene, Ōgai enriched the intellectual climate of his age, made pioneering contributions across the literary spectrum, and established a new standard of humanistic discourse. His writings constitute a vast commentary on and critique of Japan's modernization. Together with his great contemporary *Natsume Sōseki, Mori Ōgai may be said to have laid the foundation for modern literature in Japan. As a literary stylist he was without peer, and writers of every stripe have reserved the highest praise for his work and the values that he espoused. His stature as a cultural patriarch of modern Japan remains unchallenged.

Among the last generation to receive the classical Confucian education befitting his family's samurai status, young Mori Rintarō (Ōgai is a pen name) was trained as a physician at Tokyo Imperial University. While deepening his familiarity with the Chinese and Japanese literary canon, he received his medical degree and set out on a four-year course of study in Germany. During this crucial formative period, he read voraciously, absorbing the main currents of European literature, philosophy, and science. Upon his return to Japan, Ōgai embarked on a dual career in literature and medicine and achieved distinction in both areas of endeavor. The physician would eventually attain a rank equivalent to surgeon-general. A scientist with a keen analytical mind, he was at the same time a deeply committed humanist and a prodigiously talented writer. As a fledgling member of the *bundan,* the Tokyo literary establishment, Ōgai wrote fiction and poetry. (See "The Social Organization of Modern Japanese Literature.") He was a noted dramatist, essayist, and critic. Early on, he established and edited important literary journals, quickly emerging as a leading intellectual of the Meiji period. As a literary translator he had few peers.

Ōgai's debut took the form of a trilogy of stories based on his experiences in Germany. The trilogy, which reflects the romanticism of Hoffmann and Kleist, commences with *The Dancing Girl* (Maihime, 1890), a romantic novella that would rank among the best-known works of modern Japanese literature. The story tells of Ōta, a young Japanese living in Berlin who has an affair with Elise, a poor dancing girl. The couple fall madly in love, but Ōta ultimately heeds the call of duty and abandons the girl, now pregnant and on the verge of madness, and returns to Japan. The poignant tale is related in confessional style by Ōta himself as he sits in his stateroom aboard his homeward-bound ship off the port of Saigon and ponders his actions.

What so attracted the contemporary reader was not simply the exotic romance, with its undertones of Oriental "conquest," but the unmistakable autobiographical reference. "The Dancing Girl" and its two companion pieces served as models for the modern Japanese short story, gained a degree of notoriety for its young author and at the same time pointed the way to a self-referentiality that would loom large in Japan's literary future.

Having been so brilliantly innovative in his literary debut, Ōgai essentially abandoned fiction writing in favor of more congenial literary pursuits. As a critic he succeeded in elevating literary discourse to a new level of sophistication. In fact, his 1891 debate with *Tsubouchi Shōyō, a major *bundan* figure, marks the birth of modern Japanese criticism. Here, again, Ōgai continued to harvest the fruits of his intellectual tutelage in Germany, and he was instrumental in introducing the work of Nietzsche, Hartmann, and Zola to Japan. Ōgai's contribution to the establishment of a modern theater in Japan is equally noteworthy. Stagings of his translations of major plays by Ibsen, Hauptmann, and Sudermann were major events, and he himself was an accomplished playwright and theater critic.

Scholars have often remarked that literary translation was Ōgai's chief forte. Although the value of such literary labor may be hard for us to appreciate, Meiji culture grew in tandem with the work of translators. The stylistic and rhetorical innovations that Ōgai made in this area paved the way for the *development of *genbun'itchi* (vernacular written language) in the early twentieth century. In particular, his version of Goethe's *Faust* has long remained the standard, and his rendering of Hans Christian Andersen's romantic novel *Improvisatoren* was hailed as a stunning achievement.

In the realm of poetry, Ōgai oversaw the publication of *Vestiges* (Omokage, 1889), an important anthology of translated romantic verse by Byron, Heine,

and others. His own anthology *Poetic Diary* (Uta nikki, 1902–5) combines original work inspired by his wartime experience and a selection of translated verse.

The course of Ōgai's literary career was much affected by the circumstances
of his medical career, which entailed, among other things, periods of service in
both the Sino-Japanese and Russo-Japanese wars. Having distanced himself
from the late-Meiji *bundan*, which was increasingly under the sway of commercial forces and literary fads, Ōgai nonetheless found himself being drawn back
into fiction writing. In part this was in response to the rise of Japanese *naturalism, a movement that called for a literature of sincere, unadorned self-expression.
Concerned that the trend toward tawdry confessionalism and pained introspection would debase the literary currency, Ōgai countered with *Vita Sexualis*
(1909), a brilliant parody of naturalist fiction. A curiously detached and clinically dispassionate account of sexual awakening narrated by a professor concerned with writers' preoccupation with sex, the work challenges both the artistic and moral basis of the prevailing *bundan* trend. Ironically, this remarkably
inexplicit work was banned by the authorities, who evidently found the title itself sufficiently scurrilous.

Despite his long-standing ambivalence toward fiction, Ōgai could not ignore
the impressive work of writers such as Natsume Sōseki, who had raised the art of
fiction to an unprecedented level of sophistication. He wrote several novels "in
the Sōseki style," as though seeking to contest his literary rival. By comparison,
though, these experiments fell short. *Youth* (Seinen, 1910–11) manages to evoke
the emotional and intellectual mood of the late-Meiji college crowd, but it
could not match Sōseki's *Sanshirō* (1908), the work that it so closely resembles.

In spite of several failed attempts, Ōgai achieved remarkable success with
The Wild Goose (Gan, 1911), a tale of romantic longing and unrequited love. Set
in the early years of the Meiji, *The Wild Goose* tells of a young woman, Otama,
who has had to leave her poor father to become the mistress of a rich, sleazy
moneylender. Whiling away the days in her gilded cage, Otama takes notice of
a handsome university student, Okada, who regularly passes by beneath her bal-
cony. She becomes infatuated with him and the two eventually meet. However,
Okada must leave Japan to pursue his medical studies in Germany (an authorial
self-reference). Alas, the incipient romance dies on the vine, and Otama must
resign herself to her lot. But in the process she has acquired a degree of worldly
wisdom and a sense of self-worth.

Despite these novelistic forays, fiction occupies a relatively minor place in
Ōgai's oeuvre. His ambivalent stance, in part a reflection of a long-standing
Confucian denigration of literary fabrication, was shared by many of his contemporaries, most notably *Futabatei Shimei and Kōda Rohan (1867–1947).
And so, in his quest for a more congenial mode of literary expression, Ōgai
turned to the personal essay. Over several years he produced a series of ruminations on contemporary social issues, which take the measure of Japan's political
and intellectual climate while affording personal glimpses of his past. The fol-

lowing is drawn from "Casuistica" (Medical Records, 1911), a representative work in this vein:

> At first he thought that his father was leading an empty, meaningless existence. He was old, after all, and wasn't it only natural that an old man should have nothing to do? It was then that he happened to read something by [the Confucian scholar] Kumazawa Banzan. Devoted service to the state, according to Banzan, is no more a manifestation of the Way than washing one's face or combing one's hair every day.
>
> When he read this, then thought about his father's routine, it struck him. Rather than gazing off into the far distances and casually dispensing with what was close at hand, his father was devoting all of his energies to the performance of small daily tasks. And he came to understand, if only vaguely, that his father's attitude of resignation, of contentment with being a doctor in a small post-town, was in its own way a kind of enlightenment. Thereafter he began treating his father with newfound respect. (Marcus 106–107)

The death of the Meiji emperor in July 1912 and the subsequent ritual suicide of the celebrated General Nogi Maresuke (together with his wife, Shizuko) marked a crucial turning point in modern Japanese history. The events held deep significance for Mori Ōgai and his contemporaries. Whereas the final decade of Sōseki's career was devoted to fiction set in the contemporary period, Ōgai spent his last ten years exploring Japan's past through works of history and biography. General Nogi's suicide, which raised the ugly specter of Japan's feudal past and its warrior code, became the catalyst for a new literary venture—an exploration of Japanese character and values through the medium of *rekishi shōsetsu* (historical fiction). A lifelong student of history and folklore, Ōgai focused on a series of events and episodes drawn mainly from the world of the late-Edo samurai. The stories were dramatizations of these events, each one based on scrupulous research and an abiding concern for the integrity of the written record.

For instance, "The Abe Family" (Abe ichizoku, 1913) recounts with scientific precision the suicidal mania of a group of samurai retainers who in 1641 struggled for the right to take their lives following the death of their liege lord. Casting harsh light on the authoritarian underpinnings of Japanese society and a mindless adherence to barbaric codes of conduct, Ōgai stopped short of imputing motives and plumbing psyches. Rather, he allowed character to emerge from the relentless unfolding of incident. The author's ambivalent stance vis-à-vis his own samurai legacy is apparent in this and other works that question the feudal heritage of stoic fatalism and blind obedience.

In his last years, Mori Ōgai moved from historical fiction to biography. Disavowing creative license and fictional manipulation, the aging author sought to present the documentary record *sono mama*—precisely as it was. His seemingly unlikely subjects were a group of obscure nineteenth-century Confucianist physician-scholars and literati. Having come across their names in the documentary margins, Ōgai was powerfully drawn to evidence of their having been kindred spirits. He set to the task of researching these lives, a five-year endeavor that resulted in a trilogy of biographies that span centuries in the lives of its three central subjects and their large circle of colleagues and kin.

The first volume of the trilogy, *Shibue Chūsai* (1916), has been hailed as a crowning achievement of modern Japanese literature. But this is a difficult and demanding work, displaying an erudition that appears calculated to frustrate the average reader. At once an exquisitely detailed account of Chūsai and his circle, the narrative also traces the ongoing research itself, revealing a deeply spiritual bond that united the renowned biographer and his obscure subject, whom he would come to know only indirectly, through the steady accumulation of documentary evidence.

Mori Ōgai went on to pursue his biographical researches, oblivious to public disapproval and indifferent to the rising tide of popular culture, until his death in 1922. His literary legacy, perhaps increasingly hard to appreciate, contains equal measures of intellectual rigor, stylistic virtuosity, and moral integrity. Ōgai's fiction is still read, as are the essays and historical novellas. But the monumental achievement of his later years is sadly inaccessible to all but a handful of dedicated readers. One can only hope that the lofty vision of this literary giant, who so eloquently captured the spirit of his age, will not fade.

—*Marvin Marcus*

Bibliography

Bowring, Richard. *Mori Ōgai and the Modernization of Japanese Culture.* Cambridge: Cambridge University Press, 1979.

Dilworth, David, and J. Thomas Rimer, eds. *The Historical Literature of Mori Ōgai.* 2 vols. Honolulu: University of Hawai'i Press, 1977.

Marcus, Marvin. *Paragons of the Ordinary: The Biographical Literature of Mori Ōgai.* Honolulu: University of Hawai'i Press, 1993.

McClellan, Edwin. *Woman in the Crested Kimono.* New Haven: Yale University Press, 1985.

Mori Ōgai. *Vita Sexualis.* Trans. Kazuji Ninomiya and Sanford Goldstein. Tokyo: Tuttle, 1972.

——. *The Wild Goose.* Trans. Burton Watson. Ann Arbor: University of Michigan Monograph Series in Japanese Studies, 1995.

——. *"Youth" and Other Stories.* Ed. J. Thomas Rimer. Honolulu: University of Hawai'i Press, 1994.

Rimer, J. Thomas. *Mori Ōgai.* Boston: Twayne, 1975.

13

HIGUCHI ICHIYŌ
AND NEOCLASSICAL MODERNISM

In the 1890s, when Japanese literature was undergoing a modern revolution at the hands of such writers as *Futabatei Shimei, based largely on influences from Anglo-European literatures, a small number of Japanese writers worked to maintain indigenous elements from earlier periods as they created a new form of literature appropriate to the realities of Meiji Japan. Among them were Kōda Rohan (1867–1947), Ozaki Kōyō (1867–1903), and Higuchi Ichiyō (1872–1896). These writers did not work in concert, had differing ideas concerning the modernization of literature, and belonged to different literary coteries. Rohan and Kōyō had both been influenced by *Tsubouchi Shōyō's important essay *The Essence of the Novel* (Shōsetsu shinzui, 1885–86), and their experiments were consciously undertaken and based on specific principles. Nonetheless, these writers have been eclipsed in the long run by Ichiyō, a young woman of limited education who wrote fiction in an attempt to save her family from starvation. Ichiyō was "not only the first woman writer of distinction for centuries but ... the finest writer of her day" (Keene 1984, 1:183).

Ichiyō was the pen name of Higuchi Natsuko, born in Tokyo to a family that had originally been prosperous and well-educated farmers in Yamanashi Prefecture until her father brought his young wife to the capital and purchased *shizoku* (former samurai nobility) status. From early childhood Ichiyō was recognized as having extraordinary brilliance. Hoping to encourage her talent, her father sent her to a series of private schools where she learned writing, arithmetic, and poetry. Her obvious scholastic talent notwithstanding, Ichiyō was taken out of school at age eleven at her mother's insistence. For women of the Meiji period the only respectable life course and only safeguard against penury was marriage, and it was believed that too much education would make a girl less appealing as a prospective bride.

At the age of fourteen, Ichiyō entered a poetry school for wealthy young ladies, the elegantly named Haginoya (House of Bush Clover), run by a recognized woman poet, Nakajima Utako. Schools featuring cultural education were part of a young woman's preparation for marriage. It was here that Ichiyō first read the Japanese classics, such as *The Tale of Genji*, and the great poetry collection *Kokinshū*, both from the Heian period a thousand years earlier. Elements of language, imagery, and plot from these ancient texts became important components of her later fiction. (Later in her career she was also influenced by the fiction of Edo-period writer Ihara Saikaku [1642–1693].)

At the Haginoya, Ichiyō quickly showed herself to be the most talented of the students, but she suffered from a sense of inferiority because of her family's relative poverty. This intensified in 1887 as her father lost his job as a minor government official. When their father died in 1889 after having invested the last of the family's savings in a failed business venture, Ichiyō, seventeen years old, and her younger sister Kuniko became the only breadwinners for themselves and their mother.

Around this time Ichiyō experienced a series of personal betrayals, which are echoed in the social consciousness of her later fiction. A man who had promised to marry her withdrew when he saw the reversal of the family's fortunes. She was taken in by Nakajima as a servant and apprentice teacher at the Haginoya, but soon felt betrayed there, too, when it appeared that Nakajima had no intention of giving her a real teaching post.

The three Higuchi women began taking in laundry and sewing to make a living. One of their customers, a handsome widower named Nakarai Tōsui, was a well-published writer. Ichiyō, inspired by a classmate from the Haginoya who had written a novel to great acclaim, had decided to become a writer of fiction herself, to supplement the family income. Through an intermediary she obtained a formal introduction to Tōsui to solicit his help in getting started. Much has been written about Ichiyō's ambivalent relationship with Tōsui: he did help in getting her earliest stories published, and it is clear that she admired and perhaps even loved him; but in the end he, too, betrayed her, suggesting to his friends that they were having an illicit sexual affair. Ichiyō was forced to break off her relationship with him in order to preserve her reputation.

Ichiyō's determination to be a writer resulted ultimately in an extraordinary multivolume diary written in the elegant language of Heian Japan, and about twenty stories written in neoclassical language. The final ten stories were of such quality that at the time of her death at age twenty-four Ichiyō was praised as an astonishing new talent by the most revered writers and critics of the day. The most remarkable quality of her fiction was its skillful combination of elegant classical language and classical references with an acute depiction of the class and gender distinctions that underpinned Meiji society. In one story, "The Thirteenth Night" (Jūsan'ya, 1895), a young married woman runs to her parents' modest home trying to escape her hellish marriage to an upper-class man, but is persuaded to return when she realizes how much her natal family's current happiness is dependent on her husband's position and wealth. Her parents are sympathetic to her misery and express anger at her husband's cruelty, but they conclude that most rich men are selfish and brutal to their wives, and that a woman's lot is to endure such treatment as best she can. They have no alternatives to offer her.

Another story from 1895 shows that the life of a lower-class Meiji-period woman is difficult whether she becomes a wife or a celebrated prostitute, two of the very few career choices open to her. (A third choice was hard work in the textile factories under appalling conditions.) "Troubled Waters" (Nigorie) features three protagonists: Oriki, the most popular girl in a house of prostitution, the Kikunoi, in the licensed quarter of Tokyo; Genshichi, the married man Oriki loves, who has squandered all his money on visits to her and can no longer afford to see her; and Ohatsu, Genshichi's wife, struggling to keep her child fed in this new situation of poverty. As the story unfolds, the reader sees life from the point of view of each of the characters; none is portrayed as completely good or bad.

Ichiyō paints the world of the licensed quarter prostitute with no sentimentality; she makes it clear that to survive the women have to be heartless. Although Oriki had been forced into prostitution after her parents' early death, she is as capable of meaningless flirtation as any of her fellows. "She now spent her days telling lies and bantering with men who came to call. Love, compassion—in her world, these were things as flimsy as a sheet of mulberry paper, about as steady as the flickering of a firefly" (231). But Ichiyō also reveals Oriki's inner torment. In one scene she has run desperately out into the dark streets one night when her job has become too frustrating:

> "I have no choice," she whispered.... "No one's going to feel sorry for me, that much I know. If I complain about how sad I am, 'What's wrong?' people say, 'Don't you like your work?' Oh, it doesn't matter any more what happens—I haven't the slightest idea what will become of me. I might as well go on as Oriki of the Kikunoi. Sometimes I wonder if I've lost all sense of kindness and decency. No. I mustn't think such things. It won't do me any good. With my station in life and my calling and my fate, I'm not an ordinary person any more. It's a mistake to think I am. It only adds to my suffering. It's all so hopeless and discouraging. What am I doing standing here? Why did I come here? Stupid! Crazy! I don't even know myself," she sighed. "I'd better get back." (232)

Although we do not see as far into the mind of Genshichi, we come to understand that he truly loves Oriki, and wants to redeem her by buying out her contract at the Kikunoi. But most men of the merchant class cannot afford to become serious about a prostitute. Genshichi has lost his once-prospering business because of the expenses of visiting the Kikunoi to see his beloved. He suffers guilt over the ruin he has brought to his wife, Ohatsu, and their child, but also feels anger at his wife's constant nagging and utter lack of sympathy for Oriki's situation. When the reader is given a glimpse into Ohatsu's mind, we see her frustration, too; she looks old before her time from working day and night to alleviate their poverty. She tries to be kind to her husband but cannot help resenting the fact that she works so hard for the family while he only mopes after Oriki. All three characters are depicted as complex people, doing their best in social circumstances they cannot control.

Ichiyō's undisputed masterpiece is a long story called "Child's Play" (Takekurabe, 1895–96). The title, which literally means "comparing height," is a classical reference, but the story is extremely modern, tracing the destinies of children in the neighborhood of the licensed quarter. Ichiyō knew this area firsthand. In 1893 she and her mother and sister had sold off the last of their belongings and moved to a tiny house just outside the licensed prostitution district in Tokyo, the Yoshiwara, where Ichiyō opened a small shop selling sweets and sundries. Their customers and neighbors were all associated with life in the quarter in some way or other.

"Growing Up" is remarkable for its focus on the lives of children. Again there are several important characters, each of whom is depicted in complex terms. The two most memorable, however, are Midori and Nobu. Midori is destined to become a prostitute in a nearby house of pleasure where her older sister is the current favorite courtesan; she envies her sister's beautiful clothes and fame. Nobu is the son of a Buddhist priest and will enter the priesthood himself. Although his father breaks nearly all the rules of priesthood, Nobu is an earnest young man who intends to take them seriously. Both children are just on the verge of adolescence and are beginning to glimpse for the first time the realities of the lives that have been chosen for them. The story ends with Midori suddenly dressed in adult clothes, and hiding tearfully in her room instead of running around happily with her friends as before. Although no explanation is given for this abrupt change—the children who come to visit her are entirely perplexed—the reader can guess that Midori has been irrevocably confronted with some aspect of the physical reality of her situation: either she has begun to menstruate or she has been initiated as a prostitute. (Critics are divided on which of the two Ichiyō intended.) She finds inside her gate a paper flower, left by Nobu, who has left for the seminary. Although the two young people had secretly loved each other, the time has come when they must part forever to take up their lives—hers as a sexual toy and his as a sexless ascetic—in the harsh adult world.

There are no villains in this story. The tragic lives of the children and their families are the result of social forces beyond their control. Ichiyō's extraordinary achievement is in telling such a story without resorting to melodrama or overt sentimentality. All her later stories exhibit this quality: an acute depiction of the effects of the class and gender systems that were taken for granted in Meiji Japan.

Ichiyō died of tuberculosis in 1896. At the time of her death she was widely recognized in literary circles as a major talent; both famous and still up-and-coming male writers visited her for advice and discussion. She belonged to none of the literary schools (such as romanticism) or coteries of the day, but had managed to carve out a literature that was entirely original in its neoclassical modernity.

—Sharalyn Orbaugh

Bibliography

Danly, Robert L., ed. *In the Shade of Spring Leaves: The Life and Writings of Higuchi Ichiyō, a Woman of Letters in Meiji Japan.* New Haven: Yale University Press, 1981.

Higuchi Ichiyō. "Child's Play." In Robert L. Danly, ed., *In the Shade of Spring Leaves: The Life and Writings of Higuchi Ichiyō, a Woman of Letters in Meiji Japan*, 254–287. New Haven: Yale University Press, 1981.

——. "Thirteenth Night." In Robert L. Danly, ed., *In the Shade of Spring Leaves: The Life and Writings of Higuchi Ichiyō, a Woman of Letters in Meiji Japan*, 241–253. New Haven: Yale University Press, 1981.

——. "Troubled Waters." In Robert L. Danly, ed., *In the Shade of Spring Leaves: The Life and Writings of Higuchi Ichiyō, a Woman of Letters in Meiji Japan*, 218–240. New Haven: Yale University Press, 1981.

Keene, Donald. *Dawn to the West: Japanese Literature in the Modern Era.* 2 vols. New York: Holt, Rinehart and Winston, 1984.

Mitsutani, Margaret. "Higuchi Ichiyō: A Literature of Her Own." *Comparative Literature Studies* 22 (1985): 53–66.

Tsubouchi Shōyō. "The Essence of the Novel." Trans. Nanette Twine. *Occasional Papers 11.* Department of Japanese, University of Queensland, 1981.

14

SHIMAZAKI TŌSON

Shimazaki Tōson (1872–1943) was a leader in defining the standards of modern Japanese literature and poetry in the first half of the twentieth century. As one of the first Japanese authors to represent "life in the raw" (often modeled on his own experiences), he is associated with the development of Japanese *naturalism and the *shishōsetsu (personal novel). Confession as a means of revealing the private self to society and the strains within family life plays a significant role in many of his works. In essence, his writing focuses on accurately depicting the emotional truth of the individual.

In 1872 Shimazaki Haruki (pen name Tōson) was born in Magome village of Shinano Province, present-day Nagano Prefecture. His parents instructed him in classical Japanese poetry and Confucian classics and sent him to Tokyo as a young boy for a Western-style education. At Meiji Gakuin, a Christian college, he studied English literature and was introduced to Christianity; he was baptized at age sixteen. After graduating he wrote for the influential magazine *Women's Education Journal* (Jogaku zasshi), and later for the literary journal *Literary World* (Bungakukai).

He moved to Sendai to teach at Tōhoku Gakuin in 1896 and soon after published his first book of poetry, *Collection of Young Herbs* (Wakanashū, 1897). The poems were seen as modern in expressing the feelings of contemporary youth while using (albeit limited) traditional poetic language. Although Tōson gained critical acclaim for this and several subsequent poetry collections, he soon began experimenting in writing prose after moving to the town of Komoro in 1899. Here he wrote short essays that were based on his observations of nature and village life, published in 1912 as *Chikuma River Sketches* (Chikumagawa no suketchi). He developed an interest in impressionist painting and read English translations of continental European fiction and drama, including works by Tolstoy, Dostoyevsky, Flaubert, and Ibsen. Later, commenting on this period, he notes, "I was beset by a determination to see things more correctly, a determination so intense that I dropped into silence for some three years. Then I found myself writing these sketches.... I even acquired an easel which I would occasionally take out into the countryside in an effort to enrich my mind through what nature had to teach me. These sketches, then, were born from the plateau at the foot of Mt. Asama; from the lava, the sand, and the fierce winds" (*Chikuma River Sketches*, 121–122).

Tōson's first novel, *The Broken Commandment* (Hakai, 1906), was published after his move back to Tokyo, and it was recognized immediately as a groundbreaking work. The novel's main protagonist, Segawa Ushimatsu, hides the secret of his background as a *burakumin* (hereditary outcast) while living in a small town as a teacher. Ushimatsu's dilemma is whether to uphold his father's commandment never to reveal his origins or to follow the model of his intellectual mentor, Inoko Rentarō, a *burakumin* social reformer. In the end, Ushimatsu confesses his identity in front of his students and departs for Texas to begin a new life. Although some critics view *The Broken Commandment* as a social novel that addresses discrimination against *burakumin*, others read it as representing Tōson's own inner struggles for self-definition or as symbolizing the divide between the "inner self" and the "public self" in modern Japan.

Tōson modeled his next novels more directly on his own life and family. *Spring* (Haru, 1908) is based on Tōson's youthful experiences working as a writer for *Literary World*. *The Family* (Ie, 1910–11) depicts the decline of the Koizumi and Hashimoto families over a twelve-year period. Critics have considered the novel as one of the best works of Japanese naturalism for its painstaking attention to details of family life, such as financial burdens and emotional tensions that are never fully resolved. His most explicitly confessional work, *A New Life* (Shinsei, 1918–19), concerns the affair between the protagonist Kishimoto Sutekichi (based on Tōson himself) and his niece. After she becomes pregnant, he escapes to France temporarily to avoid scandal. The reactions to the work were split between those who saw Tōson's essentially autobiographical account as courageous and others who found him hypocritical and self-serving. (Tōson's niece, Komako, was sent to Taiwan for a short period after the affair became public.) Like Ushimatsu's confession in *The Broken Commandment*, Tōson's own confession through his writing reveals his desire to achieve redemption through self-expression, no matter what the cost.

Tōson's final completed work, *Before the Dawn* (Yoakemae, 1932–35), is a sweeping historical narrative of the social transformations in Japan before and after the Meiji Restoration of 1868. Based on the life of Tōson's father, the story centers on Aoyama Hanzō, who inherits the position of Magome village head-man and host for officials traveling between Kyoto and Edo (Tokyo). Hanzō, like Tōson's father, is fascinated by studies of the Edo-period Kokugakusha (na-tional learning scholars)—in particular, Hirata Atsutane—and hopes for the restoration of ancient Japan under the direct rule of the emperor. His expecta-tions, however, are ultimately disappointed and lead to his tragic downfall. In *Before the Dawn*, Tōson moved away from depicting a "self" defined by his own experiences (as in his previous works) and turned toward the past to recreate his father's life and times.

In 1943, Tōson died while working on his last novel, *Gates of the East* (Tōhō no mon, 1946). From the mid-Meiji period through the mid-Shōwa period, he moved from new-style poetry to autobiographical fiction to historical narratives. Yet his main legacy is that he helped redefine Japanese literature and poetry by depicting emotional reality in simple language. His representations of the indi-vidual vis-à-vis the family, society, and the past provide a highly personalized perspective on Japan's modern period.

—*Sayuri Oyama*

Bibliography

Fowler, Edward. *The Rhetoric of Confession:* Shishōsetsu *in Early Twentieth-Century Japanese Fiction.* Berkeley: University of California Press, 1988.

Keene, Donald. *Dawn to the West: Japanese Literature in the Modern Era.* 2 vols. New York: Holt, Rinehart and Winston, 1984.

Shimazaki Tōson. *Before the Dawn.* Trans. William E. Naff. Honolulu: University of Hawai'i Press, 1987.

——. *The Broken Commandment.* Trans. Kenneth Strong. Tokyo: University of Tokyo Press, 1974.

——. *Chikuma River Sketches.* Trans. William E. Naff. Honolulu: University of Hawai'i Press, 1991.

——. *The Family.* Trans. Cecilia Segawa Seigle. Tokyo: University of Tokyo Press, 1976.

Walker, Janet. *The Japanese Novel of the Meiji Period and the Ideal of Individualism.* Princeton: Princeton University Press, 1979.

15

NATSUME SŌSEKI

Natsume Sōseki (1867–1916) may be the best known of modern Japanese novelists. That his portrait is now featured on the one thousand-yen bill, the most common denomination, suggests his continuing stature as the most esteemed author in modern Japan.

Natsume Kinnosuke (pen name Sōseki) was born the year before the Meiji Restoration, which returned power from the shogunal government to the emperor. The reign of the Meiji emperor (1868–1912) was the period of Japan's astonishingly rapid transformation from an isolated, feudal society into a modern world power on a par with the nations of Europe and North America. Sōseki died four years after the Meiji period's end. His was a generally unhappy life, cut short in the end by ulcers—a result, perhaps, of his life-long psychological distress. He was at times plagued with tuberculosis and mental illness, as well. And yet he brought the novel, particularly the full-length novel, to a level of modernity and sophistication previously unknown in Japan. For many readers and critics these elements of Sōseki's life and work—his remarkable success coupled with internal struggles—symbolically parallel the process of modernization of the Japanese nation as a whole.

The early Meiji period afforded the young Sōseki the opportunity for a remarkable education: he excelled in both the Chinese classics of traditional instruction and the newly popular English language. At Tokyo Imperial University Sōseki took a degree in English literature and continued in the same program for graduate studies. Sōseki was particularly attracted to the robust egalitarianism he found in the essays of Mill and Spencer, the fiction of James, and the poetry of Whitman.

After a period of teaching middle-school and high-school English in rural Japan, he was sent by the Ministry of Education in 1900 to further his studies in England for two years. This was reportedly the most miserable period of Sōseki's life, as he was plagued by feelings of racial and cultural inferiority. (See "Nation and Nationalism.") Nevertheless, this period fostered in him the conviction that it was better for Japanese intellectuals to devise their own, "Japanese," solutions to the problems of modernity rather than to parrot Western ideas. His subsequent frequent public expressions of this belief were extremely influential. (See "My Individualism," for example.)

In 1903 Sōseki was appointed to a faculty position at Tokyo Imperial University teaching English. He found university teaching unfulfilling, and he quit in 1907 after having published two novels that achieved both popular and critical acclaim: *I Am a Cat* (Wagahai wa neko de aru), published serially in 1905–6, and *Botchan*, published in 1906 and loosely based on his own experiences teaching English in rural areas. Both were extremely humorous and retain much of their appeal even to contemporary readers.

At that time Sōseki took a job as the "staff novelist" for the daily *Asahi* newspaper. He was astonishingly prolific and versatile. In the course of five years from 1905 to 1910, he produced ten quite diverse novels, a collection of remarkable short stories, and works of literary criticism and theory. Sōseki is the only author of his time to produce fiction in so many different styles and in such a short period.

Unlike many of his *naturalist contemporaries, who struggled to portray their own lives as accurately as possible even if that meant confessing to squalid desires and actions, Sōseki believed in fictionality and imagination in literature. (His only excursion into semiautobiographical literature was in his final complete novel, *Grass on the Wayside* [Michikusa, 1915].) He believed that the task of the novelist was to bring order and an aesthetically pleasing structure to the chaotic flow that is human life. His male protagonists are deeply concerned with ethical questions but do not always manage to live ethical lives. Sōseki depicted the psychological struggles of such men in a world—late Meiji-period Japan—in which the moral and ethical foundations of society had undergone rapid and forceful change.

Sōseki next produced a "trilogy"—*Until After the Equinox* (Higansugi made, 1912), *The Wayfarer* (Kōjin, 1913), and *Kokoro* (1914)—culminating with the novel that many consider his masterpiece. *Kokoro*, which literally means "the heart," relies on an unusual structure: it features two first-person narrators, each of whom narrates one half of the story. The first is a young man, who identifies himself only as a student, who tells of his fascination with an older man met by chance on the seashore. The young narrator tells how he took the older man as a mentor, calling him by the honorific title *sensei*. Back in Tokyo the young man visits Sensei and his beautiful wife; he senses that something is not right between them, although they seem superficially to be a devoted couple. The student gradually comes to realize that Sensei is a deeply unhappy man, but he remains ignorant of the source of the problem. Finally, when the student is on a trip home to the countryside, he receives a letter from Sensei, which begins with the announcement that it is a suicide note and will serve to answer all the student's questions now that Sensei himself will be dead. The student instantly leaves the bedside of his dying father and rushes back toward Tokyo. On the train he reads Sensei's letter, which then comprises the second half of the novel.

The letter reveals that Sensei had been betrayed by relatives as a young man and had become bitter and cynical. Shortly thereafter he left the countryside to become a university student in Tokyo. Despite his mistrust of women he had fallen in love with his landlady's daughter, Shizu. Discovering that his fellow lodger and best friend, identified only as "K," also loved Shizu, Sensei had betrayed K's trust by hurrying to secure the landlady's permission to marry the daughter. When K had learned of this he had committed suicide, by cutting open his carotid artery.

Sensei and Shizu duly married, but Sensei has spent the rest of his life tormented by the guilt of having betrayed his friend. His wife has never known the reason for K's suicide, and consequently has no idea why her husband is so unhappy. Sensei explains to the student why he has never told his wife the truth:

> I am sure that if I had spoken to her with a truly repentant heart … she would have forgiven me. She would have cried, I know, from happiness. … I simply did not wish to taint her whole life with the memory of something that was ugly. I thought that it would be an unforgivable crime to let fall even the tiniest drop of ink on a pure spotless thing. (237)

Sensei commands that the student not reveal these matters to Shizu, either. Until she is dead, he prefers that the student not reveal his story to anyone. After that time, however, he suggests that the student should make it known to all Japan, as a cautionary tale. In the beginning of his letter he explains to the student why he has finally decided to transmit his life's story before committing suicide:

> You asked me to spread out my past like a picture scroll before your eyes. Then, for the first time, I respected you. I was moved by your decision … to grasp something that was alive within my soul. You wished to cut open my heart and see the blood flow. I was then still alive. I did not want to die. That is why I refused you and postponed the granting of your wish to another day. Now, I myself am about to cut open my own heart, and drench your face with my blood. And I shall be satisfied if, when my heart stops beating, a new life lodges itself in your breast. (128–129)

This remarkable and somewhat gory passage reminds the reader of the spurt of blood that accompanied K's earlier suicide. But it has another resonance as well. Sensei explains that his decision to commit suicide after so many years of unhappiness had been triggered by newspaper accounts of the *junshi* (a retainer following his feudal lord in death) of General Nogi Maresuke on the night of the funeral of the Meiji emperor. (See "Nation and Nationalism.") Meiji's death had marked the end of the era of Japan's successful emergence as a modern nation-state, worthy of a position among the other modern nations of the world. But Nogi's dramatic suicide to follow his lord—an act that had been outlawed for 150 years—was even more stunning to Japanese society. His anachronistic gesture, invoking the premodern "samurai code," called into question all the gains Japan had made in modernizing.

Sensei explains that he, too, feels left behind by the rapid forward thrust of modernization, and will now commit *junshi* to the spirit of the Meiji era. The blood Sensei describes as (metaphorically) drenching the student's face also therefore would call to the mind of the 1914 reader the gush of blood resulting from Nogi's cutting of his carotid artery (like K), after first making the symbolic cuts on his stomach required in traditional seppuku.

The novel ends with the end of Sensei's letter. The reader is left to wonder about the outcome of several important questions: what the student found on his arrival in Tokyo; what happened to Sensei's wife, Shizu; the consequences of the student's abandonment of his dying father; and so on. Sōseki's avoidance of an Aristotelian conclusion provided by an omniscient narrator underscores the fact that his sole intention in *Kokoro* is to explore the tormented psychology of the Meiji-period intellectual male.

After all the achievements of Meiji modernization—communications and transportation technology, reform of government systems, status as a colonizing power after victories in two wars—many people nonetheless felt a deep sense of unease, an intense need to consider questions of honor and tradition versus European-style modernization. General Nogi's suicide crystallized that dilemma. Whereas Sōseki's contemporary, *Mori Ōgai, reacted to Nogi's death by abandoning modern fiction altogether in favor of a return to Japanese history, Sōseki used the *junshi* to depict the effects of this psychological struggle; the result is *Kokoro* (Orbaugh 1996:13).

Sōseki's exploration of modern individualism is usually rational and analytical—far more than most Japanese writers of the prewar period he is known for his intellectualizing tendencies. This makes the rhetoric of blood and metaphorical reproduction in the above quotation especially striking in *Kokoro*. The passion and drama of the lives and deaths of men in this novel, symbolized repeatedly by gushing blood, is starkly contrasted with the stainless white purity of Shizu. Although Sensei wants to pass on his acquired wisdom, cynicism, and selfhood to the student through his life story, he wants to keep his wife ignorant of these peculiarly masculine struggles with modernity. From this and many of his other works it would be easy to read Sōseki as an unapologetic misogynist, in a mold common to the gender discourse of his time and not unfamiliar to scholars of Victorian England. Even among his contemporaries, however, Sōseki's problem with women is sufficiently striking that several critics have tried to explain it: Keene, quoting Sōseki's own explanation, attributes it to "a background of a thousand years of Chinese thought" (1984, 1:307); and Ueda to "an unusually pessimistic view of heterosexual relationship [*sic*]" (9). His explicitly stated admiration for the British tradition of independent thinking and public protest stops short when he writes with scorn about England's suffragettes and their "unimaginable contortions" ("My Individualism," 307–308).

But to call Sōseki a misogynist is too simple. His final complete novel, *Grass on the Wayside,* explores a painful marriage similar to his own. This novel is remarkable for the omniscient narrator's balanced portrayal of the unspoken grievances of both husband and wife, proving that Sōseki was capable of depicting the realities of life for women under the gender systems of Meiji Japan, whatever his private feelings might have been.

Sōseki died in 1916 while his next novel, *Light and Darkness* (Meian), was still being serialized.

—*Sharalyn Orbaugh*

Bibliography

Fujii, James. "Death, Empire, and the Search for History in Natsume Sōseki's *Kokoro*." In *Complicit Fictions: The Subject in Modern Japanese Prose Narratives.* Berkeley: University of California Press, 1993.

Hibbett, Howard. "Natsume Sōseki and the Psychological Novel." In Donald Shively, ed., *Tradition and Modernization in Japanese Culture,* 305–346. Princeton: Princeton University Press, 1971.

Keene, Donald. *Dawn to the West: Japanese Literature in the Modern Era.* 2 vols. New York: Holt, Rinehart and Winston, 1984.

Natsume Sōseki. *Botchan.* Trans. Alan Turney. Tokyo: Kodansha International, 1972.

——. *Grass on the Wayside.* Trans. Edwin McClellan. Chicago: University of Chicago Press, 1969.

——. *Kokoro.* Trans. Edwin McClellan. Washington, D.C.: Regnery Gateway, 1957.

——. *Light and Darkness.* Trans. V.H. Viglielmo. London: Peter Owen, 1971.

——. "My Individualism." Trans. Jay Rubin. In *Kokoro: A Novel and Selected Essays.* Lanham, Md.: Madison Books, 1992.

Orbaugh, Sharalyn. "General Nogi's Wife: Representations of Women in Narratives of Japanese Modernization." In Xiaobing Tang and Stephen Snyder, eds., *In Pursuit of Contemporary East Asian Culture,* 7–31. Boulder, Colo.: Westview Press, 1996.

Pollack, David. *Reading against Culture: Ideology and Narrative in the Japanese Novel.* Ithaca, N.Y.: Cornell University Press, 1992.

Sakaki, Atsuko. *Recontextualizing Texts: Narrative Performance in Modern Japanese Fiction*. Cambridge, Mass.: Harvard University Asia Center, 1999.

Ueda, Makoto. *Modern Japanese Writers*. Stanford: Stanford University Press, 1976.

Washburn, Dennis. *The Dilemma of the Modern in Japanese Fiction*. New Haven: Yale University Press, 1995.

Yiu, Angela. *Chaos and Order in the Works of Natsume Sōseki*. Honolulu: University of Hawai'i Press, 1998.

16

SEITŌ AND THE RESURGENCE OF WRITING
BY WOMEN

Seitō, a literary journal initially produced by five young women in Tokyo in September 1911, challenged conventional views of modern Japanese womanhood and achieved notoriety as a training ground for the *atarashii onna* ("new woman"). The use of the name *Seitō*, a rendering of "blue stocking" into Chinese characters, marked a kinship with the eighteenth-century English women's salon nicknamed the Bluestockings, and with contemporary Western use of the term as a pejorative for intellectual women. By assuming this name for themselves and their literary journal, the Bluestockings in Tokyo showed how well they knew that women's creativity would be no more welcomed in Japan than it had been in Europe.

Yet even they were astonished at the ferocity of the attacks occurring over the short span of *Seitō*'s publication. By the time *Seitō* folded in February 1916, the journal had been thrice banned, excluded from girls' schools around the nation, and denounced by prominent educators. Nevertheless, the fifty-two monthly issues of *Seitō* had provided a venue for numerous women to publish their writing. Although their notoriety as "new women" made it difficult for the Bluestockings to sustain their journal, it did enable them to turn national attention to the "woman question," making gender a controversial, much-discussed topic in the 1910s.

Understanding the controversies instigated by the Bluestockings and the themes prevalent in *Seitō* best begins with an idea of who these women were and who their society expected them to become. The five founding members,

Hiratsuka Raichō (Haruko, 1886–1971), Yasumochi Yoshiko (1885–1947), Mozume Kazuko (1888–1979), Kiuchi Teiko (1887–1919), and Nakano Hatsuko (1886–1983), were graduates of the newly established Japan Women's College. Privileged by education, position, and affluence, all could expect arranged marriages to young men with good career prospects. To the vast majority of Japanese women, who labored in fields, factories, or domestic service, these five led most enviable lives. The Bluestockings, however, took quite a different view of their position. They criticized their education for its lack of academic rigor and emphasis on domesticity. They railed against expectations that middle-class women should take up the mantle of the "good wife, wise mother," the patriotic matron who would live for educating her children, acting as helpmate to her husband, and contributing to the nation through thrifty housekeeping and concerted saving. (See "Gender, Family, and Sexualities in Modern Literature.") The Bluestockings wanted a much different life, one that embraced activity in the public realm and freedom in the private sphere.

The Bluestockings worked in this divide between themselves and others, always striving to widen rather than narrow the gap, and using bold language to accomplish this. Two pieces in the inaugural issue of Seitō set the defiant tone and have since been celebrated as landmark documents in Japanese feminism. The first, a series of verses by famed poet Yosano Akiko (1878–1942) called "Idle Thoughts in Restless Moments" (Sozorogoto), begins by cautioning the reader that women are like mountains, apparently stolid and passive but about to erupt in volcanic explosion. The other, *In the Beginning, Woman Was the Sun* (Genshi josei wa taiyō de atta), often referred to as the "Seitō Manifesto," was the first published work by Hiratsuka Raichō, who had already established herself as a rebel at age twenty-two when she became involved with author Morita Sōhei (1881–1949), a *naturalist writer and, more important, a husband and father. "Manifesto" calls on women to recover their hidden genius, the sun that blazes deep within them, and to defy all the boundaries of gender that prevent them from realizing their true selves. Significantly, neither work mentions women's rights or specific goals, yet both employ a language of high intensity and imagination that subverts the Meiji state's emphasis on order and control.

Another tactic in widening the cultural divide involved Bluestockings' writing in a confessional form popular at this time. This form required the authors to write about deeply personal, even "secret" feelings, providing an effective means to register discontent. In April 1912, Araki Ikuo's (1890–1943) story "The Letter" (Tegami) reveals a wife's dissatisfaction with her husband and her desire to continue an affair with a younger man. Similarly, Itō Noe's (1895–1923) December 1913 autobiographical story "Willfulness" (Wagamama) shows how she detests her prospective arranged marriage to a man in her Kyushu hometown and longs to be back with her sweetheart in Tokyo, a relationship that she does, in fact, realize and continues to write about in Seitō. The June 1915 story "To My Lover from a Woman in Prison" (Gokuchū no onna kara otoko e), written by

Yasuda Satsuki (1887–1933) after she read a newspaper account of a woman jailed for having an abortion, imagines the woman describing her ordeals in a letter to her lover. Notably, all three of these stories depict women defending criminal activity (adultery, fleeing one's husband, abortion), all are addressed to a sympathetic, sensitive man (a lover, but not a husband), and, by extension, to an equally sympathetic woman reader. Many *Seitō* readers responded to the confessional quality of these stories by writing the intimate details of their own lives to Hiratsuka Raichō and other Bluestockings and requesting advice.

For the censors, the truth in these stories lay in their potential to be "injurious to public morals" (Rubin 1984). Each of these three raised the censors' ire, though only the story on abortion earned *Seitō* an outright ban. Although men writers such as Tayama Katai (1871–1930) and *Shimazaki Tōson were leading the way in experimenting with confessional forms and championing sexual freedom, the prerogatives of gender afforded them an artistic license not extended to women writing in the same vein. There was no precedent for the daughters of respected families to speak out in such a public manner, to question social mores and to voice desire.

The audacity of stories such as these elicited a variety of responses. The first years saw much excitement: the number of Bluestocking members and contributors reached about 150, and volume soared from one thousand to three thousand copies per issue, with purchased issues being circulated informally among readers all over the country. Despite warnings against *Seitō* in girls' schools, women teachers appeared the most enthusiastic contributors, probably writing under assumed names. Officials condemned the journal, police in the countryside visited the homes of parents whose daughters were suspected of being Bluestockings, and the Bluestockings found difficulty in renting space for their offices. Newspaper gossip columnists exploited any hint of scandal, interpreting Bluestocking demands for freedom as nothing more than sexual promiscuity. They had particular fun with an evening's visit to the geisha quarters by a few Bluestockings and a new year's party where a "young man" visited editor Hiratsuka Raichō's room for a late-night drink. (What the press did not know was that the "man" was actually another Bluestocking, Ōdake Kōkichi [1893–1972], who was infatuated with Raichō.) By 1913 many original Bluestockings found the tension too much to bear and withdrew, leaving only those most committed to pressing their concerns in this risky cultural divide at the helm of *Seitō*.

The resulting change in group membership forced the remaining Bluestocking leaders to reevaluate their goals. Their mentor, Ikuta Chōkō (1882–1936), a literary teacher and translator and the man responsible for suggesting both the idea of *Seitō* and its name, had argued for making the discovery of women writers the group's primary purpose. Hiratsuka Raichō felt this goal too narrow, believing that the Bluestockings needed to address the broader issues of gender that *Seitō* had brought to the fore. The January 1913 *Seitō*, a special issue devoted to the woman question, made this new Bluestocking mission explicit.

Members would not run from being called "new women" but promised to adopt the label proudly and to give serious consideration to all that it might imply. Over the next few years, writers as diverse as Fukuda Hideko (1865–1927), Itō Noe, Iwano Kiyo (1882–1920), Yamada Waka (1879–1957), and Yamakawa Kikue (1890–1980) joined Hiratsuka Raichō in debating who the new woman could and should be.

Reading Seitō essays related to the woman question shows that for all their differences, the Bluestockings did share a belief that the practices of their daily lives should uphold their ideals. Some of their common demands could be found in feminist writing in any country—better education for women, more job opportunities, an equal partnership with one's mate, and the freedom to make critical life choices on one's own. But the Bluestockings did not hesitate to disagree with each other, debating such issues as abortion, prostitution, the value of chastity, and the meaning of "new woman." In crafting their arguments, the Bluestockings often looked toward the West, translating the work of Swedish eugenicist and mother advocate Ellen Key, anarchist Emma Goldman, and Russian mathematician Sonya Kovalevsky. Censors reprimanded the group for going too far in their demands on three occasions: twice censoring the work of Hiratsuka Raichō, who protested against the family system and declared that she would leave her parents' home, without their permission, to live with her younger lover, Okumura Hiroshi ("To the Women of the World" [Yō no fujin-tachi ni], April 1913, and "To My Parents on Independence" [Dokuritsu suru ni tsuite ryōshin ni], February 1914), and banning the issue carrying Fukuda Hideko's "Solution to the Woman Question" (Fujin mondai no kaisetsu, February 1913), which advocated that neither women nor men could be liberated as long as capitalism kept class hierarchies in place.

Although the radical stories and essays discussed here contributed importantly to the Bluestockings' reputation as "new women," it would be misleading to describe Seitō as uniformly confident in tone. Those who wrote regularly for Seitō also divulged their fears, their feelings of inadequacy, and the failures of their private lives. The Bluestockings rejected conventional solutions, but found searching for new ones an intellectual and emotional struggle. Even the feminist declarations in the inaugural issue by Abiko and Raichō include sentiments of self-doubt, and Itō Noe's escape from her arranged marriage, described in her February 1914 story "Flight," shows how distressed and lost the main character is in the wake of her decisive action. Two of the most touching stories in this vein are Katō Midori's (1888–1922) "Attachment" (Shūchaku, April 1912) and Ogasawara Sadako's (1887–1988) "Eastern Breeze" (Higashi kaze, April 1913) as both give vivid impressions of a woman's youthful ambitions and romantic feelings frustrated by the transition to marriage, even to a "new man," and motherhood. Such shows of vulnerability no doubt brought Seitō readers closer to these writers and increased the aura of drama surrounding the Bluestockings.

At critical junctures in postwar history, Japanese feminists have reconsidered the Bluestockings' legacy. In the wake of occupation-era reforms such as women's voting rights and other civil freedoms, some criticized the Bluestockings for not being more overtly political. More recently, others such as socialist Yamakawa Kikue deplored their lack of sympathy for working-class and poor women, while novelist Setouchi Harumi faulted their lack of attention to the tragic deaths in 1911 of Kanno Suga, hanged for attempting to kill the emperor, and Nogi Shizuko, who committed suicide in the wake of her husband General Nogi's suicide to atone for what he believed to be a dishonoring of the emperor in battle. (See "Nation and Nationalism.") Still, these women acknowledge the Bluestockings' work as an important chapter in Japanese women's history. This importance was underscored in 1971 when Hiratsuka Raichō's lengthy autobiography, which included a detailed history of the Bluestockings, was published, and in 1983 when *Seitō* was reprinted in its entirety. In the 1980s and 1990s novels, a film, and even comic books romanticized the group's more famous women, and even high-school textbooks made mention of *Seitō*. The vitality of feminist criticism at the end of the 1990s turned a different kind of critical and historical attention to *Seitō*, moving beyond the project of creating feminist heroes to questions of readership, narrative voice, publication systems, and so on. As *Seitō* nears its hundredth anniversary, the Bluestockings' poetry, fiction, drama, letters, essays, and translations continue to be read and discussed.

—Jan Bardsley

Bibliography

Andrew, Nancy. "The Seitōsha: An Early Japanese Women's Organization, 1911–1916." *Papers on Japan*, 6:45–69. Cambridge, Mass.: Harvard University East Asian Research Center, 1972.

Bardsley, Jan. *The Bluestockings of Japan: Feminist Essays and Fiction from Seitō, 1911–1916.* Ann Arbor: University of Michigan Center for Japanese Studies, in press.

Fujimura-Fanselow, Kumiko, and Atsuko Kameda, eds. *Japanese Women: New Feminist Perspectives on the Past, Present, and Future.* New York: Feminist Press, 1995.

Hiratsuka Raichō. *Genshi josei wa taiyō de atta* (In the Beginning, Woman Was the Sun). Tokyo: Otsuki, 1971.

Horiba Kiyoko. *Seitō no onnatachi* (The Women of Seitō). Tokyo: Kaien, 1975.

Lippit, Noriko. "*Seitō* and the Literary Roots of Japanese Feminism." *International Journal of Women's Studies* 2 (March–April 1979): 155–163.

Mulhern, Chieko. *Japanese Women Writers: A Bio-Critical Sourcebook.* Westport, Conn.: Greenwood, 1994.

Rubin, Jay. *Injurious to Public Morals: Writers and the Meiji State.* Seattle: University of Washington Press, 1984.

Seitō. Tokyo: Fuji, 1911–1916; rpt. 1983.

Setouchi Harumi. *Beauty in Disarray*. Trans. Sanford Goldstein and Kazuji Ninomiya. Rutland, Vt., and Tokyo: Charles E. Tuttle, 1993.

——. *Seitō*. Tokyo: Chūō kōron, 1984.

Shin Feminizumu Hihyō Kai, eds. *Seitō o yomu* (A *Seitō* Reader). Tokyo: Gakugei shorin, 1998.

Sievers, Sharon. *Flowers in Salt: The Beginnings of Feminist Consciousness in Modern Japan*. Stanford: Stanford University Press, 1983.

17

THE REVIVAL OF POETRY IN TRADITIONAL FORMS

Although many English readers may think of poetry as being far removed from the world of power, probably no form of Japanese literature has been as influenced by the political realm as verse in traditional forms. The seriousness with which such works are sometimes taken can be illustrated by two tragic events. The first occurred in 1911, when the socialist leader Kōtoku Shunsui (1871–1911) was executed along with eleven others after being convicted of plotting to assassinate the emperor. Included in the flimsy evidence against him was a poem he had composed on the *odai* (set theme) "New Year's Snow" *(shinnen no yuki)*:

bakudan no	Seeing that it is a world
furu yo to mishite	where it is bombs that fall,
hatsuyume wa	my first dream of the year is
chiyoda no matsu no	the sound of the pines of Chiyoda
yuki ore no oto	breaking under the weight of the snow.

Though it was written as a joke with an anti-imperialist aspect (Kōtoku had vigorously opposed the Russo-Japanese War), the tribunal used this verse as evidence of Kōtoku's treasonous intent (Murai 1999:280).

The second event, half a century later, was a murder at the home of the president of the publishing company Chūō kōron in 1961. The attack by a young rightist was precipitated by the publication of "The Story of a Dream of Courtly Elegance" (Fūryū mutan), written by Fukazawa Shichirō (1914–87), which, in surrealistic fashion, combines a lampoon of the writing of traditional verse with a Rabelaisian description of the execution of the imperial family. Clearly, in Japan, poetry can be a matter of life and death.

At the beginning of the Meiji period, poetry in traditional forms was seen by many to be anachronistic and inimical to modernization. Various reforms and solutions were suggested, leading ultimately into the renaming of the major genres. One was now known as tanka (literally, "short verse"—what earlier would have been called *waka*), with a metrical count of 5/7/5/7/7 syllables; and the other haiku (literally, "light verses") with a count of 5/7/5. While the metrical forms of these two genres were traditional, they were intimately implicated in the construction of the new modern imperial Japanese nation-state. Tanka was introduced into court ceremonial in the second year of the Meiji era (1869) with the reestablishment of the O-uta-dokoro (Imperial Poetry Bureau). This bureau was under the direct control of the Cabinet itself. The year 1869 also saw the establishment of the annual *uta-kai hajime* (New Year's poetry contest). In 1874 poems by commoners were accepted into the annual event, and in 1879 these poems were actually read aloud in the presence of the emperor. Finally, in 1882, the winning poems were printed in the daily newspapers, along with the compositions by the emperor, empress, and other members of the imperial household (Uchino 1988:176).

Ironically, this transformation of the New Year's Poetry Contest from a court ritual into a public event coincided with the publication of *The Book of New-Form Poems* (Shintaishi shō), which rejected the traditional form entirely, arguing that it was inherently inadequate to the modern world. This inadequacy of the poetic form was also proclaimed by *Tsubouchi Shōyō in *The Essence of the Novel* (Shōsetsu shinzui, 1885–86). However, rather than simply its form or length, greater concern was expressed about the content of tanka. Hagino Yoshiyuki (1860–1924) and Ikebe Yoshikata (1864–1923), for example, argued in their "Thesis on the Reform of National Literature and *Waka*" (Kokugaku waka kairyō ron, 1887) that the tone of tanka "should be made more masculine and conducive to a spirit of bravery" (Keene 1984, 2:10).

Standard histories of modern tanka make much out of the antagonism between the supposedly effeminate "conservatives" and militaristic "radicals." The former is represented by the court-centered Kei'en school, and the latter by the *Man'yōshū*-inspired poetry of Ochiai Naobumi (1861–1903) and his Asakasha group. The *Man'yōshū* (Collection of Ten Thousand Leaves, 759 *ante quem*) was Japan's earliest collection of native verse, and yet had been mostly ignored in later Japanese poetry from the tenth through eighteenth centuries. It had enjoyed a new revival of interest among the followers of *kokugaku* (national learning) in the late eighteenth and early nineteenth centuries, who believed that they found in it a repository of "pure" Japaneseness, unsullied by the introduction of such foreign creeds as Buddhism and the cultures of China. Yet certainly some part of the nineteenth-century imperial court had allied itself with the growing interest in the *Man'yōshū* early on, with the newly established Imperial Press issuing a deluxe 124-volume edition of the collection in 1879 (Mostow 1995:5).

However, what is generally recognized as the true modern battle cry against traditional *waka* is a series of essays entitled *Sounds Ruinous to the Country* (Bōkoku no on, 1894) by the young Yosano Tekkan (pen name of Yosano Hiroshi, 1873–1935). But literary historians have been led astray by accepting the self-proclaimed motivation of Tekkan's attack. Both he and they would have us believe that the issue was the Kei'en school's adherence to composition on set topics, in contrast to the reformers' demand that poems be written from real feelings and events. Yet, as Nagahata Michiko has pointed out, Kei'en style already showed distinct signs of having jumped on the *Man'yōshū* bandwagon and its practitioners were likewise insisting that poems came from true feelings and the things seen before one's own eyes (Nagahata 1989:82–83).

Tekkan's poetry was far overshadowed by that of his wife, Yosano Akiko (1878–1942), probably the most celebrated Japanese female poet of the twentieth century. Her most famous book is *Tangled Hair* (Midaregami, 1901), a collection of dense, complicated poems of often explicit eroticism. Its publication caused an uproar, with conservative poets such as Sasaki Nobutsuna (1872–1963) branding the poet a "whore" (Morton 2000:242). Yet the work was wildly popular and influential on a whole generation of poets.

While early Meiji politicians had made tanka a part of the imperial court's ceremonies, they early on enlisted haiku poets to fulfill an educational and moral mission toward the newly created citizenry. In 1873 the Ministry of Religious Affairs began to recruit haiku masters for the Kyōdōshoku (educational leadership committee), which aimed at the modernization of the citizenry and their morality. The year 1874 saw the establishment of Haikai Meirin Kōsha (Haikai Morality Society) and the Haikai Kyōrin Meisha (Haikai Culture Society), the latter of which published the *Haikai Morality Magazine* (Haikai Meirin Zasshi). The Edo-period master Bashō was deified by the state in 1879, and his poems were seen as sources of moral truths. Bashō was revered as the god Hana-no-moto Daimyōjin, and in 1885 a Bashō-sect of the revived Shintō state religion was formed (Horikiri 1999:381–382).

Reform in haiku was led by Masaoka Shiki (1867–1902). This revolution began in 1892 in his series "Haiku Talks from the Otter's Den" (Dassai sho'oku haiwa), where he criticized the hackneyed nature of contemporary haiku and even launched an attack on Bashō. In 1894—the same year as Tekkan's "Sounds Ruinous to the Country"—Shiki was introduced to the painter Nakamura Fusetsu (1866–1943) who, as a student of the school of *yōga* ("Western painting" in oils) made Shiki familiar with the concept of *shasei* (sketching from nature). The idea of haiku's being a form of visual realism conveyed in words became the hallmark of Shiki's innovations.

In July 1894 the Sino-Japanese War broke out, and Shiki hastened his premature death by insisting on serving as a war correspondent there. By the time of the Russo-Japanese war of 1904–5 the traditional tanka form had reestablished for itself a firm position in both the state and literary world. And whereas Emperor Meiji had not composed one poem on the topic of the Sino-Japanese War (Kimata 1971:626), during the Russo-Japanese War, in Carol Gluck's memorable phrasing, Emperor Meiji's "involvement with the war overflowed the rescripts announcing victories and urging endurance and spilled over into poetry. Of the more than ninety thousand verses the emperor is credited with, he (and perhaps the Imperial Poetry Bureau) composed 7,526 poems during the year and a half of war. This prodigious proof to his subjects of the deep imperial concern for their sacrifice included the famous poem, 'Crush the enemy for the sake of the nation, but never forget to have mercy,' but the poetic gist more commonly ran along these lines: 'When I think of those in battle, I have no heart for the flowers'" (Gluck 1985:89).

As Irokawa Daikichi has argued, "It was during the Russo-Japanese War period that the emperor was finally established as the center of *kokutai* [national polity] and the focus of elementary education." The upper division of the 1910 *Elementary Japanese Reader* (grades 4–6) included poems by Emperor Meiji, General Nogi, and Admiral Tōgō; pieces with titles such as "A Soldier of the Front"; and other works designed to inculcate loyalty and self-sacrifice (Irokawa 1985:300–305).

This elevation of Emperor Meiji as a poet, and his poems as a schoolbook for the citizenry, continued into the Taishō era. Sasaki Nobutsuna's edition of Meiji's poetry, *Heart of Japan* (Yamatogokoro, 1914), includes a seventy-page appendix with essays by such literary scholars as Haga Yaichi (1867–1927) on "The Emperor's Compositions and Education" (Gyosei to kyōiku), Hagino Yoshiyuki on "The Compositions of the Late Emperor and Filial Piety" (Sentei to onkōdō), and even essays by two scholars once opposed to the tanka form, Inoue Tetsujirō (1855–1944, one author of *The Book of New-Form Poems*) and Mikami Sanji (1865–1939). As Kimata has pointed out, the basis of selection of poems for the Taishō 11 (1922) edition of Meiji's poetry was clearly its educational content (1971:617).

By the early years of the Shōwa era, Meiji had been elevated into a *kasei* ("saint of poetry"), as seen most particularly in the writings of *Kitahara Hakushū in a 1927 article and in Saitō Mokichi's (1882–1953) book *Survey of Meiji and Taishō Tanka* (Meiji Taishō tanka shi gaikan, 1929). Mokichi, like Hakushū one of the most famous and influential poets of the period, selected in particular poems written by Meiji during the Russo-Japanese War (Kimata 1971:621). By the 1930s, Mokichi and the poetry journal associated with him, *Araragi*, devoted most of their poetic inspiration to the war effort.

The prewar years of the Shōwa period (1926–1989) witnessed considerable censorship from which tanka was not exempt and which included the suppression of not just proletarian poetry but appreciative studies of Shiki as well (Uchino 1988:33). At the same time, the form was virtually taken over as a tool of the war effort, a trend that can be said to have culminated symbolically in 1942 when Maeda Yūgure (1883–1951) abandoned writing in the "irregular" forms of modern poetry and returned to the purity of "the regular tanka form and classical language" (Keene 1984, 2:38).

In the postwar era, haiku has become a tool of internationalization and peace, especially after the inception of the international competition for school-children and others sponsored by Japan Air Lines since 1964. Contrarily, during the same period we can see the increasing reassociation of tanka with the emperor. While poets such as Kimata Osamu (b. 1906) and his journal *Yakumo* "dealt severely with tanka poets who had been wartime collaborators" (Keene 1984, 2:75), the New Year's Poetry Contest resumed after an interruption of only one year, with Saitō Mokichi among the judges.

Certainly the political is involved in the annual poetry contest, and not just in the abstract sense of supporting the emperor system: Murai Osamu notes that following the annexation of Korea in 1910, the government used poems submitted by the *shinmin* (natives of the new colonies) as evidence of their willing assimilation into the Japanese empire (1999:280). Likewise, it was only two years before Okinawa's scheduled reversion to Japan that poems from Okinawans appear among the selections (Uchino 1988:195–196).

Participation of the citizenry has continued to swell. The low point was 1953, with only 5,765 entries, but it reached a peak in 1964 with 46,908 (Uchino 1988:183–184)—the same year as the Tokyo Olympics. Poetry in both traditional and nontraditional forms has also stayed closely associated with women since Akiko's day, and many female authors best known for their fiction, such as *Ōba Minako and Tomioka Taeko (b. 1935), are also prolific poets. Akiko's continued influence can be seen in the 1998 publication by the extremely popular female poet Tawara Machi (b. 1962) of a contemporary translation of Akiko's most famous collection, *Tangled Hair—Chocolate Translation* (Midaregami chokorêtogo yaku).

—*Joshua S. Mostow*

Bibliography

Beichman, Janine. *Masaoka Shiki*. Boston: Twayne, 1982; rpt. Tokyo: Kodansha International, 1986.

Gluck, Carol. *Japan's Modern Myths: Ideology in the Late Meiji Period*. Princeton: Princeton University Press, 1985.

Horikiri Minoru. "Haisei Bashō zō no tanjō to sono sui'i" (The Image of the Saint of Haikai, Bashō, and Its Transformations). In Shirane Haruo and Suzuki Tomi, eds., *Sōzō sareta koten: Kanon keisei, kokumin kokka, nihon bungaku* (The Constructed Canon: Canon Formation, the Nation-State, and Japanese Literature), 366–392. Tokyo: Shin'yōsha, 1999.

Irokawa Daikichi. *The Culture of the Meiji Period*. Trans. Marius B. Jansen. Princeton: Princeton University Press, 1985.

Keene, Donald. *Dawn to the West: Japanese Literature in the Modern Era.* 2 vols. New York: Holt, Rinehart and Winston, 1984.

Kimata Osamu. *Hyōron Meiji-Taishō no kajintachi* (A Critique of Meiji-Taishō Poets). Tokyo: Meiji shoin, 1971.

Morton, Leith. "The Canonization of Yosano Akiko's *Midaregami.*" *Japanese Studies* 20, no. 3 (2000): 237–254.

Mostow, Joshua S. "Translating Imperialism: The Emperor System, *Waka,* and Its English Translation." *CJR Paper Series* 3. Centre for Japanese Research, Institute of Asian Research, University of British Columbia, 1995.

Murai Osamu. "Metsubō no gensetsu kūkan: Minzoku, kokka, kōshōsei" (The Discursive Space of "Vanishing": Folk, State, and Oral Tradition). In Shirane Haruo and Suzuki Tomi, eds., *Sōzō sareta koten: Kanon keisei, kokumin kokka, nihon bungaku* (The Constructed Canon: Canon Formation, the Nation-State, and Japanese Literature), 258–300. Tokyo: Shin'yōsha, 1999.

Nagahata Michiko. *Yūkoku no uta: Tekkan to Akiko, sono jidai* (A Song of Patriotism: Tekkan and Akiko and Their Time). Tokyo: Shinhyōron, 1989.

Uchino Mitsuko. *Tanka to Tennōsei* (Tanka and the Emperor System). Nagoya: Fūbaisha, 1988.

Ueda Makoto. *Modern Japanese Haiku: An Anthology.* Toronto: University of Toronto Press, 1976.

——. *Modern Japanese Tanka: An Anthology.* New York: Columbia University Press, 1996.

18

POETRY IN CHINESE IN THE MODERN PERIOD

During the Edo period, when the government espoused Confucian doctrine and encouraged the study of Chinese texts, large numbers of Japanese, particularly those of the samurai class, became proficient in the reading and writing of classical Chinese. Many of these tried their hand at composing *kanshi* or poetry in Chinese, sometimes merely as a pleasant literary pastime, at other times because they wished to treat themes that could not be handled effectively in the traditional Japanese poetic forms. Particularly in the closing years of the Edo period, *kanshi* became an important medium for decrying social or political ills or voicing opposition to the shogunate. Many of the leaders of the movement to restore power to the emperor left behind poems that, if not of outstanding literary merit, have been prized for their patriotic sentiments.

This widespread popularity of the *kanshi* form carried over into the early years of the Meiji period, and in fact reached new heights. Many of the founders of the new government were writers of *kanshi* and encouraged the use of the form. Literary societies and schools devoted to the teaching of *kanshi* flourished, modern printing methods aided the dissemination of poetry collections and works on poetic criticism, and the leading newspapers ran *kanshi* columns alongside those devoted to poetry in Japanese. New themes were essayed, and in addition to the usual hackneyed celebrations of the Japanese landscape there now appeared descriptions in Chinese verse of Niagara Falls or the Rocky Mountains, or poems on the introduction of the electric light to Japan in 1884 or the life of Maria Theresa of Austria. The opening of the country allowed Chinese scholars to come to Japan or Japanese to journey to China to study under native teachers, factors that helped to foster the spread and improvement of *kanshi* writing.

The history of Meiji *kanshi* is customarily divided into two periods. The first, from the beginning of the Meiji era in 1868 to around 1890, was essentially a continuation of the late-Edo scene. It was dominated by two men of the Seirei school, Ōnuma Chinzan (1818–1891), a disciple of the prominent Edo-period poet and supporter of the imperial cause Yanagawa Seigan (1789–1858); and Mori Shuntō (1819–1889), who had also been associated with Yanagawa Seigan at one point and was friendly with the leaders of the new government. In 1875 Shuntō founded a periodical, *New Prose and Poetry* (Shinbunshi), in which he advocated study of the Chinese poets of the Qing, particularly those who wrote in the Seirei style. He enjoyed the patronage of Itō Hirobumi and other government leaders, who published their works in his periodical. As a result, the *kanshi* of the period took on the tone of a state-sponsored literature and were often nationalistic in theme. Such official patronage no doubt lent prestige to the *kanshi* form, but it also tended to stifle any impulse toward stylistic reform or innovation.

The second period of Meiji *kanshi*, from around 1890 to 1911, represents the high point of poetry in that form. The most prominent figure was Mori Kainan (1863–1911), son of Mori Shuntō, who entered government service at an early age and thereafter held a succession of official posts. Like his father, he admired the Qing poets, taking as his model in particular the works of Wu Wei-ye (1609–1672).

Kainan's most famous work, which in many ways typifies the *kanshi* of the Meiji period, is the long poem entitled "Homeward Voyage: One Hundred Rhymes." Kainan had accompanied the statesman Itō Hirobumi on the latter's last trip to Korea in 1909 and was wounded at the time Itō was felled by an assassin's bullet in Harbin. The poem, couched in highly ornate language, eulogizes Itō's career and describes his assassination and the escorting of his body back to Japan. For students of English literature, Kainan is also noteworthy because he was Ernest Fenollosa's teacher in the reading of Chinese verse, and Fenollosa's notes on that subject formed the basis of Ezra Pound's highly influential *Cathay* translations.

Kainan had numerous outstanding disciples who carried on his work and won renown in *kanshi* circles. But by the time of his death in 1911, literary interest in Japan had shifted to the new forms and genres being introduced from the West or the newly rejuvenated tanka and haiku forms. (See "The Revival of Traditional Poetic Forms.") The study of classical Chinese had lost its place of prominence in the Japanese educational system and Chinese verse was no longer the favored medium it had once been; even the kindest of critics admit that in the late Meiji period and thereafter, *kanshi* cease to occupy a place of any real importance in Japanese literature.

The works of the professional *kanshi* poets of the Meiji period, erudite in language and largely devoid of any feeling of freshness or originality, are seldom read today and have received little critical attention. Only the Chinese poetry of such men as Masaoka Shiki (1867–1902), *Mori Ōgai, or *Natsume Sōseki, who are famous for their work in other genres, continues to attract notice. The two hundred or more *kanshi* of Sōseki, because of their relatively simple, often Zen-flavored style and personal nature, have won particular praise.

Kanshi are admired for their economy of expression and attractive appearance when inscribed in fine calligraphy, but they are not easy to compose, particularly those forms requiring tonal regulation. The rhymes and tones are not those of modern Chinese but those in use some thousand years ago, when the forms took shape. One must therefore either memorize the ancient rhymes and tones or be constantly consulting a prosody manual when composing. At present, *kanshi* are written mainly by two groups in Japanese society, scholars of Chinese language and literature and members of the Buddhist clergy. If steps were taken to simplify the prosodic requirements, or there were some unexpected resurgence of Chinese studies in Japan, the form might possibly regain some of its former popularity. Otherwise, *kanshi* writing in Japan would appear to be a dying art.

—*Burton Watson*

Bibliography

Masaoka Shiki. *Selected Poems.* Trans. Burton Watson. New York: Columbia University Press, 1997.

Nihon Yunesuko Kokunai Iinkai, ed. *Essays on Natsume Sōseki's Works.* Tokyo: Japan Society for the Promotion of Science, 1972.

Watson, Burton. *Japanese Literature in Chinese: Poetry and Prose by Japanese Writers of the Later Period.* New York: Columbia University Press, 1976.

19

MEIJI-PERIOD THEATER

The Meiji period brought about radical change in Japanese culture and theater. The virtual flood of Western influence inundating Japan after two and a half centuries of isolation spawned a dizzying atmosphere in the early-Meiji years, which came to be known as *bunmei kaika* (civilization and enlightenment). Under that rubric, the Japanese wholeheartedly accepted things Western and disdained things Japanese. At times Japanese intellectuals went to extremes of passionate advocacy for ludicrous fads, some even urging, for example, abolition of the Japanese language in favor of English and intermarriage with Westerners to improve the Japanese racial stock. Gradually, by the mid-1880s such hysteria subsided and more practical issues arising from the encounter with the West began to emerge.

That was the context for one of the central cultural developments of the era: the encounter between Japanese and Western theater. Theater in the Meiji period is best considered in this cross-cultural light. In keeping with the pervasive spirit of this new age, certain theater figures saw the necessity for a new kind of drama. Their vision took shape only gradually, refracted at first through the Theater Reform Committee (Engeki kairyō kai, est. 1887), Literary Arts Society (Bungei kyōkai, 1906–13), and Free Theater (Jiyū gekijō, 1909–19).

Yet, although Japanese culture in general became a virtual cauldron of change, the classical stage at first hewed to its deeply rooted traditions. The classical forms of Noh, Bunraku, and Kabuki, consolidated through the long years of the Edo period (1603–1867), were so entrenched by the mid-nineteenth cen-

tury that efforts to shape a new theater to fit the new age met with persistent obstacles at every turn. Noh and Kabuki actors were so entrenched in their respective styles of acting that real change was almost inconceivable. New Noh
plays were rare, and new Kabuki plays were never as popular as the old favorites.

Even such new stage expressions as *shinpa*, or new-school drama (to distinguish it from old-school drama, Kabuki), and *shinsei shinpa*, or new-life shinpa,
and *shinkokugeki*, or new national theater, and the like, though they came into
being ostensibly as alternatives to Kabuki, were so steeped in Kabuki and
Kabuki-related techniques that they hardly could be seen as modern, much less
innovative. *Shinpa* was perhaps the most vigorous of these efforts, arising in the
late 1880s largely through the initiative of Kawakami Otojirō (1864–1911) mainly
to express political views opposed to government policies. The fight scenes in
shinpa were so realistic that the plays gained brief popularity among the disaffected Kabuki crowd and those with political bones of contention. In addition,
unlike Noh and Kabuki, *shinpa* allowed women on stage (women's roles in
Noh and Kabuki are played by male actors), contemporary costumes, and even
Western music. Still, its acting and directing styles were thoroughly redolent of
Kabuki, including the actors' stylized movement and use of the *onnagata* (male
actor of female roles). Any such phenomenon as a new kind of Japanese theater
inevitably would have to break with the classical past and merge with the Western present.

Early theater-reform efforts, however, were directed at Kabuki through the
Theater Reform Committee, but there were two unfortunate results. The first
was that in pandering to the many popular Western-inspired fads, Kabuki became less traditional and stylized than it was wont to be. Some of these Kabuki
productions must have been very curious indeed. A play in 1881, for example,
featured a character sporting such Western items as a straw hat, short boots, umbrella, briefcase, and large pocket watch. Another play used foreign actors un-
trained in Kabuki technique (the arriviste producer even boasting loudly of his
modified lifestyle: he drank beer instead of sake and insisted on cooked rather
than raw fish). Still other productions featured Japanese soldiers in tight Western uniforms and Japanese women in billowing Victorian skirts.

This sort of extremism was far from the notions of idealized bravery and femininity evoked by more traditional representations and simply failed to capture
the popular Japanese imagination. Such "reform" efforts, then, merely hastened
a decline in prestige for Kabuki, relegating it to the realm of low-class entertainment for the uneducated masses. Less adherence to traditional techniques and
less stylization would surely have been necessary for a different, more realistic
kind of theater; in Kabuki such a phenomenon served only to lessen its charm.

The second unfortunate result of these attempts to reform Kabuki promoted
contemporary Western theater, and not a Japanese development, as the ideal
modern theater for Japan. Here, too, the transition was awkward. The gulf between Western and Japanese values and ideas was so vast as to hinder an easy

crossing. On matters from Christianity and democracy to individualism and women's rights, Japanese understanding was shallow at best, often totally inaccurate. Moreover, blithely structuring a Western theater form with Japanese perceptions of Western behavior or with Japanese ideas, customs, and physicality more often than not yielded awkward, even incomprehensible results. A 1902 production of *Hamlet* by the reform-minded Kawakami Otojirō, for example, had the star of the play enter the stage by riding a big-wheel bicycle down the *hanamichi* (the "flower path" that connects the rear of the Kabuki theater to stage right). And psychological identification with roles, long a staple of Western realistic, representational acting, was completely foreign to Japanese actors, trained as they were in stylized, presentational techniques. In fact, with few exceptions, this kind of conflict has been conspicuous in Japanese plays until after World War II. Until about 1960, Japanese theater can be seen quite simply as derivative of Western forms.

This was the atmosphere in 1906, when the reformers Shimamura Hōgetsu (1871–1918), who had studied theater at Oxford and the University of Berlin, and *Tsubouchi Shōyō, who had long been a major figure in reforming Japanese literature and theater and had participated in the Theater Reform Committee, reorganized the Literary Arts Society into an educational theater workshop—the first of its kind in Japan. The asserted aim of this school was to shape a new theater that would meet the needs of a new age, principally by going beyond Kabuki—a corrupt form, to Shōyō's mind—and by rendering aesthetic experiences that would serve to enlighten society. To this end, Shōyō firmly refused to accept former Kabuki actors into the workshop, preferring instead young people with no acting experience whom he could train from scratch. By staging such plays as Shakespeare's *The Merchant of Venice* (1906), *Hamlet* (1907 and 1910), *Julius Caesar* (1913)—the indefatigable Shōyō translated all of Shakespeare's plays—and Ibsen's *A Doll's House* (1911), his group successfully presented an idea of Western theater to the Japanese public. In fact, Tsubouchi revered Ibsen so much that he became the virtual god of modern theater in Japan, and Chekhov was not far behind.

A longer-lived experiment than the Literary Arts Society was the Free Theater, the name and inspiration for which came from André Antoine's Théâtre Libre (est. 1887) in Paris and Otto Brahms's Freie Bühne (est. 1889) in Berlin. The moving force behind the Free Theater was Osanai Kaoru (1881–1928), influenced early in his career by Shōyō (though Osanai later broke with him). Osanai became a staunch advocate of realism and found in the social implications of Ibsen's plays—in particular, the exposure of reality by laying bare bourgeois hypocrisies—his idea of the modern theater, prototypically naturalistic; this was the new form of theater he was seeking to establish in Japan. The intensity of his quest inevitably led Osanai and his like-minded band of Young Turks to excesses. They so revered Ibsen, for example, that they denigrated Shakespeare and sneered at the more staid Literary Arts Society. In addition,

Osanai was convinced that a new kind of theater in Japan was realizable only by breaking completely with traditional Japanese forms and importing modern Western plays. He gave an air of legitimacy to the so-called *hon'yaku jidai* (age of translation), crystallizing his approach with the famous slogan, "Ignore tradition." (In addition, he is credited with inventing the word *shingeki,* or "new theater.")

Although Osanai encouraged Japanese playwrights to write their own plays, their efforts were largely imitations of Western plays, often irrelevant to the concerns of Japanese society and lost in the blind allegiance granted the "superior" European theater. Osanai clearly preferred to stage the latest in European plays by Frank Wedekind, Maxim Gorky, Gerhart Hauptmann, Anton Chekhov, and Maurice Maeterlinck, in addition, of course, to Ibsen. Thus, the legacy of Osanai's Free Theater, as of the Theater Reform Committee and Tsubouchi's Literary Arts Society, had far more to do with transplanting Western plays than with fostering a new, indigenous Japanese theater. Yet, Osanai had incalculable influence in establishing techniques for enacting these Western plays, hence, for a new kind of theater that would emerge in Japan.

—*John K. Gillespie*

Bibliography

Bowers, Faubion. *Japanese Theatre.* New York: Hermitage House, 1952; rpt. Rutland, Vt.: Tuttle, 1974.

Horie-Weber, Akemi. "Modernization of the Japanese Theatre: The Shingeki Movement." In W. G. Beasley, ed., *Modern Japan: Aspects of History, Literature, and Society,* 147–165. Berkeley: University of California Press, 1977.

Ibaragi Ken. *Nihon shingeki shōshi* (A Short History of Japanese Shingeki). Tokyo: Miraisha, 1980.

Ortolani, Benito. *The Japanese Theatre: From Shamanistic Ritual to Contemporary Pluralism.* Princeton: Princeton University Press, 1990.

Ozasa Yoshio. *Dorama no seishinshi* (The Intellectual History of Modern Japanese Drama). Tokyo: Shinsuisha, 1983.

Rimer, J. Thomas. *Toward a Modern Japanese Theatre: Kishida Kunio.* Princeton: Princeton University Press, 1974.

20

UNO CHIYO

While in her eighties, and shortly after her best-selling, two-volume autobiography *I Will Go on Living* (Ikite yuku watashi, 1983) was published, Uno Chiyo (1897–1996) was a frequent guest on popular television interview shows. Her eyes glittering with magnified brightness behind thick glasses, Uno would regale her hosts with her insouciant views on life and love. "If ever I had a mind to do something—I would do it without a moment's thought," she has bragged. "I have never looked back. Never known a day of pain. Never even had a headache" (Copeland 1984). Uno's alleged impulsiveness is clearly manifest in her personal life. Wed thrice and divorced as often, she was never one to keep her private failures to herself. In fact, she reveled in her sexual exploits, boasting, "No one is as fortunate as a woman writer, no sooner does she break up with a man than she can write about it all without the slightest sense of shame" (Uno 1978:173). And write she did. Each of her marriages and many of her love affairs gave way to significant narratives—most conforming to the *shishōsetsu (personal novel) variety of personal narrative that then dominated the literary scene.

Uno made her debut in 1921 when a story she had submitted to a competition sponsored by the *Jiji shinpō* newspaper won first place. The story "Made-up Face" (Shifun no kao) is a slight work, but the casual spontaneity in the narrative perspective and the sensuousness that characterize it would become Uno's hallmark. By 1925 she had published five collections of short stories. Her success was stunning. She had leaped onto the literary scene without a mentor, without a supporting coterie, and seemingly without much effort. Perhaps the primary reason for Uno's meteoric rise was that she offered a fresh, sensual perspective to a literary world sated with the ponderous darkness of *naturalism and now being pounded by Marxist and socialist dogma.

Further fueling public interest in Uno's works were the successive relationships she had with well-known men and the way Uno recounted each liaison "without the slightest sense of shame." Her brief marriage to the fledgling writer Ozaki Shirō (1898–1964) netted her more than a few works of autobiographical fiction, and her five-year affair with the Western-style painter Tōgō Seiji (1897–1978) provided the material for her first novel, *Confessions of Love* (Irozange, 1935), in addition to numerous short stories. Uno's twenty-five-year marriage to Kitahara Takeo, which ended when Uno was in her sixties, yielded such outstanding works as *To Stab* (Sasu, 1966), "Happiness" (Kōfuku, 1970), for which she received the Japanese Women Writers Award, and *The Sound of Rain* (Ame no oto, 1974), among others. So volatile was Uno's life and so candid her subsequent literary production that she was soon dubbed "a writer of illicit love," a label Uno seemed as eager to deserve as her critics were to enforce.

A careful study of Uno's oeuvre, however, will reveal that this reputation for casualness and impetuosity is belied by a careful literary craft. Despite her bravado, Uno was above all an artist, her aura of nonchalance a consciously rendered performance. When *Confessions of Love* was hailed as the greatest romance in modern (prewar) Japan, Uno credited her former lover, Tōgō Seiji, and his skill as a storyteller, claiming she wrote down what he had told her about his failed romances word for word. She is equally modest with "The Puppet Maker" (Ningyōshi Tenguya Kyūkichi, 1942), her poignant account of an aging puppet carver, which she avers is little more than a transcription of the old man's soliloquy. Although she is correct in saying that the story is based on the interview she held with the eighty-six-year-old artist, the interview itself was conducted over a three-week period in 1942, when tape recorders were not available. The voice that Uno is able to create, nevertheless, of the venerable Tenguya is vibrantly authentic. The same is true of *Ohan* (1959), the recipient of both the Noma Prize and the Japanese Women Writers Award and critically acclaimed to be Uno's masterwork. Set in a provincial town at some undisclosed time in the recent past, the story, which Uno claims to have been told while poking around a secondhand shop, concerns a man who left his gentle wife Ohan to live with the brash and domineering geisha Okayo. Seven years later, the man meets Ohan again, coincidentally, and they begin a secret liaison until circumstances, perhaps fate, drive them apart. Like the earlier *Confessions of Love* and "The Puppet Maker," it is not the story alone that is important but the way it is told and the way it captures the spirit of its times. Here Uno crafts a voice for her hapless narrator that echoes the mood and rhythms of the traditional Bunraku puppet theater. Or, as critic Kobayashi Hideo (1902–1983) would note, "With a compelling use of words that outlive their power as mere words, the author invents a storybook world of fantasy, rare among contemporary novels which have surrendered completely to fact" (Okuno 1974:39).

Uno Chiyo wrote during an age when women writers, though not uncommon, were held to standards that kept them separate from the male mainstream. Women who invested too much attention in their work were often criticized as being less than womanly and for aspiring to inappropriate heights. Women who pursued their craft as a sideline by foregrounding their roles as wives and mothers were equally chastised for not being serious about their art. Uno Chiyo dealt with the double bind that confronted women of her generation by creating a persona of nonchalance. She would have her readers believe that she carelessly tossed her stories off—jotting her reflections of this or that romantic interlude; scribbling down secondhand accounts with little regard for style or narrative frame. Her subterfuge was a success. Although Uno labored over *Ohan* for ten years, for example, she is still largely remembered today as a writer of illicit love—a scandalmaker but not an artist. Perversely, this creation is perhaps Uno's greatest literary achievement.

—Rebecca L. Copeland

Bibliography

Copeland, Rebecca. Interview with Uno Chiyo, June 21, 1984.

——. "The Made-up Author: Writer As Woman in the Works of Uno Chiyo." *Journal of the Association of Teachers of Japanese* 29, no. 1 (Spring 1995): 2–25.

——. "Needles, Knives, and Pens: Uno Chiyo and the Remembered Father." *U.S.-Japan Women's Journal* 11 (1996): 3–22.

——. *The Sound of the Wind: The Life and Works of Uno Chiyo.* Honolulu: University of Hawai'i Press, 1992.

Okuno Takeo. *Joryū sakkaron* (Essays on Women Writers). Tokyo: Daisan bunmeisha, 1974.

Uno Chiyo. *Confessions of Love.* Trans. Phyllis Birnbaum. Honolulu: University of Hawai'i Press, 1989.

——. "Happiness." In Phyllis Birnbaum, ed., *Rabbits, Crabs, Etc.: Stories by Japanese Women,* 134–147. Honolulu: University of Hawai'i Press, 1982.

——. *Ohan.* In Donald Keene, ed., *The Old Woman, the Wife and the Archer,* 86–152. New York: Viking Press, 1961.

——. *The Story of a Single Woman.* Trans. Rebecca Copeland. London: Peter Owen, 1992.

——. "To Stab." (Excerpt.) Trans. Kyoko Iriye Selden. In Noriko Mizuta Lippit and Kyoko Iriye Selden, eds., *Japanese Women Writers: Twentieth Century Short Fiction,* 126–137. Armonk, N.Y.: M. E. Sharpe, 1982.

——. *Uno Chiyo zenshū* (Collected Works of Uno Chiyo). Tokyo: Chuō kōronsha, 1978.

21

TANIZAKI JUN'ICHIRŌ

The work of Tanizaki Jun'ichirō (1886–1965), an extraordinarily imaginative and experimental writer of modern Japanese fiction, is characterized by a thrilling perversity. Although Tanizaki's cultural sensibilities often followed the trends sweeping through the nation—he showed a preference for things "Western" in the 1910s and 1920s, participated in the "return to Japan" in the late 1920s and 1930s, and emerged relatively unscathed after World War II as a novelist of bourgeois life—the seeming conventionality of his choices was combined with a disturbing critical intelligence that probed the constructed nature of cultural and national ideals. This combination of traits resulted in writing that both delighted in rearticulating various cultural ideologies and analyzed such ideologies with a distinctive arsenal of critical tools: a wicked sense of irony, frequent recourse to unreliable narration undermining the assurance of essential truths, a sharp and subversive comic wit, and the relentless sexualization of cultural images.

Many of these qualities can be observed in the pages of *In Praise of Shadows* (In'ei raisan, 1934), the extended essay on Japanese aesthetics that Tanizaki wrote near the height of the nation's and his own preoccupation with things "traditional." While the work unfolds as a lyrically seductive elegy to a vanishing aesthetics of darkness and shadows, it also constantly undercuts its own seriousness with a parodic, tongue-in-cheek sense of comedy and the deliberate abstraction of cultural icons. An example of the former appears in an infamous passage, not far from the beginning, where the toilet is suddenly proposed as a supreme site for experiencing a unique poetic ethos: "I love to listen from such a toilet to the sound of softly falling rain ... there one can listen with such a sense of intimacy to the raindrops falling from the eaves and the trees, seeping into the earth as they wash over the base of a stone lantern and freshen the moss about the stepping stones" (1977:4). An example of the latter tendency toward abstraction occurs when women of the past become creatures of darkness: "The darkness wrapped her round tenfold, twentyfold, it filled the collar, the sleeves of her kimono, the folds of her skirt, wherever a hollow invited. Further yet: might it not have been the reverse, might not the darkness have emerged from her mouth and those black teeth, from the black of her hair, the thread from the great earth spider" (1977:35). A passage of this nature deals not so much with the past or women as with an exercise in pushing logic past its limits and using a language at once playful and elegant in an act of representation. The rhetoric here subverts the very national verities it proposes by baring through exaggeration the operations of cultural desire.

The writer who gloried in such doubled expressions of cultural value was born in the *shitamachi*, or the merchants' quarter of Tokyo. He was a native doomed to be displaced as Tokyo became a city of migrants and as his family lost its wealth and sank into poverty. Although he had to work for a time as a houseboy in order to support his education, his talent was evident early and he entered the Tokyo Imperial University in 1908. He began his writing career while still a student, and, though the powerful stranglehold of *naturalist realism initially blocked the publication of his flamboyantly plotted fiction, he quickly graduated from coterie magazines to mainstream journals. He established, at this time, a lifelong association with *Chūō kōron*, the respected journal of public opinion and the arts, where many of his most important pieces were to appear. This association, as well as the fact that he quickly gained and maintained a major literary reputation throughout his career, makes it evident that Tanizaki was adept at enacting a theater of marginality upon a stage located at the center. While he wrote about sexual obsession (usually in sadomasochistic and fetishistic terms), femmes fatales, abnormal psychology, confused identities, and cultural dislocation, he was also building an upwardly mobile literary career and cultivating an educated, bourgeois readership.

Tanizaki's first published short story, "The Tattooer" (Shisei, 1910), displays many of the hallmarks of his early fiction. In this febrile fantasy, set in an Edo reconfigured as exotic terrain, a tattooer searches for a woman beautiful enough to be the canvas for his ultimate creation. Once he finds the young woman, recognized by a sleek, white foot peeking out of a palanquin, the artist drugs her and proceeds to tattoo a giant black widow upon her back. This tattoo makes both the woman's beauty and her spirit supreme, and at the end the tattooer lies at the feet of his creation, begging for one last look at what he has produced. The story is a characteristic early-Tanizaki work, a tightly plotted excursion into obsession, drawing upon the popular early-Meiji fascination with *dokufu* or "poisonous women" (as well as the European fin-de-siècle preoccupation with the femme fatale), yet elevated to the realm of "literature" by its lustrous, burnished prose. Thematically, the trope of female transformation raises questions of power that will be readdressed in manifold configurations throughout Tanizaki's oeuvre: Does the woman's domination at the end signal an actual change in hierarchy, or does it merely mean that the fantasy of remaking a woman to accord with male desire, a fantasy that cannot be achieved without male power, has reached its conclusion?

Although Tanizaki's search for exotic topographies for his fictions took him in many directions—not only to the Japanese past, but also to China, and to artificially created "other worlds" indebted to Poe—his fascination in the early 1920s fastened upon the "West." This was not the West as a geographical or political reality, but rather a "West" of the imagination constructed within Japan. The writer's most acute observations and analyses of this realm occur in *Naomi* (Chijin no ai, 1925). The protagonist and narrator of this work, a seemingly conventional engineer, tells of his misadventures with a young Japanese barmaid. Initially drawn to the barmaid because she resembles Mary Pickford, the engineer sets out to transform her, with piano and English lessons, into his ideal, the "Western" woman. He succeeds so well that the barmaid, now his wife, rejects him for being too Japanese. At the end of the story, he has been convinced to move to the port city of Yokohama, so that his wife can be close to her foreign lovers. Tanizaki's accomplishment here was to create a voice of utter banality for this narration of sexual and cultural obsession. The engineer claims to be telling his story for the humdrum moral purpose of warning others who might be lured by the temptations of the foreign. But the unreliability of this claim is manifest in his enthusiasm at sharing his happy degradations. His story turns out to be not a cautionary tale but rather a celebration of a "West" that can possess and be possessed by a Japanese. His rather simple prose turns out, in the end, to be capable of narrating a passion of hallucinatory power.

This novel was both the most challenging product of Tanizaki's engagement with the "West" and a mark of its end, for his sensibility was quickly to turn toward "tradition." The historical context for this turn was the Kantō earthquake of 1923, which destroyed the cities of Tokyo and Yokohama that had supported Tanizaki's reveries of the "West." Forced to flee to the Kansai area, the region around the cities of Osaka and Kyoto associated with an older Japan, he gradually began to undergo the "return to Japan" experienced by so many writers in the 1920s and 1930s. He became engaged with classical literature, eventually translating *The Tale of Genji* three times into modern Japanese; he embraced the traditional arts, even trying to learn the samisen; and he married (after two divorces in quick succession) an Osaka woman who was to become the muse for his musings on the past.

Tanizaki's immersion in tradition, however, yielded fiction with an ironic relation to any orthodox notion of "tradition." His first major engagements with the Kansai scene occurred in two novels written almost simultaneously, *Quicksand* (Manji, 1930) and *Some Prefer Nettles* (Tade kuu mushi, 1929). *Quicksand*, a virtuoso turn in the narrative crossing of gender and regional boundaries, is told by a woman who speaks in Osaka dialect. Although some critics have identified this voice as having a traditional tone, the story that it tells is a thoroughly modern one about the instability of truth and the labyrinthine complexities of sexual identity. The narrator, a married bourgeois Osakan, tells the story of her obsessive affair with a young woman who also has her own male lover. The young woman eventually succeeds in seducing the narrator's husband and dies with him in a joint suicide. The peculiar narrative twist here is that the narrator, though confessing her sexual indiscretions retrospectively, refuses to employ the advantage of knowing how everything ends up; she tells a story rife with misrepresentations and betrayals using only the knowledge that she had at the time of the action. She thus leads the reader along on a merry chase of assertions that later prove to be false, a process that thoroughly undercuts the truth claims of the narrative. *Quicksand* shows that narration is an arbitrary act of performance, that a narrator may say anything she wants; it is the product of a writer who was to say, around this time, that only "lies" interested him (*Zenshū* 20:72). (See "The Debate over Pure Literature.")

The 1930s were the years during which Tanizaki was most heavily invested in "tradition." Along with essays such as *In Praise of Shadows*, he produced a group of novellas, set in the past or alluding to classical literature, that showed his peculiar approach to "tradition." These novellas—which include *Arrowroot* (Yoshinokuzu, 1931), *A Blind Man's Tale* (Mōmoku monogatari, 1931), *The Secret History of the Lord of Musashi* (Bushūkō hiwa, 1932), *The Reed Cutter* (Ashikari, 1932), and *A Portrait of Shunkin* (Shunkinshō, 1933)—pursue familiar recurring themes: the sadomasochistic relationship of domineering females and the men who desire them, the power relations implicit in the male wish to turn women into cultural exemplars, the longing for mother. They also show certain broad similarities in narrative structure: they are often told by a personified and thus not necessarily reliable narrator, and they are often layered narratives that juxtapose the narrative voice with accretions of documents both actual and made-up, or quotations from and allusions to classical sources. These narrative features have an impact on the "tradition" represented in these works, for they structurally reveal that the "past" is always dependent for its existence on an act of narrative intervention that selects, orders, and interprets it; any idea of "tradition" as something preexisting its articulation or produced by unmediated or natural processes is implicitly disavowed.

The late 1930s and the 1940s showed further examples of Tanizaki's doubled relations with national ideology. When he produced, in 1939, the first of his three translations into modern Japanese of the Heian classic, *The Tale of Genji*, he was both paying homage to the past and adapting it for modern contexts. The latter was true in a special, ideological sense, because Tanizaki removed, at the behest of state-connected scholars concerned about references to improprieties in the imperial line, all mention of Genji's affair with Fujitsubo, the concubine of his father, the emperor. In his forward to this translation, Tanizaki said, rather surprisingly, that the excised section "had almost no bearing on the general development of the story" (*Zenshū* 23:167)

If in this instance Tanizaki showed a too-easy accommodation of the apparatus of state ideology, he was also capable of sustained acts of resistance. In 1943, the military censors suspended the serialization of his next major novel, *The Makioka Sisters* (Sasameyuki, 1948), for being out of tune with the war effort. Despite losing his outlet, Tanizaki persevered through the rest of the war years in writing this long novel, which he published to great public acclaim during the occupation. The reasons for the anger of the wartime authorities and the enthusiasm of the postwar reader is immediately obvious in the novel: *The Makioka Sisters*, which centers on the efforts of a once-prosperous Osaka merchant family to find a husband for an unmarried daughter, is an unabashed elegy to the textures and the rhythms of bourgeois life in prewar Kansai. In its celebration of lost comforts, it was anathema to wartime censors and a balm to readers amid the ruins of defeat.

The postwar years saw a return of the writer to more complex narratives. Two masterful novellas, *Captain Shigemoto's Mother* (Shōshō Shigemoto no haha, 1950) and *The Bridge of Dreams* (Yume no ukihashi, 1959), continued and amplified the work of fictions built from layers of allusions to classical literature. The former uses references to esoteric Buddhism and the *Tales of Yamato*, a Heian-period story collection, to limn a story of longing for mother that is both sexual and sublime; the latter employs images and situations from *The Tale of Genji* to tell the story of a sexual obsession passed on from father to son.

Tanizaki opened new ground thematically and in terms of narrative in *The Key* (Kagi, 1956), a novel in the form of two juxtaposed sexual diaries written by a college professor and his wife. This novel signals an end to Tanizaki's "traditional" period and the beginning of his concern with the desires unleashed within postwar bourgeois society. This turn is evident in the various westernized accouterments of postwar life—a fluorescent light, Courvoisier brandy, a Polaroid camera—that are used by the protagonists as instruments of sexual provocation. Such a role is played as well by the parallel diary entries, which are structured to reflect the central conceit supporting the remarkable narrative experiment of the novel: the professor and his wife read each other's diaries while regularly insisting that they do not. Thus the diaries function as a means of communication between the characters, much like the letters in an epistolary novel; yet this communication can never be openly acknowledged. The narrative made up of such entries constitutes Tanizaki's most incisive and explicit exploration of writing's connection to power and truth. In effect, the reader is left guessing throughout whether the diarists write something because it is true or whether they write it in order to manipulate the other party. The result is a descent into a sexual maze that extends even beyond the death of one of the characters.

In Tanizaki, Japanese literature had a writer who used the surrounding ideological terrain as a realm for playful experimentation. In his stories the cultural aspirations of the nation emerged transfigured by their explicit joining to erotic desire and their telling through daring narratives that displaced the truth claims of standard realism. Tanizaki's writing celebrated the fictional element in narratives of culture.

—*Ken K. Ito*

Bibliography

Chambers, Anthony H. *The Secret Window: Ideal Worlds in Tanizaki's Fiction*. Cambridge, Mass.: Harvard University Council on East Asian Studies, 1994.

Golley, Gregory L. "Tanizaki Junichiro: The Art of Subversion and the Subversion of Art." *Journal of Japanese Studies* 21, no. 2 (1995): 365–404.

Ito, Ken K. *Visions of Desire: Tanizaki's Fictional Worlds*. Stanford: Stanford University Press, 1991.

Noguchi Takehiko. *Tanizaki Jun'ichirō ron* (Essays on Tanizaki Jun'ichirō). Tokyo: Chūō kōron, 1973.

Tanizaki Jun'ichirō. *In Praise of Shadows*. Trans. Thomas J. Harper and Edward G. Seidensticker. New Haven: Leete's Island Books, 1977.

——. *The Key*. Trans. Howard Hibbett. New York: Alfred A. Knopf, 1961.

——. *Makioka Sisters*. Trans. Edward G. Seidensticker. New York: Alfred A. Knopf, 1957.

——. *Naomi*. Trans. Anthony H. Chambers. New York: Alfred A. Knopf, 1985.

——. *Quicksand*. Trans. Howard Hibbett. New York: Alfred A. Knopf, 1994.

——. *The Reed Cutter and Captain Shigemoto's Mother*. Trans. Anthony H. Chambers. New York: Alfred A. Knopf, 1994.

——. *The Secret History of the Lord of Musashi and Arrowroot*. Trans. Anthony H. Chambers. New York: Alfred A. Knopf, 1982.

——. *Seven Japanese Tales*. Trans. Howard Hibbett. New York: Alfred A. Knopf, 1963.

——. *Some Prefer Nettles*. Trans. Edward G. Seidensticker. New York: Alfred A. Knopf, 1955.

——. *Tanizaki Jun'ichirō zenshū* (Complete Works of Tanizaki Jun'ichirō). 28 vols. Tokyo: Chūō kōron, 1966–70.

22

SHIGA NAOYA AND THE SHIRAKABA GROUP

Shiga Naoya (1883–1971) is the most canonical of modern Japanese writers. His style and literary techniques are considered representative of the best and most "purely Japanese" elements of modern literature. Nonetheless, Shiga has received much less critical attention in English than many of his contemporaries, and much of the criticism that does exist has been lukewarm at best. Even some Japanese writers and critics accuse Shiga of having begun several trends that led to the "stunting" of Japanese literature.

Shiga was born in a wealthy family of the elite *shizoku* (former samurai) class and attended Gakushūin (The Peers' School) for all of his early education. Having determined to become a writer, he entered the English literature faculty of Tokyo Imperial University in 1906. He did not complete his degree, withdrawing two years later to found a literary coterie, the Shirakabaha (White Birch Group) with several like-minded young men. The members of Shirakaba espoused a brand of aestheticized egoistic humanism that owed much to their elite social status, genteel upbringings, and exposure to Christianity. Their journal, *Shirakaba* (1910–1923), was the first to introduce the work of important Anglo-European writers, philosophers, and artists such as Tolstoy, Emerson, Rodin, and van Gogh.

The literary styles and themes of the various members of the Shirakaba group were widely different; what bound them was not a literary approach but a philosophy that distinguished them from both earlier writers and their contemporaries. Unlike famous predecessors such as *Futabatei Shimei or *Mori Ōgai, the Shirakaba writers did not have to struggle with the transition to the new literary language, *genbun'itchi*; they used it confidently. Confidence in the idea of themselves as modern individuals, worthy of a position in international culture, is another hallmark of this group (in contrast to *Natsume Sōseki, for example). The Shirakaba writers publicly opposed the other important literary group of the time, the *naturalists, complaining that Japanese naturalist writers were too narrow and confessional in their focus on the details of their own drab and sordid lives. Espousing an idealist, utopian philosophy, the Shirakaba group argued for a larger, more sophisticated, and more inclusive literary perspective.

It may seem ironic therefore that Shiga Naoya, the most famous of the Shirakaba writers, is best known for narratives that are tightly focused on his own life experiences. Nonetheless, Shiga's work does demonstrate a confident simplicity very different from naturalist writing, a simplicity that exerted an enormous influence over the subsequent course of Japanese literature.

Although he lived to be eighty-eight years old, most of Shiga's stories were written in the two decades between 1908 and 1928, when he was between twenty-five and forty-five years old. His oeuvre remains comparatively small: one full-length novel, three novellas, two plays, and approximately 120 short stories. Although Shiga was designated *shōsetsu no kamisama* (the god of the novel) by an admiring critic, his reputation rests as much on his shorter works as on his one novel-length publication.

Shiga's only long work, *A Dark Night's Passing* (An'ya kōro), was begun in 1912 and finally completed in 1937. Considered one of the masterworks of modern Japanese fiction, it is structured like a classic bildungsroman. The protagonist, Tokito Kensaku, is typical of many of Shiga's heroes: that is, a young man very much like Shiga himself, well born, well educated, but uninterested in the traditional life path expected of him. Like Shiga, he has a falling out with his father and marries for love against his family's wishes. Nonetheless, the marriage is rocky. At one point Kensaku shoves his pregnant wife, Naoko, off a moving train because he is angry that she "allowed herself" to be raped by a cousin in his absence. The novel ends, however, with a reconciliation and an epiphany on Naoko's part.

In the final scene Kensaku lies on a sickbed at the top of Mt. Daisen, which he had climbed in a search for some sort of enlightenment, peace for his troubled life. It seems that he has found it; the experience of sleeping outdoors the night before when he was too exhausted and weak to continue the climb has brought him a sense of mystical unity with the natural world. Naoko sees him in this state:

> She had never seen him look so tranquil. Perhaps, she thought, he is not going to live through this. But the thought somehow did not sadden her very much. As she sat there looking at him, she felt herself becoming an inseparable part of him; and she kept on thinking, "Whether he lives or not, I shall never leave him, I shall go wherever he goes." (408)

It is impossible to know how much of *A Dark Night's Passing* corresponds to events in Shiga's life. He clearly changed some facts: for example, Tokito Kensaku is an illegitimate younger son, while Shiga was the legitimate eldest son of his family. But Shiga remarked more than once that in his literary work he presented protagonists who acted as he *would* act, or would wish to act, under similar circumstances (Ueda 1976:87). In this sense all of Shiga's work is personal, if not strictly autobiographical. This philosophy distinguishes Shiga most sharply from the other writers of personal fiction, the naturalists, who strove to depict the reality of their own lives in unvarnished sordid detail. Shiga was willing to fictionalize detail to express an individual ego that demonstrated his ideal of the modern Japanese man. (The preceding excerpt may give some notion of his less interesting ideal of the modern Japanese woman.)

Several of Shiga's short stories remain required reading in the Japanese middle-school and high-school curriculum. They are thought to exemplify at least three elements that characterize the best of modern Japanese *junbungaku* (pure literature): a focus on the personal life of one man rather than sweeping accounts of public life; an avoidance of obvious fictionalization in favor of "sincerity"; and a preference for simple, even austere language rather than complex or flowery prose. (See "The Debate over Pure Literature.") In contrast, *Tanizaki Jun'ichirō, who debuted just one year before Shiga, chose to write long, obviously fictional, tightly plotted novels with dramatic tension, opulent language, and rich detail. Tanizaki remains widely read and very widely translated. Nevertheless, it is Shiga who is celebrated even today as the most "Japanese" of modern writers.

Most of Shiga's fiction fits a category that subsequently came to be called *shishōsetsu (personal novels), novels that express an extremely individualistic view of reality. Because the focalizing agent in a *shishōsetsu* is invariably the narrator/protagonist, the viewpoint provided is quite narrow, but this allows the author to explore deeply the psychology and emotions of the one main character.

Irony is a literary trope that is entirely missing from Shiga's work (and most *shishōsetsu*). In the stories considered most typical of Shiga, the distance between the "implied author," the narrator, and the protagonist is so miniscule as to give the impression that it is "Shiga himself" on the page, speaking of his own actions, thoughts and sensations exactly as they occurred. Some critics and writers, such as *Dazai Osamu and Yasuoka Shōtarō, have complained that this emphasis on writing only what one can know directly through one's own senses and experience — eschewing imagination, drama or irony — has resulted in the stunting of modern Japanese literature. Others, however, see it as a brilliant response to the problem of modern subjectivity and language raised by Japan's sudden exposure to western epistemologies. For example, writers of Shiga-style personal fiction can avoid the problem of creating an objective, omniscient third-person narrator, which violates several traditional aspects of Japanese linguistic structure. (See "The Problem of the Modern Subject.")

One of the best examples of Shiga's short fiction is his masterpiece "Night Fires" (Takibi, 1920), which opens at a mountain inn, with the narrator, the narrator's wife, an artist (called simply "S"), and the innkeeper, "K," playing cards in the narrator's room. The story follows these four through the inconsequential activities and conversations of one day until, in the evening, the group rows across the nearby lake in a small boat and builds a fire on the far shore. They talk around the fire, relating various frightening or strange incidents. Of these, the longest is a story related by K about being saved mysteriously from death. According to his story, he was attempting to return home alone one night over a mountain covered deeply in snow and was overcome on his way up by cold and exhaustion. He was saved by his mother, who inexplicably heard him calling to her for help and sent a group of men out to help him get home. At the time when his mother heard him, K was far away on the other side of the mountain pass, having told no one of his plan to return home that night.

After K's story, the members of the group begin to throw flaming brands from their fire into the lake. The narrator describes in detail the double arc made by the brands and their reflections in the water. The story ends as the group returns to the boat and begins to row back across the lake.

Although K's story occupies only about one-sixth of the whole of "Night Fires," it is clearly the focus around which the rest of the story is organized. Its theme—the mysterious power of human connection, which is only revealed under unusual circumstances—is echoed throughout the rest of the seemingly disconnected, meandering events of the tale. In this sense "Night Fires," like many of Shiga's best short works, resembles a poem more than narrative fiction. Scenes, images, conversations, and incidents, even if narrated consecutively, do not add up to a cause-and-effect sort of conclusion. Instead they intertwine or contrast to produce larger images and ideas, which reflect metaphorically the theme Shiga is trying to capture.

In the case of "Night Fires," for example, one kind of image that appears sporadically throughout the story is of a glowing object, usually as reflected in water or set against the darkness: glowworms and cigarettes in a dark forest, stars and the two campfires reflected in the lake, and the final scene of the flaming brands making double arcs in the dark sky and the water, for example. Another set of images is characterized by visual illusions, like the one that led K into making his near-fatal decision to walk home alone. The conversations among the characters at various points in the story, though seemingly random and trivial, frequently deal with topics of danger, surprise, or illusion. Taken together, they underscore the closeness of death and the human inability to grasp the complex universe clearly with our limited senses. All of these elements echo Shiga's theme of powers beyond our ken—both beneficial and dangerous—that connect people such as K and his mother even across seemingly unbridgeable distances (Orbaugh 1996:361–365).

Although some readers complain about the lack of plot, dramatic incident, and other expected structural elements in Shiga's fiction, the simple style and poetic web of metaphorical connections that characterize his best work have been praised by generations of Japanese writers. When *Akutagawa Ryūnosuke and Tanizaki Jun'ichirō engaged in their famous debate about the course of modern Japanese literature, both men extolled Shiga's fiction, though they agreed on little else. (See "The Debate over Pure Literature.") Shiga remains known as the quintessential writer of "pure literature," with an influence on the course of modern Japanese literature unparalleled by any of his contemporaries.

—*Sharalyn Orbaugh*

Bibliography

Fowler, Edward. *The Rhetoric of Confession:* Shishōsetsu *in Early Twentieth-Century Japanese Fiction.* Berkeley: University of California Press, 1988.

Keene, Donald. *Dawn to the West: Japanese Literature in the Modern Era.* 2 vols. New York: Holt, Rinehart and Winston, 1984.

Orbaugh, Sharalyn. "Extending the Limits of Possibility: Style and Structure in Modern Japanese Fiction." In Thomas Hare, Robert Borgen, and Sharalyn Orbaugh, eds., *The Distant Isle,* 337–370. Ann Arbor: University of Michigan Center for Japanese Studies, 1996.

Shiga Naoya. *A Dark Night's Passing.* Trans. Edwin McClellan. Tokyo: Kodansha International, 1976.

———. "Night Fires." Trans. William F. Sibley. In William F. Sibley, ed., *The Shiga Hero,* 186–197. Chicago: University of Chicago Press, 1979.

Suzuki, Tomi. *Narrating the Self: Fictions of Japanese Modernity.* Stanford: Stanford University Press, 1996.

Ueda, Makoto. *Modern Japanese Writers.* Stanford: Stanford University Press, 1976.

23

AKUTAGAWA RYŪNOSUKE

The writings of Akutagawa Ryūnosuke (1892–1927) provide a glimpse into a certain uncanny experience of modernity in Japan—the experience of a culture that is felt to be foreign and exterior and yet, at the same time, irrevocably internalized.

Akutagawa's writing career was comparatively brief, lasting from 1914, when he first began to publish his stories while still a student at Tokyo Imperial University, to his suicide in July 1927. During this time he wrote in a variety of genres and styles, engaging numerous themes and historical settings. He was perhaps best known for his historical fiction, which used distant settings to explore the depths of the human psyche, particularly the destructive forces of egoism and desire. In the words of Howard Hibbett, Akutagawa's writings unfolded "an elaborately varied poetic vision of human frailty and suffering" (1970:427).

Underlying this heterogeneous corpus, however, was a continually evolving negotiation of the condition of modernity—this seemingly alien cultural formation that, by the early decades of the twentieth century, could no longer be strictly identified as foreign. For Akutagawa, the demarcation of this space of Japanese modernity was both a personal question and a pressing historical issue.

One part of this negotiation was, for Akutagawa, the assimilation, translation, and rewriting of foreign literature as well as of classical Japanese narratives. Over the years, scholars have identified a remarkable number of his stories as having been based on prior texts, ranging from slight indications of event or character to entire narratives (Yu 1972:20–22). Commentators tended to cite this reliance on previous writings as a mark of Akutagawa's unoriginality: "He was likened, even by admiring critics, to a mosaicist, piecing together fresh masterpieces out of the materials gleaned from many books" (Keene 1984, 1:565). One of his friends, the writer Kume Masao (1891–1952), remarked after his death that Akutagawa might have been better suited to scholarship than to writing.

Beyond any indication of antiquarian tastes, however, this activity of rewriting and translating other texts can be seen as a performance of the formation of modern culture in Japan, one that involves the grafting of the fragments of the past and of the foreign other onto a new context. It may be, as his critics claimed, a process of imitation, but it is also one of appropriation and incorporation, something that Akutagawa himself suggested was the construction of an artificial subjectivity.

The process of modernization was in fact one of the key themes of Akutagawa's fiction, although this was not always apparent on the surface. His early works were often set in premodern Japan, yet his concerns were ultimately contemporary (Yoshida 1958:174). He was in particular fascinated with the Japanese converts to Christianity at the end of the sixteenth and early seventeenth centuries. He saw in them the basis for modern Japanese civilization, embodiments of a primal encounter between East and West and representatives of an age in which Japan was most opened up to the outside.

In his story "The Martyr" (Hōkyōnin no shi, 1918), for example, the encounter between different civilizations is figured literally by the body of Lorenzo, a young acolyte at the Santa Lucia church in Nagasaki in the sixteenth century. Lorenzo, who had been found at the doorsteps of the cathedral as a boy, is accused of fathering a child with a young woman living nearby. He never denies the accusation and is banished from the church, forced to live at the edge of the city among the outcasts. Then, when a fire breaks out in Nagasaki and consumes the woman's house, Lorenzo rushes in to save the child from the inferno, only to perish himself. As he dies, however, his burned and tattered clothing reveals to the surprised onlookers the body of a woman—together with Lorenzo's innocence. The revelation of sexual difference in this final scene of the story serves as a vehicle for expressing an underlying, bodily transformation—the incorporation of a foreign faith.

Akutagawa's Meiji-era stories also present a nostalgic view of a culture opened up to the outside. In one, "Husband of the Enlightenment" (Kaika no otto, 1919), Akutagawa looks back on Meiji as a time when aspects of foreign civilizations mingled appealingly with the native. The work opens in the present-day Ueno Museum at an exhibition of "early Meiji civilization." The narrator remarks on a copperplate engraving contained in one of the display cases:

Tokyo Bay inscribed with mica-like waves, steam-ships flying various flags, images of European men and women strolling the avenues, a row of Hiroshige-style pines spreading their branches towards the sky in front of

an Occidental house—in both subject and technique, there was a blending of East and West then, a beautiful harmony specific to the art of early
Meiji. Since then, this harmony has been forever lost to our art. It has
even disappeared from the city of Tokyo we inhabit. (*Zenshū* 3:4)

For Akutagawa, Meiji Japan—the era in which he had been born—had already become a museum piece, an object of nostalgia (Keene 1984, 1:570). In
Akutagawa's view, the "blending" and the "harmony" between East and West
was possible only to the extent that the two were perceived to have a separate existence at the time. By the Taishō period, after Japan's victories in two major
wars, its annexation of Korea and the consolidation of a formal empire, as well
as its rapid economic expansion and industrialization, "the West" was no longer
something entirely external, but had also become an integral part of Japanese
life. Elsewhere, for example, Akutagawa wrote that "today's Japanese women are
too Japanese for Western dress, and too Westernized for Japanese dress" (*Zenshū*
7:228). The type of cultural authenticity that he saw in (or perhaps projected
onto) the early Meiji period—when distinctions between inside and outside, between native and foreign, could, he imagined, still be clearly discerned—had
all but dissipated in his own time. The sense of a sharp divide between Japan
and the West that had haunted such older writers as *Natsume Sōseki or *Mori
Ōgai troubled Akutagawa far less, but the blurring of borderlines—as his late
fiction would show especially—constituted its own crisis.

Akutagawa's well-known work "The Ball" (Butōkai, 1920) sketches another
scene from the early days of Japan's modernization. The story is set at the
Rokumeikan, the Western-style building in Tokyo that became a symbol of the
assimilation of European manners among the Meiji elite. Here Akutagawa
stages an encounter between a French naval officer and a young aristocratic
Japanese woman named Akiko. The story is filtered through the perspectives of
both characters. For the Frenchman, this Japanese woman with her "charming
rose-colored evening gown" and "light-blue ribbon tastefully adorning her
neck" is an amusing example of mimicry of the West (1999:72). Even as he sees
her in Western dress, he cannot help but evoke the exotic images of her living in
a house of paper and bamboo, eating with steel chopsticks. For Akiko, on the
other hand, the event signifies entry into a cosmopolitan world:

> From time to time, he whispered flattering words in French into her ear.
> As she responded to his kind words with embarrassed smiles, she glanced
> around the ballroom where they danced. Beneath the purple banner im-
> printed with the Imperial crest and the Chinese flag, with its image of a
> bare-clawed dragon, the chrysanthemums in their vases shone among the
> waves of people in bright silver and melancholy gold. The waves of peo-
> ple were fanned by the breeze of German orchestral melodies that flowed
> out like champagne. (73–74)

The Rokumeikan is thus presented as a space of intoxication and enjoyment, characterized by the intermingling of different cultural fragments and artifacts.

In the coda to the work—set in the Taishō period, when the dreamlike atmosphere of the Rokumeikan has long faded—the Frenchman is revealed to be the writer Pierre Loti, author of *Madame Chrysanthème* (1887). In fact, Akutagawa's story is based on a chapter from Loti's book *Japoneries d'automne* (1889) that describes his attendance at a birthday celebration for the Meiji emperor, as well as his encounter with a Japanese woman there. Akutagawa thus transformed Loti's sketch (itself filled with dismissive portrayals of the Japanese) into his own narrative of a moment in the history of Japan's modernization. In this sense, Akutagawa was in fact staging, through this story, a textual encounter between Loti and himself—between the Western gaze and the gaze that returns, appropriates, and transforms it.

Yet the encounter with the other was not only depicted through the kind of nostalgia found in Akutagawa's "Enlightenment" stories. It also led him to more anxious depictions of doubling, of replication, and ultimately of the fragmentation of consciousness. He wrote a number of times, for example, about the doppelganger, the uncanny figure that upsets the integrity of ego and bodily boundaries. Such works include his epistolary work "Two Letters" (Futatsu no tegami, 1917), which chronicles the destruction of a man's family and social standing because of the untimely appearances of his double.

Toward the end of his life, Akutagawa began to publish a number of autobiographical stories, a genre he had long resisted. Yet this personal fiction ultimately did not succeed in framing a coherent narrative of his life, but instead can be seen to narrate the internal fragmentation of consciousness. In one of his last pieces of criticism, part of a famous polemical exchange with *Tanizaki Jun'ichirō, Akutagawa introduced the concept of the novel without plot, which he also defined as the destruction of the novel. (See "The Debate over Pure Literature.") It represented a rejection of his earlier attention to structure and plot in his stories and signified the dissolution of a certain conception of literature. If his earlier work had been based on a process of assimilating other texts, his final writings seem to constitute a reverse process, one of disintegration. The autobiographical work "A Fool's Life" (Aru ahō no isshō, 1927), found at his deathbed, for example, is a fragmentary, aphoristic account of the last fifteen years of his life. It is divided into fifty-one scenes that describe significant moments of this period, some of which are little more than a few lines in length. The work resists categorization into any single genre, for it contains elements of the film scenario, confessional story, autobiography, prose poem, and lyric poem.

"A Fool's Life" is perhaps the prime example of what Akutagawa termed the destruction of the novel, but it also marks the dissolution of a subjectivity formed through the appropriation of foreign culture. One of its central images is of Akutagawa as Icarus, fashioning "artificial wings" through the reading of European philosophy and literature, yet ultimately soaring too high into the sky toward an impending death. In another work published the same year, Akutagawa wrote, "Having been born in modern Japan, I cannot help but feel countless divisions inside me, both artistically and personally" (*Zenshū* 9:60).

Akutagawa's suicide by an overdose of sleeping medication in July 1927 was no doubt an eminently personal and private catastrophe, yet it also became an historical one in its impact on the literary world and on the culture at large. Coming little more than half a year after the end of Taishō and the beginning of Shōwa, it was perceived by many as the end of an era. In his suicide note, Akutagawa had written of a "vague sense of anxiety" about the future (Yu 1972:110). This statement was taken by many critics to indicate the anxiety of the bourgeois intellectual in the face of rising class struggle and the promise of proletarian revolution. Yet soon, as the left was crushed by government pressure and internal conflicts and as the nation moved increasingly toward the consolidation of a fascist state apparatus and military expansion in Asia, this anxiety came to signify a general unease within society. To this extent, then, Akutagawa's last works are as "historical" as his early writings; as Borges remarked of these writings: "Thackeray declared that to think about Swift is to think about the collapse of an empire. A similar process of vast disintegration and pain operates in Akutagawa's last works" (1999:viii). Ultimately, as Borges's statement suggests, these writings can be inscribed into a general crisis within Japanese modernity, one that would take an exceptionally violent form only a few years after his death.

—*Seiji Lippit*

Bibliography

Akutagawa Ryūnosuke. *Akutagawa Ryūnosuke zenshū* (Complete Works of Akutagawa Ryūnosuke). Tokyo: Iwanami, 1977.

——. *The Essential Akutagawa.* Ed. Seiji M. Lippit. New York: Marsilio, 1999.

——. *A Fool's Life.* Trans. Will Peterson. New York: Grossman, 1970.

——. *Japanese Short Stories.* Trans. Takashi Kojima. New York: Liveright, 1952.

——. *Rashomon and Other Stories.* Trans. Takashi Kojima. New York: Liveright, 1961.

——. *The Spider's Thread and Other Stories.* Trans. Dorothy Britton. Tokyo: Kodansha International, 1987.

——. *Tales Grotesque and Curious.* Trans. Glenn W. Shaw. Tokyo: Hokuseidō, 1930.

Borges, Jorge Luis. "Foreword." In Seiji M. Lippit, ed., *The Essential Akutagawa.* New York: Marsilio, 1999.

Hibbett, Howard S. "Akutagawa Ryūnosuke and the Negative Ideal." In Albert M. Craig and Donald H. Shively, eds., *Personality in Japanese History,* 425–451. Berkeley: University of California Press, 1970.

Keene, Donald. *Dawn to the West: Japanese Literature in the Modern Era.* 2 vols. New York: Holt, Rinehart and Winston, 1984.

Lippit, Seiji M. "The Disintegrating Machinery of the Modern: Akutagawa Ryūnosuke's Late Writings." *Journal of Asian Studies* 58, no. 1 (February 1999): 27–50.

O'Brien, James. *Akutagawa and Dazai: Instances of Literary Adaptation.* Tempe: Arizona State University Center for Asian Studies, 1988.

Yoshida Seiichi. *Akutagawa Ryūnosuke.* Tokyo: Shinchōsha, 1958.

Yu, Beongcheon. *Akutagawa: An Introduction.* Detroit: Wayne State University Press, 1972.

24

THE DEBATE OVER PURE LITERATURE

In 1927, the last year of his life, *Akutagawa Ryūnosuke engaged in a public debate with *Tanizaki Jun'ichirō over the standards for judging modern Japanese fiction. Both men were highly regarded and popular authors. Each was arguing a position held by illustrious predecessors and contemporaries. Yet, when Akutagawa committed suicide on July 27 of that year, contemporaries attributed it partly to his despondence over having "lost" the debate over this literary issue: the nature and importance of *junbungaku* (pure literature). The questions that arose in this debate have resonated throughout Japanese literary criticism and are implicated in the larger issues of modernity and "Japaneseness."

The debate began when Akutagawa remarked in a magazine interview that he considered truth more important than imagination in fiction. He believed that authors had become obsessed with producing a complex plot, and he wanted to downplay the importance of plot in favor of "personal truth." Akutagawa stressed that literature could be interesting without the razzle-dazzle of a fancy plot.

Tanizaki then wrote a rebuttal to Akutagawa's remarks, defending the place of imagination in fiction. He said that in his own work he was addicted to what Stendhal had called "beautiful lies"; anything that was not patently fictional was uninteresting to him. In typically hyperbolic fashion, Tanizaki wrote that fiction's "lies" should be as gnarled and twisted as possible to allow readers to revel in artifice. He mentioned *chanbara* (swashbuckling historical fiction), which he found terrifically enjoyable, as an example of "good" literature.

Akutagawa responded with dismay. He objected particularly to the *chanbara* example—wasn't this advocating a return to the worst faults of Edo-period (that is, premodern) fiction? Wasn't Tanizaki demonstrating an irresponsible disregard for all the progress made by modern Japanese fiction since *Tsubouchi Shōyō's and *Futabatei Shimei's early experiments? It was now recognized that the novel was a serious form of literature, capable of expressing profound aspects of human life. Wasn't Tanizaki risking a return to the notion of the novel as nothing more than trivial entertainment?

To the reader familiar with the works of both Akutagawa and Tanizaki, the heat with which this debate was joined may have been puzzling. Both had a healthy disregard for the literary establishment, and both had written successful works in various styles—semiautobiographical/personal narratives and completely fictional, fanciful stories. Moreover, the two men were friends and maintained cordial relations throughout the debate.

Tanizaki's next installment argued that the novel was the literary genre that was uniquely effective for making maximum use of plot; why should authors waste this inherent strength of the form? He emphasized the potential for "architectural beauty" in the novel, and used as an example the work of *Shiga Naoya, which he said exhibited "stamina." Most Japanese authors, he declared, were weak in terms of "stamina" and structural beauty.

Akutagawa's reply seemed to demonstrate his discomfort with the position he was now forced to defend. In it he repeatedly emphasized that there are many good kinds of fiction—he did not mean to exclude the possibility of architectural beauty. But just as there are good paintings with clear, representational pictures and also good paintings that are more abstract, it should also be possible to see value in various kinds of novels, including those that are more "abstract." A novel with no real story line, that merely followed the miscellaneous events of the main character's life, could be very "pure," and worthwhile, he argued. As an example he mentioned Shiga Naoya's short work "Night Fires" (Takibi, 1920), which he admired for its poetic simplicity of language and lack of obvious plot.

Akutagawa wanted to advocate a serious literature with a serious readership. While any reader could be seduced and dazzled by a fancy plot, a serious reader would be willing to look for more than entertainment. The serious reader would be willing to pay attention to stories of simple characters living relatively undramatic lives—and would derive from these stories true insight into the writer's heart (and, presumably, though Akutagawa does not say so, into the nature of humanity). Though he conceded that plot was the structural backbone of a novel, he insisted again that too much attention to plot obscured other important literary elements. Here Akutagawa likened "plot" in a narrative to "line" in drawing—these are the elements that provide the most simplistic kind of structure. He raised the example of French painter Cézanne: just as Cézanne had moved away from line in order to make maximum use of the possibilities of color in depicting the elements of a scene, he wanted to write fiction that did away with the surface structure provided by plot in order to concentrate on other literary elements.

One of the issues being addressed in this debate is the place of the authorial persona in fiction. Tanizaki emphasized that the writer's own personality should be obliterated in his work, in favor of a completely convincing *created* world. Earlier examples of this sort of author would include *Higuchi Ichiyō and *Natsume Sōseki, who created believable protagonists utterly unlike themselves. In contrast, *naturalist writers, proletarian movement writers, and advocates of the *shishōsetsu* (personal novel) subgenre felt that the most important task of literature was to present the unvarnished, unmediated experiences of the author himself. (This style of writing was usually seen as a purely masculine pursuit.)

In the former case, the writer is somewhat godlike in his or her ability to create an entirely fictional world. But in the latter case the author is also godlike, in that the image of his persona, built up over many "personal" works, is the sole focus of attention and value. The "world" the reader sees in such works is the limited, solipsistic world of the author. Nonetheless, it was believed by many writers and critics that even such a narrow viewpoint was valuable in its ability to reveal human "truth." Unlike Tanizaki's obvious fabrications, *this* view of the world was seen as "sincere" and "pure": truthful.

Tanizaki, however, insisted that human truth could be more readily invoked through artifice. Raising the example of the Japanese traditional puppet theater, Bunraku, in which large puppets are manipulated by three men in full view, he argued that the puppets are capable of expressing more humanity than a human actor can, because the "shadows" and implications of art(ifice) can stimulate the imagination of the audience to an unusual degree of receptivity and sensitivity. He argued that most people had weak imaginations, and therefore were unable to apprehend the conditions of another person. Authors, on the contrary, were people of strong imagination who could use their powers to stimulate the minds of ordinary people to greater understanding of others.

This disagreement relates back to issues raised in the earliest attempts to create a modern language and literature in Japan. Because in normal (nonliterary) contexts the Japanese language has no way of directly expressing the feelings of another person, the creation of an omniscient narrator, able to narrate the innermost feelings and thoughts of a fictional character, seems unnatural, epistemologically invalid, to many readers and critics. (See "The Problem of the Modern Subject.")

In contrast, it *is* possible to express *one's own* feelings and thoughts; writers who concentrated on their own inner worlds have therefore been seen as more readily believable. So believable, in fact, that most works by naturalist, proletarian, and *shishōsetsu* writers are usually read by Japanese critics as transparent autobiography; incidents in literary works are taken as facts about the author's life, even if those incidents cannot be independently verified. Some such writers, such as *Hayashi Fumiko, narrated the same event differently in different stories, and writers like Shiga Naoya obviously shaped their narratives to fit specific thematic purposes; nonetheless, the "unmediated" veracity of their accounts is rarely questioned. Neither Tanizaki nor Akutagawa raises this linguistic/epistemological issue explicitly, but it is at the heart of their disagreement.

Finally, the debate comes down to questions of modernity vs. premodernity and the place of Japan in an international literary discourse. Natsume Sōseki had advocated maintaining Japanese standards in the face of an Anglo-European discourse that took itself to be hegemonic. But Sōseki implicitly situated his writing within that larger discourse, and he wrote "Western-style" novels—fully fictional, carefully plotted structures with interesting and believable characters. This is his vision of the modern *and* Japanese novel. Tanizaki echoes Sōseki's stance, but with even greater confidence. When he praises the "stamina" in Shiga's work ("powerful breathing, muscular arms, robust loins" [Karatani 1993:161]), he invokes a clearly masculine image for the place of Japanese writing in literary discourse, whether international or otherwise. On the contrary, the stance of the writer of the "personal novel"—in its intentionally limited viewpoint, and its appeal to a purely *Japanese* linguistic and lyrical tradition—struck Tanizaki perhaps as unnecessarily "feminine" and weak in international terms.

In contrast, advocates of the personal novel argued that in order to be appropriate to a genuinely *Japanese* modernity (not merely an apish imitation of western paradigms), the *shōsetsu* should reflect the strengths of the Japanese literary and linguistic traditions, even if this resulted in a form that would not be appreciated by outsiders. This stance thus takes up an aggressive attitude toward the international literary scene, demanding to be understood on its own terms. (It must be noted, however, that the exclusivity implied by outsiders' inability to understand such works is extended even to those *within* Japan but outside the *bundan* as well.)

This split is symptomatic of the positions taken up by intellectuals ever since the Meiji opening of the country: Tanizaki represented the school of thought that took for granted the legitimacy of Japan's place in the international literary world, and envisioned that place in strong, masculine terms. Akutagawa—however reluctantly—represented what appeared to be a more defensive idea: that a truly Japanese modern literature could only and should only be appreciated by those few willing to take its idiosyncrasies and solipsism seriously, even if this kept Japan from participating in international literary discourse. The two positions continue to be debated today.

—*Sharalyn Orbaugh*

Bibliography

Akutagawa Ryūnosuke. "Bungeitekina, amari ni bungeitekina" (Literary, All Too Literary). In *Akutagawa Ryūnosuke zenshū* (Complete Works of Akutagawa Ryūnosuke), 9:3–80. Tokyo: Iwanami, 1977–78.

Karatani Kōjin. *Origins of Modern Japanese Literature*. Trans. Brett de Bary. Durham, N.C.: Duke University Press, 1993.

Keene, Donald. *Dawn to the West: Japanese Literature in the Modern Era*. 2 vols. New York: Holt, Rinehart and Winston, 1984.

Lippit, Noriko Mizuta. *Reality and Fiction in Modern Japanese Literature*. London: Macmillan, 1980.

Tanizaki Jun'ichirō. "Jōzetsu roku" (Record of Loquacity). In *Tanizaki Jun'ichirō zenshū* (Complete Works of Tanizaki Jun'ichirō), 20:69–166. Tokyo: Chūō kōron, 1981.

25

NATURALISM AND THE EMERGENCE
OF THE *SHISHŌSETSU* (PERSONAL NOVEL)

The literary form known as the *shishōsetsu* or *watakushi-shōsetsu* (I will use *shishōsetsu* throughout) is the most important and most problematic in modern Japanese literature. Usually translated as "I-novel" or "personal novel," the term was evidently invented as a translation of the German *Ich-Roman* (I-novel) to describe a genre of writing that flourished in the 1910s and 1920s. One way to begin to understand the problems with this form is to examine the name itself. It is made up of two parts: *shi* or *watakushi*, and *shōsetsu*. The first part is a Chinese character that means "I" when pronounced "watakushi," and that means something like "personal" or "private" when pronounced "shi. In this sense it would seem to parallel the "Ich" of Ich-Roman. But the "I" referenced by *watakushi* is not straightforward, for in Japanese there are many words for the first-person singular pronoun, and each is appropriate only within a limited context (Fowler 1988:5). *Watakushi* is used by both men and women (unlike most Japanese first-person pronouns, which are strictly gender-coded) exclusively in formal situations. Unlike "I" or "Ich," which can be used regardless of context, *watakushi* is not an appropriate pronoun when speaking to a friend, a colleague, a child, a lover, or oneself.

The second half of the term, *shōsetsu*, is a Chinese word adopted by *Tsubouchi Shōyō in 1885–86 to describe the modern novel—the literary form that readers were discovering as they eagerly read and translated Western literature. Shōyō advocated the invention of an analogous literary form for Japan, stressing the need for plot, realistic characterization, a modern language, and so on.

The mature *shōsetsu*, however, though certainly an expression of modernized Japan, differed from most Anglo-European novels in many important respects. The Japanese "I-novel" form, therefore, has neither "I" nor "novel" as conventionally understood. Nor is it a category whose defining characteristics are clear and widely agreed upon. Nonetheless, the *shishōsetsu* form is described by critics as "the most salient and unique" in modern Japanese literature (Suzuki 1996:1).

Perhaps the *shishōsetsu's* most important characteristic is the fact that, as Tomi Suzuki points out, "it was formulated on a polar axis that contrasted the Western novel with its Japanese counterpart" (1996:3). Characterizing the Anglo-European novel as fictional and impersonal, advocates of the *shishōsetsu* emphasized its unmediated directness and veracity, claiming that these elements had long distinguished Japanese literary forms. The *shishōsetsu* writer was believed to record his or her own personal experience, whether the narration was in the first or the third person. (Many of the most famous works considered *shishōsetsu*, such as *Shiga Naoya's A Dark Night's Passing [An'ya kōro], are indeed narrated in the third person but are still believed to refer directly to the author's own life. The fact that in *A Dark Night's Passing* many of the details of the protagonist's life are verifiably different from Shiga's does not alter that belief.) The *shishōsetsu* form is single-voiced, with (usually) a single focalizer, as opposed to the sometimes polyvocal novel incorporating multiple points of view that is common in the West (and among Japanese writers of non-*shishōsetsu*).

The definition of the *shishōsetsu* as a self-referential, unmediated work has proved problematic for Western readers who might therefore expect the genre to be synonymous with autobiography. In many cases the distinction between the two forms may be unclear, but in some cases it is glaring. For example, many *shishōsetsu* writers returned again and again to the same event, narrating it with significant differences each time. (See, for example, "Hayashi Fumiko.") Others clearly crafted their narratives for maximum literary effect; although the surface may have appeared simple and unmediated, closer reading revealed obvious authorial sculpting. (See "Shiga Naoya.") Although writers of autobiography must also exercise judgment and narrative skill in choosing what to relate of a complex life and how to structure that narration, the degree of "artistic license" demonstrated by many *shishōsetsu* may be disconcerting to the reader expecting autobiography.

The *shishōsetsu* is often reported to have grown out of the Japanese naturalist movement, which is usually said to begin in 1907 with Tayama Katai's *The Quilt* (Futon). *The Quilt* concerns a married writer, Takenaka Tokio, who falls in love with his female protégé and is devastated when she takes his advice about individualism and romantic love seriously enough to run off with a young male acquaintance. In the infamous final scene, Takenaka buries his face in her used bedding to recapture her scent. This slight work was extremely influential, primarily because of its "confessional" quality. As the literary world knew, Tayama himself had had a similar relationship with a young woman, Okada Michiyo, who had left his tutelage in favor of a more appropriate suitor. The fact that Tayama would reveal the erotic details of a sordid episode in his own life was considered revolutionary—if not always in a positive sense—by contemporaries. (*Shimazaki Tōson was another writer who is considered a member of the Japanese naturalist school because of several novels in which he confessed sordid sexual affairs.) Rather than the pitiless, objective, "scientific" tone and wide lens of European naturalists as they turned their gaze on society's seamier areas, the Japanese naturalists concentrated on small-scale perversions, always with a personal connection to the author's life. It was the focus on unpleasant, embarrassing, even shameful aspects of modern life that made the Japanese naturalists so influential—this was a break indeed from the moralizing didacticism of premodern prose.

Although the fashion for sordid confession lasted only into the 1920s, the popularity and critical valorization of "personal" novels that straddled the divide between autobiography and fiction lasted much longer, well into the postwar period. Some critics have related this to the Japanese linguistic and epistemological preference for reporting only the phenomena to which the speaker has direct access through his or her own senses. (See "The Problem of the Modern Subject.") The veracity, accuracy and sincerity—the truth value—of a narrative based on the author's own life experiences could be trusted. The truth value of an obviously fictional narrative could not. (See "The Debate over Pure Literature.")

It is clear, however, that to fully appreciate the force of the author's personal confession it was necessary that readers *recognize* facts from the author's life—even in a third-person narrative whose protagonist might bear a different name. In the 1910s and 1920s the *bundan* (literary world) may have been small and insular enough to make that recognition possible. (See "The Social Organization of Modern Japanese Literature.") But in subsequent decades, as education steadily increased the numbers of writers and readers, male and female, from various class and geographical backgrounds, an author could no longer assume that readers would be able to distinguish confession from fiction. As Suzuki argues, however, the concept of the *shishōsetsu* had taken such firm hold in Japanese literary consciousness by the end of the 1920s that readers thereafter could be counted on to *assume* a connection between the author and his or her protagonist unless given obvious clues to the contrary. The *shishōsetsu* became defined, therefore, more as a mode of *reading* than of writing (Suzuki 1996:10). Through the reading of several works by one writer, all of which featured a similar protagonist (of the same gender and roughly the same age as the author) the reader could derive an image of an authorial persona—the "I" of the I-novel—that appeared to underwrite the veracity of the narrated experience, whether or not the reader knew the facts of the author's life well enough to recognize them in the literary works.

Despite the large and increasing numbers of translations into English of Japanese fiction since the end of World War II, there have so far been very few translations of *shishōsetsu*. For English-language readers, unfamiliar with the implicit contract that binds *shishōsetsu* authors and their audience, and perhaps less concerned with issues of veracity and sincerity, the solipsistic worldview and undeveloped plot and characterization of the *shishōsetsu* often prove disappointing (Fowler 1988:xix–xx; Orbaugh 1996:339–340). No modern writer has focused exclusively on the *shishōsetsu* form, but from the canonization of many of the writers whose oeuvre contains a large percentage of *shishōsetsu* (among them Shiga Naoya, Shimazaki Tōson, Hayashi Fumiko, Kanbayashi Akatsuki, *Dazai Osamu, and Ozaki Kazuo), we can see that this form cannot be ignored in any consideration of modern Japanese literature.

—*Sharalyn Orbaugh*

Bibliography

Fowler, Edward. *The Rhetoric of Confession:* Shishōsetsu *in Early Twentieth-Century Japanese Fiction.* Berkeley: University of California Press, 1988.

Hijiya-Kirschnereit, Irmela. *Rituals of Self-Revelation:* Shishōsetsu *As Literary Genre and Socio-Cultural Phenomenon.* Cambridge, Mass.: Harvard University Council on East Asian Studies, 1996.

Orbaugh, Sharalyn. "Extending the Limits of Possibility: Style and Structure in Modern Japanese Fiction." In Thomas Hare, Robert Borgen, and Sharalyn Orbaugh, eds., *The Distant Isle*, 337–370. Ann Arbor: University of Michigan Center for Japanese Studies, 1996.

Suzuki Tomi. *Narrating the Self: Fictions of Japanese Modernity.* Stanford University Press, 1996.

Tayama Katai. *The Quilt and Other Stories.* Trans. Kenneth Henshall. Tokyo: University of Tokyo Press, 1981.

26

KAWABATA YASUNARI

One of the first modern writers to be extensively translated into English, Kawabata Yasunari (1899–1972) was—not coincidentally—the first Japanese writer to be awarded the Nobel Prize in literature, in 1968. His unexpected and unexplained suicide four years later ended a life characterized by contradictions: a seemingly shy, withdrawn, and bookish man, from the 1930s until his death he was active in Japanese and international literary societies, literary prize committees, and even local politics; despite extensive and apparently willing cooperation with Japan's militaristic wartime government, he was hardly taken to task by postwar critics who were extremely harsh to other literary collaborators; and, known from his early days as a member of the Shinkankakuha (the New Sensationalists) coterie, whose writing explored the modernist and sometimes surrealist territory marked out by James Joyce and the like, the majority of Kawabata's work is in a simple, straightforward, realist vein.

This life of contradictions began in Kawabata's childhood. He was orphaned by age three and sent to live with his grandparents. His grandmother died when he was seven, his only sister when he was nine, and his grandfather when he was still a young teenager. Nonetheless, throughout his life he declared that he felt no particular deprivation or sadness from the tragic events of his childhood.

In the early 1920s, as Kawabata was beginning his career, the New Sensationalist school of writers was advocating a literature that emphasized the phenomenology of human sensation or perception. Rather than an artificially produced coherence of both dialogue and narrative structure, this group experimented with a style that more closely replicated the inchoate, fragmentary, free associative nature of human speech, thought, and experience. Several of Kawabata's earliest published works show the influence of this school, and he remained associated with it in the minds of some critics throughout his career. It is important to point out, however, that in his case at least the significance of New Sensationalism was its art-for-art's-sake, conservative stance against the Marxist and proletarian writers coming into prominence at the time. Though Kawabata soon abandoned the "experimental" prose style of the New Sensationalists, throughout his life he maintained a more generally modernist, conservative and elitist view of literature as necessarily aesthetically pleasing and accessible only to the reader sensitive enough to appreciate "purity" and beauty. In this he echoed *Akutagawa Ryūnosuke's position in the famous 1927 *debate over pure literature, though he is rarely associated with Akutagawa on any other basis. He favored the simple, aesthetically pleasing nature of much of *Shiga Naoya's short fiction, and disliked the artifice and playfulness of *Tanizaki Jun'ichirō (Ueda 1976:176).

After several experimental stories, Kawabata produced in 1926 a short work that more closely foreshadowed the shape of his later novels: "The Izu Dancer" (Izu no odoriko). Made into a movie at least three times, this story is still the one considered Kawabata's masterpiece by many readers. It shows virtually no influence of the New Sensationalists school; the story has a coherent plot expressed in straightforward language.

"The Izu Dancer" is narrated by a Tokyo higher school student on a walking tour alone on the Izu peninsula. He has met a group of itinerant performers—a despised occupation at the time—and developed an erotic attraction to the young dancing girl of the troupe. He befriends the group as part of his plan to possess the girl sexually. Before he can do so, however, he sees her run naked from the bath at a hot springs resort to wave to him, and realizes that she is still a child, much too young and innocent to be the object of his lust. The narrator's reaction is, surprisingly, relief and joy. He continues with the troupe happily— on the road witnessing the discrimination with which they are treated—and leaves them only when he must return to Tokyo for school. The story ends with the narrator's ingenuous tears as he recalls the friendship the dancer and her family had shown him.

This story encapsulates a number of themes that were to recur in much of Kawabata's later fiction: an emphasis on purity of emotion, unconsummated (or impossible to consummate) love, and the special beauty of innocent young girls. It is noteworthy that Kawabata's earlier memoir of a 1918 trip to Izu during which he met such an itinerant troupe depicts them as far less "pure" and appealing. "The dancer's elder brother and his wife suffered from malignant tumors, apparently caused by venereal disease." The young dancer herself was far from beautiful (Ueda 1976:185). Another characteristic of Kawabata's work is evident in this contrast between his actual experience in Izu and his depiction of it in fiction: unlike the *naturalist writers of the previous generation, Kawabata strove to produce idealized characters, the essence of his notions of beauty and purity. In "The Izu Dancer" Kawabata depicts the overcoming of class barriers as a matter of sensitivity and a return to honest emotions—the narrator's eventual preference for "purity" and "niceness" over lust. This was in direct contrast to the naturalists' attempts to explore a very different definition of honesty, which more often treated class barriers and other problems as intractable because of rigid social structures and human venality. Kawabata's positive depiction of human interaction is certainly more appealing than that of an author who wallows in the inevitability of unhappiness, but might also be regarded as overly simplistic and thus antagonistic to social reform.

The poignant beauty of the protagonist's desire for an unattainable object, seen in "The Izu Dancer," is probably Kawabata's most common theme, and in that story we see the theme introduced with a common Kawabata trope: passage through a tunnel—literal or figurative—leading into a realistic, but somehow separate universe on the far side. The inhabitants of the far side of the tunnel are purer, more genuine, more vulnerable, and therefore more beautiful than those in the protagonist's "normal" universe. By far the most famous instance of this trope is the opening scene in the novel *Snow Country* (Yukiguni, 1935–48), where the protagonist, Shimamura, a jaded Tokyoite, gets his first glimpse of Yōko, the snow country girl who becomes the object of his fascination and desire. But because Yōko has a dying lover, Yukio, whom she tends, she is unavailable to Shimamura, unaware of his interest. The novel opens: "The train came out of the long tunnel into the snow country. The earth lay white under the night sky" (1956:11). In the long flashback that follows, Shimamura recalls the last few hours on the train, during which he has gazed at Yōko's face, reflected in the windows of the train, blending beautifully with the light and the scenery behind it:

> In the depths of the mirror the evening landscape moved by, the mirror and the reflected figures like motion pictures superimposed one on the other. The figures and the background were unrelated, and yet the figures, transparent and intangible, and the background, dim in the gathering darkness, melted together into a sort of symbolic world not of this world. Particularly when a light out in the mountains shone in the center of the girl's face, Shimamura felt his chest rise at the inexpressible beauty of it. (1956:15)

As with many of his novels and short works, Kawabata experimented with different endings for *Snow Country*, adding segments from 1937 to 1948 (Keene 1984, 1:801–815; Miyoshi 1974:102–103). His final choice is more ambiguous than some of the earlier ones. At the beginning of the novel Shimamura is returning to the snow country of western Japan to meet a hot springs geisha, Komako, with whom he had been intimate on a previous trip. The novel traces his generally undramatic interactions with and observations of Komako, Yōko (who turns out to be Komako's friend), and Yōko's dying lover. In the final scene, Yōko leaps from a burning building to what may or may not be her death. As Komako cradles her body, the novel ends with Shimamura watching from a distance. "As he caught his footing, his head fell back, and the Milky Way flowed down inside him with a roar" (1956:142). In considering the effect of Yōko's death or injury and Komako's desperation on Shimamura, it is up to the reader to interpret the meaning of this metaphor (see Ueda 1976:205). This is in line with Kawabata's practice in general: when he experimented with diverse endings he tended to move from relatively clearer denouements to those that were more picturesque and beautiful, but also more ambiguous.

The use of a mirror to create an alternate, preferable universe can be seen again in one of Kawabata's most lovely short works, "Moon on the Water" (Suigetsu, 1953). The protagonist of "Moon on the Water" is Kyōko, whose husband is slowly dying of tuberculosis. Set shortly after the war, when food was very scarce, the story describes Kyōko working all day in her vegetable garden, leaving her husband alone in his bed on the second floor of their house. One day she hits upon the idea of giving him her hand mirror so that he can see her reflection as she works, a happy inspiration that drastically improves his life. Besides watching his wife work, he also gazes at the sky, the flowers in the fields, and the moon reflected in the mirror. Kyōko enjoys looking into it with him at times, and she is struck by the unusual beauty of the (alternate) world as reflected in the mirror. She knows that she is similarly beautiful when viewed by her husband in the mirror as she works outside. In fact, this part of the story is all told in flashbacks. Kyōko, recently remarried after the death of her first husband, cannot help comparing the sad and nonsexual but somehow beautiful life they had shared, and the love-filled alternative universe they had created, with her new life with the second husband who is strong and vigorous.

Kawabata believed that there were three types of people best able to discover pure beauty, and therefore best as narrators, protagonists, or focalizers for his stories: "little children, young women, and dying men" (Ueda 1976:186). "Moon on the Water" is focalized through Kyōko, who is struggling with the tension between her feelings of satisfaction in her sexually active and "normal" second marriage and her longing for the purity and beauty of her first. This same dynamic is found in one of Kawabata's finest works, the novel *The Sound of the Mountain* (Yama no oto, 1954). In this case the narration is focalized through Ogata Shingo, a sixty-two-year-old man who feels death to be very close by. Shingo lives with his wife (the homely sister of the beautiful woman he had really loved), his son, and the son's wife, Kikuko. Only his relationship with the young and innocent Kikuko gives Shingo any sense of life and happiness. Kikuko, like Kyōko, struggles with the tension between her erotic love for her husband and her purer feelings for her father-in-law, but in this case the story is told not from her point of view but from that of the "dying" Shingo. Kawabata explores to brilliant effect the psychology and thought processes of an older man, in whose mind the events of yesterday are instantly forgotten but the smallest details of a long-ago love are vivid and significant.

Throughout his life Kawabata was a generous critic of aspiring authors; he is credited with discovering and encouraging Okamoto Kanoko (1889–1939), *Ibuse Masuji, and *Mishima Yukio, among many others. When Mishima committed suicide so dramatically in 1970, many people speculated that part of his motivation was disappointment at not winning the Nobel Prize in literature in 1968. The prize had gone instead, of course, to Mishima's mentor, Kawabata. Kawabata was shocked at Mishima's suicide, and he may have felt guilty at his unwitting part in it. But he had shown interest in and admiration for suicidal men before, including the writer Akutagawa and former Olympic athlete Tsuburaya Kōkichi, whose 1968 suicide moved Kawabata to write that "he felt ashamed at his own writings" when compared with the purity and simplicity of Tsuburaya's suicide note (Ueda 1976:199). In the end it is impossible to know what caused Kawabata's suicide at the end of a long and extraordinarily distinguished career.

—*Sharalyn Orbaugh*

Bibliography

Kawabata Yasunari. "The Izu Dancer." Trans. Edward Seidensticker. In *The Izu Dancer and Other Stories*. Rutland, Vt.: Tuttle, 1974.

——. "Moon on the Water." Trans. George Saito. In Ivan Morris, ed., *Modern Japanese Stories*, 245–257. Tokyo: Kodansha International, 1962.

——. *Snow Country*. Trans. Edward Seidensticker. New York: Alfred A. Knopf, 1956.

——. *The Sound of the Mountain*. Trans. Edward Seidensticker. New York: Alfred A. Knopf, 1970.

Keene, Donald. *Dawn to the West: Japanese Literature in the Modern Era*. 2 vols. New York: Holt, Rinehart and Winston, 1984.

Miyoshi, Masao. *Accomplices of Silence: The Modern Japanese Novel*. Berkeley: University of California Press, 1974.

Pollack, David. *Reading against Culture: Ideology and Narrative in the Japanese Novel*. Ithaca, N.Y.: Cornell University Press, 1992.

Ueda, Makoto. *Modern Japanese Writers and the Nature of Literature*. Stanford: Stanford University Press, 1976.

Washburn, Dennis. *The Dilemma of the Modern in Japanese Fiction*. New Haven: Yale University Press, 1995.

27

FREE VERSE IN THE TAISHŌ ERA

Taishō-era free verse developed from the new-style poetry of the final years of Meiji, and the key figures are Kitahara Hakushū (1885–1942), *Takamura Kōtarō, and Hagiwara Sakutarō (1886–1942). Hakushū did not excel in the genre, but his command and untraditional use of the classical idiom and traditional metrics expanded the new-style form and pointed the way for Takamura and Hagiwara, the two recognized early masters of colloquial free verse.

Hakushū came to prominence in 1907 while a member of Yosano Hiroshi's (pen name Tekkan, 1873–1935) and Yosano Akiko's (1878–1942) Shinshisha (New Poetry Society) and publishing in their journal *Morning Star* (Myōjō). Late that year, however, Hakushū led a rebellion against Tekkan's rule, with the result that *Morning Star* folded in November 1908. The antinaturalist literary lion *Mori Ōgai worked to mend the rift, and in January 1909 *The Pleiades* (Subaru) arose in *Morning Star*'s place. Organized around Ōgai, a steadily expanding Pleiades group produced a journal filled with new-style and traditional poetry, prose fiction, drama, artistic reviews, and critical essays.

Hakushū's focus, no less than that of the naturalists, was on the present physical reality. Rather than strip the human animal of its myths of the past, however, and expose the human beast's basest (and usually sexual) desires in all their ugliness, he attended to his present as the site of endless sensual discovery. His first collection, *The Heathen Faith* (Jashūmon, 1909), gives expression to the Pleiades poets' collective desire for a life of hedonistic fin de siècle decadence and sensual indulgence. Accordingly, the opening poem, "Secret Psalm of the Heathen Faith" (Jashūmon hikyoku), an eclectic concatenation of foreign collocations, exoticized cultural artifacts, and intoxicatingly sensual detail, declares any spiritual, chemical, or technological means welcome so long as it "defamiliarizes" everyday reality.

Being more than pure hedonism, however, Hakushū's best poetry often focuses on his personal past to discover those experiences that nurtured his desire and the supersensitivity that fed it. Such poetry fills his second collection, *Memories* (Omoide, 1911). Where the sensuality of *Heathen Faith* can seem gratuitous, that of *Memories* is compellingly convincing. Take, for example, the poem "Red Fruit" (Akaki mi):

> I know not what day,
> Nor do I know a place,
> But with one who seemed a beautiful child
> I crawled close—
> Peaches perhaps, or perhaps *ikuri*,
> On a crimson lacquered tray mounded high.
> More I do not know,
> Nor do I know a name.
> Likely just a dream—
> But even so, though dimly indistinct,
> On a crimson lacquered tray mounded high
> That which there I saw
> Was red fruit.

To this Hakushū adds a note: "The fruit of the *ikuri* is somewhat smaller than a plum but slightly larger than an apricot, and the color of blood." Despite hazy imprecision concerning its circumstances, the memory gains in power by its lack of delimiting detail. The exotic and foreign-seeming *ikuri* is as a lexical item empty of any verifiable meaning, which suggests that words fail to comprehend and convey experience. As irrecoverable sensual memory, however, *ikuri* stands as a marker for an absence that can never be filled, becoming a perfectly realized symbol for the object of human desire, which forever recedes before the outstretched hand of memory. And the poem's speaker cannot explain his desire's significance, but Hakushū's annotation dimly suggests an underlying physiological factor when he links the fruit through its color to blood.

Hakushū's new-style poetry represented a large step toward greater metrical and linguistic freedom. His imaginative and skillful interweaving of foreign and other nontraditional items into traditional rhythms no doubt helped give poetic legitimacy to and demonstrate the poetic possibilities of the materials presented by this generation's daily lives. More important, Hakushū taught his contemporaries that with sufficient attention to nuance and aural detail, the music of poetry could realistically mirror the workings of human sense and suggest the manner in which human consciousness develops.

Though born but a year after Hakushū, Hagiwara Sakutarō debuted almost a decade later. Publishing often in magazines edited by Hakushū, his self-chosen mentor, Hagiwara first produced traditional tanka, then new-style verse, and finally, forging a new metrical and colloquial idiom for Japanese lyric poetry, free verse in the modern language. His first collection, *Howling at the Moon* (Tsuki ni hoeru, 1917), brought together metered and free verse in both the classical and the colloquial, sometimes within the same poem, but always in a voice recognizably his own.

Blue Cat (Aoneko, 1923), Hagiwara's second collection, brings together free verse composed wholly in the colloquial. Dwelling on a personal sense of despair, Hagiwara captures an aural beauty previously believed possible only in the classical idiom and meter. "Moonlit Night" (Tsukiyo) exemplifies his characteristic music and theme:

> heavy and large the wings they beat and
> ah, what faint feeble hearts they bear!
> to the moonlight night bright like a flower-gas globe
> see these life-forms a flow of white!
> their quiet direction!
> see the feeling single and wounding, possessing these life-forms!
> with the moonlit night like a bright flower-gas globe
>   lamentably sad, the riot of the butterflies!

The drive to write poetry, or to forge into uncharted territory in any field of knowledge, Hagiwara conceived as the product of *shiseishin*, or poetic spirit. To explain his conception, he invoked a platonic world of originary perfect forms that all life seeks to rejoin. This is the light that, like the butterflies here, all living forms unfailingly gravitate toward, an urge inscribed in all being that he terms elsewhere "nostalgia." This urge, however, dooms life to failure because its goal is unobtainable. Most often, moreover, the desperate struggles of these "butterflies" will culminate in their finding not the moon but rather some life-extinguishing flame; yet because the motivating drive is physiologically based and prior to conscious thought, the organism cannot avert this fate. For the same reason, though, lyric poetry is this spirit's perfect expression, inasmuch as lyric depends, Hagiwara argued, upon feeling and sensation rather than conscious thought for its material (Ueda 1983:138–147).

The Ice Land (Hyōtō, 1934), Hagiwara's last collection, makes a "shameful retreat" to the classical language and traditional meters to give expression to intense personal anger at his life. For such poems, Hagiwara felt the modern colloquial inappropriate if the result were still to be perceived as poetry, and critical opinion has diverged widely in its estimate of the collection (Ueda 1983:179). Hagiwara spent his remaining years writing various commentaries, criticism, collections of aphorisms, and studies of Japanese culture. He died in 1942, the same year as Kitahara Hakushū and that other *Morning Star* giant, Yosano Akiko.

—Charles Fox

Bibliography

Fukasawa, Margaret Benton. *Kitahara Hakushū: His Life and Poetry.* Ithaca, N.Y.: Cornell University East Asia Program, 1993.

Hagiwara Sakutarō. *Face at the Bottom of the World and Other Poems.* Trans. Graeme Wilson. Tokyo and Rutland, Vt.: Tuttle, 1969.

———. *Howling at the Moon: Poems of Hagiwara Sakutarō.* Trans. Hiroaki Sato. Tokyo: University of Tokyo Press, 1978.

———. *Principles of Poetry.* Trans. Chester C.I. Wang and Isamu P. Fukuchi. Ithaca, N.Y.: Cornell University East Asia Program, 1998.

Keene, Donald. *Dawn to the West: Japanese Literature in the Modern Era.* 2 vols. New York: Holt, Rinehart and Winston, 1984.

Ueda, Makoto. *Modern Japanese Poets and the Nature of Literature.* Stanford: Stanford University Press, 1983.

28

TAKAMURA KŌTARŌ

Though primarily a sculptor, Takamura Kōtarō (1883–1956) is remembered
more for his poetry. Scholars credit him, together with Hagiwara Sakutarō (see
"Free Verse in the Taishō Period"), with having produced the first successful
colloquial free verse in Japanese, but the common reader would likely point to
his 1941 collection *Selections on Chieko* (Chieko shō) as his highest achievement. Hiroaki Sato, their translator, has described these poems, which chronicle Takamura's relationship with Naganuma Chieko (1886–1938) from their first
meeting and eventual marriage to her death and the years immediately following, as the "longest running best-seller in modern Japanese poetry." Takamura's
work has a further significance when one considers his unwavering commitment to the ideal of the ultimate value of art and its capacity to give expression
to truths unique to a particular individual. Contradictorily, however, the poet
actively supported Japanese aggression against Asia and its all-out war against its
rivals in the Pacific, the United States and Great Britain, voluntarily producing
three volumes of poetry on predominantly public, war-related topics. Takamura
was not alone in his inability to comprehend the anti-individualistic, cruelly im-
perialistic policies of the Japanese government, and he is emblematic of many
of his contemporaries, an unwitting accomplice in and ultimately victim of
nineteenth- and twentieth-century cultural power politics.

Born in Tokyo, the son of sculptor Takamura Kōun (1852–1934), Takamura
Kōtarō was educated to succeed his father, first in Kōun's studio, later in the
Tokyo School of Fine Arts, where Kōun also taught, and from 1906 in New

York, London, and Paris, where he studied Western art. In France Takamura's interest in the work of Auguste Rodin flamed into a passion that centered his artistic aspirations, and he discovered poetry as well through the works of Charles Baudelaire, Émile Verhaeren, and others. At the same time, however, the young sculptor suffered a disillusionment that had its basis in a sense of racial inferiority and a belief in the cultural backwardness of Japan. At the end of his 1947 poem "Paris" (Pari) he looks back on that dilemma, saying:

> In Paris I awakened for the first time to sculpture,
> had my eyes opened to the reality of poetry,
> and in each and every person living there
> could see the reasons underlying culture.
> Saddened, helpless,
> I sensed how great the drop from that unmatchable height.
> Everything Japanese, its customs and its ways,
> I longed for nostalgically while denying all.

On returning home in 1909, Takamura's intellectual suffering led him into devil-may-care decadence, but unlike the deliciously sensual poems of *Kitahara Hakushū (see "Free Verse in the Taishō Era"), often his companion in revelry, Takamura's poetic expressions of world-weariness seem unfeigned, his descriptions of mental suffering convincing. With utmost earnestness, he threw himself into dissipation while simultaneously seeking deliverance. Chieko became that salvation. These two sides of his passion, stated in straightforward, precise terms, filled the pages of *Along the Path* (Dōtei, 1914), the first of six collections of free verse. First come poems focused on the speaker's dissipation, his personal despair, and his impatience to be "purified." Love arrives, however, in the form of an unnamed representation of Chieko, and the latter part of the collection gives expression to renewed devotion to art and a sense of a pioneering personal quest into uncharted territory. Representative of these is the title poem:

> Before me lies no path
> Behind me lies what path there is
> Ah, Nature
> Father
> you who set me off alone, boundless Father
> watch over me, never taking your eyes away
> May I be always filled with Father's spirit
> all along this far-reaching path
> all along this far-reaching path

Sculpture, translation (the sayings of Rodin, poetry by Verhaeren, Whitman, and others), and commentaries on Western art filled the next decade. Poetry served, however, as a "safety valve," as Takamura says in his 1923 "Thorny Epigrams" (Togetoge epiguramu), providing a release, one might infer, of creative steam that in his view could not attain meaningful expressive form otherwise.

The world of two that he and Chieko formed centered his life and art, but in 1928, the first signs of the schizophrenia that would eventually rob Chieko of her sanity appeared, and she died ten years later. *Chieko's Sky*, Takamura's second collection, pulls together poems written sporadically over thirty years and lyrically transforms her into an unforgettable literary presence. In "To Someone" (Hito ni, 1912) the speaker importunes a young, birdlike representation of Chieko to mimic nature and the seasonal round, with which their love by implication accords by not yielding to family pressure for an arranged marriage to an unknown man. "Beneath the Trees" (Juka no futari, 1923) finds the externally heard, assonantly incantatory voice of the speaker's lover in counterpoint to his own internal meditation on his attraction to this woman and her native landscape, which the speaker views as having literally given birth to her. "Chieko Riding the Wind" (Kaze ni noru Chieko, 1935) describes with understated feeling this same Chieko, now "mad," having "quit being human," as she wanders in and out among the trees, communicating only with birds and this by signs. In "Lemon Elegy" (Remon aika, 1939) Chieko, now on her deathbed, bites into a slice of lemon proffered by the speaker and regains for an instant her old clarity just before her "engine simply stopped." And "To One Who Died" (Naki hito ni, 1939) finally transforms the deceased lover into a presence that inhabits nature, that nature indeed itself now mimics.

Immediately following the war, some within Japan argued that Takamura should be prosecuted as a war criminal. *Epitome* (Tenkei, 1950), his final collection, answers by presenting its speaker as emblematic of the entire culture's wrong turn: a sufficiently intelligent and well-meaning, and at one time healthily rebellious, member of society who falls victim nevertheless to cultural myths propagated throughout Japan's modern era. The twenty-poem autobiographical sequence *A Brief History of Imbecility* (Angu shōden) in essence summarizes his personal history and gives expression to a desire for expiation. Such motivation had led Takamura to impose upon himself a seven-year exile from Tokyo after the war in order to live alone in a mountain hut in Japan's cold north. He finally returned to Tokyo to work on a large bronze nude of Chieko for the shores of Lake Towada in northern Honshū. The artist completed this piece in 1954 and died of tuberculosis in 1956.

—*Charles Fox*

Bibliography

Keene, Donald. *Dawn to the West: Japanese Literature in the Modern Era*. 2 vols. New York: Holt, Rinehart and Winston, 1984.

Takamura Kōtarō. *A Brief History of Imbecility*. Trans. Hiroaki Sato. Honolulu: University of Hawai'i Press, 1992.

———. *Chieko's Sky*. Trans. Soichi Furuta. Tokyo: Kodansha International, 1978.

———. *Chieko and Other Poems of Takamura Kōtarō*. Trans. Hiroaki Sato. Honolulu: University of Hawai'i Press, 1980.

Ueda, Makoto. *Modern Japanese Poets and the Nature of Literature*. Stanford: Stanford University Press, 1983.

29

TAISHŌ AND PREWAR SHŌWA THEATER

The tone of Japanese theater in the Shōwa era was set by the Jiyū gekijō, or Free Theater, a group established by Osanai Kaoru (1881–1928) with the collaboration of the Kabuki actor Ichikawa Sadanji II (1880–1940) and active from 1909 to 1919. Osanai strove to continue the kinds of reforms already set in motion by *Tsubouchi Shōyō and the Literary Arts Society (Bungei kyōkai, 1906–13), though Osanai was impatient with Shōyō's gradualist approach. He had traveled to Europe in 1912–13, witnessing the work of Max Reinhardt in Berlin and of Stanislavski in Moscow. (Sadanji had in fact gone to Europe earlier, becoming the first of the progenitors of *shingeki*, or new theater, to see plays there firsthand.) That exposure worked a profound impact on the approach taken by the Free Theater.

Osanai's productions, however, revealed the dual-edged nature of virtually all efforts to reform Japanese theater. On one hand, he mounted translated Western plays that crystallized his vision of what modern Japanese theater should be; on the other hand, his actors, including women (who never acted in traditional Japanese dramatic forms), were all trained in Kabuki acting techniques. Osanai's very first production, for example, Ibsen's *John Gabriel Borkman* in 1909, while pointedly staged to honor Ibsen—whom both Shōyō and Osanai revered almost as a divinity of theater—featured Sadanji in the main role and had the unmistakable look and feel of recycled Kabuki. Nevertheless, this production at the Yūrakuza, the most modern theater building in Japan at the time, struck those in attendance as a new departure for Japanese drama; it can be said to be the first *shingeki* production.

Osanai's approach was, of course, detrimental to native playwrights, wrestling as they were with the onslaught of new techniques and ideas gleaned from Western theater. Still, by incrementally inculcating Western methods for actor training and emphasizing the kind of social realism rendered in plays by Ibsen, Chekhov, Hauptmann, Wedekind, and others, Shōyō and Osanai paved the way for a new kind of Japanese theater—*shingeki*—that would be truly creative and expressive of the new age.

As the Free Theater was approaching dissolution, two other reform-minded companies were in the offing. The first was called *shinkokugeki*, or New National Theater, developed by Sawada Shōjirō (1892–1929) around 1917. *Shinkokugeki* could be seen as a kind of successor to *shinpa*, or new-school drama, which had reached its zenith in the first decade of the twentieth century. Sawada aimed to support his audiences, for whom Western theater was, he felt, too advanced and strange. To ease the transition of his audiences' aesthetic sensitivities, he strove with his company's productions to build a bridge over the yawning gap between Kabuki and Western plays. His calculated attempt at this was mainly to feature acrobatics and sword fights. Unfortunately, his efforts were strikingly reminiscent of *shinpa* and, as a result, produced little in the way of innovation.

The other reform-minded company was the Tsukiji shōgekijō, or Tsukiji Little Theater, founded by Osanai himself in 1924 with Hijikata Yoshi (1898–1959), who had studied drama in Berlin and Moscow. In a milestone lecture at Keiō University, prior to inaugurating their new theater, Osanai declared that he would produce only translated Western plays because contemporary Japanese plays did not measure up. His productions included Shakespeare's *Julius Caesar*, Chekhov's *The Cherry Orchard*, Ibsen's *Ghosts* and *An Enemy of the People*, Kaiser's *From Morn to Midnight*, Strindberg's *Miss Julie*, O'Neill's *Beyond the Horizon*, Rolland's *Les Loups*, and Pirandello's *Six Characters in Search of an Author*.

For Japanese theatergoers in the Meiji and Taishō periods, who were weaned on the traditional Japanese forms of Noh, Bunraku, and Kabuki, translated Western plays were startlingly new and different. Modern theater in Japan can be said in effect to begin with such plays, and the early images of a modern society and people on the Japanese stage are based on the characters in those translated plays—principally on Shakespeare's tragic heroes, Chekhov's fading aristocrats, and above all Ibsen's rebellious spirits. For the Japanese, these characters were larger than life, aggressive, self-assertive, even superior—images that in some sense have persisted in modern Japanese plays. By the late Meiji and into the Taishō period, when Japanese playwrights began to write their own plays and even occasionally to see them performed, the almost universal fascination with things Western extended not only to themes and dramaturgy (especially Ibsen's) but, indeed, at times to Westerners themselves and to their social behavior.

Then, in March 1926, Osanai placed another milestone on the road to *shingeki*, at last staging a Japanese play, *The Hermit* (En no gyōja), written by Shōyō. The play is fairly dense going, rendering the classic struggle of man—here a Buddhist monk—against the forces of evil. This production was a springboard to staging other works by Japanese writers. The Tsukiji Little Theater subsequently nurtured many Japanese playwrights, directors, and actors. With this legacy, Osanai can be said to have had the single greatest impact on the early modernization of Japanese theater. He died suddenly at the end of 1928, and the company disbanded the next year.

Still, Western theater by the mid-1920s was as much liability as inspiration. New Japanese theater would have to outgrow dependence on Western plays before it could become creative and vital. Japanese playwrights would have to distinguish between what was Western, on one hand, and what was modern, on the other.

At this point, *shingeki* hit a fork in its incipient path, one direction informed more by political ends, the other more by aesthetic ones. The key figure on the left fork was Hijikata, who after Osanai's death organized the Shin-tsukiji gekidan, or New Tsukiji Drama Group. His experience in Europe, especially seeing the work of Meyerhold, who artfully melded spectacle and political message, inspired Hijikata to create a similar kind of theater in Japan. Hijikata persisted in this effort through more than a decade and considerable ups and downs—including government censorship of virtually every play script—mounting proletarian plays that appealed to labor unions and the intelligentsia. Most of these plays were fairly dull political tracts and could hardly withstand objective critical scrutiny. Yet, they were done in the realistic *shingeki* style, and several fine examples were created, by such leftist playwrights as Kubo Sakae (1901–1958) and Miyoshi Jūrō (1902–1958). Even more important than the approach taken in the plays was the fact that they were original efforts by Japanese playwrights, thus giving further impetus to the creation of a new theater that was truly Japanese. As the war approached and governmental harassment became rampant, the New Tsukiji Drama Group and others like it were disbanded; not cowed, Hijikata was finally arrested for his activities and spent the war years in jail.

The most prominent guide in the other fork in *shingeki*'s path was one of Osanai's associates, Kishida Kunio (1890–1954), who had worked with the renowned Jacques Copeau in France in the early 1920s. Kishida envisioned himself to be like Copeau in Japan; that is, he wanted nothing less than to completely revamp Japanese dramatic literature. After he returned to Japan, Kishida worked with Osanai at the Tsukiji Little Theater (1924–28), the successor group to the Free Theater, which had disbanded in 1919. Kishida ultimately disagreed with Osanai's almost exclusive use of translated Western plays and vigorously encouraged Japanese playwrights to write their own. He practiced what he preached, writing a number of plays himself, but he was far more successful and influential as a leader and champion of *shingeki*. Leading up to the war, he worked with a number of small *shingeki* troupes, providing guidance in choice of repertory, in stage techniques, and in all-purpose theater know-how. To the Scandinavian, German, and Russian inclination of Osanai, he added awareness in Japan of French and English theater. He advocated the relatively natural style Copeau sought in uttering lines on stage, as opposed to the far more stylized declamation common in Japan. Above all, Kishida led the way to a serious and professional native theater that would be characterized by aesthetic, not political, standards. His vision became the foundation for the Bungakuza, or Literary Theater, established in 1936, which, having no political agenda, continued through the war and long into the postwar period. The Literary Theater staged the work of perhaps the most prominent prewar *shingeki* playwrights, Kubota Mantarō (1889–1963) and Morimoto Kaoru (1912–1946).

Kishida was clearly the most influential *shingeki* figure in the 1930s and 1940s. When he died in 1954, his legacy was secure as perhaps the key architect of *shingeki*. His work came full circle with postwar playwrights, especially the generation that came of age in the underground theater of the 1960s. For the first time, Japanese playwrights, directors, and producers created new plays that were critical successes in their own right, no longer derivative of Western forms. Today, the eponymous Kishida Prize for playwriting (Kishida Gikyokushō) is granted each year to the outstanding new Japanese play.

—*John K. Gillespie*

Bibliography

Bowers, Faubion. *Japanese Theatre.* New York: Hermitage House, 1952; rpt. Rutland, Vt.: Tuttle, 1974.

Horie-Weber, Akemi. "Modernization of the Japanese Theatre: The Shingeki Movement." In W. G. Beasley, ed., *Modern Japan: Aspects of History, Literature, and Society,* 147–165. Berkeley: University of California Press, 1977.

Ibaragi Ken. *Nihon shingeki shōshi* (A Short History of Japanese Shingeki). Tokyo: Miraisha, 1980.

Ortolani, Benito. *The Japanese Theater: From Shamanistic Ritual to Contemporary Pluralism.* Princeton: Princeton University Press, 1990.

Ozasa Yoshio. *Dorama no seishinshi* (The Intellectual History of Modern Japanese Drama). Tokyo: Shinsuisha, 1983.

Rimer, J. Thomas. *Toward a Modern Japanese Theatre: Kishida Kunio.* Princeton: Princeton University Press, 1974.

Shea, George Tyson. *Leftwing Literature in Japan.* Tokyo: Hosei University Press, 1964.

Takaya, Ted T., ed. *Modern Japanese Drama: An Anthology.* New York: Columbia University Press, 1979.

30

HAYASHI FUMIKO

Hayashi Fumiko (1903–1951) was an especially prominent and prolific novelist and poet who at certain points in her career "was the most popular writer in the country" (Keene 1984, 1:1142). Hayashi was best known for her ostensibly autobiographical "diaries" and as the indefatigable chronicler of resilient characters, predominantly women, who occupy the underside of Japanese society. The appeal of her best work today is twofold: by depicting the ever-baffled, ever-resurgent aspirations of those operating largely outside societal norms or, at least, middle-class conventions, she subverted stereotypes associated with female identity; and by adopting a vivid, accessible style, incorporating written-as-spoken imagery and peripheral dialects with original similes and onomatopoeia that departed, strikingly, from the literary language of the era, her works retain an immediacy and vibrancy for contemporary readers.

As a poor, provincial female who made her origins and early hardships a central theme of her writing, Hayashi crafted an original literary voice that was often at odds with dominant literary tendencies and always reflected the contradictions of her place in popular culture as a woman writer *(joryū sakka)* or writer of women's literature *(joryū bungaku)*. Her breakthrough best-seller *Diary of a Vagabond* (Hōrōki, 1928–30) invoked the idioms and themes of classical women's diaries while depicting the catch-as-catch-can travails of a young female protagonist principally in the gritty urban underbelly of Tokyo. In contrast with earlier literary depictions of the helpless resignation of the poor and powerless, typically composed at considerable intellectual and physical distance by university-educated male elites, Hayashi wrote from bitter personal experience, yet she adopted an upbeat, optimistic tone in the face of grinding destitution and bleak prospects. Hayashi's approach, often characterized as *minshuteki* ("of the people"), collided with the increasingly politicized art championed by the proletarian-literature movement, and in the late 1930s it would run afoul of the escalating state repression and censorship of any writing found to contain unflattering portraits of Japanese society. Despite a notable drive to embrace opportunities as a "woman writer"—including not only commissions for publications, but also lecture tours, celebrity fêtes, and even plane relays—that often meant catering to the expectations of her readership in women's magazines and newspapers, Hayashi consistently sought to establish herself as a writer of serious fiction in mainstream literary journals. Her detailed depictions of everyday life, a characteristic of so-called women's literature, were usually drab or desperate, if not nasty and brutish, and had nothing especially feminine about them. And despite the considerable distance she sought to place between herself and the openly feminist journal *Women's Arts* (Nyonin geijutsu), where her prose debuted, she might be considered a feminist in spite of herself for portraying women as irrepressibly autonomous agents, castigating manipulative males, and celebrating female relationships as the principal locus of altruism and affection.

Hayashi began her literary career as a poet. In the early 1920s, she published a series of poems in Hiroshima prefectural newspapers under the name Akinuma Yōko and, from 1925, under her own name when one of her poems appeared in Shinchōsha's literary journal *Prose Club* (Bunshō kurabu). Even before she had secured critical recognition, her 1927 poem in the special issue on female poets of *Literary Forum* (Bungei kōron) stood apart in its departure from standard imagery and allusions and for its unabashed celebration of herself as the measure of all things (Mori 1992:11–12). In her first poetic anthology, *I Saw a Pale Horse* (Aouma o mitari, 1929), Hayashi's self-representations combined sharply contrasting postures—humble and defiant, plaintive and bombastic—and expressed a tough sentimentality that reflected her position as young, female, and unconstrained, if not unbridled (Brown 1997:115–135). Her poems "Lament" (Kurushii uta) and "My Ship Has Sailed" (Noridashita fune dakedo), among many others, were indicative of the bright, irrepressible, unrepentant optimism that she adopts, defiantly, in harsh environments and bleak circumstances.

Hayashi's transition to prose occurred initially in *Diary of a Vagabond*, serialized in *Women's Arts*, in a form that echoed *uta monogatari* (classical poetic tales). Her diary entries combined a mixture of ostensibly autobiographical anecdotes, introspection—including her own neurotic anxieties—and self-realized bits of wisdom, and they frequently included poetry written by herself or Ishikawa Takuboku (1886–1912) or half a dozen other modern poets. Hayashi wrote unvarnished accounts of encounters with an assortment of literary figures, reflecting the roman à clef style often seen in the *shishōsetsu* (personal novel). The clarity and immediacy with which she portrays a Japanese underclass, especially women in highly unstable environments with tenuous holds on employment, residence, or relationships, cut loose and scrambling to find any means to survive, stand out in Japanese letters.

Once *Diary of a Vagabond* had made Hayashi a public figure, she wrote for an audience that wanted to know more about her. In successive sequels as well as dozens of other works that similarly adopted a confessional diary format and a lyrical style, Hayashi recounted and celebrated her life, often returning to the same incidents from the mid-1920s, providing either more or less incriminating detail. Hayashi also published many commentaries on her work (see, for example, Fesseler 1998:159–170) that typically combined mildly self-deprecating humor, defensiveness, and still more details about personal hardships. She repeatedly employed the trope of "no food for two days" in order to contrast herself with male elites. Yet her commercial success supported ostentatious pretensions—notably, in enrolling her adopted son in Gakushūin, the Peers School—and incurred condemnation for snobbish, social-climbing aspirations of the nouveau riche. Nakamura Mitsuo would observe after her death that Hayashi's garish tastes and unsophisticated affectations were themselves of the people (1957:24). Biographers have tended to accept Hayashi's assertions about her own life at face value, to treat her confessional writing as unadorned autobiography, and to correlate episodes from her fiction with incidents in her own life. However, like many male authors, Hayashi was perfectly capable of dissembling her past and recasting herself to fit the times.

Hayashi sought to project a public persona as a brash, irrepressible, sometimes flamboyant libertine. As portrayed in *Diary of a Vagabond*, she took several "husbands" in the early and mid-1920s, but without the formality of entering the man's family's register (only in 1944 would Ryokubin, her lover since 1926, take Hayashi's surname, and in the same year she would adopt an infant boy). She was a forceful and occasionally outrageous personality and went some distance to purvey sensational, if not salacious, intimacies to her reading public. She could sail close to the winds of scandal while for the most part gauging correctly what was permissible and popular. During periods of increased state censorship, her account of her personal life was far more circumspect and the depiction of her poverty far more muted. Hayashi was somewhat reckless in her personal life, but much of what went into print was cut from whole cloth.

Hayashi's penchant for revisiting and revising her work—to say nothing of incidents in her life—was evident from the outset. Her initial poetry publications were reworked successively (Mori 1992:11–23) and then recast as prose passages in diary entries. Her *Diary of a Vagabond* was revised in minor ways between its initial serialization and publication as a book, and again, more substantially, in a 1939 revised edition, including the emendation of sixty passages of pseudo-classical grammar. However, the most noteworthy transformation in Hayashi's writing was a self-conscious shift toward "objective fiction" and the adoption of more standard, composed, and complex grammatical construction with a clearly delineated narrative structure.

Hayashi received considerable notoriety when, writing for the *Mainichi* newspaper in December 1937, she was the first Japanese woman to enter Nanjing after it fell to Japanese troops. Despite failing to note any atrocities and hardly making any observations about Nanjing, Hayashi's renown as a war reporter was assured. In 1938 she and Yoshiya Nobuko (1896–1973) were picked by the Ministry of Information for the "Pen Squadron"—a group of popular writers who were to tour the front and write about the circumstances and sacrifices of soldiers. Hayashi's collaboration with state-sponsored propaganda was the focus of much postwar criticism. She was singled out in a 1946 editorial of *Akahata*, the Communist Party newspaper, which condemned writers' wartime collaboration. In contrast with other writers, Hayashi never rationalized her actions or apologized for her participation in the war effort. But just as she had joined in the general enthusiasm for the war effort, when the war was over she raised her voice against the dislocation and misery caused by the war. Although several of her postwar stories, such as "Splendid Carrion" (Uruwashiki sekizui, 1947), were explicitly antiwar, they focused on postwar dilemmas of repatriated soldiers, unwelcome, rootless, and lost, or of war widows fending for themselves often after only the most fleeting of relationships with their spouses.

Hayashi's postwar fiction resonated with much of what was best in her earlier works, exploring themes of wandering, abandonment, bare subsistence, and disillusioned intimacy, tempered by irrepressible resiliency. Her writing captured the imaginations of a generation who found their experience reflected in it. In "Late Chrysanthemum" (Bangiku, 1948), which won the Women's Literary Prize, Hayashi effectively evokes the weary disillusionment of the times through the succession of false hopes that a remarkably well-preserved former geisha and a once-dashing young officer embrace at the sour end of a relationship. In "Downtown" (Dauntaun, 1949) Hayashi adopts a dark tone in presenting the bleak circumstances and unpleasant choices confronting her female protagonist. But unlike other nihilistic authors who also write of desperate poverty and disillusionment, Hayashi stands out in presenting the feints and false starts that fractured personalities suffer. Her characters internalize the ambiguities and conflict that characterize the uncertainties of the era. Through their interior monologues Hayashi captures their conflicting desires: how they struggle with these desires, rather than what they do or how low they descend, is what elicits the reader's sympathy.

"Narcissus" (Suisen, 1949) is representative of Hayashi's postwar sophistication of language and tightness of narrative. "Narcissus" presents the irreconcilable differences and bitter recriminations between a mother and her son. The unrelenting petty insults and bickering between two selfish, vain, and irresponsible characters conveys an especially pessimistic assessment of human relationships. Unlike Hayashi's early works, this story lacks even a hint of sentimentality:

at the final parting of the two characters, the mother thinks her son looks pathetic, and he quickly releases her hand. For her the final parting is a liberation.

Edward Seidensticker (1963) heralds this closing scene from "Narcissus" as among the most memorable of postwar literature. In contrast to rigid conformity of governmentally orchestrated "good wife, wise mother" perspectives or the didactic moralizing of *katei shōsetsu* (domestic fiction), "Narcissus" depicts a world bereft of righteousness. By focusing on the most common and revered of personal relations, between a mother and her son, Hayashi reveals a dark underside of ordinary life, and she suggests that, however resilient the human spirit, the real exercise of free will is in choosing between distasteful choices. As in most of her later works, the language is more standard and composed, and the structure more clearly delineated, in contrast with the fragmented, discontinuous narrative of *Diary of a Vagabond*.

In her last complete novel, *Drifting Cloud* (Ukigumo, 1949–51), Hayashi chronicled a wandering, ill-fated love affair from the highlands of wartime Indochina to the unrelenting downpours on remote Yakushima, an island south of Kyushu. Mizuta's analysis of this work perceptively underscores how vagabondage and wandering are a central experience not only for Hayashi but also in the works and lives of most modern women writers (see also Vernon 1988). Freedom, in this view, is possible for Japanese women only outside of the constraints of marriage and the family. Japanese men were free to explore other countries and cultures, but women, if they wanted to wander, had to move beyond the conventions of the Japanese social system. Renewed interest in Hayashi's writing, as seen in recent republications of her works, no doubt reflects its ability to convey the capacity for autonomous female agency and to suggest a range of human experience that transcends middle-class conventions.

—*Joan Ericson*

Bibliography

Brown, Janice. "Reading *I Saw a Pale Horse*." In Hayashi Fumiko, *I Saw a Pale Horse and Selected Poems from Diary of a Vagabond*, 115–135. Ithaca, N.Y.: Cornell University East Asia Program, 1997.

Fesseler, Susanna. *Wandering Heart: The Work and Method of Hayashi Fumiko*. Albany: State University of New York Press, 1998.

Hayashi Fumiko. *Diary of a Vagabond*. Trans. Joan E. Ericson. In Joan E. Ericson, *Be a Woman: Hayashi Fumiko and Modern Japanese Women's Literature*, 119–219. Honolulu: University of Hawai'i Press, 1997.

——. *The Floating Clouds*. Trans. Yoshiyuki Koitabashi and Martin C. Collcott. Tokyo: Hara, 1965.

——. *I Saw a Pale Horse and Selected Poems from Diary of a Vagabond*. Trans. Janice Brown. Ithaca, N.Y.: Cornell East Asia Program, 1997.

———. "Late Chrysanthemum." Trans. John Bester. *Japan Quarterly* 3, no. 4 (October–December 1956): 468–486. Also translated as "A Late Chrysanthemum." Trans. Lane Dunlop. In Lane Dunlop, *A Late Chrysanthemum: Twenty-One Stories from the Japanese*, 95–112. San Francisco: North Point Press, 1986.

———. "Narcissus." Trans. Kyoko Iriye Selden. In Noriko Mizuta Lippit and Kyoko Iriye Selden, eds., *Japanese Women Writers: Twentieth Century Short Fiction*, 49–61. Armonk, N.Y.: M. E. Sharpe, 1991. Also translated as "Narcissus." Trans. Joan E. Ericson. In Joan E. Ericson, *Be a Woman: Hayashi Fumiko and Modern Japanese Women's Literature*, 223–235. Honolulu: University of Hawai'i Press, 1997.

———. "Splendid Carrion." Trans. Shioya Sakae. *Western Humanities Review* 6, no. 3 (Summer 1952): 219–228.

———. "Tokyo." Trans. Ivan Morris. In Donald Keene, ed., *Modern Japanese Literature*, 415–428. New York: Grove Press, 1956. Also translated as "Downtown." Trans. Ivan Morris. In Ivan Morris, ed., *Modern Japanese Stories*, 350–364. London: Spottiswoode, 1961.

———. "Vagabond's Song." Trans. Elizabeth Hanson. In Yukiko Tanaka, ed., *To Live and to Write: Selections by Japanese Women Writers, 1913–1938*, 105–125. Seattle: Seal Press, l987.

Keene, Donald. *Dawn to the West: Japanese Literature in the Modern Era*. 2 vols. New York: Holt, Rinehart and Winston, 1984.

Mizuta, Noriko. "In Search of a Lost Paradise: The Wandering Woman in Hayashi Fumiko's *Drifting Clouds*." In Paul Gordon Schalow and Janet A. Walker, eds., *The Woman's Hand: Gender and Theory in Japanese Women's Writing*, 329–351. Stanford: Stanford University Press, 1996.

Mori Eiichi. *Hayashi Fumiko no keisei—sono sei to hyōgen* (The Evolution of Hayashi Fumiko: Life and Expression). Tokyo: Yūseidō, 1992.

Nakamura Mitsuo. "Hayashi Fumiko bungaku nyūmon" (Introduction to the Literature of Hayashi Fumiko). *Bungei* 14, no. 7 (June 1957): 20–27.

Seidensticker, E. G. "Hayashi Fumiko." *Jiyū* 5 (1963): 122–131.

Vernon, Victoria. "Between Osan and Koharu: The Representation of Women in the Works of Hayashi Fumiko and Enchi Fumiko." In *Daughters of the Moon: Wish, Will, and Social Constraint in Fiction by Modern Japanese Women*, 137–169. Berkeley: University of California Institute of East Asian Studies, 1988.

31

MIYAMOTO YURIKO AND SOCIALIST WRITERS

Born in Tokyo to an affluent family as Chūjō Yuri, Miyamoto Yuriko (1899–1950) was a prolific writer whose works reflect the social turbulence of Japan as it grappled with modernization and militarism during the early part of the twentieth century. Her works are compiled in thirty volumes, two of which are devoted solely to writings about women's issues. Yet despite the copious amount of material she wrote and the significance of her works as literary documents of Japan's social history, especially pertaining to socialism and women's rights, to date only four English translations of Miyamoto Yuriko's works exist. Three of the four translations are excerpts from her novels *Nobuko* (1924–1926), *The Banshu Plain* (Banshū heiya, 1946) and *The Weathervane Plant* (Fūchisō, 1946). The only work translated in its entirety is her short story "The Family of Koiwai" (Koiwai no ikka, 1934).

Miyamoto Yuriko had two strikes against her as a writer in the early part of the twentieth century: she was a socialist and a woman. A writer identified with either category tended to be relegated to the margins of scholarly attention unworthy of canonization. Proletarian literature has been criticized for being tedious and flat due to its emphasis on conveying a political message rather than focusing on plot and character development. Miyamoto Yuriko's works stand out from those of male peers such as Kobayashi Takiji (1903–1933) because her stories usually focus on women's rather than men's participation in Japan's socialist movement. In general male proletarian writers were fighting for the improvement of social conditions in Japan, but not necessarily interweaving their concerns with women's issues. Miyamoto Yuriko addressed both (Lippit 1980:146).

To be labeled a *joryū sakka* (woman writer) also relegated one's works to the margins of *junbungaku* (pure literature). The problem with the term *joryū bungaku* (women's literature) is that it implies a single style that all women writers share because of their gender, ignoring differences of history, socioeconomic background, and education. Husband Miyamoto Kenji's biography of Miyamoto Yuriko purposely avoids the term *joryū sakka* out of concern that this label would cause readers to overlook her intellectual contribution to Japan's progressive political movements (Ericson 1996:94–95).

The unfortunate consequence of both categorizations is that Miyamoto Yuriko's works have not been given the attention they deserve as literary documents of social history. She spent her adult life trying to free herself from her privileged but traditional background and to fight for social equality as Japan struggled to become modern. Early works had an inward focus, exploring her awakening as a young woman trying to free herself from the traditions of the patriarchal marriage and family system, a relic from Japan's neo-Confucian feudal past. Later works reflect a more outward orientation, concerned with sociopolitical issues aimed at improving all people's lives, both male and female. Through her travels in the Soviet Union and postwar Europe, Miyamoto Yuriko realized that the advancement of the social position of women in Japan would occur only when a general respect for humanity was instituted so all people regardless of social status and wealth could lead fulfilling existences. Marx's social revolution was the vehicle, she believed, to eradicate social inequalities in early twentieth-century Japan. As she became more involved in Japan's socialist movement during the war years, however, she realized the sexist paradox of men working to improve laborers' conditions but still treating women as second-class citizens.

Throughout her writing career she had three major concerns: the question of consciousness and practice; a woman's ability to be happy and creative; and the merging of politics with literature (Lippit 1980:147). Most of her stories are written in the traditional *shishōsetsu (personal novel) style. What makes her semiautobiographical fiction significant, Katō Shuichi argues in *The History of Japanese Literature* (1983), is that her travel in the Soviet Union and her life experiences as a Communist, lesbian, and divorced woman opened up arenas in Japanese literature that had previously been marginalized or completely ignored (234).

Honda Shūgo, a prominent Japanese literary critic, divides Miyamoto Yuriko's writing career into five periods. The first, considered her "apprenticeship as a writer" period, extends from 1916 to 1918. Her debut novel, *A Flock of Poor People* (Mazushiki hitobito no gun, 1917), is about her own experience spending summers with her grandparents in a poor rural area of northern Japan and the unfairness of the landowner system toward peasants. *Tsubouchi Shōyō endorsed this novel, thus launching her writing career (Lippit 1980:148). Following this success, Miyamoto left university after only one semester to focus full-time on writing.

The second period begins in 1918, when she went to New York City with her father on an extended study tour at Columbia University, and it ends in 1927 when she traveled to the Soviet Union with her female companion Yuasa Yoshiko (1896–1990), a Russian scholar. This is considered her "rebellion against the family" period. It includes her first marriage in 1919 to Araki Shigeru, a scholar of ancient Persian, and their 1924 divorce. This relationship is described in *Nobuko*, the first in a trilogy of semiautobiographical novels. Published serially from 1924 to 1926 in the journal *Reconstruction* (Kaizō), *Nobuko* is about a young girl's awakening as an individual and the obstacles marriage can pose to attaining personal satisfaction and creative achievement. It is often cited as the Japanese version of Ibsen's *A Doll's House*.

The protagonist, Nobuko, rebels in two ways. The first rebellion is against her family: she refuses to marry the man they have chosen and selects her own husband, a social inferior. The second rebellion is against Japanese society: she seeks a divorce at a time when, though legal for women, divorce was a choice to be avoided because of the lack of familial or social support. Noriko Mizuta Lippit argues that this is one of the first novels to depict the development of the modern woman's ego and that it parallels Meiji literary treatments of the male ego in works such as *Natsume Sōseki's 1914 *Kokoro* and *Shimazaki Tōson's 1906 *The Broken Commandment* (150); and it has been read as a bildungsroman for Japanese women (Kobayashi 1991:58). Another novel of this period, *One Flower* (Ippon no hana, 1927), based on Miyamoto Yuriko's eight-year relationship with Yuasa Yoshiko, also touches on an unspoken topic: same-sex love.

The third period extends from 1927, the beginning of her travel in the Soviet Union with Yuasa, and ends in 1933 when she married Miyamoto Kenji, the leader of Japan's Communist Party. Miyamoto Yuriko became a convert to the Communist movement while traveling through the Soviet Union. She was particularly struck by how involved Soviet women were with the political process. Moreover, she was appalled by the inequalities between the rich and poor observed while traveling through Europe; when she returned to Japan in 1930, she dedicated herself to promoting socialism in Japan as a means to eradicate the societal ills of capitalism and in turn improve women's socioeconomic condition.

Miyamoto Yuriko's romance with Miyamoto Kenji began when she joined the illegal Japanese Communist Party (Nihon kyōsantō) in 1931, as well as several other proletarian writers' groups. In February 1932 they married. During this time, the government—increasingly militaristic following the 1931 invasion of Manchuria—intensified its suppression of literary groups. On March 26, 1932, Yuriko was arrested and Kenji was forced to go underground. This would be the first in a series of ten arrests for her over the next thirteen years. A year later, in December 1933, Kenji was arrested, accused of murdering an ex-

Communist member who had become a police informer. He spent thirteen years in a Hokkaido jail and was not released until the occupation forces revoked the 1925 Maintenance of Public Order Act (Chian iji hō) on October 9, 1945. The correspondence between Kenji and Yuriko was published from 1950 to 1952 as *Twelve Years of Letters* (Jūni nen no tegami).

The fourth period, though rife with political turmoil, was ironically one of her most prolific and is considered her "rebellion against the country" period. It begins in September 1934, when the proletarian movement was disbanded, and ends with Japan's defeat in World War II. As Japan became more militaristic with its invasions into China's mainland, government pressure on writers to commit *tenkō* (political conversion) increased. Miyamoto Yuriko refused to do this and was prohibited from writing from 1938 to 1939, and later from 1941, the beginning of the Pacific War, until 1945. When she was able to write, her works were often censored.

It is during the fourth period that the six-chapter novella *Breasts* (Chibusa, 1935) and the short story "The Family of Koiwai" were written. Both works are prime examples of her political fiction, which presents a critical picture of the proletarian movement and its treatment of women. In both cases, soon after publication, she was arrested.

"The Family of Koiwai" is about the wife of a Communist poet who is forced · to go underground due to his devotion to his political literary movement. The protagonist, Otome, whose name means "young maiden," becomes the epitome of strength and endurance. She must become an independent woman actively participating in a world where traditional conventions regarding family duty have been dismantled and the hierarchy of the feudal family system in which men rule but also protect is crumbling. Otome must endure the loneliness and poverty in which she and her husband live because of his insistence on writing political poetry that earns little money. To survive, Otome puts aside her pride and takes work as a barmaid. Eventually the husband leaves the family so as not to endanger their safety. Otome is left alone with her in-laws and daughter to survive police harassment and wartime poverty. It becomes increasingly clear to Otome that unless she participates in her husband's political movement, she and her husband will grow apart.

While the stories of this period are often rather somber accounts of the proletarian movement, by the fifth period, which begins at the end of World War II in 1945 and ends with Miyamoto Yuriko's death in 1950, her writings became more optimistic. She was finally able to write without any fetters. To make up for the years she was in prison and the censorship of her writing, the last five years of her life saw no rest in terms of her commitment to socialist and feminist causes. She wrote *Women's History* (Josei no rekishi, 1948) and continued her participation in the Communist Party, traveling around the country giving lectures on socialism and peace movements. She wrote more than fifty essays, was a member of the Broadcasting Bureau (Hōsō iinkai) and Publication Bureau

(Shuppan iinkai), and was editor of *Working Woman* (Hataraku fujin), a journal of the newly formed Democratic Japanese Cultural Association (Nihon minshū shugi bunka renmei).

During this final period she produced two postwar novels, *The Banshu Plain* and *The Weathervane Plant*. The significance of both stories is that they are early depictions of postwar Japan. She also completed her autobiographical trilogy with the publication of *Two Gardens* (Futatsu no niwa, 1948) and *Signposts* (Dōhyō, 1949–50).

Miyamoto Yuriko clearly had a voice that deserves reexamination. Initially her writing focused on women's issues in novels such as *Nobuko* and *One Flower*, where she advocated that women find their identities by breaking free from Japan's feudal family system. Later her voice became more political, as evidenced in "The Family of Koiwai," where she asks all people, men and women, to cooperate and become friends blind to social status and gender. The inner psychological struggles of her characters are symbols of the greater social struggle occurring in Japan in the early part of the twentieth century as it grappled with modernization and militarism. As literary documents of this significant time in Japan's social history, Miyamoto Yuriko's thirty volumes of essays, fiction, and letters deserve to be rescued from the margins of modern Japanese literature where proletarian and women's writing are often placed.

—Anne Sokolsky

Bibliography

de Bary, Brett. "After the War: Translations from Miyamoto Yuriko." *Bulletin of Concerned Asian Scholars* 16, no. 2 (1984): 40–47.

Ericson, Joan E. "The Origins of the Concept of 'Women's Literature.'" In Paul Gordon Schalow and Janet A. Walker, eds., *The Woman's Hand: Gender and Theory in Japanese Women's Writing*, 74–115. Stanford: Stanford University Press, 1996.

Katō Shūichi. *A History of Japanese Literature*, vol. 3, *The War Years*. Trans. Don Sanderson. London: Macmillan, 1983.

Keene, Donald. "The Barren Years: Japanese War Literature." *Monumenta Nipponica* 33, no. 1 (Spring 1978): 67–112.

Kobayashi Fukuko. "Women Writers and Feminist Consciousness in Early Twentieth-Century Japan." *Feminist Issues* 11, no. 2 (Fall 1991): 43–64.

Lippit, Noriko Mizuta. "Literature and Ideology: The Feminist Autobiography of Miyamoto Yuriko." In *Reality and Fiction in Modern Japanese Literature*, 146–162. Armonk, N.Y.: M. E. Sharpe, 1980.

Mikals-Adachi, Eileen. "Miyamoto Yuriko." *Dictionary of Literary Biography: Japanese Fiction Writers, 1868–1945*. Detroit: Bruccoli Clark Layman, 1997.

Miyamoto Yuriko. "The Banshu Plain." (Excerpt.) Trans. Brett de Bary. *Bulletin of Concerned Asian Scholars* 16, no. 2 (1984): 41–45.

——. "Chibusa" (Breasts). In *Sangatsu no dai yon nichiyō hoka*. Tokyo: Shin nippon shuppansha, 1934.

———. "The Family of Koiwai." In Noriko Mizuta Lippit and Kyoko Iriye Selden, eds., *Japanese Women Writers: Twentieth Century Short Fiction*, 3–19. Armonk, N.Y.: M.E. Sharpe, 1991.

———. *Nobuko*. Tokyo: Shinchōsha, 1928. Excerpts published in Yukiko Tanaka, ed., *To Live and to Write: Selections by Japanese Women Writers*, 1913–1938, 41–64. Seattle: Seal Press, 1987.

———. "The Weathervane Plant." (Partial translation.) Trans. Brett de Bary. *Bulletin of Concerned Asian Scholars* 16, no. 2 (1984): 46–47.

32

NAGAI KAFŪ

The work of Nagai Kafū (1879–1959) encompasses two of the principal themes of Japanese modernity: a sincere and enduring interest in Western civilization and a search for an authentic, or at least aesthetically viable, Japanese culture located in the past. For Kafū, this meant an early and decisive encounter with French literature, notably the works of Zola, Maupassant, and Baudelaire, followed by what many critics have described as the classic "Return to Japan" (Nihon kaiki) and a long, eccentric career cultivating the pose of an Edo-period *bunjin*, or man of letters. Much of the interest of Kafū's work, however, lies in the way he combines these two strands, seeking to create a recognizably Japanese modern literature, informed by an ongoing reading of French fiction, in the idiom of Edo-period arts.

Nagai Sōkichi (Kafū was one of a number of pen names and sobriquets) was born on December 3, 1879, in Tokyo to parents of considerable social position and literary pedigree. His father, Nagai Hisaichirō (or Kagen), was the son of a wealthy landowner from Owari Province, and his mother, Tsune, was the daughter of the renowned Confucian scholar Washizu Kidō, who was also Hisaichirō's teacher. Before Kafū's birth, the family had moved to Tokyo, where Hisaichirō had a successful career at the Ministry of Education, and later in industry. Kafū's upbringing reflected his father's unorthodox combination of strict Confucian training and a taste for Western culture, what Edward Seidensticker has called "newness without liberation" (Seidensticker 1965:6), and it is hardly surprising that the young Kafū grew to be a rebel. His checkered academic career, marked by a greater aptitude for indulgent amusements than for study, ended in 1899 when he was expelled from the Foreign Language School in Tokyo for failure to attend classes. He turned to traditional *kiyomoto* singing and the study of the *shakuhachi* flute and even tried his hand at *rakugo* storytelling before approaching the *Ken'yūsha (Friends of the Inkstone) novelist Hirotsu Ryūrō. Ryūrō refused to accept Kafū as a disciple but did help him to publish some early stories in the Romantic Ken'yūsha style, thereby launching his literary career.

The important milestones in Kafū's career are relatively few and occur largely in the early years. In 1900 he apprenticed himself to Fukuchi Ōchi (1841–1906), founder and chief playwright of the Kabuki Theater, following him into newspaper work a year later. Fukuchi introduced Kafū to the writings of the French naturalist author Émile Zola, who inspired Kafū's first three novels: *Ambition* (Yashin, 1902), *Flowers of Hell* (Jigoku no hana, 1902), and *Woman of the Dream* (Yume no onna, 1903). These works established Kafū as a pioneer of the emerging Japanese *naturalist movement, though they are closer in intent to French naturalist attempts to depict society at large than to the authorial self-revelation that characterized the school in Japan. In 1903 Kafū's father sent him to America, where he remained until 1907, when he was finally allowed to go to France, the object of his literary and aesthetic interests. In 1908 he returned to Japan, never to leave again, but he recorded his experiences abroad in two works that placed him squarely in the literary avant-garde and made his reputation as a novelist: *American Stories* (Amerika monogatari, 1908) and the famously banned *French Stories* (Furansu monogatari, 1909). In the years following his return to Japan, Kafū divided his energies between teaching French at the forerunner of Keiō University, editing a journal that served as the voice of the so-called antinaturalist movement, and publishing strident criticisms of what he saw as the superficiality of Japanese westernization and modernization. He was often numbered among the members of the *tanbiha* or "aesthetic school" for works such as "The River Sumida" (Sumidagawa, 1909). But by 1916 his involvement in the *bundan* (literary establishment) had waned, and he began the reclusive, eccentric, peripatetic existence that would characterize his life and works until the end. He pursued a desultory study of Edo-period arts and literature designed to enhance his writerly persona, lived in houses named to reflect his cantankerous attitude (Danchōtei, or Dyspepsia House; Henkikan, or Eccentricity House), kept company with waitresses, actresses, and prostitutes, and published infrequently but steadily until his death in 1959.

Kafū's literary reputation is enhanced by his essays, translations (most notably of French poetry), and his important diary, *Daily Records of Dyspepsia House* (Danchōtei nichijō), kept from 1917 to 1959. But it is for his fiction, generally brief and often autobiographical in inspiration, that he is best known, particularly for a handful of works from the first four decades of the twentieth century: *American Stories, Geisha in Rivalry* (Udekurabe, 1917), *Dwarf Bamboo*

(Okamezasa, 1918), *During the Rains* (Tsuyu no atosaki, 1931), and "A Strange Tale from East of the River" (Bokutō kidan, 1937). The earliest of these, *American Stories,* is generally considered Kafū's first mature literary work. The stories and sketches that make up the collection show considerable influence from Kafū's reading of Maupassant during his time in the United States, emphasizing as they do experiments in narrative form, principally varieties of framed narratives, a generally decadent tone, and demimonde motifs. Stories such as "Women of the Night" (Yoru no onna), "Shelter from the Snow" (Yuki no yadori), and "Chinatown" (Chainataun) inaugurate Kafū's career-long thematization of prostitution at the same time that they offer a startlingly confident and astute portrait of America in the first decade of the twentieth century.

Geisha in Rivalry, on the other hand, already postdates Kafū's ostensible "return to Japan" and is set in and around the traditional entertainment district of Shinbashi in Tokyo. The novel follows the progress of an ambitious geisha named Komayo through a complicated series of affairs with patrons and conflicts with fellow geisha, focusing on the mediated and ultimately hollow nature of relationships in the demimonde. In one of his earliest and most successful weddings of foreign and native sources, Kafū in effect creates a traditional *gesaku* (an Edo-period fiction style, usually translated as "frivolous writing") setting for a work whose emotional and spiritual content might have been provided by Baudelaire. The narrative alternates between brutally naturalistic passages describing the victimization of Komayo and more lyrical interludes typical of Kafū's elegiac evocations of the Tokyo cityscape—an imaginative topography in which he was searching for the remnants of Edo culture. At the same time, the success of *Geisha in Rivalry* is due in large part to the character of Komayo, who is among Kafū's most vivid and convincing creations, and to the beauty of Kafū's style, which Donald Keene has called "a glory of modern Japanese literature" (Keene 1984, 1:420).

A year after *Geisha in Rivalry* appeared, Kafū published the work that many consider his most carefully plotted and exciting sustained fiction. *Dwarf Bamboo* shares many themes with *Geisha in Rivalry*—competitive desire, prostitution, the decline of contemporary culture—but Kafū sets the novel closer to home, in the bourgeois neighborhoods of the Yamanote district of Tokyo, near the Azabu home he would himself occupy in 1920. The story concerns an unexpected run of good fortune enjoyed by a hack painter, Uzaki Kyoseki, and the corresponding misfortunes of those around him. The principal characters are corrupt artists and their equally corrupt art dealers on one hand and prostitutes and procurers on the other, and Kafū makes the analogies between the activities of the two groups explicit. The aesthetic pleasures provided by the traditional setting and lyrical interludes in *Geisha in Rivalry* are absent in this later novel, leaving only a stinging portrait of the decadence of bourgeois culture. Amid the general tawdriness established by the coming of unlicensed brothels to the upper-class neighborhoods, Kafū has Uzaki stumble upon a forgery done by the master painter who had served as his mentor, a tryst between a governor's wife and her houseboy, and the fact that his master's son has married an illegitimate daughter. The humorous irony of the work (indeed, Kafū called this his *kokkei shōsetsu*, or "comic novel") is that each of these inadvertent discoveries leads to considerable financial gain for Uzaki and allows him to pursue his own erotic adventures in the encroaching demimonde. Beyond its interesting plot, however, the work gives evidence of Kafū's growing concern with the nature of narrative structure, and in particular with modernist experiments with self-referential fiction. Kafū employs a number of devices to manipulate the reader's response to his story, raising and then subverting expectations for a mystery plot, a comedic novel, and a naturalist fiction. *Dwarf Bamboo* is full of classic narrative feints—misdirected letters, mistaken identities, foreshadowed doom—none of which delivers its intended effect, a fact that Kafū emphasizes with his larger theme of forgery. The novel inevitably draws attention to its own narrative processes, a self-conscious theme that Kafū takes up again two decades later in the work that many consider his masterpiece, "A Strange Tale from East of the River."

"A Strange Tale from East of the River" was labeled a "comeback" work by an older writer who had not published much fiction during the 1920s. It is a peculiar work that has been called "slight" and "misshapen" and is often considered more autobiography than fiction. But it is almost certainly Kafū's best known and best loved work, and one that he clearly intended as the summation of a career. It tells the story of a writer, Ōe Tadasu, who pursues a desultory affair with a prostitute named O-Yuki in the grimy brothel district of Tamanoi (east of the Sumida River) while he is writing a novel entitled *Shissō* (Whereabouts Unknown), featuring a character named Taneda Junpei. Portions of the latter text, which functions as a parody of the *shishōsetsu (personal novel) form, are included as chapters in "A Strange Tale," as are miscellaneous poems, passages from old romances, and other "found" texts. The effect of the novel-within-a-novel structure and these other pastiche-like elements is to remind the reader of the constructed nature of the work; that is, that the subject of narration is always narration itself.

Kafū worked under the influence of a number of muses in writing "A Strange Tale." He pays tribute in a long aside to *ninjōbon* (Edo-period sentimental tales) writer Tamenaga Shunsui (1790–1843) who was himself a master of the self-conscious narrative aside; and near the end there is a reference, perhaps ironic, to the power of Pierre Loti's *Madame Chrysanthème*. But the most important debt is to André Gide (1869–1951), and in particular to his novels *Paludes* (1920) and *Les Faux Monnayeurs* (The Counterfeiters, 1925), both of which feature the novel-within-a-novel device that Gide called *mise en abîme*. Kafū exploits the *mise en abîme* to insist on the thematic significance of the act of narration, choreographing a complex and highly self-referential dance between himself as implied author, his writer-character (Ōe), and his character-character (Taneda).

Yet another prostitute-character, the brilliantly portrayed O-Yuki, emphasizes the long-standing analogy in Kafū's work between the artificial desire created by the prostitute and the reader's desire evoked in the act of narration. "A Strange Tale" weds Kafū's twin concerns: an elegiac tale of vanishing Japanese culture, unearthed in the seedy alleys of Tamanoi, that is nonetheless told in the form of a modernist experimental fiction as sophisticated as any to be found in the Japanese literature of the 1930s.

During World War II Kafū withdrew still further from the literary world, seeing almost no one but his old friend and protégé, *Tanizaki Jun'ichirō, and recording his opposition to the war effort, and particularly to the German occupation of Paris, in his diary. In the postwar years, he enjoyed a resurgent popularity based largely on his newly fashionable antimilitarist reputation, and in 1952 he was awarded the Bunka kunshō (Order of Cultural Merit). But Kafū continued to prefer the company of actresses in the burlesque theaters that sprang up in Asakusa or the waitresses in Ginza cafés, and he continued to set the remaining stories he published among them. He died during the night of April 29, 1959, alone in his house on the eastern edge of the city, leaving behind, as the citation for his imperial decoration suggests, a legacy that included his pioneering research in Edo literature and an important role in bringing foreign literature to Japan.

—Stephen Snyder

Bibliography

Isoda Kōichi. *Nagai Kafū*. Tokyo: Kōdansha, 1979.

Keene, Donald. *Dawn to the West: Japanese Literature in the Modern Era*. 2 vols. New York: Holt, Rinehart and Winston, 1984.

Nagai Kafū. *American Stories*. Trans. Mitsuko Iriye. New York: Columbia University Press, 2000.

———. *During the Rains & Flowers in the Shade*. Trans. Lane Dunlop. Stanford: Stanford University Press, 1994.

———. *Geisha in Rivalry*. Trans. Kurt Meissner. Tokyo: Tuttle, 1963.

Seidensticker, Edward. *Kafū the Scribbler: The Life and Writings of Nagai Kafū, 1879–1959*. Stanford: Stanford University Press, 1965.

33

WARTIME FICTION

The most important fact to keep in mind about Japanese literary prose written during the war is that it was written during the war—that is to say, whether or not the war itself was the predominant subject of such works, they were written according to tenets defined by, and under the strict supervision of, the government. The Japanese government, which was dominated by the military beginning in the early 1930s, designated very specific guidelines about what could be written and published in Japan and maintained an extensive censorship regime that not only examined magazine articles and books for acceptable content before publication, but also could ban the distribution of specific books and specific issues of magazines even after they had been published and distributed to bookstores and newsstands.

This is not to say that Japanese writers resisted the government's strict regulation of literary activity. Indeed, most writers saw it as their patriotic duty to support the nation's military enterprise in their work. Almost all major writers—including those who were harshly critical of wartime collaborators after the war—participated in literary trips to China and other Japanese-occupied areas sponsored by the government and joined government-sponsored literary organizations. Only two major writers, *Nagai Kafū and *Tanizaki Jun'ichirō, and a few committed Communists who spent much of the wartime period in prison, are commonly recognized as having withdrawn from the war effort and refrained from supporting Japan's military activities (Keene 1971:301). But the roster of writers and intellectuals who did take part in government-sponsored activ-

ities and supported the war more or less enthusiastically included the stars of
the Japanese literary establishment, such as writers Ozaki Shirō (1896–1964)
and Yoshiya Nobuko (1896–1973), critics Kobayashi Hideo (1902–1983) and
Hirano Ken (1907–1978), and other important figures such as editor Kikuchi
Kan (1888–1948). Many writers who had been members of the Communist
Party, or were at least sympathetic to leftist causes, were encouraged or coerced
by the government to make public statements repudiating their leftist politics
and, implicitly, endorsing the authoritarian state. This renunciation, commonly
referred to as *tenkō* (conversion), was an experience shared by so many writers
and intellectuals that it would be a major focus of the literary world's debates
over the war experience in the postwar period.

The most notable prose literary genre practiced during the war was a form of
documentary autobiographical prose that came to be called *jūgunki*, or "campaign accounts." These were first-person descriptions of the experiences of Japanese soldiers at the front, and often on the battlefield itself, in China and other
places Japan's aggressive expansion reached. Many *jūgunki* were written by literary celebrities flown to the front in China for periods as short as a few days, put
up in luxury accommodations and wined and dined by Japanese military escorts.
But more popular credence was extended to *jūgunki* written by actual soldiers on
the battlefield, the most famous of whom was Hino Ashihei (1907–1960).

Hino had been an aspiring poet and writer, studying English literature at the
elite Waseda University in Tokyo, and a supporter of labor unionism in his native Kyushu, even journeying with a band of Kyushu longshoremen to support
labor strikes in Shanghai in 1932. Hino was drafted as a regular soldier in 1937
and had already been sent into combat in China when a novel he had completed just before entering the army won the prestigious Akutagawa Prize. His
ensuing celebrity prompted the army to transfer him from his combat unit
to the Army's Information Bureau, which disseminated Japanese propaganda
abroad and provided inspiring war information to the home front. After a few
months with the Information Bureau, Hino published a campaign account of
his experiences accompanying a Japanese platoon as it advanced through southern China. The book, *Wheat and Soldiers* (Mugi to heitai, 1937), became the
best-selling volume of the war, along with the two companion volumes that
formed "the Soldier Trilogy," eventually racking up sales of 1.2 million copies.

Hino's acclaim was based on his sentimental, heartwarming descriptions of
individual Japanese soldiers—the *heitai* of the title, which carries the unpretentious, common-man connotations that the term *GI* does in reference to U.S. soldiers. His soldiers plodded through the vast Chinese wheat fields, usually hungry
and tired, but always dedicated, devoted to the emperor, and warmly supportive
of each other. They were kind to but disdainful of the Chinese farmers and
refugees they encountered, considering them childish, ignorant, and dirty and in
need of guidance from their "big brother," Japan. Hino presented himself as one
of the *heitai*, simple and patriotic—glossing over his elite education and literary

fame. His narrator loves a good beer and a good bath, and he often finds an opportunity for comradeship by sharing one or the other with fellow soldiers. He unabashedly describes incidents that demonstrate his own clumsiness or ignorance, describing with relish, for example, how his unit unwittingly used an elegant chamber pot they found in an abandoned house to cook in.

Hino's unpretentious narrative persona was quite different from another well-known soldier-writer of the period, Hibino Shirō (1903–1975), whose novella *Wusun Creek* (Wusun kurîku, 1939), described his combat experiences dramatically, but clearly from an elite perspective: Hibino carries his copies of the classical texts the *Manyōshū* and *Saikontan* with him on the battlefield, and says he would sooner abandon his rifle than his books (*Zenshū* 2:225). Equally cultured but less impressed with himself, *Ibuse Masuji described his experiences as an Information Bureau officer in Japanese-occupied Singapore in the novella *City of Flowers* (Hana no machi, 1942). Other writers whose accounts of their military experiences, whether in combat or as members of an occupying force, were well received in Japan included Takami Jun (1907–1965), for works such as his short story "About Nokana" (Nokana no koto, 1943), and Satomura Kinzō (1902–1945), whose death in combat in the Philippines in 1945 cut short his literary career after he published only a few books describing his military service in China.

Not so well received was the novel *Living Soldiers* (Ikite iru heitai, 1938), by another Akutagawa Prize-winning author, Ishikawa Tatsuzō (1905–1985). Ishikawa was dispatched by the literary and intellectual magazine *Chūō kōron* to accompany a Japanese military unit that participated in the infamous siege and capture of Nanjing in December 1937. It is surprising that the editors of the magazine thought that Ishikawa's lurid depiction of the brutal killing of both enemy soldiers and civilians and the cynical attitudes of Japanese soldiers would meet the government's approval. The editors' miscalculation resulted in the recall of the entire issue and the conviction of Ishikawa and some editors for violations of the Peace Preservation Law, and the incident certainly weighed heavily in the government's decision to ban publication of the magazine in 1944. (Issued in December 1945 by the publisher Kawade shobō, *Living Soldiers* was one of the first works to be published in postwar Japan.)

Although few writers were as bold in their representation of atrocities by Japanese soldiers as Ishikawa was, careful readings of many wartime texts reveal elements that could be read as critical of or resistant to the wartime state. Ibuse's gentle but pointed descriptions of the inefficiencies and ineptitude of Japanese administration in Singapore in *City of Flowers* and Takami's criticism of racial prejudice by Japanese soldiers against darker-skinned natives in "About Nokana" are examples of this subtle resistance. And even some of the wartime writings of Hino, anathematized as a "cultural war criminal" after the war, suggest revulsion at the excesses of some Japanese soldiers. Indeed, significant portions of Hino's works depicting such war crimes as the execution of prisoners of war were cut from his wartime works by military censors.

The *jūgunki* form, as practiced by Hino, Ishikawa, and others, had much in common with the dominant prose genre of the prewar period, the **shishōsetsu*, or personal novel. Like the *shishōsetsu*, the *jūgunki* was typically narrated in the first person and could encompass both purportedly factual documentary accounts and works that seemed to be fiction. In either case, however, both the *jūgunki* and the *shishōsetsu* were conventionally read as the actual experiences of the author, who was equated with the narrator of the text. As many modern explorations of the *shishōsetsu* have revealed, they were often heavily fictionalized and mediated for literary effect, despite being presented as unmediated experience. *Jūgunki*, too, claimed authority for their narratives based on the credibility of their authors' experience in the war: much of Hino's acclaim, for instance, was based on the fact that he had been in fact a common soldier, and he consciously sought to enhance this effect by suppressing from his texts aspects of his identity as an educated man of letters.

One crucial difference between the *shishōsetsu* and the *jūgunki*, though, was the social commonality of the subject matter they depicted. *Shishōsetsu* authors moved in rarefied literary circles, and emphasized their detachment from mainstream society. Their texts emphasized the solitary and individual character of their experiences. Chronicles of the war, however, described events and experiences that millions of Japanese would share.

—David Rosenfeld

Bibliography

Hibino Shirō. *Wusun kurīku* (Wusun Creek). In Hirano Ken, ed., *Sensō bungaku zenshū* (Complete Works of War Literature), 2:5ff. Tokyo: Mainichi shinbunsha, 1971–72.

Hino Ashihei. *Wheat and Soldiers.* Trans. Shidzue Ishimoto. New York: Rinehart, 1939.

Ibuse Masuji. *Black Rain.* Trans. John Bester. Tokyo: Kodansha International, 1969.

Keene, Donald. *Landscapes and Portraits: Appreciations of Japanese Culture.* Tokyo: Kodansha International, 1971.

34

ATOMIC FICTION AND POETRY

The 1945 atomic bombings of Hiroshima (August 6) and Nagasaki (August 9), together with their related themes of subsequent nuclear weapon development and testing, the Cold War "balance of terror," and the nuclear power industry, have been important and even urgent topics for Japanese writers from World War II to the present. Although examples of such writing can be found in other countries, principally the United States and the Republic of Korea (where sizeable numbers of *hibakusha*—that is, atomic-bomb survivors—relocated), the unique deployment of fission weapons on Japanese soil is why only Japanese literary history can legitimately speak of a genre of *genbaku bungaku* (atomic-bomb literature). It is a major postwar theme that has spawned works in many guises: not just poetry, fiction and drama, but film, music, and even *manga* ("comic" books; see, for example, Nakazawa Keiji's [1938–] *Barefoot Gen* [Hadashi no Gen, 1973]).

Nonetheless, it is also true that Japanese writers attempting this theme have encountered intense critical resistance to this often angry or even nihilistic literary and historical topic. It was not until the 1980s, for instance, that a multivolume anthology of atomic-bomb writing was published in Japan. In recent years, however, new attention has been paid to these writers and their works in Japan and in other countries, thanks to translation into foreign languages and the publication of a major critical study in English (Treat 1995).

Atomic-bomb writers in Japan can be divided into two groups: writers who are themselves survivors of the bombings, and those who are not. Straddling these two categories are writers who are natives of Hiroshima or Nagasaki but were not present when they were bombed, such as Nagasaki's Sata Ineko (1904–1998). This distinction, though not the only one that can be made, is key. The former group has an experience to tell that they often doubt can, in fact, ever be comprehended by nonsurvivors, whereas the latter must struggle to find the means to imagine nuclear war without misappropriating the memories belonging to those who actually survived it—two ethical and technical conundrums not unknown, for instance, in the literature of the Holocaust in Europe or of slavery in the western hemisphere.

It is also important to note that not all survivor-writers are professional writers. Indeed, most of the testimonies and the poetry—the two most voluminous types of atomic-bomb writing—were written by literary amateurs motivated by a need to express, perhaps for themselves as much as for others, the experiences they underwent but only partially comprehend. Perhaps the crude naiveté for which so much atomic writing has been faulted by professional critics is characteristic of any literature, Japanese or otherwise, that is produced by modern technological violence perpetrated on masses of ordinary people.

The first and in many ways still the most impressive atomic-bomb memoirist was Hara Tamiki (1905–1951), a professional poet and short-story writer in Hiroshima whose vivid, raw account of August 6 and its immediate aftermath, *Summer Flowers* (Natsu no hana, 1949), owes much of its power to the moment in which it was written—only days and weeks after the bombing. A triptych whose second part is the "Summer Flowers" memoir of August 6, it was published in 1947 despite the occupation-era censorship that prevented the appearance of other atomic-bomb writing in Japan. It begins with a sentence famous in Japanese literature precisely because of its banality: "I was saved because I was in the toilet." Only seventeen pages long, "Summer Flowers" captures the consternation and horror of an event whose causes and extent were unknowable at the time, and it remains the most gruesome eyewitness account of either bombing.

Another Hiroshima native and professional writer, Ōta Yōko (1903–1963), is Japan's most important *hibakusha* novelist. Her best-known works are *City of Corpses* (Shikabane no machi, 1948), *Human Rags* (Ningen ranru, 1951), and *Half Human* (Han-ningen, 1954). Though each of these novels differs in its narrative point of view and degree of fictional content, collectively they constitute the single most sustained attempt by any survivor-writer to record in prose the experience and import of Hiroshima, an attempt inspired by her rhetorical question: Just what would constitute a "successful work" *(ii sakuhin)* of post-Hiroshima literature? How can a subject such as this ever inspire the pleasure of reading? The anger and bitterness of her writing inspired considerable criticism of her work, but by the time she died of what may have been bomb-related health problems, she had justly earned her reputation as Japan's most significant "A-bomb writer."

The two most important atomic-bomb poets are also Hiroshima natives. Tōge Sankichi (1917–1953) was a left-wing activist and writer before the war and wrote in the few years of life left him after the bombing the most widely read polemic poetry to come out of Hiroshima, his *Poems of the Atomic Bomb* (Genbaku shishū, 1951). The most famous poem in the collection, "Give Me Back My Father" (Chichi o kaese), is carved into a stone memorial that stands prominently in Hiroshima's Peace Park:

> Give me back my father. Give me back my mother.
> Give me back the old people.
> Give me back mankind.
> Give me back the children.
> Give me back myself. And all those people
> Joined to me, give them back.
> Give me back mankind.
> Give me peace.
> A peace that will not shatter
> As long as man, man is in the world.

Tōge died, like Ōta, of bomb-related causes, but still alive and writing today is poet and essayist Kurihara Sadako (1913–). Her collection of poems *Black Eggs* (Kuroi tamago, 1946) was the first book of atomic-bomb literature published in Japan. A more affecting if less political collection than Tōge's, it expresses Kurihara's optimistic hopes for a literal revival of human values after the bombings: the collection's most famous poem, "Let Us Be Midwives!" (Umashimen ka na), describes the birth of a baby among Hiroshima survivors crowded in a makeshift shelter.

The most critically acclaimed work of atomic-bomb literature in Japan today is also a work that offers the possibility of a human resilience that survives even nuclear war. Written by *Ibuse Masuji, one of Japan's major writers since the 1920s but not himself a bomb survivor, *Black Rain* (Kuroi ame, 1966) has become the atomic bomb's equivalent, at least in terms of worldwide circulation and critical stature, of Anne Frank's Holocaust diary. In the opinion of many intellectuals in Japan polled in the late 1980s, *Black Rain* is the single most important book, in any genre and on any topic, published in Japan since 1945.

"For several years past, Shizuma Shigematsu, of the village of Kobatake, had been aware of his niece Yasuko as a weight on his mind" (9). So starts *Black Rain*, with a sentence whose understatement will only become clear when, by the end of the novel, Yasuko faces an imminent death as a result of her presence in Hiroshima on August 6. The story Ibuse tells is assembled through diaries that Shigematsu, his wife, niece, and other survivors kept of their experiences as *hibakusha*. The novel—made into an award-winning 1989 film by noted director Imamura Shōhei—is a masterful quasi-documentary of man-made suffering never far from nature's capacity for regeneration. Despite criticism from the left, which was suspicious of *Black Rain*'s failure to examine the question of blame for the atomic bombings, and from *hibakusha* activists who question the success of a novel written by a nonsurvivor, *Black Rain* remains the most widely read and popular work of atomic-bomb literature around the world.

At approximately the same time as Ibuse was writing *Black Rain*, the 1994 Nobel laureate for literature *Ōe Kenzaburō was publishing a series of essays later collected under the omnibus title of *Hiroshima Notes* (Hiroshima nōto, 1965). Based on several trips made to Hiroshima over two years to observe political demonstrations against the global arms race, *Hiroshima Notes* has been hailed as Japan's most influential collection of essays since the end of the war. *Hiroshima Notes* is an existentialist meditation on how Hiroshima survivors have embraced their victimhood and thereby retrieved their dignity in the face of near-certain failed health and eventual death. It remains an important work for its refusal—atypical for atomic-bomb literature—to relegate *hibakusha* to the status of passive, pathetic victims.

Although *Black Rain* and *Hiroshima Notes* remain the most widely disseminated works of atomic-bomb literature, it is important to note that Nagasaki, the second city to be bombed, has also produced its own, if less voluminous or well-known, literature. Despite the use of a more powerful weapon over Nagasaki, the hilly geography of the city produced fewer victims and consequently fewer atomic-bomb writers. Nonetheless, Nagasaki offers many works—memoirs, poetry, short stories, plays, and novels—similar to those of Hiroshima. Hara's *Summer Flowers*, for instance, finds its Nagasaki parallel in Ishida Masako's *Masako Will Not Succumb: An Account of the Nagasaki Atomic Bomb* (Masako taorezu: Nagasaki genshi bakudan ki, 1949). Inoue Mitsuharu, in his work *People of the Land* (Chi no mure, 1963) describes the postwar degradation of *hibakusha* in terms reminiscent of Ōta Yōko's novels. But because many of Nagasaki's *hibakusha* were Christian, a small minority in Japan, it is a place that has produced a rather different literature from Hiroshima's. Tanaka Chikao's drama *The Head of Mary* (Maria no kubi, 1959) describes how a local cult of the Virgin Mary appeals to her power to heal Nagasaki *hibakusha*. Nagai Takashi's famous first-person documentary account *The Bells of Nagasaki* (Nagasaki no kane, 1949) links the historical persecution of his native city's Christian followers with both the biblical persecution of God's chosen people and Nagasaki's own twentieth-century martyrdom on August 9, 1945.

The atomic-bomb writers most associated with the bombing of Nagasaki today, however, are not Christian, and in fact their work steadfastly refuses to find any comfort in or rationale for their city's fate. The late Sata Ineko's *The Shade of Trees* (Juei, 1972) is the tragic story of a second-generation Chinese woman in Nagasaki who dies of radiation disease after years of tending to the health of her fellow *hibakusha* and married lover, a Japanese. It is perhaps the most powerful work of Japanese atomic-bomb literature in describing the psychology of denial in bomb victims who only gradually realize and come to terms with their abbreviated mortality. Hayashi Kyōko (b. 1930) has written many stories and novels—the most famous "Ritual of Death" (Matsuri no ba, 1975)— that often describe the fate of survivors, especially those who are women and must fear for the health of their children, in cynical terms that allow no room for the succor that, for example, a Christian perspective might have provided.

The most recent major writer to have taken up the atomic bombings is Oda Makoto (b. 1932), one of Japan's most prominent left-wing writers and activists who, though not a *hibakusha*, published in 1980 a long novel entitled simply *Hiroshima*. It is an ambitious epic work of Hiroshima not as an atrocity unique to Japan but as one that involves the entire "nuclear age" in which all the world lives today. Its characters include not only native Japanese but also Americans of many ethnicities and wartime colonial subjects in Japan, such as Koreans and Southeast Asians.

Hiroshima is perhaps the best example of what might be called Japan's "post-Hiroshima" literature. The novel places the specific violence visited on Japan in 1945 within the global context of mass technological warfare and the political, ethical will of modern nation-states to use it. For that reason, Oda makes the narrator of his key scene—the detonation of the bomb on August 6—an American prisoner of war in Hiroshima rather than a Japanese civilian. Named Joe, this young symbol of the enemy, killed by his own compatriots, is the vehicle through which Oda explores twentieth-century atrocity as an international, rather than strictly national, phenomenon.

—*John Whittier Treat*

Bibliography

Hara Tamiki. *Summer Flowers*. Trans. Richard H. Minear. In Richard H. Minear, ed., *Hiroshima: Three Witnesses*, 41–113. Princeton: Princeton University Press, 1990.

Hayashi Kyōko. "Ritual of Death." In Marty Sklar, ed., *Nuke Rebuke: Writers and Artists against Nuclear Energy and Weapons*, 21–57. Iowa City: The Spirit That Moves Us Press, 1984.

Ibuse Masuji. *Black Rain*. Trans. John Bester. Tokyo: Kodansha International, 1969.

Kurihara Sadako. *Black Eggs*. Trans. Richard H. Minear. Ann Arbor: University of Michigan Center for Japanese Studies, 1994.

Oda Makoto. *The Bomb*. Trans. D. H. Whittaker. Tokyo: Kodansha International, 1990.

Ōe Kenzaburō. *Hiroshima Notes*. Trans. David L. Swain. Tokyo: YMCA Press, 1981.

Ōta Yōko. *City of Corpses*. Trans. Richard H. Minear. In Richard H. Minear, ed., *Hiroshima: Three Witnesses*, 143–273. Princeton: Princeton University Press, 1990.

Tanaka Chikao. *The Head of Mary*. Trans. David G. Goodman. In David G. Goodman, ed., *After Apocalypse: Four Japanese Plays of Hiroshima and Nagasaki*, 105–181. New York: Columbia University Press, 1986.

Treat, John Whittier. *Writing Ground Zero*. Chicago: University of Chicago Press, 1995.

35

OCCUPATION-PERIOD FICTION

At noon on August 15, 1945, after the atomic bombings of Hiroshima (August 6) and Nagasaki (August 9), the emperor of Japan went on the radio to announce to the Japanese people the government's plans to surrender. On September 2 the documents of surrender were formally signed on a U.S. battleship anchored in Tokyo Bay. From that moment until April 28, 1952, nearly seven years later, Japan was under the control of the Allied occupation.

The occupation government, SCAP (Supreme Command for the Allied Powers), was headed by U.S. General Douglas MacArthur. Although it was formed by a coalition of Allied nations, the occupation of Japan was from the beginning primarily an American enterprise, responding to American attitudes and policies toward Japan and the larger world. During the nearly seven years of occupation, the American advisors working for SCAP imposed comprehensive structural changes on Japan's existing economic, political, educational, and judicial systems (Iokibe 1992:91–106; Passin 1992).

SCAP's first official directive after the surrender, issued on September 3, 1945, established its general right to perform censorship. This was followed in subsequent weeks by censorship directives regarding the mail, press, and radio, all of which stressed the responsibility of the Japanese organizations involved to conform to certain general prohibitions. In particular "destructive criticism" of the Allied forces was outlawed. These directives were matched by others that promoted free speech and civil liberties; earlier Japanese government restrictions and censorship codes were removed.

From September 1945 until September 1947, the Civil Censorship Detachment (CCD) of SCAP was responsible for the "precensorship" of all printed matter in Japan: newspapers, magazines, books (fiction and nonfiction), dramatic scripts, and so on. Precensorship meant that all these materials had to be submitted to SCAP prior to their publication. As of October 1947 most books and magazines were transferred to "postcensorship." Although CCD's responsibilities continued formally until October 1949, very few items were even subjected to examination after December 1948 (Mayo 1991).

Prewar and wartime censorship within Japan had been capricious and punishments sometimes severe, with leftist sentiments and "pornography" its most frequent targets (Rubin 1985). In contrast, SCAP was seen as surprisingly lenient toward sexual explicitness and freedom of political expression, although anything that appeared to be "ultranationalist" was expressly prohibited. Some writers took advantage of the new freedom to explore the sexual body in ways that had been impossible in prewar Japan. Tamura Taijirō, for example, wrote the notorious *Gate of the Flesh* (Nikutai no mon) in 1947, depicting the lurid activities of a group of feral prostitutes and criminals. Despite explicit sexual content, this story was not liable to CCD censorship.

There were, however, relatively severe limits placed on depictions of the atomic bombings (Braw 1991). Some *hibakusha* (survivors of the atomic bombings) writers' accounts of their experiences were written soon after the bombings, but could not be published until 1949 (Treat 1995:93; Mayo 1991:150–151; Rubin 1985:88–89). (See "Atomic Fiction and Poetry.") Graphic depiction of food shortages, fraternization between soldiers and Japanese citizens, or Allied soldiers' involvement with the black market were also forbidden.

One group of young writers that emerged prominently during this period was known as the *daisan no shinjin* (the third generation of new writers). They were for the most part young men with military experience. They included Yasuoka Shōtarō (b. 1920), Kojima Nobuo (b. 1915), and Shimao Toshio (1917–1986). In general, the occupation-period writing of these young men can be characterized as dark, sometimes humorous, sometimes surrealistic, but always expressing a sense of disempowerment and degradation—it is sometimes known, in fact, as "the literature of humiliation." A typical story is Kojima's 1948 "On the Train" (Kisha no naka). The protagonist, Sano, is a teacher, whose material well-being and social status have been decimated by the war. On a long train ride from the countryside, where he has obtained black market rice, Sano experiences multiple incidents of humiliation and discomfort while his impatient wife berates him for being feckless and ineffectual. In the end he is robbed of his hard-won rice by a man who had pretended to be sympathetic and helpful throughout the journey. During the war the Japanese people had frequently been figured in propaganda as *ichioku* ("the hundred million"), moving and thinking as one entity with one glorious goal. In this story that putative unity is shown to be shattered, with every person out for himself or herself. Sano's final wish is simply to disappear into nothingness—a conclusion reached by many male protagonists in the literature of humiliation.

Yasuoka Shōtarō's "Prized Possessions" (Aigan, 1952) is another example of this genre. The young male protagonist has returned whole from the war but is bedridden because of spinal tuberculosis. He wears a plaster-of-paris body cast. His parents have also both survived the war, but the family is struggling to survive under the difficult circumstances of the immediate postwar period. The protagonist's father decides to raise angora rabbits for their fur. Soon he is obsessed with the rabbits, constantly devising new homes for them and new methods of encouraging fur growth. Though it appears at first that the family may be moving toward security under the leadership of a newly reawakened paternal strength, that rosy picture soon breaks down. The rabbits take over the house; their fur and droppings are everywhere: in the human's food, in the protagonist's bed (with the fur getting inside his cast and making him nearly insane with itchiness), in his father's nostrils. In fact, the father begins increasingly to resemble the rabbits in the protagonist's eyes. He even makes a pitiful bleating sound in his sleep that resembles both the rabbits and, as the protagonist recalls, the sound of the emperor's voice on the radio as he announced the surrender. In the end the family discovers that there is no market for rabbit fur and is forced to sell the rabbits to a butcher. He berates them for their gullibility in thinking they could make a go of the rabbit business. At that point the rabbit the butcher is holding bites him, and the protagonist is delighted, feeling that his family and the rabbits who symbolize them have been avenged against the butcher, who represents those brutal, occupation-identified elements of Japanese society thriving in the postwar period. But the butcher then easily crushes the rabbit's skull. This story, too, underlines social fragmentation and the psychologically oppressive conditions of occupation, and it ends in humiliation.

These young male writers explicitly address the psychological effects of life under foreign occupation, particularly the loss of masculine authority, usually as represented by the postwar father and the emperor. They explore in common the question: to whom should one profess loyalty in this confusing situation? One's fathers, who were directly responsible for the war? The leftists, who had resisted the war but were later thrown in prison by the occupation officials? Japanese women, who seem to have forged an entente with the occupation unavailable to young men? To Douglas MacArthur, the new model of adult manhood? Clearly none of these options is possible, and these writers express the resulting confusion and sense of absurdity. Their stories are exaggerated, clearly allegorical, sometimes even surreal.

In contrast, the fiction produced by women writers during this period tends to focus on the day-to-day realities of life—the difficulty of surviving and caring for children alone in the ruined cities, in the midst of food shortages worse than any of wartime. Women's fiction also explores the new types of families being created after the chaos of war. A typical example is *Hayashi Fumiko's "Downtown" (Dauntaun, 1948) which features a young widowed mother, Riyo, struggling to survive with her son in the ruins of downtown Tokyo. Riyo meets a repatriated soldier whose wife had left him while he was imprisoned in the Soviet Union after the end of the war. The two begin to forge a new life and a new definition of family, but when the man is suddenly killed in an accident, Riyo once again has to struggle on alone. Despite her feelings of despair, Riyo finds hope in the kindness of other struggling female survivors.

In this and many other stories by Hayashi Fumiko and Hirabayashi Taiko (1905–1972), the two most prolific women writers of the period, the occupation as such is almost never mentioned. Instead the focus is very much on the daily and personal struggles of women and families to survive in the difficult conditions of the immediate postwar.

In contrast, male writers wrote many stories that depicted occupation personnel, such as Yasuoka Shōtarō's "House Guard" (Hausu gâdo, 1953), *Glass Slipper* (Garasu no kutsu, 1951), and "Gloomy Pleasures" (Inkina tanoshimi, 1953) and Kojima Nobuo's "American School" (Amerikan sukūru, 1954). It should be noted, however, that Kojima's story was published after the occupation had ended, and Yasuoka's stories were written while the occupation was still in power but were published only after CCD censorship had ended. In contrast, Ishikawa Jun (1899–1987) is one writer who depicted occupation soldiers directly very early in the period. His 1946 story "Golden Legend" (Ōgon densetsu) concerned a first-person male protagonist at war's end who has only three desires: to fix his watch, which had unaccountably stopped running during one of the air raids; to find a good hat to replace the one he had lost in an evacuation; and to find a woman, the widow of a friend, who epitomized gentle Japanese womanhood. One day, wandering in the black market, he finds the perfect hat. A little later, in a small, seedy black-market bar he sees the woman. She is loud and somewhat vulgar, dressed differently than he remembered. They walk out together toward a train station, when suddenly she runs away from him—and into the arms of an African American soldier, someone with whom she has obviously consorted previously. The narrator is shocked, but as he turns and hurries away his watch once more begins to tick.

Ishikawa's somewhat farcical depiction of how conditions have changed for genteel, middle-class Japanese after the war was not appreciated by CCD. The story slipped through the approval process and was published in its entirety at first. But when "Golden Legend" was scheduled to be reprinted in a collection of stories later that year, CCD insisted that the final scene, depicting the liaison between the Japanese woman and the black soldier, be cut. Ishikawa refused, and the story was not reprinted.

During the occupation few men, including returned soldiers, wrote stories that explicitly described the brutality of Japanese soldiers' behavior. With the

Tokyo War Crimes trials still ongoing, men perhaps feared the consequences of evincing too much knowledge of wartime atrocities. (After 1952 there were several novels by, for example, *Endō Shūsaku, Noma Hiroshi, and Ōoka Shōhei, that deal explicitly with Japanese war crimes.) One exception to this silence was female writer Hirabayashi Taiko, whose 1946 "Blind Chinese Soldiers" (Mō chūgoku hei) was one of the first pieces of fiction to indict the Japanese populace in the brutal treatment of enemy prisoners.

After the occupation ended Japanese writers were free to express their experiences of war and its aftermath any way they chose. However, many of the master narratives and tropes that emerged in the specific conditions of the occupation continued to influence postwar fiction.

—Sharalyn Orbaugh

Bibliography

Braw, Monica. *The Atomic Bomb Suppressed: American Censorship in Occupied Japan.* Armonk, N.Y.: M. E. Sharpe, 1991.

Etō Jun. *Tozasareta gengo kūkan: Senryogun no ken'etsu to sengo nippon* (The Closed Space of Language: Occupation Army Censorship and Postwar Japan). Tokyo: Bungeishunjū, 1989.

Gessel, Van C. *The Sting of Life: Four Contemporary Japanese Novelists.* New York: Columbia University Press, 1989.

Hayashi Fumiko. "Downtown." Trans. Ivan Morris. In Ivan Morris, ed., *Modern Japanese Stories: An Anthology,* 349–364. Rutland, Vt.: Tuttle, 1962. Also translated as "Tokyo." Trans. Ivan Morris. In Donald Keene, ed., *Modern Japanese Literature,* 415–428. New York: Grove Press, 1956.

Hirabayashi Taiko. "Blind Chinese Soldiers." Trans. Noriko Mizuta Lippit. In Noriko Mizuta Lippit and Kyoko Iriye Selden, eds., *Japanese Women Writers: Twentieth Century Short Fiction,* 41–45. Armonk, N.Y.: M. E. Sharpe, 1991.

Iokibe Makoto. "Japan Meets the United States for the Second Time." In Carol Gluck and Stephen R. Graubard, eds., *Shōwa: The Japan of Hirohito,* 91–106. New York: W.W. Norton, 1992.

Kojima Nobuo. "American School." Trans. William Sibley. In Howard Hibbett, ed., *Contemporary Japanese Literature,* 119–144. New York: Alfred A. Knopf, 1977.

Mayo, Marlene. "Literary Reorientation in Occupied Japan: Incidents of Civil Censorship." In Ernestine Schlant and J. Thomas Rimer, eds., *Legacies and Ambiguities: Postwar Fiction and Culture in West Germany and Japan,* 135–161. Washington, D.C.: Woodrow Wilson Center Press, 1991.

Passin, Herbert. "The Occupation—Some Reflections." In Carol Gluck and Stephen R. Graubard, eds., *Shōwa: The Japan of Hirohito,* 107–129. New York: W.W. Norton, 1992.

Rubin, Jay. "From Wholesomeness to Decadence: The Censorship of Literature under the Allied Occupation." *Journal of Japanese Studies* 11, no. 1 (1985): 71–103.

Sparling, Kathryn. *"The Sting of Death" and Other Stories by Shimao Toshio.* Ann Arbor: University of Michigan Center for Japanese Studies, 1985.

Treat, John Whittier. *Writing Ground Zero.* Chicago: University of Chicago Press, 1995.

Yasuoka Shōtarō. "Gloomy Pleasures." Trans. Kären Wigen Lewis. In *A View by the Sea*, 77–90. New York: Columbia University Press, 1984.

——. "Prized Possessions." Trans. Edwin McClellan. In Howard Hibbett, ed., *Contemporary Japanese Literature*, 110–118. New York: Alfred A. Knopf, 1977.

36

DAZAI OSAMU, SAKAGUCHI ANGO,
AND THE *BURAI* SCHOOL

After the defeat in World War II, Japan's economic, political and social systems were reorganized by the American occupation forces. (See "Occupation-Period Fiction.") As a result, an entirely new set of values was introduced, and Japanese lives were completely restructured. In the midst of this chaos, a group of young writers called the *Buraiha* (Decadent School) became very popular. Their novels portrayed the changing lives of the postwar Japanese people, the anxieties, the despair, and the confusions. The term *burai*, which generally refers to conduct that transgresses social norms, captures the writers' tendency to describe characters who overtly disregard social conventions. In private, these writers embodied the "decadence" they portrayed in their fictional works. They spent time in bars, took narcotic drugs, and had relationships with bar women at the expense of their families. They were in all senses of the word "decadent."

Although the name *Buraiha* includes the term *ha* (school), its membership has never been clearly defined. In any discussion of the *Buraiha*, however, Dazai Osamu (1909–1948) and Sakaguchi Ango (1906–1955) are introduced as the two most prominent writers of the group. Critics also refer to Oda Sakunosuke (1913–1947) and Ishikawa Jun (1899–1987) as members of this school. Unlike the *Shirakaba school, whose members identified themselves as a literary circle, *Buraiha* writers never actively started a literary movement. In this sense, the success of the *Buraiha* was not strictly a literary phenomenon. Rather, it reflected the historical circumstances of the contemporaneous Japanese readership, which needed to establish new social norms and moral criteria through reading and discussing *Buraiha* works.

Dazai was, and still is, the most popular among the *Buraiha* writers. The son of a wealthy landowner, he was born in Aomori in 1909. He lived a comfortable life until he was disowned by his father for an attempted love suicide. (Dazai is famous for a total of five suicide attempts, the last of which was successful.) The event is thematized in his earlier stories such as "Flowers of Buffoonery" (Dōke no hana, 1935) and "The God of Farce" (Kyōgen no kami, 1935). In these autobiographical works, Dazai followed the *shishōsetsu (personal novel) tradition in which the author makes explicit use of his personal experiences. At the same time, however, he went against this tradition by using a technique of metafiction he learned from the French novelist André Gide (1869–1951). In "Flowers of Buffoonery," for example, the writer "Dazai" intrudes in the novel and comments on the autobiographical plot, exposing the fact that it is fictional and hence by no means an "authentic" reproduction of his life. Even at the beginning of his literary career, Dazai was a *burai*, a violator of conventions.

Although Dazai had already been an up-and-coming writer before the war, it was not until 1946 that he became a best-selling novelist. He produced masterpieces such as "Villon's Wife" (Viyon no tsuma, 1947), *The Setting Sun* (Shayō, 1947), and *No Longer Human* (Ningen shikkaku, 1948) successively. In these novels, he portrayed people whose lives underwent great transformations owing to the reforms carried out by the occupation forces. "Villon's Wife" is a story of a woman in an unregistered marriage, a status that was legally protected under the prewar system. With the revision of the Civil Code, however, unregistered marriage was denied previously instituted legal protection, and the woman finds herself struggling to live in the new world. In *The Setting Sun*, Dazai described an aristocratic family whose privileges were taken away due to the abolition of its class.

In the last novel, *No Longer Human*, Dazai tackled the issue of what it is to be "human." *No Longer Human* features the memoirs of a man named Ōba Yōzō who regards himself as a failed human. Yōzō's misery, which is caused by an acute awareness that he is different from others, makes the reader question the criteria with which people define humanity. As much as this inquiry appears universal, it is also historically bound. With *No Longer Human*, Dazai posited the crucial question of how the Japanese should live in the new world. All in all, these works thus capture the transitional and chaotic environment of the postwar era.

The other leading member of the *Buraiha*, Sakaguchi Ango, was born and raised in Niigata Prefecture. In 1931, he published "Doctor Wind" (Kaze hakase). Its plot is completely "unrealistic" and its style full of wordplay and nonsensical humor; it is experimental given the fact that the autobiographical personal novel was still the norm in mainstream literary practices. With his success in "Doctor Wind," Ango gained a reputation as a writer of playful works.

Contemporaneous critics identified similarities between Ango's experimental style and Dazai's earlier works that ridiculed the personal-novel convention, and as such, Ango and Dazai were also categorized as *shin-gesakuha* (the New Gesaku School), named after the Edo genre that featured subversive humor and playfulness. This label was replaced by *Buraiha* as their more "serious" works grew popular in the postwar period.

Ango's fame was established with the essay *Decadence* (Daraku ron, 1946). This is often associated with French existentialist Jean-Paul Sartre, whose works became best-sellers in 1946. In his essay, Ango argued that life is fundamentally absurd and provocatively urged the Japanese to consciously live a "demoralized" life. *"Ochi yo"* ("Debase yourselves") was his slogan. He tried to build a new value system by destroying the prevailing values of the time. His desperate plea fascinated the postwar intellectuals who were acutely aware that prewar values needed to be discarded to build new ones. In "The Idiot" (Hakuchi, 1946), a fictional rendering of decadence, Ango described an explicit physical relationship between an intellectual man and a demented woman, thereby destroying old family values. His works criticized not only the prewar Japanese values but also the newly introduced American values of democracy that quickly replaced the old. In his postwar works, Ango consistently problematized the prevailing social norms and conventions, especially those regarding sexuality, and he remained faithful to his slogan.

—*Richi Sakakibara*

Bibliography

Dazai Osamu. *No Longer Human.* Trans. Donald Keene. New York: New Directions, 1958.

——. *The Setting Sun.* Trans. Donald Keene. New York: New Directions, 1956.

——. "Villon's Wife." Trans. Donald Keene. In Donald Keene, ed., *Modern Japanese Literature: From 1868 to the Present Day,* 398–414. New York: Grove Press, 1956.

Keene, Donald. *Dawn to the West: Japanese Literature in the Modern Era.* 2 vols. New York: Holt, Rinehart and Winston, 1984.

Sakaguchi Ango. "Doctor Wind." In Robert A. Steen, "To Live and Fall: Sakaguchi Ango and the Question of Literature." Ph.D. diss., Dartmouth College, 1995.

——. "The Idiot." Trans. George Saito. In Yoshinobu Hakutani and Arthur O. Lewis, eds., *The World of Japanese Fiction,* 232–262. New York: Dutton, 1973.

Wolfe, Alan. *Suicidal Narrative in Modern Japan: The Case of Dazai Osamu.* Princeton: Princeton University Press, 1990.

37

ABE KŌBŌ

Abe Kōbō (1924–1993) is widely considered one of the canonical Japanese novelists of his generation. But, appropriately for a writer who abhorred boundaries, categories, and stereotypes of all kinds, Abe does not fit neatly into any of these boxes: "novelist," "canonical," or even "Japanese."

Abe is widely known for his fiction, but his work ranges across the artistic spectrum, from poetry to early experiments with electronic music. He made important contributions to the visual literary genres of film and theater, most notably the Abe Kōbō Studio, an experimental theater group he formed and directed in the 1970s. He also wrote a number of film and television screenplays, among them an adaptation of his novel *The Woman in the Dunes* (Suna no onna, 1962), directed by Teshigahara Hiroshi, that has been hailed as a classic of Japanese cinema. His distinctive visual sensibility is further revealed in a large and striking body of photographic work that has recently begun to receive increased critical attention.

But the portion of Abe's work most readily available to English-speaking audiences is his novels, and to a surprising extent it is these Western translations—and Abe's foreign reception in general—that have defined his reputation in Japan. His stories have been read and studied from Scandinavia to Latin America, and particularly in Russia and Eastern Europe; in Japan he is frequently characterized as an "international author," both because of his foreign success and because his literary influences consist largely of authors outside the Japanese tradition. But one sometimes suspects that Abe has been relegated rather than elevated to this international status by Japanese critics, who have written relatively little about his work, particularly his difficult later novels, in a sense leaving him to the attentions of foreign scholars.

This may be an appropriate and not even unhappy legacy for an author who has always stood at the edge of Japanese society and the Japanese nation. Abe's grandparents were Meiji-era settlers on Japan's northern frontier of Hokkaido, and his parents moved to the even more distant frontier of Manchuria, where Abe's father worked as a doctor. Born in Japan, Abe spent his childhood in Mukden, Manchuria, and received part of his later schooling in Japan, eventually graduating from the Tokyo Imperial University Medical School, though he never practiced medicine. With Japan's defeat in 1945 came the end of the Japanese empire in China and the radical reconstruction of the Japanese state—the disappearance, in effect, of Abe's two homes. He was, in his own words, "a person with no homeland" (*Zenshū* 20:92).

These experiences provided the material for early novels such as *On the Sign at the End of the Road* (Owarishi michi no shirube ni, 1948), which contemplates the idea of home and personal origins against the backdrop of Manchuria and the war's end. Many critics see this as the point of departure for a lifetime of literature that probes the issues of homeland and homelessness, frontier and empire, belonging and escape. Abe's novels treat this theme of community at all levels, from the perilous negotiations of the sexual relationship to the anonymity of the city and even the future of the species.

No matter what its scope, community in Abe's work always embodies both promise and threat. It offers companionship and belonging, but it also carries the risks of nationalism and parochialism as well as politics and obligations that threaten to manacle or suffocate Abe's characters ("Obligation is a man's passport among his fellow men," says the hero of *The Woman in the Dunes* [127]). In contrast, the loneliness and isolation of the natural or urban wilderness—the barren desert or the impersonal city—frequently metamorphose into the freedom and independence of a new frontier. This divided attitude toward community makes it possible to interpret Abe's work in different and even diametrically opposed ways: either as a radical rejection of all society and the identities it imposes, or as an attempt to rediscover a lost sense of community and self.

Of course, the ambiguous status of homeland that makes Abe's life and work "international" also connects him with other postwar and even Meiji Japanese authors who have been influenced by similar feelings and experiences: suspicion of the state fueled by autocracy or militarism; rapid westernization or Americanization that alters Japan's cultural identity; and life in an increasingly international but also progressively more generic and anonymous urban geography. What distinguishes Abe's work is his suggestion that one can embrace this identity crisis as a means to make a new life.

Abe probed the dilemmas of community and identity most successfully in a series of novels written in the 1960s and early 1970s. In *The Woman in the*

Dunes, the protagonist is an amateur insect collector who takes a vacation from his job and obligations in the city to travel to a remote seacoast in search of spec-imens. There he comes across an isolated village whose buildings are con-structed amid the dunes, many of them at the bottom of deep pits formed by these blown walls of sand. Before he knows it, the man has been kidnapped by the villagers and imprisoned with a woman in a house at the bottom of one of these pits, where every day he is forced to work shoveling sand to shore up the shifting walls of the hole and prevent the house from being buried.

Abe's novel takes this Sisyphean image of vain existence and unexpectedly weaves it into a kind of existentialist thriller, deftly combining a sense of in-evitability and futility attached to the man's situation with a sustained suspense over his fate. On the novel's opening pages we read that the man never returns to the city; but much of the story still revolves around whether and how he can es-cape, and, eventually, whether he still wants to. While the novel maintains this fragile balance, it also juxtaposes the different communities of the city, the vil-lage, and this odd household in the sand pit. In this way Abe takes the image of a futile existence as a cog in society and turns it into a more nuanced treatment of the issue of freedom versus community. The novel's suspenseful but foregone conclusion and the interrelationship of escape and obligation are both summed up in the epigraph: "Without the threat of punishment there is no joy in flight."

The contrast between the existential fable that is this work's premise and the suspense of its tight plotting is seen in Abe's other novels, several of which take the form of intricately crafted detective stories with foregone conclusions that finally undercut or sidestep the mystery. In *The Ruined Map* (Moetsukita chizu, 1964), the protagonist is a detective hired to find a woman's missing husband. None of the many clues lead anywhere until the novel's dreamlike conclusion, in which the detective reveals the man's fate by merging with him, traveling for-ward or back in time to reenact the man's life with the wife and his final flight. The mystery is not so much solved as elided; the map of events that the detec-tive and reader have been searching for is finally irrelevant.

Time is manipulated even more explicitly in *Inter Ice Age 4* (Dai yon kan-pyōki, 1959), a murder mystery with a time-traveling detective who discovers that he has been split into his own present and future selves to become the murderer, the detective, and the victim all at once. "I was caught in a vicious circle," he says, "as if I were divining my own fortune with a coin the two faces of which were the same" (209). The cause and effect of a conventional mystery thus give way to a series of paradoxes in time and causality, producing a tale of suspense that is actually over before it begins.

Abe could warp the conventions of the mystery novel in this way and com-bine them with elements from science fiction because at the time both were still pliable, largely imported genres. He capitalized on the resulting freedom. The juxtaposition of the logical reasoning that characterizes mysteries and sci-ence fiction with the erosion of reason seen in surrealism and other avant-garde literature is a hallmark of his style. This competition between sense and non-sense is also related to the issue of community and belonging, for the most limiting of the societal bonds that Abe's characters struggle against are the everyday ideas and experiences that constitute sense or common sense in the society in which we live. It is this wall of convention (to use one of Abe's favorite images) that his texts and characters are struggling to pierce, often by resorting to violence against society, its rules, or its members.

This juxtaposition of reason and fantasy is nowhere more apparent than in Abe's language. Despite their dreamlike, poetic, or surreal elements, all of the novels mentioned above rely on exactingly realistic descriptions, frequently employing highly technical scientific and mathematical vocabulary. Inevitably, though, Abe and his narrators employ this language and its logic in ways that finally seem to undermine common sense, revealing a creative or poetic side to science as they lead the reader one logical step at a time down a road to fantasy.

For example, in *The Woman in the Dunes* the sand is described using scientific language, which details everything from its fluid mechanical characteristics to the diameter of individual grains—"a Gaussian distribution curve with a true mean of 1/8 mm" (13). But as the sand's remarkable properties are revealed or invented by the author (one is never entirely certain which), the dunes begin to seem more and more like a wonderland, the sand a magic force that can scour away not only conventional society but also all conventional thought.

In Abe's later novels, the balance shifts decisively toward the surreal or fantastic end of the spectrum. The narrators' worlds become progressively more marginal and hermetic, ruled by their own idiosyncratic logic. Abe's novel *Secret Rendezvous* (Mikkai, 1977) is a pivotal example. The story opens with another eerie disappearance: "One summer morning an ambulance suddenly drove up, although no one remembered having sent for one, and carried away the man's wife" (8). The protagonist tracks her to a strange hospital where bizarre experiments are conducted, following a trail of clues that includes tapes from an elaborate surveillance system that records every conversation in the hospital. But instead of finding his wife, the man himself becomes lost in this world of recorded fragments and twisted logic.

Some readers and critics have had difficulty making sense of these later works, whose plots often seem to lack a conclusion or even a unifying thread. But novels like *Secret Rendezvous* arguably represent the culmination of Abe's ideas about language, technology, community, and meaning. The power to eavesdrop with the surveillance system promises the novel's protagonist a way to participate in society while avoiding its obligations. But despite or because of the system's elaborate technology—including "a special one-track (all one direction) six-channel recording system" (71) that allows the eavesdropper to listen to multiple conversations simultaneously—the recorded sounds never resolve themselves into a coherent account. The novel thus repeats Abe's point that even when it is captured and analyzed by science, language cannot help but give birth to the unexpected or the surreal.

But *Secret Rendezvous* also updates Abe's ideas. The motif of electronic surveillance links the novel's linguistic chaos with the specter of media technology, so that in contrast to *The Woman in the Dunes*, with its relentlessly geographical emphasis, *Secret Rendezvous* addresses the emerging new community shaped by mass media, a force that today both forms and fractures our language, our identities, and our sense of place. The danger Abe's novels face as they try to portray this world is that they themselves will become part of the media flow, a pastiche of images without coherence or direction. This is what makes Abe's later novels so challenging. But seen in the context of the author's whole career, they represent the climax of a long, striking literary experiment.

—*Christopher Bolton*

Bibliography

Abe Kōbō. *Abe Kōbō zenshū* (Complete Works of Abe Kobo). 29 vols. to date. Tokyo: Shinchōsha, 1997– .

——. *Inter Ice Age 4.* Trans. E. Dale Saunders. New York: Alfred A. Knopf, 1970.

——. *The Ruined Map.* Trans. E. Dale Saunders. New York: Alfred A. Knopf, 1969.

——. *Secret Rendezvous.* Trans. Juliet Winters Carpenter. New York: Alfred A. Knopf, 1979.

——. *The Woman in the Dunes.* Trans. E. Dale Saunders. New York: Alfred A. Knopf, 1964.

Shields, Nancy K. *Fake Fish: The Theater of Kobo Abe.* New York: Weatherhill, 1996.

Watanabe Hiroshi. *Abe Kōbō.* Tokyo: Shinbisha, 1976.

38

ŌE KENZABURŌ

Ōe Kenzaburō (b. 1935) won the Nobel Prize in literature in 1994, the second Japanese writer to be so honored. (*Kawabata Yasunari was the first, in 1968.) Ōe's writing is harsh and challenging, always concerned with difficult moral questions arising from the context of life in post–World War II Japan. More specifically, Ōe is concerned with the meaning of being Japanese in a postwar national and international context. The worlds he creates, however, are focused to such a degree on the human, psychological dilemmas of the protagonists that the narratives transcend their specific temporal and national settings.

Ōe is a decidedly modernist (as opposed to postmodernist) writer. The themes and issues that concern him are grounded in a morality that acknowledges only one standard for right and wrong; moral relativism does not interest him. Moreover, his protagonists, particularly in his early work, personify the postwar male subject: humanist, secular, individual, but with a strong sense of responsibility toward family and often some larger collective. The tension between the desires of the individual and the duty toward a collective is at the heart of many of Ōe's novels. At the same time, Ōe's morality is never simplistic, and the living of a moral life is something not easily achieved. There may be only one standard for right and wrong, but clearly grasping that standard is not always possible for his protagonists.

This complex view of morality is no doubt related to the historical events of Ōe's formative years. As a child during the war he had to vow allegiance to the emperor every day in school, promising to die for him if necessary. Ōe has written that the idea of his own death terrified him, no matter how much he might wish to express his loyalty (Ōe 1977:xiii–xiv). When the war ended he was ten years old and thus was a teenager during the years of the Allied occupation (1945–1952). In the first years after the war there was an eager sense of optimism about Japan's new democratic process. The egalitarianism that had eluded the earlier framers of Japan's constitution of 1890 would be achieved with Douglas MacArthur's postwar constitution; the rights of the individual, rather than the family or nation, would be paramount. But in 1947 the occupation government underwent a "reverse course," and those liberal democratic ideals were publicly subverted. Men who had originally been purged from government for their fascism or war crimes were reinstated, and others who had resisted the war were now purged for their alleged communist connections. As the Korean War loomed the occupation intensified its anticommunist stance, leading to more infractions on civil liberties; there was even talk of using the atomic bomb on Korea. In the eyes of many, the moral credibility of the United States (which dominated the Allied forces in the occupation) was severely compromised.

It is perhaps no surprise that, coming out of this politically turbulent era, Ōe chose to study French literature, particularly Sartrean existentialism, at Tokyo University. His work often features protagonists who are faced with a set of impossible, mutually conflicting circumstances and yet must find a way to "freely choose," and then live out, an impossible destiny. His interest writings about the *hibakusha*—the survivors of the atomic bombings of Hiroshima and Nagasaki—often explore the theme of those who have "resolved to be free" despite their undeniable ties to an ongoing tragedy. (See "Atomic Fiction and Poetry.")

Although many of his novels and short stories are clearly based on experiences from his own life, Ōe is in no sense a *shishōsetsu (personal novel) writer. His works demonstrate a clear, carefully considered structure, and usually end with a striking final message.

He began his writing career in 1956 while in his second year at Tokyo University. One of his earliest stories, "Prize Stock" (Shiiku, 1958), was awarded the prestigious Akutagawa Prize for fiction in 1958. Like many of his other earliest works, "Prize Stock" was loosely based on Ōe's experiences as a child during the war and the occupation.

"Prize Stock" is set in a village on the island of Shikoku, the smallest of Japan's four main islands. Ōe grew up in rural Shikoku himself, but the depiction of this unnamed village is too mythologized to be considered a realistic picture of his childhood home. The protagonist is a young boy, about the age Ōe would have been during the final years of the war, when this story is set. Together with his father and beloved younger brother, he lives a primitive and squalid life in a remote village, supported by his father's hunting and tanning. Far from feeling misery at his lot, the young first-person protagonist describes a rich, extravagantly sensuous world. Into this isolated world falls an African

American soldier who had parachuted out of his plane when it was about to crash. Up to this time the villagers have managed to remain apart from the war raging throughout the rest of Japan and the larger world, but the presence of this enemy alien destroys that privileged isolation.

While the village adults wait for word to come from the faraway military authorities concerning their "catch," they imprison him in the basement of the converted storehouse where the protagonist lives. The children of the village are terrified of this large and racially different man, but eventually they "adopt" the soldier, whom they come to view as a "beautiful animal," caring for his every need and even taking him out of his "prison" to bathe in the local spring. They are oblivious to the ramifications of his enemy status; for them he is merely a new and wondrous addition to the prelapsarian world of nature in which they bask. Ōe's depiction of the soldier adds to this impression: the man never speaks (although he sometimes sings sad songs), and at the spring with the pubescent children he pretends to have sex with a goat, to the children's delight. The story ends tragically, as word finally arrives from the nearby town that the soldier is to be killed. The young protagonist tries to warn the soldier but ends up taken hostage when the soldier understands his danger. When the protagonist's father comes to rescue him, the boy's hand and the soldier's head are simultaneously shattered by one blow of the father's axe. The story ends with the protagonist partially recovered from his wound but forever changed by the trauma of the incident.

Through this story, Ōe is dealing allegorically with a number of issues, including the "loss of the father" that many Japanese felt when the Shōwa emperor, who in the prewar and wartime period had been figured legally and metaphorically as deified father of the nation, was demoted to the status of a human individual thereafter. But this story is not just about loss; here the father, despite his intention of saving the son, actually betrays him by killing the beloved soldier and permanently wounding the boy. This, too, is allegorically linked to a feeling experienced by many young Japanese men after the war of having been betrayed by those elder statesmen, personified by the emperor, who had led the nation into such a destructive path.

"Prize Stock" engages another issue found throughout Ōe's work: the profoundly disruptive nature of American influence on Japan, here seen in the way the soldier's sudden presence destroys the prelapsarian community of the village. The sudden influx of "the Other" into a homogeneous community evokes both love/desire and hatred/revulsion, and that familiar literary theme is beautifully played out in this story.

This is a brilliant work of literature, but one troubling to the North American reader on several counts. The explicit and unapologetic sexuality of the adolescent children, the brutality of human relations in the village, and particularly the racist depiction of the African American soldier are elements that many readers find disturbing. Ōe has written often of his fondness for Mark Twain's

The Adventures of Huckleberry Finn, given to him by his father when he was a boy, and there are obvious links between Huck's relationship with the slave Jim and the protagonist's relationship with the soldier. The primitive sensuality of the scene at the spring is reminiscent of the scenes of Huck and Jim lolling naked on the raft, for example. In Ōe's story, however, the utopian vision of harmony between peoples who are politically divided is not permitted to remain utopian. Ōe shows the inevitably tragic consequences of the involuntary conjunction of politically divided humans: the soldier dies, the protagonist loses his hand, and the boy's relationship with his father and other Japanese paternal figures is permanently shattered. As opposed to Twain's failure (or refusal) to confront the true ramifications of Jim's experience, Ōe, by rewriting *Huck Finn* in the setting of Japanese wartime village, reveals the harsh, brutal truth of any set of human relations that is based on differential power. Other stories from this time, such as "Human Sheep" (Ningen no hitsuji, 1958), are similar in their insistence on depicting the inhuman treatment experienced by disempowered people—in this case ordinary Japanese citizens under Allied occupation.

In 1960 Ōe married, and in 1963 his first son was born with serious brain damage. Over the next decade Ōe wrote one novel and several shorter works that revolve around a protagonist interacting with a handicapped child or young man. The most famous of these is the 1964 novel *A Personal Matter* (Kojintekina taiken), in which the adult male protagonist, Bird, comes to terms with the birth of his severely handicapped first child. As his wife lies in the hospital, recovering from the birth, Bird struggles frantically to escape his new reality: he gets repeatedly drunk, has violent sex with an old girlfriend and makes plans to run away with her to Africa, and schemes to have the baby removed to an abortionist's clinic where it will be starved to death. Finally, however, Bird reaches an epiphany about family and responsibility and decides to keep the baby and become the mature, dutiful adult he has never been. Some critics have complained that the happy ending is incongruous after the ruthlessly realistic depiction of a tormented man trying to escape responsibility by every ugly means he can muster. Nonetheless this novel, together with other works written at the same time, solidified Ōe's reputation in modern Japanese literature.

Ōe's work from the 1960s and 1970s frequently addressed (if sometimes indirectly) the issue of Japan's political position in the larger world. *The Silent Cry* (Man'en gannen no futtobōru, 1967) evokes the previous hundred years of Japanese history from the time of the country's forced opening by Commodore Perry and his black ships through the U.S.-Japan Security Treaty riots of the late 1950s and early 1960s. One of the two protagonists, Takashi, brings his experiences from a period living in the United States back to his natal village, where he attempts to foment a revolution to reinstate a premodern Japanese sense of community, just as one of his ancestors had done. The novel implicitly criticizes the role of the United States as Japan's big brother, but it also accepts the implications of the now-inevitable ongoing relationship between the two countries. As in "Prize Stock," the otherness of the United States is figured in both positive and negative terms in *The Silent Cry*.

But it is Africa that represents a place of real opportunity for Ōe's male protagonists; Africa is depicted here as still primitive by international standards and therefore in need of aid from a newly prosperous Japan, but also a place of adventure, danger and challenge, where a man might achieve true maturity. It is for these reasons that Bird, in *A Personal Matter*, dreams of escaping to Africa: he wishes to find a masculine, heroic identity that is not constrained by the tedious responsibility of family and social obligation that characterizes modern Japan. Bird eventually makes the more heroic (and existential) decision to remain where he is and fully shoulder his responsibilities. In *The Silent Cry*, however, Takashi's passive and negative older brother Mitsusaburō finally achieves maturity through a decision to do relief work in Africa. Unlike many of his literary forebears, Ōe depicts protagonists who live in a world configured by possibilities and pressures beyond the borders of Japan.

The postwar emperor and emperor system are also subjects of repeated exploration in Ōe's fiction. One of his most difficult and challenging works is the 1972 novella *The Day He Himself Shall Wipe My Tears Away* (Waga namida o nuguitamau hi), narrated by a dying and possibly insane man. The novella was evidently written in response to *Mishima Yukio's suicide and final novel, *Runaway Horses*, which Ōe read as a call to arms on behalf of the emperor system. "The Day" is not, however, a straightforward criticism of the emperor or of Japanese attitudes toward him. It is a complex, at times multivoiced, tirade recalling the narrator's father and his failed attempt to "save the emperor from himself" by murdering him in the final days of World War II (Napier 1991:168). The distortions of written history and painful consequences of historical events are two of the themes of this work, but more important, it is structured as conflicting and ambiguous explicitly to oppose the romanticized single-minded fanaticism that Ōe saw in Mishima's view of the emperor. Ōe once again insists on reintroducing "harsh reality" in all its grotesque complexity to an otherwise oversimplified and sanitized topic.

In the 1980s and 1990s Ōe continued his confrontational engagement with social and political issues, focusing in recent years on the issue of new religions in Japan. When the members of the Aum Shinrikyō cult launched their terrorist attack with sarin gas in the Tokyo subway in 1995, Ōe was moved to wonder what could motivate young, well-educated Japanese men to join such a group. He addresses this question in novels such as the trilogy *The Burning Green Tree* (Moeagaru midori no ki), which explores the frustration felt by many Japanese young men at their inability to see a viable future for Japan (or for themselves) in an international context, and their resulting sociopathic attitude. That this lack of purpose should find its solace in a religious affiliation is not surprising; many Japanese authors have explored the appeal of Christianity at times of political and social upheaval, among them *Endō Shūsaku, *Dazai Osamu,

*Shiga Naoya, and Takahashi Takako. Ōe's interest is not in Christianity per se, but rather in the new, hybrid, eclectic cults that mix Buddhist, Shinto, and Christian elements and their messianic, apocalyptic messages. The characters explored in these novels make choices that are diametrically opposed to those of the atomic-bomb survivors: in a world of plenty they choose mass destruction (including self-destruction) and doom, rather than the existential choice of life even under impossible circumstances that characterized many of the *hibakusha*.

—*Sharalyn Orbaugh*

Bibliography

Napier, Susan. *Escape from the Wasteland: Romanticism and Realism in the Fiction of Mishima Yukio and Ōe Kenzaburō.* Cambridge, Mass.: Harvard University Council on East Asian Studies, 1991.

——. *The Fantastic in Modern Japanese Literature: The Subversion of Modernity.* London: Routledge, 1996.

Ōe Kenzaburō. *A Personal Matter.* Trans. John Nathan. New York: Grove Press, 1969.

——. *Rouse Up O Young Men of the New Age!* Trans. John Nathan. New York: Grove Press, 2002.

——. *The Silent Cry.* Trans. John Bester. New York: Kodansha International, 1974.

——. *Teach Us to Outgrow Our Madness.* Trans. John Nathan. New York: Grove Press, 1977.

Pollack, David. *Reading against Culture: Ideology and Narrative in the Japanese Novel.* Ithaca, N.Y.: Cornell University Press, 1992.

39

IBUSE MASUJI

Ibuse Masuji (1898–1993), one of Japan's most acclaimed modern novelists, was born in Kamo, a small farming village nestled in a narrow valley in eastern Hiroshima Prefecture. Ibuse is best known outside of Japan for his novel *Black Rain* (Kuroi ame, 1965–66), a moving portrayal of a family in the aftermath of the atomic bombing of Hiroshima. However, it is Ibuse's spare yet evocative style and his portrayal of simple pleasures and everyday people that endears his writing to the Japanese.

Although Ibuse left his country home at age nineteen and lived in Tokyo for the rest of his life, he wrote far more about the people and scenery he had encountered during his childhood in rural Hiroshima. Like many Japanese authors, Ibuse produced a wide range of works in many different styles and genres, including fantasy, semiautobiographical essays, and historical fiction. Much of his writing employs natural imagery, and his love of water is revealed in his many essays and stories on fish and his lifelong passion for fishing. Like the hero of *Dr. Doolittle*, which he translated into Japanese, Ibuse's fiction clearly shows affection for animals, and creatures such as cats, snakes, and various amphibians are common in his essays and short descriptive sketches.

Ibuse, whose family were well-to-do landholders for many generations, was raised on Japanese and Chinese classics, and much of his later interest in history and military tales stems from his early contact with these genres. However, he hoped first to be a painter, and maintained his interest in painting throughout his life.

Ibuse left his family home in 1917 to study French literature at Waseda University in Tokyo, although he never graduated. In 1923 he published his first short story, "Confinement" (Yūhei), which was later revised into the beloved "The Salamander" (Sanshōuo, 1926). In "The Salamander," a work frequently anthologized in Japanese school textbooks and representative of the wryly humorous tone for which Ibuse is well known, a giant salamander finds himself unable to escape his hiding place in a rock cave because he has become too fat. He bemoans his situation, but when a frog unwittingly enters the cave, the salamander traps the creature, thinking that if he must suffer another will share his fate. A battle of wits ensues, and the story ends when the frog resigns himself to the situation, admitting that he "doesn't hate the salamander."

Many of Ibuse's other early works, such as "Kuchisuke's Valley" (Kuchisuke no iru tanima, 1929), portray life in the countryside with warmth, compassion, and humor, often conveyed through local dialect. Ibuse continued to write through the politically difficult era of the 1930s, and instead of riding the wave of proletarian literature he kept to the modes for which he had become famous: the pastoral, such as "Life at Mr. Tange's" (Tange shi tei, 1931), and historical fiction, including *John Manjiro, the Castaway* (Jon Manjirō hyōryūki, 1937), the story of a shipwrecked Japanese man who visited the United States in the mid-nineteenth century. The novel won Ibuse the Naoki Prize in 1938. In that year he completed *Waves: A War Diary* (Sazanami gunki, 1938), a coming-of-age novel based on *The Tale of the Heike*.

In 1941 Ibuse was drafted as a war correspondent and sent to Singapore. Upon his return to Japan a year later, he published several chronicles of his colonial experiences, including *City of Flowers* (Hana no machi, 1942), "An Account of My Voyage South" (Nankū taigaiki, 1943), and "A Young Girl's Wartime Diary" (Aru shōjo no senji nikki, 1943). (See "Wartime Fiction.") After the war, Ibuse again converted his experiences into narrative in "Lieutenant Lookeast" (Yōhai taichō, 1950), a story of a junior army officer who maintained an almost religious reverence for the emperor by having his troops bow to the east (a reference to the rising sun and Japan's emperor) whenever a battle was won. However, the lieutenant receives head injuries and spirals into madness. Even after he is repatriated and the war ends, he maintains his peculiar habit. Ibuse thus illustrates through a single individual the "madness" that struck Japan during the war.

However, it is Ibuse's epic novel *Black Rain*, the story of one family's efforts to deal with the aftermath of the atomic bombings of Hiroshima, on which his reputation primarily rests. For his accomplishment Ibuse received the Noma Prize, as well as the Order of Cultural Merit in 1966. The novel, written twenty years after the events it depicts, offers a view of the events in Hiroshima tempered with the perspective of time and told, in part, through the eyes of everyday people whose lives were inexorably altered by the events of August 6, 1945. (See "Atomic Fiction and Poetry.")

The novel takes a two-tiered approach. One story is narrated through the diary entries of a man named Shizuma Shigematsu and concerns what seems to be a rather prosaic problem: how to find a husband for his niece, Yasuko. In counterpoint is another documentary-like narrative, describing in dry but gruesome detail the terrifying power of the atomic bomb and its physical and mental effects. However, these two narratives are closely intertwined, for Yasuko had been in Hiroshima shortly after the bomb was dropped and had been exposed to so-called black rain, sooty rain containing nuclear fallout. She is therefore viewed as "contaminated" by potential marriage partners, who fear that the radiation may have rendered her infertile. Thus, although rain, as in the title, is generally viewed as life-giving, positive, and healthy, in Ibuse's novel the rain not only stains Yasuko's skin but also taints her reputation and future. Similarly, for the residents of Hiroshima, life after the bomb is turned upside down, rendered senseless and beyond comprehension.

During his long life, Ibuse served as an important literary mentor to several writers, including *Dazai Osamu. Ibuse outlived most of his literary contemporaries, however, and died at his home in Tokyo in 1993 at the age of ninety-five. A museum, archive, and library complex was built in honor of Ibuse in his hometown of Fukuyama in the late 1990s.

—*Gretchen Jones*

Bibliography

Cohn, Joel R. *Studies in the Comic Spirit in Modern Japanese Fiction.* Cambridge, Mass.: Harvard University Asia Center, 1998.

Ibuse Masuji. *Black Rain.* Trans. John Bester. Tokyo: Kodansha International, 1969.

——. *John Manjiro, the Castaway: His Life and Adventures.* Trans. H. Kaneko. Tokyo: Hokuseido Press, 1941.

——. "Kuchisuke's Valley." Trans. John Treat. In Van C. Gessel and Tomone Matsumoto, eds., *The Shōwa Anthology: Modern Japanese Short Stories,* 1–20. Tokyo: Kodansha International, 1985.

——. *Lieutenant Lookeast and Other Stories.* Trans. John Bester. Tokyo: Kodansha International, 1971; rpt. (as *The Salamander and Other Stories*) 1981.

——. *Waves: Two Short Novels.* Trans. David Aylward and Anthony Liman. Tokyo: Kodansha International, 1986.

Keene, Donald. *Dawn to the West: Japanese Literature in the Modern Era.* 2 vols. New York: Holt, Rinehart and Winston, 1984.

Treat, John Whittier. "Ibuse Masuji and the Material of History." In Dennis Washburn and Alan Tansman, eds., *Studies in Modern Japanese Literature: Essays and Translations in Honor of Edwin McClellan,* 261–281. Ann Arbor: University of Michigan Center for Japanese Studies, 1997.

——. *Pools of Water, Pillars of Fire: The Literature of Ibuse Masuji.* Seattle: University of Washington Press, 1988.

40

ENDŌ SHŪSAKU

Following the international acclaim accorded his novel *Silence* (*Chinmoku*, 1966), the depiction of Endō Shūsaku (1923–1996) as the "Japanese Graham Greene" gained rapid currency. The epithet was certainly convenient and derived in no small measure from the author's own accounts of his reluctant conversion to Christianity as a child, his subsequent struggle to come to terms with "the great flow of European culture" experienced during two and a half years spent in France studying French Catholic novels in the early 1950s, and his consequent determination to address in his literature the issues raised by his affiliation to the faith. Equally well documented was his wish to seek a literary reconciliation between "his desire as author to scrutinize human nature" and "the Christian yearning for purity" (*Zenshū* 12:96).

As with so many convenient labels, however, the depiction fails to do justice to the unique qualities of Endō's art. Moreover, as Endō himself was first to acknowledge, the tension was further exacerbated by the need to operate within "a cultural and spiritual framework that provides less encouragement for the development of literary themes dealing with the spiritual drama of the relationship between God and man." Endō portrayed the ensuing "trichotomy" in the following terms: "As a Christian, Japanese and an author, I am constantly concerned with the relationship and conflict created by these three tensions.... Unfortunately, these three tensions continue to appear as contradictory in my mind" (*Zenshū* 12:300).

The challenge for Endō was to make of his adopted faith, frequently depicted as an "ill-fitting Western-style suit," something better suited to his identity as Japanese—to "find God on the streets of Shinjuku and Shibuya, districts which seem so far removed from Him" (*Zenshū* 12:380), and to give expression to this in literary as opposed to theological terms. It is as a novelist steeped in a unique literary heritage yet well versed in the Western prose narrative tradition that Endō's literary legacy is best considered.

The predominant narrative form during Endō's formative years was that of the *shishōsetsu* (personal novel), in which the boundary between the "real" world of the author's life and its "fictional" reenactment is constantly subverted. For Endō and fellow members of the *daisan no shinjin* (third generation of new writers) who rose to prominence in the aftermath of defeat in World War II, this legacy could not be ignored and it is as much to this, as to any determination to emulate the various Western narratives he had studied, that Endō's concerted examination of his spiritual journey in his literature may be attributed. (See "Occupation Period Fiction.") To be sure, Endō's novels are a far remove from the "unmediated reality" on offer in so many of the prewar *shishōsetsu*. The desire to transcribe lived experience and the concomitant attempt to plumb the depths of the self is nevertheless pronounced, resulting in some of the most concerted considerations of individual psychology available in Japanese literature.

Raised in occupied Manchuria, Endō returned to Japan at the age of ten with his mother following his parents' divorce. Offered hospitality by his aunt, a devout Catholic, he found himself bewildered by the austere, judgmental god to whom he was introduced by the family priest. But awareness of the satisfaction his mother would derive from his compliance proved overwhelming, and, blissfully unaware of the significance of his act or of how it would shape the rest of his life, he was baptized in 1934. From that moment on, he would subsequently claim, his chief task as a writer was to "retailor" the foreign suit of Western Christianity to fit his Japanese body (*Zenshū* 12:394).

In literary terms, this process of reconciliation assumes the guise of a gradual subversion of initial appearances and a concomitant fusion of qualities, initially established as in opposition. In several of the early texts, including *White Man* (*Shiroi hito*) and *Yellow Man* (*Kiiroi hito*), the two novellas for which Endō was awarded the prestigious Akutagawa Prize in 1955, the central dichotomy is that between East and West, with the distance between the two, initially depicted as unfathomable, subtly undermined as a result of the author's increasing focus not on external distinctions but on internal similarities that allow for meaningful communication across various national, religious, and cultural divides. This quality was to become more pronounced in *Silence* and the subsequent *The Samurai* (1980). In *Silence*, the trait is embodied in the figure of Rodrigues, initially portrayed as fired by an insatiable missionary zeal to nurture the growth of the "sapling of Christianity" even in the "mudswamp" of Japan and entirely confident of his own inner resources. Confronted by the choice, imposed on him by the Japanese shogunal authorities, between adherence to his faith (and the consequent death of the Japanese converts being tortured before his eyes) and renunciation of all that his life to date had stood for, Rodrigues ultimately succumbs and tramples on the crucifix *(fumie)* in an outward act of apostasy. Internally, however, there is evidence, supported textually by the erosion of the apparently irreconcilable distinction between the "strong" martyr and the "weak" apostate, of a protagonist possessed of a more personal relationship with God at the end of the novel. Far from dismissing Kichijirō, his erstwhile Japanese interpreter who had betrayed him to the authorities, therefore, Rodrigues agrees to hear his confession, confident in the knowledge that "even if he was betraying [his fellow priests], he was not betraying his Lord. He loved him now in a different way from before. Everything that had taken place until now had been necessary to bring him to this love" (298).

A similar process can be seen at work in *The Samurai*, a novel in which the distance between the "Western" missionary, Velasco, and the lower-ranking samurai, Hasekura, symbol of "Eastern" values, is initially portrayed as unfathomable. As the novel progresses, however, so Endō's narrator succeeds in breaking down the various obstacles to reconciliation. In the case of Velasco, initially so dismissive of the samurai who has been selected to accompany him on a mission to Europe to secure better trading rights for their feudal lord's domain, such rapprochement takes time—but leads to his eventual recognition, born of his unconscious, that "it was as if a firm bond of solidarity had formed between the envoys and myself" (186). A similar process can be seen at work in Hasekura. Initially scornful of the wretched figure he sees on the ubiquitous crosses he confronts in Nueva España, his repeated attempts to convince himself that the baptism into which Velasco cajoles him is "not from the heart.… It is merely for the sake of the mission" (175) are nevertheless undermined by the voice of more objective reason that argues tellingly, "If this were a mere formality, there was no need to keep repeating the same words to himself over and over again" (176). By the conclusion of the novel, Hasekura is ready and willing to embrace death alongside Velasco as a martyr to a faith that he is still unable to espouse at the conscious level: the initial perception of an unfathomable divide between the two men has been eroded as a result not of any dramatic change of heart but of concerted focus on evidence of a greater complexity to their beings than initially countenanced, evidence that, try as they might, they are ultimately unable to deny.

It is a similar focus on a steady growth of self-awareness that characterizes Endō's next major novel, *Scandal* (Sukyandaru, 1986), a work that, in its depiction of Suguro, a successful Catholic author, overtly parodies the self-referential tenor of the earlier *shishōsetsu*. With Suguro disturbed at the outset of the novel by a man he attempts to dismiss as either a deliberate impostor or chance lookalike, the central narrative focuses on the protagonist's emerging conviction that, in reality, this being represents none other than his own doppelganger:

"What he had seen … had been no illusion, no nightmare…. That had been no stranger, no pretender. It had been Suguro himself. It had been another side of himself, a separate self altogether. He could no longer conceal that part of himself, no longer deny its existence" (221).

The critic Moriuchi Toshio was not alone in his assessment of *Scandal* as "leaving too much unfinished business" and in acknowledging his fascination as to "whether, in the future, Suguro would intone the music of destruction or of rebirth" (*Tosho shinbun*, 12 April 1986). In response, Endō resolved to write a novel with a "focus, not on the psychological worlds of the characters, but on the issues that trouble their souls" (Endō and Kaga 1993:7). It is in this context—as an exploration of the possibilities for "rebirth" of the individual—that Endō's final novel, *Deep River* (Fukai kawa, 1993), is perhaps best appreciated. The first indication within the novel of the significance to be attached not merely to the process of evolving self-awareness, but to the desire for rebirth born of renewed optimism, is provided by Endō's title: the African American spiritual with its dream of rebirth in the promised land is cited as a prologue. Thereafter, in keeping with precedent established in the earlier novels, the narrative focuses on a group of Japanese tourists to India, initially established as complete strangers, yet increasingly drawn to share in their respective journeys of self-discovery. Each of the tourists is portrayed as engaged in a search born of intensely personal experience, a search for "something" to alleviate the sense of frustration and loneliness that pervades their everyday lives. For some, the search assumes concrete form: Isobe, troubled by his wife's desperate plea from her deathbed ("I'll be reborn somewhere in the world. Look for me…. Find me … promise!" [17]), is determined to track down an Indian girl whom an American psychologist has identified as the possible "reincarnation" of a Japanese woman; Kiguchi is determined to find a suitable venue beside the Ganges to offer prayers for his comrades who died during the desperate retreat along the Burma Road at the end of the war. For others, most notably Mitsuko, the focus of the search remains intangible: she has "no real sense of what she wanted to see in India" (32), and participates in the tour in response to an impulse, unfathomable even to herself, to be near to Ōtsu, the outcast Japanese priest, whom she had consistently "trifled with" during their student days but to whom she now finds herself inexorably drawn. Learning that Ōtsu, having struggled to reconcile himself with European Christianity, is now spending his days dressed as a Hindu monk carrying the dying to bathe in the Ganges, she joins the tour on a whim. Much happens during the course of the tour, but none of the tourists is portrayed as bringing their search to a satisfactory conclusion: in a very real sense, all appear destined, at the end, to leave India as empty-handed as when they had arrived. There is, however, a deeper level of narrative—one that seeks to capture the inner worlds of the characters—and it is here, as one by one they stand on the banks of the "deep river," that each shows signs of a heightened self-awareness, in the form of a previously unconscious awareness of a spiritual dimension to their being.

Receipt from the Japanese government of the Order of Cultural Merit in October 1995, awarded as he battled terminal illness, was widely seen as fitting reward for a career in which Endō had offered some of the most moving examinations of the search for spiritual roots in all of Japanese literature. The search for a universal faith, one that transcends sectarian boundaries but that allows for belief at a more personal level, had assumed a variety of guises and upset many traditionalists within the Catholic community. As suggested by the breadth of his readership (*Silence* sold more than two million copies in Japanese alone, *Deep River* some one million), however, the impact of this lifelong quest for a literary portrayal of reconciliation was profound, and Endō's position within the mainstream of twentieth-century Japanese literature long since assured.

—*Mark Williams*

Bibliography

Endō Shūsaku. *Deep River*. Trans. Van C. Gessel. London: Peter Owen, 1994.

———. *Endō Shūsaku bungaku zenshū* (Complete Works of Endō Shūsaku). 15 vols. Tokyo: Shinchōsha, 1999–2000.

———. *The Girl I Left Behind*. Trans. Mark Williams. London: Peter Owen, 1994.

———. *The Samurai*. Trans. Van C. Gessel. London: Peter Owen, 1982.

———. *Scandal*. Trans. Van C. Gessel. London: Peter Owen, 1988.

———. *The Sea and Poison*. Trans. Michael Gallagher. Tokyo: Tuttle, 1973.

———. *Silence*. Trans. William Johnston. Tokyo: Sophia University/Tuttle, 1968.

Endō Shūsaku and Kaga Otohiko. "Saishinsaku *Fukai kawa*: Tamashii no mondai" (The Question of the Soul in the Recent Novel *Deep River*). *Kokubungaku* 38, no. 10 (1993): 6–21.

Gessel, Van C. "Silence and Voices." *Journal of the Association of Teachers of Japanese* (April 1993): 57–89.

———. *The Sting of Life: Four Contemporary Japanese Novelists*. New York: Columbia University Press, 1989.

Kasai Akio and Tamaki Kunio. *Sakuhin ron: Endō Shūsaku* (Endō Shūsaku: A Study of His Works). Tokyo: Sōbunsha, 2000.

Quinn, Philip. "Tragic Dilemma, Suffering Love and Christian Life." *Journal of Religious Ethics* 17 (Spring 1989): 151–183.

Williams, Mark. *Endō Shūsaku: A Literature of Reconciliation*. London and New York: Routledge, 1999.

Yamagata Kazumi. *Endō Shūsaku: Sono bungaku sekai* (Endō Shūsaku: His Literary Worlds). Tokyo: Kokken shuppan, 1997.

41

ENCHI FUMIKO

Enchi Fumiko (1905–1986) was born Ueda Fumi in Asakusa, Tokyo. She grew up reading the Japanese classics in the extensive collection of her father, prominent linguist Ueda Kazutoshi, and enjoyed Kabuki, Bunraku, Noh, and Edo-period fiction (1600–1867) through her paternal grandmother. At age seventeen she quit school to study English, French, and classical Chinese with private tutors. She particularly enjoyed the work of Izumi Kyōka (1873–1939), *Nagai Kafū, *Tanizaki Jun'ichirō, Oscar Wilde, Edgar Allen Poe, and E. T. A. Hoffmann, all of whom wrote with a gothic or sensual style that she later incorporated into her own fiction.

She wrote drama for the stage and radio for the first ten years of her career and published essays, commentaries, and modern Japanese translations of classical works (including *The Tale of Genji*) throughout her life. However, her reputation rests chiefly on the short stories and novels she produced from the 1950s until her death. She was awarded nearly every major literary prize: the Women Writer's Prize in 1954, the Noma Literary Prize for *The Waiting Years* (Onnazaka, 1957), the Women's Literature Prize for *A Tale of False Fortunes* (Namamiko monogatari, 1965), the Tanizaki Prize in 1956, the Japanese Literature Grand Prize for *Wandering Spirit* (Yūkon, 1970), and the Order of Cultural Merit in 1985.

Enchi has also been among the most frequently translated of Japanese authors, male or female. In addition to the aforementioned translations of her work, the following are also available in English: *Masks* (Onnamen, 1958); "Enchantress" (Yō, 1956); "Skeletons of Men" (Otoko no hone, 1956); "Love in Two Lives—The Remnant" (Nise no en—shūi, 1957); "The Old Woman Who Eats Flowers" (Hana kui uba, 1974); "Blind Man's Buff" (Mekura oni, 1962); "Boxcar of Chrysanthemums" (Kikuguruma, 1967); "The Wicket Gate" (Kuguri, 1970); and "Metamorphosis" (Keshō, 1964).

Her career as a playwright began at age twenty-one, when she staged *Hometown* (Furusato, 1926) at the Tsukiji Little Theater founded by Osanai Kaoru (1881–1928). (See "Taishō and Prewar Shōwa Theater.") In 1928 she met proletarian writers such as Hirabayashi Taiko (1905–1972), Nakamoto Takako (1903–1991), and *Hayashi Fumiko and published her plays and essays in left-wing as well as literary journals. In 1930 she married journalist Enchi Yoshimatsu, and she gave birth to a daughter, Motoko, in 1932. She left the theater in 1935 after releasing *Passionate Spring* (Seishun), a collection of thirteen of her previously published plays.

Critics writing about Enchi's work often refer to her personal life as a woman—whether as the daughter of her famous father, as a wife in a loveless marriage, or as the survivor of a 1938 mastectomy and 1946 hysterectomy. Her narratives are also often debated in terms of her political commitment (or, more often, the lack thereof) and her feminist credentials. Regardless of one's views on her political engagement, it is should be noted that Enchi is one of the few women writers to earn the regard of the male-dominated literary world even while maintaining close relationships to feminist writers (such as Hirabayashi) and writing bold representations of sexual politics.

Enchi's fame in fiction writing began in late 1949 with the serialization of her novel *The Waiting Years* (completed in 1957). This story, set in the Meiji period, relates the jealousy and anguish experienced by the wife and concubines of an upper-class politician. Like most of Enchi's narratives, *The Waiting Years* deals with the conflict between a woman's sexual desires and the kind of behavior expected of her in contemporary society. After a lifetime of catering to her husband's every wish—even going so far as to select and care for his concubines—the protagonist, Tomo, manages to "split [her husband's] arrogant ego in two" with her final wish of having her body dumped into the sea in place of a proper burial (203).

Enchi wrote strictly realist narratives and those featuring fantasy, but nearly all of her fiction aims toward a blurring of the line between the true and the false, particularly regarding ideas about female sexuality. Whether she employs flashbacks, intertextual references to classical Japanese literature, stories within stories, or an unreliable narrator, Enchi shows that deception by loved ones and illusions about ideal love can victimize women. However, she uses fantasy also to show that empowerment through understanding is possible at an individual level. The fantastic emerges directly from the sexual relationships between men and women in order to problematize socialized gender roles. In *A Tale of False Fortunes* (recasting the eleventh-century classic *A Tale of Flowering Fortunes*), for example, the intense love between Emperor Ichijō and Empress Teishi is a threat to Regent Fujiwara Michinaga's political dominance. Michinaga stages a false spirit possession of the daughter he wants to make empress, in order to convince Ichijō that Teishi's jealous spirit is trying to harm her rival. Eventually Teishi's own spirit, proclaiming to Ichijō her love and innocence, inhabits the false shaman during one of these staged possessions. An example of a woman using the weapon of "true" spirit possession, demonstrating her sincerity, succeeds in revealing the manipulative and politically motivated nature of the masculine false spirit possession.

Critical views of Enchi's fictional love relationships point to the fundamentally helpless situation of her women characters, who can only fantasize about empowerment. The protagonist of *Masks*, however, does carry out a plot to avenge her husband's past infidelity when she creates her own maternal genealogy through spirit possession. Mieko successfully challenges patriarchal dominance in the family structure by having her daughter-in-law act as a "medium" to trick her lover into impregnating Mieko's mentally deficient daughter, but the end of the story suggests a fate of isolation as a woman who cannot escape the "ghosts" in her bitter past.

Fantasy in Enchi's fiction effects an understanding of the way oneself and others behave in a culture where power is wielded in sexual terms. As the haziness of true and false in her narrative technique attests, her characters and readers can resign or resist, but the questioning continues.

—*Marilyn Bolles*

Bibliography

Bargen, Doris G. "Translation and Reproduction in Enchi Fumiko's 'A Bond for Two Lifetimes—Gleanings.'" In Paul Gordon Schalow and Janet A. Walker, eds., *The Woman's Hand: Gender and Theory in Japanese Women's Writing*, 165–204. Stanford: Stanford University Press, 1996.

Enchi Fumiko. "Blind Man's Buff." Trans. Beth Cary. In Makoto Ueda, ed., *Mother of Dreams and Other Short Stories: Portrayals of Women in Modern Japanese Fiction*, 165–177. Tokyo: Kodansha International, 1986.

——. "A Bond for Two Lifetimes—Gleanings." In Phyllis Birnbaum, ed., *Rabbits, Crabs, Etc.: Stories by Japanese Women*, 25–47. Honolulu: University of Hawai'i Press, 1983.

——. "Boxcar of Chrysanthemums." Trans. Yukiko Tanaka and Elizabeth Hanson. In Yukiko Tanaka and Elizabeth Hanson, eds., *This Kind of Woman: Ten Stories by Japanese Women Writers 1960–1976*, 76–89. New York: Putnam, 1982.

——. "Enchantress." Trans. John Bester. In Dorothy Shimer, ed., *Rice Bowl Women: Writings by and about the Women of China and Japan*, 69–86. New York: Meridian, 1986.

————. "The Flower-Eating Crone." Trans. Lucy North. In Theodore Goossen, ed., *The Oxford Book of Japanese Short Stories*, 172–181. New York: Oxford University Press, 1997.

————. "Love in Two Lives—The Remnant." Trans. Noriko Mizuta Lippit. In Noriko Mizuta Lippit and Kyoko Iriye Selden, eds., *Japanese Women Writers: Twentieth Century Short Fiction*, 97–111. Armonk, N.Y.: M.E. Sharpe, 1991.

————. *Masks*. Trans. Juliet Winters Carpenter. New York: Alfred A. Knopf, 1983.

————. "Metamorphosis." Trans. S. Yumiko Hulvey. *Manoa* 10, no. 1 (1998): 101–110.

————. "The Old Woman Who Eats Flowers." Trans. S. Yumiko Hulvey. *Manoa* (Winter 1994): 162–168.

————. "Skeletons of Men." Trans. Susan Matisoff. *Japan Quarterly* 35, no. 4 (1988): 417–426.

————. *A Tale of False Fortunes*. Trans. Roger K. Thomas. Honolulu: University of Hawai'i Press, 2000.

————. *The Waiting Years*. Trans. John Bester. Tokyo: Kodansha International, 1971.

————. "The Wicket Gate." Trans. S. Yumiko Hulvey. *Manoa* 9, no. 2 (1997): 160–167.

Gessel, Van C. "The 'Medium' of Fiction: Fumiko Enchi as Narrator." *World Literature Today* 62, no. 3 (Summer 1988): 380–385.

Hulvey, S. Yumiko. "Enchi Fumiko." In Chieko Mulhern, ed., *Japanese Women Writers: A Biocritical Sourcebook*, 40–60. Westport, Conn.: Greenwood, 1994.

————. "The Intertextual Fabric of Narratives by Enchi Fumiko." In Steven Heine and Charles W. Fu, eds., *Japan in Traditional and Postmodern Perspectives*, 169–224. Albany: State University of New York Press, 1995.

42

MISHIMA YUKIO

Mishima Yukio (1925–1970) never won the Nobel Prize in literature, but he did attain celebrity status both in Japan and abroad as has no other Japanese novelist. His unprecedented fame developed partly because of his compelling and controversial novels, films, and plays, but it can be attributed more to his flamboyant personal lifestyle and especially to his shocking and dramatic suicide in 1970.

Born in 1925 in Tokyo, Hiraoka Kimitake (Mishima Yukio being his pen name) was the eldest son of a middle-class family. He attended Gakushūin, an elite private school, and later Tokyo Imperial University. He published his first story, "A Forest in Full Flower" (Hanazakari no mori), in 1941, while still in his teens. During World War II the bookish Mishima received a draft notice, but he never served in the military because he failed the physical examination.

The 1949 *Confessions of a Mask* (Kamen no kokuhaku) propelled Mishima to prominence in the literary world. The novel explores the tortured inner world of a young man who is erotically obsessed with men, beauty, and violence. While the protagonist struggles outwardly to lead a conformist, heterosexual life, he secretly adores paintings of St. Sebastian that depict the martyr with his hands bound and his bare torso shot through with arrows, as well as the sight of the muscular nightsoil man working in the neighborhood. *Confessions* is commonly regarded as an autobiographically inspired novel. Whether the sadomasochistic fantasies that dominate the mask's inner life are Mishima's confessions of his own feelings is less significant than the identification between

Mishima and his protagonist's relentless quest to prove himself special, destined for martyrdom, a fate "proud and tragic ... even radiant." Indeed, such a vision guided Mishima in both his writing and his life.

Never content with being a docile novelist, Mishima traveled extensively · during the 1950s in the United States, Europe, and Latin America, where he lectured, hobnobbed with editors and writers, and immersed himself in the theater. It was also during the 1950s that Mishima started doing his famous body-building workouts. His disciplined physical regimen at first reflected Mishima's intense desire to fashion himself into a strong masculine presence in the public eye, as well as his devotion to the ideal of the classical Greek male body. Throughout the 1950s and 1960s, the media was filled with photographs of Mishima wearing only a loincloth and wielding a sword in the snow, snapshots of Mishima in the gym lifting weights, and later, Mishima seminude and draped with roses.

From the 1950s through the following decade, Mishima distinguished himself by his diverse activities in the literary and performing arts: he produced plays for the modern theater and for the traditional Noh theater, starred in *yakuza* (gangster) movies, and penned criticism and essays. Notable among his prose writings of this period is the novella *Patriotism* (Yūkoku, 1961), which portrays in astonishing detail the eroticized and aestheticized ritual double suicide of a young military officer and his wife in the aftermath of a 1936 military coup attempt. Although this prophetic story stands out in hindsight, Mishima showed his versatility and breadth with novels such as *The Temple of the Golden Pavilion* (Kinkakuji, 1956), the story of a monk so obsessed with the beauty of a temple that he is driven to destroy it. Mizoguchi, the protagonist, stutters and feels ugly. As a Buddhist acolyte, he discusses the meanings of Zen koans and other philosophical points with his friend Kashiwagi, whose deformed leg signals that he, like Mizoguchi, is profoundly alienated. Mizoguchi, rather than finding liberation in the transcendent beauty represented by the Golden Pavilion, discovers that it blocks his way to the recognition of other types of beauty such as the love of women, and he also feels threatened by the temple's defiance of beauty's usual ephemerality as it survives even the war. Although written as a first-person narrative, *Temple* was inspired by an actual incident and shows a marked shift away from the confessional mode of *Confessions of a Mask*. As with much of Mishima's serious literature, the style of this work tends to challenge the reader because Mishima purposely employed difficult and rare *kanji* characters and arcane vocabulary. He also frequently launched into philosophical musings in many of his novels. Many critics have praised *The Temple of the Golden Pavilion* as one of Mishima's greatest narrative achievements.

Other works of this period include the novels *After the Banquet* (Utage no ato, 1960), the story of the downfall of a powerful Tokyo politician and his relationship with his entrepreneurial wife; *Silk and Insight* (Kinu to meisatsu, 1962), a tragic tale of business, labor, and paternalism; and *The Sailor Who Fell from*

Grace with the Sea (Gogo no eikō, 1963), with its romantic adolescent fantasy; as well as critical writings such as *On Hayashi Fusao* (Hayashi Fusao ron, 1963), a study of the ideologically fickle intellectual and former war criminal. Hayashi's romantic reverence of the emperor as transcendent had a profound influence on Mishima. Notably, Mishima's focus on nationalism in works such as *Patriotism* and *On Hayashi Fusao* followed close after the social protest occasioned by the 1960 renewal of the U.S.-Japan Security Treaty.

Mishima expressed his interest in right-wing politics in works such as *The Voices of the Spirits of the War Dead* (Eirei no koe, 1966–67) and *Defense of Culture* (Bunka bōeiron, 1969). The former evokes the narrative stance of fallen kamikaze pilots and other heroic figures, who bemoan the emperor's declaration that he is an ordinary man, not a god. Mishima's *Defense* explains the decline of Japan in gendered terms—specifically pointing to the "feminization" of culture that accompanied Japan's post-Edo modern age. That Mishima was no ordinary conservative can be seen in works from the same period such as the play *Madame de Sade* (Sado kōshaku fujin, 1965), the extended essay *Sun and Steel* (Taiyō to tetsu, 1968), and the play *My Friend Hitler* (Waga tomo Hittora, 1968), all of which exhibit his fascination with eroticism, the body, and nihilism. Mishima also took the leftist student movement seriously enough that he joined in lengthy and vigorous debates with its members in the late 1960s.

Beginning in 1966, Mishima pursued two parallel courses of action that would culminate in his suicide. On the artistic side, he completed the novel *Spring Snow* (Haru no yuki, 1966), the first volume of his famous tetralogy, *The Sea of Fertility* (Hōjō no umi). In the autumn of that same year, Mishima transformed his interest in the sword and the military into decisive action by signing up to train with the Jieitai (Japan Self Defense Force, JSDF). Signs of Mishima's growing passion for the aesthetic of violent death and for the way of the warrior can be seen in his choice to play the role of the young officer in the cinematic version of *Patriotism* (released first abroad in 1965 and in Japan in 1966), and his increasingly frequent association with right-wing neonationalists.

By 1967, Mishima had completed the second volume of the tetralogy: *Runaway Horses* (Honba), published serially in 1968, which portrayed the ultranationalist Isao battling the status quo in the 1930s. Mishima had long aimed at winning the Nobel Prize in literature by choosing his translators and tending carefully to his relations with foreign journalists, critics, and publishers. In October 1968, however, he learned that his old friend and mentor *Kawabata Yasunari had been awarded the prize instead.

Mishima took another step toward realizing his fantasy of living the aestheticized warrior's life in 1968 when he founded his private army, called the Tate no kai (Shield Society). Many members of the public and the media regarded this group, composed of unarmed right-leaning college students (who, like Mishima, professed allegiance to the emperor), as a joke, but the JSDF allowed Mishima and his cadets to train in its boot camp.

By spring of 1970 Mishima had completed the serialization of *The Temple of Dawn* (Akatsuki no tera), the third volume of the tetralogy. As massive demonstrations and public discussions surrounding the pending renewal of the U.S.-Japan Security Treaty raged, Mishima commenced what would be the final tasks in both the military and literary spheres of his life. With a core group of Shield Society members, he plotted decisive political action in reaction to Japan's peacetime constitution. He also worked feverishly on the last book of the tetralogy, *Decay of the Angel* (Tennin gosui), which he completed that year.

Although Mishima rehearsed his death many times and made clear in his writings, films, plays, and photographs his fascination with the "aesthetics of beautiful death" (Peterson 1979:203), few people expected that he would actually cross the line that separated the performance of seppuku in front of a movie camera or on the printed page and the act of taking his own life. But Mishima surprised the world when, on November 25, 1970, he went with his loyal Shield Society followers to the Ichigaya (Tokyo) headquarters of the Self Defense Forces, held captive a general, and demanded the presence of the troops. Mishima spoke to those assembled about the wrongs of the postwar constitution, the United States, and resistance in the name of the emperor. Then he stepped back inside and slit open his own belly, after which one of his cadets beheaded him. His most loyal follower, Morita Masakatsu, with whom he had an erotic bond, followed him in death.

Mishima's great final multivolume work, *The Sea of Fertility*, depicts the entangled lives of five main characters over the span of the twentieth century, and it ranges in setting from Nara to Thailand. Emphasizing the themes of reincarnation and transmigration, Mishima traces the life of a man named Honda from youth (in the romantic *Spring Snow*) to old age (in *Decay of the Angel*), as he encounters and searches for the four people who are reincarnations of a single being. A mole on the arm functions as the sign of authentic reincarnation. In the first volume, this being is manifest in Kiyoaki, a beautiful rich boy in love with Satoko, a woman promised to someone else; in *Runaway Horses*, perhaps the most dramatic volume, it is Isao, a right-wing youth involved in a 1930s rebellion in the name of the emperor. Mishima traveled to Thailand to do research for *The Temple of Dawn*, which features a Thai princess bearing the mark of reincarnation. The final volume shows Honda facing disillusionment when Tōru, the man who seems to be the reincarnation of Kiyoaki, may be a fake, and Satoko, now an elderly nun at a Buddhist temple, asserts that Kiyoaki never existed. At the end of *The Decay of the Angel*, Honda stands in a temple garden: "The garden was empty. He had come, thought Honda, to a place that has no memories, nothing. The noontime sun of summer flowed over the still garden" (236). This famous closing passage echoes Mishima's choice for the paradoxical title of the tetralogy—the Sea of Fertility, which is in fact a dry, lifeless area of the moon—as well as the nihilism that tempted Mishima all his life. Throughout his career, Mishima held a place in the mainstream of Japanese literature, but he also flirted heavily with the margins. His choice of an anachronistic public form of death allowed him to present himself as an ultimate Nietzschean man of action and to exit the stage as the spectacular performer that he had always been, but it also meant that his literary oeuvre would forever be read in the shadow of that final act.

—Ann Sherif

Bibliography

Mishima Yukio. *After the Banquet.* Trans. Donald Keene. New York: Alfred A. Knopf, 1963.

———. *Confessions of a Mask.* Trans. Meredith Weatherby. New York: New Directions, 1958.

———. *Decay of the Angel.* Trans. Edward Seidensticker. New York: Alfred A. Knopf, 1974.

———. *Madame de Sade.* Trans. Donald Keene. New York: Grove Press, 1967.

———. *Patriotism.* Trans. Geoffrey W. Sargent. In *Death in Midsummer and Other Stories.* New York: New Directions, 1966.

———. *Runaway Horses.* Trans. Michael Gallagher. New York: Alfred A. Knopf, 1973.

———. *Spring Snow.* Trans. Michael Gallagher. New York: Alfred A. Knopf, 1972.

———. *Sun and Steel.* Trans. John Bester. Tokyo: Kodansha International, 1970.

———. *The Sailor Who Fell from Grace with the Sea.* Trans. John Nathan. New York: Alfred A. Knopf, 1965.

———. *The Temple of Dawn.* Trans. E. Dale Saunders and Cecilia Segawa Seigle. New York: Alfred A. Knopf, 1973.

———. *The Temple of the Golden Pavilion.* Trans. Ivan Morris. New York: Alfred A. Knopf, 1959.

Napier, Susan J. *Escape from the Wasteland: Romanticism and Realism in the Fiction of Mishima Yukio and Ōe Kenzaburō.* Cambridge, Mass.: Harvard University Press, 1991.

Nathan, John. *Mishima: A Biography.* Boston: Little, Brown, 1974.

Noguchi Takehiko. *Mishima Yukio no sekai* (The World of Mishima Yukio). Tokyo: Kodansha, 1968.

Petersen, Gwenn Boardman. *The Moon in the Water: Understanding Tanizaki, Kawabata, and Mishima.* Honolulu: University of Hawai'i Press, 1979.

Scott-Stokes, Henry. *The Life and Death of Yukio Mishima.* New York: Farrar, Straus & Giroux, 1974.

Starrs, Roy. *Deadly Dialectics: Sex, Violence and Nihilism in the World of Yukio Mishima.* Honolulu: University of Hawai'i Press, 1994.

Yourcenar, Marguerite. *Mishima: A Vision of the Void.* Trans. Alberto Manguel. New York: Farrar, Straus & Giroux, 1986.

43

THE 1960S AND 1970S BOOM
IN WOMEN'S WRITING

The 1960s and 1970s represent a pivotal period in the history of Japanese women's writing. Dubbed by critics as the *saijo jidai* (age of talented women) and as a "Little Heian" after the great Heian period of women writers in the tenth and eleventh centuries, the 1960s and 1970s saw a dramatic increase in the number of women achieving critical acclaim and winning literary prizes. As a result, more women were able to publish their work than ever before. This period represents not only a quantitative change in women's writing, but also a qualitative change in terms of the subjects, themes, and styles chosen by women writing during that time.

A consideration of literary prizes provides a clear example of the change in how women writers were viewed. A look at the oldest and arguably the best-known award for literature in Japan, the Akutagawa Prize, reveals that, until the 1960s, women writers were barely represented. The prize, begun in 1935, is awarded twice yearly to new authors who show literary talent and promise; receipt of the prize is often credited with launching new writers on a successful career. (See "The Social Organization of Modern Japanese Literature.") In the nearly thirty years from the prize's inception in 1935 until 1963, only three women—Nakasato Tsuneko (1909–1987) in 1938, Shibaki Yoshiko (b. 1914) in 1941, and Yuki Shigeko (1902–1969) in 1949—had ever received the prize. In 1963, however, author Kōno Taeko (b. 1926) received the prize for her short story "Crabs" (Kani). Following this, women authors won the prize three more times in the 1960s, including Tanabe Seiko (b. 1928) in 1964, Tsumura Setsuko (b. 1928) in 1966, and *Ōba

Minako in 1968, and six times in the 1970s, by Yoshida Tomoko (b. 1934) in 1970, Yamamoto Michiko (b. 1936) and Gō Shizuko (b. 1929) in 1972, Hayashi Kyoko (b. 1930) in 1975, and Shigekane Yoshiko (b. 1927) and Mori Reiko (b. 1928) in 1979. Beginning in the 1980s, a woman won the prize nearly every year, including such well-known writers as Takagi Nobuko (b. 1946), Kometani Fumiko (b. 1930), and the Korean-Japanese author Lee Yangji (b. 1955). To sum up, before 1960 women authors represented less than 10 percent of the total number of recipients, while in later years nearly half the winners are women. Using the receipt of this prize as a gauge, we can thus locate a marked change beginning in the early 1960s in the way the literary establishment, which was responsible for choosing a winner, perceived women authors and their literary output.

Several interrelated factors are responsible for the striking increase in visibility and recognition of women authors and their access to literary venues. Before World War II, Japanese women writers such as *Hayashi Fumiko, Hirabayashi Taiko (1905–1972), and *Miyamoto Yuriko had attracted critical attention and attained moderate success. However, during the war the creative impulse of many authors, both male and female, was effectively silenced by the increasingly repressive government of wartime Japan. Although some women, such as Hayashi and Yoshiya Nobuko (1896–1973), continued to write during this time, their output was quite limited compared to their postwar effort. (See "Wartime Fiction.")

Following the war, authorities of the Allied occupation under General Douglas MacArthur also censored print materials, and paper shortages made publishing difficult. While the immediate postwar period represents a boom in literary production, the rejuvenated literary environment was strikingly gendered, with new male writers greatly outnumbering their female counterparts. Women writers who had established themselves before the war, such as Miyamoto, Hirabayashi, and Hayashi, continued to write, yet few new female faces emerged on the literary scene during the occupation. Nonetheless, the occupation incorporated social changes that would provide, in part, a platform for the rise of women authors in the coming years. Among the many social reforms encouraged (and even implemented) by occupation authorities were several significant policies that affected the social status of women, including the new 1947 Japanese constitution.

Although the new constitution laid the ground for more equality between the sexes, the 1950s brought several major changes that led to increased opportunities for women writers. Perhaps most important was access to education, which was universal for both boys and girls and became increasingly coed as well. These educational opportunities implemented immediately after the war took time to have an effect, but by the late 1950s and 1960s had led to a greater degree of literacy and autonomy for women. The emphasis on equality also allowed women to be more assertive and active in public society, and, likewise, society was forced to acknowledge the potential of women in a variety of public occupations, including those related to the media and literary activities.

Another factor was high economic growth brought on by the conflict in Korea in the early 1950s. This resulted in the development of an increasingly consumerist society. The capitalism of the late 1950s and 1960s required the creation of new markets, and women were seen as an important and as yet unexplored population. Fiction written by women for women thus became a new product to market and sell; as more women wrote and read, the larger the constituency became. The changing economic picture also had a direct impact on the material conditions women faced. Increasing affluence and advances in industry resulted in machines (such as the washing machine and refrigerator) that substantially freed women from the daily burden of domestic duties and allowed them to engage in other pursuits.

Additionally, there was an increasing movement toward a more populist society. Developments in media provided a greater number of potential publishing forums in which writers of both genders could have their work published. At the same time, the reading public, both men and women, developed an almost voracious appetite for the printed word. Translations of foreign literature and *bungaku zenshū* (collected works of a particular author) as well as a broad range of literary magazines enjoyed tremendous popularity, and all of these provided previously unavailable opportunities for women to seek publication.

The combination of these changes led to a flowering of literature written by women during the 1960s and 1970s. However, these decades are notable not only for the large numbers of women writers who suddenly debuted. In terms of theme and subject matter, the 1960s represent another important landmark in this map of women's writing in Japan as women authors began writing in ways that sharply differed from most of their literary predecessors. Works by Kōno Taeko, Ōba Minako, Kurahashi Yumiko (b. 1935), and other women feature utopian and fantasy worlds, parody, satire, and a focus on the grotesque—modes that stand in opposition to the previously accepted norms for women's writing: autobiography, confession, and realistic or historical fiction. Furthermore, much of the fiction written by women in this era seems fixated on the abnormal, and, in particular, on "deviant" sexuality, including masochism, pedophilia, incest, partner-swapping, homosexuality and sexually motivated murder, all wrapped up in an oblique, often impenetrable narrative style. Stories involving dreams, madness, and sexual fantasies are common, as well as a preoccupation with myth and the antirational, mystical side of life.

Rejection of typical female norms, including motherhood and heterosexual, monogamous marriage is another common feature of 1960s and 1970s women's writing. Kōno, Kurahashi, and later, Tomioka Taeko (b. 1935), Takahashi Takako (b. 1932), and *Kanai Mieko frequently portray single women, often without children. Kōno and Takahashi further question the link between women and motherhood by integrating fantasies of violence toward children into their characters' psyches.

Women's writing from the 1960s and 1970s seems to be a search for delineating a revised identity more befitting the new age. The quests on which these women embark range from self-discovery to outright rejection of social or cultural norms. The use of deviant modes of behavior seems intentional, however, and reflects a deliberate effort to defy norms or at least to force readers to reconsider preconceived notions of femininity and womanhood.

Though many women wrote in this manner, not all women's writing in the 1960s and 1970s had these characteristics. Historical fiction, biography, and the *zuihitsu* (personal essay) continued to be genres explored by women writers. For example, the work of Ariyoshi Sawako (1931–1984), who wrote primarily realist fiction, focuses on the role of women within history, and her work continues to enjoy tremendous popularity. Many of her novels are available in English.

Nonetheless, it was the activities of Kōno Taeko, Kurahashi Yumiko, Takahashi Takako and other radical women writers of the 1960s and 1970s that have had the broadest effect in forging new directions for fiction. A brief introduction to some of these authors follows.

KŌNO TAEKO

Born in Osaka, Kōno Taeko was dispatched to work in a munitions factory when she was just sixteen, during the height of World War II. She thus spent her youth engaged in Japan's war effort and the aftermath that followed defeat. Although Kōno had literary ambitions from a young age, her first story to receive critical attention, "Toddler Hunting" (Yōjigari, 1961), was not published until she was in her mid-thirties. During her career, Kōno has won, in addition to the prestigious Akutagawa Prize in 1963 for "Crabs," nearly every major literary prize given in Japan. "Toddler Hunting," "Crabs," and several other short stories are available in English, French, and German translation. Perhaps the most significant sign of her success is that she was nominated to the Akutagawa Prize jury itself a few years ago, one of the first women to hold such an influential position.

Kōno's writing is not easily apprehended; she demands that her readers grapple with many difficult, and often abhorrent ideas and images. For example, "Toddler Hunting" is the story of Akiko, an unmarried woman in her thirties who loves little boys but has a profound fear and dislike of little girls. Childless herself, Akiko goes to great lengths to seek out the company of little boys, often giving them gifts. Akiko engages in masochistic sex with her boyfriend, but when he is away, Akiko has a recurring, and strikingly lurid sexual fantasy in which a little boy is beaten to an extreme degree. The story gestures to the strict differentiation of gender roles in 1960s Japan, and to the complex set of emotions a woman, unmarried and childless, might feel in such a society. The violence of the fantasy, in which it seems that Akiko is both a participant and an onlooker, beater and the beaten one, is also indicative of the complex relationship between dominator and dominated. In this way, "Toddler Hunting," and indeed, much of Kōno's fiction, unveils hierarchies and exposes the inner workings of power. Kōno's stories "Ants Swarm" (Ari takaru, 1964), "Night Journey" (Yoru o yuku, 1963), and "Bone Meat" (Hone no niku, 1969) all take up masochism from a woman's point of view. In 1990 Kōno completed a long novel, *The Bizarre Tale of the Mummy Hunter* (Miira tori ryōkitan), which explores the converse: it portrays a male masochist who "trains" his wife to please him and ultimately, to kill him according to his wishes.

KURAHASHI YUMIKO

Kurahashi Yumiko also uses sexually transgressive themes, including incest, to challenge ideas about women and sexuality. Like other women authors of this time, Kurahashi's imagery is often grotesque, and seems designed to question or deny not only conventional moral values but also social and literary norms.

Kurahashi was born in 1935 in Shikoku—the same year and location as Nobel Prize winner *Ōe Kenzaburō. Although her father was a dentist and wanted Kurahashi to follow him in her profession, Kurahashi herself had other ideas and entered the Department of French at Meiji University in Tokyo without her father's knowledge. Her first work of critical note, "Parutei" (1960), was nominated for the Akutagawa Prize and bears traces of French existentialism while exploring gender relations in the Japanese Communist Party.

In her later work Kurahashi began to consider such relationships from a far more radical position, challenging sexual mores in particular. Following "Parutei," her next enthusiastically received short story, "The End of Summer" (Natsu no owari, 1960), is a story of two sisters who plot to murder a male lover whom they share. Other stories that defy conventional monogamous heterosexuality include *Divine Maiden* (Seishōjo, 1965), "Scorpions" (Sasori tachi, 1963), and *The Floating Bridge of Dreams* (Yume no ukihashi, 1970). Kurahashi is also known for her use of myth and traditional drama, both Western and Japanese, and for such shocking themes as sibling incest and sex with aliens. Her short story "To Die at the Estuary" (Kakō ni shisu, 1970), one of a group of five stories published together under the title of *Antitragedies* (Hanhigeki, 1971), incorporates both the Oedipus myth and themes from classical Japanese literature. Kurahashi has also produced several collections of short stories, including a reworking of traditional fairy tales in her *Cruel Fairy Tales for Adults* (Otona no tame no zankoku dōwa, 1984). Recently a book-length collection of her stories called *The Woman with the Flying Head* has been released in English translation.

MORI MARI

Mori Mari (1903–1987) was the eldest daughter of Meiji author *Mori Ōgai. Although her father was an illustrious author and statesman, Mori did not begin writing until she was over fifty and her father had died. Her first work, titled "My Father's Hat" (Chichi no bōshi) and published in 1957, was a well-received recollection about her famous father. She won the Tamura Toshiko Prize two years later in 1961 for her "Lovers' Woods" (Koibito-tachi no mori), which deals with a male homosexual relationship that culminates in murder. *Mishima Yukio praised Mori for her treatment of the world of homosexuals in Japan and unique style. Several other works, all written in the 1960s and 1970s, similarly challenge sexual mores by employing the fantastic mode and portraying homosexuality and death. Mori died alone in her small room in a Tokyo suburb in 1987.

SETOUCHI HARUMI

Setouchi Harumi was born in 1922 on the island of Shikoku. In 1973 she became a Buddhist nun and since then has been known as Setouchi Jakuchō. Setouchi's career began with an acclaimed literary biography of the modern woman writer Tamura Toshiko (1884–1945), for which she won an award. One of her first stories, "Pistil and Stamen" (Kashin, 1957), was criticized and even labeled by some as pornography because of its explicit use of the word "uterus," thus earning Setouchi the unenviable sobriquet *shikyū no sakka* (writer of the womb). Setouchi, like other women writers of her era, also writes of women pushing the limits of propriety, and many of her stories involve promiscuity, especially triangular love affairs. Setouchi is the most recent Japanese author to produce a modern-language translation of *The Tale of Genji*.

TAKAHASHI TAKAKO

Takahashi Takako is yet another female author whose fiction "has continued to enchant and alarm readers with its hallucinatory explorations of women's secret subversive proclivities" (Mori 1996:29). Takahashi Takako was born in Kyoto in 1932. After attending Kyoto University and studying French literature, she graduated and soon thereafter married Takahashi Kazumi, a well-known literary figure. In the 1960s, Takahashi Kazumi became an ideological leader in the student protest movement; he died in 1971 of cancer. After her husband's death, Takako's career was firmly launched with a volume of her first short stories. In 1972, she received the first of many literary prizes for *To the End of the Sky* (Sora no hate made). In 1975 she converted to Catholicism and in 1986 entered a convent in Paris.

   Much of Takahashi's fiction denies the existence of a link between female sexuality and motherhood. For instance, "Congruent Figures" (Sōjikei, 1971), like Kōno's "Toddler Hunting," is a story of a woman's profound ambivalence toward her own daughter. Takahashi frequently writes of women alone (her 1977 series of linked short stories is even titled *Lonely Woman* [Ronri ūman]) who engage in dream world fantasies that often take a violent turn. Many of her short story collections, such as *Lonely Woman*, consist of linked stories that follow a similar theme or involve the same character and are intended to be read together.

TOMIOKA TAEKO

Tomioka Taeko (b. 1935) is well known in Japan as a multitalented author, writing poetry, screen plays, fiction, and feminist literary criticism. Born in Osaka in 1935, Tomioka was raised in a single-mother household. Tomioka's literary interests were first in poetry, and she published several prize-winning collections of poetry in the late 1950s and early 1960s. In 1968, Tomioka wrote the screenplay for director Shinoda Masahiro's stunning *Double Suicide* and is heard offscreen at the beginning of the film. Her first fictional work, "Facing the Hills They Stand" (Oka ni mukatte hito wa narabu, 1971), uses an unusual narrative style reminiscent of the puppet theater. Later stories such as "Straw Dogs" (Sūku, 1980) explore a female sexuality that is completely separate from motherhood and reproduction. In 1989, along with critic/scholars Ueno Chizuko and Ogura Chikako, Tomioka coauthored a path-breaking book of essays called *On the Male School of Literature* (Danryū bungaku ron, a play on the commonly used term *joryū bungaku*, or "women's literature") that analyzes canonical male writers including *Tanizaki Jun'ichirō, *Kawabata Yasunari, and Mishima Yukio from a female and feminist point of view.

Kōno, Kurahashi, Mori, Setouchi, Tomioka, and other women writers rose to critical acclaim in the 1960s and 1970s, often defying both sexual mores and literary norms. In the process, they questioned stereotypical roles for women and created new, alternative, and often subversive subject positions. Yet the trends described above did not end with the 1970s. A consideration of writing of the 1980s and 1990s reveals that many Japanese authors, male and female alike, continue to question gender roles, and the boundaries between fantasy and reality, the body and the external world.

—*Gretchen Jones*

Bibliography

Aoyama, Tomoko. "A Room Sweet As Honey: Father-Daughter Love in Mori Mari." In Rebecca L. Copeland and Esperanza Ramirez-Christensen, eds., *The Father-Daughter Plot: Literary Women and the Law of the Father*, 167–193. Honolulu: University of Hawai'i Press, 2001.

Kōno Taeko. "Ants Swarm." Trans. Noriko Mizuta Lippit. In Noriko Mizuta Lippit and Kyoko Iriye Selden, eds., *Japanese Women Writers: Twentieth Century Short Fiction*, 112–125. Armonk, N.Y.: M. E. Sharpe, 1991.

———. "Bone Meat." Trans. Lucy Lower. In Howard Hibbett, ed., *Contemporary Japanese Literature: An Anthology of Fiction, Film, and Other Writing since 1945*, 41–52. New York: Alfred A. Knopf, 1977.

———. "Crabs." Trans. Phyllis Birnbaum. In Phyllis Birnbaum, ed., *Rabbits, Crabs, Etc.: Stories by Japanese Women*, 99–131. Honolulu: University of Hawai'i Press, 1982.

———. *Toddler Hunting and Other Stories*. Trans. Lucy North. New York: New Directions, 1996.

Kurahashi Yumiko. *The Woman with the Flying Head and Other Stories*. Trans. Atsuko Sakaki. Armonk, N.Y.: M. E. Sharpe, 1998.

———. "To Die at the Estuary." Trans. Dennis Keene. In Howard Hibbett, ed., *Contemporary Japanese Literature: An Anthology of Fiction, Film, and Other Writing since 1945*, 247–281. New York: Alfred A. Knopf, 1977.

Mitsutani, Margaret. "Renaissance in Women's Literature." *Japan Quarterly* 33, no. 3 (July–September 1986): 313–319.

Mori, Maryellen Toman. "The Subversive Role of Fantasy in the Fiction of Takahashi Takako." *Journal of the Association of Teachers of Japanese* 28, no. 1 (April 1994): 29–56.

———. "'Jouissance' in Takahashi Takako's Texts." In Paul Gordon Schalow and Janet A. Walker, eds., *The Woman's Hand: Gender and Theory in Japanese Women's Writing*, 205–235. Stanford: Stanford University Press. 1996.

Mulhern, Chieko. *Japanese Women Writers: A Bio-Critical Sourcebook*. Westport, Conn.: Greenwood, 1994.

Muta, Orie. "Aspects of Love in Contemporary Japanese Fiction by Women Writers." *Hecate* 16, no. 1 (1990): 151–163.

Orbaugh, Sharalyn. "Arguing with the Real: Kanai Mieko." In Stephen Snyder and Philip Gabriel, eds., *Ōe and Beyond: Fiction in Contemporary Japan*, 245–277. Honolulu: University of Hawai'i Press, 1999.

———. "The Body in Contemporary Japanese Women's Fiction." In Paul Gordon Schalow and Janet A. Walker, eds., *The Woman's Hand: Gender and Theory in Japanese Women's Writing*, 119–164. Stanford: Stanford University Press, 1996.

Sakaki, Atsuko. "(Re)canonizing Kurahashi Yumiko: Toward Alternative Perspectives for "Modern" "Japanese" "Literature." In Stephen Snyder and Philip Gabriel, eds., *Ōe and Beyond: Fiction in Contemporary Japan*, 153–176. Honolulu: University of Hawai'i Press, 1999.

Schierbeck, Sachiko. *Japanese Women Novelists in the 20th Century: 104 Biographies, 1900–1993*. Copenhagen: Museum Tusculanum Press, 1994.

Setouchi Harumi. *The End of Summer: Stories*. Trans. Janine Beichman. Tokyo: Kodansha International, 1989.

Takahashi Takako. "Congruent Figures." Trans. Noriko Mizuta Lippit. In Noriko Mizuta Lippit and Kyoko Selden, eds., *Japanese Women Writers: Twentieth-Century Short Fiction*, 168–193. Armonk, N.Y.: M. E. Sharpe, 1991.

Tanaka, Yukiko, and Elizabeth Hanson, eds. *This Kind of Woman: Ten Stories by Japanese Women Writers, 1960–1976*. Stanford: Stanford University Press, 1982.

Tomioka Taeko. *The Funeral of a Giraffe: Seven Stories by Tomioka Taeko*. Trans. Kyoko Iriye Selden and Noriko Mizuta. Armonk, N.Y.: M. E. Sharpe, 2000.

———. "Straw Dogs." Trans. Yukiko Tanaka. In Yukiko Tanaka, ed., *Unmapped Territories: New Women's Fiction from Japan*, 120–151. Seattle: Women in Translation, 1991.

Vernon, Victoria. *Daughters of the Moon: Wish, Will and Social Constraint in Fiction by Modern Japanese Women.* Berkeley: University of California Institute of East Asian Studies, 1988.

Williams, Mark. 1999. "Double Vision: Divided Narrative Focus in Takahashi Takako's *Yosōi seyo, waga tamashii yo.*" In Stephen Snyder and Philip Gabriel, eds., *Ōe and Beyond: Fiction in Contemporary Japan,* 104–129. Honolulu: University of Hawai'i Press, 1999.

44

ŌBA MINAKO

Among prominent Japanese writers of the late twentieth century, Ōba Minako (b. 1930) is noted for her provocative female voice, one that combines literary and critical acumen with an uncommon global perspective. Focusing on issues of power, nation, and gender, Ōba creates fictional female figures who, though Japanese, often reside abroad or return to Japan after many years in a foreign country. Through their intercultural experience, these characters examine old ideas and express new viewpoints that challenge long-held assumptions about the roles of women and men in Japan and elsewhere. Although Ōba's exploration of female subjectivity, sexuality, and cross-cultural experience have placed her somewhat outside the mainstream of modern Japanese literature, she has won several prestigious literary prizes and is one of only two women to serve on the Akutagawa Prize committee, one of the most important literary prizes in Japan. In her later years, Ōba has acquired distinction not only as a literary figure but also as a social commentator.

Ōba began her career late and from an unexpected direction. The wife of a Japanese salaryman living in Sitka, Alaska, Ōba published her first story, "The Three Crabs" (Sanbiki no kani) in 1968, when she was thirty-eight years old. Awarded the Gunzō Prize for New Writers and the Akutagawa Prize in the same year, Ōba suddenly found herself rubbing shoulders with the elite of the Japanese literary world. Since then she has continued to write profusely, producing both short and long fiction as well as poetry and essays. In 1990, her writings of the 1970s and 1980s were compiled in a ten-volume collected works.

The appeal of Ōba's early works, including "The Three Crabs," may be attributed in part to situations and characters drawn from her own experiences abroad. In "The Three Crabs," for example, the female protagonist, Yuri, lives with her husband and young daughter in a gloomy, rain-soaked Northwest coast locale. In addition to the description of a Japanese family in an exotic foreign setting, the depiction of Japanese and non-Japanese interacting as friends, acquaintances, and lovers was an entirely new literary perspective for late 1960s Japan. The alienated Japanese housewife as protagonist also provided a fresh vantage point. In "The Three Crabs," Yuri's perceptive yet caustic criticism of her conventional existence rips away the social veneer; describing her nausea at having to host yet another bridge party, Yuri soon escapes the gathering on a pretext. Wandering aimlessly through an amusement park, she meets a local man, and the two have sex under the letters of a glowing neon sign that reads: "The Three Crabs." Later Yuri discovers the man has stolen some money from her purse. The sharp observations, biting dialogue, coolly observant female protagonist, and offbeat characters make "The Three Crabs" stand out not only as an intriguing debut story but also as an initial statement of the themes and concerns that would continue to occupy Ōba in her writing—the stultifying social codes of contemporary society, the lack of communication between the sexes, and the social dangers resulting from psychosexual repression of the female.

In the late 1960s and early 1970s, Ōba began to incorporate elements of fantasy and reverie in her exploration of gender and its power over the female unconscious. Many of these works invoke the familiar Pacific Northwest setting, as in "Fireweed" (Higusa, 1969). Set in a mythical past among the native tribes of the Alaska coast, this story focuses on the destructive side of female appetite and desire. Other works, such as "The Pale Fox" (Aoi kitsune, 1973), retain the twilight atmosphere of Ōba's rainforest but encompass the urban areas of modern Japan. In "The Pale Fox," Ōba constructs a dreamlike montage in which a woman imagines her lover as a fox, a notorious trickster figure in Japanese legend. Unexpectedly, her fantasy becomes entwined with memories of her parents, particularly her senile father who, like the shape-shifting lover, slips in and out of reality.

Throughout the 1970s and into the 1980s, Ōba drew inspiration increasingly from ancient Japanese tales, which she utilized in various ways in her writings of the period. "The Smile of a Mountain Witch" (Yamanba no bishō, 1976) is based on legends of the demonic female figure, *yamanba*. In this story, Ōba portrays a stereotypically self-sacrificing wife and mother whose inner nature is revealed to be that of the terrifying female ogre. In the long fiction *Urashimasō* (1977) Ōba takes the Rip van Winkle-like tale, Urashima Tarō, for her motif. Similar to Urashima Tarō, who visits the Dragon King's palace under the sea only to find on his return home that he has been gone three hundred years, the female protagonist, Yukie, is a modern day traveler who returns to Japan from America after an absence of more than a decade. Yukie finds appalling changes within her family and uncovers old secrets linked to the war and the bombing of

Hiroshima. Awakening to the realities of her native country, Yukie is forced to confront a troubling mix of horror, memory, and family trauma resulting both from the war and from the binding of women to an uncompromising patriarchal system. Present as a young girl in the aftermath of Hiroshima, Ōba seldom wrote of the events she witnessed prior to this treatment of the bombing. *Urashimaso* thus represents Ōba's attempt to come to terms with the traumatic past and to rework that past in a way that has meaning for her as a writer and for contemporary society.

In the 1990s Ōba's writings often exhibited inspiration from classical Japanese literature. Chief among these works is *Long Ago, There Was a Woman* (Mukashi onna ga ita, 1994), a collection of prose and poetry that parodies the tenth-century *Tales of Ise* (Ise monogatari) and its male narrator. The rewriting of classical literature from the perspective of a contemporary female indicates yet another new direction for this writer.

— *Janice Brown*

Bibliography

Brown, Janice. "Ōba Minako—Telling the Untellable." *Japan Quarterly* 45, no. 3 (July–September 1998): 50–59.

Ōba Minako. "Fireweed." Trans. Marian Chambers. *Japan Quarterly* 28, no. 3 (July–September 1981): 403–427.

——. "Long Ago, There Was a Woman." Trans. Paul Schalow. In Paul Gordon Schalow and Janet A. Walker, eds., *The Woman's Hand: Gender and Theory in Japanese Women's Writing*, 34–40. Stanford: Stanford University Press, 1996.

——. "The Pale Fox." Trans. Stephen W. Kohl. In Van C. Gessel and Tomone Matsumoto, eds., *The Showa Anthology: Modern Japanese Short Stories*, 337–347. Tokyo: Kodansha International, 1986.

——. "The Smile of a Mountain Witch." Trans. Noriko Mizuta Lippit. In Noriko Mizuta Lippit and Kyoko Iriye Selden, eds., *Japanese Women Writers: Twentieth Century Short Fiction*, 194–206. Armonk, N.Y.: M. E. Sharpe, 1991.

——. "The Three Crabs." Trans. Yukiko Tanaka and Elizabeth Hanson. In Yukiko Tanaka and Elizabeth Hanson, eds., *This Kind of Woman: Ten Stories by Japanese Women Writers, 1960–1976*, 87–113. Stanford: Stanford University Press, 1982.

——. *Urashimaso*. Trans. Yu Oba. Tokyo: Josai University Center for Intercultural Studies and Education, 1995.

Orbaugh, Sharalyn. "A Female Urashima Tarō: Ōba Minako's Return to Japan." In Yoichi Nagashima, ed., *Return to Japan from "Pilgrimage" to the West*, 300–319. Aarhus: Aarhus University Press, 2001.

——. "Ohba Minako and the Paternity of Maternalism." In Rebecca Copeland and Esperanza Ramirez-Christensen, eds., *The Father–Daughter Plot: Japanese Literary Women*, 265–291. Honolulu: University of Hawai'i Press, 2001.

Wilson, Michiko. *Gender Is Fair Game: (Re)thinking the (Fe)male in the Works of Ōba Minako*. Armonk, N.Y.: M. E. Sharpe, 1999.

45

MURAKAMI RYŪ

The career of Murakami Ryū (b. 1952) reflects the late twentieth-century Japanese cultural landscape perhaps as well as any other contemporary novelist. Having published more than thirty works of fiction (only three of which are so far available in English translation), he ranks among the most prolific and popular writers of his generation; yet he has also been a highly visible figure in media culture, hosting a late-night talk show, working as a disk jockey, establishing his own record label, and writing and directing a number of films, including *Tokyo Decadence* (1991). His work, like that of contemporaries such as *Murakami Haruki and *Yoshimoto Banana, consistently problematizes traditional distinctions between high and popular culture.

Murakami Ryūnosuke (later shortened to Ryū) was born in 1952, in the western city of Sasebo, home to a large U.S. naval base. He recalls childhood memories of a nearby brothel patronized by American sailors and the shame and fascination he associated with the women who worked there. This intimate interaction with the negative influences of American culture has shaped much of his work, beginning with his debut novel, the sensational *Almost Transparent Blue* (Kagirinaku tōmei ni chikai burū, 1976). A semiautobiographical account of youth culture focused on drugs and promiscuous sex, *Almost Transparent Blue* shocked the conservative literary establishment by winning both the Gunzō Prize and the seventy-fifth Akutagawa Prize in 1976. The novel is set in the Tokyo suburb of Fussa, site of a U.S. Air Force base, prompting the critic Karatani Kōjin to label the work a "basically base novel based upon the base"

(Karatani 1991:84). It chronicles the adventures of Ryū and his friends, who support themselves by arranging orgies for black soldiers. The graphic depictions of decadent sex and drug use are couched in a language that at times approaches the lyrical, but that also inaugurates a "nominalization" of Japanese prose style in which traditional emphasis on adjectives and adverbs is replaced by sentences heavily larded with nouns, principally loan words written in *katakana*. Thematically, the novel embodies Murakami's principal concerns: alienation within contemporary Japanese society and the violent and deviant responses of the marginalized.

In 1980 Murakami published *Coin Locker Babies* (Koinrokkaa beibīzu, 1980), an ambitious fantasy that has been called the best summation of the Japanese experience of the 1970s. *Coin Locker Babies* is a dark parable of the abandonment of Murakami's postwar generation, symbolized by two boys, Kiku and Hashi, who are left at birth in coin-operated lockers. The babies, raised together as brothers, embark on separate careers: Kiku as a disaffected and vengeful pole-vaulter, and Hashi as a bisexual pop star in search of a vaguely remembered primordial sound (revealed finally to be the maternal heartbeat). The narrative is peopled with numerous idiosyncratic minor characters (Murakami's specialty), including Anemone, Kiku's sociopathic fashion-model girlfriend who keeps a pet crocodile in her condominium. The intricate, at times unwieldy, plot consists of alternating chapters of the protagonists' stories, brought together at the climax in the destruction of Tokyo by nerve gas released by Kiku—a scene often cited as having prefigured the gassing of the Tokyo subway in 1995 by the alienated youth of the Aum Shinrikyō cult. During the 1980s, Murakami published a number of other important works, including *69* (1987), an ironic account of a young man who attempts to bring a parodic version of urban campus unrest to his provincial high school, and *Fascism of Love and Fantasy* (Ai to gensō no fashizumu, 1987), the farcical story of Suzuhara Tōji's attempt to "return man to animal" by depopulating the planet and allowing the strong to rule. The explicit violence of this and other texts from this period earned Murakami's style the label *dōbutsuteki* (animal-like).

More recently, Murakami has continued to explore themes of sexual depravity and violence, often mixing the two in works such as *Ecstasy* (Ekusutashī, 1993), which follows a jet-setting drug smuggler as he travels between Tokyo, New York, and Paris in a search for ever-escalating thrills, and *Piercing* (Piasshingu, 1994), which pairs a homicidal man and a suicidal woman for an evening of grisly misunderstandings. *In the Miso Soup* (In za miso sūpu, 1997), which won the Yomiuri Prize, concerns an American serial killer loose in Tokyo who leads a young sex-tour guide on a "romp" through the contemporary Japanese demimonde. Despite the relentlessly explicit nature of works such as these, many commentators detect a serious intent beneath Murakami's provocative surface: a critical challenge to the normative, conservative mainstream of Japanese society in the form of insistent representation of extreme violence and sexuality.

At the same time, Murakami continues to develop the fantasy/science fiction motifs first seen in *Coin Locker Babies* in works such as *The World Five Minutes After* (Gofungo no sekai, 1994) and its sequel, *Hyūga Virus* (Hyūga uirusu, 1996). These novels explore the adventures of a protagonist from contemporary Japan who finds himself inexplicably transported to a parallel universe, five minutes behind our own, in which Japan never surrendered and continues fifty years later to fight against Allied invaders from its last remaining stronghold, an elaborate system of tunnels dug beneath Mount Fuji. *The World Five Minutes After* gives voice to an ongoing rhetorical posture in Murakami's work, a mixture of xenophobia and nationalism that is at once parodic and in earnest.

In addition to his filmmaking, Murakami continues to publish fiction, most recently the novel *Rain* (Line, 1998), and is active as well in other genres. His nonfiction works include a three-volume edition of collected essays and *E. V. Café* (1989), a series of discussions with the musician Sakamoto Ryūichi and various guests, among them critics Yoshimoto Takaaki and Asada Akira. Murakami's literary career, though far from over, has already embodied a number of themes central to the Japanese cultural imaginary in the last decades of the twentieth century: social disaffection born of exhaustion following the student movements of the 1960s, opposition to the deadening forces of Japanese consumer culture conceived in the form of extreme behaviors, and the ongoing problematic of defining a Japanese identity in the face of American cultural hegemony.

—*Stephen Snyder*

Bibliography

Karatani Kōjin. "Sōzōryoku no beesu" (Base of Imagination). In *Ryū Book*, 84–89. Tokyo: Shinshosha, 1991.

Murakami Ryū. *Almost Transparent Blue*. Trans. Nancy Andrews. Tokyo: Kodansha International, 1977.

——. *Coin Locker Babies*. Trans. Stephen Snyder. Tokyo: Kodansha International, 1995.

——. *Sixty-Nine*. Trans. Ralph F. McCarthy. Tokyo: Kodansha International, 1993.

Snyder, Stephen. "Extreme Imagination: The Fiction of Murakami Ryū." In Stephen Snyder and Philip Gabriel, eds. *Ōe and Beyond: Fiction in Contemporary Japan*, 199–218. Honolulu: University of Hawai'i Press, 1999.

46

MURAKAMI HARUKI

Murakami Haruki (b. 1949) is one of the most widely discussed of contemporary Japanese authors. A leading writer of postmodern fiction, Murakami's works often fall outside the parameters of established categories such as "serious" and "popular" and seem to represent a mixture of the formulaic styles of fantasy or adventure literature and more inventive, artistic fiction.

Born in the early years of the postwar era, Murakami belongs to the generation of Japanese who reached maturity at the climax of the student counterculture movement in Japan, known as Zenkyōtō, and who witnessed its subsequent, rapid collapse. This is a crucial point in understanding the author's work, for while his experiments in style and structure have varied during the first twenty years of his career, his awareness of the vacuum of identity left in the wake of Zenkyōtō has remained evident in his work throughout.

Although consciousness of an identity crisis in Japan may be traced at least to the early decades of the Meiji period, the nature of this crisis differs for Murakami's generation, and each successive one thereafter. Murakami highlights the identity crisis experienced by a generation of young people growing up in the relative affluence of the rapid growth period beginning in the mid-1950s. Lacking the concrete national goals that shaped previous generations (rebuilding the nation, competing economically with the West, and so on), Japanese youth in the 1950s and 1960s, like their counterparts throughout the industrialized world, turned to political activism for self-definition. With the collapse of these movements in the early 1970s, however, and the subsequent relaxation of political tensions between right and left, most reentered the dominànt mainstream culture and accepted the identity of worker-consumer. This fact remains as true today as it was thirty years ago and suggests one explanation for the author's continued popularity among young Japanese seeking to define themselves.

Murakami began to write about his generation's post-Zenkyōtō disillusion-ment in his first work, *Hear the Wind Sing* (Kaze no uta o kike, 1979), in which the first-person protagonist ("Boku") struggles to maintain connectivity with his best friend and alter-ego, "Rat," who represents, psychologically, his inner self. By the end of the book Boku and Rat are separated, and one could say that Murakami has spent the remainder of his writing career trying to bring them back together. The result of such a union would be, presumably, the reforma-tion of a "complete" self for the Murakami protagonist and, by analogy, for every generation to emerge since the collapse of Zenkyōtō in 1970.

The author has experimented with a variety of methods and styles to this end during the past twenty years. One of the earliest and most enduring features in his writing has been the "magical realist" universe. In Murakami's case this most commonly manifests itself as the protagonist's ability to enter his own un-conscious and revisit memories of people and things he has lost. In this way he achieves partial reunion with his inner self by recovering, temporarily, a portion of his historical past.

We see this clearly in Murakami's second work, *Pinball 1973* (1973-nen no pinbōru, 1980), in which the protagonist's obsession to recover lost friends leads him to conjure them in unlikely forms: twin girls with no names and a pinball machine that speaks. A similar obsession for Rat leads to the quest for a semi-mythical sheep in the third novel, *A Wild Sheep Chase* (Hitsuji o meguru bōken, 1982), in which Murakami allegorizes the Zenkyōtō movement in gen-eral, pitting Rat (counterculture) against the Sheep (mainstream culture).

This opposition between the individual and mainstream culture—repre-sented in Murakami's fiction as a coalition of politicians, businessmen, and the mass media—has become the basic structure of Murakami's fiction. Certainly this is the case in *Hard-Boiled Wonderland and the End of the World* (Sekai no owari to hâdo-boirudo wandârando, 1985), a futuristic work in which the pro-tagonist finds himself at the mercy of a pitiless state engaged in a war for infor-mation. His final fate is chillingly reminiscent of real life for contemporary Jap-anese: he becomes a prisoner of the Japanese "system" of high technology.

A similar structure supports *The Wind-Up Bird Chronicle* (Nejimakidori kuronikuru, 1994–96), which, like previous Murakami novels, is about loss and attempted recovery. In this case the protagonist, Okada Tōru, attempts to re-cover his missing wife. Eventually we learn that her brother Noboru, a politi-cian, has removed her "core identity." Only Tōru, who possesses the magical ability to restore identity, can counter Noboru's action. It is not difficult to read this work, also, as a metaphor for the control exerted by the contemporary con-sumerist Japanese state over the minds of its people. The individual self must be sacrificed for the good of the consumerist economy that drives the Japanese state.

Murakami's role as a major Japanese writer was cemented in 1990–91 with Kodansha's release of an eight-volume collection of his fiction from 1979 to 1989. In addition to chronicling the decline of the individual self in contemporary Japan, Murakami has written nonfiction works concerning major current events. In 1997 he published *Underground* (Andâguraundo), in which he interviews survivors of the Aum Shinrikyō cult's poison gas incident of 1995, attempting to understand the victims as real people rather than mere statistics in the newspapers. In a more controversial sequel, *Underground 2* (1998), he interviews members of the cult itself in an attempt to historicize their motivations in the context of contemporary Japanese society.

Most recently Murakami has returned to writing fiction about loss and psychological alteration. In *Sputnik Sweetheart* (Supūtoniku no koibito, 1999) he explores the sacrifice of individuality for love, and in his latest work, *All the Gods' Children Dance* (Kami no kodomotachi wa mina odoru, 2000), he examines a form of post-traumatic stress following the Kobe earthquake of 1995. Additionally, Murakami has written travelogues detailing his various travels throughout the world, several books of essays, and a guidebook intended to help young readers appreciate Japanese short fiction.

—*Matthew Strecher*

Bibliography

Murakami Haruki. *Hard-Boiled Wonderland and the End of the World*. Trans. Alfred Birnbaum. New York: Vintage International, 1991.

——. *Hear the Wind Sing*. Trans. Alfred Birnbaum. Tokyo: Kodansha International, 1987.

——. *Murakami Haruki Zensakuhin, 1979–1989* (Complete Works of Murakami Haruki, 1979–1989). 8 vols. Tokyo: Kodansha, 1991.

——. *Pinball 1973*. Trans. Alfred Birnbaum. Tokyo: Kodansha International, 1985.

——. *Sputnik Sweetheart*. Trans. Philip Gabriel. New York: Alfred A. Knopf, 2001.

——. *Underground: The Tokyo Gas Attack and the Japanese Psyche*. Trans. Alfred Birnbaum and Philip Gabriel. London: Harvill Press, 2000.

——. *A Wild Sheep Chase*. Trans. Alfred Birnbaum. New York: Plume, 1989.

——. *The Wind-Up Bird Chronicle*. Trans. Jay Rubin. New York: Alfred A. Knopf, 1997.

Rubin, Jay. *Haruki Murakami and the Music of Words*. London: Harvill Press, 2002.

Strecher, Matthew C. *Dances with Sheep: The Quest for Identity in the Fiction of Murakami Haruki*. Ann Arbor: University of Michigan Center for Japanese Studies, 2002.

47

NAKAGAMI KENJI

Through works of fiction and criticism, Nakagami Kenji (1946–1992) worked to build a counternarrative of modern Japanese literature by redefining the term *monogatari* (a tale), which had formerly been reserved for premodern narrative texts. Beginning with the 1977 series of essays *The Genealogy of the Tale* (Monogatari no keifu), Nakagami translates *monogatari* into an organizing principle for a postwar mode of literary historiography that draws attention to the narrative operations of a historical relation to the past. *Monogatari* is explicitly counterposed to the sets of texts, reading practices, and institutions that compose the discipline of *kokubungaku* (literally "national literature," referring to Japanese literature as it came into formation alongside other nation-building infrastructures and ideological fantasies in the 1890s).

In contrast to the sovereign individual subject, which Nakagami says has been retrofitted to serve as the origin of *kokubungaku*, he proposes *monogatari*, whose depictions of "law and system" reintroduce themes, tropes, and characters that are constitutive of history and literary historiography yet cannot be named. Crucial figures in this genealogy are the ethnologist Origuchi Shinobu, fiction writers *Enchi Fumiko and *Tanizaki Jun'ichirō, poet Satō Haruo (1892–1964) and Edo-period writer of ghost stories Ueda Akinari (1734–1809). Narrative, redefined as *monogatari*, is seen to move constantly between documentary and fiction, demonstrating both the possibilities (a politics of transfiguration, or the utopian refiguring of social modes of practice and imaginary worlds) and limitations (a politics of fulfillment, or the demand that the state deliver on the promises of its social contract with its citizens) of a postwar enlightenment project.

Born in the folklore-rich region of Wakayama, Nakagami moved to Tokyo in 1965 and served as an editor on the small-press *dōjin zasshi* (literary coterie magazine) *Literary Capital* (Bungei shuto) while working as a baggage handler at Haneda Airport. Beginning with this stint of manual labor, the embodied subjectivity of the narrator in Nakagami's works, as experienced through sound, smell, touch, and the memory of heterogeneous time, takes on an important role in depicting his characters' relation to history. Early stories such as "On Japanese" (Nihongo ni tsuite, 1968) and "JAZZ" (1966) typically took place in the highly mythologized space of the Shinjuku area of Tokyo of the 1960s and 1970s. These stories used a *shishōsetsu (personal novel)-like fractured first-person grammar influenced by the masculine iconoclasm of African American free jazz virtuosos. Nakagami's first collection of stories, *The Map of a Nineteen-Year-Old* (Jūkyūsai no chizu, 1975), signaled the beginning of the topological imagination that continued to surface in resignified variations throughout his career and underscored his claim to undertake the conceptual equivalent of Faulkner's works within the context of *kokubungaku*. Subsequent works shifted from Tokyo to the southern periphery of Japan, Kumano, to form a story cycle that developed a parallel cosmology to *kokubungaku* in the ethnically fluid space of the *roji* (an alley neighborhood discursively similar to a *hisabetsu buraku*, or outcast neighborhood).

Nakagami's fictions draw on the broader use of the term *monogatari* as "narrative" by 1960s translators of narratological and structuralist-anthropological writings. Writers of anthropology such as Yamaguchi Masao translated works of structuralist literary criticism, such as those of Todorov and Lévi-Strauss, and applied the analysis of narrative and strategies of semiotic close reading to a postwar critique of the emperor system and its center-periphery structure. Beginning with *Kishū: Country of Trees, Country of Roots, Monogatari* (Kishū: ki no kuni, ne no kuni, monogatari, 1977), the fieldwork of a road trip and reportage on narratives of discrimination in Kishū *buraku* (outcast villages) written for the leftist weekly *Asahi Journal*, Nakagami developed this critique by showing how practices of "reading" extend beyond encounters with texts.

The three-volume Kishū saga, composed of the Akutagawa Prize-winning *The Cape* (Misaki, 1976), *The Sea of Withered Trees* (Karekinada, 1977) and *The Ends of the Earth, Sublime Time* (Chi no hate, shijō no toki, 1983), featured an interlocking set of characters. The cluster of stories revolves around Hamamura Ryūzō, the dissolute and charismatic construction-company owner, from "who knows what bone of what horse," and the son he fathered shortly before being incarcerated, Takehara Akiyuki, a construction worker and pretender to his father's seemingly invincible authority. The swings of social mobility enabled by the diffusions of capital that peaked under Prime Minister Tanaka Kakuei (1972–1974) are legible in the Kishū saga. However, the stories in the cycle refuse conventions of ethnographic and psychological realism that had previously rendered the space of the *buraku* into textual form.

The Kishū saga dramatizes and critiques the patriarchal impulses of postwar, nationalist narratives of development: the creation of fabulated ancestors as legitimizations of empire-building, and the son's desire to both spurn and transcend the father. The interstices of these three volumes feature a different series of short stories, longer fictional works, and reportage. These stories investigate possibilities of narrative storytelling alternative to the modern oedipal subject. Sometimes located in characters reminiscent of the female *kataribe* storytellers of classical oral narrative, a utopian and ever-shifting metaphysics of alterity exists in tension with the organizing principles of nation and the cultural legacies of the emperor system. The newspaper serial *Hosenka* (1980) depicted the maternal melodrama as constitutive of history yet outside its representation. Beginning with *A Thousand Years of Pleasure* (Sennen no yuraku, 1982), a six-part story of six striking youths of the *buraku* who all die tragically young, the "roots" of Japanese literature become grafted onto the "routes" of pan-Asian thought. The transnational and cultural-comparative dimension of Nakagami's writings becomes more prominent as he extends the critique of the center-periphery structure of *kokubungaku*, incorporating alliances of countercultural characters from other Asian contexts and spending more time investigating contemporary Korean literary production. Several of Nakagami's works have been made into films.

—*Anne McKnight*

Bibliography

Cornyetz, Nina. *Dangerous Women, Deadly Words: Phallic Fantasy and Modernity in Three Japanese Writers*. Stanford: Stanford University Press, 1999.

Nakagami Kenji. *The Cape and Other Stories from the Japanese Ghetto*. Trans. Eve Zimmerman. Berkeley: Stone Bridge Press, 1999.

Zimmerman, Eve. "In the Trap of Words: Nakagami Kenji and the Making of Degenerate Fictions." In Stephen Snyder and Philip Gabriel, eds., *Ōe and Beyond: Fiction in Contemporary Japan*, 130–152. Honolulu: University of Hawai'i Press, 1999.

48

KANAI MIEKO

Nineteen-year-old Kanai Mieko (b. 1947) saw her first published story, "Love Life" (Ai no seikatsu, 1967), not only come in second place for the third annual Dazai Osamu Prize but also receive warm praise from respected writers Ishikawa Jun (1899–1987) and Yoshida Ken'ichi (1912–1977). The next year she won a poetry prize for "The House of Madame Juju" (Madamu Juju no ie, 1971). From that moment on, Kanai knew that she would be a writer. Subsequently, in the late 1960s and throughout the 1970s, Kanai moved in the circles of prominent and even infamous figures on the arts scene: Yoshioka Minoru (1919–1990), Shibusawa Tatsuhiko, Yotsuya Simone, and *Nakagami Kenji, to name a few. In the early 1970s Kanai joined established authors testifying against censorship at the obscenity trial of Nosaka Akiyuki (b. 1930) whose publication of a "pornographic" *Nagai Kafū story had caused an uproar. The unusual success that launched Kanai's career at a young age has prompted literary critics to describe her as a *sōjuku na sakka* (a "writer who bloomed early"), implying a continuing "success" that remains better appreciated among intellectuals and other writers, and even foreign scholars, than among the reading public in Japan.

Indeed, Kanai found great literary inspirations outside of Japan: artists Jasper Johns and Robert Rauschenberg; writers Gustave Flaubert, Jorge Luis Borges, Michel Foucault, and Roland Barthes; filmmakers Godard, Renoir, and Ford. Among Japanese literary influences, she invariably mentions writers Ōoka Shōhei (b. 1909), *Sakaguchi Ango, and Ishikawa Jun and poets Yoshioka Minoru, Amazawa Taijirō (b. 1936), and Irizawa Yasuo (b. 1931). Although she won the seventh annual Izumi Kyōka Literature Prize for "Platonic Love" (Puratonteki ren'ai, 1979) and the Japanese Women's Literature Prize for *Tama, and More Tama* (Tamaya, 1987), and although her essays and film criticism regularly appear in major newspapers, women's magazines, and literary journals, Kanai strikes a singular pose among women writers; this is perhaps due to her experimental and difficult prose as well as to her outspoken rejection of the popular label *joryū sakka* (woman writer). (See "Gender, Family, and Sexualities in Modern Literature.") The very quality and diversity of her prolific literary output—even including children's stories such as *Fleas, Off to the Circus* (Nomi, sâkasu e yuku, 1997), illustrated by her sister Kanai Kumiko, and her critical assessment of children's picture books, *The Finger That Turns the Page* (Pêji o mekuru yubi, 2000)—do not make for easy categorization and may not endear her to literary purists.

Kanai's best known works in English include the early short stories "Rabbits" (Usagi, 1972), "Rotting Meat" (Funiku, 1972), and "Platonic Love"; the poem "The House of Madame Juju"; and several stories from her later story-cycle novel *Treading on Soft Earth* (Yawarakai tsuchi ni funde, 1997). In 1992 her many short stories were collected in the three-volume *Complete Short Works of Kanai Mieko* (Kanai Mieko zentanpenshū), while her longer works of fiction were republished first in 1995 with *Sea Without Shores* (Kishibei no nai umi, 1974) and then in 1999 with *Writing Class* (Bunshō kyōshitsu, 1985) and *Indian Summer* (Koharubiyori, 1988). The two-volume *Love's War Stories* (Ren'ai taiheiki, 1995) alludes to classical literature as well as works by *Tanizaki Jun'ichirō in tracing the everyday, contemporary lives and loves of four sisters. *Dizzy Spells* (Karui memai, 1997) concentrates an almost excruciating focus on the quotidian in a woman's urban lifestyle, deploying long, lyrical sentences to suggest that the boring and familiar can be extraordinary, even "dizzying," to perceive up close.

Kanai's short fiction is well represented in English translation. In "Rabbits" and "Rotting Meat," for example, we find boxed structures made up of internal and external narratives, and stories whose metafictional qualities are heightened by nameless, allegorical characters and settings, by wordplay, and by rich allusions to fables and children's stories. "Rabbits" plays on the multiple levels of childlike innocence and adult fantasy seen in Lewis Carroll's *Alice's Adventures in Wonderland* and *Through the Looking Glass*, while the untranslated story "The Story of the Air Man" (Kūki otoko no hanashi, 1974) rewrites Franz Kafka's parable-like "Hunger Artist" to make the protagonist not a fasting artist but rather one who eats insatiably in his striving to personify a perfectly sublime roundness. In "Rotting Meat," when the unnamed male narrator tells us about the apartment he once moved to and the woman he found there, the embedded narrative becomes dreamscape as a tale of metonymic equivalences and savagely ironic punning depicts a prostitute who confuses consumption and violence with love, and herself and her lovers with "meat." The end returns us to the narrator confessing his desire to be consumed by the woman he can no longer find, transgressing boundaries between past and present, internal and external narrative, fantasy and reality: as a writer himself struggling with words, the narrator is as consumed by the endless regression of signifiers for "meat" as he is seduced by desire for the female flesh with which he wishes to merge. "Platonic Love," on the other hand, describes a more "realistic" but no less metafictional story: it situates the reader in modern Japan with a woman writer who finds herself receiving anonymous letters from a woman writer whom she increasingly fears is indistinguishable from herself. Not simply autobiographical, "Platonic Love" simultaneously invokes and parodies the *shishōsetsu (personal novel) in order to problematize narrative point of view and forms, as well as to render strange our obsession with conventional writerly "intentions" and readerly "expectations." Kanai's latest work, *Rumor's Daughter* (Usawa no musume, 2002), derives its stylistic innovations from cinema, both in its shaping of time and space and in its preoccupation with allusion and melodrama.

Kanai's novels evince postmodernist concerns with writing as a self-reflexive activity in which author, reader, and other texts are inextricably entangled and mutually informing of a particular story's meaning. Indeed, Kanai frequently reminds her readers and critics that "It is about writing that I write," and this strategy of *écriture* is amply present in the fiction Kanai herself feels to be most representative of her literary project, *Sea Without Shores* and *Treading on Soft Earth.*

—*Mary A. Knighton*

Bibliography

Kanai Mieko. "Fiction's Language of the Extraordinary." In *Japanese Book News* 19 (Fall 1997): 22.

——. "The House of Madame Juju." Trans. Christopher Drake. In Howard Hibbett, ed., *Contemporary Japanese Literature: An Anthology of Fiction, Film, and Other Writings since 1945*, 342–343. New York: Alfred A. Knopf, 1977.

——. *Kanai Mieko Zentanpenshū* (Complete Short Fiction of Kanai Mieko). 3 vols. Tokyo: Nihon Bungeisha, 1992.

——. "Platonic Love." Trans. Amy Vladeck Heinrich. In Van C. Gessel and Tomone Matsumoto, eds., *The Shōwa Anthology: Modern Japanese Short Stories*, 375–382. Tokyo: Kodansha International, 1979.

——. "Rabbits." Trans. Phyllis Birnbaum. In Phyllis Birnbaum, ed., *Rabbits, Crabs, Etc.: Stories by Japanese Women*, 1–16. Honolulu: University of Hawai'i Press, 1982.

——. "Rotting Meat." Trans. Mary A. Knighton. In *Fiction International* 29 (1996): 110–115.

——. "Treading on Soft Earth." Trans. Sarah Teasley. *TriQuarterly* 99 (Spring–Summer 1997): 7–27.

Orbaugh, Sharalyn. "Arguing with the Real: Kanai Mieko." In Stephen Snyder and Philip Gabriel, eds., *Ōe and Beyond: Fiction in Contemporary Japan*, 245–277. Honolulu: University of Hawai'i Press, 1999.

——. "The Body in Contemporary Women's Fiction." In Paul Gordon Schalow and Janet A. Walker, eds., *The Woman's Hand: Gender and Theory in Japanese Women's Writing*, 119–164. Stanford: Stanford University Press, 1996.

Schierbeck, Sachiko Shibata. *Japanese Women Novelists in the 20th Century: 104 Biographies, 1900–1993*. Copenhagen: Museum Tusculanum Press, 1994.

49

TSUSHIMA YŪKO

Tsushima Yūko (b. 1947, daughter of *Dazai Osamu) is perhaps best known as a writer of semiautobiographical prose narratives and short stories about single-parent mothers. She has also written nonautobiographical narratives, short essays, and book-length studies of Japanese classical literature. Evincing her tremendous success are the many awards she has won: the Izumi Kyōka Award in 1977, the Women Writers Award in 1978, the Noma New Writers Award in 1979, the Kawabata Yasunari Award in 1983, the Yomiuri Award for Literature in 1986, the Hirabayashi Taiko Award in 1990, the Itō Sei Award for Literature in 1996, and the Tanizaki Jun'ichirō Award in 1999. Two novels and many of her short stories have been translated into English.

Much has been written about her work. Japanese and Western literary critics discuss her focus on mundane household objects and activities, her attack on the traditional concept of motherhood, and her portrayal of female sexuality. They note that her narratives frequently blend dream and memory with present-time events, creating a highly subjective sense of reality. Japanese critics characterize her work of the mid- to late 1980s as "therapeutic," a means by which the author endured the death of her son, and therefore written without the benefit (or detriment) of distance from her subject. And both Japanese and Western readers note the many Tsushima narratives that include a character who is mentally challenged.

Such characters represent what she terms "the idiot." It is clear that idiocy, both as a recurring motif and as a discursive mode, is an important locus of identity for the Tsushima heroine. There is also a parallel between the idiot and the female mountain-demon, or *yamanba*, of Japanese folklore, with which Tsushima heroines are likewise identified; the idiot and *yamanba* are intersecting subjectivities.

The idiot paradigm in Tsushima's work may be traced to experiences that she had growing up with her brother, who had Down's syndrome and who died when she was thirteen. In a number of Tsushima's writings, the heroine likewise has an "idiot brother" who lives in a world without language. Examples include "Requiem: For a Dog and an Adult" (Rekuiemu—inu to otona no tame ni, 1968), "Mother in the House of Grass" (Mugura no haha, 1974), "A Bed of Grass" (Kusa no fushido, 1977), *Child of Fortune* (Chōji, 1978), "The Bath" (Yokushitsu, 1983), and *Toward Noon* (Mahiru e, 1988).

All but one of these texts, *Requiem*, features an adult heroine whose brother has long since died. The heroine misses her late brother, who had been her "best ally" whom she could "trust completely" ("A Bed of Grass" 233). She felt that she could know no happiness without him and the world she experienced through him, which was "peaceful and free, a fairy-tale world" (*Child of Fortune* 127).

That fairy-tale world, a world belonging solely to the idiot, was sustained, at least in part, by his freedom from language. The heroine's communication with him was direct, based on simple words augmented by nonverbal cues such as hand gestures, facial expressions, touch, taste, and smell. Idiot consciousness is rooted outside of the realm of the Symbolic, to borrow Lacanian terminology, a stage in human psychological development that is marked by the introduction of language. Language ushers a child into social discourse, with its host of symbols that differentiate one thing, and one person, from the next.

Because he did not participate in the realm of the Symbolic, then, the idiot brother saw and responded to the world straightforwardly, without the filter of socially constructed interpretation. His "emotions were unclouded: what pleased him meant joy, what displeased him meant anger" (*Child of Fortune* 82). The same may be said of the idiot children in "Island of Joy" (Yorokobi no shima, 1977), who were delighted, much to the dismay of their adult caretakers, by the garbage that used to be dumped near their institution. The children did not know about the worthlessness of "garbage"; they only knew the pleasure they took in what got dumped.

The idiot is entirely divorced from, indeed cannot comprehend, the historically created conventions and discursive codes that people adopt and wear as though they were garments. The idiot's metaphorical lack of such clothing is represented in these texts by his actual nudity. The heroine in "Bed of Grass" thought that her brother had seemed cleanest when he was undressed, because his garments were perpetually soiled. The idiot brother did not engage in activities such as creating a social persona for himself, and in that sense he did not belong in clothing.

Tsushima heroines such as Kōko (*Child of Fortune*) and Sachi ("Pregnant with a Fox" [Kitsune o haramu], 1972) loved playing in the nude with their brothers. Each seemed to crave contact with her brother's body. This attraction contrasts sharply to the repulsion others felt toward him. Kōko's older sister Shōko was ashamed of him. The idiot's "nakedness" made him ill fit to interact with other members of society. But to Kōko, the idiot's nakedness represented the quintessential "bare human being" that she desired.

Idiot-identified Tsushima heroines never fully understand why others do not accept them. Takiko, the teenage-mother heroine of *Woman Running in the Mountains* (Yama o hashiru onna, 1980), does not seem capable of comprehending the directives that make her fellow workers keep a "shocked distance" from her when she continues to work during her pregnancy (23). And as a child, Kōko had been "unable to understand what made [her mother and sister] find fault with her grades, her manners, her language" (*Child of Fortune* 78). As "bare human beings," these two heroines are baffled by the socially constructed behavior of the people around them.

A poignant metaphor for the alienation of these heroines may be found in the short Tsushima narrative "The Bath," in which the heroine fears that her idiot brother cannot understand that he is dead. In her dreams night after night, he draws near the translucent bath window wanting to be let back in the house, only to be confused and saddened when he is not. Unable either to live or to die, he is forced to linger in a kind of purgatory. Like him, the heroines hover at the margins of society, unable to participate fully, yet unable to depart.

Also hovering on earth in a kind of purgatory is the *yamanba*, the female demon of Japanese folk legend, who serves as another locus of identification for the Tsushima heroine. *Yamanba* legends are told throughout Japan and in China and Korea and can be linked to similar archetypes around the world. The body, not the mind, governs the *yamanba* of the oral folk tradition. Her physical drives define her in the same way that his nude body defines the idiot. Indeed, a Rabelaisian-style emphasis on her carnality is characteristic of *yamanba* tales. The *yamanba* of the widely told tale "The Yamanba and the Pack Driver," for instance, eats the poor driver's entire basket of fish, then his cow, and then she tries to eat the driver himself. In the end, however, the driver kills the *yamanba*. The large size of her appetite is echoed in the large size of her body, which towers seven feet tall, and her large mouth, which stretches from ear to ear.

Tsushima's texts, too, emphasize the heroine's carnally defined nature. Thus, Takiko feels most comfortable at the job where she handles pots of plants, which heightens her awareness of the muscles in her body. Outside of work, her life is made up of physical brawls with her father, caring for her baby's bodily needs, and meeting her own needs. Sometimes she attends to her own physical needs and desires before her baby's. She sleeps, has sex, or rifles through the refrigerator while he cries.

Coupled with the emphasis on Takiko's physical existence is her inability to acquire the accoutrements of socially constructed womanhood. She is hopelessly clumsy at applying makeup to her face, and fails miserably as a cosmetic saleswoman. She is as unsuited to wearing cosmetics as the idiot is to wearing clothing. Neither of them seems to belong in the company of the socially cloaked world.

Alienation from society is another hallmark of the *yamanba*. The alienation shared by the heroine, the *yamanba*, and the heroine's mother, is developed in the short story "The Mother in the House of Grass," where the heroine recalls the *yamanba* tale that her mother frequently told her as a child—one very similar to the tale of "The Yamanba and the Pack Driver." The "House of Grass" version of the tale begins with a traveler entering the *yamanba*'s house while she is away, eating all of her food, and then falling asleep. She comes home, finds him, and is about to eat him when he pokes her eyes out with a dried fish. He escapes, and the *yamanba*, "shedding red tears from her wounded eyes," runs after him calling "Wait! Wait!" (276). She keeps on chasing him like that forever.

The man's trespassing on the *yamanba*'s property and stealing her food demonstrates his presumed power over her from the outset. He does not kill her, as in the traditional tale, but he attacks her with the phallic dried fish, with which he pierces her eyes. He thus "blinds" her to everything but her desire to catch him, gaining dominion over her consciousness.

The *yamanba* and mainstream/male realms are in an eternal deadlock. The fact that if the man stays he will be eaten by the *yamanba* suggests that living in her world would result in his self being assimilated into hers, an archetypal result of being eaten. He will never allow it. Nor can she live in his world, where her being is subject to violation.

"House of Grass" draws a distinct parallel between the intratextual *yamanba* and the heroine's mother, who are conflated in the heroine's mind. The heroine likes the *yamanba* but also fears becoming one. She likes her mother's *yamanba* tale because the *yamanba* keeps running after the man without realizing that he is gone. The blood in her eyes does not allow her to see it, and her idiot subjectivity does not allow her to perceive it. She is blind to her own unhappiness, which gives her the strength that the heroine admires.

Like the *yamanba*'s endless chase, and the idiot's reverie, the Tsushima heroine's subjective experience defines her reality. Tsushima's characteristic blending of memory, fantasy, and present-time reality supports this subjective, or idiot's, sense of reality. All of her texts are, in this sense, discourses of idiocy.

As she refocuses her recent writing onto Ainu poetry, fictional works set in distant times and places, and reflections on the Japanese classics, Tsushima may leave the discourse of the idiot behind. But recent novels such as *Mountain of Fire* (Hi no yama, 1998), which invokes the Great Mother image, related to the *yamanba*, and essays such as "The End of Magic" (Mahō no owari, 1999),

which describes the idiot's reappearances in the narrator's life, suggest otherwise. Idiot subjectivity is likely to remain an integral part of Tsushima's writing
for some time to come.

—*Amy Christiansen*

Bibliography

Copeland, Rebecca L. "Motherhood As Institution." *Japan Quarterly* 39 (January–
   March 1992): 101–110.
Tsushima Yūko. "The Bath." Trans. J. Martin Holman. In Michael J. Rosen, ed., *The
   Company of Animals*, 133–157. New York: Doubleday, 1993.
———. "A Bed of Grass." Trans. Yukiko Tanaka. In Yukiko Tanaka and Elizabeth
   Hanson, eds., *This Kind of Woman: Ten Stories by Japanese Women Writers*,
   1960–1976, 140–155. Stanford: Stanford University Press. 1982.
———. *Child of Fortune*. Trans. Geraldine Harcourt. Tokyo: Kodansha International,
   1983.
———. "Island of Joy." Trans. Lora Sharnoff. *Japan Quarterly* 27 (1980): 263–269.
———. "Mother in the House of Grass." Trans. Sara Dillon. *The Literary Review* (1987)
   30: 265–296.
———. "The Marsh." Trans. Yukiko Tanaka. In Yukiko Tanaka, ed., *Unmapped Territo-
   ries*, 152–168. Seattle: Women in Translation, 1991.
———. *Moeru kaze* (Burning Wind). Tokyo: Chūkō bunko, 1985.
———. *The Shooting Gallery and Other Stories*. Trans. Geraldine Harcourt. New York:
   Pantheon, 1988.
———. *Woman Running in the Mountains*. Trans. Geraldine Harcourt. New York: Pan-
   theon, 1991.
Viswanathan, Meera. "In Pursuit of the Yamamba." In Paul Gordon Schalow and
   Janet A. Walker, eds., *The Woman's Hand: Gender and Theory in Japanese Women's
   Writing*, 239–261. Stanford: Stanford University Press, 1996.

50

SHIMADA MASAHIKO AND SHIMIZU YOSHINORI

Shimada Masahiko (b. 1961) and Shimizu Yoshinori (b. 1947) are representative Japanese postmodernist writers, a group that includes, among others, Takahashi Gen'ichirō (b. 1951), Kobayashi Kyōji (b. 1957), Ogino Anna (b. 1956), and *Yoshimoto Banana, all of whom came to prominence in the 1980s and early 1990s. No matter how one defines "postmodernist fiction," critics agree that Shimizu, a master of pastiche, and Shimada, Japan's own literary enfant terrible, are postmodernist in style, thematic concerns, and overall approach to literature.

Shimizu Yoshinori was born in Nagoya in 1947 and graduated from Aichi Teachers College. Since his literary debut in 1981 he has continued to publish prolifically, most notably short humorous pieces in popular magazines such as *Weekly Fiction* (Shūkan shōsetsu) and *Contemporary Fiction* (Shōsetsu gendai). Prominent among these works are "Soba vs. Kishimen Noodles" (Soba to kishimen, 1984); "Japanese Entrance Exams for Earnest Young Men" (Kokugo nyūshi mondai hisshōhō, 1988), for which Shimizu won the Yoshikawa Eiji Literary Prize for New Writers; "Jack and Betty Forever" (Eien no Jakku & Beti, 1988); and "Growing Down" (Guroingu daun, 1989). Shimizu has continued to publish numerous collections of shorter works, and, more recently, full-length parodies of such subjects as religion (*Siesta of the Gods* [Kamigami no gosui, 1995]), and world literature (*Collected Works of the World* [Sekai bungaku zenshū, 1995]).

Besides being one of the most prolific of contemporary Japanese writers, Shimizu is also known for the variety of styles he employs, his stories mimicking everything from advertising copy, screenplays, and academic treatises to bureaucratic documents and classical Japanese tales. He is arguably one of the funniest and most inventive writers in Japan today, the range of his imagination and his linguistic playfulness rivaling that of Tsutsui Yasutaka (b. 1934). The word most often associated with Shimizu—pastiche—should not be understood in Fredric Jameson's negative sense of "blank parody," but as something closer to classical parody and satire. The novelist Maruya Saiichi (b. 1925) argues that Shimizu's work revives a tradition of parodic writing reaching back to the Edo period, a tradition that, since the late Meiji period, has been held in check by the continuing influence of a serious, confessional, naturalist approach to literature (Maruya 1990:247–248).

Perhaps most interesting to the foreign reader are Shimizu's parodies of the world of Japanese education and academia. "Japanese Entrance Exams for Earnest Young Men," for instance, in the guise of a story of a tutor and pupil preparing for the Japanese-language section of entrance examinations, lampoons the typical multiple-choice and short-answer questions on exams—and indeed the whole institution of entrance exams. In "Footnote Tale" (Chūshaku monogatari, 1990) Shimizu parodies the type of endnotes and commentary beloved of academics, producing, with its interplay of text and commentary, a short work reminiscent of Vladimir Nabokov's *Pale Fire*. And in "Preface" (Jobun, 1986) Shimizu satirizes the *Nihonjinron* (cultural nationalist) discourse of the 1980s with its search for the "uniqueness" of the Japanese language. Here Shimizu presents, couched in the style of an academic monograph, the whimsical argument (based on such similar pairs as *namae*/name, *boya*/boy) that the English language is historically derived from Japanese.

In two of his best-known works, "Jack and Betty Forever" and "Growing Down," Shimizu explores, in his typically humorous way, the kind of critique Asada Akira makes of Japan as a nation characterized by "infantile capitalism." In "Growing Down," a fantasy in which time has inexplicably begun to flow backward (with the characters growing progressively younger and historical events occurring in reverse order), Shimizu sketches a sense of nostalgia for an earlier Japan, one that predates Japan's economic dominance of the late 1980s and early 1990s. In "Jack and Betty Forever" Shimizu portrays the reverse, contrasting an infantile, healthy Japan with a "mature" United States that is ailing (Gabriel 1999:222–226).

Shimada Masahiko was born in Tokyo in 1961 and graduated from the Tokyo University of Foreign Languages, majoring in Russian. While still a university student he began writing fiction, with his first work the novella *A Divertimento for Gentle Leftists* (Yasashii sayoku no tame no kiyūkyoku, 1983), which was nominated for the Akutagawa Prize. (Shimada has been nominated six times for the Akutagawa, tying the record, though he has never won the award.) After graduating from university in 1984 Shimada became a professional novelist, and he has continued to publish a steady stream of novels, short stories, plays, and essays. His works of fiction include *Cries and Mutters of the Refugee Travelers* (Bōmei ryokōsha wa sakebi tsubuyaku, 1984); *Music for a Somnambulant Kingdom* (Muyū ōkoku no tame no ongaku, 1984), awarded the Noma New Writer's Award; *I Am an Artificial Man* (Boku wa mozō ningen, 1985); *Heaven Is Tumbling Down* (Tengoku ga futte kuru, 1985); *Donna Anna* (1986); *Unidentified Shadowing Object* (Mikakunin bikō buttai, 1987); *Dream Messenger* (Yume-tsukai, 1989); *Rococoville* (Rococo-chō, 1990); *King of the Armadillos* (Arumajiro ō, 1991); *The Name of the Prophet* (Yogensha no namae, 1992); *Professor Equinox* (Higan sensei, 1992), winner of the Izumi Kyōka Prize; and *From Exile with Love* (Ryūkeichi yori ai o komete, 1995). Shimada has also published several essay collections, including *Don't Speak, Sing* (Katarazu, Utae, 1987) and *A Colonial Alice* (Shokuminchi no Arisu, 1993), and a book of essays on *Natsume Sōseki (Sōseki o kaku, 1993). In addition, he has been active in writing and producing plays, *Ulalume* (Urariumu, 1988, based on the poem of the same name by Poe), and *Luna* (Runa, 1990, inspired by Dante), and more recently he has been involved in music, acting as narrator on the recording of Otomo Yoshihide's *My Dear Mummy* (1996).

Shimada writes in a playful, yet intellectual style, his literature influenced by his readings of writers as varied as Dante, Poe, and Witold Gombrowicz. His fictional characters are typically those on the edges of society—rebels, orphans, and refugees. In his early works "A Divertimento for Gentle Leftists" and "Momotaro in a Capsule" (Kyapuseru no naka no Momotarō, 1983), Shimada traces the infertile ground for political or social rebellion faced by youth in 1980s Japan. "Divertimento" depicts radical student politics transformed into a kind of after-school club. Ideology has been replaced by "gentleness," radical political activity reduced to the level of a fashion statement. In "Momotaro in a Capsule" Japan is a "land of Potemkin villages and papier-mâché people" (123), where the "walls of control [are] covered in velvet" (125). The college student protagonists, "cell-cultured in a capsule of a massive housing development" (121), can only throw a feeble "tantrum" against the state (131), concluding that "maybe revolution *should* be in the mind" (145).

In other works Shimada more openly foregrounds questions of individual and national identity. "A Callow Fellow of Jewish Descent" (Yudayakei aonisai, 1991), for example, depicts a young Japanese schizophrenic who feels split by a "civil war at [his] nerve center" (9) between himself and his genes, which are "using me, a machine, for their own survival" (5). In an attempt to cure his schizophrenia and regain a stable identity, the protagonist goes to France, where he works for a refugee agency run by a Jewish man, Mr. Penman. Penman expresses envy for the youth's yet-to-be-fixed identity: "You are wonderfully zero" (19), he remarks, yet the conclusion reveals that Penman's identity as a Jew is not what it seems: he has "translated" himself into being Jewish (22).

The work that most fully encompasses Shimada's range of literary themes— identity, rebellion, and marginality—is the novel *Dream Messenger*. Written upon Shimada's return from a year as a visiting writer at Columbia University, *Dream Messenger* (subtitled "A Rental Child's New Tale of Two Cities") presents a more positive vision of the postmodern condition than either the earlier "The Legend of Saint Akahito" (Sei Akahito den, 1984) or the later novel *Rococoville*, both of which view the postmodern world less as utopian than as dystopian. The main character of *Dream Messenger*, Matthew/Masao, straddles boundaries of sexual, linguistic, and national identity as he works first as a "rental child" (one of a group of trained children who change identity to suit the needs of the families who rent them), then, as an adult, as a professional companion and lover. Despite the presence of this main character, the novel is, in postmodern fashion, decentered, featuring a large array of characters who relate their life stories and fade from view. Through these *Dream Messenger* treats a number of interesting motifs, all of which develop Shimada's postmodern concerns with the possibilities of diversity in modern Japan: life on the most remote of islands, the creation of independent countries within Japan, and the presence of a subculture of descendants of the Heike. The final pages of the novel, a rewriting of the creation story, posit the world as a work in progress—the chaotic result of "unprogrammed, free play."

Shimada has continued to experiment with a variety of themes and genres, writing stories on AIDS, religion, and supercomputers, and in his latest work, "Francisco X," beginning to work in the genre of the historical novel.

—*Philip Gabriel*

Bibliography

Asada Akira. "Infantile Capitalism and Japan's Postmodernism: A Fairy Tale." In Masao Miyoshi and H. D. Harootunian, eds., *Postmodernism and Japan*, 273–278. Durham, N.C.: Duke University Press, 1989.

Gabriel, Philip. "Dream Messengers, Rental Children, and the Infantile: Shimada Masahiko and the Possibilities of the Postmodern." In Stephen Snyder and Philip Gabriel, eds., *Ōe and Beyond: Fiction in Contemporary Japan*, 219–244. Honolulu: University of Hawai'i Press, 1999.

Maruya Saiichi. "Kaisetsu" (Commentary). In Shimizu Yoshinori, *Kokugo nyūshi mondai hisshōhō* (How to Pass Entrance Exam Questions in Japanese), 244–250. Tokyo: Kodansha, 1990.

Shimada Masahiko. "A Callow Fellow of Jewish Descent." Trans. Hiroaki Sato. In Helen Mitsios, ed., *New Japanese Voices: The Best Contemporary Fiction from Japan*, 1–22. New York: Atlantic Monthly Press, 1991.

——. *Dream Messenger*. Trans. Philip Gabriel. Tokyo: Kodansha International, 1992.

——. "Momotaro in a Capsule." Trans. Terry Gallagher. In Alfred Birnbaum, ed., *Monkey Brain Sushi: New Tastes in Japanese Fiction*, 113–146. Tokyo: Kodansha International, 1991.

Shimizu Yoshinori. *Jack and Betty Forever.* Trans. Frederik L. Schodt. Tokyo: Kodan-sha International, 1993.

——. "Japanese Entrance Exams for Earnest Young Men." Trans. Jeffery Hunter. In Alfred Birnbaum, ed., *Monkey Brain Sushi: New Tastes in Japanese Fiction,* 239–259. Tokyo: Kodansha International, 1991.

51

YOSHIMOTO BANANA

Although Yoshimoto Banana's (b. 1964, pen name of Yoshimoto Mahoko) place in the spotlight of literary stardom lasted for only a decade, her career and writings represent an important stage in Japanese cultural history. Banana's first published work, the novel *Kitchen* (Kitchin, 1987), propelled her to instant fame and sold tens of millions of copies. In the postwar period, neither youthful fame nor women writers are unusual, but Banana's entrance onto the cultural scene resulted in no less than the *Banana genshō* (Banana phenomenon).

What distinguishes Banana's success from that of other best-selling authors? First, her novels fueled a widespread public debate in Japan that raised significant questions about gendered categories of identity, subjectivity, the family, and nationalism. Another major sign of Banana's significance is her overwhelming and nearly instant commercial and critical reception and acceptance outside of Japan. By 1995, only eight years after her debut, thirty-nine translations of her major works had appeared in English, Italian, French, Korean, Spanish, and other languages, and she received much critical attention and even foreign literary prizes. Significantly, Banana's publishers, editors, and even the Japanese Foreign Ministry promoted her fiction abroad as having an international style, rather than as exotically Japanese, as had been the case with Nobel Prize-winner *Kawabata Yasunari, *Mishima Yukio, and other successful translated authors. Banana was marketed as being hip and in step with global youth culture.

Banana's most famous work, *Kitchen*, concerns the coming of age of one Sakurai Mikage. At the beginning of the novel, Mikage finds herself utterly alone after her grandmother's recent death (her parents having died in an accident years earlier) and looks for comfort in the familiar sights and sounds of her kitchen. Mikage is not alone for long, however, because Tanabe Yūichi, a young male friend of her grandmother, invites her to stay at his family's home during her mourning. When Mikage discovers the wonders of the Tanabes' attractive home, and especially their kitchen, she moves in and distracts herself from grief by doing what she enjoys most—cooking in a well-designed kitchen for appreciative eaters. For Mikage, the presence of Yūichi's transsexual mother (formerly father) Eriko enhances the warm atmosphere of her new environment. The three grow closer, and Mikage, fortified by her new family, goes to work as an assistant in a cooking school and moves out of the Tanabe house. Later, Mikage learns that Eriko has been murdered by an erstwhile admirer who became unhinged on learning of Eriko's sex change. After a second period of mourning and separation from Yūichi, Mikage decides that she wants to see him again. In the famous final passage, Mikage takes a long, expensive taxi ride to deliver a delicious bowl of *katsudon* (fried breaded pork on rice) to Yūichi, and the two are reunited.

Why have *Kitchen* and Banana's other early novels such as *Tsugumi* (1989) earned such attention? Critics point to Banana's nonchalant approach to provocative subjects such as the non-nuclear family, sexual orientation, incest, spirituality, new religions, death, violence, the single person, and AIDS, and her ability to make these often threatening themes palatable to readers. The comforting details of daily life dominate the novels, while the threatening specters of disease, spiritual confusion, and death maintain a muted presence. In *Kitchen*, the orphaned young people comfort themselves with deliciously described bowls of food, and, strikingly, their love remains on a platonic level, although the sensuality of food and its consumption assume an erotic dimension. Rather than portraying dystopian or alienating views of society, as is the case in the works of many well-known postwar authors such as *Ōe Kenzaburō or *Murakami Haruki, Banana typically offers readers comforting and upbeat spiritual solutions or means of emotional healing. In addition, Banana's prose is exceedingly easy to read and occasionally lyrical, winning the allegiance of many readers.

The Banana phenomenon encompassed an outpouring of discussions and writing about the *shōjo*, or premarriage female, and the ways that Banana's works were instrumental in evoking as appealing the subjectivity of heterosexual girlhood. Some readers interpreted the widespread acceptance of the *shōjo* as evoked in Banana's novels and of the genre of *shōjo* narratives as a privileging of female experience and expression, and thus a sign of rising feminism. Others saw the *shōjo* narratives as an escape from the responsibilities and burdens of adult working, family, and reproductive life, and thus figured the subjective realm of the *shōjo* as a social imaginary available to mature women and even men. Banana's novels further found their roots in *shōjo* culture because of their undeniable stylistic, conceptual, and thematic ties to *manga* (comic books), and in particular those aimed at a young female audience.

Yoshimoto Banana attended Nihon University, where her novella *Moonlight Shadow* (Munraito shadō) won a prize. Soon after graduation in 1987, her first published work, *Kitchen*, was awarded both the Izumi Kyōka Literary Prize and the Kaien Newcomer Award. Following the tremendous commercial and critical success of *Kitchen*, Banana wrote many other best sellers, such as *Tsugumi*, *N.P.* (1990), *Sad Prediction* (Kanashii yokan, 1988), *Deep Sleep* (Shirakawa yofune, 1989), *Lizard* (Tokage, 1993), and *Amrita: The Water the Gods Drink* (Amurita, 1994).

Banana was well acquainted with the ways writers work and live from childhood because of her father Yoshimoto Takaaki's (b. 1924) highly successful career as a poet, intellectual, and critic. In contrast to the philosophical and political seriousness of her father's writings, Yoshimoto Banana loved popular fiction (Stephen King and Japanese *manga* comics being among her favorites). The careers of the father and daughter form a striking contrast: Takaaki, who stood out as a relentless voice of political consciousness concerning wartime guilt and complicity in the early postwar, engaged with the U.S.-Japan Security Treaty protests of the 1960s and 1970s, and critiqued the postindustrial, high capitalist global consumer culture of the 1980s and 1990s; and Banana, whose narrative realm seems naive when it comes to domestic and global political concerns. Banana's links to popular culture—through the *manga* and her love of pop music and pulp fiction, East and West—rather than to elite art and thought, made many critics nervous even as they praised and speculated about the importance of her writing.

—Ann Sherif

Bibliography

Awaya Nobuko and David P. Phillips. "Popular Reading: The Literary World of the Japanese Working Woman." In Anne E. Imamura, ed., *Re-imaging Japanese Women*, 244–270. Berkeley: University of California Press, 1996.

Matsuoka Tsuneo. *Ajia no shūen: Yoshimoto Takaaki to Yoshimoto Banana no aida*. Tokyo: Yamato, 1990.

Sherif, Ann. "Japanese without Apology: Yoshimoto Banana and Healing." In Stephen Snyder and Philip Gabriel, eds., *Ōe and Beyond: Fiction in Contemporary Japan*, 278–301. Honolulu: University of Hawai'i Press, 1999.

Treat, John Whittier. "Yoshimoto Banana's Kitchen, or the Cultural Logic of Japanese Consumerism." In Lisa Skov and Brian Moeran, eds., *Women, Media, and Consumption in Japan*, 275–308. Honolulu: University of Hawai'i Press, 1995.

——. "Yoshimoto Banana Writes Home: Shōjo Culture and the Nostalgic Subject." *Journal of Japanese Studies* 19, no. 2 (1993): 353–387.

Yoshimoto Banana. *Amrita: The Water the Gods Drink*. Trans. Russell Wasden. New York: Grove Press, 1997.

——. *Kitchen*. Trans. Megan Backus. New York: Grove Press, 1993.

——. *Lizard*. Trans. Ann Sherif. New York: Grove Press, 1995.

——. *NP*. Trans. Ann Sherif. New York: Grove Press, 1994.

52

YAMADA EIMI

Yamada Eimi (b. 1959, pen name of Yamada Futaba) and her fiction are part of a particular phenomenon belonging to the 1980s and early 1990s, known as "the bubble," that gave rise to stories about young middle-class women who work in the sex trade for large amounts of money and a high-class lifestyle. Eimi, who has herself been a sex worker, started out as a *manga* (comic book) artist but soon moved into fiction. Her first novel, *Bedtime Eyes* (Beddo taimu aizu, 1985), won the Literary Arts Prize, and she has been publishing prodigiously since.

Her stories are famous for their sexual explicitness and assertive female characters, who are more often than not Japanese women in relationships with African Americans. Her work is controversial in both Japan and North America because it breaks many taboos in its openness about women, sex, sexuality, and sex work and because it deals with these themes in interracial, intercultural, and cross-class settings. It may not be the sex, but the money with the sex (and the gender of the author) that is creating the controversy, inasmuch as sex with prostitutes is a common enough theme in Japanese literature. The main arguments critics make are based on deciding whether Eimi's work and her values are feminist and liberatory or colonial and racist, yet the texts seem to support both arguments. Even though American and Japanese critics tend to take opposing stands, they all comment on the fact that Eimi's fiction contains what is variously described as vacillation or ambivalence. Though North Americans seem to see this as an instability in Eimi's personal politics, this vacillation or ambivalence is part of almost all of her work and is usually noted by Japanese critics as a change in the reader's feelings or thinking. It is clear that this movement is not there by accident or because of ambivalence in the author's own values, though it may speak of a definition of "power" that is specific to Eimi. The stories are set up so that nothing is ever in one position for long enough to be "pure" anything. Characters move from "sadist" to "masochist," prey to hunter, or buyer to bought in the space of a page. Women act like men and men act like children. Similar relationships may be set in different countries; all of the power references get switched ("bottoms" become "tops"); and assumptions about what is normal in any sexual relationship are questioned. Even the style of Eimi's writing reflects this vacillation; although it is very literary in its grammar and the aesthetic quality of the imagery, the content and the plethora of English loanwords that give authenticity to her worldly characters are more akin to pop fiction. It is possible to argue that this motion, the vacillation between extremes, creates the tension that drives the plot of most of her stories.

Like the singer Madonna, Eimi has worked very hard to create a public persona that is sold along with her novels. In *After School Keynotes* (Hōkago no kīnōto, 1989), a collection of short stories that was serialized in a young women's fashion magazine called *Olive*, Yamada explains to high-school girls how to be a cool, stylish woman like herself. This same didactic element runs through all of Eimi's works, though not always as explicitly as in *After School Keynotes*. On a fundamental level, Eimi's stories attempt to play on basic insecurities. Readers have to want to some degree at some time to be beautiful, popular, or sexually desirable. Eimi captures these feelings—the desire and the derision the desire produces—and harnesses them into stories. As the characters move from paroxysms of pleasure to the pits of despair and back again, the readers, too, enjoy their own agony. The lifestyle of the beautiful ones is held out like a proverbial carrot, making the readers feel hopeful and hopeless all at once.

Another frequent element of Eimi's fiction is physical attraction between women. Most of her stories are centered on the relationship between the female narrator and a female friend. The relationship is always described in older sister-younger sister, or *senpai-kōhai* (senior-junior) terms. The older sister is usually "different" in some way, and it is the narrator's secret yearning for this difference, or sexual maturity, that draws them together. "Bedtime Eyes" (one section of *Bedtime Eyes*) a story about protagonist Kim's love for an African American soldier, is framed by her relationship with "Maria Oneesan" (older sister Maria), the stripper who introduced her to the world of foreign men. At the climax of the story, when Kim finds Maria in bed with her man, Maria claims that she did it because she loved Kim but had no other way to get closer. *Kneel Down and Lick My Feet* (Hiza mazuite, ashi o oname, 1988), a bitterly angry critique of the Japanese publishing world that is reputed to be semiautobiographical, is about a Tokyo S/M queen who becomes a prizewinning writer. This story, too, is told through the relationship between the heroine and a "senior" at work with many comments between them about going beyond platonic friendship.

Whether the relationships between the women are sexually consummated or are openly lesbian, the female relationships form the central structure of the narratives and are, therefore, at least as important as the protagonist's relationships with male lovers. These are stories about sex, and it is the *stories* that are traded between women. This complicates any simple arguments critics might make about the racial colonialism of Eimi's fiction. The racism is not in having sex with black American soldiers, just as the liberation is not in wearing red Chanel lipstick; the "othering" and the "selfing" are in the writing and the reading, the producing and consuming of these signs. Both sides are there in the same story as Yamada Eimi gives readers both a body and a mind and the hope to be the woman with the story to tell one day.

—*Alwyn Spies*

Bibliography

Yamada Eimi. *After School Keynotes.* Trans. Sonya L. Johnson. Tokyo: Kodansha International, 1992.

———. "Bedtime Eyes." Trans. Charles M. DeWolf. *Japanese Literature Today* 11 (1986): 309–318.

———. *Kneel Down and Lick My Feet.* (Excerpt.) Trans. Terry Gallagher. In Alfred Birnbaum, ed., *Monkey Brain Sushi: New Tastes in Japanese Fiction,* 184–202. Tokyo: Kodansha International, 1991.

53

POSTWAR POETRY

Japan's "modern poetry" is postwar poetry. The country's defeat in World War II was not only complete in the material sense but also entailed a seemingly complete reversal in values. Demilitarization replaced militarism, and democratization replaced thought-regimentation. The majority of intellectuals, poets among them, had sided, willingly or under duress, with their country's militaristic causes during the war. As a result, many were harshly denounced as enemies of the people for their *sensō sekinin*, or "war responsibility." And most intellectuals quickly reversed themselves, many trying to erase their wartime pronouncements and writings from the record.

Symbolic of the material and psychological devastation was the second formation, in 1947, of a poets' group called Arechi (The Waste Land). The original Arechi group was formed in 1939 with the aim of rejecting Romantic tendencies, and it folded in 1940. In contrast, its reincarnation was built on the simple premise that Japan in its defeat was a wasteland, both materially and spiritually. The second group was as short-lived as the first, but it had an enduring influence. Representative of the Arechi view was Tamura Ryūichi (1923–1998). The title poem of his first book, *Four Thousand Days and Nights* (Yonsen no hi to yoru, 1966), is typical, and begins:

> For a piece of poetry to be born,
> we must kill

must kill many people,
we shoot, assassinate, poison many people we love.

And "Sunken Temple" (Shizumeru tera, 1956), one of a sequence of nine prose poems, begins: "People all over the world want proof of death. But no one has ever witnessed death. In the end, people may be a mere illusion, and reality the greatest common divisor of such things."

Another Arechi poet, Ayukawa Nobuo (1920–1986), also typified the spirit of the time. The first two stanzas of his poem "The Dead Man" (Shinda otoko, 1947), which announced the advent of postwar poetry, may be translated:

> For example, out of the fog
> and the footfalls on every staircase,
> an executor vaguely emerges.
>
> A distant yesterday ...
> we would sit on the chairs in a dark bar,
> not knowing what to do with our distorted faces,
> turning a letter envelope inside out.
> "In reality, no shadow, no form?"
> —Having failed to die, that certainly was the case.

The severity of social conditions began to ease in the 1950s, and as this happened the "wasteland" view of the world started losing its imaginative hold—although Tamura, Ayukawa, and some others maintained their view of the world long after Japan recovered from the war devastation. At any rate, if the fault line between prewar and postwar poetry lies in the absence or presence of "anxiety and suffering felt unconsciously or vaguely that can't be ratiocinated," as the poet-critic Yoshimoto Takaaki (b. 1924) has put it, the Arechi group embodied such "anxiety and suffering."

Along with the Arechi, the Rettō (Archipelago) group, which came into being in 1952 with several motley poets' groups banding together, played an important role in the formative years of postwar poetry. Basically left-leaning, it defined itself as "a gathering of poets with the intent to carry the fate of the folk on their backs." Among the contributors to its magazine, *Rettō*, published from 1952 to 1955, there are some surprises. *Abe Kōbō went on to write internationally renowned avant-garde fiction and plays. Andō Tsuguo (b. 1919), trained in French literature, became an outstanding commentator on *haikai* (Edo-period verse composed in the vernacular). The presence of at least one Korean poet, Kyo Nanki (Huh Nam-ki, 1918–1988), should also be noted.

Hasegawa Ryūsei (b. 1928), one of the several Rettō poets who have remained prominent since the group's dispersal, has written some of the more foreboding poems reflecting that turbulent period. For example, the title poem of his first book, *Pavlov's Cranes* (Paburofu no tsuru, 1957), begins:

> Beating sturdy feathers,
> exerting the power of flight,
> severing and rebounding
> the mist in space,
> their oar, wings, a single motion,
> thousands of migrant birds, their vibrations,
> begin to echo in the depth of my ear.

Just about the time the Rettō group was disintegrating, a distinct voice emerged. Oda Kyūrō, who founded the influential poetry monthly *Modern Poetry Notebook* (Gendaishi techō) in 1959 and started an unparalleled paperback series for modern poets in 1968, has recollected the great excitement created in 1954 by a poem submitted to the magazine of which he was editor. Called "Night's Invitation" (Yoru no shōtai), the poem begins:

> Outside the window, a pistol shot,
> the curtain instantly
> set on fire
> and so comes the hour I waited for:
> night, like a regiment,
> framed with cellophane—
> France, be reconciled with Spain.

The writer was Ishihara Yoshirō (1915–1977), who had only a year earlier returned from eight years in Siberian concentration camps. Though he had little grounding in poetry writing and would not publish his first book of poems, *Sancho Panza's Homecoming* (Sancho Pansa no kikyō, 1963), until he was forty-eight, Ishihara went on to write, in taut language, some of the more memorable poems haunted by the war and its aftermath. Invariably counted among postwar masterpieces is his "Funeral Train" (Sōshiki ressha, 1955). It begins:

> What station we started from
> no one remembers.
> Only, through a strange land where it's always midday on the right
> and midnight on the left
> the train goes on running.

Among other poets, Takarabe Toriko (b. 1933), three of whose books have won prizes (the latest, *Nonexistent People* [Uyū no hito, 1998], received the Hagiwara Sakutarō Prize), continues to write poems colored directly or indirectly by her girlhood in Manchuria and the loss of her father and sister while the family was fleeing the puppet state after Japan's defeat. Koyanagi Reiko (b. 1935), has also written poems haunted by the war. Her sixth book, *Rabbit of the Nether World* (Yomi no usagi, 1989), is an attempt to lay to rest the ghosts from her war-ravaged girlhood through a collage of prose and poems.

There have, of course, been poets seemingly unaffected by the war or various postwar ideologies. The first to attract attention in this group was Tanikawa Shuntarō (b. 1931), who at age twenty-one debuted with *Two Billion Light-Years of Solitude* (Nijū-oku kōnen no kodoku, 1952). It opened with a poem called "Growth" (Seichō, 1972), a parody of a Confucian statement, and reads in its entirety:

> Three years old:
> I had no past.
>
> Five years old:
> My past went as far as yesterday.
>
> Seven years old:
> My past went as far as topknots.
>
> Eleven years old:
> My past went as far as dinosaurs.
>
> Fourteen years old:
> My past was as textbooks said it was.
>
> Sixteen years old:
> I stared at the infinity of my past frightened.
>
> Eighteen years old:
> I did not know what time was.

Tanikawa went on to become an exceedingly popular and prolific poet—one of a handful capable of making a living solely as a poet. Among his lines often quoted are,

> Shall I speak the truth?
> I pretend to be a poet,
> but I'm not a poet.

This deadpan lucidity is one characteristic that makes Tanikawa attractive.

In 1955 Yoshioka Minoru (1919–1990) published *Still Life* (Seibutsu), with its title poem:

Within the hard surface of night's bowl
Intensifying their bright colors
The autumn fruits
Apples, pears, grapes, and so forth
Each as they pile
Upon another
Goes close to sleep
To one theme
To spacious music
Each core, reaching its own heart
Reposes
Around it circles
The time of rich putrefaction
Now before the teeth of the dead
The fruits and their kind
Which unlike stones do not strike
Add to their weight
And in the deep bowl
Behind this semblance of night
On occasion
Hugely tilt

With this poem Yoshioka, called "a nonsurrealist surrealist," opened up an unusual poetic vista. Someone who started out as a romantic tanka poet à la Kitahara Hakushū (see "Free Verse in the Taishō Era"), he went on to etch daily scenes of modern life with sensual, often grotesque details that verge on abstraction.

Japanese poetry today covers a wide ground. At one end there is Yoshimasu Gōzō (b. 1939), whose shamanistic, incantatory poetry does not come alive until you actually hear him; and at the other end there is Shinkawa Kazue (b. 1929), who records daily comings and goings with quiet wonder. Here I want to mention three other distinctive voices that emerged from the 1950s to the 1960s: Shiraishi Kazuko (b. 1931), Tomioka Taeko (b. 1935), and Takahashi Mutsuo (b. 1937).

Shiraishi, born in Vancouver, joined the avant-garde poetic group VOU, led by Kitazono Katsue (1902–1978), in her teens and later shocked some with her sexual explicitness. Her 1970 book *The Season of the Sacred Lecher* (Seinaru inja no kisetsu), which describes a jazz-enveloped sexual adventure, has such passages as:

even now wet with men's semen
burnt by the flames of their penises
getting high, continuing to be wet

and

all, the penises continuing to weep
caressing like petals
the wombs continuing to laugh.

The book won the Mr. H. Prize. Shiraishi has remained at the forefront of the movement to combine poetry with jazz.

Tomioka—"a native of Osaka, resident of Tokyo, and visitor to New York, she has the big city dweller's savvy and refusal to be awed by affectation or cant," as Burton Watson put it in introducing a selection of her poems in English, *See You Soon*—created an oeuvre of chatty, "pronoun-infatuated" poetry in a span of a dozen years before quitting the genre in the early 1970s in favor of fiction and drama. (See "The 1960s and 1970s Boom in Women's Writing.") Among her poems is "Let Me Tell You about Myself" (Minoue-banashi), which begins:

Because both Dad and Mom
Even the old midwife
In fact every single prophet
Bet that I'd be a boy
I tore out of the placenta determinedly a girl.

Takahashi Mutsuo became Japan's first poet to celebrate homosexuality openly. Debuting with *Mino, My Bull* (Mino watashi no oushi, 1959), he collected highly dramatic, finely structured poems, long and short, in several volumes, among them *Sleeping, Sinning, Falling* (Nemuri to okashi to rakka to, 1965), the one thousand-line paean to the male body *Ode of Praise* (Homeuta, 1971), and *Self-Portraits* (Watakushi, 1975). Although he later turned to more or less nonsexual themes, he also stands out among postwar Japanese poets for doing equally well in tanka and haiku, winning prizes in those traditional genres as well.

Two of the great literary events in recent years have had to do with poetry collections that returned to these two traditional poetic forms. (See "The Revival of Poetry in Traditional Forms.") *Salad Anniversary* (Sarada kinenbi, 1987), the book by the tanka poet Tawara Machi (b. 1962), sold a staggering 2.6 million copies, while *Summer on Side B* (B-men no natsu, 1994), the book by the haiku poet Mayuzumi Madoka (b. 1965), sold sixty thousand copies (unprecedented for a haiku book) and thrust the author into media stardom. Both books light-heartedly describe a love affair.

—*Hiroaki Sato*

Bibliography

Guest, Harry, Lynn Guest, and Kajima Shōzō, eds. *Postwar Japanese Poetry*. London: Penguin, 1972.

Kijima, Hajime, ed. *The Poetry of Postwar Japan*. Ames: University of Iowa Press, 1975.

Kimura Nobuko. *The Village Beyond*. Trans. Hiroaki Sato. Middletown Springs, Vt.: P.S., A Press, 2002.

Koyanagi Reiko. *Rabbit of the Nether World*. Trans. Hiroaki Sato. Winchester, Va.: Red Moon Press, 1999.

Lueders, Edward, and Koriyama Naoshi. *Like Underground Water: Poetry of Mid-Twentieth Century Japan*. Port Townsend, Wash.: Copper Canyon Press, 1997.

Nagashima Minako. *The Girl Who Turned into Tea*. Trans. Hiroaki Sato. Middletown Springs, Vt.: P.S., A Press, 2000.

Ōoka, Makoto, and Thomas Fitzsimmons. *A Play of Mirrors: Eight Major Poets of Modern Japan*. Muncie, Ind.: Katydid, 1987.

Sato, Hiroaki, and Burton Watson, eds. *From the Country of Eight Islands: An Anthology of Japanese Poetry*. New York: Doubleday, 1981.

Shiffert, Edith Marcombe, and Yūki Sawa, eds. *Anthology of Modern Japanese Poetry*. Rutland, Vt., and Tokyo: Charles E. Tuttle, 1972.

Shinkawa Kazue. *Not a Metaphor*. Trans. Hiroaki Sato. Middletown Springs, Vt.: P.S., A Press, 1999.

Shiraishi Kazuko. *Let Those Who Appear*. Trans. Samuel Grolmes and Tsumura Yumiko. New York: New Directions, 2002.

Takahashi, Mutsuo, and Hiroaki Sato. *Sleeping. Sinning. Falling*. San Francisco: City Lights Books, 1992.

Tamura Ryūichi. *Poems, 1946–1998*. Trans. Samuel Grolmes and Tsumura Yumiko. Palo Alto, Calif.: CCC Books, 2000.

Tawara Machi. *Salad Anniversary*. Trans. Juliet Winters Carpenter. Tokyo: Kodansha International, 1990.

Thwaite, Anthony, ed. *The Penguin Book of Japanese Verse*. London: Penguin, 1964.

Tomioka Taeko. *See You Soon*. Trans. Hiroaki Sato. Chicago: Chicago Review Press, 1979.

54

POSTWAR EXPERIMENTAL THEATER I: *ANGURA*

A search for national and personal identity unifies the diverse performance and playwriting styles in Japan after World War II. In the wake of traumatic social changes, intellectuals and artists pondered the very foundations of reality. Young theater artists rebelled against Western-style, primarily realistic *shingeki* (new drama). *Shingeki*'s ideals had been inspired by Western dramatists such as Ibsen and Stanislavski. Consequently, many postwar Japanese theater artists viewed it as politically corrupt, morally bankrupt, and artistically dead.

These younger artists identified with the outrageous, sexually ambiguous, outcast actors of early seventeenth-century Kabuki, called *kawara kojiki* (riverbed beggars). They laced their productions with aspects of previously disparaged indigenous culture such as magic, shamanistic practices, and traveling rural performance genres. They rejected standard concepts of beauty, disdained commercial theater buildings, embraced political protest, encouraged anguished personal narrative, sanctioned sexually or socially shocking performance, and championed marginalized or outcast groups. Some dramatists reenvisioned or refashioned aspects of Euro-American avant-garde theater.

Despite phenomenal economic prosperity, many intellectuals harbored a complex love-hate relationship with the United States. Others remained conflicted about or disturbed by prewar Japanese militarism and imperialism. Political events of the 1960s to early 1970s galvanized an entire generation. Widespread anger over the 1960 ratification of the U.S.-Japan Security Treaty escalated to massive protests against the Vietnam War in 1968–1969. In 1972, the

Japanese left was utterly confused and demoralized by the spectacle of Japanese Red Army terrorists committing murder at the Tel Aviv Airport.

ANGURA: 1960s–1970s

The "first generation" of Japanese avant-garde theater is termed *angura*, an abbreviation of the English "underground." *Angura* plays are among the most vital of the past fifty years. Numerous works critique Japanese materialism or American-style popular culture. Others explore the legacy of the atomic blasts. Often the sociopolitical content is submerged in theatricality or metaphor.

Japan's lyrically grotesque *butō*, the postwar "dance of darkness" created by Hijikata Tatsumi (1928–1986) and Ōno Kazuo (b. 1906), has philosophical connections with *angura*. (See "*Butō* and Performance Art.") For early *butō* artists, the goal was to break out of culture-bound aesthetic concepts and to seek the primeval essence of the human soul. They embraced all that is human, without regard for nationality, race, time, or gender—even things considered foul, diseased, vulgar, or ugly. *Butō* also influenced *angura*'s performance style. For example, *butō* performers often shave the hair from their heads and bodies, paint themselves white all over, appear nearly naked, and practice contortions that challenge standard concepts of human endurance and beauty.

Most scholars identify *The Elephant* (Zō, 1962) by Betsuyaku Minoru (b. 1937) as the first significant *angura* play. Betsuyaku was influenced by the theater of Samuel Beckett and by the compressed, allusive poetry of Noh. *The Elephant* concerns a man and his uncle, both victims of the atomic blasts, who await the inevitable symptoms of contamination. They are frozen in an emotionless void, unable to feel affection or hatred, clinging to memories and fantasies as they await death. The uncle remembers a time just after the war when strangers would pay to see or touch his gruesome keloid scar. He would smear it with oil to make it glisten. Nowadays, people seem indifferent. He can no longer earn a living by displaying his contaminated body. His nephew floats unconsciously through life, unable even to test the direction of the wind. In one sequence (placed in the middle of the play like the *ai-kyōgen*, or comic/explanatory interlude, of a Noh play), a man insists on a deadly duel with a stranger. There is no reason; he does not know his victim, nor has the stranger done anything to provoke him. The killing is without malice, arbitrary, merely a force of nature. The victim's incomprehension is not unlike the reactions of children and other civilians exposed to the atomic bombs.

Betsuyaku has written more than seventy plays and won numerous awards. Among his major works are *The Little Match Girl* (Matchi-uri no shōjo, 1966), which uses Hans Christian Andersen's fairy tale to suggest painful yet nostalgic wartime memories. *The Legend of Noon* (Shōgo no densetsu, 1973) invokes the meaninglessness of clinging to discredited political or militarist beliefs. *A-bubblin', A-boilin'* (Aabukutatta, niitatta, 1976) treats the empty lives of contemporary office workers. *The Story of Two Knights Traveling around the Country* (Shokoku o henrekisuru futari no kishi no monogatari, 1987) combines aspects of Cervantes's *Don Quixote* with Beckettian themes. Unlike many *angura* dramatists, Betsuyaku accentuates dramatic text rather than performance.

In 1966 Betsuyaku joined director-theorist Suzuki Tadashi (b. 1939) and others to found the Waseda Little Theater (Waseda shōgekijō). Suzuki, who had directed *The Elephant* in 1962, is internationally renowned for creating an intense, physical actor-training method emphasizing rhythmic movements of the lower body and feet. He maintains that this physical connection to the earth is primal, and he sees his method as opposed to overly realistic, intellectual, psychological *shingeki*. For inspiration, Suzuki turned away from Western drama. Instead, he uses physically strenuous Asian training methods, including unique variations of Kabuki, Noh, and Indian *kathakali*.

Many of Suzuki's directorial works are radical revisions or deconstructions of Western classics, such as Greek tragedies or the plays of Shakespeare. His interest lies both in the power of performance and in finding the Japanese and universal aspects of mythic tales. Through the late 1980s, the powerful, deep-voiced actress Shiraishi Kayoko (b. 1941) often starred in his internationally acclaimed works. *The Trojan Women* (Toroiya no onna, 1974) shifts between ancient Troy and war-devastated Japan. As a Buddhist deity helplessly watches, the spirits of Hecuba and Cassandra possess an anguished beggar woman, portrayed by Shiraishi, who experiences rape and murder anew. Ragged bands of starving, defeated soldiers roam the land in this passionate antiwar play. In 1984 Suzuki's troupe moved to remote Toga, taking the English name SCOT (Suzuki Company of Toga). SCOT hosts an annual international theater festival in the summers.

Actor-director-playwright Kara Jūrō (b. 1940) founded the precursor to his Situation Theater (Jōkyō gekijō), now called Kara and Company (Kara gumi), in 1963. He set up a huge, portable red tent at Kyoto's Shijō–Kawaramachi intersection, where Okuni is said to have performed her first Kabuki dance around 1600. The Situation Theater's red tent had no permanent location, reflecting the outcast status of Kabuki's early "riverbed beggars." Kara's scripts—idiosyncratic, comedic, often bawdy retellings of well-known Japanese or Western tales—mingle past and present in allegorical, sometimes surreal, nonlinear plots. Kara feels that his style reflects the psychosocial disorientation of postwar Japan. *John Silver: The Beggar of Love* (Jon Shirubâ: Ai no kojiki, 1970) takes place simultaneously in a bombed-out toilet in postwar Japan and in a cabaret in Japanese-occupied Manchuria. John Silver has been transformed into a rogue Japanese imperialist. The play focuses on the legendary pirate's (and thus Japan's) craving for forgiveness. *Two Women* (Futari no onna, 1979) shifts supernatural events from the *Tale of Genji* (c. 1000) to a psychiatric ward. As in *John Silver* and other plays, characters are transformed and combined. For example, a single actress plays three roles. These include the vindictive Lady Rokujō, who possesses the soul of her rival in love Aoi, only to find Aoi pursuing her until the two souls/bodies mingle. In the end, the mad woman/women hangs/hang herself/themselves by leaping from a rafter. Kara suggests that the classical certainties of identity, madness and sanity, even right and wrong are no longer valid in the postwar era. Kara is interested in communicating his political and artistic ideas to the developing world and has toured to Bangladesh and Korea and to Palestinian refugee camps.

Terayama Shūji (1935–1983) was unquestionably Japan's most experimental postwar dramatist, devoted to testing the limits of theater. Terayama disdained leftist politics. He wanted to create "revolution through imagination." This internationally acclaimed, award-winning poet, playwright, director, filmmaker, essayist, and photographer also wrote provocative essays encouraging adolescent rebellion. Some productions provoked scandal and legal actions due to nudity or alleged violence to audience members.

Terayama founded the theater laboratory The Peanut Gallery (Tenjō sajiki) in 1967 and the journal *Underground Theater* (Chika engeki) in 1969. Early plays such as *The Hunchback of Aomori* (Aomori-ken no semushi otoko, 1967), *La Marie Vison* (Kegawa no Marî, 1967; also called *Mink Marie*), *Inugami: The Dog God* (Inugami, 1969), *Jashūmon* (1971; also known as *Gate of the Heretics*), and his finest film, *Cache-Cache Pastorale* (Den'en ni shisu, 1975; also known as *Death in the Countryside*), evoke a nightmarish world of fictional (or imagined) autobiography in which a young boy confronts demonic mother figures, circus freaks, forbidden sexuality, rural superstitions, and death. These plays often have subtextual, anti-American references. For example, *The Hunchback of Aomori* reworks the Oedipus story, set in rural Japan during the Taishō era. A poor hunchbacked thief is sexually assaulted and possibly murdered by the grotesque, westernized mother (herself a victim of rape by her master's son) who had abandoned him. The child can be seen as traditional Japan (spiritually thirsty and innocent, yet deformed because of the horrific facts of his conception), while the mother can be interpreted as both the hated/desired West and as the appalling result of Japanese infatuation with the West.

In various versions of *Throw away Your Books, Go out into the Streets* (Sho o suteyō, machi e deyō, 1967, 1968; film 1971), Terayama's teenage disciples recited their own anguished, autobiographical poetry. *Directions to Servants* (Nuhikun, 1979) featured nearly naked, white-painted actors performing bizarre, apparently sexual behavior with complex machines to encourage rebellion against authority. Plays such as *A Journal of the Plague Year* (Ekibyō ryūkōki, 1975) experimented with "invisible theater" or total darkness, forcing audiences into cramped, dark corners while scenes were enacted for only a few. In contrast, "town dramas" such as *Man-Powered Plane Solomon* (Jinriki hikōki soromon, 1970) were performed all over the city by "guerrilla" actors simultaneously accosting unsuspecting citizens. In both cases, Terayama's goal was to awaken imagination. The Peanut Gallery troupe regularly toured Europe and performed occasionally in America. It disbanded after Terayama's death, though his provocative plays are still performed by other troupes.

AFTER *ANGURA*

Theater in the 1980s highlighted the cool, hip, "postmodern" attitude of affluent, complacent youth. Writer-director Noda Hideki (b. 1955) offered fast-paced science fiction, parodies, and plays styled like *manga* (comic books). His works include *The Demigod* (Hanshin, 1986) and *Beneath a Forest of Cherry Blossoms: A Parody* (Gansaku sakura no mori no mankai no shita, 1989). Kawamura Takeshi (b. 1959) founded Daisan Erotica, which presented brutal, futuristic visions such as *Nippon Wars* (Nippon wōzu, 1984).

After 1989 playwrights turned inward in reaction to economic recession, disillusionment with government, and natural and man-made disasters. These playwrights disdained raucous theatricality and playfulness. Iwamatsu Ryō (b. 1952) is a major force in this "quiet theater." Plays such as his *Tea and a Lecture* (Ocha to sekkyō, 1986) and *Futon and Daruma* (Futon to Daruma, 1988) seek reality in minutely observed details of ordinary life. "Quiet theater" uses minimal plot. Other notable "quiet theater" works include *Fireflies* (Kami o kakiageru, 1996) by Suzue Toshirō (b. 1963) and *Citizens of Seoul* (Sōru shimin, 1989) by Hirata Oriza (b. 1962).

—*Carol Fisher Sorgenfrei*

Bibliography

Goodman, David. *After Apocalypse: Four Plays of Hiroshima and Nagasaki*. New York: Columbia University Press, 1986.

——. *Japanese Drama and Culture in the 1960s: The Return of the Gods*. Armonk, N.Y.: M. E. Sharpe, 1988.

Japan Playwrights Association. *Half a Century of Japanese Theater I: The 1990s, Part 1*. Tokyo: Kinokuniya, 1999.

Ortolani, Benito. *The Japanese Theatre: From Shamanistic Ritual to Contemporary Pluralism*. Leiden: E.J. Brill, 1990; rev. ed. Princeton: Princeton University Press, 1994.

Rolf, Robert, and John Gillespie, eds. *Alternative Japanese Drama: Ten Plays*. Honolulu: University of Hawai'i Press, 1992.

Senda Akihiko. *The Voyage of Contemporary Japanese Theater*. Trans. J. Thomas Rimer. Honolulu: University of Hawai'i Press, 1997.

Suzuki Tadashi. *The Way of Acting: The Theater Writings of Tadashi Suzuki*. Trans. J. Thomas Rimer. New York: Theatre Communications Group, 1986.

Takaya, Ted T., ed. *Modern Japanese Drama: An Anthology*. New York: Columbia University Press, 1979.

55

POSTWAR EXPERIMENTAL THEATER II:
BUTŌ AND PERFORMANCE ART

Japanese theatrical experimentation began in the late 1950s and flowered in the 1960s, inspired in large part by Hijikata Tatsumi (1928–1986). The frenetic creativity and the manic performances of what he would eventually call *ankoku butō* (dance of darkness), had a tremendous influence on the experimental theater and dance performances that were to follow.

The *butō* movement Hijikata created has become the only true Japanese theatrical export of the twentieth century. The *butō* performance style, in its truest form never a fixed mode of expression, was initially a number of challenging stylistic experiments performed by Hijikata Tatsumi, Ōno Kazuo (b. 1906), and Kasai Akira (b. 1955). Though the elder statesman and initial master of the group was Ōno, who continues to dance internationally well past the age of ninety, the *auteur* of the group was Hijikata. With a devoted following in Tokyo subculture, Hijikata created a series of performances in which his own mesmerizing dances became the vortex for performative experimentation. The year 1959 saw the creation of *Forbidden Colors* (Kinjiki), based on the novel of that name by *Mishima Yukio. Hijikata's disturbing work flew in the face of the structured beauty of conventional dance.

Although *butō*'s pioneers tried to distance themselves from Western modern dance, the influence of German *Neue Tanz* (new dance) and 1960s "happenings" was evident in Hijikata's early *butō* works. A compelling performer, he found support among young Japanese theater people and the Japanese artistic elite in the tumultuous 1960s. With artistic revolution in the air, *butō* flourished alongside new and exotic forms of theater it helped to inspire. "[Hijikata's] haggard body, apparently at the nadir of ignoble impotence, moving with an extreme slowness reminiscent of Noh was the visible epitome of everything that was opposed to the comfortable intelligibility of modern culture. His art was at once a critique of modernity and a manifesto of a new aesthetics rooted in the 'darkness' within the Japanese body and psyche" (Rolf and Gillespie 1992:6). By the 1970s, in performances such as 27 *Nights for Four Seasons* (performed on twenty-seven consecutive nights in 1972), Hijikata's *butō* style was fully developed. Exemplified by a shaven head and face painted white (to hide his expression), Hijikata's appearance is what overseas audiences have come to expect from all *butō* performers. In Hijikata's performances, budding theater artists saw an otherworldly display of gathered energy; muscles and sinews taut, ribs, jaws, and limbs straining to break free of flesh in an often slow-motion display of disciplined body language. He was a performer working against his own body and against accepted norms of Japanese performance. Hijikata continued to choreograph and direct after he stopped giving public performances, working mainly with female *butō* performers seldom seen outside Japan, and his death in 1986 left an absence that contributed to a splintering of styles as the students he and others inspired went beyond their teachers in search of their own voices.

Butō has been diversifying in style since its inception. It is now an aesthetic dance form known for creating a strangely evocative and deformed world of images tinged with disconcerting humor, and featuring cross-dressing, skeletal dancers whose bodies are seemingly at war with themselves. Ōno Kazuo has preserved Hijikata's *butō* style at its purest; Dairakudakan (Great Camel Battleship), Byakkosha (White Tiger Brigade), and the women's *butō* group Hakutobo (founded by Hijikata) have evolved their own styles as Hijikata's descendents; Min Tanaka is a self-made maverick and leader of Maijuku; and Sankaijuku (Mountain-Ocean School), together with its leader Amagatsu Ushio—formerly of Dairakudakan—works predominantly in France and Japan and is perhaps the most famous troupe worldwide. Solo performers include Fukuhara Tetsurō, Goi Teru, Iwana Masaki, Katsura Kan, Kim Itō, Mori Shigeya, and Ōno Kazuo, among others. There are also troupes based in the United States, France, and Germany.

THE EXPERIMENTAL THEATER/
LITTLE THEATER MOVEMENT

Hijikata inspired theater artists as well as dancers, and the large-scale social unrest of the 1960s may have further inspired many individuals to follow his lead. Although theater artists themselves had and have strong opinions about how their work should be viewed, critics and scholars still do not agree on terminology to describe experimental Japanese theater. *Shingeki* (new drama) most often refers to realistic, Western-based modern drama, but it is often the generic term used to distinguish contemporary works from traditional forms like Noh and Kabuki. In the 1960s, *angura (an abbreviation of the English word "underground") was a term used to refer to new experimental dramas springing up outside of regular playhouses and known modes of modern expression. Eventually, the totality of experimental troupes came to be referred to as the *shōgekijō undō* (little theater movement—in reference to the types of small, nontraditional theater spaces used), although this is also sometimes called the "post-*shingeki* movement." The confusion and sometimes hostility over what to call themselves and each other continues and has very real consequences when it comes to organizing associations that could help with financing, for example. Regardless of the terminology used, most experimental performances are decidedly anti-*shingeki*, and as such interested in creating a drama far from realism.

The long-time experimental theater critic Senda Akihiko looks at experimental theater generationally. He has credited the first generation of *shōgekijō* artists with a number of achievements: the creation of a contemporary theater with a Japanese identity; companies that created original works or at the very least created unique styles of interpretation; a movement away from realistic plays tracing the linear flow of time in ordinary life; emphasis on actors' bodies, as in Kara Jūrō's "privileged body theory" and Suzuki Tadashi's "Suzuki Method"; performance spaces not limited to conventional playhouses; and attempts to close the distance between traditional and contemporary theater (Senda 1997). Senda delineates the production styles of four generations of such artists, and his collection of reviews is probably the most valuable look at the variety and vitality of experimental theater in Japan.

The predominant production structure for experimental performances is theater troupes. Groups of artists, inspired by the first generation and their near cultlike devotion to troupe leaders, spend years together developing their individual voices and approaches to theater. Nevertheless, a structure gaining more use, although in existence since the 1970s, is the so-called producer system. This is analogous to the way Broadway productions are assembled, a production mode that gathers individual artists and technicians for a particular performance set. More and more artists with some experience are turning to this mode over the long, and in some ways limiting, experiences within a particular troupe.

Also worth noting is an increase in experimental drama outside the hothouse of Tokyo. Other than barnstorming tours that became almost a staple for radical troupes in the late 1960s and early 1970s, during the second half of the twentieth century Japan saw theatrical activities center almost exclusively on the capital city. In the early 1990s, however, local governing bodies began to show an interest in constructing theaters and supporting local theatrical activities. Exemplary among practitioners is first generation artist Suzuki Tadashi, who has long organized an annual gathering of experimental performances in the remote mountain village of Toga. He was appointed art director of the ACM Theater, built by the city of Mito, and more recently, art director of four prefectural theaters in Shizuoka Prefecture.

Experimental Japanese theater involves young people who choose to participate in a public spectacle best described not as amateur, but rather as not quite professional. A structured system of sponsoring institutions and related professionals feeds off performances, while the performers themselves receive little immediate monetary compensation. There are leagues that look out for their own, realignments, and constantly shifting policy debates. Ancillary personnel and landowners profit. A willing public is entertained. The groups performing are often subsidized, however inadequately, by the government or private parties. The lack of a formal theatrical education (only three colleges in Japan have theater in the curriculum, and none concentrates on practical theater), the lack of unifying forces of consistent intellectual criticism, a need for theatrical self-expression that has grown through at least four generations, and a performer-centered rather than audience-centered approach to experimental theatrical creation has resulted in a theater landscape much different from that of the West. Experimental artists are spinning out personal, quirky, idiosyncratic dramatic visions that can be added to this landscape.

—*Brett Johnson*

Bibliography

Blackwood, Michael. *Butoh: Body on the Edge of Crisis.* Videotape. Michael Blackwood Productions, 1990.

Goodman, David G. *Japanese Drama and Culture in the 1960s.* New York: An East Gate Book, 1988.

Klein, Susan Blakeley. *Ankoku Buto: The Premodern and Postmodern Influences on the Dance of Utter Darkness.* Ithaca, N.Y.: Cornell University Press, 1988.

Ortolani, Benito. *The Japanese Theatre: From Shamanistic Ritual to Contemporary Pluralism.* Leiden: E. J. Brill, 1990; rev. ed. Princeton: Princeton University Press, 1994.

Rimer, J. Thomas. *Toward a Modern Japanese Theatre: Kishida Kunio.* Princeton: Princeton University Press, 1974.

Rolf, Robert T., and John K. Gillespie, eds. *Alternative Japanese Drama: Ten Plays.* Honolulu: University of Hawai'i Press, 1992.

Senda Akihiko. *The Voyage of Contemporary Japanese Theater.* Trans. J. Thomas Rimer. Honolulu: University of Hawai'i Press, 1997.

Theater Year-Book. Tokyo: Japan Centre of International Theater Institute. Published annually.

Tsuboike, Eiko, ed. *Theater Japan: A Who's Who Guide to Theater and Dance in Japan.* 2d ed. Tokyo: Japan Foundation, 1993.

56

MODERN OKINAWAN LITERATURE

Okinawa's modern literature occupies an ambiguous position in relation to the literature of Japan's main islands. On one hand, there are compelling reasons for viewing it as a subset of Japanese literature rather than as a separate literary tradition. First, Okinawa became part of the Japanese nation in 1879, seven years after the Meiji state forcibly annexed the Ryukyu Islands and abolished the Ryukyu kingdom. Second, the vast majority of Okinawan literary works published since that time have been written in standard Japanese rather than in local dialect, although several of today's writers incorporate dialect into their works while providing glosses for mainland Japanese readers. Third, the modes of representation that have dominated Okinawa's twentieth-century literature (the personal novel and various forms of realism and modernism) were introduced to local writers mainly through Japanese literary works and through Japanese-language translations of European literature. Finally, most Okinawan critics and writers themselves continue to measure literary "success" by the response of the Tokyo-based literary establishment.

Yet if Okinawa's twentieth-century literature is best understood within the broader rubric of modern Japanese literature, it is nonetheless more than just one among many regional literary traditions in Japan. The islands' tropical topography offers the most tangible testimony to Okinawa's difference from Japan's main islands. But significant cultural differences remain as well. The Ryukyu kingdom was, after all, a separate political entity that for centuries engaged in direct relations with both China (especially Fujian Province) and

Japan (especially the Satsuma domain in Kyushu). In addition, the kingdom at one time maintained an active trade with Korea as well as with peoples of Southeast Asia and the Pacific.

Not surprisingly, such cultural differences are less pronounced today than they were in the early decades of the twentieth century, when Okinawa's modern literature began to take shape. Many Japanese at the time treated Okinawans much as they treated Koreans and Taiwanese: as foreign colonial subjects in need of ideological and cultural enlightenment. In fact, Okinawans who moved to the Japanese mainland were often discriminated against when seeking housing or work, and these migrants reported seeing signs that read, "No Chinese, Koreans, or Ryukyuans admitted." Several stories from the 1920s and 1930s relate such experiences while exploring the interrelated problems of colonialism, ethnic discrimination, and assimilation. Ikemiyagi Sekiho's (1893–1951) "Officer Ukuma" (Ukuma junsa, 1922) and Kushi Fusako's (1903–1986) "Memoirs of a Declining Ryukyuan Woman" (Horobiyuku Ryūkyū onna no shuki, 1932) are especially critical of elite Okinawans whose powerful desire to assimilate leads them to reject not only their cultural heritage but also their own families. As both stories suggest, such a rejection ultimately entails the denial of self and the affirmation of the state's colonial and imperial ideology. Nowhere is such self-denial more apparent than in "Mr. Saitō of Heaven Building" (Tengoku biru no Saitō-san, 1938), a story by Okinawa's best-known poet, Yamanokuchi Baku (1903–1963). The main character in this story is a Korean who assumes the Japanese name Saitō in an unsuccessful effort to conceal his birthplace and to "pass" as Japanese. Yamanokuchi's 1935 "A Conversation" (Kaiwa) addresses the problem of Okinawan assimilation more directly: the poem's young Okinawan narrator lives in mainland Japan and avoids discussing his origins, even with the Japanese woman he hopes to marry.

Works about discrimination and assimilation represent one prominent theme in Okinawa's literature of the 1920s and 1930s. They appear to draw on the experiences of the writers themselves, most of whom had moved to Japan's main islands and were confronted with these issues in their daily lives. Clearly, this strain of Okinawan literature has much in common with *zainichi bungaku*, the literature in Japanese by writers of Korean descent, and it is tempting to view this body of writing as comprising, in part, a "Japanese minority literature." But few Okinawan writers seem comfortable with the label "minority," which threatens not only to marginalize their literary tradition but also to diminish the role of those writers, who rarely wrote about Okinawa itself or about Okinawan identity. Two such writers active in Tokyo in the 1920s and 1930s were poets Nakamura Kare (1905–1951) and Tsukayama Issui (1905–1981). Neither man achieved the critical acclaim or popularity of Yamanokuchi Baku, but each left behind a small, ambitious body of work that attests to his participation in Japan's modernist movement.

From the late 1930s until the end of World War II, Okinawan writers published comparatively little. In contrast to their counterparts in mainland Japan, they also produced few literary works during the immediate postwar years. The war had taken an especially devastating toll on Okinawa, and in its aftermath there was little leisure to write. It is often forgotten, for example, that an October 1944 air raid destroyed 90 percent of the capital city of Naha, leaving a thousand people dead and fifty thousand homeless nearly six months before the Battle of Okinawa even began. The battle itself developed into the deadliest of the Pacific War: approximately 230,000 people were killed, including 147,000 Okinawans, most of them civilians. The number of Okinawan casualties is roughly equivalent to one-fourth of the island's prewar population and includes hundreds of people who were indoctrinated by the Imperial Japanese Army to commit suicide rather than be captured by the enemy. After the battle ended, nearly every survivor on the main island of Okinawa was placed in an American internment camp, where they were totally dependent on the occupiers for food, clothing, and shelter—no currency was even put in place until 1946. Life in the camps was not easy, but American food rations and medicines helped stave off mass starvation and disease.

By the early 1950s a group of radical student writers at University of the Ryukyus was revitalizing Okinawan literature with a small magazine named *University of the Ryukyus Literature* (Ryūdai bungaku). This magazine, started by the students, initially served as a forum for publishing their own fiction and poetry, but it quickly became a lightning rod for debates about the nature of literature and the responsibility of the writer living under foreign military occupation. *University of the Ryukyus Literature* gained notoriety for excoriating several established Okinawan writers whom the magazine's editors accused of pursuing a vapid aestheticism instead of a politically engaged literature. The editors advocated socialist realism as the literary approach most suitable for addressing the political problems Okinawa faced at that time (Okamoto 1981).

Of utmost concern to the students was the perpetuation of American control over Okinawa as sanctioned by the San Francisco Peace Treaty, which ended the American occupation of Japan's main islands while ceding most of the Ryukyu Islands to the United States. At the same time, the Korean War had led to the rapid expansion of American military bases on Okinawa. Although the base expansion program created new jobs, it also entailed expropriating private land from Okinawan farmers for "rental" payments. Not all farmers were willing to part with their land, and those who resisted were sometimes threatened by American soldiers wielding bayonets while others waited with bulldozers. By the middle of the decade, the land seizures had sparked an islandwide protest movement consisting of a coalition of farmers, labor activists, teachers, and students. The editors of *University of the Ryukyus Literature*, who had already caught the eye of occupation authorities for their anti-American rhetoric, were among the movement's organizers. In 1956, without submitting the magazine to occupation censors for the requisite prepublication clearance, the editors published an issue of *University of the Ryukyus Literature* that contained several controversial poems, including Arakawa Akira's (b. 1931) "The Colored Race" (Yūshoku jinshu-shō, sono ichi, 1956). In response, American authorities closed down the magazine for six months and, with the cooperation of university administrators, arranged for four of the editors to be expelled (Kano 1987).

Although *University of the Ryukyus Literature* ultimately published few works of fiction and poetry that continue to be read today, several of its editors went on to become leading figures in postwar Okinawan intellectual circles. Okamoto Keitoku, for example, became one of the preeminent scholars of modern Okinawan literature and is a respected critic in his own right. But it was poet, critic, and journalist Arakawa Akira, together with his coeditor Kawamitsu Shin'ichi (b. 1932), who was the driving force behind the magazine in the early 1950s. Both men later worked at *The Okinawa Times*, one of the region's two major newspapers, and eventually rose to the positions of president and vice president, respectively. Arakawa and Kawamitsu established reputations not only as politically minded poets and powerful journalists but as influential social critics who regularly engaged in dialogues with *Ōe Kenzaburō and other writers from mainland Japan. In 1966 Arakawa and Kawamitsu launched *New Okinawan Literature* (Shin Okinawa bungaku), which remained the region's premier forum for publishing fiction, poetry, and criticism until the magazine's demise in the early 1990s.

Among the earliest pieces published in *New Okinawan Literature* were two works of fiction that helped establish the reputation of Ōshiro Tatsuhiro (b. 1925), postwar Okinawa's most prolific and best-known writer: *Cocktail Party* (Kakuteru pâti, 1967) and "Turtleback Tombs" (Kame no kō baka, 1966). *Cocktail Party* focuses on the rape of an Okinawan girl by an American soldier and on the myriad injustices sanctioned by occupation rule. This was the first Okinawan work to be awarded the Akutagawa Prize, which generated enormous excitement in local literary circles—not only because the award committee recognized an Okinawan writer for the first time, but also because this recognition also seemed to validate Okinawan literature's place within Japan's postwar literary tradition even while the region remained under American occupation.

Publication of *Cocktail Party* coincided with the "reversion movement," which demanded an end to American rule and the islands' return to Japan. The vast majority of mainland Japanese as well as Okinawans favored reversion, and the movement was given added impetus by widespread opposition throughout Japan to the Vietnam War (the United States relied heavily on its bases in Okinawa, especially as it intensified its bombing campaign in the late 1960s). Thus *Cocktail Party*'s appeal can be attributed partly to its contemporary relevance. Yet this novella is equally critical of Japan's historical exploitation of Okinawa and of the Japanese government's complicity with the American occupiers. Ōshiro's story further suggests that before Okinawans can claim to be victims of the American occupation, they must first confront their own complicity with Japanese imperialism during the war.

Despite *Cocktail Party*'s timeliness and critical acclaim, Ōshiro himself has always considered "Turtleback Tombs" to be a better work of literature. Built into the ground to form cavelike structures resembling tortoiseshells, these large and copious ancestral tombs, together with the island's natural caves, served as a refuge for both Okinawan civilians and Japanese soldiers during the Battle of Okinawa. Ōshiro's novella depicts an Okinawan family that hides in their ancestral tomb while shells from America's naval bombardment explode outside. Local dialect is interspersed throughout the dialogue portions of the narrative, which contains many references to traditional religious practices and explores how Okinawa's traditions as well as its people were under siege.

From the 1970s through the present day, Okinawa's novelists and poets, in contrast to their counterparts in mainland Japan, continued to write often about the war and postwar occupation. This is partly because Okinawans, unlike mainland Japanese, experienced the war as a battle fought on their homeland. Their ongoing concern with life under occupation can also be attributed to their particular experience of American occupation, which lasted twenty years longer than on the mainland. As a result, several generations of Okinawan writers spent much—if not all—of their childhood under occupation. Those who grew up near one of the many U.S. military bases (which take up 20 percent of the land of Okinawa's main island) regularly encountered American soldiers on their streets and in their shops. Writers such as Higashi Mineo (b. 1938) and Matayoshi Eiki (b. 1949) describe American soldiers in bars, strip clubs, and brothels that catered to the occupation forces. Countless stories about the occupiers feature these establishments, the most famous of which is Higashi's novella *Child of Okinawa* (Okinawa no shōnen, 1971).

Of course, not all works of Okinawa's postwar literature address the war and occupation. Beginning in the 1970s, a new generation of writers emerged, broadening both the thematic scope and narrative approach of the region's literature. In the realm of fiction, Nagadō Eikichi (b. 1932) and Matayoshi Eiki led the way, and both men continue to publish stories that attract both mainland Japanese and Okinawan readers. During the 1980s several women writers, including Sakiyama Tami (b. 1954), Nakawaka Naoko (b. 1948), Yamanoha Nobuko (b. 1941), and Yoshida Sueko (b. 1947), published award-winning stories. Few women had been active in Okinawan letters until that time, and these writers— each with her own thematic concerns and stylistic conception—brought added variety to Okinawa's literary landscape. The 1990s will be remembered in Okinawan letters as the decade when the Akutagawa Prize was awarded to local writers two years in a row. Matayoshi Eiki was awarded the prize in 1996 for his novella *Pig's Revenge* (Buta no mukui), and Medoruma Shun (b. 1960) received it in 1997 for his story "Droplets" (Suiteki). When Matayoshi was awarded the prize, cynical observers attributed the decision to Okinawa's prominence in the news at that time. Less than a year earlier, three American servicemen had abducted and raped a twelve-year-old Okinawan girl, and this led to massive protests that threatened to become a full-blown diplomatic crisis for Japan and the United States. But when Medoruma was awarded the prize the following year, political considerations alone could not explain the selection committee's decision. On the contrary, the committee strives to avoid choices that could invite accusations of favoritism based on "nonliterary" considerations, and because Okinawa Prefecture comprises only 1 percent of Japan's population, the choice of an Okinawan writer for the second consecutive year seemed unlikely. Several critics have concluded that Okinawa is simply producing a higher proportion of noteworthy writers than elsewhere in Japan. Whatever one's view of literary prizes and their significance, it is undeniable that Okinawan writers today have preserved their separate identity while at the same time becoming increasingly integrated into Japan's modern literary tradition. This entails a delicate balancing act, for these writers must maintain their distinct cultural heritage while ensuring that their work is accessible to readers in mainland Japan.

Matayoshi Eiki and Medoruma Shun have been especially successful in writing works grounded in Okinawa's cultural particularity while making them accessible to mainland Japanese readers. Like nearly all postwar Okinawan writers, both men continue to live in Okinawa and to write stories set almost exclusively on their home island. They often infuse these works with local dialect, refer to religious and cultural practices unfamiliar to mainland readers, and probe the nuances of social memory—and national amnesia—through the prism of Okinawa's twentieth-century history. Okinawa's modern literature was largely shaped by this history, which includes the experience of Japanese colonialism, the war's deadliest battle, and prolonged American occupation. It remains to be seen whether the region's writers will manage to preserve their distinctive literary tradition, and whether history will treat their islands more kindly in the twenty-first century than in the last.

—Michael Molasky

Bibliography

Johnson, Chalmers, ed. *Okinawa: Cold War Island.* Cardiff, Calif.: Japan Policy Research Institute, 1999.

Kano Masano. *Sengo Okinawa no shisō-zō* (Postwar Okinawan Thought). Tokyo: Asahi shinbunsha, 1987.

Molasky, Michael S. *The American Occupation of Japan and Okinawa: Literature and Memory.* London: Routledge, 1999.

Molasky, Michael S., and Steve Rabson, eds. *Southern Exposure: Modern Japanese Literature from Okinawa.* Honolulu: University of Hawai'i Press, 2000.

Nakahodo Masanori. *Okinawa no bungaku: 1927–1945* (Okinawan Literature, 1927–1945). Naha: Okinawa taimusu-sha, 1991.

———. *Kindai Okinawa bungaku no tenkai* (Forms of Modern Okinawan Literature). Tokyo: San'ichi shobō, 1981.

Okamoto Keitoku. *Gendai Okinawa no bungaku to shisō* (Contemporary Okinawan Literature and Thought). Naha: Okinawa taimusu-sha, 1981.

Rabson, Steve. *Okinawa: Two Postwar Novellas.* Berkeley: University of California Institute of East Asian Studies, 1989.

PART III

China

KIRK A. DENTON, ASSOCIATE EDITOR

Thematic Essays

57

HISTORICAL OVERVIEW

The question of the origins of modern Chinese literature is very much inter-twined with politics and politicized definitions of modernity. The conventional view, initially promoted by May Fourth-movement literary critics and later propagated by their Marxist inheritors before and after the 1949 revolution, is that modern Chinese literature erupted suddenly in 1918 with the publication of Lu Xun's short story "Diary of a Madman" (see "The Madman That Was Ah Q"). The "birth" of this socially and culturally engaged literature was portrayed as the beginning of a telos that leads to the revolutionary literature of the late 1920s and 1930s and the establishment of a class-based literature of political util-ity in Yan'an, the Communist base during the war against Japan, which in turn became the model for literature in the People's Republic of China (PRC). Since the early 1980s, however, literary historians in China have assailed this canonical May Fourth / Maoist view of the origins of modern Chinese literature and consciously sought to "rewrite literary history" *(chongxie wenxue shi)* (see "Modern Chinese Literature As an Institution"), a project that has restored many writers excluded or marginalized from the Maoist canon and that has cre-ated a far more diverse and heterogeneous picture of literary development. Chi-nese and Western critics have questioned the narrative of May Fourth as origins, its faith in "enlightenment," and looked to "alternative modernities" repressed by its hegemonic voice, including late Qing fiction (Wang 1997) and popular fiction (Chow 1991:34–83).

Any periodization of literary history will whitewash tensions, complexities, and ambiguities; yet it is still useful to delineate periods as a means of understanding how and why literature evolves and changes. We should recognize, however, that the very structure one uses to divide literature into periods—and, for that matter, into schools and styles—is never empty of political and ideological motive (see "Modern Chinese Literature As an Institution"). In what follows I will sketch a history of modern Chinese literature that draws from conventional PRC representations while at the same time trying to focus attention on and question the politics of this representation.

LATE QING: IMAGINING THE NATION (1895–1911)

The history of nineteenth century China was shaped by two important and intertwined forces: imperialism and internal social disintegration. To a great degree, although of course by no means absolutely, these forces determined the nature of literary production in the late Qing and through the rest of the twentieth century. As the sovereignty of their country was increasingly threatened by Western and Japanese imperialism, particularly economic imperialism, over the course of the nineteenth century, Chinese intellectuals began to look for explanations for their country's weakness relative to the global powers of the time. Initial responses—such as borrowing Western science and technology in order to increase Chinese "wealth and power"—were grounded in a faith that Western materiality would not destroy the essence of Chinese spiritual and cultural values. With the humiliating defeat by Japan in the Sino-Japanese War (1894–95), however, intellectuals began to extend this reflection to the sacrosanct realm of ideas and culture. Was there something inherent in Chinese culture, they asked, that inhibited national strength and prevented China from acting on equal terms with other nations?

For the most part, late Qing intellectuals questioned aspects of tradition from within a traditional set of assumptions; their goal was not to destroy tradition but to invigorate it by shedding it of its negative characteristics and renewing it with an infusion of Western ideas. The effect of their labors, however, was often to make tradition appear even less relevant. A good example of someone who sought this revamping of tradition is Kang Youwei (1858–1927), whose reinterpretations of Confucian texts transformed Confucius from someone who looked back nostalgically on a lost golden age to a forward-looking, progressive reformer, a transformation that could not have occurred without the aid of Darwinian, evolutionary thought. Tan Sitong (1865–1898), another late Qing reformer, sought to revive Confucianism by attacking what he saw as its dominant ethics of *li* (the prescriptive ethical guidelines for social relations).

Central to the dissemination of Western thought in China was, of course, translation. Two translators, Lin Shu (1852–1924) and Yan Fu (1854–1921), stand far above the rest. Yan Fu translated a host of Western works of sociology, economics, and philosophy, including Adam Smith's *Wealth of Nations*, Montesquieu's *The Spirit of Laws*, John Stuart Mill's *On Liberty*, and, most influential of all, Thomas Huxley's *Evolution and Ethics*. As these works were read and discussed by intellectuals in the crisis atmosphere of the late Qing, their ideas were appropriated and shaped into a Chinese discourse of modernity centered around such terms as evolution and progress, individualism, liberty, law, nation, and national character. Lin Shu's translations of more than two hundred, mostly Western European, novels were extremely popular in intellectual circles. They seemed to give narrative form to aspects of this discourse of modernity, presenting tales of individualist heroes, for example, and to offer a new, more politically engaged role for fiction in nation-building.

The spread of this discourse of modernity could not have occurred without the rise of a commercial print culture, which blossomed especially after 1905 when the civil service examination system was abolished and intellectuals were forced to search for new careers. Western style newspapers, literary journals and literary supplements to newspapers, popular magazines, women's magazines, and the like became national forums for the shaping and dissemination of this discourse of modernity. Key to this new print culture was the figure of *Liang Qichao (1873–1929), who founded and edited many newspapers and journals and contributed his own very influential writings to them. These writings introduced to a national Chinese readership knowledge of the West, critiqued aspects of the Chinese tradition and the national psychology it instilled, and promoted political, social, and literary reform. The professional writer is a phenomenon that appeared first, at least on a large scale, during this period. Writers could potentially live off the proceeds of their writing, although in reality this was seldom the case and most relied on more steady incomes from teaching or jobs as editors in publishing houses.

Interconnected with these events in the intellectual and print spheres were important changes in literature. Even within the dominant Tongcheng and Wenxuan schools, which advocated traditional styles of classical prose, important changes were occurring. The Tongcheng school of prose, of which the translators Yan Fu and Lin Shu were a part, sought to revive traditional values through a restoration of "ancient-style prose" *(guwen)* modeled on the prose masters of the Tang and Song dynasties. When Lin Shu translated Western novels into Chinese, he did so not in the vernacular but in ancient style. He did this to make the Western novel respectable, but also because he wanted to reinvigorate the ancient style with some of the dynamism that the Western novel seemed to offer. Ultimately, readers were far more interested in the exotic content of the novels than the prose style into which they were translated (Huters 1987, 1988). The Wenxuan school promoted a highly ornate parallel prose as the embodiment of an indigenous national culture and as a revolutionary stance against the

Qing, a foreign dynasty. Outside of these traditional literary schools, more profound changes were taking place. A *"poetry revolution" led by Liang Qichao and Huang Zunxian proposed reinvigorating classical poetry by incorporating into it Western terms, folk motifs, vernacular language, and new themes. In prose, Liang was instrumental in developing a style called "new prose" (*xin wenti*), a blend of classical syntax, vernacular language, and foreign load words, that would exert an important influence on the formation of a modern vernacular language in the May Fourth period.

Liang Qichao's most influential contribution to literature was his promotion of fiction as an instrument of national reform. With its particular power of immersing the reader in its world, Liang believed that fiction could "renovate" morality, politics, social customs, learning and arts, and the human mind itself (Denton 1996:74). In seeing fiction as a didactic vehicle, Liang was being both traditional and modern. His modernity lies in promoting fiction—traditionally a genre on the low end of the literary hierarchy—for the serious moral and political purposes conventionally ascribed to poetry and prose. Following Liang's call for a new "political" novel was an unprecedented boom in fiction writing (see "Late Qing Fiction"). Thousands of novels in many styles and on a wide variety of themes were produced in the final decade of the Qing: sentimental love stories, detective novels, satires of corruption, science fiction, allegories about China. Strikingly different from the premodern novel in writing about contemporary society, these novels also bear the structural properties of their premodern progenitors, although some scholars argue that they also show narrative modes and plot structures of the Western novel (Doleželová-Velingerová 1980). Of course, the novels produced during this period were tremendously varied in form and content; some embodied Liang's call for a new political novel, but many were far more concerned with entertaining and titillating.

Broadly speaking, the late Qing was a transitional period in which there was a gradual move away from traditional concepts of *wen*—writing in a wide variety of prose genres and poetic forms performed by literati not for profit but for their own moral self-cultivation or that of civilization as a whole—to a modern, Western-influenced concept of *wenxue*—a belletristic view of literature as a field distinguished from other areas of society and limited to the genres of fiction, poetry, and drama (Huters 1987).

MAY FOURTH: ICONOCLASM
AND THE DISCOURSE OF MODERNITY (1915–25)

The meaning of "May Fourth" and its relation to the formation of literary modernity is so contested as to provoke at least one scholar (Hockx 1999) to question its validity as a category. But May Fourth is still a necessary tool with which to discuss literary modernity in China. The term derives from the May Fourth Incident of 1919, when in response to the humiliating terms of the Treaty of Versailles, which would have ceded control to Japan parcels of Chinese territory, thousands of university students in Beijing marched to Tiananmen Square in protest. The term *May Fourth* is also used to describe a broader cultural movement (sometimes also called the New Culture movement) that was both different from and closely related to the anti-imperialist nationalism expressed in the student demonstrations and the nationwide patriotic movement that followed.

The May Fourth cultural movement deepened and developed the discourse of modernity conceived by the late Qing. Antitraditionalism, democracy, science, enlightenment, individualism, evolution, nation, and revolution, a hodge-podge of sometimes conflicting concepts derived from a range of Western cultural-historical periods, were the rhetorical tools with which these intellectuals attempted to pry themselves and their compatriots free from the "iron house" of tradition. Central to this discourse was iconoclasm, a totalistic attack on tradition. Wu Yu (1871–1949), *Lu Xun (1881–1936), Chen Duxiu (1880–1942), Gao Yihan (1885–1968), Yi Baisha (1986–1921), and other westernized intellectuals focused their iconoclasm on the Confucian ethical system *(lijiao)*, which they saw as deadeningly hierarchical and oppressively authoritarian. Lost in the constricting web of Confucian social relations was the individual; liberating the individual would unleash a new dynamic force that would serve society and the nation well. Key to May Fourth iconoclasm was the question of language. Denying the significant vernacularization that had already occurred in the final years of the Qing, May Fourth intellectuals like Hu Shi and Chen Duxiu (in Denton 1996) made grand appeals for an end to the hegemony of the classical language—the very bearer of tradition—and for the adoption, in all forms of writing, of a modern vernacular language. Because it was closer to what people actually spoke, these language reformers tell us, the vernacular could better portray social and emotional realities and serve as the new national language (see "Language and Literary Form").

The literary production that emerged following these calls for reform was highly diverse and heterogeneous. Poets were among the first to heed the call (see "Form and Reform"). Working against the powerful force of a long and glorious poetic tradition that favored highly structured forms, Hu Shi, Zhou Zuoren (1885–1967), Xu Yunuo (1893–1958), Xu Zhimo (1895–1931), Bing Xin (1900–1998), Yu Pingbo (1899–1990), and Guo Moruo (1892–1978), for example, experimented with the vernacular in free verse forms (Hockx 1994). In fiction, some writers wrote in a style they labeled "realism," exposing a reality that traditional ideology concealed as a way of demystifying the naturalness of that ideology's worldview. *Lu Xun's fiction, especially his first collection of stories *Call to Arms*, is often seen in this light. Others saw themselves in the romantic mode of literature as self-expression; *Yu Dafu, in fiction, and Guo Moruo, in poetry, became the icons of this romantic position. The romantic and realist positions—and the Creation Society and Literary Association that promoted them, respectively—were not nearly so at odds as conventionally thought; more often than not, the romantic and realist ethos coexisted within individual writers. Still other writers in the May Fourth movement placed emphasis not so much on writing about reality or expressing the self as they did on language, style, and form—the aesthetics of the literary text. All writers in this early period were participating in the formation of the new national literary language—a mélange of premodern vernacular, Liang Qichao's "new style," Western and Japanese grammatical forms, foreign loanwords, and even remnants of classical Chinese.

May Fourth writers, in all their variety, shared a disdain for entertainment fiction, which was extremely popular at the time and which they deprecatingly labeled *"Mandarin Ducks and Butterflies" fiction. Butterfly fiction came in many forms, including knight-errant novels (see "Martial-Arts Fiction and Jin Yong"), detective fiction, comedic satires, and sentimental love stories. Even as they denounced the didactic tradition of "literature as a vehicle for the Dao," May Fourth writers asserted their own serious high-mindedness by positioning themselves apart from the popular writers, with whom they competed for an urban readership (Hockx 1998). They also differed from the Butterfly writers in terms of language and literary form; whereas the latter retained some of the forms of premodern fiction, the former developed a highly Westernized, or Japanized, prose style and experimented with the narrative modes, poetic forms, and dramatic styles of the modern West (Gunn 1991).

As Michel Hockx discusses in his essay below, literary societies (and their journals) were important phenomena of the early twentieth century. These journals offered a place for publication of members' writings and were forums for manifestos and polemics that declared to the literary world a society's position. Until 1949, societies debated amongst themselves, sometimes vociferously and with venom, as they vied for positions within the literary field.

Another important phenomenon of this period was the emergence of women writers (see "Reconsidering the Origins of Modern Chinese Women's Writing"). Although Dorothy Ko (1994) and Susan Mann (1997) have shown us that women writers were active in the late imperial period—a fact that undermines received views, largely created by the May Fourth itself, that women had been completely silenced by a patriarchal tradition—it is nonetheless true that women writers emerged on the May Fourth literary scene to a much greater degree and in a much more public way than ever before. Not surprisingly, this first generation of modern women writers were from the economic elite, daughters of wealthy families whose parents allowed them at least some access to Western-style education. Bing Xin, Chen Hengzhe (1893–1976), Huang Luyin (1889–1934), and Ling Shuhua (1904–90) are among the most significant members of this first generation of women writers. Unlike their male counterparts, they tended to write about love and domestic life, perhaps because they felt excluded from the new male discourse of modernity or because they consciously struggled against its patriarchal implications.

LEFTIST LITERATURE OF THE 1920s AND 1930s: CLASS AND NATION

Although the degree to which writers adhered to the leftist revolutionary cause has been dramatically overemphasized by Marxist literary historians, it is true that many May Fourth writers and a new generation of younger writers willingly embraced a political role for literature by the 1920s and into the 1930s. This turn to the left has everything to do with political and historical circumstances: the success of the revolutionary Northern Expedition (which united most of Chinese territory in 1928 after years of warlord domination), the rise of Japanese imperialism after 1930, and Guomindang fascism and its inattention to social problems. This leftward swing in literature began with a critique of the May Fourth movement by such leftists as Qu Qiubai (1899–1935), who perceptively attacked the May Fourth writers for their elitism, particularly their use of westernized language and literary forms, which Qu labeled "Western eight-legged essays" *(yang bagu)*, referring to the traditional abstruse and formulaic examination system essay. Qu promoted the use of street vernacular and favored popular performance arts that would be more accessible to the masses and hence more effective as tools of social change (see "Language and Literary Form"). Some of these radical critics went so far as to attack Lu Xun, widely regarded as the father of modern literature and the embodiment of May Fourth enlightenment values. Qian Xingcun (1900–1977), for example, claimed that the age of Ah Q was "bygone" (Denton 1996:276–288) and that what China needed was not the gloomy and difficult moods of Lu Xun's prose poems in *Wild Grass* (Yecao, 1927) but a more positive and optimistic literature that pointed to a bright revolutionary future.

The critics promoting this *"revolutionary literature"—a literature written about the masses and in their interests—and the writers they addressed were from bourgeois or gentry backgrounds. According to the logic of Marxist determinism, bourgeois writers could not but write in the interest of their own class, a predicament critics circumvented by claiming that bourgeois writers could "transcend" or "sublate" their class backgrounds by entering into and experiencing the lives of the lower classes. Many of the debates that arose in the leftist camp in the 1930s centered on this question of what role the bourgeois writer could have in the production of a revolutionary literature (Denton 1996:48–49).

Attempting to end the rhetorical battles in the leftist literary world, the Chinese Communist Party (CCP) established the League of Left-Wing Writers (1930–36), which promoted Marxist literary theory and published leftist literature in its many official journals. Not surprisingly, the literary practice of left-leaning writers was a very imperfect realization of Marxist theoretical prescriptions. The generally engaged nature of this writing can be seen in the dominance of the literary modes of realism and satire. Writers such as *Mao Dun, who had since May Fourth promoted "naturalism," wrote realistic novels and short stories about, for instance, the economic hardship of peasants or the inner workings of capitalism in Shanghai. Zhang Tianyi (1906–1985) and Wu Zuxiang (1908–1994) offered satirical portraits of a decadent gentry class. Romantic writers of the Creation Society, who were the most histrionic in their "conversions" to the revolutionary cause, publicly decried their former individualism, only to continue to uphold a romantic view of the power of literature to participate in the revolutionary movement and to transform the world. The modern spoken drama *(huaju)* (see "Performing the Nation"), a new form that developed in the 1920s against a powerful operatic tradition, came into its own in the 1930s, particularly in the hands of *Cao Yu (1910–1966), and was largely associated with the leftist movement.

Leftist literature was only one element of the literary field in the late 1920s and 1930s. Butterfly fiction continued to be highly popular. Writers like Zhang Henshui reached a readership unimaginable to most of the progressive writers, the one exception being *Ba Jin, whose novel *Family* (Jia, 1933) reached a wide readership, although this is precisely because it contains many conventions from the Butterfly tradition. A small group of writers associated with the journal *Les Contemporains* (Xiandai) promoted and wrote literary works that were self-consciously at odds with those demanded by the proponents of revolutionary literature. These writers have been referred to as the *New Sensationists, after the Japanese modernist school (the Shinkankakuha, usually translated as "New Sensationalists") that one of its members, Liu Na'ou (1900–1939), followed while in Japan. Modernist tendencies were also very strong in poetry. Dai Wangshu (who was connected with *Les Contemporains*) and Li Jinfa (1900–1976), for example, experimented with symbolist modes of poetry. Much ink has been spilled on the question of whether these Chinese modernists constitute true modernism. One scholar (Lee 1990) argues that modernism, at least as it was formulated in Western Europe and America, could not develop fully in China because of the radically different historical circumstances: "Cultural modernity" arose in the West as a critique of "historical modernity" (capitalism, science, progress, civilization, and the like); in China, however, culture was usurped by the cause of bringing about historical modernity. Based in a narrow Euro-American view of modernism that ignores the possibility of alternative varieties, this view is nonetheless valuable in delineating how and why literature was made to serve the cause of nation building in China.

The 1930s also gave rise to writers like *Shen Congwen (1902–1988) and Feng Wenbing (1901–1967), whose works depict in a lyrical and nostalgic mode life in rural areas. These works are void of political jargon and the heroic revolutionary themes being promoted by leftist critics; instead, their language gives off a folk quality, even as it is studiously modern, and their plots have the universal appeal of primitive themes. Literary historians have often depicted Shen as a "nativist" writer, a writer whose work consistently recounts his native region (in Shen's case, West Hunan). But Shen also wrote romantic short stories (in the manner of Yu Dafu) and modernist-style fiction. In any case, his body of work resisted, sometimes quite self-consciously, the literary prescriptions emanating from the leftist camp, which is one of the reasons it is so popular today.

With the historical pressures of the war against Japan and the increasingly strident calls for social realism from the revolutionary camp, these various attempts to steer literature away from politics faded, but did not disappear, by the late 1930s.

WAR PERIOD: LITERATURE AND NATIONAL SALVATION (1937–45)

The war period, during most of which China was divided into three distinct political regions (the Communist-controlled area around Yan'an in the northwest, the Japanese-occupied coast, and the Guomindang-held southwest), has been seriously misrepresented in literary histories. Marxist literary historians in the PRC have often portrayed the war period as one of great homogeneity: writers happily abandoned their personal motivations for writing and devoted themselves and their pens to the political cause of national salvation. They arrived at this view by emphasizing the theory and practice in Yan'an and ignoring or underemphasizing work produced in the Guomindang-held areas and in territory under Japanese control. When taking all three areas into consideration, however, the Chinese literary scene during the war appears quite heterogeneous. Yet, at the same time it is clear that the war period also marked a shift toward cultural homogenization: realism, romanticism, modernism, regionalism, and popular literature seemed to be making their "last stands" against the tide of revolutionary and national salvation literature (Anderson 1989). The May Fourth notion of the writer as the voice of "critical consciousness," an ideal embodied in the figure of Lu Xun, also came under assault during this war.

In the early years of the war, writers caught up in the euphoria of resistance did seem to devote themselves voluntarily to propaganda work. The All China League of Resistance Writers (and its many local branches)—an umbrella cultural organization established in Wuhan in 1938 to unite cultural workers from all political persuasions—directed this promotion of anti-Japanese propaganda work. Writers and other cultural workers were encouraged to produce works that were readily accessible to a mass audience (see "Language and Literary Form"). This meant using "national forms" (*minzu xingshi*) or "old forms" (*jiu xingshi*)—literary, performance, and visual forms that had indigenous roots and were appealing to a rural as well as urban audience. These forms included storytelling, ballads, New Year's prints, local opera, and Peking drum singing. New forms such as "street plays" (*jietou ju*), short propaganda dramas performed in villages around the country, were also developed; the most famous of them was

Put Down Your Whip (Fangxia nide bianzi, 1936). The war was also a period in which the modern spoken drama flourished and came to maturity.

That writers willingly engaged in propaganda work is not to say that there was no debate in literary circles during the war, or that literary practice was homogeneous. In the face of what they saw as a degrading retreat from the May Fourth ideal of a modern, cosmopolitan literature, some critics such as Hu Feng (1902–1985) denounced "national forms." Other voices (Shen Congwen and Liang Shiqiu) even criticized as destructive the usurpation of culture by politics and political figures. By the early 1940s, moreover, the national literary scene became increasingly heterogeneous. In the Guomindang-controlled areas, realism and romanticism returned as writers shifted their attentions away from the war (which had stalemated by this time) and the external enemy toward domestic and cultural issues. Writers such as Sha Ting (1904–92) wrote fiction that exposed the social problems under Guomindang rule. Lu Ling (1923–1994), in a radically subjective style, wrote about the psychological effects of oppression.

In Beijing and Shanghai, the Japanese occupiers sought to stem political dissent and largely succeeded in doing so. Although historical costume dramas were occasionally used allegorically to promote resistance, popular-entertainment fiction and escape were the rule of the day. This is not to say that there were not serious writers. *Eileen Chang's (1921–1995) *Romances* (Chuanqi, 1943), a collection of short stories, is among the most sophisticated and important works of modern Chinese literature. Although the war does not figure directly in them and they seem to be self-consciously reacting against the heroic historical narratives that dominated the literary scene outside Shanghai, her fiction nonetheless reveals in subtle ways how history imprints itself on the psyche. Shi Tuo (1910–1988) wrote lyrical essays and experimental fiction that further belie the stereotype of war literature as uniformly propagandistic.

In Yan'an, CCP cultural policy promoted "national defense literature" and the use of "national forms." Urban, bourgeois writers like *Ding Ling, who had idealistically made their way to Yan'an to participate in the revolution, found life there far from the promise they had held for it and experienced difficulty abandoning May Fourth notions of the role of literature. With Communist Party backing, in the spring of 1942 they began to publish essays and short stories that exposed problems in Yan'an society: Party privilege, the unequal place of women, thought reform of intellectuals, absence of freedom of speech, and the like. Mao Zedong, who had since 1935 been head of the Chinese Communist Party but whose political position was not completely secure, was surprised by the depth and extent of the criticism that he himself had unleashed. He decided to hold a conference for cultural workers, at the end of which he gave two speeches, collectively called the *"Yan'an Talks," that summed up Communist Party cultural policy: literature is subservient to political interests and writers should write for and about the masses of workers, peasants, and soldiers. Even as he invoked his name, Mao countered everything *Lu Xun stood for: intellectual autonomy and the critical consciousness of the writer. The "Talks" are significant for setting the draconian cultural policy after the establishment of the PRC in 1949.

Although often skipped over in literary histories, the brief period after the war and before the establishment of the PRC, was highly active. The period saw the appearance of many excellent full-length novels, including Qian Zhongshu's (1910–1998) satirical *Fortress Besieged* (Weicheng, 1946), although film and drama were perhaps the most important cultural forms.

EARLY POSTREVOLUTIONARY PERIOD: REVOLUTIONARY ROMANTICISM (1949–66)

After the revolution, the CCP began to impose systematically the dictates of Mao's *"Yan'an Talks." Although many writers enthusiastically embraced the cultural policy of the new regime, others balked at abjuring their roles as cultural critics. The Party attempted to impose literary uniformity in two primary ways: institutions and cultural campaigns. The publishing industry was nationalized and journals were brought under state control. Writers were organized into the Chinese Writers Association (Zhongguo zuojia xiehui), which "served the complementary functions of providing the Party with a means of monitoring and controlling creative writing and of establishing a clear-cut ladder of success for writers within the socialist literary system" (Link 2000:119). The pluralist literary field of the Republican period—with its privately owned journals and publishing houses, competing literary societies, and stylistic heterogeneity— was effectively destroyed. Censorship (see "Literary Communities and the Production of Literature") was exerted by not approving manuscripts for publication, but more often than not writers internalized party guidelines (as best they could interpret them in the ever-changing political climate). When writers crossed the line, public criticism could follow. The 1950s, even before the radical excess of the Great Leap Forward and the Cultural Revolution, were dotted with periodic campaigns against wayward writers and intellectuals (for example, the campaign against the Hu Feng clique in 1955). The effect of these campaigns was to break down intellectuals' lingering sense of autonomy and critical consciousness and instill in them a notion of what the party would and would not tolerate.

Even under such effective means of control, the literary products of the first "seventeen years" of the PRC, as they are often called on the mainland, were not just uniform political propaganda. There were moments of relaxation in cultural policy, such as the *Hundred Flowers (1956–57), when writers were encouraged to write about problems in the new socialist society. This they did with a forthrightness that Mao, who launched the movement in 1956, could never have foreseen. After just a few short months, the Communist Party reversed its policy and attacked the very writers and intellectuals it had encouraged to speak out. At least 100,000 writers and intellectuals were targeted during the subsequent Anti-Rightist Campaign (1957–58), the most virulent cultural campaign to date and a harbinger of the radicalism and anti-intellectualism of the Cultural Revolution to come.

In terms of literary production, writers were expected to follow the "worker, peasant, soldier" formula established by Mao in his *"Yan'an Talks." Socialist realism and then "revolutionary romanticism combined with revolutionary realism" were the prescribed literary models (see "Revolutionary Realism and Revolutionary Romanticism"). Although much of the resulting literary practice was dull and uninspiring, readers sincerely enjoyed and were moved by some of the better works. Novels such as Yang Mo's *Song of Youth* (Qingchun zhi ge, 1958), Zhou Erfu's *Morning in Shanghai* (Shanghai de zaochen, 1958), Qu Bo's *Tracks in the Snowy Forest* (Linhai xueyuan, 1957), Liu Qing's *The Builders* (Chuangye shi, 1959), and Luo Guangbin and Yang Yiyan's *Red Crag* (Hongyan, 1961) were extremely popular with readers for varying reasons, including sentimental description of love and revolution *(Song)*, sense of adventure *(Tracks)*, heroic sacrifice *(Red Crag)*, and optimism for building a new society *(The Builders)*, elements that derive in part from the popular literary tradition (Link 2000:210–248). Poetry (much of it narrative) was promoted by the state, as was traditional style operatic theater, but neither gained the wide audience enjoyed by fiction.

CULTURAL REVOLUTION: CLASS STRUGGLE (1966–76)

Although bald politics—he had lost control of the vast CCP bureaucracy to the more pragmatic wing of the party leadership—was at the core of Mao Zedong's motivation for launching the Cultural Revolution in 1966, there was also a sincere desire to radically revamp a culture that had, Mao felt, become complacently mired in bourgeois values. The Cultural Revolution was an attempt to destroy remnants of both the feudal culture of China's past and Western bourgeois culture. The campaign attacking the "four olds" (ideas, culture, customs, habits), carried out sometimes by marauding Red Guards burning library books or destroying temples, was one element of this revamping of culture. Many of the writers associated with the May Fourth tradition were attacked, sometimes physically, and their works were disparaged. Lu Xun, poster boy for the leftists, was one of the few Republican-era intellectuals to escape critique during the radicalism of the Cultural Revolution. During this time, educational and cultural institutions were closed. Swept up in the political fervor of the times or simply trying to survive, most writers stopped writing. Those who did write and publish generally belonged to a younger generation. They churned out short stories, essays, and reportage that praised the Cultural Revolution and supported its class-struggle ideology. Hao Ran was the best known of the Cultural Revolution novelists, and his *Bright and Sunny Days* (Yanyang tian, 1965) and

The Golden Road (Jinguang dadao, 1972–74) exemplify the Cultural Revolution aesthetics of heroism and class struggle.

By far the most important cultural products of the Cultural Revolution were the *model plays *(yangban xi)*: Peking operas (for example, *Taking Tiger Mountain by Strategy, The Red Lantern*) and ballets (such as *The White-Haired Girl* and *Red Detachment of Women*) designed to embody the class-struggle values of the radical leftist position. The *Model Theater was the domain of Jiang Qing, Mao Zedong's wife; through it, she supported Maoism, exerted herself in the cultural field, and, some scholars argue, propounded a feminist agenda with strong revolutionary heroines. Stylized and propagandistic as they are, with their colorful costumes and set designs, songs, dance, and acrobatics, these plays were genuinely enjoyed by audiences.

Mostly in the form of hand-copied manuscripts, works of popular fiction circulated underground throughout the Cultural Revolution. That people would take the serious risk of being caught with these "dregs" of bourgeois culture attests to the powerful appeal of literature as pure entertainment (Link 2000:193–197).

POST-MAO: THE RETURN OF MODERNITY (1977–89)

The death of Mao, the end of the Cultural Revolution, and the liberalization of Party cultural policy unleashed a flowering of Chinese literature that has often been compared to the May Fourth movement. The parallels are striking. Like the May Fourth writers, who portrayed themselves as emerging from the shackles of a deadening Confucian tradition, post-Mao writers saw themselves as struggling against the legacy of an equally oppressive Maoist system. Early post-Mao writers, like their May Fourth counterparts, discovered and experimented with romantic self-expression, modernist literary styles, critical realism, and the avant-garde; they did so at least in part to pry themselves from the Maoist discourse and its ideological assumptions. Just as May Fourth writers saw a need to develop a new vernacular language free of traditional ideology, so too did post-Mao writers attempt to develop a language untainted by Maoism. As in the May Fourth movement, women writers (the most famous of whom is *Wang Anyi) reemerged on a large scale in the post-Mao period.

The development of post-Mao literature has often been seen in terms of literary movements:* Misty poetry (modernist-style poetry that was intensely personal and lyrical in contrast to the highly politicized narrative poetry that dominated the Maoist era), *scar literature (fiction that depicted the psychological wounds suffered during the Cultural Revolution), *roots-seeking literature (fiction that sought a return to China's indigenous cultures, although often marginalized ones, in reaction to a century of rupturing iconoclasm), and the *avant-garde (postmodern fiction that questions modernity's basic discourse of self, progress, realism, and enlightenment in a language self-consciously denuded of Maoist tropes). Of course, not all writing produced in the 1980s fit neatly into these movements, and some literary genres were more closely associated with movements than others. As a whole, the development from movement to movement shows an intensification of criticism of the socialist system: whereas scar literature in the late 1970s and early 1980s was superficial in its treatment of the Cultural Revolution, often laying blame with the Gang of Four and falling back on the stereotypical representation of characters seen in Cultural Revolution writing, by the late 1980s the avant-garde, with its radical formal and linguistic experiments, questioned the values at the heart of socialist ideology. This radicalization in the cultural sphere contributed to the 1989 protest movement.

Another significant phenomenon in the 1980s was the arrival on the mainland of Taiwan and Hong Kong commercial culture (film, pop music, television programs, and fiction). *Qiong Yao and *San Mao, Taiwanese women writers of popular romance, led the way in this literary invasion. Their novels and shorts stories were extremely popular in the mainland and can be said to have helped to usher in the commercialization of cultural production of the 1990s.

POST-TIANANMEN: THE RISE
OF CONSUMER CULTURE (1989–)

The violent crackdown on the 1989 movement was followed by what Barmé (1999) describes as a "soft" cultural suppression. Wang Meng (b. 1934), an important writer of fiction in the 1980s who had risen in the cultural bureaucracy to become minister of culture, was removed from his post and, eventually, criticized for allowing cultural pluralism to flourish during his tenure. Conservative cultural figures crawled out of the woodwork and began to call for a return to the socialist culture that the late 1980s had so effectively erased. Some writers involved in the movement were arrested, others fled the country. Exile literature, or a literature of the PRC *diaspora, emerged at this time. *Jintian* (Today), an underground journal associated with the Democracy Wall movement of 1978–79, was resurrected abroad and became the leading vehicle for the publication of exile writing. Exiles also published in journals and newspapers in Hong Kong and Taiwan.

But by far the most significant phenomenon of the 1990s cultural scene was the commodification of culture (see "Wang Shuo and the Commercialization of Literature"). Because of market reforms and the influx of capital from Taiwan and Hong Kong, cultural institutions in the PRC (journals, publishing houses, film studios, and the like) were forced to turn a profit and compete in the cultural marketplace. Some writers responded by popularizing their work. The literary figure who best embodies this commercialization phenomenon is the novelist and scriptwriter *Wang Shuo (b. 1958). Credited with establishing *pizi wenxue* or *liumang wenxue* (punk literature), fiction about hooligans, the laid-off, and the disenfranchised, Wang Shuo both made use of popular fiction forms and tapped into a social discontent that made him extremely popular with young readers, as well as intellectuals. This is not to say that all writers have succumbed to commercialization and given into popular culture. To the contrary, some poets have created of poetry a "cult," a bastion from the relentless onslaught of commercial culture (Yeh 1996). Whereas Wang Shuo embraces the commercialization of culture and its popular forms, poets like Xi Chuan (b. 1963) position themselves as purveyors of pure art against the stench of the popular (Van Crevel 1999). Still other writers, such as Su Tong, have attempted to negotiate a position somewhere between the avant-garde and the popular (Xu 2000). The protagonist in Jia Pingwa's controversial novel *City in Ruins* (Feidu, 1993), notorious for its explicit description of sex, is emblematic of intellectuals' struggle to find a new role in the rapidly changing society of 1990s China.

The 1990s also saw a return to realist fiction. Liu Heng (b. 1954), He Dun (b. 1958), Chen Ran (b. 1962), Qiu Huadong (b. 1969), and others have created a new *urban fiction that attempts to describe realistically the problems of living and coping in the new market economy.

TAIWAN

Literature in Taiwan and Hong Kong developed along paths independent of, but not disconnected from, that of the mainland. Unlike the mainland, Taiwan and Hong Kong were colonies, the former of Japan and the latter of Britain. Taiwan (with Korea) was given over to Japanese control under treaty terms following the defeat of the 1894–95 Sino-Japanese War. It remained under Japanese occupation until the end of World War II. Under the influence of the May Fourth movement and literary developments on the mainland, "new literature" emerged in Taiwan around 1924 and developed as a form of nationalist (both Chinese and Taiwanese) resistance to Japanese colonialism. This first generation of modern writers, represented by Lai Ho (1894–1943), was more Chinese than Taiwanese in its cultural consciousness (Chang 1999:269). The next generation, having been educated primarily in Japanese, was more culturally hybrid. Many wrote in Japanese. *Kominka* literature, or literature written by Chinese in Japanese, has been conventionally treated very unkindly by Taiwan literary historians, who have equated it with political or moral collaboration. Recently, however, some have begun to find in these texts a form of agency and resistance to the colonial oppressors (Chang 1997). Chinese publications were banned outright by the colonial government during World War II.

Not many years after the Japanese left Taiwan, the Nationalists, defeated by the CCP in the civil war on the mainland, retreated there. Many Taiwanese view this as yet another colonial occupation, especially after the Guomindang brutally suppressed a Taiwanese protest movement on February 28, 1947. This ushered in a period of three decades of suppression of intellectual dissent. Writers were cut off from the leftist literary tradition of the previous three decades, and had for indigenous literary models only the more lyrical strand of May Fourth writing (Xu Zhimo, Zhu Ziqing, and others). The Guomindang actively promoted anticommunist literature and tolerated popular romances, which dominated the literary scene. T. A. Hsia upheld realism in the pages of the journal he edited, *Literary Review* (Wenxue zazhi, 1956–60), but had a hard time attracting works for publication as well as readers. In the politically repressive environment of the 1950s and 1960s, writers turned for influence to the West and to a particularly aesthetic form of Western modernism. The leading journal promoting modernism was *Modern Literature* (Xiandai wenxue, 1960–73), founded by students of T.A. Hsia: Bai Xianyong (b. 1937), Wang Wenxing (b. 1939), Ouyang Zi (b. 1939), and Chen Ruoxi (b. 1938). The journal systematically introduced Western modernist writing and promoted experimentation in literary form (see "The Taiwan Modernists"). Modernism encountered criticism from nationalist critics. In defense of the modernist position, Wang Wenxing wrote: "If someone would say that this Chinese effort to experiment with modernism betrays a mentality of adulating foreign things, we cannot tolerate [this charge]. Are Chinese not permitted to create new forms? … In the opinion of some people, Chinese cannot write psychological or symbolist fiction or novels of fantasy, nor should they experiment with surrealism or accept existentialism. These people are like fathers who forbid their children's activities—no ball-playing, no running, no singing, no riding bicycles, no listening to radios—all because of one reason: that they are foreign things. Dear reader, if you meet such a father, please give him some good advice" (in Faurot 1980:16).

As in the mainland, there was a reaction against this modernist literature. In some sense, it was a natural reaction against the westernization of literature, but it was also the product of an abrupt shift in global politics. Nations around the world, including the United States, were beginning to recognize the government on the mainland as the sole legitimate Chinese nation, leaving Taiwan in a state of political limbo. This contributed to the Taiwanese nationalist movement, which in turn engendered a *"nativist" *(xiangtu)* literature that was realist in its focus on rural Taiwan society and that attempted to capture in language and form a Taiwanese consciousness. The 1970s literary scene was dominated by such nativist writers as Huang Chunming (b. 1939), Wang Zhenhe (b. 1940), and Chen Yingzhen (b. 1937).

The lifting of martial law in 1986 and the remarkable democratization of Taiwan political life that followed has led to a heterogeneous literary scene. As in post-Mao China and contemporary Hong Kong, recent writing in Taiwan has become so varied as to undermine any attempts to impose on it neat literary categories. This heterogeneity has much to do with capitalism and the global commercialization of culture, as well as with a more general postmodern or postcolonial decentering of culture. Tied to an ever-changing and volatile market, writers have had to find a niche that makes them identifiable and marketable. Some writers, such as Li Yongping, have gone the avant-garde route taken by the likes of Su

Tong (b. 1963), Ge Fei, and Yu Hua on the mainland. Popular culture has found its way into elite literature in the works of women writers such as *Qiong Yao (b. 1938) and *San Mao (1943–1991), whose romances were extremely popular in the 1980s and 1990s. Indeed, one of the characteristics of recent writing in Taiwan is the breakdown of clear distinctions between elite and popular literature. Others like Zhang Xiguo have used satire to draw attention to problems in Taiwan's urban society. A flourishing queer literature exists (see "Same-Sex Love in Recent Chinese Literature"), as does a self-consciously feminist body of work (for example, Li Ang [b. 1952]). Although, as everywhere, serious literature faces the challenge of a marketplace dominated by popular, commercial culture, in its heterogeneity Taiwan literature has perhaps never been healthier.

HONG KONG

Like Taiwan, Hong Kong's cultural development is inseparable from its colonial history and from its close proximity to the mainland. The British were colonial overlords of Hong Kong from after the Opium War (1839–42) until 1997, when it "returned" to the mainland to much media fanfare. Unlike the Japanese in Taiwan, the British took a laissez-faire approach to the production of culture in Hong Kong (Tay 1995). Although some writers and editors were influenced by the new literature being produced on the mainland in the 1920s and 1930s and attempted to develop this realist, engaged literature in Hong Kong (the journal *Red Beans* [Hongdou, 1933] being its most important forum), writers who identified with tradition and traditional literary forms dominated the literary scene. This traditionalism was perhaps a product of the colonial environment; writers resisted the colonial government by asserting their Chineseness through upholding and recreating their literary tradition. But in its apolitical stance it was inherently conservative.

Over the years, the cultural scene in Hong Kong has been greatly influenced by writers who came from either Taiwan or the mainland. An influx of writers from the mainland during the war against Japan and again during the civil war that followed stirred up the literary scene, and Hong Kong became a hotbed of modern, often leftist, literature. Some critics argue that this period marks the real birth of Hong Kong modern literature, although this reflects a mainland-centric perspective. Many of these mainland writers stayed only temporarily and Hong Kong did not figure substantially in their works. Others, such as Liu Yichang (b. 1918), an émigré from the mainland, and Yu Kwang-chung (b. 1928), from Taiwan, integrated issues of Hong Kong identity into their writing, and they have consequently been adopted as Hong Kong writers. The postwar period also saw the rise of martial-arts fiction, whose most famous exemplar is the prolific *Jin Yong.

Hong Kong's cultural scene flourished with its development as a major global metropolis in the 1970s. By the 1980s, new writing, much of it vaguely modernist in its experimentation with form, proliferated. Writers were beginning to concern themselves with issues of Hong Kong identity—what it means to live in a space that is neither Chinese nor British. A self-consciously Hong Kong-oriented literature developed further, ironically, when the looming event of Hong Kong's 1997 "return" to the mainland reared its head (see "Voices of Negotiation in Twentieth-Century Hong Kong Literature"). Writers such as *Xi Xi (b. 1938), Dung Kai-cheung (b. 1967), and Leung Ping-kwan (b. 1949) self-consciously wrote Hong Kong in their works. Leung's poetry collection *A City at the End of Time* (1992) beautifully conveys a sense of Hong Kong's spatial marginality—between the mainland and Taiwan—and its cultural hybridity—Chinese, colonial, British, cosmopolitan. "We need a fresh angle, / nothing added, nothing taken away, / always at the edge of things and between places," wrote Leung, expressing Hong Kong's search for identity in the postcolonial period. In some sense, Hong Kong's marginal status as a "city at the end of time" can be taken as a metaphor for the postmodern condition itself, a condition Hong Kong shares with both China and Taiwan.

It is not clear yet to what extent the "return" of Hong Kong to the mainland has affected the cultural sphere. Early indications are that it has not led to a stifling of literary dissent. A more significant influence perhaps has been the downward turn in the economy, which has hit the cultural world hard.

—*Kirk A. Denton*

Bibliography

Note: For extensive bibliographies of translations and studies of modern Chinese literature, see MCLC Resource Center (http://deall.ohio-state.edu/denton.2/biblio.htm).

Anderson, Marston. "Realism's Last Stand: Character and Ideology in Zhang Tianyi's *Three Sketches.*" *Modern Chinese Literature* 5, no. 2 (Fall 1989): 179–196.

Barmé, Geremie. *In the Red: On Contemporary Chinese Culture.* New York: Columbia University Press, 1999.

Chang, Sung-cheng Yvonne. "Beyond Cultural and National Identities: Current Reevaluation of the Kominka Literature from Taiwan's Japanese Period." *Journal of Modern Literature in Chinese* 1, no. 1 (1997): 75–107.

——. "Literature in Post-1949 Taiwan, 1950s to 1980s." In Murray A. Rubenstein, ed., *Taiwan: A New History,* 403–418. Armonk, N.Y.: M.E. Sharpe, 1999.

——. *Modernism and Native Resistance: Contemporary Fiction from Taiwan.* Durham, N.C.: Duke University Press, 1993.

Chow, Rey. *Woman and Chinese Modernity: The Politics of Reading between West and East.* Minneapolis: University of Minnesota Press, 1991.

Denton, Kirk A., ed. *Modern Chinese Literary Thought: Writings on Literature, 1893–1945.* Stanford: Stanford University Press, 1996.

Doleželová-Velingerová, Milena, ed. *The Chinese Novel at the Turn of the Century.* Toronto: University of Toronto Press, 1980.

Faurot, Jeannette L. *Chinese Fiction from Taiwan: Critical Perspectives.* Bloomington: University of Indiana Press, 1980.

Gunn, Edward. *Style and Innovation in Twentieth-Century Chinese Prose.* Stanford: Stanford University Press, 1991.

Hockx, Michel. "Is There a May Fourth Literature? A Reply to Wang Xiaoming." *Modern Chinese Literature and Culture* 11, no. 2 (Fall 1999): 40–52.

———. "The Literary Association and the Literary Field of Early Republican China." *China Quarterly* 153 (March 1998): 49–81.

———. *Snowy Morning: Eight Chinese Poets of Early Modern China.* Leiden: CNWS, 1994.

Hsia, T.A. *The Gate of Darkness: Studies on the Leftist Literary Movement.* Seattle: University of Washington Press, 1968.

Hung, Chang-tai. *War and Popular Culture: Resistance in Modern China, 1937–1945.* Berkeley: University of California Press, 1994.

Huot, Claire. *China's New Cultural Scene: A Handbook of Changes.* Durham, N.C.: Duke University Press, 2000.

Huters, Theodore. "From Writing to Literature: The Development of Late Qing Theories of Prose." *Harvard Journal of Asiatic Studies* 47, no. 1 (June 1987): 50–96.

———. "A New Way of Writing: The Possibility for Literature in Late Qing China, 1895–1908." *Modern China* 14, no. 3 (1988): 243–276.

Kinkley, Jeffrey, ed. *After Mao: Chinese Literature and Society, 1978–1981.* Cambridge, Mass.: Harvard University Council on East Asian Studies, 1985.

Ko, Dorothy. *Teachers of the Inner Chambers: Women and Culture in Seventeenth-Century China.* Stanford: Stanford University Press, 1994.

Larson, Wendy. *Literary Authority and the Modern Chinese Writer: Ambivalence and Autobiography.* Durham, N.C.: Duke University Press, 1991.

———. *Women and Writing in Modern China.* Stanford: Stanford University Press, 1998.

Lee, Leo Ou-fan. "In Search of Modernity: Some Reflections on a New Mode of Consciousness in Twentieth-Century Chinese History and Literature." In Paul Cohen and Merle Goldman, eds., *Ideas Across Culture: Essays on Chinese Thought in Honor of Benjamin I. Schwartz,* 109–135. Cambridge, Mass.: Harvard University Council on East Asian Studies, 1990.

———. *The Romantic Generation of Modern Chinese Writers.* Cambridge, Mass.: Harvard University Press, 1973.

———. *Shanghai Modern: The Flowering of a New Urban Culture in China, 1930–1945.* Cambridge, Mass.: Harvard University Press, 1999.

Link, Perry. *Mandarin Ducks and Butterflies: Popular Fiction in Early Twentieth Century Chinese Cities.* Berkeley: University of California Press, 1981.

———. *The Uses of Literature: Life in the Socialist Chinese Literary System.* Princeton: Princeton University Press, 2000.

Liu, Lydia. *Translingual Practice: Literature, National Culture, and Translated Modernity—China, 1900–1937.* Stanford: Stanford University Press, 1995.

Mann, Susan. *Precious Records: Women in China's Long Eighteenth Century.* Stanford: Stanford University Press, 1997.

McDougall, Bonnie, and Kam Louie. *The Literature of China in the Twentieth Century.* London: Hurst and Co., 1997.

Tang, Tao. *History of Modern Chinese Literature*. Beijing: Foreign Languages Press, 1993.

Tay, William. "Colonialism, the Cold War Era, and Marginal Space: The Existential Conditions of Four Decades of Hong Kong Literature." In Sung-sheng Yvonne Chang and Michelle Yeh, eds., *Contemporary Chinese Literature: Crossing the Boundaries*, 141–147. Austin: Literature East and West, 1995.

Van Crevel, Maghiel. "Xi Chuan's 'Salute': Avant-garde Poetry in a Changing China." *Modern Chinese Literature and Culture* 11, no. 2 (Fall 1999): 107–149.

Wang, Ban. *The Sublime Figure of History: Aesthetics and Politics in Twentieth-Century China*. Stanford: Stanford University Press, 1997.

Wang, David Der-wei. *Fictional Realism in Twentieth-Century China: Mao Dun, Lao She, Shen Congwen*. New York: Columbia University Press, 1992.

——. *Fin-de-Siècle Splendor: Repressed Modernities of Late Qing Fiction, 1849–1911*. Stanford: Stanford University Press, 1997.

Wang, Jing. *High Culture Fever: Politics, Aesthetics, and Ideology in Deng's China*. Berkeley: University of California Press, 1996.

Wang, Xiaoming. "A Journal and a Literary Society: A Reappraisal of the May Fourth Tradition." *Modern Chinese Literature and Culture* 11, no. 2 (Fall 1999): 1–39.

Wang Yao. *Zhongguo xiandai wenxue shi gao* (A Draft History of New Chinese Literature). Hong Kong: Bowen shuju, 1972 [1951].

Xu, Jian. "*Blush* from Novella to Film: The Possibility of Critical Art in Commodity Culture." *Modern Chinese Literature and Culture* 12, no. 1 (Spring 2000): 115–163.

Yeh, Michelle. "The 'Cult of Poetry' in Contemporary China." *Journal of Asian Studies* 55, no. 1 (1996): 51–80.

58

LANGUAGE AND LITERARY FORM

Modern Chinese literature emerged from a more general, sweeping cultural transformation that spanned the last decades of the Qing dynasty to the aftermath of the World War I (roughly 1841–1921). This transformation was initiated in large part by late Qing literati influenced by Western thought and deeply concerned about China's survival in a hostile, competitive world. In part because it was traditionally the literati who guided and governed the nation, the responses they offered to this crisis were more often intellectual than practical. The transformation culminated in the May Fourth movement, which in many ways defined the character of Chinese cultural modernity, and its principal achievements were the establishment of a standard written vernacular language *(baihua wen)* and the launching of a new Chinese literature, under the influence of European forms, that used this language as a vehicle. The standardization of *baihua* led to unforeseen rigidity under the influence of leftism, nationalism, and war, but the inherent diversity of the Chinese language returned to fracture the bonds of conformity and bring about unprecedented formal innovation.

ESTABLISHING THE LANGUAGE
AND FORMS OF MODERN WRITING

During the 1890s, the first attempts were made in literature and education to develop and use some sort of written vernacular language (as well as to standardize the spoken language) (Doleželová-Velingerová 1977:19–22). The classical or literary language *(wenyan)* that served as the only written medium for official purposes had changed little over two millennia. It was vastly different from modern-day spoken Chinese in both structure and vocabulary and very difficult to learn. Moreover, many literati decried the artificiality of formal prose, the principal mode of written expression in the late imperial period. This genre had been nicknamed "eight-legged essay" *(baguwen)* for its tight formal constraints, and the term continued to be used throughout the twentieth century to refer to slavish adherence to literary formulas and stereotypes. However, the absence of clear alternatives to *wenyan* made the development of a practical modern written language a long and difficult process.

As early as the medieval period a written vernacular much closer to the language of speech began to appear in popular literature (Buddhist sutras and short stories based on the performances of professional storytellers), and continued to develop especially in fiction and drama of the Ming and Qing dynasties. However, it was not until the end of the nineteenth century that educational reformers and publishers began to publish *baihua* journals and primers on practical matters—especially for women and others just learning to read. At the same time, a group of poets emerged who attempted to combine a greatly simplified style with lively emotional, political, and social content (see "The Late Qing Poetry Revolution"). Although the still classical idiom of this poetry halted its development at the turn of the century, one of its practitioners—Liang Qichao—turned his attention to other strategies for achieving linguistic and literary modernity.

Liang Qichao played a crucial role in linking the educational, political, and literary uses of *baihua* (see "The Uses of Fiction"). Educated in both traditional Chinese and modern European cultures, Liang was convinced that the key to cultural modernization and national strength lay in the publishing industry, in the newspaper in particular. Newspapers published by foreign missions and businessmen had existed in treaty ports and foreign concessions throughout most of the nineteenth century; even the earliest of these modified *wenyan* by simplifying the structure and using a limited vocabulary. Observing this phenomenon and its influence, Liang Qichao entered the publishing industry himself, but with a nationalist mission: his newspapers would educate and enlighten their readers to become informed citizens who would help build a strong, modern China. To this end, he developed a hybrid of *wenyan* and *baihua*—called "new style prose," or *xin wenti*—that was a more lucid means of expression than other prose forms of the turn of the century, and which became the standard for newspaper Chinese for more than a generation. In addition, he joined with other prominent modernizers such as Xia Zengyou and Yan Fu to do something that would set the course of modern Chinese literature for most of the twentieth century: he promoted the use of political fiction in the popular press for the civic indoctrination of readers.

There was also experimentation with European style poetry and drama in the 1890s (see "Performing the Nation") and 1900s, but by the 1920s fiction came to dominate modern Chinese letters. According to one literary history, the predominance of fiction over poetry and drama was intimately tied up with matters of language and form (Doleželová-Velingerová 1977:26–31). Attempts to modernize drama were hampered by the tradition of performing in regional dialect, whereas poetry was mired in a formal legacy antithetical to vernacular expression. Late imperial fiction, however, had already been developing for two centuries in the direction advocated by the literary reformers and had a readership much broader than that of purely elite essays and poetry. By the last decades of the Qing, traditional-style novels had already incorporated themes of social critique and were often conceived by their writers as a means of public indoctrination, so as a mode of expression the novel fit right in to the ambitions of turn of the century advocates of new literature.

The Literary Revolution of 1917 and the ensuing New Culture movement attempted to go much farther: leading intellectuals like Hu Shi and Chen Duxiu advocated the complete abandonment of *wenyan* and set the unification of writing and speech as one of the stylistic goals of modern literature. The May Fourth movement merged with the New Culture movement and established a role for these modern intellectual reformers at the forefront of social change and at the center of a new literary arena. The translation of Western literature and the creation of a new, modern vernacular literature became the principal concerns of writers in the 1920s. This set the stage for the emergence of modern China's first major writers, *Lu Xun, Ye Shengtao, and Bing Xin, as well as China's first important modern literary organization, the Wenxue yanjiu hui (Literary Association).

Within fiction, realism took on the role almost of an ideological norm. The preference for fictional realism reveals much about the adoption of the vernacular language and what was at stake. Despite the earnest passion to modernize literature, language, and society, there was still a very traditional faith that the proper form of writing would capture the truth immanent in reality. Literature was not in essence a creative enterprise, but rather a vehicle for the author to bring his readers closer to the truth: the adoption of fictional realism was a modern phase of this age-old concern, one that dominated the first half of this century.

THE ENTRENCHMENT OF REVOLUTIONARY LANGUAGE AND FORM

The written vernacular of the May Fourth intellectuals reflected their education and their social profile. It was not long before writers with revolutionary dreams of uniting with the broad masses of common people began to feel that this new vernacular was still too sophisticated to serve the needs of the general population. By the mid-1920s, further transformation was called for to forge an even more common and popular vernacular idiom. Qu Qiubai was one of the most outspoken and radical advocates of the "massification" (*dazhonghua*) of the modern language and its literature (Pickowicz 1977). As left-wing writers multiplied and influenced the literary mainstream, the League of Left-Wing Writers (est. 1930) helped direct the process by promoting activities and forums that would bring modern literature closer to the working class, linguistically and otherwise. This massification effort also involved experimentation with new forms like reportage and "wall newspapers" *(bibao)* in order to educate the working class and make its members not only consumers of literature but also producers in their own right.

The war against Japan (1937–45) gave leftists the opportunity to exploit widespread anti-Japanese sentiment to popularize their literary initiatives, with the only cost to them being toning down the less popular themes of class struggle and social critique. Inasmuch as business as usual in the publishing industry became impossible, especially after the November 1937 fall of Shanghai, the headquarters of the Chinese publishing industry, the war made unique new demands on writers. The idea that literature was a weapon for struggle gained greater popularity, and its propaganda potential became more important, at least in the short term, than issues of literary quality. The demand for moral seriousness in literature, formerly met with soul-searching complexity and profundity of thought, was under these conditions met by the sincere determination to use literature as a weapon in the effort to resist Japan's invasion. Now even more than in the revolutionary phase of the late 1920s and early 1930s, the audience of contemporary literature had to be maximized, expanded throughout the broad public, even to the illiterate.

Modern writers confronted with this challenge put the 1930s debate on the use of national forms for revolutionary ends into high gear. National forms— premodern popular forms such as folk theater and storytelling—were important vehicles for crossing the literacy gap that had hindered the success of revolutionary literature over the past two decades. Theatrical performances with new patriotic scripts were performed to all kinds of audiences, including the rural peasantry, throughout the regions of the (unoccupied) rear (Holm 1991). The troupes that performed these plays, especially those dispatched from the remote Communist base areas, also penetrated into the front-line battle zones and occupied regions. These plays, as well as dramatic harangues on current events called "living newspapers" *(huobao)*, often had no texts, or only a rudimentary outline. They were performing arts and were often rehearsed into shape in a collective and active process rather than carefully crafted beforehand. Many of the actors, directors, production assistants, and especially writers and organizers of such performances were themselves novelists, poets, and playwrights before the outbreak of the war. The Communist base areas were attractive and relatively safe training grounds for such "cultural workers" (as they came to be called), but the literary record has left behind only a fraction of their interventions into the wartime cultural scene (Hung 1994).

The prolific novelist *Lao She makes an interesting case in point. Although not regarded as a leftist writer when he assumed leadership of the newly formed All China League of Resistance Writers, Lao She confronted the need to adapt both the language and the form of his creative intervention to the needs of the times. He dabbled in the creation of theatrical pieces based on the traditional performing arts. By his own account, these efforts, although determined by the urgent needs of the times, had the effect of reforming his literary imagination, and his subsequent efforts clearly bore the marks of traditional popular forms (Kao 1980).

If standard *baihua* or the "national language" *(guoyu)* was the distinctive product of the Literary Revolution and the May Fourth movement, there would be further, more profound transformations of both the written and spoken languages as a result of "massification," revolutionary literature, the war against Japan, and especially the emergence of a socialist society in the Communist base areas during the war and its subsequent expansion throughout China during and after the civil war. The forces of radical change—militant students, revolutionary organizers, leftist journalists, and officers and soldiers in the Red Army—began by the late 1920s to imagine and legitimize their experience in purely military terms. Courage, determination, even ruthlessness became exalted qualities in every field of endeavor, and written discourse among these groups became suffused with a standardized rhetoric of battle, weapons, front lines, and enemies. By the time of the outbreak of war, such rhetoric, because it had been available to the reading public for some years already, spread very quickly to become a principal medium of discourse, at least for the war experience. Even writers engaged in inquiries not directly related to the war, if writing introductions or prefaces or engaging in a public discussion, almost invariably peppered their words with militant and patriotic catchphrases.

In the Communist base areas, the militarization of the language of everyday life was blended with politically correct Maoist jargon: "class background," "bad elements," and "counterrevolutionary" all became household words. Becoming a good citizen in Mao's republic largely meant acquiring the special language and concepts of Chinese Communism and being able to tell the story of one's own life adeptly using this language and these concepts. The Communist Party learned that perhaps the most effective way to guarantee political conformity was to recreate knowledge and language in their own image and impose it upon their citizens (Apter and Saich 1994).

The regimentation of language in the Maoist era had its literary counterpart in orthodox styles such as socialist realism and "revolutionary romanticism"—in effect, modern-day "eight-legged essays." This is an ironic development, considering that fictional realism was originally viewed in China as a vehicle through which sincere writers would bring readers closer to the truth immanent in historical experience. People learned to hide their true feelings and thoughts behind a mask of political correctness in the interest of self-preservation and the protection of their families. In the tragically frequent political campaigns that enforced conformity throughout the history of the People's Republic at least until the Cultural Revolution (1966–76), these words and concepts (just as the accidents of one's past history) became landmines that could suddenly incriminate the unwitting and weapons to attack those who had made themselves vulnerable through honesty or humanity. This strange political/linguistic process may very well have taken place unconsciously; there were probably only a few cases in the divisive campaigns from the Anti-Rightist movement to the Cultural Revolution of individuals who stood back and said to themselves, "What am I saying?"

Only years after the Cultural Revolution, after the death of the Great Helmsman (Mao Zedong) in 1976 and the birth of the era of reform and opening, did it occur to critics to name the use of this stilted Communist jargon in literature and life "Maoist discourse" and try hard to move beyond it. In fact, one of the principal goals of mainland writers since the mid-1980s has been to wrest themselves and the Chinese reading public free from the stultifying shadow of Maoist discourse, to enrich the language anew and make it once again into a viable medium for the creation of modern literature (Li Tuo 1993). The trend of *"roots-seeking" *(xungen)* literature in the 1980s, many of the works of which were made into prominent films such as *Yellow Earth* and *The King of Children*, registered a profound ambivalence toward the meaning and legitimacy of Maoist discourse: critiquing it and yet still largely caught within its own terms. A more radical break was accomplished by *avant-garde fiction writers such as Can Xue and Yu Hua, who launched an assault on not only conventional language but also the very moral compass and standards of intelligibility that accompanied the legacy of socialist culture. It should come as no surprise that this shift coincided with an unprecedented resurgence of poetry led by writers such as Bei Dao whose defiant ambiguity led conservative critics to label them *"Misty Poets." Indeed, the departure from realism and the linguistic and symbolic enrichment of fiction since the 1980s should be in part attributed to the influence of "misty" and "post-misty" poetry.

REGIONAL SPEECH AND THE FRACTURE OF STANDARDS

The topic of regional speech involves the literatures of Taiwan and Hong Kong as well. To return briefly to the late Qing, regional dialect was one of the principal obstacles to both the standardization of spoken and written modern Chinese and to the establishment of certain forms of modern literature. Apart from what we now call Mandarin, which is spoken widely across the northern half of China but is based largely on the Beijing dialect, there are also the Cantonese spoken in Guangdong Province and in Hong Kong, the Wu and Min dialects of southeastern China, Shandong dialect, Sichuan dialect, and so on. Before language reform and new literature, these dialects were used locally, especially in commerce, everyday speech, and theatrical performances, to the exclusion of official Mandarin (*guanhua*). Even as the modern language and literature were standardized, dialect-based literature persisted in its appeal to regional audiences. One example is the traditional-style vernacular novel *Flowers of Shanghai* (Haishang hua), which was originally written in the Wu (Shanghai) dialect and later became more prominent after its translation into Mandarin by the famous writer *Eileen Chang (Zhang Ailing). These local literatures and performing arts were marginalized by the overwhelming force of standardization during the first half of the twentieth century. But in the wake of the civil war, which ended in 1949, dialects took on a new significance as vehicles of regional identity resisting linguistic and literary standardization with both cultural and political overtones.

For example, the distinction between modernist and nativist literature in Taiwan, usually approached from the point of view of content or theme, can also be illuminated by the issues of language and form. Although the official language of the Republic of China on Taiwan has been Mandarin since its move there in 1949, most of the people (including both immigrants from southeastern China and Chinese-speaking natives of Taiwan) speak variations of the Min dialect. In Taiwan this issue has become more than a linguistic one, as the people indigenous to Taiwan as well as non-elite immigrants from mainland China often feel alienated from the Mandarin-speaking elite associated with the nationalist Guomindang. Rural poverty and ethnic minority issues found expression in the use of dialect-inflected speech in *"nativist" (*xiangtu*) literature (Gunn 1991:154–161). And with the liberalization of the print media in 1986, regional speech has become more conspicuous on the Taiwanese cultural scene. It is worth noting here that a similar inclination toward regional speech in the *"roots-seeking" fiction of the 1980s in mainland China was instrumental in breaking the grip of standard Maoist discourse (Gunn 1991:164–176).

Similar issues surrounded the emergence of Cantonese written literature in Guangzhou and Hong Kong, particularly after World War II (Gunn 1991:48–49). The manifestations of Cantonese inflections in the written language appeared first and continued to be most numerous in newspapers. One of the easiest places to find such special characters to represent idiomatic particles is in political cartoons: the dialogue in the cartoons was often expressed in writing in heavily inflected Cantonese, almost indecipherable to a reader who does not understand Cantonese and a perfect vehicle for political satire when government officials do not speak the local language. Cantonese popular music has become widespread throughout the Chinese-speaking world and has led to an interest in Cantonese expressions and other aspects of popular culture in Taiwan and mainland China as well.

Although a standard written and spoken vernacular based on Beijing dialect is in place, and many had a stake in affirming its authority, forces inherent in actual usage and in literature undermined that authority and continued to threaten its stability throughout the twentieth century. That it has been unable to be completely standardized is testimony to the diversity and vitality of modern spoken Chinese. Similarly, realistic fiction has loosened its hold on modern literature, making room for the proliferation of both nonfictional forms and more adventurous approaches to fiction. This vital diversity will nourish the language and forms of Chinese literature as it enters a phase of unprecedented accomplishment.

—*Charles Laughlin*

Bibliography

Apter, David, and Tony Saich. *Revolutionary Discourse in Mao's Republic.* Cambridge, Mass.: Harvard University Press, 1994.

Doleželová-Velingerová, Milena. "The Origins of Modern Chinese Literature." In Merle Goldman, ed., *Modern Chinese Literature in the May Fourth Era*, 17–35. Cambridge, Mass.: Harvard University Press, 1977.

Gunn, Edward. *Style and Innovation in Twentieth-Century Chinese Prose.* Stanford: Stanford University Press, 1991.

Holm, David. *Art and Ideology in Revolutionary China.* Oxford: Clarendon, 1991.

Hung, Chang-tai. *War and Popular Culture: Resistance in Modern China, 1937–1945.* Berkeley: University of California Press, 1994.

Kao, George, ed. *Two Writers and the Cultural Revolution: Lao She and Ch'en Jo-hsi.* Hong Kong: The Chinese University Press, 1980.

Li, Tuo. "The New Vitality in Modern Chinese." In Wendy Larson and Anne Wedell-Wedellsborg, eds., *Inside Out: Modern and Postmodernism in Chinese Literary Culture*, 65–77. Aarhus: Aarhus University Press, 1993.

Pickowicz, Paul. "Qu Qiubai's Critique of the May Fourth Generation: Early Chinese Marxist Literary Criticism." In Merle Goldman, ed., *Modern Chinese Literature in the May Fourth Era*, 351–384. Cambridge, Mass.: Harvard University Press, 1977.

59

LITERARY COMMUNITIES AND THE PRODUCTION OF LITERATURE

The texts of modern Chinese literature, as with those of any other modern literature, circulate within a professional community of writers, editors, publishers, booksellers, critics, educators, and readers, all of whom share and uphold the conviction that literature is a significant part of culture. In China, as in the United States, this community began to take shape in the second half of the nineteenth century as a direct result of revolutionary changes in the system of education and in the techniques of printing and publishing. However, the ways in which this community organized itself, produced literary works and defined their value, and interacted with the state and other communities has often been very different from other countries. Understanding the habits and beliefs of the members of this community is an important condition for understanding and appreciating the literary works that they shared.

Working with texts has always been the trademark of the Chinese elite. Traditional Chinese education strongly emphasized the reading and memorizing of an array of canonized philosophical, historical, and literary texts. A thorough knowledge of the literary tradition and the ability to write in various literary forms were indispensable for any man wishing to pass the imperial examinations and work his way up the social ladder. Women were not allowed to take part in the examinations, but literacy was very common among upper-class women and there have been women writers throughout Chinese history.

During the second half of the nineteenth century, the Qing government confronted mounting threats to the unity and integrity of the country because of both internal problems (rebellions and uprisings) and external pressure (the on-slaught of Western and Japanese imperialism). In order to cope with these threats, many within government and the local elites believed that the education system should be reformed and offer a wider variety of practically oriented courses. New schools were set up at all levels, offering a Western-style curriculum consisting of various topics in the sciences and humanities (including foreign languages). The importance of literary skills and the significance of the imperial examinations decreased rapidly. Finally, the system of imperial examinations was abolished in 1905 and replaced by a nationwide, state-supported system of primary, secondary, and tertiary education.

With literary skills no longer promising a successful career in government, intellectuals with an interest in textual work were forced to explore new career paths. Many of them took advantage of the mushrooming of new schools all over the country to pursue careers as educators. Many others were attracted by the booming print and publishing industry in major cities, especially Shanghai.

The Chinese, of course, invented the art of printing, and large-scale printing and publishing houses had existed in China from at least the Ming dynasty. However, during the second half of the nineteenth century, the introduction into China of a number of new printing techniques developed in the West (for instance, steam printing and lithography) created the possibility to reproduce texts, photographs, and illustrations in very large quantities and at very low cost. These new techniques enabled the establishment of large, commercial publishing houses and the publication of newspapers, journals, and cheap books. In other words, this was the beginning of modern print culture in China. The new industry was badly in need of writers, translators, proofreaders, editors, and the like, creating many career opportunities for intellectuals.

It was in these two novel sectors of society (the new schools and the new publishing industry) that the modern Chinese literary community began to take shape. Starting out as journalists or teachers, modern Chinese literary intellectuals during the first decades of the twentieth century gradually managed to turn literature into an independent discipline by founding literary organizations, launching literary publications, and promoting literary education. Apart from periods of extreme political repression in mainland China during the 1960s and 1970s, the modern Chinese literary community in the whole of Greater China has displayed a number of stable characteristics.

ORGANIZATIONS

Modern Chinese literary practice throughout the twentieth century has been characterized by a high level of organization. During the first half of the century, most writers clearly preferred working in various kinds of collectives, a preference that was institutionalized by the authorities in mainland China after 1949, with the establishment of the Chinese Writers' Union (*Zhongguo zuojia xiehui*). The most common types of literary organization have been literary-sphere organizations, public-sphere organizations, political organizations, and professional organizations.

A literary-sphere organization is a small society *(shetuan)* mainly involved in the editing of a literary journal meant for the publication of members' own works. Membership is limited to those involved in running the journal. A manifesto is published in the journal's first issue. Members' financial contributions are used to fund the printing and distribution of the journal, although more successful societies of this type have tended to cooperate with publishing houses. Many Chinese writers of the Republican era (1911–49) began their literary careers in such societies and continued to organize similar ones during later stages of their careers. An active organizer was the famous writer *Lu Xun. In the 1920s and 1930s, there were literally hundreds of small societies. In later decades, societies continued to be prominent on the literary scenes of Hong Kong and Taiwan.

A public-sphere organization is a literary association with a relatively formal structure and a public function that extends beyond the literary community. Collectives of this kind depend on a large membership or on shareholders for funding a variety of (publishing) activities, including literary journals, literary series *(congshu)*, and literature textbooks. Their public visibility derives from factors such as the hosting of receptions and dinner parties; the establishment of an official location (a bookshop, printing shop, or clubhouse carrying the name of the society); the publication of announcements in large newspapers; and the signing of general political or cultural manifestos. This type of society is almost exclusively a phenomenon of the Republican era and played a large role in the public acceptance of new literature *(xin wenxue)* and its literary scene *(wentan)*. Important examples are the Literary Association (Wenxue yanjiu hui, 1920–47) and the Creation Society (Chuangzao she, 1921–30).

A political organization is one whose literary activities are determined by the agenda of a government or political party. Its literary significance is usually limited, but for the sponsoring party its value may be considerable. A typical example is the League of Left-Wing Writers (1930–36), which was established by the Communist Party.

A professional organization provides the basis for its members' livelihood. Many small drama societies of the Republican era were of this type, but the most important example is the Chinese Writers' Union, the main literary institution of the People's Republic of China (PRC), a government organization under the auspices of the Ministry of Culture. It has subdivisions on the provincial and local levels. It provides writers with a steady income, housing, and social benefits in return for their loyalty to party principles concerning literature. The system has consolidated the status and well-being of writers, but it has also restricted their freedom, especially at times of extreme ideological pressure. In the 1990s, when a privatized market for literature began to develop, many writers ceased to be dependent on the union. However, it continues to play an important role in the literary life of the PRC.

PUBLICATIONS

Partly because of this preference for collective organization, the most important medium for the publication of literary works in modern China has always been the literary journal. Literary journals are periodical publications devoted in their entirety to the theory and practice of literature. In twentieth-century China, these include both literary magazines and literary supplements of newspapers. The first literary journals appeared in Shanghai in the late nineteenth century. They were mainly commercial fiction journals aimed at a broad readership of literati and city-dwellers, although many of them included contributions in other genres written for a more limited audience. A further change occurred in the late 1910s and early 1920s, with the influx of large numbers of graduates from the new education system into the publishing business and the rapid spread of the new literature. The new literature journals, often run by literary societies, had a more highbrow and less commercial image, although most of them were business ventures catering to the tastes of the younger generation. These new literature journals come closest to the Western definition of a "serious" literary journal. It should be kept in mind, however, that journals containing more traditional forms of (popular) literature continued to appear and draw a substantial readership throughout the twentieth century.

In China, unlike in many Western countries, books have never really replaced journals as the primary avenue for publication of literary work. In the present-day PRC, even full-length novels by famous writers are often first serialized in literary journals before they are presented in book form. The dominance of this mode of literary production merits consideration, particularly of its general effects on literary writing and literary texts. For the writer, regular contribution to journals has important financial advantages (journals usually pay by the word). This can lead to a tendency to write large numbers of short works, or very large works in many short installments. During the Republican era, the shorter genres were extremely popular, while somewhat longer works, such as *Lu Xun's seminal "The True Story of Ah Q" (Ah Q zhengzhuan, 1922), clearly bear the traces of publication in installments in the form of cliffhangers and other devices meant to keep the audience's attention. If financial pressure or pressure from the editors is high, journal publication can also lead to fast or sloppy writing. This phenomenon was especially prevalent during the Republican era, but is not entirely absent today because the PRC Writers' Union demands regular productivity from its members. Finally, because most literary journals are commercial in orientation (for instance, because they rely on income from advertisements) and reach relatively large audiences, writers may be inclined to take their perception of readers' tastes and needs strongly into account, which can result in populist or moralizing writing and in a reluctance to experiment.

The exact influence of journal publication on modern Chinese reading habits has not been investigated. Although readers will read journals selectively, rather than from cover to cover, it is not unlikely that, besides the individual reputation of an author, the collective reputation of a journal or a literary society will play some role in readers' approaches to and appreciation of literary works. This assumption is supported by the prominent role commonly assigned to groups, schools, societies, and journals in histories of modern Chinese literature, both in mainland China and in Taiwan.

LITERARY EDUCATION

Although the introduction of a modern education system in China from the late nineteenth century onward brought about a significant drop in the cultural value of literary skills, the study of literary texts continued to be part of the school curriculum. However, emphasis in teaching shifted from memorization and reproduction to the reading and analysis of literary texts. Under the influence of the modern Western concept of literature (encompassing fiction, poetry, and drama), literary education began to include the study of vernacular genres, such as the novel.

Education was the key to the success of the new literature. Whereas the first generation of literary reformers, including people like *Liang Qichao (1873–1929), were "journalist-littérateurs" (Lee 1973) who wielded their influence mainly through journals and newspapers and gave modern literature an audience, the second generation, including people like Hu Shi (1891–1962), Chen Duxiu (1880–1942), and Zhou Zuoren (1885–1967), were "literary intellectuals" (McDougall and Louie 1997), active in schools and universities, who gave modern literature its status. Within years after the Literary Revolution of 1917 (see "Language and Literary Form"), works of new literature were being included in school textbooks and were well on their way toward canonization.

A very influential canon of modern Chinese literature was the one established in the PRC after 1949 (see "Modern Chinese Literature As an Institution"). In line with Mao Zedong's opinions on the nature and function of literature, standard textbooks from both before and after the Cultural Revolution made literary development subservient to political development (for instance, adopting periodizations based on the various stages of the "revolution") and placed great emphasis on the political correctness of the contents of literary works. Although this canon of revolutionary literature has come under increasing attack since the 1980s, the idea that the mainstream of modern Chinese literature should consist of socially engaged, realist writing remains a commonplace among scholars and students of modern Chinese literature, both in China and elsewhere.

In post-1949 Taiwan, for various, mainly political, reasons, modern Chinese literature was not commonly taught in Chinese departments of universities. Although the discipline was finally established in the 1980s, its significance has been overshadowed by the more pressing concerns for the historiography of and education in modern Taiwanese literature, referring to texts written during the twentieth century by writers living on Taiwan and writing either in Japanese, in Taiwanese, or in Mandarin Chinese. The problems involved in writing and teaching the history of Taiwanese literature continue to divide the Taiwanese literary community into "China-oriented" and "nativist" groups (see Martin 1995).

In Hong Kong under British rule, the teaching and study of Chinese literature was long marginalized. Modern Chinese literature, especially, was considered a minor subject, for, unlike classical literature, it could not be employed to transmit the Chinese cultural heritage. As in Taiwan, the topic of local identity, intertwined with issues of colonialism and postcolonialism and of language (English, Cantonese, Mandarin), played an important role in the study of modern literature in Hong Kong in the last two decades of the twentieth century.

Education in modern Chinese literature in all areas of Greater China strongly affirms the relationship between works of literature and sociopolitical reality, with relatively less emphasis placed on the aesthetic function of literature. Although this is an overgeneralization, it is safe to say that many Chinese readers and critics have great tolerance for political and didactic statements in literary texts, and that this taste has been partly inculcated by the canonization practices of literary education.

CENSORSHIP

All literature published in China during the twentieth century and all literature published in Taiwan until the late 1980s was produced under conditions of state censorship. This means that for most modern Chinese writers, unlike for modern writers in most Western countries, censorship is the norm, and knowing how to deal with censorship authorities an essential skill.

During the first three decades of the twentieth century, censorship of literature was normally carried out after publication, with regulations differing from region to region and censors erratically deciding to ban certain books or journals, or to raid certain shops or publishing houses. In the 1930s, the Nationalist government attempted to establish a system of prepublication censorship, forcing publishers to submit all book manuscripts to censorship authorities for inspection and possible revision. One of the main (although surely unintended) results of this policy was the further rise in popularity of literary magazines, which, due to the time constraints on their production, were exempt from censorship prior to publication. Main targets of censorship in the 1930s were works referring to the (then outlawed) Communist movement and works critical of the government's policy toward Japanese aggression. Although the Nationalist government attempted to launch its own literary movement, its censorship system was more prohibitive than prescriptive, not telling writers what to write but what *not* to write. The 1930s were a good period for apolitical, modernist writers in that the censorship system had nothing against their works, whereas it significantly limited the impact on cultural circles of prescriptive Communist ideology.

Around the same time on Taiwan, under Japanese rule, the authorities were carrying out what has become known as the "assimilation policy" aimed at fully integrating Taiwan (and Korea as well) into the Japanese empire. In the literary realm, this policy demanded a type of writing that has since become known as *kominka* literature, written in Japanese and emphasizing themes such as loyalty to the Japanese emperor, Taiwanese men volunteering for the Japanese army, as well as co-prosperity in general. Although most Taiwanese writers of the time ended up conforming to the policy in one way or other (the alternative being not to publish at all), various expressions of resistance or ambiguity can and have been read into their works.

When the Nationalist government relocated to Taiwan in 1949, it established a prohibitive censorship system similar to that of mainland China in the 1930s. The main target of censorship was still leftist writing, but a second important target, especially in the 1950s and 1960s, was *Taiwanese nativism. Most important literary publications were initially controlled by intellectuals who had moved from the mainland and brought along and continued the new literary tradition, but with an even greater emphasis on modernism, both through translation of Western modernist works and theories and through original creation. After the extended debates between *"modernists" and *"nativists" in the late 1970s, and especially after the introduction of civil rights, including freedom of speech, in 1987, nativist critics pointed out the ambiguous relationship between the modernist trend and government cultural policy at the time. On one hand, modernist writing was politically safe, for the censors had no interest in it. On the other hand, through its language (standard Chinese) and its background (building on mainland Chinese literary history), it also helped to further the government's attempts to suppress expressions of local Taiwanese culture.

By far the most repressive system of censorship, however, was established in mainland China by Communist authorities after 1949. Adopting Mao Zedong's *"Yan'an Talks" as its basic credo, the Communist authorities assumed a prescriptive approach and installed a system of total prepublication censorship. All publishing houses were brought under state control, and all writers were assembled in the Writers' Union. In theory, nothing that did not live up to the doctrine of socialist realism could be published. The reason so many writers were persecuted and so many books banned during the first three decades of the PRC was not that the censorship system did not work properly, but rather that official views of what could or could not be permitted kept changing. Many writers who were imprisoned or killed for their writing earnestly believed that they had been following the official policies and indeed enthusiastically supported them (as in the case of the *Hundred Flowers movement of 1956–57). Policies were most extreme during the Cultural Revolution (1966–76), when cultural authorities drew up long lists of requirements for literary form and content aimed at preventing any possible confusion about, for instance, who were the heroes and who were the villains in a particular work (see "The Cultural Revolution Model Theater").

During the Cultural Revolution, other types of literature than the officially sanctioned ones managed to survive through the apparently spontaneous development of a network of underground distribution of texts and books, which were often copied out by hand and exchanged among young intellectuals throughout the country. After the Cultural Revolution, some of these underground writers, such as the poet Bei Dao (pen name of Zhao Zhenkai, b. 1949) (see "Misty Poetry"), soon rose to prominence both inside and outside China. During the last two decades of the twentieth century, censorship in the People's Republic gradually became more relaxed, but occasional campaigns continued to be leveled against writers or works perceived to have directly attacked the leadership of the Party, insulted national minorities, or violated "good taste." Prepublication censorship mechanisms are still in place and many problems with the authorities are avoided by editors preemptively cutting out possibly objectionable passages from authors' manuscripts. In general, there now seems to be a status quo in which writers censor themselves, in a way, by choosing not to write on topics known to be problematic while fully exploring all the topics (such as, for instance, sex) that were once taboo and are now permissible.

Meanwhile, however, the increase in contact between the mainland and Taiwan has opened up important avenues of publication for mainland authors. Many new works by leading writers from the PRC are now often first published in Taiwan or Hong Kong, which has the double advantage of freeing authors from censorship and giving them substantially higher fees and royalties. The emergence of a Greater China literary community, as well as the increased participation of Chinese writers in a global literary community through, for instance, international festivals and prizes, and of course through translation are important developments that will no doubt influence the course of Chinese literature in the twenty-first century.

—*Michel Hockx*

Bibliography

Denton, Kirk A., ed. *Modern Chinese Literary Thought: Writings on Literature, 1893–1945*. Stanford: Stanford University Press, 1996.

Hockx, Michel. *Questions of Style: Literary Societies and Literary Journals in Modern China*. Leiden: E. J. Brill, 2003.

——, ed. *The Literary Field of Twentieth-Century China*. Honolulu: University of Hawai'i Press, 1999.

Lee, Leo Ou-fan. *The Romantic Generation of Modern Chinese Writers*. Cambridge, Mass.: Harvard University Press, 1973.

Link, Perry. *The Uses of Literature: Life in the Socialist Chinese Literary System*. Princeton: Princeton University Press, 2000.

Martin, Helmut. *The History of Taiwanese Literature: Towards Cultural-Political Identity. Views from Taiwan, China, Japan and the West*. Bochum: Ruhr University, 1995.

McDougall, Bonnie, and Kam Louie. *The Literature of China in the Twentieth Century*. London: Hurst and Co., 1997.

60

MODERN CHINESE LITERATURE AS AN
INSTITUTION: CANON AND LITERARY HISTORY

Literary history is a reconstruction of the past in writing, an interpretative practice informed in varying degrees by the literary historian's chosen theoretical paradigm as well as his (rarely her in modern China) ideological purpose at a specific historical moment (Zhang 1994:348). Different artistic or ideological agendas, as well as changing political circumstances, often determine the model of literary development and the selection of literary writers and works in literary histories.

The first phase of the formation of a modern Chinese literary history, from the 1920s to the 1940s, I call the "experimental phase." This phase is characterized by efforts to institute modern literature as a legitimate subject worthy of special attention due to its close tie to contemporary life. In 1922, Hu Shi published a survey of Chinese literature from the previous fifty years and instituted an evolutionary paradigm by endorsing "new literature" *(xin wenxue)* as "living literature" that would replace "dead" or "half-dead" classical literature (Hu Shi 1953: 165–66). Contrary to Hu's model of a linear development toward a certain telos, Zhou Zuoren envisioned in 1934 a pattern of wavelike movement, with "literary as a vehicle of the Dao" *(wen yi zai dao)* and literature as an "expression of intention" *(yan zhi)* as two alternating currents that rise and fall with literary developments. With the publication of Wang Zhefu's 1933 history, Chinese literary historiography embarked on a genuine search for methodology. Most literary historians adopted Wang's narrative method of combining theoretical discussion, historical account, and detailed analysis of individual writers in subsequent years. On the other hand, Li Helin's 1939 book signaled the starting point from which issues of periodization and the ideological "nature" of modern Chinese literature became polemical. For Li, the first period began with the May Fourth movement (1919), and all his other periods were demarcated by significant sociohistorical events such as the Japanese invasions of Manchuria and Shanghai. Li's model carries the serious implications that literary development is directly affected by historical events, and that historical events must further be subject to correct political interpretation. Another notable work of this period is A Ying's 1937 study of late Qing fiction, which proposed a sociological model by classifying social themes in fiction and treating literature as "reflecting" social conditions.

Scholarship on modern Chinese literary history from the 1920s to the 1940s may be characterized as experimental in that it rarely aspired to a comprehensive coverage of all aspects of literary developments and sought, instead, to develop certain historical visions, theoretical paradigms, or narrative methods. In other words, a full-scaled institutionalization of literary history was not attempted until after the founding of the People's Republic of China (PRC) in 1949, which marks the beginning of phase two in the formation of modern Chinese literary historiography. One immediate cause of the new efforts at canon formation was pedagogical, for leading universities were in urgent need of curriculum development for their Chinese programs. The official release of the first volume of Wang Yao's comprehensive history in 1951 marked a founding moment in this sense. Wang Yao adopted Li Helin's scheme of periodization and improved Wang Zhefu's methodology. Like Hu Shi before him, Wang Yao also implemented an evolutionary paradigm, but this time modern Chinese literature was shown to "progress" toward the ends legitimized by Mao Zedong's 1942 *"Yan'an Talks," namely, literature must serve Party politics and appeal to the masses.

In spite of its ideological efforts, Wang Yao's history was harshly criticized in 1952 for neglecting revolutionary writers and proletarian leadership, and the result of official intervention was the increasing politicization of modern Chinese literature. Ding Yi's 1955 history, which soon became available in English translation (Ding Yi 1959), defined realism as the mainstream, integrated class analysis into its discussion, and clearly labeled writers as "revolutionary" (for example, Jiang Guangci and Hu Yepin), "progressive" (for example, *Lao She and *Ba Jin), and "bourgeois" (for example, Xu Zhimo and *Shen Congwen). The prerogative of "political correctness" was evident in subsequent literary histories, such as Liu Shousong's (1956), which reclassified writers into two opposing camps, the "enemy's" (*di*) and "ours" (*wo*) and devoted three chapters to *Lu Xun, redefined as "a great Communist" writer. Compared with the experimental spirit that characterized the founding phase of literary historiography, the second phase in the PRC was marked by a monolithic voice and by extreme intolerance. For instance, women's writings and stories about private or "humanistic" concerns are denounced as petit bourgeois and are written out of standard history. Toward the mid-1960s, only a handful of "revolutionary" writers (for example* Lu Xun, Guo Moruo, and *Mao Dun) survived rigid political scrutiny, and scholars such as Wang Yao and Liu Shousong were severely criticized during the Cultural Revolution (see sample criticisms collected in Wang Yao 1972).

The historiography of phase three focuses on canon revision, and its beginnings can be traced back to the 1970s. Outside the PRC, scholars slowly began to revise the canon set up by the Communist ideological apparatuses. While Li Huiying's history—published in Hong Kong in 1970—attempted to reclaim the tradition of intellectual openness of the first phase, Liu Xinhuang's—published in Taiwan—redirected attention to the New Literature movement and expanded coverage to include Taiwan literature. It was not until 1975–78 that a substantial challenge to the Communist canon was posed by Sima Changfeng's three-volume history, which is distinguished by its meticulous documentation, its nonpartisan position, its wide selection of "marginal" or women writers (for example, Mu Shiying and Xu Xu, or Luo Shu and Lin Huiyin), and its organic model of literary development from "birth" through "fruition" to "decline" and "stagnancy." Although he shared Sima's pessimism by declaring that modern Chinese literature had turned into a "wasteland" by the 1960s, Zhou Jin (1980:9) nonetheless launched with Taiwan Chengwen Books in 1980 an ambitious forty-volume book series, which covered or "rediscovered" neglected literary schools and societies (such as *Crescent Moon), writers (for example, Qian Zhongshu, *Xiao Hong, and Su Xuelin), and intellectuals (for example, Lin Shu, Wu Mi, and Mei Guangdi). The fact that Zhou Jin's series openly deals with the Creationists (many of them Communists), for instance, reveals the increasing freedom Taiwan scholars were allowed in the early 1980s.

The 1980s also witnessed a proliferation of literary histories in the PRC, most of them fruits of collective efforts, and nearly all of them intended for use as college textbooks. As represented by Tang Tao's three-volume history, this new crop of histories inherited certain "genetic" traits from their precursors, and periodization was done strictly in accordance with the sociohistorical paradigm. Gradually, however, a revision of the canon was underway, particularly in the project of rewriting literary history *(chongxie wenxue shi)* in the late 1980s (Zhang 1994:371). Three separate works by Beijing University professors—in the fine tradition of literary scholarship exemplified by Wang Yao and Tang Tao—are worth mentioning: Qian Liqun and his colleagues' 1987 history of modern literature reclaimed the tradition of intellectual openness, although political jargon still props up from time to time; Chen Pingyuan's 1989 history of late Qing fiction returned to A Ying's pioneering exploration of the late Qing as the beginning period of modern Chinese literature; and Yan Jiayan's 1989 history of modern fiction recommended a new historiographic paradigm, one that traces the formation, divergence, and convergence of various literary schools or trends *(liupai)* in modern China (see Zhang 1991 for a review).

Two other points regarding literary historiography merit further attention. First, in the 1980s, periodization schemes were greatly loosened up, and the starting dates of modern Chinese literature were pushed back to late Qing (see also David Wang 1997). Second, from studies of literary schools initiated by Yan Jiayan and pursued by many others (for example, Shi Jianwei 1986), the Chinese modernism of both the Beijing and Shanghai schools of the 1920s and 1930s, which had been proscribed in most previous PRC literary histories, emerged as a viable alternative to mainstream realism. Rather than grouping writers according to their alleged political or ideological affiliations, which had been the practice, literary historians paid more attention to other connections in terms of gender (for example, women writers), geographical area (for example, Northeastern writers), literary styles and themes (for example, the *New Sensationists [*xin ganjue pai*] and psychoanalytic fiction). To a great extent, Yang Yi's three-volume history of modern Chinese fiction represents the best product of the canon revision taking place in this third phase of literary historiography, and Huang Xiuji's (1995) history of modern Chinese literary historiography provides an overview of major books, historians, and problems.

LITERARY HISTORY OF TAIWAN AND HONG KONG

In terms of either quantity or quality, scholarship on Taiwan and Hong Kong literatures pales in comparison to that for mainland literature. This unfortunate situation may have resulted not just from the geopolitically (though not economically) marginal status of both Taiwan and Hong Kong, but from other factors, such as the Nationalist (GMD) government's investment in the revival of traditional Chinese culture in Taiwan, and the British colonial government's discouragement of reflections on local culture and history in Hong Kong.

In spite of the flourish of *"nativist literature" (xiangtu wenxue), modernist poetry, and popular fiction (for example, *Qiong Yao), the history of Taiwan literature did not receive much scholarly attention until the 1970s. Li Shaoting's 1977 work represents one of the earliest book-length treatments of the subject. After years of archival research and critical discussion, the picture of the Japanese occupation period—when writers published in both Chinese and Japanese—became clearer. In a 1987 history of Taiwan literature, Ye Shitao (b. 1925), a long-time advocate for nativist literature, starts his discussion with the influence of traditional Chinese literature on the island and the development of the new literature movement in the 1920s and the 1930s. From the 1940s to the 1980s, Ye periodizes by decade and examines both literary and sociohistorical events. In 1995, Xu Junya's doctoral dissertation on Taiwan fiction of the occupation period was published in book form. This work contains a wealth of information on and analyzes not just literary societies and journals but also writers, themes, styles, dialects, and characters. A new development in the 1990s was the debate on Taiwan identity, and scholars have drawn on theories of anthropology and postcolonial criticism to inform their historical research (for example, Chen Zhaoying 1998; Lin Ruiming 1996).

Several histories of Taiwan literature have been published in the PRC, among which Gu Jitang's *History of the Development of New Poetry in Taiwan* (Taiwan xinshi fazhan shi, 1989) also appeared in a Taiwan edition. Like Ye Shitao, Gu also adopts decades as his periodizing scheme and surveys the rise of fiction in Taiwan (for example, Lai Ho as "Taiwan's Lu Xun"), its uneven developments through anticommunist fiction of the 1950s, *modernist fiction (for example, Bai Xianyong and Wang Wenxing) of the 1960s, *nativist fiction (for example, Chen Yingzhen and Huang Chunming) of the 1970s, and its diversification in the 1980s. As true of most other PRC histories, the two-volume history compiled by Liu Denghan and his associates in 1991 aspires to a comprehensive treatment, tracing roots back to ancient Taiwan culture, oral literature of the aboriginals, through the Ming and Qing dynasties, to the early occupation period. In the United States, very few book-length studies of Taiwan literary history are available; other than a collection of critical studies (Faurot 1980) and numerous articles scattered around, Yvonne Chang's *Modernism and the Nativist Resistance* (1993) stands nearly alone. One encouraging sign, however, is that both Columbia University Press and the University of Hawai'i Press have published many books of Taiwan literature in English translation in the 1990s.

Even more underdeveloped is the research on the history of Hong Kong literature. According to Leung Ping-kwan, a noted Hong Kong poet and scholar, only in the 1990s does the study of Hong Kong literature emerge with the appearance of book-length studies, most of which are "compiled by mainland Chinese scholars" and informed by "a predominantly mainland Chinese perspective" (Leung 1998:78). Nonetheless, it is interesting to note that Hong Kong scholars published a number of anthologies and bibliographies of Hong Kong literature in 1996–97, right before the colony's return to China's sovereignty.

SOME DEVELOPMENTS IN THE WEST

In 1961, C. T. Hsia published the first history of modern Chinese fiction written in English and explained that his "main intention has been to contradict rather than affirm the communist view of modern Chinese fiction" (Hsia 1961:498). Focusing on the art of individual writers, Hsia elevated *Shen Congwen, *Eileen Chang, Qian Zhongshu, and Shi Tuo to a level comparable to, if not better than, PRC canonized writers such as *Lu Xun, *Mao Dun, *Lao She, and *Ba Jin. Hsia's radical challenge to the PRC canon triggered a polemical exchange between him and Jaroslav Prušek over ideological functions of literature and literary study (Prušek 1961; Hsia 1963; see also Zhang 1993: 820–21). From his firm Marxist stance, Prušek denounces Hsia's preference of minor writers over socially committed masters of letters. Although Hsia's author-centered approach to literary history might have influenced Leo Ou-fan Lee's (1973) study of the romantic generation of Chinese writers, Hsia's interest in New Criticism finds echoes in Edward Gunn's close readings of some "minor" writers—labeled as "unwelcome muses"—marginalized by the PRC scholars for years (Gunn 1980). Perhaps not originally intended, Perry Link's study of popular urban fiction of the *Butterfly school has also challenged the rigid divide between "serious literature" and popular urban culture (Link 1981). In fact, fifteen years later, images of the city and urban culture have come to great prominence in literary-historical research (Zhang 1996; Lee 1999), and the blurring of high and low culture has fundamentally changed the institution of literary history in modern China (D. Wang 1998).

Two other works contributed to the paradigm shift during the 1990s. Marston Anderson (1990) interrogates the canonical practice of realism in modern Chinese literature by revealing the social and moral impediments to pure representation, whereas Rey Chow (1991) proceeds from the margins of literary history and redirects our attention to textual details that challenge the entrenched habits of interpretation in modern Chinese literature. Although itself more a critical intervention than a historical study, Lydia Liu's 1995 book seeks to replace the influence model of comparative literature with one that is squarely situated in historical situations in modern China. Also related to literary history of modern China is Kirk Denton's 1996 anthology of modern Chinese literary criticism, which contains an extensive introduction to major problematics in literary study from 1893 to 1945. However, despite numerous English studies of modern Chinese literature (listed in Chow 1998:1–2), the only ambitious literary history in English to follow Hsia's is the 1997 book coauthored by Bonnie McDougall and Kam Louis, which, while comprehensive in its coverage (including poetry and drama from 1900 to 1989), is nevertheless limited by its lack of in-depth critical analysis of representative writers and works.

Literary history is an ongoing project of constructing the past in literary production and reception. As a result, canon formation and revision is an open-ended process in and through which generations of literary critics and historians compete in verifying evidence, supplying interpretations, and negotiating their own production and distribution of knowledge and power.

—*Yingjin Zhang*

Bibliography

A Ying. *Wan Qing xiaoshuo shi* (A History of Late Qing Fiction). Beijing: Renmin wenxue, 1980.

Anderson, Marston. *The Limits of Realism: Chinese Fiction in the Revolutionary Period*. Berkeley: University of California Press, 1990.

Chang, Sung-cheng Yvonne. *Modernism and the Nativist Resistance: Contemporary Fiction from Taiwan.* Durham, N.C.: Duke University Press, 1993.

Chen Pingyuan. *Ershi shiji Zhongguo xiaoshuo shi* (A History of Twentieth-Century Chinese Fiction), vol. 1. Beijing: Beijing daxue, 1989.

Chen Zhaoying. *Taiwan wenxue yu bentuhua yundong* (Taiwan Literature and the Nativization Movement). Taipei: Zhengzhong shuju, 1998.

Chi, Pang-yuan and David Der-wei Wang, eds. *Chinese Literature in the Second Half of a Modern Century: A Critical Survey.* Bloomington: Indiana University Press, 2000.

Chow, Rey. *Ethics after Idealism: Theory-Culture-Ethnicity-Reading.* Bloomington: Indiana University Press, 1998.

———. *Woman and Chinese Modernity: The Politics of Reading between West and East.* Minneapolis: University of Minnesota Press, 1991.

Chow, Tse-tsung. *The May Fourth Movement: Intellectual Revolution in Modern China.* Cambridge, Mass.: Harvard University Press, 1960.

Denton, Kirk A., ed. *Modern Chinese Literary Thought: Writings on Literature, 1893–1945.* Stanford: Stanford University Press, 1996.

Ding Yi. *A Short History of Modern Chinese Literature.* Peking: Foreign Languages Press, 1959.

———. *Zhongguo xiandai wenxue shilüe* (A Brief History of Modern Chinese Literature). Beijing: Zuojia, 1955.

Faurot, Jeannette L. *Chinese Fiction from Taiwan: Critical Perspectives.* Bloomington: University of Indiana Press, 1980.

Goldman, Merle, ed. *Modern Chinese Literature in the May Fourth Era.* Cambridge, Mass.: Harvard University Press, 1977.

Gu Jitang. *Taiwan xiaoshuo fazhan shi* (A History of the Development of Taiwan Fiction). Taipei: Wenshizhe, 1989.

———. *Taiwan xinshi fazhan shi* (A History of the Development of New Poetry in Taiwan). Taipei: Wenshizhe, 1989.

Gunn, Edward. *Unwelcome Muse: Chinese Literature in Shanghai and Peking, 1937–1945.* New York: Columbia University Press, 1980.

Hsia, C.T. *A History of Modern Chinese Fiction.* New York: Columbia University Press, 1971 [1961].

———. "On the 'Scientific' Study of Modern Chinese Literature: A Reply to Professor Prušek." *T'oung Pao* 50, nos. 4–5 (1963): 428–474.

Hu Shi. *Wushinian lai Zhongguo zhi wenxue* (Chinese Literature in the Past Fifty Years). Taipei: Yuandong tushu, 1953 [1922].

Huang Xiuji. *Zhongguo xin wenxue shi bianzuan shi* (A History of the Historiography of Modern Chinese Literature). Beijing: Beijing daxue, 1995.

Lee, Leo Ou-fan. *The Romantic Generation of Modern Chinese Writers.* Cambridge, Mass.: Harvard University Press, 1973.

———. *Shanghai Modern: The Flowering of a New Urban Culture in China, 1930–1945.* Cambridge, Mass.: Harvard University Press, 1999.

Leung, Ping-kwan. "Two Discourses on Colonialism: Huang Guliu and Eileen Chang." *Boundary 2* 25, no. 3 (1998): 77–96.

Li Helin. *Jin ershinian zhongguo wenyi sichaolun* (An Essay on Chinese Ideological Currents in Literature and Arts over the Past Twenty Years). Xi'an: Shanxi renmin, 1981 [1939].

Li Huiying. *Zhongguo xiandai wenxue shi* (A History of Modern Chinese Literature). Hong Kong: Dongya shuju, 1970.

Li Shaoting. *Taiwan xin wenxue yundong jianshi* (A Concise History of the New Literary Movement in Taiwan). Taipei: Lianjing, 1977.

Lin Ruiming. *Taiwan wenxue de lishi kaocha* (A Historical Investigation of Taiwan Literature). Taipei: Yunchen, 1996.

Link, Perry. *Mandarin Ducks and Butterflies: Popular Fiction in Early Twentieth Century Chinese Cities*. Berkeley: University of California Press, 1981.

Liu Denghan, Zhuang Mingxuan, Huang Chongtian, and Lin Chenghuang, eds. *Taiwan wenxue shi* (A History of Taiwan Literature). 2 vols. Fuzhou: Haixia wenyi, 1991.

Liu, Lydia. *Translingual Practice: Literature, National Culture, and Translated Modernity—China, 1900–1937*. Stanford: Stanford University Press, 1995.

Liu Shousong. *Zhongguo xin wenxue shi chugao* (A Draft History of New Chinese Literature). 2 vols. Beijing: Renmin wenxue, 1979 [1956].

Liu Xinhuang. *Xiandai zhongguo wenxue shihua* (A History of Modern Chinese Literature). Taipei: Zhengzhong shuju, 1971.

McDougall, Bonnie, and Kam Louie. *The Literature of China in the Twentieth Century*. London: Hurst and Co., 1997.

Prušek, Jaroslav. "Basic Problems of the History of Modern Chinese Literature and C.T. Hsia, *A History of Modern Chinese Fiction*." *T'oung Pao* 49, nos. 4–5 (1961): 357–404.

Qian Liqun, Wu Fuhui, Wen Rumin, and Wang Chaobing. *Zhongguo xiandai wenxue sanshinian* (Three Decades in Modern Chinese Literature). Shanghai: Shanghai wenyi, 1987.

Shi Jianwei. *Zhongguo xiandai wenxue liupai lun* (On Literary Schools in Modern Chinese Literature). Xi'an: Shanxi renmin, 1986.

Sima Changfeng. *Zhongguo xin wenxue shi* (A History of New Chinese Literature). 3 vols. Hong Kong: Shaomin, 1975–78.

Tang Tao. *History of Modern Chinese Literature*. Beijing: Foreign Languages Press, 1993.

——, ed. *Zhongguo xiandai wenxue shi* (A History of Modern Chinese Literature). 3 vols. Beijing: Renmin wenxue, 1979–80.

Wang, David Der-wei. *Fictional Realism in Twentieth-Century China: Mao Dun, Lao She, Shen Congwen*. New York: Columbia University Press, 1992.

——. *Fin-de-Siècle Splendor: Repressed Modernities of Late Qing Fiction, 1849–1911*. Stanford: Stanford University Press, 1997.

Wang Yao. *Zhongguo xiandai wenxue shi gao* (A Draft History of New Chinese Literature). Hong Kong: Bowen shuju, 1972 [1951].

Wang Zhefu. *Zhongguo xin wenxue yundong shi* (A History of the Movements of New Chinese Literature). Beijing: Jiecheng yinshuju, 1933.

Xu Junya. *Riju shiqi Taiwan xiaoshuo yanjiu* (A Study of Taiwan Fiction during the Japanese Occupation Period). Taipei: Wenshizhe, 1995.

Yan Jiayan. *Zhongguo xiandai xiaoshuo liupai shi* (A History of the Schools of Modern Chinese Fiction). Beijing: Renmin wenxue, 1989.

Yang Yi. *Zhongguo xiandai xiaoshuo shi* (A History of Modern Chinese Fiction). 3 vols. Beijing: Remin wenxue, 1986–91.

Ye Shitao. *Taiwan wenxue shigang* (A History of Taiwan Literature). Taipei: Wenxuejie zazhishe, 1987.

Zhang, Yingjin. "Four Recent Histories of Modern Chinese Fiction in the PRC." *Journal of Asian Studies* 50, no. 4 (1991): 923–925.

——. *The City in Modern Chinese Literature and Film: Configurations of Space, Time, and Gender.* Stanford: Stanford University Press, 1996.

——. "The Institutionalization of Modern Literary History in China, 1922–1980." *Modern China* 20, no. 3 (1994): 347–377.

——. "Re-envisioning the Institution of Chinese Literary Studies: Strategies of Positionality and Self-Reflexivity." *Positions* 1, no. 3 (1993): 816–832.

Zhou Jin. *Zhongguo xinwenxue jianshi* (A Concise History of New Chinese Literature). Taipei: Chengwen, 1980.

Zhou Zuoren. *Zhongguo xinwenxue zhi yuanliu* (The Sources of New Chinese Literature). Beijing: Renwen shudian, 1934.

Authors, Works, Schools

61

THE LATE QING POETRY REVOLUTION:
LIANG QICHAO, HUANG ZUNXIAN,
AND CHINESE LITERARY MODERNITY

The *shijie geming* (poetry revolution), a term that first appeared in Liang Qichao's (1873–1929) *Record of Travel* (Hanman lu), a diary of his ocean voyage from Yokohama to Honolulu in December 1899 (Chen 1985:321–340), has been the object of a great deal of attention by Chinese writers and literary scholars. In their pioneering works on the history of modern Chinese literature, Hu Shi (1891–1926) and Chen Zizhan (1898–1990) praised the poetry revolution for its utilitarian and populist vein, and especially for its role in transforming poetic language from the classical to the vernacular, which directly contributed to the May Fourth "literary revolution" (Tang 2002:256–257). Marxist literary scholarship in the People's Republic of China (PRC) has treated the poetry revolution as an important chapter in modern Chinese literary history, recognizing it as a progressive literary school with an antifeudal and anti-imperial program, but limited by a political and literary conservatism. Although the term *shijie geming* may not have been used until 1899, most scholars agree that the poetry revolution took place between 1894 and 1897, when reformers Huang Zunxian (1848–1905), Liang Qichao, Tan Sitong (1865–1898), and Xia Zengyou (1863?–1924) discussed and experimented with new literary forms as part of their nationalist political agenda. However, Huang Zunxian's revolutionary poetic practice preceded the "revolution" itself by several years.

The poetry revolution is inseparable from the late Qing reform movement, which was initiated out of the shock and humiliation felt by intellectuals after China's defeat in the Sino-Japanese war. With Kang Youwei (1858–1927) and

Liang Qichao in the lead, the reformers were a group of protean intellectuals, well armed with classical scholarship and current Western knowledge. Unlike the participants in the earlier "self-strengthening movement" *(yangwu yundong)*, they planned to make China wealthy and powerful by turning to the West not only for technology but also for ideas and culture. During the Hundred Days Reform (1818), they undertook a nationwide movement at all levels, making policy at the imperial court and enlightening the populace through local institutions. Their strategy was to remold the nation and its people and modernize Chinese culture. They viewed literature as a viable medium through which to awaken patriotism and forge a new national soul, and yet felt its current styles too archaic and elitist to do so. The print media, which was undergoing a boom at this time, offered them a national forum in which to propose revisions of literature in terms of its social function and communicative potential. It was no accident that their first successful literary experiment was the "new-style prose" *(xin wenti)* Liang Qichao developed in his journalist writings.

Despite its casual style, Liang's "Record of Travel" is no less than a manifesto of Chinese literary modernity. It prophetically proclaims that Chinese "poetic destiny" *(shiyun)* can be saved from doom only by accepting the modern challenge and breaking with the past. The diary is an amalgam of politics and aesthetics, nationalism and cosmopolitanism, tradition and modernity, fact and fantasy. This prophetic voice arises from a rare moment of crisis for Liang Qichao and his country, reflected in the poems he wrote during the sea journey. In "Self-Encouragement" (Zili), for example, he depicts himself as a tragic hero with the mission of enlightening the Chinese by introducing Western ideas. He feels lonely in his desperate struggle against tradition and the ignorance of his four hundred million compatriots. In "A Song for the Twentieth Century on the Pacific Ocean" (Ershi shiji Taiping yang ge), his sense of destiny is more acutely expressed as he finds himself located at a particular historical time and global space: between the old and new century, and between a reformed Japan in Asia and the advanced democracy in America.

The new "poetic revolution" signified a crucial inversion of traditional Chinese "revolutionary" discourse. To a reformer like Liang, talking about "revolution" was taboo; in the context of Confucian political culture, the word *geming* meant the divine legitimization of a new dynasty usually born from violent overthrow of the old regime. In his intense study of the Meiji experience, Liang became fascinated with the Japanese translation of the English word "revolution," whose meanings includes "change in all societal affairs." The term *poetry revolution* carried with it complex connotations of world political revolution, ideas that had begun to exert an influence in China. Rather than advocate a poetry revolution for its own sake, Liang wanted to mobilize literary forces to rescue China. At the end of the diary, he hints at political violence when he predicts an advancing "revolutionary army" and calls new poets to join its ranks. A rumor circulated that Liang was at the time under the influence of Sun Yat-sen (1866–1925), head of the anti-Manchu revolutionary movement, and that Liang was forced by his mentor Kang Youwei, who feared Liang's stay in Tokyo would further involve him with the revolutionaries, to leave for America (Chen 1999:366–370).

The diary begins with Liang's apology for his lack of poetic talent; these days, however, he is so inspired by the splendor of the ocean scenery that he has written many poems. Liang then describes the Chinese poetic tradition as spoiled by more than a millennium of parrotlike poets who emulate past masters and know nothing of true poetry. He calls for an end to this shame:

> Therefore, in our present age, one should not have to bother with poetry unless it is to become a Columbus or Magellan in the poetic realm. As it happened in Europe that the fertility of soils became exhausted and overly exploited, the Europeans had to seek new land in America and the Pacific coastal regions. Those who want to be a Columbus or Magellan of the poetic realm must follow three principles: first, a new world of perceptions; second, new vocabularies; and third, incorporating the two into the styles of the ancients. Only made in this way can it be poetry.... If one can satisfy these three principles, then he will become a poetic king of twentieth-century China.... Although I am not a talented poet, I will do my best to introduce European spiritual thought, so that it can serve as poetic material for future poets. In short, Chinese poetry is doomed if there is no poetry revolution. However, poetry can never die and a revolution is just around the corner. A Columbus or a Magellan will soon appear on the horizon. (Liang 1900: 2280–2281)

Liang's vision of poetry revolution clearly encompasses things beyond the poetic realm, such as colonial adventure, economics, technology, and spirituality. Liang uses foreign names and images with ingenious eloquence. The figures of Columbus and Magellan, for example, become metaphors for the kind of intrepid spirit of discovery needed by the poetry revolution. In another metaphor—the "poetic king of twentieth-century China"—poetic modernity is constructed as the promise of China's future, an imagined totality of Chinese modernity in all its diversity and global scale. The author predicts a poetic destiny, one that implies memories of Chinese imperial history and an optimistic reception of Western enlightenment and colonialism. If modern Chinese literature was born from and nourished by national crises, then the poetry revolution was an important moment for Chinese literary modernity and its radical rupture with the past. Liang advocates a poetry revolution that implies a decisive break with the literary and cultural tradition.

The "poetic king" will emerge as a literary spokesman only by adhering to Liang's three revolutionary poetic principles, which form the core of his text. Interrelated and in tension with each other, the three principles constitute a poetics, based on Liang's newly accepted theoretical dichotomy of content and form. The principle of "new vocabularies" seemingly contradicts that of "ancient styles," and the "new world of perceptions" suggests a whole aesthetic effect that will occur with a synthesis of the former two principles. "New vocabularies" refer to the neologisms that came to China through Japanese translations of Western books—for instance, such terms as *ziyou* (freedom) and *pingquan* (equality). Liang strongly believes that simply using loanwords can offer a shortcut to modernization of the Chinese mind. In the poetic realm, however, the use of new vocabularies would violate traditional poetics. In China, poetic style was considered from not only aesthetic but also political perspectives, and the use of poetic language was governed by stylistic canons. For example, Gong Zizhen (1792–1841), forerunner of the late Qing poetry revolution, emancipated poetry by using Buddhist terms, for which orthodox Confucians condemned him as a heretic. Liang's obsession with neologism can also be traced back to the mid-1890s, when he, Tan Sitong, and Xia Zengyou experimented with a kind of "new poetry" *(xinshi)* using unintelligible terms from the translated Bible.

Although his intention was not to create a movement, Liang's repetition of the phrase "poetry revolution" resulted in an efflorescence of revolutionary poems appearing in the poetry sections of *Discussion of China* (Qingyi bao) and *New Citizen* (Xinmin congbao), reform journals published in Yokohama. Between 1900 and 1905 thousands of poems were published, although not all of them expressed revolutionary ideas. To better articulate the role of the poetic revolution in his propaganda agenda, in 1902 Liang established a column called "Poetry Talks from the Ice-Drinking Studio" (Yinbingshi shihua), serialized in *New Citizen*, in which he developed a theory of poetry revolution. Of his comments on numerous poets, the most influential are on Huang Zunxian, Jiang Zhiyou (1865–1929), and Qiu Fengjia (1864–1912), whom he praised as "three masters of the poetry revolution."

With the poetic revolution, a modern literary field emerged built by the interactive forces of the print industry, circulation networks, and a national literary fellowship. Its formation as a literary movement provided the necessary experience for reformers to launch a "fiction revolution" (see "The Uses of Fiction" and "Late Qing Fiction") three years later, leading national literature into a new phase. The "poetic king" Liang called for became a symbol of national literature, around which poets scattered in mainland China, Japan, Taiwan, Hong Kong, Singapore, and Malaysia would share a poetic vision of imagined nationhood. The poetic revolution, beyond its advocates' expectations, greatly supported the anti-Manchu movement, best evidenced by Jiang Zhiyou's "Rousseau" (Lu Sao), which was widely cited by the revolutionaries of the time. The second quatrain of the poem says:

> We do our utmost to pave the way for equality,
> And shed our blood on the flower of freedom.

The day will come when our words come true,
And the revolutionary flood sweeps across the world!

Huang Zunxian is generally recognized as the leading figure of the poetic revolution. Despite Huang's reservations about the slogan itself, Liang praised him as the spirit of the poetry revolution. If we take a closer look at Huang's poetic theory and practice, we can see not only a broader historical and global perspective of the poetry revolution, but also better understand the controversy over poetic form and the modern spirit. Huang was born in 1848 in Meizhou, in northeastern Guangdong Province, which became a frontier for contact with the West in the mid-nineteenth century. He grew up in a recently established scholar-official family that was still close to its peasant roots. As a child, Huang was educated by his great-grandmother, who taught him, among other things, to sing Hakka folk songs. As his early poem "Mixed Emotions" (Zagan) shows, he radically criticizes the Confucian worship of antiquity and the eight-legged essay that suffocated free thinking. He exposes the Tang and Song scholars' idea of "truth" in their exegesis of Confucian classics as simply a projection of their own desires. Ancient sages, he asserts, speak merely with a language of their own time, which then appears antique to later generations. So he boldly claims "I intend to write in my very own language / And refuse to be limited by ancient fashions" (Huang 1981:42; Schmidt 1994:225). With this historical sense, Huang explored in his later years a "new-style poetry," characterized by contemporaneity and free use of poetic language.

In 1877 Huang decided to pursue a diplomatic career rather than climb higher on the examination ladder, as his family wished, and he went to Japan to serve as an assistant in the Chinese embassy. Over the next two decades, Huang's diplomatic career took him to America, Europe, and parts of Asia, where he continuously wrote poetry and developed his new poetics. His many intellectual interests and observations of a diverse, contingent world are interwoven into his poetry, giving it a radiant and kaleidoscopic quality. The poems refract, vividly and colorfully, his curious view of the world: how he envisions and revisions China's past, present, and future within the global context, how he moves from sinocentrism to nationalism, and how he develops a broad concern with the human condition.

During his stay in Japan, Huang wrote "Assorted Quatrains on Japan" (Riben zashi shi), praising various achievements brought by the Meiji reformation. While admiring such Western-style institutions as fire departments, newspapers, and women's normal schools, he was bewildered by and skeptical of Japan's fervent embrace of Western culture (Huang 1981:1097–1159; Schmidt 1994:238–241). Yet, late in his life, the sinocentrism faded out of his poetic vision of historical China as he became increasingly aware of China's decline in the world. Influenced by the political and legal philosophy of Rousseau and Montesquieu, he became convinced that China would eventually follow the road of democracy. This conviction was more evident in a couplet of one of his latest poems, addressed to Liang: "People say that in the twentieth century / No one will tolerate the imperial system any more" (Schmidt 1994:207). More than a historical mirror or social commentary, Huang's poetry serves as a medium of self-reflection. He uses satire and irony as rhetorical devices mediating his doubt, anger, or uncertainty about modern reality.

National feeling grows more poignant in Huang's poetry when he witnesses the overseas Chinese living in poor, tragic conditions and appeals strongly for a China of wealth and power. But it is worth noting that his nationalist ethos tends to contradict with or yield to broader humanist concerns and a cosmopolitan perspective. In poems about the Chinese government's 1881 decision to withdraw students from the United States and the American government's 1882 Exclusion Act prohibiting Chinese immigration, Huang criticizes both policies for a lack of cultural open-mindedness. His assertion that all human beings are brothers is rooted in the Confucian ideal of "great union" *(datong)*, yet he cherishes even more an ideal of global community in harmony and diversity regardless of nation and race. In "Overseas Merchants" (Fanke pian) he depicts, jubilantly and sympathetically, an overseas Chinese wedding ceremony on a South Pacific island, in which different races and cultures happily mix. He shows a larger concern with the diaspora of those minor nationalities in world history when he compares overseas Chinese to Jews (Huang 1981:608).

Perhaps what aroused his contemporaries' interest the most were Huang's passionate and creative representations of the metropolitan, exotic, and novel in foreign lands in such poems as "A Song of Cherry Blossoms" (Yinghua ge), "The Great London Fog" (Lundun da wuxing), "On Climbing the Eiffel Tower" (Deng Pali tieta), and "The Suez Canal" (Suyishi he). These poems were unprecedented in conveying the meaning of modernity, suggesting a new fashion in pursuit of new space, individual expression, and literary creativity. In representing an "alternative poetic world" *(bie chuang shijie)* with his new poetics, Huang's works invoke the tension between maintaining a traditional style and modern spirit. While successfully creating the sensation of newness by breaking with outworn poetic forms, his new poetics nonetheless exposes an incompatibility or disturbance within traditional poetic structure, which can be attributed to the use of translated terms from Western sources. As early as the 1870s, Shanghai newspapers published numerous "bamboo twist ballads" *(zhuzhi ci)* describing Western-style novelties in the foreign concessions. New words such as *qiqiu* (balloon), *dianbao* (telegraph), and *dihuo* (gas) were highly fashionable, showing great curiosity for the modern. Fascinated by these novelties though he was, Huang was cautious about using these new terms for fear of losing traditional poetic flavor. For example, in a series of poems from 1875 that refer to Western science and technology, translated terms are excluded from the poems and yet treated in the notes (Huang 1981:160–169). If those bamboo ballads were not taken seriously by literati because of their folk style, Huang's saturation with the Western modern and his poetic experiments posed a challenge to the literary mainstream of the time and to his own identity as well. It seems that by the early 1890s his "new-style poetry" matured in terms of both theory and practice.

The praise for Huang's "Modern Parting" (Jin bieli) in the early 1890s might be attributed to the widely accepted formula of the essence *(ti)* and means *(yong)* at the time (most intellectuals felt that China must be modernized by adopting Western technological means and yet at the same time must keep her cultural essence) (Schmidt 1994:269). The three poems in this series describe separated lovers longing for each other, and each poem has as subject a Western innovation—the steamship, train, and telegraph. In describing how the separated lover is ecstatically dramatized by means of modern communications, the poetic convention is attractively refreshed by new images and metaphors. In this work, Huang masterfully proves the potential of traditional poetics to cope with literary modernity, for it symbolically holds up the essences of both cultures: eulogizing the technological power of the modern and at the same time keeping the poetic form intact and integral.

In 1891, Huang compiled an anthology of his poems called *Poems from the Hut in the Human World*. In the preface he emphasizes the power of poetic tradition: "Among my predecessors, well over a hundred can be considered masters of poetry. My goal is to rid myself of their flaws and free myself from their bondage. This is a difficult task indeed" (Huang 1996:69). Huang's iconoclast claim to rid himself from the "bondage" of the past predicted the literary modernity implicit in Liang's poetry revolution, though his practical approach to poetic reform differed from the latter's. Huang was more concerned with formal and aesthetic problems of poetic modernity. In the preface, he asserts that new poetry must freely use all kinds of language, whether classical or colloquial, official or dialectical. This understanding of poetic language was more sophisticated than Liang's prioritization of "new vocabularies."

Naturally enough, because Liang had always been fascinated by Western learning, he showed dissatisfaction with the lack of new thought in Huang's poems; for his part, Huang kept silent about the poetic movement, and he even expressed uneasiness at Liang's toying with the idea of revolution. A compromise seemed to take shape between them in 1902. Huang sent Liang his new poem "Military Songs" (Chujun ge) and other works, indicative of his support for the poetic revolution. In turn influenced by Huang's warning about political radicalism, Liang removed the principle of "new vocabularies"; in other words, in revising the revolutionary poetics he no longer prioritized Western ideas and what he emphasized were only the principles of a world of perceptions and ancient styles. In turn, Liang applauded Huang's poetry as the highest achievement of the poetry revolution. However, their compromise in a way embodied the significance of the poetry revolution. They both agreed to encourage the use of colloquial language, as Huang's "Military Songs" showed, so that poetry would be more accessible to common readers. Largely for this reason, the May Fourth literary revolutionaries took the late Qing poetry revolution as a legacy.

—*Jianhua Chen*

Bibliography

Chen, Jianhua. "Chinese 'Revolution' in the Syntax of World Revolution." In Lydia H. Liu, ed., *Tokens of Exchange: The Problem of Translation in Global Circulation*, 355–374. Durham, N.C.: Duke University Press, 1999.

——. "Wan Qing 'Shijie geming' fasheng shijian ji qi tichang zhe kiaobian" (A Textual Study of the Time and Advocacy of the Late Qing Poetry Revolution). In *Zhongguo gudian wenxue congkao*, 321–340. Shanghai: Fudan daxue, 1985.

Huang Zunxian. "Hong Kong." Trans. T. C. Lai. *Renditions* 29–30 (1988): 63.

——. "Preface to *Poems from the Hut in the Human World.*" Trans. Michelle Yeh. In Kirk A. Denton, ed., *Modern Chinese Literary Thought: Writings on Literature, 1893–1945,* 69–70. Stanford: Stanford University Press, 1996.

——. *Renjinglu shicao jian zhu* (Poems from the Hut in the Human World). Ed. Qian Zhonglian. Shanghai: Guji, 1981.

Levenson, Joseph R. *Liang Ch'i-ch'ao and the Mind of Modern China.* Berkeley: University of California Press, 1967.

Liang Qichao. *Hanman lu* (Record of Travels). *Qingyi bao* 35 (February 1900): 2280–2283.

Liu, Wei-p'ing. "The Poetry Revolution of the Late Ch'ing Period: A Reevaluation." In A. R. Davis and A. D. Stefanowska, eds., *Austrina: Essays in Commemoration of the Twenty-Fifth Anniversary of the Founding of the Oriental Society of Australia,* 188–199. Sydney: Oriental Society of Australia, 1982.

Schmidt, J.D. *Within the Human Realm: The Poetry of Huang Zunxian, 1848–1905.* Cambridge: Cambridge University Press, 1994.

Tang, Xiaobing. "'Poetic Revolution,' Colonization, and Form at the Beginning of Modern Chinese Literature." In Rebecca E. Karl and Peter Zarrow, eds., *Rethinking the 1898 Reform Period: Political and Cultural Change in Late Qing China,* 245–265. Cambridge, Mass.: Harvard University Press, 2002.

62

THE USES OF FICTION:
LIANG QICHAO AND HIS CONTEMPORARIES

Liang Qichao (1873–1929) is generally considered one of the most significant theorists of literature in nineteenth- and twentieth-century China. He is credited with the popularization of a literary prose style that was easy to read, a reevaluation of the function and effects of vernacular fiction in the literary sphere and in society more generally, and the establishment in 1902 of one of the earliest fiction magazines, *The New Fiction* (Xin xiaoshuo). In addition, he began but never completed a novel set in a future China, wrote extensively on his impressions of travels in the United States and Europe, and completed an influential study of Qing-dynasty intellectual history. Liang is often depicted as an iconoclast: breaking decisively with long-standing conceptions of the novel and the short story as lowly literary genres, he declares in his 1902 essay "On the Relationship between Fiction and the Government of the People" (Lun xiaoshuo yu qunzhi zhi guanxi) that fiction is literature's "highest vehicle." A more balanced understanding of the originality of his theories of literature, however, requires careful attention to the work of Chinese commentators on fiction in preceding centuries.

In late sixteenth-century China, long vernacular fiction began to appear in commentary editions; over the next three hundred years, the commentaries to novels became more lengthy and more elaborate, constituting a complex system of aesthetic standards and establishing new expectations for the novel as a genre. The best-known novels of this period—not only the six considered to be "classics" of the genre, but many others as well—circulated in editions that included at least one and occasionally as many as three or four distinct commentaries. The insights found in these commentaries are scattered and occasionally fragmentary, but this does not mean that Qing commentators on long vernacular fiction had no coherent theories of literature. These commentators frequently discussed the ways in which novels, when read properly, could have a positive moral influence, and they reflected on the reasons for and effects of their broad appeal. In addition, they were interested in the ways in which a well-written novel could teach one to read more thoroughly and write better literary prose, including the "eight-legged" essays for the civil-service examinations. Fiction could make one not only a better person but also a better reader and writer (Rolston 1997:1–21).

Important insights into the structure, function, and effects of fiction continued to appear in prefaces and commentaries in the decades preceding Liang Qichao's writings. A preface to a narrative translated from English and printed in *Shenbao* in the 1870s introduced "leisure" as an important component within a didactic theory of the novel: in the hustle and bustle of everyday affairs, the novel provided a chance for the reader to distance himself or herself from ordinary worries and enter a more relaxed and receptive state. Writing in 1892, the author, journalist, and critic Han Bangqing proposed a new aesthetic of the novel in which multiple plot lines progress simultaneously throughout the work, with no single central character or group of characters, anticipating the "novels of exposure" and "social fiction" that would play a central role in Chinese literature of the first two decades of the twentieth century. In a commentary to his own novel *Lives of Shanghai Flowers* (Haishang hua liezhuan, 1892), Han emphasized the care with which all of the different narrative threads are woven together and called on his readers to read both behind and beyond the text he provides to get the full story. New commentaries and reader's guides (*dufa*) to novels continued to appear into the early 1900s.

Liang Qichao's fiction criticism breaks with this interpretive tradition in two respects. The most obvious difference is in the format of his analysis: whereas previous critics worked primarily within the commentary form, alternating briefly stated general principles of fiction writing with extremely specific notes on concrete features of the text, ad hominem attacks, and lists of characters or characteristics, Liang instead develops his observations in the form of a lengthy and systematic argument. Second, he shows no interest in the specific features of narrative organization that had been understood to determine the literariness of works of fiction. Although Liang discusses narrative content and its effects in detail, he ignores the forms that structure that content, passing over textual features like point of view, flashback and alternation, and strategic repetition with little comment. This active suppression of inquiry into literary technique conveniently erases the link that many earlier commentators had seen between quality fiction and superior organization in more orthodox genres such as the civil-service examination essay, which Liang despised. It is in fact this active counterposition of fiction against more "orthodox" prose forms that is Liang's most radical innovation.

In addition to the structural features of the text, Qing commentators were interested in the broad appeal of novels and the potential that novels offered as tools for moral renovation. Liang Qichao adopted both of these interests: in "On the Relationship between Fiction and the Government of the People" and "Foreword to the Publication of Political Novels in Translation" (1898), he emphasized the ease with which the common person with basic literacy could pick up fiction and find it interesting, and he went on to claim that fiction could serve as the vehicle for moral uplift. "On the Relationship Between Fiction and the Government of the People" begins with the following striking assertions:

> If one intends to renovate the people of a nation, one must first renovate its fiction. Therefore, to renovate morality, one must renovate fiction; to renovate religion, one must renovate fiction; to renovate politics, one must renovate fiction; to renovate learning and the arts, one must renovate fiction; and to renovate even the human mind and remold its character, one must renovate fiction. Why is this so? This is because fiction has a profound power over the way of man. (74)

What gives fiction this power? Liang first tries two explanations—that fiction is easy to understand, and that it is pleasurable—but he finds objections to these explanations, and dismisses them as inadequate. He concludes instead that the nature of fiction's power is twofold: first, it can show individuals what other worlds are like; and second, it can give voice to those conscious or subconscious feelings that its readers themselves cannot articulate. Novels and short stories can tell us something about the lives of others, and also something about ourselves ("On the Relationship" 74–76). But Chinese fiction up until this point had wasted its powers, or worse, used them to persuade its readers to behave improperly; the answer was to translate healthier novels, short stories, and plays from abroad and to encourage Chinese authors to learn from these models in their own writing.

The degree to which Liang Qichao reproduces ethical assessments of the nature of fiction that had already been in circulation for more than two centuries can be seen in his frequent imprecations against "seditious and pornographic" *(huidao huiyin)* literature. Writing "A Warning to Novelists" (Gao xiaoshuo jia) in 1915, more than a decade after his influential campaigns on behalf of fiction as a literary form, Liang made extensive use of the rhetoric of retribution that appears in eighteenth- and nineteenth-century texts advocating censorship of fiction and dramatic productions. Authors writing novels that led the youth of the nation astray were warned that they risked divine punishment visited on them or their descendants, whether in this world or the next, just as moralizing intellectuals of the previous century had delighted in retailing accounts of the afflictions visited upon the sons and grandsons of famous novelists such as Shi Nai'an—accounts that were as imaginative as they were lacking in textual foundation. But whereas earlier critics saw the danger of "seditious and pornographic" fiction in its attack on the social order, with no reference to an exterior beyond that order, Liang worried instead about the effect of this fiction on China as a nation among nations. The moral uplift that ethical fiction could produce refers not to the salvation of the individual, but rather to the relation between the individual and a new type of social formation, the nation.

One type of fiction in particular, the "political novel" *(zhengzhi xiaoshuo)*, was to lead this transformation of Chinese subjects into citizens of a new nation. Liang based his faith in this literary form largely on the developments in Meiji-era Japan: political novels first began to appear in Japan in the 1880s, as intellectuals interested in reform were inspired by translations of novels by such English public figures as Benjamin Disraeli and Edward Bulwer-Lytton. A contemporary critic wrote of these novels that they "mainly describe the situation in the political world, and most of them are by politicians who tacitly make propaganda for their party policies" (Kockum 1990:170). Several of these political novels were subsequently translated into Chinese; two of the better-known examples, *Unexpected Encounters with Beauties* (Kajin no kigû) and *Worthwhile Chats on Statecraft* (Keikoku bidan) appeared under Liang's auspices in his journal *Qingyi bao*. In 1902, Liang began a political novel of his own, *An Account of the Future of New China* (Xin Zhongguo weilai ji), of which only the first few chapters appeared (Kockum 1990:168–182; Hsia 1978:231–236, 251–256). It is interesting to note that in his faith in the novel as a means for the production of new citizens with nationalist consciousness, Liang not only echoes Christian missionaries of the nineteenth century but also anticipates twentieth-century scholars of nationalism like Benedict Anderson. The condemnation of all previous works of fiction as an introduction to an account of the virtues of the particular novel in question is a familiar trope in premodern commentaries to vernacular fiction; Liang appropriates this evaluative maneuver, but puts it more broadly. What he is interested in praising is not a single work, but an entire genre in translation (the political novel) or even an entire new universe of genres that he hopes to call into existence (including the new novel and short story).

Liang Qichao was not the only turn-of-the-century intellectual to advocate fiction as a means of national salvation; in 1897, Xia Zengyou and the famous translator Yan Fu published a manifesto called "Why Our Newspaper Will Print a Fiction Supplement" (Benguan fuyin shuobu yuanqi, 1897). Explaining that fiction preserves accounts of heroic deeds and romantic experiences that would otherwise fade from memory, these authors maintained, as Liang Qichao would in the following year, that fiction had broad social appeal and could lead its readers to more moral behavior. Although many intellectuals writing on fiction in the first decade of the twentieth century echoed Liang, Yan, and Xia's general approach, there were critical responses. Wang Zhongqi, writing in 1907, presented a defense of four Ming and Qing novels considered to be classics (*The Water Margin, The Three Kingdoms, The Golden Lotus, and The Dream of the Red Chamber*), arguing that they, too, were in fact "political" novels and that the value of translated fiction should not be overestimated (Kockum 1990:199–200; A Ying 1989:34–39). In an early attempt to read European fiction and Chinese fiction comparatively at the aesthetic level, Wang found the multiple narrative lines and characters of Chinese vernacular fiction to be more than the equal of Western fiction that he characterized as centered on a single person and single event.

Lin Shu, one of the earliest and probably the best-known translator of European and American fiction into Chinese, articulated a slightly different position on the uses of fiction in his prefaces to translations of works by Charles Dickens, H. Rider Haggard, and others. In these prefaces, fiction is represented as a mirror that reports on the failings and corruption present in a given society. Whereas Liang saw fiction as the means for the production of new citizens, and therefore a new nation, Lin instead sees fiction as a tool for encouraging introspection and reform at all levels of society. Whereas Liang ignores narrative structure in his discussion of the novel, Lin Shu emphasizes it, judging Dickens's *David Copperfield* according to aesthetic standards drawn from the practice of literary Chinese (including the civil-service examination essay) and earlier vernacular fiction (Lin 1996; A Ying 1989:196–278).

The most important alternative to a utilitarian theory of literature aimed at renovating the nation during this period is to be found in the works of Wang Guowei (1877–1927): "A Critical Discussion of *The Dream of the Red Chamber*" (Honglou meng pinglun, 1904), *Talks on Verse in the Human World* (Renjian cihua, 1906–1910), and "Incidental Remarks on Literature" (Wenxue xiaoyan, 1906). Wang argued that genuine literature inevitably "conflicts with prevailing societal and political concerns" and is a "playful enterprise" that cannot coexist with the "struggle for existence" or constitute a professional means of support (Wang 1996:90–91, 95). He was absolutely opposed to the idea that literature should be used as a means of consolidating national feeling or increasing a nation's power among other nations. Instead, drawing on Schopenhauer's metaphysics, he maintained that the task of literature is to express the fundamental philosophical truth that the will to live leads inevitably to suffering. In a lengthy and sophisticated discussion beginning from this premise, Wang concluded that of all the Chinese novels past and present, *The Dream of the Red Chamber* best captures the tragic character of ordinary human life (Bonner 1986:81–88, 91–127).

Liang Qichao's conception of fiction as a means to remake the nation and the citizenry has had immense influence on theories of literature in twentieth-century China: from May Fourth authors to Mao Zedong (see "Literature and

Politics") to the writers of *scar or wound literature in the late 1970s and early
1980s, the conviction that fiction works best as a tool for civic reconstruction
persists. But the pervasiveness of this view of fiction at the discursive level does
not necessarily entail a corresponding dominance in practice: indeed, as we
look at the many and varied forms of literary production in the Chinese language over the course of the twentieth century, it becomes evident that alternative ideas of how and why one should write fiction continue to flourish.

—Alexander Des Forges

Bibliography

Anderson, Benedict. *Imagined Communities: Reflections on the Origin and Spread of
Nationalism.* London and New York: Verso, 1983.

A Ying, ed. *Wan Qing wenxue congchao xiaoshuo xiqu yanjiu juan* (Anthology of Late
Qing Literature: Research Materials on Fiction and Drama). Beijing: Xin wenfeng
chuban gongsi, 1989.

Bonner, Joey. *Wang Kuo-wei: An Intellectual Biography.* Cambridge, Mass.: Harvard
University Press, 1986.

Denton, Kirk A., ed. *Modern Chinese Literary Thought: Writings on Literature,
1893–1945.* Stanford: Stanford University Press, 1996.

Hsia, C.T. "Yen Fu and Liang Ch'i-ch'ao as Advocates of New Fiction." In Adele
Rickett, ed., *Chinese Approaches to Literature from Confucius to Liang Ch'i-ch'ao,*
221–257. Princeton: Princeton University Press, 1978.

Kockum, Keiko. *Japanese Achievement, Chinese Aspiration: A Study of the Japanese Influence on the Modernization of the Late Qing Novel.* Löberöd, Sweden: Plus Ultra,
1990.

Lee, Leo Ou-fan, and Andrew Nathan. "The Beginnings of Mass Culture: Journalism
and Fiction in the Late Ch'ing and Beyond." In David Johnson, Andrew J. Nathan,
and Evelyn Rawski, eds., *Popular Culture in Late Imperial China,* 360–395. Berkeley: University of California Press, 1985.

Liang Qichao. "Foreword to the Publication of Political Novels in Translation." Trans.
Gek Nai Cheng. In Kirk A. Denton, ed., *Modern Chinese Literary Thought: Writings on Literature, 1893–1945,* 71–73. Stanford: Stanford University Press, 1996.

——. "Gao xiaoshuo jia" (A Warning to Writers of Fiction). In A Ying, ed., *Wan Qing
wenxue congchao xiaoshuo xiqu yanjiu juan* (Anthology of Late Qing Literature:
Research Materials on Fiction and Drama), 19–21. Beijing: Xin wenfeng chuban
gongsi, 1989.

——. "On the Relationship Between Fiction and the Government of the People."
Trans. Gek Nai Cheng. In Kirk A. Denton, ed., *Modern Chinese Literary Thought:
Writings on Literature, 1893–1945,* 74–81. Stanford: Stanford University Press, 1996.

Lin, Shu. "Preface to Part One of *David Copperfield.*" Trans. Yenna Wu. In Kirk A.
Denton, ed., *Modern Chinese Literary Thought: Writings on Literature, 1893–1945,*
84–86. Stanford: Stanford University Press, 1996.

Rolston, David. *Traditional Chinese Fiction and Fiction Commentary: Reading and Writing between the Lines.* Stanford: Stanford University Press, 1997.

Tsau, Shu-ying. "The Rise of 'New Fiction.'" In Milena Doleželová-Velingerová, ed., *The Chinese Novel at the Turn of the Century*, 18–37. Toronto: University of Toronto Press, 1980.

Wang, Guowei. "Incidental Remarks on Literature." Trans. Kam-ming Wong. In Kirk A. Denton, ed., *Modern Chinese Literary Thought: Writings on Literature, 1893–1945*, 90–95. Stanford: Stanford University Press, 1996.

63

LATE QING FICTION

The last years of the Qing dynasty were a time of tremendous social and political crisis. The empire had sustained numerous disastrous military and cultural confrontations with the Western powers since the Opium War of 1839–42, as well as internal social strife and mass dislocation caused by the Taiping Rebellion (1851–64) and the Boxer Uprising (1900). The defeat at the hands of the new imperial power of Japan (1895) sent fresh shock waves across the country, further intensifying the sense of national and cultural crisis. This crisis — the Chinese experience of the crisis of modernity — is inscribed in myriad ways in the many novels and short stories of the late Qing, a period during which fiction experienced an incredible boom. From approximately 1898 to 1911, by a conservative estimate, more than a thousand fictional works were published (A Ying 1935). Not only did regular newspapers routinely carry fiction supplements, but there were also more than twenty periodicals devoted to fiction. In order to understand what part late Qing fiction played in the unfolding of Chinese modernity, it is necessary first to outline three crucial historical factors that contributed to its emergence: the politicization of fiction, the translation of Western literature, and the commercialization of fiction writing.

Around the turn of the century, "revolution in the realm of fiction" was a popular phrase among intellectuals interested in political and cultural reform. In 1897, the preeminent translator Yan Fu and his friend Xia Zengyou first championed the social utility of fiction in the modern world as they set forth the power of fiction to affect the largest possible reading public. In 1902 the reformer *Liang Qichao further politicized fiction by explicitly harnessing it for the cause of national reform: "If one intends to renovate the people of a nation, one must first renovate its fiction" (Denton 1996:74). Liang Qichao's conclusion is in part derived from his experience in Japan, where translations of works such as those by the politician-novelists Bulwer-Lytton and Benjamin Disraeli had been popular after the Meiji Restoration. More important, it is ultimately for political advantage that Liang invoked the myth of "great European intellectuals" who turn to the writing of fiction, claiming that "a newly published book could often influence and change the views of the whole nation" (Denton 1996:73). For indeed, although Disraeli did intend his fiction to influence public opinion and social legislation, his own works hardly had the effect that he himself or Liang wished for. Thus, borrowing the term *new fiction* from Japanese, reform-minded intellectuals such as Liang gave a powerful legitimization for fiction writing. As a genre, fiction was thus suddenly promoted from its previously marginal position in the Chinese literary landscape to "the highest form of literature."

It may appear strange that despite its undisguised political instrumentality, New Fiction was repeatedly proclaimed "the highest form of literature." Indeed, Liang himself condemned traditional fiction for its lack of moral value, as it does nothing but "incite lust and robbery." New Fiction, on the other hand, could ascend the generic hierarchy precisely because it was given a moral imperative as the best vehicle for national reform. In regarding literature as a tool in cultural transformation, Liang at once harkens back to the Confucian conception of "culture as the vehicle of moral philosophy," and prefigures the 1920s leftists' motto "literature for life." Thus, during the late Qing, progressive intellectuals called for the translation of political fiction from abroad, and many attempted writing New Fiction themselves. Typically these Chinese experiments in the political novel are set in the near future, where the protagonists debate at length over the advantage of the parliamentary system or expound on John Stuart Mill's views on the equality of the sexes. The majority of fiction produced at the time is not political fiction, strictly speaking, but rather falls into the subgenres of social exposé, detective stories, science fiction, and courtesan tales.

The late Qing saw an unprecedented flourishing of translation. At its height—between 1902 and 1907—more than six hundred translations were published, a number that exceeded original works (Tarumoto 1998). Interest in translation was first ignited soon after the Opium War, notably by Commissioner Lin Zexu, who ordered the translation of international law, geopolitical surveys of the world, and various topics on "Western opinions on Chinese affairs" gleaned from Western newspapers. In the 1860s government-sponsored translation houses were established. The translation of western literature burgeoned with the immense success of Lin Shu's translation of Dumas's *La Dame aux camélias* in 1899. Works by Charles Dickens, Victor Hugo, and Sir Walter Scott followed. Rather than the advocated "political fiction," however, the most popular of translated fiction were Dumas's book, fiction by Rider Haggard, and the detective stories of Arthur Conan Doyle. In their translated—and often drastically transformed—states, these works of popular entertainment nonetheless offer new ways of imagining the modern through an allegory of individual passion and conventional censorship, for example, or through a tale of social justice and scientific investigation.

A third important factor in the sudden prosperity of fiction was the commercial printing industry. The modern technology of the letterpress made it cheaper and therefore commercially profitable to print large quantities of popular reading materials. Beginning in the second half of the nineteenth century, newspapers also became immensely popular, thus adding a major medium for the wide dissemination of fiction (Lee and Nathan 1985). Of the many periodicals devoted to fiction, four are most important: *New Fiction* (Xin xiaoshuo, 1902), edited by Liang Qichao; *Illustrated Fiction* (Xiuxiang xiaoshuo, 1903), edited by Li Boyuan; *Monthly Fiction* (Yueyue xiaoshuo, 1906), edited by Wu Jianren; and *Forest of Fiction* (Xiaoshuo lin, 1907), edited by Zeng Pu. All but *New Fiction*, which was launched in Yokohama, Japan, were published in Shanghai, the hub of the new printing technology and the heart of cultural production in the late Qing. That fiction was the only form of writing for which the newspaper houses recompensed authors illustrates the profitability of fiction and serves as index of the rapid professionalization of fiction writers. This is especially significant because the abrogation of the civil-service examination system in 1905 effectively terminated the major professional route that had been in existence for centuries for the literati class. Indeed, many of the late Qing fiction writers, such as Li Boyuan and Wu Jianren, came from families of literati-officials; some had themselves been reasonably successful in the examination system, such as Liang Qichao and Zeng Pu.

Although the heyday of New Fiction did not last much longer than a decade, it produced an amazingly rich literary legacy with unparalleled diversity of subject matters and fascinating formal innovations. How to interpret this cultural phenomenon has been a matter of scholarly debate, one that is important because it concerns how we understand modernity as well as historical change. May Fourth intellectuals typically claimed their generation as the harbinger of modernity and its radical break with the past, thus consigning late Qing fiction to the dustbin of "tradition" (much as Liang Qichao had done a few decades earlier with fiction that preceded his generation). More recently, scholars have argued that "the crucial burst of modernity came in the late Qing" rather than in the May Fourth era (Wang 1997:17). Certainly many of the key questions addressed in May Fourth literature had made their appearance in late Qing fiction. For example, the question of how to balance the need for close social engagement with the demand for formal experiment in literary representation is a central problematic in late Qing and much of twentieth-century Chinese literature. How to overcome the simplistic tendencies of "imitating the West" or "adhering to pure Chinese tradition" is another difficult task with which both late Qing and May Fourth writers had to contend. In answering these questions, however, late Qing fiction often indicated other "trajectories" that did not become mainstream in later development, trajectories that may very well suggest alternative models of thinking through modernity (Wang 1997).

The rest of this essay will illustrate the implications of this debate through a discussion of specific examples of late Qing fiction, including *Strange Events Eyewitnessed over Twenty Years* (Ershi nian mudu zhi guai xianzhuang, 1903–5), *A Brief History of Modern Times* (Wenming xiaoshi, 1903), *Flower in a Sea of Retribution* (Nie hai hua, 1905–7), *The Travels of Lao Can* (Lao Can youji, 1903), and *The Sea of Regret* (Hen hai, 1906).

One striking characteristic, shared by many late Qing fictional works, is its satirical engagement with contemporary society. In *Strange Events Eyewitnessed over Twenty Years*, for example, the author Wu Jianren (1866–1910) portrays the decaying empire in all its putrid aspects, a world of utter moral squalor full of corrupt officials, degenerate literati, and unscrupulous businessmen. *A Brief History of Modern Times* by Li Boyuan (1867–1906), on the other hand, exposes the pretense of those who espouse the latest trends and newest ideas, a world of fake reformers and phony progressives. Both writers made their careers in Shanghai as newspapermen, and their novels, serialized in popular fiction periodicals, have been described as social exposés in which all aspects of a corrupt society, whether of the ancient regime or of the new elite, are targets for satirical treatment. Lu Xun, the preeminent cultural critic of the May Fourth movement, condemned this kind of writing for its superficiality, lack of subtlety, and exaggeration (1976:352–357). This harsh proscription dominated the evaluation of late Qing fiction until recently, when scholars tried to reverse the verdict by arguing for the thematic and formal complexity of the so-called exposé novels. Some scholars argue that these novels experiment extensively with narrative techniques, such as introducing the first-person perspective, and that this experimentation addresses the larger problem of the writing subject, a problem that continued to plague writers for generations to come (Doleželová-Velingerová 1980; Chen 1990; Huters 1997). Others favor the grotesque realism in exposé novels as an alternative to the critical realism that dominated the landscape of Chinese literature for the next few decades (Wang 1997). Furthermore, Lu Xun's criticism may reflect his own inability to accept the lack of a worldview, a grand scheme that writers such as Wu Jianren did not or were not willing to offer (Huters 1997).

Another prominent feature of late Qing fiction is its constant awareness of global geopolitics, a feature well showcased in Zeng Pu's *Flower in a Sea of Retribution*. An ambitious novel aimed at capturing the history of the last three decades of the Qing dynasty, *Flower* recounts the diplomatic journey of a Qing ambassador and his concubine, both characters modeled after real historical figures. Although the novel met with immediate popularity upon the publication of its first twenty chapters in 1907, the next fifteen chapters took twenty-five years to appear, and the novel was never finished. The novel's attempt to capture the rapidly changing times is both its success and failure. It is as though the crisis of modernity produced a similar crisis in narrative, a burden so great that any artistic resolution proved elusive. This lack of fictional closure, incidentally, is not uncommon among late Qing novels. Given that the author Zeng Pu (1872–1935) was a traditionally trained man of letters and had worked hard at reeducating himself with Western learning, it is not surprising that the primary concern of the novel is the role of the traditional scholar caught in a drastically different world. This figure is represented by the scholar-ambassador Jin Wenqing, whose erudition in traditional learning is contrasted with his utter ignorance of current affairs. This results in a catastrophic mistake: he presents the court with a questionable collection of border maps, resulting in serious territorial losses for the Qing in its border dispute with Russia. Significantly, this blunder is not presented as an unfortunate mistake but as an inevitability for the traditional scholar and the deficient and antiquated system to which he belongs. The courtesan cum concubine Fu Caiyun, who travels with Jin, embodies another chief undercurrent of the fictional narrative: the reconfiguration of the "woman's place" in relation to the newly conceived world order and in relation to the incompetent scholar. Although in many ways a descendant of countless courtesans portrayed in traditional fiction and drama, Caiyun departs from the conventional figure through her extensive travels. In those moments when she transforms herself into a "Lady of the camellias" or is studying German with a Russian anarchist, Caiyun's literal border crossing and transgressions of gender and class boundaries are intimately intertwined, with one enabling the other. Hardly what we would now associate with the new woman of China, she nonetheless prefigures several qualities later to be cherished by the May Fourth generation, albeit without the sublimation to a noble cause: an eagerness for education, an appetite for all things new and Western, and a demand for sexual autonomy, to name just a few.

Even further beyond the mainstream of twentieth-century Chinese fiction, the next two novels are harder to categorize. Unlike most late Qing fiction writers, Liu E (1857–1909), the author of *The Travels of Lao Can*, was not a professional writer but a practicing physician and sometime entrepreneur, particularly known for effective flood control on the Yellow River. His novel is modeled on travelogue; we follow the footsteps of the protagonist, the intellectual-physician Lao Can, as he tries to "cure" physical as well as social ills with his many unconventional skills. In its critique of contemporary society, *The Travels of Lao Can* shares some characteristics with the typical exposé novel. At the same time, it has been lauded (and sometimes criticized) for its lyrical passages, allegorical structure, and experimentation with techniques from detective fiction. Unlike many other works of the time, *The Travels of Lao Can* exhibits some of the refinement of the traditional literati culture (such as art connoisseurship and rhapsodic prose); the refinement, however, is typically employed to depict folk rather than elite culture. Similarly, the most profound moral philosophy in the novel comes out of the mouth of a courtesan-nun.

The Sea of Regret, another important novel by Wu Jianren, was perhaps the most popular novel of romance and sentimentality in the late Qing. Set against the backdrop of the tumultuous days of the Boxer Uprising and its aftermath, it portrays a young woman's devotion for a wastrel to whom she has been betrothed since childhood. In its response to the theme of love and marriage in the modern world, the novel exhibits an ambivalent morality. Most striking are the excessiveness of the female protagonist's virtue and the melodramatic manner with which she conforms to the wifely ideals of Confucianism. Thus, a seemingly simple allegory of doomed love and female sacrifice becomes a vehicle by which to explore the advent of modernity, with its rapidly changing relations between men and women and between parents and children.

Late Qing fiction marked a reaction to the national and cultural crisis at the end of the dynasty. Spurred by the urgent need of renovating the citizenry and reinvigorating the nation, the political champions of New Fiction offered a heady moment of new hope. In the practice of fiction writing, however, the resulting product is far more diverse and less instrumental than the reformers would have hoped. Yet, in its unflinching ways of depicting the coming modern world in all its aspects, in its ambiguous, sometimes conflicting portrayals of the old, the new, the Chinese, and the Western, late Qing fiction exhibits an amazing richness and a creative vigor quite unparalleled before or after.

—*Ying Hu*

Bibliography

A Ying. *Wanqing xiaoshuo shi* (A History of Late Qing Fiction). Beijing: Renmin wenxue, 1980 [1935].

Chen Pingyuan. *Ershi shiji Zhongguo xiaoshuo shi* (A History of Twentieth-Century Chinese Fiction), vol. 1, 1897–1916. Beijing: Beijing daxue, 1989.

Denton, Kirk A. ed. *Modern Chinese Literary Thought: Writings on Literature, 1893–1945*. Stanford: Stanford University Press, 1996.

Doleželová-Velingerová, Milena, ed. *The Chinese Novel at the Turn of the Century*. Toronto: University of Toronto Press, 1980.

Hsia, C.T. "Yen Fu and Liang Ch'i-ch'ao as Advocates of New Fiction." In Adele Austin Rickett, ed., *Chinese Approaches to Literature from Confucius to Liang Ch'i Ch'ao*, 221–257. Princeton: Princeton University Press, 1978.

Hu, Ying. *Tales of Translation: Composing the New Woman in China, 1899–1918*. Stanford: Stanford University Press, 2000.

Huters, Theodore. "The Shattered Mirror: Wu Jianren and the Reflection of Strange Events." In Theodore Huters, R. Bin Wong, and Pauline Yu, eds., *Culture and State in Chinese History*, 277–299. Stanford: Stanford University Press, 1997.

Lee, Leo Ou-fan, and Andrew J. Nathan. "The Beginning of Mass Culture: Journalism and Fiction in the Late Ch'ing and Beyond." In David Johnson, Andrew J. Nathan, and Evelyn S. Rawski, eds., *Popular Culture in Late Imperial China*, 360–395. Berkeley: University of California Press, 1985.

Li, Boyuan (Li Po-yüan). *Modern Times: A Brief History of Enlightenment.* Trans. Douglas Lancashire. Hong Kong: Research Centre for Translation, The Chinese University of Hong Kong, 1996.

Lu, Xun (Lu Hsün). *A Brief History of Chinese Fiction.* Trans. Yang Hsien-yi and Gladys Yang. Beijing: Foreign Language Press, 1976.

Liang Qichao. *Yinbingshi heji—wenji* (Collected Writings from the Ice-Drinker's Studio: Collected Essays). 24 vols. Shanghai: Zhonghua shuju, 1936.

Liu, E (Liu T'ieh-yün). *The Travels of Lao Ts'an.* Trans. Harold Shadick. New York: Columbia University Press, 1990.

Tarumoto, Teruo. "A Statistical Survey of Translated Fiction, 1840–1920." In David Pollard, ed., *Translation and Creation: Readings of Western Literature in Early Modern China, 1840–1918*, 37–42. Amsterdam: John Benjamins, 1998.

Wang, David Der-wei. *Fin-de-siècle Splendor: Repressed Modernities of Late Qing Fiction, 1849–1911.* Stanford: Stanford University Press, 1997.

Wei Shaochang. *Wanqing sida xiaoshuojia* (Four Great Novelists of the Late Qing). Taipei: Shangwu, 1993.

Wu, Jianren (Wu Wo-yao). *The Sea of Regret: Two Turn-of-the-Century Chinese Romantic Novels.* Trans. Patrick Hanan. Honolulu: University of Hawai'i Press, 1995.

——. *Vignettes from the Late Ch'ing: Bizarre Happenings Eyewitnessed over Two Decades.* Trans. Shih Shun Liu. Hong Kong: The Chinese University of Hong Kong, 1975.

Zeng Pu (Tseng P'u). "A Flower in a Sinful Sea." (Partial translation.) Trans. Rafe De Crespigny and Liu Ts'un-yan. In Liu Ts'un-yan, ed., *Chinese Middlebrow Fiction from the Ch'ing and Early Republican Eras*, 137–192. Hong Kong: The Chinese University Press, 1984.

64

ZHOU SHOUJUAN'S LOVE STORIES
AND MANDARIN DUCKS
AND BUTTERFLIES FICTION

The Mandarin Ducks and Butterflies school (*yuanyang hudie pai*; henceforth Butterfly) has its origins in the mid-1910s boom in commercial periodicals. Disillusioned with Yuan Shikai's government and the 1911 Republican revolution, this new wave of popular print culture seemed to continue the reform agenda of the late Qing "fiction revolution" (see "The Uses of Fiction") advocated by *Liang Qichao (1873–1929), although it was more commercially oriented and better articulated the everyday life of the metropolis (Lee 1999:43–81). In its narrow sense, Butterfly fiction refers to the sentimental romances or love stories that blossomed during the 1910s. Most popular and representative of these romances was Xu Zhenya's (1889–1937) *Jade Pear Spirit* (Yuli hun, 1914), which describes a tragic love affair between a chaste widow and a young scholar in a style of classical parallelism. More broadly, the term came to refer to all popular literature that developed in multiple forms in the first half of the century, mostly in Shanghai.

Other writers associated with this school were Bao Tianxiao (1876–1973) and his *Eastern Times* (Shibao) circle and Wang Dungen (1888–1950), and Chen Diexian (1879–1940) and Zhou Shoujuan (1884–1968) with their weekly magazine *Saturday* (Libailiu). In addition to the love stories of Xu and Zhou, the most notable writers and genres were Li Hanqiu (1874–1923) and Bi Yihong's (1892–1926) social fiction, Xu Zhuodai's (1880–1958) comic fiction, Cheng Xiaoqing's (1893–1976) detective stories, Xiang Kairan's (1890–1957) knight-errant fiction, and Zhang Henshui (1895–1967) as a master of diverse genres. According to Perry Link's (1981:16) estimate, the volume of published popular fiction between 1912 and 1949 (including translations) must have reached the equivalent of five or ten thousand novels of average length—that is, about two hundred pages or 100,000 characters.

The place of Butterfly fiction in literary history has been tenuous, tied to the political vicissitudes of the century. The revival of Butterfly literature in 1990s China—with many works reprinted and with sympathetic academic reevaluations—seems to be more than a mere literary phenomenon. It signals a resurgence of popular print culture, a longing for reading pleasure and generic pluralism, a nostalgia for the bygone splendor of urban life, and a freedom from Communist ideology. In the field of literary criticism, this revival—an ironic one, given the suppression and neglect of Butterfly fiction for more than half a century—renews nonetheless the polemics of old and new, popular and literary and forces us to confront once again such basic questions as what is literature and what is Chinese literary modernity.

Butterfly fiction has not always been received so positively. The name "Mandarin Ducks and Butterflies" was coined in the late 1910s by May Fourth writers, shortly after their "literary revolution" (see "Language and Literary Form") was launched. The term mocked the inseparable lovers (symbolized by Mandarin ducks and butterflies) in Butterfly fiction and was later disparagingly used to refer to all popular literature rooted in late nineteenth-century courtesan novels. As a result, Butterfly fiction was canonically excluded from "literature" (*wenxue*), a new form of vernacular writing the May Fourth movement promoted to replace the classical language. This advocacy went hand in hand with the conceptual dichotomy of new and old, progressive and backward that underpinned their worldview. Obsessed with linear time and the notion of progressive history, May Fourth intellectuals wanted to legitimize their concept of "new literature" or "literature" itself in terms of the universal codes of world literature. Butterfly fiction fit poorly into this new category of literature; it was, from the May Fourth perspective, no more than a mixture of feudal and colonial cultures associated with a decadent and money-grubbing Shanghai. Zhou Zuoren (1885–1967) and Qian Xuantong (1887–1939), in particular, criticized Butterfly fiction as the residue of "old culture," backward and amoral. In a series of essays, Zhou accused *Jade Pear Spirit* and other sad love stories of "decay and absurdity" in content and form. Examining how the "Butterfly" label was invented, circulated, and interpreted reveals how "literariness" as a canonical code ideologically articulated literary fields and empowered intellectual discourses in modern China.

Feeling the pressure from the advocates of new literature, the Butterfly writers tried to raise their voices. In early 1921, after Mao Dun (1896–1981) took over the *Short Story Magazine* (Xiaoshuo yuebao) and turned it into a bastion of the new literature, Butterfly writers opened fire in newspapers and periodicals such as Zhou Shoujuan's *Free Talk* (Ziyou tan), Bao Tianxiao's *Sunday* (Xingqi), and Yu Daxiong's *The Crystal* (Jingbao). Compared with Mao Dun, Zheng Zhenduo (1898–1958), and other May Fourth theorists, their orchestrated voices seemed less theoretical and combative. Many Butterfly writers identified themselves with the *old* stance and questioned the linguistic, literary, and cultural legitimacy of the new literature. But within their cultural conservatism lies a paradox. While espousing Western literature on one hand, they feared losing their cultural identity on the other. In emphasizing pleasure and happiness as the core of literary production (Denton 1996:243–246), they endeavored to mediate Western modernity—largely on the level of quotidian materialism—through traditional literary forms, conventions, and poetics. In this sense, their literature not only functioned to create psychological comfort for the petit-bourgeoisie (Link 1981:197) but also served their politics: internalizing Western modernity through native values. Rather than endorse a utopian ideal, it catered to urban desires that were deeply embedded in a liberal ideology and a constitutional Republican government and that emphasized social divisions and the functions of the individual, family, and state.

Butterfly fiction did not lose its dominance in the popular literary market until 1949, best evidenced by the sustained popularity of Zhang Henshui's *Fate in Tears and Laughter* (Tixiao yinyuan, 1930), a love story mixed with social and knight-errant elements. Nor did Butterfly fiction give up its hallmark—the pleasure principle—until the late 1930s, when the whole nation was plunged into war. Nevertheless, after the 1920s debate between May Fourth and Butterfly writers, the latter lost their claim on "literature" both ideologically and institutionally. Ideologically, they were never legitimated by the "new culture," nor did they adopt notions of "progressive history" or "revolutionary literature." They were fatally labeled "old" because of their continued association with the classical language. Most Butterfly writers did not wholly embrace the new vernacular language that had come to dominate the literary field with the May Fourth movement and the officially implemented "national language movement" *(guoyu yundong)*. Even in the 1940s, Zhou Shoujuan claimed that his magazine *The Violet* (Ziluolan) was impartial with respect to the vernacular and classical. Institutionally, Butterfly writers seemed not to see beyond their commercial success and paid little attention to their place in literary history. In contrast, May Fourth writers tied the formation of "literature" to the educational field, including universities, and the production of literary history. An example of this May Fourth self-promotion is the 1935 publication of *Compendium of Modern Chinese Literature* (Zhongguo xin wenxue daxi), which erected a historical monument not only to "new" literary creation but also to the enterprise of "literature" *(wenxue)* as a progressive institution in modern China. Butterfly literature was, of course, nowhere to be found. In late-1950s Communist China, a younger generation of Marxist literary historians in Beijing and Shanghai universities rewrote modern Chinese literary history, severely criticizing Butterfly literature as a "countercurrent" against the progressive May Fourth "new literature." This view of Butterfly fiction dominated until the revisionism of the 1980s and 1990s.

Zhou Shoujuan was one of the key figures in the Butterfly school, best known as the "king of the sad love story." In many ways he contributed to the formation of modern Chinese literature in its early phase: even before the May Fourth literary movement, he had experimented with using the vernacular in fiction, drama, and translations. Many of his love stories appearing in *Saturday* in the mid-1910s were infused with new narrative techniques borrowed from Western fiction and exerted influence in his time. He translated numerous works of Western fiction by Dickens, Maupassant, Zola, Tolstoy, Conan Doyle, and many others; his *Anthology of Famous European and American Short Stories*, published in 1917 in three volumes, was praised by Lu Xun and given an award by the Education Bureau. In addition Zhou edited many popular magazines, among which *Saturday, Semi-Monthly* (Banyue), and *The Violet* were often best-sellers. From 1919 to 1932 he also edited the daily literary page "Free Talk" in *Shenbao*, the largest newspaper in Shanghai, and contributed critiques on current politics.

In his early literary career, Zhou fervently assimilated Western ideas of love. Topics in his writings ranged from the love stories of world celebrities, such as Napoleon, Hugo, Byron, Lincoln, and Washington, to how to kiss, date, or write love letters. While promoting modern ideas of love, the world of love in his fiction is nonetheless shattered rather than harmonious, mirroring complexities and conflicts in semicolonial and multicultural Shanghai. In Zhou's stories, love is entangled with hatred, a hatred that derives perhaps from a trauma in his childhood. As he recalled it, his father died in 1900, tortured by illness and angered by national shame: having heard of the Boxer Uprising and the Western forces invading Beijing, he jumped down from his deathbed and shouted to his sons: "You are men, go fight!" Then he died. Zhou writes with resentment, "So, unexpectedly, the familial disaster and national humiliation befell the six-year-old boy" (Fan and Fan 1996:98).

The loss of his father made him love all the more his widowed mother, who single-handedly raised four children by working as a seamstress. In his early, sad love stories, women often appear as extraordinary patriots, sacrificing their lives to save the country. However, more heartrending are his descriptions of the conflicts between patriotism and women's repressed desire. The famous short story "We Shall Meet Again" (Xing zai xiangjian, 1914) describes a girl falling in love with a young British officer in the service of the consulate in Shanghai. As her uncle recognizes, he is the man who killed her father during the Allied invasion of Beijing in 1900; finally, she obeys her uncle and murders him by poison. But bending over her lover's corpse, her last words, "We shall meet again," reveal that her act had been a reluctant one. The split between her love and revenge implies that nationalism and ethical responsibility are legitimate and yet horrible (Link 1976:14–18).

Zhou's moral didacticism reminds one of Confucian ethics, but passion, as a supreme force capable of subverting the social order, is equally strong in his stories. In his 1911 vernacular drama *The Flower of Love* (Ai zhi hua), female desire is represented more sympathetically. The heroine, Manyin, who has an extra-marital affair with a young military officer, curses the state that sends him to war. Influenced by Lin Shu's (1852–1924) translation of *La Dame aux camélias* (Chahua nü, 1898), the drama ends in tragedy when Manyin commits suicide in her bedroom after unwittingly eating her lover's heart. In this rewriting of a modern French drama, the heroine embodies the ideal of love and is victimized by the patriarchal order: both her husband and her lover are depicted nega-tively, identified with the power of the nation-state and alien to true love.

For Zhou, love is a kind of discursive practice through which to reconcile tra-dition and modernity. Following his romantic predecessors Lin Shu, Xu Zhenya, and Su Manshu (1884–1918), he refashions the Chinese discourse of "true passion" *(zhenqing)*, together with the poetic tradition of sentimental-erotic literature (Hsia 1984:199–253). But Zhou departs from them not only in using the vernacular; more significantly, he also changes traditional values and codes to suit modernity. Such a merger is not always easy, as we see in his fa-mous short story "A Gramophone Record" (Liushengji pian, 1921), in which a young couple dies "for true love" *(wei qing er si)* after a long and painful separa-tion caused by the feudal marriage system. A grotesque effect is evoked when the woman dies next to a gramophone after listening to a record sent by her lover exiled on an island in the Pacific Ocean, a record that magically delivers his dying message. The broken heart/fragile record metaphor symbolizes West-ern technology as both happiness for and threat to China's modern fate. An-other story, "In the Nine-Flower Curtain" (Jiuhua zhang li, 1917), is in the form of the author's "pillow talk" to his bride on their wedding night. This comic piece contains generic elements of diary, love-letter, confession, and autobio-graphical fiction and is representative of Zhou's early experiments with first per-son narratives (Fan 1994:177). While the narrator passionately expresses his modern ideal of love and family, the lyricism and theatricality owe much to tra-ditional rhetoric and poetics.

Zhou's literary discourse reflects changing ideas of love, marriage, and family in a transitional society; he reshapes the public and private spaces in which modern technology and communication play a crucial role. His characters are no longer the stereotyped "talent and beauty" but urbanites from all walks of life. The boy and girl meet in open spaces in colorful city landscapes—at the Bund, in tramcars, public parks, shops, or medical clinics—unlike the trysts in the back gardens or inner chambers in traditional romances. *The Intimate Beauty* (Hongyan zhiji), a novella published in 1917, gave birth to the modern romance that celebrates free contact and love between man and woman in urban space, and at the same time creates an "intimate realm" for fantasy and daydream. Yichen, a young novelist, meets Minghua (whose name sounds like that of a famous flower) at the Bund one night. He manages to meet her again by advertising in a newspaper. Through free contact and mutual understanding,

they fall in love and finally get married. This blissful description of their relationship eulogizes modern love and free communication and departs radically
from traditional modes of representation. Zhou opens up literary dimensions in
which love and compassion convey new meanings by relying on modern communicative modes; at the same time, he carves out an intimate sphere in the
imagined community of his public readership. Thus "intimacy" plays a crucial
role in the story; the episode in which Yichen daydreams in a train about the
broach Minghua gave him as a token of intimacy is also significant in evoking
an erotic fantasy in urban space.

Zhou's own real-life romance was more than just a failed first love, for it was intertwined with a complex of personality, collective psychology, and cultural production. As the story goes, when Zhou was eighteen he came to know a girl in his
neighborhood, and they fell in love by exchanging letters. A year later, however,
the girl's parents arranged for her to marry a rich man. Zhou never recovered from
this loss, and for the remainder of his life he was obsessed with the violet, which
was his lover's Western name. The violet becomes a prism that mirrors the split of
his self into public and private spaces. Zhou embodies a paradigm shift in terms of
the male attitude toward marriage: in contrast to the debauched literati who adopt
concubines or frequent the pleasure quarters, he becomes a sincere monogamist
in real life. As a public figure, he speaks for patriotism and family values, but privately he always lives with the fantasy and alienation related to Violet—his ideal
lover. Haunted by images of Violet, Zhou is torn by the conflict of morality and
passion, the real and the ideal. He enjoys a happy family life, and yet he dreams of
the *other* woman in his fiction. In 1943, on his fiftieth birthday, the magazine *The
Violet* published his *Confessions of Love* (Ai de gongzhuang), consisting of a hundred classical poems with detailed commentaries about his love affair with Violet.
Even in the mid-1950s, Zhou recalled this affair nostalgically in his essay "My
Lifelong Worship of Violet" (Yisheng dishou Ziluolan, 1956).

Evoking the classical aesthetics of flowers, Violet is identified with a pretty,
educated woman—a symbol of modernity. The figure of violet becomes a
medium through which the female body and social norms of gender and sexuality are represented, privately and publicly. One of the phenomena unique to
literary culture in 1920s Shanghai, the popular print media favored the violet as
a symbol of the modern woman for its sustained power to arouse the urban
imagination. An inquiry into this phenomenon in terms of sexuality, politics,
and aesthetics reveals how Butterfly literature embodied the reform ideology of
the early Republican nation-state. It functioned in educating, regulating, and
transforming urban mentality and culture through literary production and consumption, and created private and public space in which the autonomy of the
individual was nourished and practiced. Here the central issue is how Zhou's
love discourse bares his vision of gender roles in private space and his cultural
politics in public space. The popularity of his writing also served to transform
the private space of his own sentiment into a public space of print media, in

which women's fate was envisioned in terms of the conflict between domesticity and publicity. Zhou treated all the problems faced by women of the time: abuse by the old family system, free contact with men, public education, new familial roles, social responsibility, and national identity.

Beginning with *late Qing fiction, the "new woman" became the focus of various kinds of literary representations. In Zhou's love stories, woman is a contested site of nationalism and romanticism, emblematic of the chasm between tradition and modernity in the early Republican period. Like most Butterfly writers, Zhou was more concerned with women's role in domestic space, which was closely tied to his advocacy of the "small family," a new social development in urban China. Butterfly writers' reform agenda and gender politics were expressed in articles in the *Semi-Monthly* and *The Violet*, specifically in special issues on "family," "lovers," "divorce," and the "problem of prostitution."

In the late 1920s, *The Violet* presented a unique visual image of the new woman: an extra frame was added around the face of a pretty woman on the magazine's cover, making the women's image doubly shaped by the male gaze. The making of *The Violet* in social space must thus be connected to the larger issue of publicizing women through the power of visuality. On the one hand, Zhou used the female body to invoke male desire; on the other hand, his magazines enormously enhanced the social mobility of women. Many woman writers, for example, were published in his magazine. After *Eileen Chang's first story, "Aloewood Ashes: The First Brazier" (Chenxiang xie: Diyi lu xiang), appeared in *The Violet* in 1943, she rose to fame overnight.

This visual *Violet*, imbued with desire for and anxiety about the modern, was indebted to the spread of photography and cinema in Shanghai. Photography and cinema often appeared figuratively in Zhou's fiction, serving diverse rhetorical purposes. The Butterfly writers had a strong faith in a kind of "photographic realism," asserting that fiction should represent life as accurately as a camera does. In reality, of course, their fiction was hardly as mimetic as they intended it to be. They often toyed with frames, "camera" angles, dramatic effects, theatricality, the seen and the unseen, best exemplified by the story "The Opposite Window" (Duilin de xiaolou, 1925; Fan 1996:59–66), in which the way the author looks at the changing life behind the opposite window comes from the idea of a movie theater.

Zhou's vision of gender roles and family values should be linked to the ideology of the new Republic and its conceptions of citizenry, privacy, and the modern nation-state. Whereas Zhou frequently satirized in *Free Talk* the Republican presidents and provincial warlords for their vile deeds and scandals, he and other Butterfly writers spread knowledge of citizenship, law, voting rights, the economy, and domestic life in the pages of *Common Sense* (Changshi), another supplement to *Shenbao*.

The semiotic web of violet/Violet/*The Violet* is interwoven into a complex representation of urban identities. It designates Zhou's own writing persona, his ideal goddess of love, his home, and the magazines he edited, as well as the images of women on the magazine's front cover. From such excessive use of the figure of violet arises a variety of issues about Zhou's identity and its literary representations. As a circulated commodity, *The Violet* was the object of city dwellers' daydreams, engendering anxiety or aspiration for a better life. Linking up the multiple facets of the flower and beauty, the magazine created an intimate dialogue between authors and readers, sharing the pleasure of the erotic gaze, fantasy, gossip, and secrecy. In searching for the figure of violet in Zhou's and his friends' writings, in magazines and newspapers, we are drawn into a semiotic labyrinth, moving from mental space to textual space and from production space to social space. In examining the kaleidoscopic representations of the violet in the process of circulation and mass reproduction, we cross the boundaries between literature and culture, aesthetics and politics, gender and visuality, popularity and publicity, urban space and perception. Crossing these boundaries in turn reveals how authorship and readership in the practice of literature were being redefined by Zhou and his fellow literati.

Zhou's imagined intimate sphere seemed to meet an urgent moral need. Since the late 1910s, prostitution in Shanghai had drawn serious attention from social critics as a degenerate behavior that resulted in an epidemic of diseases. Although *The Violet* was founded on the pleasure principle, it also served a moral function. Through literary and visual innovations, the magazine transformed the world of literati, courtesans, and "flowers" into an aesthetic world of love and compassion (interestingly enough, Zhou's editing principle—"renewing the fashion" [*huayang fanxin*]—was borrowed from the jargon of late Qing brothels). The "violet" phenomenon, as a modern vision of women, sex, family, and daily life combined with the aesthetics of pleasure and intimacy, implies the author's agenda to reform urbanites' sexual tastes and behavior to save China from moral corruption.

—*Jianhua Chen*

Bibliography

Chen, Diexian. *The Money Demon: An Autobiographical Romance*. Trans. Patrick Hanan. Honolulu: University of Hawai'i Press, 1999.

Chow, Rey. *Woman and Chinese Modernity: The Politics of Reading between West and East*. Minneapolis: University of Minnesota Press, 1991.

Fan Boqun. "Zhu, yi, bian jie jing de 'wenzi laogong'—Zhou Shoujuan pingzhuan" (A Laborer of Literary Writing, Translating, and Editing: Zhou Shoujuan). In Fan Boqun, ed., *Zhongguo jin xiandai tongsu zuojia congshu* (Anthologies of Modern Chinese Popular Writers), 163–180. 10 vols. Nanjing: Nanjing, 1994.

Fan Boqun, ed. *Zhongguo jin xiandai tongsu wenxue shi* (A History of Modern Chinese Popular Literature). Nanjing: Jiangsu jiaoyu, 2000.

———— and Fan Zijiang, eds. *Zhou Shoujuan daibiao zuo* (Representative Works of Zhou Shoujuan). Nanjing: Jiangsu wenyi, 1996.

Hsia, C. T. "Hsu Chen-ya: *Yu-li hun:* An Essay in Literary History and Criticism." In Liu Ts'un-yan, ed., *Chinese Middlebrow Fiction: From the Ch'ing and Early Republican Era,* 199–253. Armonk, N.Y.: M. E. Sharpe, 1984.

Lee, Leo Ou-fan. *Shanghai Modern: The Flowering of a New Urban Culture in China, 1930–1945.* Cambridge, Mass.: Harvard University Press, 1999.

Link, E. Perry. *Mandarin Ducks and Butterflies: Popular Fiction in Early Twentieth-Century Chinese Cities.* Berkeley: University of California Press, 1981.

Liu Yangti. *Liubian zhong de liupai—Yuanyang hudie pai xinlun* (The Schools in Change: A New Study of the Mandarin Duck and Butterfly School). Beijing: Zhongguo wenlian chubanshe, 1997.

Wang, Dungen. "Remarks on the Publication of *Saturday.*" Trans. Gilbert Fung. In Kirk A. Denton, ed., *Modern Chinese Literary Thought: Writings on Literature, 1893–1945,* 243–244. Stanford: Stanford University Press, 1996.

Wang Zhiyi. *Zhou Shoujuan yanjiu ziliao* (Research Materials on Zhou Shoujuan). Tianjin: Tianjin renmin chubanshe, 1993.

Wei Shaochang. *Wo kan Yuanyang hudie pai* (My View of the Mandarin Ducks and Butterflies School). Taipei: Commercial Press, 1992.

————. *Yuanyang hudie pai yanjiu ziliao* (Research Materials on the Mandarin Duck and Butterfly School). Shanghai: Shanghai wenyi, 1984.

Yuan Jin. *Yuanyang hudie pai* (On the Mandarin Ducks and Butterflies School). Shanghai: Shanghai shudian, 1994.

Zhang, Henshui. "Fate in Tears and Laughter." (Excerpt.) Trans. Sally Borthwick. In Liu Ts'un-yan, ed., *Chinese Middlebrow Fiction: From the Ch'ing and Early Republican Era,* 255–287. Armonk, N.Y.: M. E. Sharpe, 1984.

————. *Shanghai Express: A Thirties Novel by Zhang Henshui.* Trans. William Lyell. Honolulu: University of Hawai'i Press, 1997.

Zhou, Shoujuan. "Congratulations to *Happy Magazine.*" Trans. Gilbert Fung. In Kirk A. Denton, ed., *Modern Chinese Literary Thought: Writings on Literature, 1893–1945,* 245–246. Stanford: Stanford University Press, 1996.

————. "We Shall Meet Again." Trans. Perry Link. In John Berninghousen and Ted Huters, eds., *Revolutionary Literature in China: An Anthology,* 12–19. New York: M.E. Sharpe, 1976.

65

FORM AND REFORM:

NEW POETRY AND THE CRESCENT MOON SOCIETY

In considering the invention of Chinese new poetry *(xin shi)* in the 1910s, it is well to keep in mind that although early modern poets did indeed come up with something quite new in the context of the long history of Chinese literature, the type of poetic project they envisioned had by that time experienced a distinct global history of its own. This is a history that can be traced from German polymath Johann Gottfried Herder's revival of native poetics and folk song in the late eighteenth century on through any number of nationalist cultural revival movements that have taken place—and are still taking place—in various quarters of Europe, Africa, the Americas, the Pacific, and Asia. Loosely unifying these many poetic renaissances is an emphasis on values consonant with those of nationalist thought. Among these is the belief that poetry, like the nation itself, must be reborn through liberation. Thus, where a new nation would throw off the political and psychological shackles of a colonial power or its own premodern past, the nation's new poetry was to reassert its identity and relevance by shaking off the formalist fetters of codified prosodies and outmoded conventions.

China's classical poetic tradition lent itself well to such a program. For those who sought to emulate the Tang poetic virtuosos, writing poetry often meant writing regulated verse *(lüshi)* with lines of either five or seven monosyllables that adhered to fixed patterns of tonal contrast and followed set end-rhyme schemes. Another popular genre, *ci* or lyric meters, allowed some flexibility in line length, but only within the format of fixed templates that the poet filled in with his or her own selection of tonally appropriate monosyllables. By the late Qing, the mainstream of poetry being written in China was vulnerable to criticism for its reliance upon a fixed repertoire of inherited forms, and, within these forms, its tendency to draw from a rather narrow range of conventionalized diction, allusion, and theme. Yet most damning of all, at least in the eyes of China's twentieth-century literary reformers, was that almost without exception Chinese poetry was the domain of the archaic classical language rather than the spoken vernacular.

Like many thinkers since the era of romantic philology, the intellectuals promoting a modernized New Culture for China in the late 1910s tended to identify language with culture. Working from this premise, they underscored the difference between the learned, written register of classical Chinese and a vernacular register that approximated everyday speech. The literary program they began to formulate was conceptually parallel to those forwarded by nineteenth- and twentieth-century scholar-poet nationalists in regions with similarly "diglossic" linguistic situations. In Turkey and Greece, for example, modernizing literati made the same distinction between a "dead" written register—for them associated with cultural traits of elitism, antihumanism, and repression—and a "living" vernacular, which they promoted as the medium for a potentially modern and democratic culture to be founded upon that most primary constituent of the nation, the people. Poetry, so often understood as the quintessence of any language, represented all that was worst or best in either of these coexisting linguacultures.

Given the close relation between culture, language, and poetry, it should come as little surprise that Hu Shi (1891–1962), one of the flag bearers of the New Culture movement in China, should have been both a language reform activist and the proclaimed father of Chinese new poetry. Hu first turned his attention toward poetic renewal while he was living in New York in 1915 and 1916. At the time an overseas graduate student, Hu was a voracious reader, an avid though amateurish poet, and a cultural cosmopolitan well acquainted with New York's intellectual elite, including the "long-haired men and short-haired women" who frequented the tea parties held at the home of Hu's scholarly mentor at Columbia University, John Dewey (Hu 1981:92). Among the intellectual trends Hu encountered around this time was America's own literary renaissance, and in particular the movement against the conventional and derivative verse of the Victorian genteel tradition.

A convincing amount of circumstantial evidence points to Hu's awareness of the poetic innovations then afoot in America. We know he was familiar with the keystone journal of Anglo-American new verse, Harriet Monroe's *Poetry*, and Hu's earliest prescriptions for Chinese new poetry, his famous "Eight Don'ts," seem at least partially inspired by Amy Lowell's "Imagist Credo" of 1915 (Wong

1988:44–47). It is also worth noting that one of Hu's first outright declarations on poetic revival, "Where does revolution in the Kingdom of Poetry begin? Poetry must be written like prose" *(shi guo ge ming he zi shi, yao xu zuo shi ru zuo wen),* penned while riding the train into New York City in September 1915, echoes Ezra Pound's assertion that "poetry should be written at least as well as prose" (Hu 1947:790; Pound 1914:115).

As a rule, however, Hu downplayed the influence of the foreign avant-garde on his poetic thought. For a home audience that still had to be convinced of the validity of Chinese vernacular free verse, he emphasized the new genre's supposed indigenous origins. In the 1919 theoretical essay "On New Poetry," for instance, he proposed that the history of poetry in China had been one of unconscious "liberations" in line length. Thus, poetic form evolved from the four-syllabic line of the *Book of Poetry* (Shi jing), to five- and seven-syllabic ancient-style poetry *(gushi)* and regulated verse, and on through the patterned verse of Song lyric meter and Yuan dynasty dramatic verse *(qu).* According to Hu, the free-verse revolution marked a conscious transcendence of tradition, a breaking of the "shackles" of the spirit that allowed "abundant material, precise observation, high ideals, and complex feeling and emotion" to enter poetry (Hu 1935:295). The appeal of Hu's rather simplistic historical-evolutionary narrative of poetic liberation lay in how it worked rhetorically to link him and his immediate contemporaries to their poetic past even as they sought to carry the nation into a new era of historical consciousness.

After Hu's first new-style poems appeared in *New Youth* (Xin qingnian) in 1917, nearly all the intellectuals promoting the New Culture movement began to try their hand at the infant genre, thus registering a vote of confidence in Hu's program and at the same time affirming their own status as progressive men of letters. Although most of these writers produced only a handful of poems for *New Youth* and other reformist journals such as *Renaissance* (Xinchao) and *Young China* (Shaonian Zhongguo), the more ambitious among them began to publish single-author collections and multi-author anthologies. The new poets struck out in many directions. Thematically their poems ranged from social protest and sympathy with the downtrodden to nature worship, travel, love, metaphysical despair, and patriotic outrage. They eschewed fixed forms, experimenting with everything from lengthy prose poems *(sanwen shi)* to haikulike "short poems" *(xiao shi),* allegorical narrative poems, and poems styled loosely on folk song, a genre that had begun to attract its own band of enthusiasts. Diction in these poems ranged from the colloquial to the archaic and from local dialect to the insertion of foreign words. Hu Shi's own best effort, published in his own poetry collection *Experiments* (Changshi ji, 1922), was perhaps "Dream and Poetry" (Meng yu shi):

> All ordinary experience,
> All ordinary images,

Surging by chance into dream,
They are transformed into many a remarkable pattern!

All ordinary feelings,
All ordinary words,
Encountering by chance the poet,
They are transformed into many a remarkable verse!
Drink to know wine's strength,
Love to know passion's intensity: ——
You cannot write my poem,
Just as I cannot dream your dream.

"Dream and Poetry" demonstrates a restraint and structural integrity lacking in much poetry of its time. According to Hu, it describes his theory of "poetic empiricism," the idea that poetry must be grounded in concrete, individual experience. Such a message may seem banal from today's perspective, but at the time it framed the poem as a programmatic statement against what Hu and his cohort often denounced as a lack of genuine self-expression in the traditional, form-bound literary mind.

Yet the cult of self-expression that left its thematic and formal impress on so much May Fourth era new poetry is best represented not by Hu, but by another poet inspired while studying abroad, Guo Moruo (1892–1978). Under the influence of Bengali poet Rabindranath Tagore, Guo had in fact begun writing modern vernacular poetry at least one year before news of Hu Shi's poetic revolution reached him in Japan (Roy 1971:65–68). Soon afterward Guo discovered another poetic soul mate in Walt Whitman. Where the American bard assumed the task of poetic spokesman for the United States, Guo, in poems such as "Heavenly Hound" (Tiangou, 1920), established himself as the poet of an effusive, unfettered "I" (the word *Energy* appearing in English in the original):

I am the Heavenly Hound!
I swallow the moon,
I swallow the sun,
I swallow all the stars,
I swallow the entire universe,
I am I!
I am the light of the moon,
I am the light of the sun,
I am the light of all the stars,
I am X-ray beams,
I am the amassed *Energy* of the entire universe!

The exuberant egotism, celebration of freedom, and disdain for conventional form that marked this and other poems included in Guo's *The Goddesses*

(Nüshen, 1921) won him instant fame and numerous imitators. There were, however, those who began to wonder if this new poetry could persist on raw spontaneity, undigested foreignisms, and bristling exclamation marks. In the early and mid 1920s, even as interest in the genre began to sag among some of the original new poets, others began to draw inspiration from the poetics of French symbolism, Russian revolutionary poetry, and, in the case of the Crescent Moon Society (Xinyue she), English-language verse. The society, which took its name from a poetry collection by Tagore, formed initially around 1923 at a Beijing social club for returned students, professors, and other elements of China's urban intellectual elite. Literary inclinations ran strong among members, and over the ensuing ten years the seventeen or so poets affiliated with the society and its publications generated a varied yet stylistically distinctive corpus of poetry.

A stated goal of the Crescent Moon poets was to continue the renewal of Chinese culture through poetry, but to do so through stanzaic and metric discipline. As the society's informal leader, the irrepressible poet and socialite Xu Zhimo (1896–1931), wrote in 1926, "We believe that without a proper style of poetic expression the current spiritual liberation or spiritual revolution of our people will be incomplete." The poet's duty, Xu continued, was "to hammer out an appropriate form through the discovery of new patterns and prosodies," because "perfection of outer form is the means towards expressing perfection of spirit" (Xu 1935:119).

True to this mission, the Crescent Moon poets applied themselves to inventing poetic forms amenable to the Chinese vernacular. They experimented with and improvised on the meters, rhymes, and rhythms offered by a variety of imported stanzaic patterns. The playful Xu Zhimo, for example, was not averse to setting a love poem to what an English reader would mark as the comic limerick format, as seen in his "By Chance" (Ouran, 1926). Although the Chinese version does not—and, because of linguistic difference, cannot—adhere precisely to the metrics of the limerick, the poem lends itself well to a "reverse" translation:

> You and I met one black night at sea,
> Our courses were set, you and me,
> You may think of it yet,
> Better, though, to forget,
> How we shone one on one brilliantly!

To be sure, the turn to strict poetic form so soon after the critique of traditional verse required a defense. Wen Yiduo (1899–1946), an American-trained painter and poet in whose bohemian artist's studio poets would gather to declaim and polish their work, pointedly denounced the free-verse excesses of recent new poetry in his 1926 essay "Form in Poetry." Formal technique, Wen argued, was an aid to artistic expression, not an obstacle, and thus poetry can only attain perfection when the poet learns to "dance in fetters." He took care, however, to identify the difference between old forms and new forms, noting that, "The format of Regulated Verse has been determined for us by our predecessors, whereas the format of New Poetry is decided upon spontaneously according to the artist's predilection" (Wen 1996:324). Consequently, the new poet controls form, not form the new poet, leaving the modern poetic personality free to impose structure without sacrificing personal creative autonomy.

But Wen was much more than a theorist. He demonstrated his aesthetic principles throughout his poetic works, but nowhere more strikingly than in "Stagnation" (Sishui, 1926). In the original Chinese, each line of this five-stanza poem measures nine syllables, creating a visual effect of stanzaic "blocks" impossible to replicate in English. Wen attains to something akin to poetic "feet" by subdividing each nine-syllable line into two- and three-syllable semantic clusters. Such patterning begins to allow for interlinear grammatical and rhythmic parallelism, effects that Wen enhances with subtle alliteration, assonance, and internal rhyme. A partial translation that observes at least some of these features might read:

> A hopeless ditch of stagnation,
> Where the breeze cannot stir half a riffle.
> Just dump in scrap copper and iron,
> Or pour in slops, leavings, and offal.
> That copper may green into jade,
> Those cans rust to peach blossom petals;
> So let the grease weave a silk plait,
> And scum steam the cloud-glow of nightfall.

Opinions vary as to what Wen might be addressing here, but most commentators see in it an irony-tinged despair over China's deeply corrupt political situation. Although this may be so, Wen's deliberate blurring of the line between decay and beauty, together with the desire to contain this "noble rot" within an exacting architectonic symmetry, speaks less to the politics of warlords and imperialists than to the subtler aesthetic politics of fashioning the raw, intractable stuff of language into a self-sufficient corpus of modern national poetry.

—*John A. Crespi*

Bibliography

Acton, Harold, and Chen Shih-hsiang, eds. *Modern Chinese Poetry*. London: Duckworth, 1936.

Guo, Moruo (Kuo Mo-jo). *Selected Poems from* The Goddess. Beijing: Foreign Languages Press, 1978.

Hockx, Michel. *Snowy Morning: Eight Chinese Poets on the Road to Modernist.* Leiden: Research School, CNWS, 1994.

Hsu, Kai-yu, ed. *Twentieth Century Chinese Poetry: An Anthology.* Ithaca, N.Y.: Cornell University Press, 1963.

Hu Shi. *Hu Shi koushu zizhuan* (An Oral Autobiography of Hu Shi). Trans. Tong Te-kong (Tang Degang). Taipei: Zhuanji wenxue, 1981.

———. *Hu Shi liuxue riji* (Hu Shi's American Diary). Taipei: Shangwu, 1947.

———. "Tan xinshi" (On New Poetry). In Zhao Jiabi, ed., *Zhongguo xinwenxue daxi* (Compendium of Chinese New Literature), 1:294–311. Shanghai: Liangyou, 1935.

Lin, Julia C. *Modern Chinese Poetry: An Introduction.* Seattle: University of Washington Press, 1972.

Pound, Ezra. "Mr. Hueffer and the Prose Tradition in Verse." *Poetry* 4, no. 6 (1914): 111–120.

Roy, David Tod. *Kuo Mo-jo: The Early Years.* Cambridge, Mass.: Harvard University Press, 1971.

Wen, Yiduo. "Form in Poetry." Trans. Randy Trumbull. In Kirk A. Denton, ed., *Modern Chinese Literary Thought: Writings on Literature, 1893–1945*, 318–327. Stanford: Stanford University Press, 1996.

———. *Wen Yiduo: Selected Poetry and Prose.* Beijing: Panda Books, 1990.

Wong, Yoon Wah. *Essays on Chinese Literature: A Comparative Approach.* Singapore: Singapore University Press, 1988.

Xu Zhimo. 1935. "*Shikan* bianyan" (Foreword to *Poetry Journal*). In Zhao Jiabi, ed., *Zhongguo xinwenxue daxi* (Compendium of Chinese New Literature), 2:117–119. Shanghai: Liangyou, 1935.

Yeh, Michelle, ed. *Anthology of Modern Chinese Poetry.* New Haven: Yale University Press, 1994.

66

RECONSIDERING THE ORIGINS
OF MODERN CHINESE WOMEN'S WRITING

The "problem" of women has been one of the more enduring hallmarks of Chinese modernity, and the problem of literary women is no exception. Beginning in 1916, with the publication of Xie Wuliang's pioneering *Literary History of Chinese Women* (Zhongguo funü wenxue shi), countless discussions have centered on the issue of women as writers. The expanding influence of women's studies on the field, coupled with the post-Mao fascination with those aspects of the literary and cultural past marginalized by dominant Communist Party historiography, is helping to fuel yet another surge of interest, and the recent proliferation of reprints and reference materials (including bibliographies, biographical dictionaries, and new translations) and a growing corpus of textual and theoretical analyses will continue to shape the critical discourse on literary women for years to come.

Not surprisingly, one topic that has sparked renewed interest is women's writing in the May Fourth and post–May Fourth eras (1915–37). Conventionally deemed the moment when women were newly empowered with a voice of their own, May Fourth has long been privileged as a formative moment in the history of the female literary experience in China. According to this account, a Western-inspired movement for cultural enlightenment alerted modern male intellectuals like Lu Xun to the plight of Chinese women, a subject that thereafter found extensive coverage in the articles and fiction that they—and, soon, a small legion of newly emancipated women—published in the urban press. Recent research, though continuing to affirm the historic significance of May Fourth to the Chinese women's literary tradition, has brought to light new evidence that paints a somewhat different picture of the "rise" of women's writing. What follows does not exhaust the wealth of recent archival findings or critical discussion on this topic; it does, however, attempt to reintroduce this pivotal historical juncture in light of recent scholarship.

To begin with, it has become increasingly clear that the flurry of female literary activity in the 1920s and 1930s has roots in much earlier developments. Signs of a reconfiguration of the relationship between women and literature are apparent by the late 1890s, if not much earlier. Archivists have unearthed a substantial body of writing by women before the twentieth century—poetry, drama, *tanci* (ballads), religious scriptures, essays, criticism, and fiction—and it is now evident that by late imperial times female poets enjoyed public recognition for their work (Widmer and Chang 1997). As the nineteenth century drew to a close and the Qing dynasty teetered on the brink of collapse, well-to-do female activists like Qiu Jin (1875–1907), Chen Xiefen (1883–1923), and Luo Yanbin (1869–?) began launching magazines to serve as a political forum for women to discuss such issues as women's subordinate status, China's weakness vis-à-vis foreign powers, and the need to press for reforms to remedy both. Because of the nationalist inflection of the contents of these early women's magazines *(nübao)*, they have been examined primarily in the context of late Qing politics (Beahan 1975). But from the standpoint of women's literary history, the experiments with genre, rhetorical style, and ideological content in these and other late Qing publications represent an important precursor to the literary innovations of May Fourth women writers. *Stones of the Jingwei Bird* (Jingwei shi, 1907), for example, a revolutionary *tanci* Qiu Jin intended for publication in her magazine *Chinese Women's Paper* (Zhongguo nübao), combines classical storytelling techniques and newly imported political terminology to tell a story of five young ladies who escape the secluded confines of their Confucian families. Wang Miaoru's *Flowers of the Women's Prison* (Nü yu hua, 1904), a fantasy novel composed in simple vernacular prose addressed to a female audience, analyzes female education as the key to an egalitarian Chinese future. Late Qing writers tended to display a more didactic bent than those that followed, but they clearly shared an understanding of print culture not just as means for self-expression but as means of social change.

By the 1920s and 1930s women had begun to flourish in the literary marketplace, both as producers and consumers of the new vernacular writing advocated by liberal reformers such as Hu Shi and as ideas and images animating the myriad print debates about Chinese modernity. The much-vaunted literary revolution, fueled by desires to supplant a supposedly decrepit traditional order with a brand new textual practice, designated femininity as an integral part of the "new knowledge." Concubinage, prostitution, female morality, foot binding, domesticity, and myriad other topics identified as "women's problems" *(funü wenti)* were fervently debated in the press, and women themselves increasingly asserted their own authority in these matters. Social reforms, including initiatives dating back to the mid-nineteenth century to improve female literacy, also helped pave the way for the flowering of women's writing in the May Fourth movement. Advances in education, for instance, spawned a much larger pool of educated young women capable of reading and writing modern vernacular texts and, to the extent that newly founded schools provided an alternative to the sheltered domesticity of orthodox Confucian women, bred an entire generation of self-styled "new women" *(xin nüxing)*. Through modern academic institutions (which soon encompassed coed universities), a growing number of urban middle- and upper-class women came to interact socially and politically with a broader range of people, and they were exposed to the new magazines and foreign literature that espoused the key ideas and ideologies of the day. Hence when young women began venturing into the burgeoning literary scenes of Beijing and Shanghai as creative writers—or journalists, critics, editors, and publishers—they came well equipped to collaborate in the making of China's "new culture," bringing to the enterprise both a profoundly altered sense of feminine roles and an unprecedented confidence that included writing as a legitimate modern vocation.

Among the most salient themes these women writers tackled was the nature of the new womanhood itself. Bing Xin and Lu Yin, the first two women to have work featured in the prestigious May Fourth literary journal *Short Story Magazine* (Xiaoshuo yuebao), dramatized the quest of educated, semiwesternized heroines for independence and meaningful lives. Social obstacles, including Confucian mothers (Feng Yuanjun's "Separation" [Gejue, 1923]), financial constraints (Chen Xuezhao's *Dream of Southern Winds* [Nanfeng de meng, 1929]), deceitful lovers (Bai Wei's play *Lin Li* [1926]), and unwanted pregnancy (Chen Ying's "Woman" [Nüxing, 1929]) loom large in the realist narratives female authors favored at this time, but increasingly, psychological factors began to be explored as impediments to the new women's happiness. Lu Yin's novel *The Heart of Women* (Nüren de xin, 1934) features a depressed young heroine who is stuck in a loveless arranged marriage and feels wracked by guilt when she falls in love with a classmate. In "Miss Sophie's Diary" (Shafei nüshi de riji, 1928), the short story that brought *Ding Ling overnight fame, the protagonist's ambivalence over what (or whom) she desires plunges her to the depths of loneliness, despair, and self-loathing. And Shi Pingmei, in a story that challenged the increasingly familiar dichotomy between the traditional and the modern woman, highlights the internal moral struggle of a duty-bound wife who admires her self-sufficient sister-in-law yet remains trapped by her own internalized sense of filial obligation ("Lin Nan's Diary" [Lin Nan de riji, 1928]).

Central to the emergent (and highly textualized) conceptions of the modern female self was the notion of literary authority itself. The 1920s and 1930s witnessed a concerted effort to weld positive links between women and literature and to overcome cultural paradigms of the literary as a fundamentally masculine domain (Larson 1998). In countless works of fiction and autobiography, the literary act figures prominently in the new woman's resistance to inherited gender roles by emphasizing connections between writing and self-definition, authorship, and autonomy. Feng Yuanjun's "Separation," for instance, following the popular epistolary structure, comprises a letter by a young woman whose parents have locked her up lest she defy an impending arranged marriage. In addition to containing a spirited defense of her disobedience, the letter represents the key to her escape, for it is to be delivered to the lover who will (supposedly) rescue her. Conceptions of modern women's writing were further consolidated by marketing devices of publishers that highlighted the author's gender, as well as women's histories and literary histories that delimited female literature (*nüxing wenxue; funü wenxue*) in terms of gender difference. Paradoxically, though, the May Fourth discourse on women's writing was also partially responsible for painting a bleak picture of women's literary past, for, in the process of applauding the creative freedoms women were thought to enjoy in the present, critics and theorists often dwelled on the restrictions women writers faced in earlier times, rather than their creative accomplishments. Contrasting the "authentic" voice of the liberated new woman was the stereotype of the repressed poetess of the past who survived hostile cultural conditions by confining herself to private poetic forms or by upholding orthodox Confucian views. Yi Zhen, a contributor to *On Contemporary Women Writers* (Dangdai Zhongguo nü zuojia lun, 1933), for instance, begins with a quotation from the famous Song female poet Zhu Shuzhen on the incompatibility between women and writing to illustrate the extent to which traditional patriarchal values were internalized by women themselves:

> When a woman dabbles in literature, that is truly evil
> How can she "intone the moon" or "chant into the wind"?
> Wearing out the inkstone is not our business
> Let us rather be skilled at needlework and embroidery.

Given such views and women's limited access to literary training, it is not altogether surprising, according to Yi Zhen, that so few women "writers" emerged in the course of China's long literary tradition. (Yi Zhen and the many others who echoed his view fail to acknowledge the sharp irony that underlies Zhu's poem, which flouts the very message it ostensibly delivers.) The popular notion that modern literary culture gave "birth" to women's writing, in other words, is a myth that originated in the specific context of May Fourth debates on gender reform.

Just as research on late imperial literary history is helping to better contextualize May Fourth discourses on women's writing, a broader engagement with authors and texts excluded by the modern canon has also begun to challenge prevailing views of the period and to uncover forgotten dynamics. Names such as Bai Wei (1894–1987), Lu Yin (1898–1934), Shi Pingmei (1902–1928), Lu Jingqing (1907–1993), Su Xuelin (1989–?), Luo Shu (1903–1938), Chen Xuezhao (1906–1991), and Chen Ying (1907–1986)—popular and in many cases prolific authors who had virtually vanished from the historical record—are again surfacing in discussions of women's writing. Such recoveries are valuable not merely because they defy the picture of a meager literary output by women writers of this era, but because they offer the chance to interrogate the assumptions underlying the critical paradigms that led to their marginalization in the first place. They reveal, for example, that fiction—the form most typically hailed as the preeminent modern form—was but one of many genres with which women writers experimented. Chen Xuezhao, who paid for graduate studies in France from her writing, published numerous essay collections, many of which went into multiple printings. Bai Wei and Lu Yin collaborated with male partners to produce collections of love letters, a new genre that tapped into the wide public interest in new-style romance. And Xie Bingying, Xiao Hong, and Bai Wei, to name just a few, all wrote full-length autobiographies that were well received by contemporary readers. In addition to these forms, drama, poetry, reportage, travel writing, children's fiction, and translation were all part of the literary practices of "modern" women writers.

If formal diversity attests to a high degree of creative experimentation, more important is the cultural import of this diversity, especially in relation to the recurring subject around which most of it swirled: namely, the female self. The aforementioned developments undoubtedly enabled women to speak with unprecedented authority about their experiences. Yet women's literature competed with other emergent cultural discourses as a site where gendered knowledge and identities were produced (Barlow 1994; Larson 1998). Visual media, most notably cinema and advertising, textbooks, and foreign publications, also provided enormously important channels through which new representations and theories of femininity were introduced. Intellectuals such as Zhou Zuoren hailed the new women writers as the emancipated voice of the hitherto repressed and silenced "female self," but in fact they were more complex than this formulation implies: they were beings whose identities were in the process of being reconfigured by China's new urban culture at the same time as they themselves actively rewrote gender as a category (Dooling and Torgeson 1998:1–38).

The horizon of gender representations expanded dramatically during the early twentieth century as social, political, and cultural roles beyond those sanctioned by orthodox Confucianism became possible in both the real and ideal worlds. The newness of May Fourth discourse, however, had limits. In spite of their progressive stance on the "woman problem," the writings of many male intellectuals evinced startling continuities with traditional gender assumptions (Yue 1993:54). Fictional accounts of female suffering that appeared to contest repressive social practices, often relied on rhetorical strategies that supported, rather than subverted, male authority. Throughout the 1920 and 1930s, moreover, conspicuous male advocacy of women's liberation and the formation of male mentor/female protégé relationships (between, for instance, Lin Yutang and Xie Bingying, Zheng Zhenduo and Lu Yin, and *Lu Xun and *Xiao

Hong), suggest a deeply paternalistic logic underlying the new gender order. Yet women were never merely empty signifiers of male debate. In the essays and fiction they published, literary women of the early twentieth-century reveal a high degree of self-consciousness about their authority (or lack thereof) in inscribing women and the meanings of feminine experience(s). In a series of articles in *The New Woman* (Xin nüxing), Chen Xuezhao accused China's "new" men of hypocritically spouting feminist rhetoric. In addition, despite the fact that women undoubtedly benefited from ties to prominent men, women intellectuals also increasingly took on mentor roles for women themselves. For example, as joint editors of a widely read newspaper supplement in the 1920s, Shi Pingmei and Lu Jingqing, both students at the newly founded Beijing Women's Normal, recruited female friends and readers to contribute. And, in the early 1930s, one of the most active presses to promote writing by and about women was the Women's Bookstore (Nüzi shudian) in Shanghai, whose early members included Huang Xinmian, Chen Baibing, and Zhao Qingge (Zhao 1999).

The legacy of May Fourth women's writing has yet to be appreciated fully. In a view first promoted by leftist critics and perpetuated by mainstream literary historians, the May Fourth generation of women writers ultimately failed to live up to their full historic potential. Specifically, they became so narrowly fixated on the realm of personal experience that they missed the boat when literature veered toward the left and assumed a revolutionary course in the late 1920s and 1930s. Scholars of women's literary history, citing writers such as Ge Qin (b. 1907), who wrote about laborers and bosses in the Jiangsu pottery kilns, and Luo Shu, whose stories provided vivid sketches of the Sichuan salt works, have disputed this finding, yet they also regard May Fourth as the thwarted beginning of modern women's literature: for no sooner had women begun to use literature to explore issues of female sexuality, subjectivity, and feminism than the national emergency dictated that they suppress questions of gender difference. In this view, not until the post-Mao era has China witnessed a second "blossoming" of women's literature (Yue 1989). Insofar as both accounts rest on predetermined assumptions about what constitutes "women's writing," important questions remain unanswered: what does the abiding interest in the domestic and personal among women writers of that generation suggests about their relationship to the national sphere? How did new definitions of revolutionary literary practice render invisible the work of women writers at a specific moment in history? How much can the archive be reimagined to account for such elisions?

—*Amy D. Dooling*

Bibliography

Barlow, Tani, ed. *Gender Politics in Modern China: Writing and Feminism.* Durham, N.C.: Duke University Press, 1993.

——. "Theorizing Woman: *Funü, Guojia, Jiating.*" In Angela Zito and Tani Barlow, eds., *Body, Subject and Power in China*, 253–289. Chicago: University of Chicago Press, 1994.

Bing, Xin. *The Photograph*. Beijing: Panda Books, 1992.

Beahan, Charlotte. "Feminism and Nationalism in the Chinese Women's Press, 1902–1911." *Modern China* 1, no. 4 (October 1975): 379–416.

Chen Jingzhi. *Xiandai wenxue zaoqi de nüzuojia* (Early Modern Women Writers). Taipei: Chengwen, 1980.

Chow, Rey. *Woman and Chinese Modernity: The Politics of Reading between West and East*. Minneapolis: University of Minnesota Press, 1991.

Ding, Ling. *I Myself Am a Woman: Selected Writings of Ding Ling*. Eds. Tani Barlow and Gary Bjorge. Boston: Beacon Press, 1989.

Dooling, Amy, and Kris Torgeson, eds. *Writing Women in Modern China: An Anthology of Women's Literature from the Early Twentieth Century*. New York: Columbia University Press, 1998.

Larson, Wendy. "The End of Funü Wenxue: Women's Literature from 1925 to 1935." In Tani Barlow, ed., *Gender Politics in Modern China: Writing and Feminism*, 58–73. Durham, N.C.: Duke University Press, 1993.

——. "Female Subjectivity and Gender Relations: The Early Stories of Lu Yin and Bing Xin." In Liu Kang and Xiaobing Tang, eds., *Politics, Ideology and Literary Discourse in Modern China*, 124–143. Durham, N.C.: Duke University Press, 1993.

——. *Women and Writing in Modern China*. Stanford: Stanford University Press, 1998.

Lu, Tonglin, ed. *Gender and Sexuality in Twentieth-Century Chinese Literature and Society*. Albany: State University of New York Press, 1993.

Meng Yue and Dai Jinhua. *Fuchu lishi dibiao* (Emerging on the Horizons of History). Zhengzhou: Henan renmin, 1989.

Ng, Janet, and Janice Wickeri, eds. *May Fourth Women Writers: Memoirs*. Hong Kong: Renditions Press, 1997.

Qiao Yigang. *Zhongguo nüxing de wenxue shijie* (The Literary World of Chinese Women). Wuhan: Hubei jiaoyu, 1993.

Wang Jialun. *Zhongguo xiandai nüzuojia lunwang* (A Discussion of Modern Chinese Women Writers). Beijing: Zhongguo funü, 1992.

Widmer, Ellen, and Kang I-sun Chang. *Writing Women in Late Imperial China*. Stanford: Stanford University Press, 1997.

Xiao, Hong. *Selected Short Stories of Xiao Hong*. Trans. Howard Goldblatt. Beijing: Chinese Literature Press, 1982.

Xie, Bingying. *Autobiography of a Chinese Girl*. Trans. Tsui Chi. London: Pandora Press, 1986.

Yue, Mingbao. "Gendering the Origins of Modern Chinese Fiction." In Tonglin Lu, ed., *Gender and Sexuality in Twentieth-Century Chinese Literature and Society*, 47–66. Albany: State University of New York Press, 1993.

Yue Shuo. *Chidao de chaoliu: Xin shiqi funü chuangzuo yanjiu* (Belated Trend: Research on Women's Writing in the New Era). Zhengzhou: Henan renmin, 1989.

Zhao Qingge. *Changxiang yi* (Forever Recalling Each Other). Shanghai: Xuelin, 1999.

67

ROMANTIC SENTIMENT AND THE PROBLEM
OF THE SUBJECT: YU DAFU

One of the principal characteristics of late nineteenth- and early twentieth-century literature in China is its emotionality, its emphasis on subjective expression. What makes this modern phenomenon different from the premodern tradition of "poetry expresses intention" *(shi yan zhi)* or "poetry expresses feelings" *(shi yuan qing)* is primarily the type of emotions being expressed and the lack of restraint with which they are expressed. How do we account for this dramatic and obsessive interest in exposing the self in early modern literature? How do we deal with the sentimental, melodramatic, sometimes maudlin, character of these works? What are the cultural and historical motivations for this obsessive desire to emote and express the self? These questions can be looked at in terms of a larger problem of subjectivity in Chinese modernity, but before I do so some background is necessary.

In the crisis atmosphere of the late Qing and early Republican periods, intellectuals searched for causes for China's national impotence. Many explained this weakness in cultural terms: traditional culture had emasculated the Chinese people by rigorously enforcing submission to authority and rigidly codifying ethical behavior. The heart of this transitional generation's construction of the past was Confucianism and its concept of *li*, or ritualized ethical behavior, which intellectuals from Tan Sitong to Liang Qichao and Chen Duxiu fashioned into the central problem of Chinese culture. Of course, the self was never conceived of in the past as these and other reformers and iconoclasts made out. The heterogeneity of the past—its many contending intellectual and philosophical schools, its regional variations, and its class disparities—was reduced to a monolithic and all-powerful Confucianism—the better to attack it by. This ethical system created a nation of passive individuals, so the discourse went, subordinated to familial and state authority, whose very identities were seen to be constructed through hierarchical social relations, who as such lacked the kind of dynamic, willful, aggressive, and autonomous personalities needed to build a strong nation and repel the advance of imperialism. Whereas tradition was portrayed in feminine terms, modernity and the new self were seen as masculine. One of the central crises faced by intellectuals in the early twentieth century, then, was the question of how to recreate the self so that it could participate in national renovation and the global march to modernity. Self and nation were from the beginning of Chinese modernity inextricably tied together (Liu 1995:87–89), and literature was one of the important means of exploring new modes of selfhood and its relation to imagined national and global communities.

For many of the radical thinkers of the transitional generation, the Chinese tradition offered no models for this new masculine selfhood, so they sought models from outside. Precedents for this modern anti-Confucianism can be found in late Ming individualism and its cult of *qing* (love, emotion, sentiment), suggesting perhaps that traumatic historical moments give rise to reconceptualizations of the self, but the radical quality of the late Qing and early Republican writers' attack on Confucian hierarchy and authoritarianism was unprecedented. As Leo Lee (1973:46) has shown, Lin Shu and Su Manshu were at the forefront of this new interest in sentiment *(qing)*, although to Lin "sentiment ... is more than the inner reflection of propriety *(li)* as prescribed in the *Analects*; sentiment is morality." Rather than draw from late Ming antecedents, however, Lin Shu looked to graft the models of the colonizing West onto traditional Chinese ethics, forging Dickens's sentimentality, for example, onto traditional Confucian conceptions of filial piety. Su Manshu was an early romantic poet and China's first translator (with Chen Duxiu) of Byron, who became in the May Fourth movement an emblem of a dynamic and revolutionary romantic individualism China was seen to lack.

Whereas late Qing thinkers such as Lin Shu were still attached to the Confucian tradition, by the May Fourth period that tradition had lost any sort of resonance with their world for many intellectuals. They turned instead to a wide variety of Western thought and literature as a way of resolving practically and psychologically the problems of a rapidly changing society. Science and democracy were the buzzwords of this generation, but these were merely two of many Western terms to enter the cultural vocabulary of May Fourth China. "Self" *(wo)* was being refashioned into a Western sense of an isolated and unique entity (Liu 1995:77–99). Central to this new self was the concept of self-consciousness *(zijue)*, sometimes translated as autonomy (Schwarcz 1986:26). Self-consciousness meant developing a sense of intellectual and political autonomy from the power and authority of the state, but it also meant becoming aware of layers of the self buried by tradition, recovering the fullness of one's humanity.

By exposing areas of mind and personality, writers of fiction such as Yu Dafu, Guo Moruo, *Mao Dun, and *Ba Jin broadened conceptions of self, reimagined the self's relation to the cultural whole (now called "nation"), and rewrote the national character. Love and eros, for example, were discussed and expressed in May Fourth literary works as a reaction, at least partly, to the relative denial of these things in the elite literary tradition. Excavating dark recesses of the mind set modern writers apart from their traditional counterparts who were less interested in the unconscious, of which they likely had no conception, than they were in the social and moral mind, that part of the mind linked to other minds through the divine.

Yet Chinese writers seeking to rewrite the self appropriated this Western model of an autonomous self with difficulty. There is a profound anxiety at the heart of the experience of modernity, an anxiety that is perhaps best seen in the writing of Yu Dafu, arguably the representative voice in the male May Fourth strain of sentimental fiction. Yu was a founding member of the Creation Society—a literary group formed in Japan in 1921 with Cheng Fangwu, Guo Moruo, Zhang Ziping, and Tian Han—and shared with these writers a romantic-aesthetic view of literature that emphasized self-expression and promoted notions of the writer as genius. Yu Dafu's fiction sought to lay bare the private, to expose what had been traditionally repressed: sexual desire, alienation, despair, guilt, anxiety, insecurity, and paranoia. "My heart is thus inclined," Yu wrote in 1923, "to discharge myself once and for all of the sin of insincerity, I can only reveal my inner self in all its nakedness" (*Wenji* 7:155–157). His fiction consistently sought to make a public display of the private and psychological, what Leo Lee (1985:282–307) has called the "externalization of the self," and as such it exposes the very deepest levels of the experience of modernity of Chinese intellectuals. Here is how Yu described, in 1933, the origin of his early stories:

> In youth, one always passes through a romantic lyrical period, when one is still a mute bird but wants nonetheless to open one's throat and sing out, especially those full of emotion. This lyrical period was spent in that sexually dissolute and militarily oppressive island nation [Japan]. I saw my country sinking, while I myself suffered the humiliations of a foreigner. Everything Yufu felt, thought, experienced, was essentially nothing but despair and suffering. Like a wife who had lost her husband, powerless, with no courage at all, bemoaning my fate, I let out a tragic cry. This was "Sinking," which stirred up so much criticism. (*Yu Dafu yanjiu ziliao* 1:216–220)

All critics agree that one of the most prominent characteristics of Yu Dafu's writing is its autobiographical tenor. Yu is famous in China for his invocation of the notion that "literature is nothing but the autobiography of the author" (*Wenji* 7:180). His fictional prose tends to draw from the events of his own life and is peopled with characters resembling those in his life: his domineering mother, his arranged wife Sun Chuan (whom he essentially abandoned but about whom he often wrote with a strong sense of guilt), members of the Creation Society, and Wang Yingxia (his long-time lover and a famous Chinese beauty). Indeed, so autobiographical is his fiction that scholars often disagree in designating particular works fiction or autobiographical prose. Yu also wrote a great deal of explicitly autobiographical writing and published his letters and diaries. In its autobiographical nature, Yu's fiction is typical of his generation. Writers of all literary persuasions in the May Fourth, those who saw themselves as romantics and those who saw themselves as realists, drew quite directly from their own lives for fictional material; indeed, the appeal and power of their works derive precisely from that fact. Even the supreme ironist Lu Xun borrowed much fictional material from his own experiences.

Although some have seen in Yu's stories parallels with traditional "talent and beauty" *(caizi jiaren)* fiction, the psychological probing of the self makes them modern. They exhibit, moreover, a decadent quality in their obsession with sexual fetishes, masochism, masturbation, homosexuality, excessive drinking, and guilt. The minds revealed in his fiction are modern minds wracked by contradictions and paradoxes, unable to recapture a sense of unity with the landscape of their pasts. Yu's characters can be read as emblems of modernity's tensions between desires for an autonomous self and traditional desires for stability defined within a shared cultural meaning system. What makes this experience of modernity so difficult and traumatic is that neither desire is in and of itself in any way satisfying. The modern intellectual is homeless in a very profoundly psychological way (Denton 1992).

Many of Yu Dafu's stories center on the return of male intellectuals to their homes, most often in small-town Jiangnan. These stories tell us much about the problematic of leaving home, a spatial trope that implied a temporal separation from tradition, a trope that begins with Hu Shi's translation of Ibsen's *Doll House.* Leaving home was the paradigmatic act of modernity for May Fourth writers and their fictional alter egos. Yu Dafu, by contrast, was far more obsessed in his writing with returning home. A good example of this is Yu's autobiographical prose work called "Record of Returning Home" (Huan xiang ji, 1923). The story relates the narrator's feelings and fantasies as he awakens in the metropolis of Shanghai, takes the train to Hangzhou (where he stays overnight), and finally boards a boat for his hometown up the Qiantang River. As the story opens, he awakens suddenly in a "sensitive psychic state," bothered by lingering feelings from his early morning sleep, and vaguely recalls that he was supposed to go somewhere that day (to return home). His room faces the Shanghai racetrack and the clock that looms above it, emblems of modernity in Republican China (Lee 1999:31), and the contrast between home as a disturbing memory and the space and time of modernity sets the theme of the story as the conflict between tradition and modernity.

"Sinking" (Chenlun, 1921) is Yu's most famous story, and it displays many of the characteristics for which he was so well known and notorious. The nameless hero in the story is a student studying in a Japanese university. He is torn by sexual desires and finds little pleasure and much guilt in daily masturbation and spying voyeuristically on his landlord's daughter as she bathes and on a couple making love in the woods. When an opportunity for real sexual intercourse with a Japanese prostitute presents itself, he gets drunk and passes out. Intertwined with this sexual insecurity is the protagonist's convenient blaming of his country's weakness for his own sexual inadequacies. Perhaps the most blatant example of sublimation in the history of modern Chinese literature, this deep-felt linking of the self to the state of the nation was something shared by many young Chinese at the time. What makes this story modern is not its interest in sexuality or even deviant sexuality, for there was a long tradition in China of erotic literature, but describing that sexuality from a psychological perspective, through a tortured mind. But the story also enacts in spatial terms and through literary allusions the irresolvable modern tension between a radically alienated consciousness attempting to understand itself in social isolation and a nostalgic longing to return to the comfort of a traditional community of like minds in a unified moral cosmos (Denton 1992:177).

Psychic conflict in Yu's characters is also played out in terms of human relations. "Wisteria and Dodder" (Nuoluo xing, 1923), usually classified as a prose work (the story is in the form of a letter addressed to Yu's arranged wife, Sun Chuan), expresses the protagonist's misery in his marital relationship. Addressing his wife, the narrator writes, "Woman whom I must love and woman whom I cannot love! I despise the world because I despise myself for all my savagery to you" (247). Yu Dafu's characters also play out their psychic anxiety through others who are weaker and more powerless, often lower class characters. The poverty and oppression experienced by these lower class characters becomes a reflection of the first-person intellectual narrator's identity crisis. Perhaps the most famous examples are "Nights of Spring Fever" (Chunfeng chenzui de wanshang, 1923) and "Humble Sacrifice" (Bodian, 1924), stories favored, not surprisingly, by leftist literary critics for their sympathetic portrayal of the working class.

Most of Yu Dafu's protagonists are loners who do not fit into society, alienated wanderers constructed through a filter of Western literary images of self (Rousseau, Oblomov, Turgenev, Ernest Dowson, and so forth). There is a marked tendency in Yu Dafu's fictional/autobiographical writings toward confession, something that some critics have argued was absent in premodern times and that Yu may have discovered with reading of Rousseau and Japanese naturalism. As Mau-sang Ng (1980) has discussed, Yu's characters are drawn after character types from the Russian literary tradition, in particular, the superfluous man, a type seen most prevalently in Turgenev's fiction. Like the Russian model, the superfluous man in Yu's fiction both scorns society and is bothered by his out-of-placeness. So the awkward homelessness displayed by Yu's characters can be seen not only as a product of Chinese intellectuals' particular experience with modernity, but also as a universal tendency in global literary modernism.

Some of Yu's characters indulge in a self-pity that makes them disagreeable. It is often difficult to determine authorial attitude to these self-pitying characters. At times there seems to be a close identification between author and character; at others, the reader senses an ironic distance between the two, implying authorial criticism of the character's lack of self-awareness. Yu's stories lack the kind of rigorous irony seen in the stories of Lu Xun, who seemed always to question intellectual self-indulgence, but this does not mean that we should dismiss the suffering of the characters in Yu's stories as mere self-pitying. Rather, the mawkish sentimentality and the confessional urge we see in Yu's prose reveal much about the traumatic nature of modernity for Chinese intellectuals.

—*Kirk A. Denton*

Bibliography

Denton, Kirk A. "The Distant Shore: The Nationalist Theme in Yu Dafu's Sinking." *Chinese Literature: Essays, Articles and Reviews* 14 (1992): 107–123.

Doleželova, Anna. *Yu Ta-fu: Specific Traits of His Literary Creation.* Bratislava: Publishing House of the Slovak Academy of Sciences, 1970.

Egan, Michael. "Yu Dafu and the Transition to Modern Chinese Literature." In Merle Goldman, ed., *Modern Chinese Literature in the May Fourth Era,* 309–324. Cambridge, Mass.: Harvard University Press, 1977.

Feuerwerker, Yi-tsi Mei. "Text, Intertext, and the Representation of the Writing Self in Lu Xun, Yu Dafu, and Wang Meng." In Ellen Widmer and David Wang, eds., *From May Fourth to June Fourth: Fiction and Film in Twentieth-Century China,* 167–193. Cambridge, Mass.: Harvard University Press, 1993.

Ko, Dorothy. *Teachers of the Inner Chambers: Women and Culture in Seventeenth-Century China.* Stanford: Stanford University Press, 1994.

Lee, Leo Ou-fan. *Shanghai Modern: The Flowering of a New Urban Culture in China, 1930–1945.* Cambridge, Mass.: Harvard University Press, 1999.

——. "The Solitary Traveler: Images of the Self in Modern Chinese Literature." In Robert Hegel and Richard Hessney, eds., *Expressions of Self in Chinese Literature,* 282–307. New York: Columbia University Press, 1985.

——. "Yu Ta-fu." In *The Romantic Generation of Modern Chinese Writers,* 81–123. Cambridge, Mass.: Harvard University Press, 1973.

Liu, Lydia. *Translingual Practice: Literature, National Culture, and Translated Modernity, China 1900–1937.* Stanford: Stanford University Press, 1995.

Ng, Mau-sang. *The Russian Hero in Modern Chinese Fiction.* Albany: State University of New York Press, 1980.

Prušek, Jaroslav. "Mao Tun and Yu Ta-fu." In *The Lyrical and the Epic: Studies in Modern Chinese Literature*, 121–177. Bloomington: Indiana University Press, 1980.

Schwarcz, Vera. *The Chinese Enlightenment: Intellectuals and the Legacy of the May Fourth Movement of 1919*. Berkeley: University of California Press, 1986.

Yu, Dafu. "Blood and Tears." In S. R. Munro, trans. and ed., *Genesis of a Revolution: An Anthology of Modern Chinese Short Stories*, 158–175. Singapore: Heinemann Educational Books, 1979.

———. "Class Struggle in Literature." Trans. Haili Kong and Howard Goldblatt. In Kirk A. Denton, ed., *Modern Chinese Literary Thought*, 263–268. Stanford: Stanford University Press, 1996.

———. "Intoxicating Spring Nights." In Harold Isaacs, trans. and ed., *Straw Sandals*, 68–83. Cambridge, Mass.: MIT Press, 1974.

———. *Nights of Spring Fever and Other Writings*. Beijing: Panda Books, 1984.

———. "Sinking." Trans. Joseph Lau and C. T. Hsia. In Joseph Lau and Howard Goldblatt, eds., *Columbia Anthology of Modern Chinese Literature*, 44–69. New York: Columbia University Press, 1995.

———. "Wisteria and Dodder." In Edgar Snow, ed., *Living China*, 247–263. New York: Reynal and Hitchcock, 1937.

———. *Yu Dafu wenji* (Collected Writings of Yu Dafu). 12 vols. Guangzhou: Huacheng, 1982.

———. *Yu Dafu yanjiu ziliao* (Research Materials on Yu Dafu). 2 vols. Tianjin: Tianjin renmin, 1982.

68

THE MADMAN THAT WAS AH Q: TRADITION AND MODERNITY IN LU XUN'S FICTION

There is perhaps no better example of the modern Chinese intellectual's problematic of self than can be found in a comparison of Lu Xun's "Diary of a Madman" (Kuangren riji, 1918) and "The True Story of Ah Q" (Ah Q zhengzhuan, 1921). The Madman is the modern independent subject: self-conscious, discarnate, a romantic proclaiming his independence from the outside world he aspires to transcend. Ah Q is the May Fourth notion of the trapped traditional self, the unselfconscious self that does not act but reacts to the calamities and consequences of the outside world without memory or vision. The Madman is the modern enlightened savior; Ah Q is a symbol of China's national character and tradition. Ah Q is the disease embodied; he suffers from a malady that leaves him hypersensitive to the outer world and empowers society and tradition to interfere with and even to mold his actions. He is selfless and exists only in orientation to the other. The Madman, on the other hand, is the model of the modern Western, independent self. He is the archetypal romantic cure for that debilitating disease called tradition. In Lu Xun's paradoxical moral vision, however, there is no precise dichotomy between the two; tradition and modernity do not exist in strict opposition. This is no more obvious than in the conclusions to "True Story" and "Diary," as Ah Q emerges a victim and the Madman realizes that he too may be a cannibal (Denton 1998:58–59).

Although "Diary" and "True Story" may best illustrate the paradox of tradition versus modernity, Lu Xun's other fictional works, "Kong Yiji" (1919), "Medicine" (Yao, 1919), "Soap" (Feizao, 1924), "In the Wine Shop" (Zai jiulou shang,

1924), and the stories in *Old Tales Retold* (Gushi xinbian, 1936), respond in differing ways to the problematic self, the brutality of tradition, and a sometimes irreconcilable modernity, contributing again and again to the wavering tightrope of discourse that connects the traditional to the modern in China.

Lu Xun (Zhou Shuren, 1881–1936) must be understood against the backdrop of the concept of literary modernity that prevailed in the May Fourth era. May 4, 1919 represents a watershed in modern Chinese literary history. On this day, student representatives in Beijing drew up five resolutions in response to the Versailles Treaty, which had transferred Germany's rights to parts of China's Shandong Province to Japan. The nationalism of the student movement, accompanied by a growing discussion of Social Darwinist ideas and the rise of interest in Communist ideology, were symptomatic of a cultural upheaval that was spreading throughout China. The term *May Fourth movement* refers both to the demonstrations that took place on May 4, 1919 and to the complex cultural and political developments that preceded and followed them.

The most striking change brought about by the May Fourth movement in literary terms was that most writers discarded native literary language in favor of a language explicitly based on the grammatical construction, sentence cohesion, narrative forms, and rhetoric invention of Western models. The discourse of Chinese literature since the May Fourth period dwells on the notion of a singular, belated modernity, a modernity at once at odds with the classical Chinese literary tradition and simultaneously in awe of it. Hailed as the first modern fiction in Chinese history, short stories such as Lu Xun's "Diary" represented Chinese tradition, and its linguistic and literary forms, as cannibalistic. Lu Xun's story begins with a preface written in classical Chinese, the written language of the literati, and continues in the vernacular in the diary proper. The ironic juxtaposition of these two languages in the story was revolutionary: the Madman's vernacular diary, with its enlightenment discourse, implicates the classical language of the preface for blinding Chinese to the violent reality of their tradition.

First published in *New Youth* (Xin qingnian), "Diary of a Madman" reveals most concisely Lu Xun's attitude toward tradition. Suffering from a "persecution complex," the Madman imagines that all those around him, including his family members, are plotting to kill him and consume his body. To authenticate his suspicions, he resorts to the pages of a Chinese history book:

> In ancient times, as I recollect, people often ate human beings, but I am rather hazy about it. I tried to look this up, but my history has no chronology, and scrawled all over each page are the words: "Virtue and Morality." Since I could not sleep anyway, I read intently half the night, until I began to see words between the lines, the whole book being filled with the two words—"Eat people." (1977:10)

Although the rhetoric of virtue and morality echoes through the annals of Chinese history, that rhetoric is undermined by a tradition of cannibalism. Officials cannibalize lower officials who cannibalize those beneath them, and so on. Even the Madman, the reader is told in the introduction, "recovered some time ago and has gone elsewhere to take up an official post" (1977:7); attaining sanity means that the Madman rejoins a cannibalistic society. The Madman is the curative for the disease of tradition, but a curative incapable of doing away with tradition itself. Lu Xun is nevertheless not completely hopeless. At the conclusion to the story, the Madman makes the now famous plea: "Perhaps there are children who have not eaten men? Save the children" (1977:18).

Ah Q, the protagonist of "The True Story," represents the very disease the Madman diagnoses. Living in the final years of the Qing dynasty, Ah Q is poor and homeless, the very bottom of the social stratum of the village in which he lives. Rather than sympathize with him, though, Lu Xun uses Ah Q as a symbol of what is wrong with the Chinese national character (*guominxing*). For example, Ah Q invents "spiritual victories" as a way of rationalizing defeat at the hands of those who bully him; he then turns around to torment those who are weaker than he is. He wallows in a physically abusive (but mentally oblivious) world of self-deception, consoling himself after each catastrophe and claiming victory in the face of glaring defeat. "True Story" is, then, a scathing reminder of China's weakened position in world politics and the encroachment of Western modernity. It is also, however, a cunning criticism of how revolution, particularly the Republican revolution, forced tradition into a binary and ultimately unsuccessful relationship with modernity.

At the end of the story, Ah Q's longing to join the revolution leads to his death. After angering the most important family in the village, he travels to the city and drifts among a gang of thieves where he hears rumors of the anti-Manchu revolution. Each time he returns to the village to sell his stolen goods, he boasts about the revolution as if he were a soldier himself. He does this both to amplify his reputation and to intimidate those who have abused him. He naively masquerades as a revolutionary because he is superficially aware that revolution changes things—it produces new opportunities and resolves old grievances. Ironically, however, when the revolutionary forces enter the village, they collude with the local gentry to try Ah Q for his suspected part in a robbery. The hero dies a victim of the revolution, but the "Ah Q spirit" lives on to haunt a feudal society that ignores the potential of Ah Q and those like him. Tradition and modernity stand in murky contrast to illustrate Lu Xun's still ambiguous stance, as the "traditional" Ah Q embodies far more revolutionary potential than his revolutionary accusers epitomize modernity.

Lu Xun's paradoxical moral vision, his constant probing of the tortuous relationship between tradition and modernity, and attempts to understand what to him was the misguided, defective Chinese national character are reflected in other stories. "Kong Yiji" and "Medicine" ridicule traditional society while casting just as critical an eye at the point and practice of revolution. "Kong Yiji" is a poignant yet perfunctory portrayal of a minor literati figure who has taken to thieving. Narrated by a boy who warms drinks in the tavern, the story recounts how Kong Yiji, dressed in a tattered scholar's gown, lectures to tavern customers in highbrow language on the differences between stealing and stealing books. Having never gotten very far with the civil service examination, Kong Yiji nonetheless considers himself a scholar, even as he steals to support his drinking and his laziness. Kong Yiji (who shares a surname with Confucius, Kongzi) clings desperately to the image and empty scholarship of the Confucian literati class whose demise he represents. As such, the story criticizes both feudal society and the complicity of the intellectual in it. Yet the story is not without sympathy for Kong; as Kong's plight becomes increasingly pitiful through the course of the story, Lu Xun seems to shift his satirical scorn away from Kong and toward the crowd in the tavern, which shows no compassion for Kong's suffering, and perhaps even toward the boy who narrates Kong's story and remains unmoved by it.

"Medicine" is both a realistic interpretation of traditional life and a symbolic parable on revolution and modernity. A youth named Xia has just been beheaded for participating in the anti-Qing revolution. Meanwhile, a young boy surnamed Hua is dying of consumption. Hua's aged and superstitious father buys a piece of bread soaked in the dead revolutionary's blood from the executioner in the belief that this blood will cure his ailing son. Hua the younger eats the bread but dies nonetheless. The two boys have died very different deaths: Xia as the martyr of a hopeful cause and Hua as the victim of ignorance. Their mothers, however, feel a common pain. One cold, early spring morning, as they visit adjacent graves to mourn their dead sons, the mothers face each other in shared sorrow.

Lu Xun speaks to the complexity of nation, tradition, revolution, and the modern in "Medicine." As indicated by their names, *Huaxia* being a poetic synonym for China, the two young men represent the hope and failure of Chinese society. Hua's failure to survive even after he has drunk Xia's blood symbolizes the demise of the feudal order, but it also shows Lu Xun's desolate view of modernization by revolution in China. Yet Lu Xun allows Xia's grief-stricken mother an enduring protest over her son's unjust execution. Upon visiting his grave, his mother is baffled to find a Western-style wreath of red and white flowers on the burial mound. Although his revolutionary comrades probably placed the wreath there, she imagines that it could be a prodigious sign from her son indicating a soul not yet at peace. The mother laments, "I know ... they murdered you. But a day of reckoning will come, Heaven will see to it. Close your eyes in peace.... If you are really here, and can hear me, make that crow fly on to your grave as a sign" (1977:32–33). A mother's desperate belief in the justice of Heaven becomes a symbolic enquiry into the meaning and future of the revolution. "The crow, his head drawn back, perched among the straight boughs as if it were cast in iron," is completely unresponsive to the mother's cries.

It is with the short story "Soap," written three years after "True Story," that Lu Xun abandons, if only briefly, the doubt that once accompanied his interrogations of the connection between tradition and modernity. Siming, the protagonist of "Soap," returns home one evening with a bar of scented soap for his wife, an article extravagant beyond her expectations. Though he calmly accepts her thanks, he is obviously irritated by the day's events. He had not understood the English profanity flung at him by students while he was comparing soaps at the pharmacy. When he asks his son to translate the phrase ("O-du-fu" or "old fool") into Chinese and the boy cannot, Siming unleashes a tirade against modern education, claiming the traditional Confucian education is far superior. To prove his point, he evokes a scene from earlier in the day in which a young beggar girl ministers to her blind grandmother—for Siming a perfect example of traditional piety. Yet passersby remark lasciviously, "If you buy two cakes of soap, and give her a good scrubbing, the result won't be bad at all!" (1977:169). Siming's wife, naturally, makes an immediate connection between the purchase of the soap and the encounter with the beggar girl, understanding all along that in buying her the soap her husband has transferred his lascivious thoughts from the beggar girl to herself. Such a realization calms her, and the earlier quarrel is all but forgotten. Lu Xun's clever symbolism in "Soap" sustains a satire the depth of which is rarely seen in his fictional works. The shabbily dressed beggar girl represents the ragged Confucianism that Siming seems to champion, while the image of her clean, nude body symbolizes the reality that lies behind the façade of Confucian values, the far-flung hope to which he surrenders. For a moment, the binary between tradition and modernity is cast aside to reveal pretension for what it really is.

"In the Wine Shop" is based on a visit Lu Xun made to his hometown, Shaoxing, during the winter of 1919–20. While sipping wine alone in a restaurant, the narrator encounters an old classmate and former colleague at the Shaoxing middle school whom he has not seen in years. No longer the energetic reformer he once was in his youth, Lü Weifu has returned home from a distant province to carry out his mother's request that he move her younger son's grave, which has been inundated with water. Although no remains of his brother could be located, Lü "wrapped up in some cotton some of the clay where his body had been, covered it up, put it in the new coffin, moved it to the grave where father was buried, and buried it beside him" (1977:149). Lü Weifu goes on to recount that he has also returned, again at the request of his mother, to give a gift of red and pink artificial velvet flowers to Ah Shun, the daughter of a boatman he once knew. The girl has died, so Lü gives the flowers instead to her sister. Upon his return, he will tell his mother "that Ah Shun was delighted with them, and that will be that" (1977:153). A little deception seems worth the price of his mother's happiness.

Conscious that had he maintained his faith in the new culture he would not have been quite as nostalgically filial, Lü Weifu is unable to hide his shame as he reveals his adventures to the narrator. Lu Xun's intention in "In the Wine Shop" was obviously to portray the old classmate as a failure who had abandoned the revolution and bargained with the enemy, the old society. "When I have muddled through the New Year I shall go back to teaching the Confucian classics as before," concludes Lü. "I could never have guessed that you would be teaching such books," the narrator retorts (1977:154). Yet, although Lü Weifu appears to be quite deplorably a failure, his compassion and piety affirm the positive aspects of traditional society, traditional strengths that enchanted a nostalgic Lu Xun in spite of his nonconformist beliefs. "In the Wine Shop" is both a critique of compromise and a fictional affirmation of the author's own ambivalence and hesitation, a microcosm of Lu Xun's paradoxical moral vision.

The collection of eight stories entitled *Old Tales Retold* includes fiction begun during the early 1920s as well as his only fiction written after 1926. Although it has been labeled by critics as "marking the sad degeneration" (Hsia 1971:46) of his talent, the project reflects Lu Xun's ongoing revision of the forever arguable relationship between tradition and modernity. "As for historical stories," Lu Xun begins in his 1935 preface to the collection, "those based on extensive research with sound evidence for every word are extremely hard to write, even though they are sneered at as 'novels smacking of the schoolroom' *(jiaoshou xiaoshuo)*; whereas not much skill is needed to take a subject and write it up freely, adding some coloring of your own" (1961). It is by reading the void between *jiaoshou* (professorial) *xiaoshuo* (novels) and "adding some color" that the reader arrives at an understanding of the complexity and meaning of "old tales retold."

The tales in this collection recount events taken from ancient texts, including *Book of History, Huainanzi, Classic of Mountains and Seas, Imperially Reviewed Encyclopedia of the Taiping Era* (Taiping yulan), *Mencius, Mozi, Zhuangzi, Arrayed Marvels* (Lieyi zhuan), and *Records of the Search for Spirits* (Soushen ji), but in a style that is self-consciously anachronistic. They make use of modern language, with words such as *youdai* (to give preferential treatment to) and Western phrases such as "good morning" and "how do you do." There are also frequent allusions to Lu Xun's contemporaries: a former student, Gao Changhong, in "Flight to the Moon" (Benyue, 1926), the Creation Society in "Gathering Vetch" (Cai wei, 1935), and several well-known scholars and writers in "Curbing the Flood" (Li shui, 1935).

There is no question that *Tales* negotiates its most powerful ironic effects through allusions and references to traditional Chinese texts. But reading, writing, and decoding earlier texts no longer have the same significance they had in Lu Xun's iconoclastic "Diary of a Madman" phase, and it seems to take second place to his more urgent need to penetrate and fathom what was happening around him. At a time when literature had already undergone a spectacular (yet fitful) transformation, when Lu Xun was attacking *New Sensationist author Shi Zhecun for his fascination with the "skeleton," to reread and rewrite traditional tales was at once radical and extremely conservative. To dare confront both the past and the present with satire, the uncanny, and a good dose of humor was radical. To rely on the verisimilitude granted by the exploitation of the traditional in order to ponder the present was, at most, conservative. If, as Leo Ou-fan Lee has argued, the Madman could be "regarded as an artistic version of Lu Xun's inner voice" (1987:53), then so too could Mozi and Mencius be treated as components of Lu Xun's alter ego. To describe these retold tales as autobiographical, however, would be to oversimplify the purpose and implications of the project.

Published first in 1922 under the title "Bu Zhoushan," the first story in the collection, "Mending Heaven" (Bu tian), presents the mythological character of Nüwa and her tale of repairing heaven. The details of the original story can be traced to a number of texts: the narrative of how Nüwa created humans from mud can be found in the *Taiping Yulan* (ca. A.D. 990); Nüwa repairing heaven with five-colored stones exists in the Han dynasty *Huainanzi*; and the particulars of Gong Gong cracking his head against the mountain, the fire in an ancient forest on Kunlun Mountain, and the many search parties ordered by a succession of emperors to find the Fairy Mountains are all chronicled in Sima Zhen's Zhou-era *Supplement to the Records of the Grand Historian* (Bu Shiji), the *Classic of Mountains and Seas*, and the *Records of the Grand Historian* itself. What separates Lu Xun's rewriting of the Nüwa myth from those original tales is his complicated portrayal of Nüwa. "I've never been so bored!" Nüwa claims upon waking. She bends down and kneads some mud to create her first human beings. Satisfied with her creations and lulled by their laughter, Nüwa falls off to sleep again, only to be awakened by a crash. Zhuan Xu, a descendant of the Yellow Emperor, and the giant Gong Gong, in their struggle for power, had cracked heaven and split the earth. Nüwa begins mending heaven, expending all of her energy and eventually taking her last breath as her mission is concluded. The humans she had created had "covered their bodies in the most curious fashion, and some of them had snow-white beards growing from the lower part of their faces." Another was hung "from head to foot … with thick folds of drapery, with a dozen or more supernumerary ribbons at his waist." A creature held forth a black oblong board that stated, "Your lewd nakedness is immoral, an offence against etiquette, a breach of the rules and conduct fit for beasts!" The very creatures that she had forged now stood in judgment of her nakedness. Only later, on a bitterly cold day, does a group of soldiers encamp on Nüwa's stomach, announcing themselves to be the "true descendants of the goddess" and altering their standard to read "The Entrails of Nüwa" (1961:1–13).

This rewriting of the traditional story of creation has many possible readings. Was the Freudian reworking of Nüwa a commentary on the May Fourth spirit? More likely it seems a covert critique of the relationship between the old vanguard and later generations, between Lu Xun and younger revolutionaries, between those who have paved the way and those who have come after. Such commentary pervades the collection of retold tales, at times more obviously than at others. When in "Gathering Vetch," for example, Lu Xun recounts the travels of Boyi and Shuqi, a story that can be traced to the *Book of History, Records of the Grand Historian,* and so on, he cannot resist a far more obvious response to and critique of the Creation Society aesthetic of "art for art's sake" in the words of Lord Xiaoping: "They went to the Old People's Home ... but they wouldn't steer clear of politics. They came to Shouyang Mountain ... but they would insist on writing poems. They wrote poems, all right! But they would express resentment, instead of knowing their place and producing 'art for art's sake'" (1961:78).

In "Curbing the Flood," Lu Xun appropriates the classics in a biting criticism of Pan Guangdan (a well-known eugenicist), Gu Jiegang (a scholar and expert on folk songs), Lin Yutang (an advocate of a return to the classics and their inherent "spiritual values"), Chen Xiying, the poet Xu Zhimo, and Du Heng (coeditor of the Shanghai journal *Les Contemporains*). Though the story seems a superficial reworking of the story of Yu, the curber of the floods and founder of the Xia Dynasty, first written in the *Records of the Grand Historian,* Lu Xun wastes little time getting to his point: the problem is not the "flood," but the scholars assembled on Mount Culture. The obvious referent was a group of scholars who, in 1932, had petitioned the Guomindang to declare Beijing a "city of culture," moving all military institutions out of the capital. Lu Xun discussed the folly of such a plan, as well as what he believed to be the Guomindang's betrayal of the nation, first in a 1933 essay "Notes on False Freedom" (1993, 5:12–13). Peppered with phrases such as "Good morning" and "How do you do," parodying westernized scholars of the period, "Curbing the Flood" jabs constantly at the scholars' responses to the catastrophes of the time. Upon return from a trip to the flooded areas, a group of officials settles in for dinner and drink, coming almost to blows over a few samples of calligraphy. First place is finally granted to the inscription: "The state is prosperous, the people at peace." "For not only was the calligraphy so ancient as to be almost undecipherable, with a rude antique flavor about it, but the sentiments were thoroughly appropriate, worthy to be recorded by imperial historians" (1961:43), even as the country drowns in the floodwaters.

Yu is told in part three of the story that the "powers of endurance" of the common people "are famed throughout the world." "The most urgent matter, however ... is to send a squadron of large rafts forthwith to fetch the scholars to the higher ground ... culture is the life blood of a nation and scholars the soul of a culture. So long as culture exists, China will exist. All the rest is secondary" (1961:46). There is perhaps no lamentation more evocative of Lu Xun's personal plight than the phrase uttered by a member of the "lower orders" who had been chosen as a representative: "Death is better than being a spokesman!" (1961:39).

Though obviously burdened by his position in society and struggles of the early 1930s, Lu Xun manipulates the classics in ways that undermine the modernity of his project. His methods, especially those employed in *Old Tales Retold*, lay bare the often-ignored complexities of his very revolutionary existence. Tales from ancient texts become the bare-bones script behind what often appears as no more than a failed contemporary romance. What can be said about a Lu Xun who critiques a Lin Yutang or a Shi Zhecun for his fascination with the classics, but resorts himself to those same texts in order to contemplate contemporary skirmishes? Does the reader gain a better understanding of Nüwa, Mozi, and Laozi? Or does Lu Xun instead reveal the darker, more genuine corners of his own existence via his revisions of these characters? In the end Nüwa provides but a fertile piece of ground on which soldiers might camp. Mozi, in "Opposing Aggression" (Fei gong, 1934), successfully saves the Song from the Chu, only to be stopped and interrogated by "National Salvation Collectors"; then "outside the South Gate he ran into a storm, and when he tried to take shelter under the city gate two patrolmen armed with spears chased him away. He was soaked to the skin, with the result that he suffered for over ten days from a heavy cold" (1961:135–136). Laozi, in "Leaving the Pass" (1935), laments Confucius' departure: "He will never come back nor ever call me master again. He will refer to me as 'that old fellow,' and play tricks behind my back" (1961:110). Laozi's fate is no better at the pass when asked to lecture to the guards. When a combination of his accent and his toothless diction make his words difficult to understand, he spends a day and a half recording his ideas for the pass guards. Laozi leaves in a cloud of yellow dust, abandoning the warden, copyist, and accountant to a discussion of what to do with the manuscript. What is the fate of Laozi's day and a half of writing? "Warden Xi dusted his desk with his sleeve, then picked up the two strings of tablets and put them on the shelves piled high with salt, sesame, cloth, beans, unleavened bread and other confiscated goods." The musings of the philosopher, whether he be Laozi or Lu Xun, are no longer worthy of recording in the *Book of History* or the *Zhuangzi*, but instead are relegated to the dusty corners of the storeroom of time.

The same conflict that Lu Xun denigrated in the likes of Shi Zhecun and Lin Yutang—their fascination with the "skeleton"—seems to haunt Lu Xun in his retelling of old tales. For how an author mirrors himself in Mozi and Laozi, all the while harboring doubts as to the efficacy of their philosophies and the purpose of their missions, indicates a complexity of tradition and modernity that far surpasses that evidenced in "Diary of a Madman." It is a complexity, however, that goes misunderstood and misplaced, a complexity that can be disentangled only by the less burdened pens of the likes of Shi Zhecun and Shen Congwen.

After years of adulation during the Mao era, the publication of his sixteen-volume complete works, and numerous scholarly manuscripts dedicated to analyzing his life, philosophy, and writing, Lu Xun remains for many not only the father of modern Chinese literature but also the greatest modern Chinese writer. When Mao Zedong claimed in *The New Democracy* (1940) that "the direction of Lu Xun is the direction of the new Chinese culture," he was making a powerful prediction. Although the Madman seemed to be the modern curative for a diseased traditional Ah Q, Lu Xun in his constant probing of old and new in stories such as "Kong Yiji," "Medicine," "Soap," and "In the Wine Shop" and in *Old Tales Retold* reminds readers that modernity is never the true antithesis of tradition, and that the Madman was also an Ah Q.

—*Ann Huss*

Bibliography

Anderson, Marston. "Lu Xun's Facetious Muse: The Creative Imperative in Modern Chinese Fiction." In David Wang and Ellen Widmer, eds., *From May Fourth to June Fourth: Fiction and Film in Twentieth-Century China*, 249–268. Cambridge, Mass.: Harvard University Press, 1993.

Denton, Kirk A. *The Problematic of Self in Modern Chinese Literature: Hu Feng and Lu Ling*. Stanford: Stanford University Press, 1998.

Hsia, C. T. *A History of Modern Chinese Fiction*. New Haven: Yale University Press, 1971.

Hsia, Tsi-An. *The Gate of Darkness: Studies on the Leftist Literary Movement in China*. Seattle: University of Washington Press, 1968.

Lee, Leo Ou-fan. *Lu Xun and His Legacy*. Berkeley: University of California Press, 1985.

———. *Voices from the Iron House: A Study of Lu Xun*. Bloomington: Indiana University Press, 1987.

Lu, Xun. *Diary of a Madman and Other Stories*. Trans. William Lyell. Honolulu: University of Hawai'i Press, 1990.

———. *Lu Xun quanji* (Collected Works of Lu Xun). 16 vols. Beijing: Remin wenxue, 1993.

———. *Old Tales Retold*. Beijing: Foreign Languages Press, 1961.

———. *Selected Stories*. Trans. Yang Hsien-yi and Gladys Yang. New York: W. W. Norton, 1977.

Lyell, William A. *Lu Hsün's Vision of Reality*. Berkeley: University of California Press, 1976.

69

FEMINISM AND REVOLUTION:
THE WORK AND LIFE OF DING LING

Ding Ling (pen name of Jiang Bingzhi, 1904–1986) was one of the major Chinese writers of the twentieth century. She wrote in times of great social and political upheaval, and she and her literary reputation suffered many vicissitudes of fortune during those times. She remains a highly controversial figure.

Ding Ling is known especially as a feminist and a revolutionary. Yet many critics, especially Western feminists, believe that after Mao's *"Yan'an Talks" in 1942 she betrayed feminism in favor of the socialist struggle. Indeed, when she emerged again in the early 1980s after more than twenty years of silence following her denunciation as a rightist in 1957, she decried Western feminism and showed a remarkable faith in the future of socialism. But it may be more accurate to say that Ding Ling's feminism grew away from the concern with individual self-expression that is central to most Western conceptions of the aim of feminism. She came to think of Western feminism as self-indulgent and to believe that the best interest of women (as of all people) lay in socialism, not in liberal individualism. Ding Ling's work raises many profound questions. How does it reflect the theme of feminism and revolution? Are there serious tensions between feminism and social progress in her writing? How does someone who begins as a champion for women's individuality and selfhood—as she was in her early writings and in her courageous challenge to the patriarchal order in Yan'an—change into a genuine believer that women's issues are only part of the social question and that the national interest should come before the personal?

Ding Ling's early life shares features with the lives of many writers of the May Fourth generation and even with many of the characters in their stories: she came from the declining gentry class in the countryside and fled her hometown in defiance of an arranged marriage to seek a new life in a big city, where she pursued a writing career. Quite unusual, however, was that Ding Ling was brought up by an unconventional and rebellious mother who, widowed when Ding Ling was three years old, got a degree in education and made her own living by teaching at newly reformed schools. Such activities were virtually unthinkable for a gentry-class widow at that time. Ding Ling's unfinished story "Mother" (Muqin, 1933) is thought to draw from the model of Ding Ling's own mother, telling of a mother and her sworn sisters who unbind their feet, abandon their gentry-class way of life, take part in a movement for social reform, and learn to put the interest of the nation before their own interest. Ding Ling grew up in Hunan Province, with its ancient Chu culture, a region that was vigorously pursuing educational reforms at the time of Ding Ling's youth, well ahead of other provinces. Growing up among reformers and young rebels, Ding Ling devoured Western books and new ideas about democracy and freedom. A rebel at heart, she published her first essay in the local newspaper, exposing the unsavory deeds of her maternal uncle, a local despot, and denouncing the social system to which her uncle belonged. To avoid her prearranged betrothal to this man's son, she fled with the help of her mother to Shanghai.

In the early 1920s, the large treaty port of Shanghai was on its way to becoming an international metropolis. It had all the allure of a modern city: uprooted people could remain anonymous and did not have to rely on clan networks. Here she adopted the name Ding Ling for its brevity and simplicity (the Chinese character *ding* has only two strokes) and began her life as a "modern girl." In 1921 she attended a women's college set up by Chen Duxiu and Li Dazhao, two of the founders of the Chinese Communist Party. A year later she and her friends enrolled in the Department of Chinese Literature at Shanghai University, a school known as a gathering place for left-wing intellectuals. Free from the watchful gaze of elders, she and her friends lived a bohemian life, spending most of their time in extracurricular activities. In 1924, Ding Ling went to Beijing and took private lessons in painting; and a year later she met Hu Yepin, a young poet whom she eventually married.

In 1927 Ding Ling published her first short story, "Mengke" (a transliteration of the French *mon coeur*, my heart). In the same year her second story, "Miss Sophie's Diary" (Shafei nüshi riji), became an instant success. Many of Ding Ling's early works are about "modern girls"—educated young urban women— and their desires, frustrations, aspirations, and hopes. Ding Ling was particularly praised by the critics for the psychological complexity and sexuality of her female characters. "Miss Sophie's Diary" touches on the forbidden topic of female erotic desire and records Sophie's tortured self-scrutiny. It was characterized by Mao Dun as "representative of the contradictory psychology regarding sexual love found in young women liberated since May Fourth" (Feuerwerker 1982:43).

"Miss Sophie's Diary" remains a landmark in Chinese women's writing of the May Fourth period. In writings by the May Fourth generation of women writers, platonic love was perhaps the dominant theme. Narratives tended to be sentimental, lyrical, and romantic, as in the writings of Bing Xin, Lu Yin, and Su Xuelin. Feng Yuanjun was the boldest of them all, but even she had not broken through the confines of traditional moral propriety. Although Ding Ling was not among the first women writers to publish in the May Fourth generation, she was perhaps the first to portray female sexual desire. Her literary success was achieved by moving beyond lyricism, introducing to the Chinese literary scene the autonomous and intelligent sensibility of someone like Nora in Ibsen's *Doll's House* or Emma in Flaubert's *Madame Bovary*, two works that caused a splash in China at the time. Part of the success of "Miss Sophie's Diary" also lay in its use of the diary form, which diminished the sense of distance between the writer and the reader and appealed to readers' voyeuristic desires.

The influence of Western literary works is conspicuous in Ding Ling's early writings. For instance, many of the protagonists in her early stories have foreign names: Mon Coeur in "Mengke," Sophie in "Miss Sophie's Diary," Wendy in "A Woman and a Man" (Yige nüren he yige nanren, 1928), and Mary in "Shanghai, Spring 1930" (Yijiusanling nian chun Shanghai, 1930). More substantively, her psychological approach to the construction of female characters bears resemblance to those in Western and Russian novels. Ding Ling used Western themes and motifs to break new literary ground. For example, "Miss Amao" (Amao guniang, 1928) may be read as a Chinese version of *Madame Bovary* (and surely the protagonist's name is meant to suggest Emma). Amao, a country girl, is married into a middle-class family near the city of Hangzhou. Dissatisfied with the life of a housewife and dreaming of glamour, she leaves her husband's home and ventures into the city. But her dream is beyond her reach, and she eventually commits suicide. Amao's progression from innocence through insatiable desire to destruction parallels that of Emma. Still, Ding Ling's Amao is a psychologically convincing picture of a rural woman suffocated by a glamorous but small-minded urban society and her inability to rise above it. What is original and important about this story is the way Ding Ling brings Flaubert's Emma into play as a direct response to most previous constructions of rural women by May Fourth writers: miserable, helpless female figures largely devoid of inner life, such as Sister Xianglin in *Lu Xun's "New Year's Sacrifice" (Zhufu, 1924). In contrast, Ding Ling creates an image of a Chinese rural woman with westernized individuality. Ironically, this figure is destroyed by her passionate desire for material wealth in the city.

At the beginning of the 1930s, Ding Ling's writing began to shift from expressing the subjective life of her characters toward portraying their social milieu. This transition began with two stories, "Weihu" (1930) and "Shanghai,

Spring 1930." She brings together the two themes—the personal and the social—through the "love and revolution" formula, which was popular at that time among young leftist writers in Shanghai. This formula marked a modest politicization of the passion and subjectivism of 1920s romanticism, still focusing on the emotional conflicts and torments of the intellectual protagonists and very different from "social realism." Nevertheless, the formula helped Ding Ling and other writers gradually transfer their literary focus from "love" to "revolution."

As the 1930s progressed, the general narrative paradigm among Chinese writers shifted from portraying the lonely individual to depictions of society at large, from personal psychological exploration to a focus on broad social and political issues. Ding Ling was at the vanguard of this new kind of literature. She became one of the most influential left-wing authors of the 1930s and worked as editor-in-chief of *Big Dipper* (Beidou), an organ of the League of Left-Wing Writers. She also began to write stories in the social-realist mode. "Water" (Shui, 1931), published in the first issue of *Big Dipper*, is representative of her work during this period and has been regarded as a leading work of social-realist fiction in China. The story was inspired by the floods of 1931, but it focused on the impact of the natural disaster on the political consciousness of a rural community. Instead of viewing the event from a single protagonist's perspective, the narrative evokes the collective, the community as a whole, and sympathetically depicts its uprising against the corrupt local officials as inevitable.

With Ding Ling's deepening involvement in left-wing circles, political tragedies fell upon her. In early 1931, Ding Ling's husband Hu Yepin and four other young League writers were captured and murdered by the Guomindang. Ding Ling herself was kidnapped and put under house arrest by the Guomindang in 1933. In 1936, she escaped from her imprisonment in Nanjing and arrived in Yan'an, where the Communist Party was located and where her writing career took another turn. In Yan'an, Ding Ling taught Chinese literature at the Red Army Academy and was given responsibilities for political training. Despite her efforts to conform to party ideology, Ding Ling, as a keen observer of her surroundings, chose not to remain silent about the Communist treatment of women in the revolutionary base. Two stories published in 1941, "When I Was in Xia Village" (Wo zai Xiacun de shihou) and "In the Hospital" (Zai yiyuan zhong), dwell on the dark side of the revolutionary experience and raise the question of women's position within the revolutionary community.

Ding Ling had her first taste of party criticism after she published an essay on the eve of the International Women's Day: "Thoughts on March Eighth" (Sanba jie you gan, 1942). This very direct feminist essay criticizes the unequal treatment of women in the "liberated areas." Ding Ling uses the official Communist policy that men and women are equal partners in the revolutionary cause to criticize the practice in Yan'an where women were subordinate to men in revolutionary organizations and were assigned social status according to the status of their husbands. Ding Ling thus points out the revolutionary women's dilemma: even where class oppression is lifted, gender oppression remains. For this essay she was severely criticized and forced to retract its ideas and apologize for its potential divisive effect. Her essay, along with others critical of life in Yan'an, including Wang Shiwei's "Wild Lilies" (Yebaihehua), prompted Mao Zedong to convene a forum on culture, at the end of which he presented two lectures (the *"Yan'an Talks") that laid down Communist Party cultural policy: literature and art should be subordinate to politics, writers should overcome their remaining petit-bourgeois subjectivism and write works about and for the "masses" (workers, peasants, and soldiers) in order to mobilize them in the struggle against the Japanese, and writers should make use of Chinese national forms and folk traditions.

Guided by Mao's redefinition of the role of the writer, Ding Ling joined a reporters' group and later a propaganda team and went to the battlefront in the war against Japan. She wrote plays and performed on stage for soldiers and villagers. In order to communicate with the often illiterate masses, the cultural workers utilized popular traditional forms such as drum songs, clapper talk, two-man acts, and comic cross talk. Ding Ling's own writing from this period shows a radical change of style and theme. No longer focusing on just one or two protagonists, her fiction begins to paint a broad scroll of a village or of other collectives. Her socialist-realist novel *The Sun Shines over Sanggan River* (Taiyang zhao zai Sanggan he shang, 1948), which took second place in the 1951 Stalin Prize competition, was based on material collected when she took part in a village land reform.

Ding Ling held a leading position in Beijing cultural circles after the founding of the PRC. During this period she wrote essays, literary criticism, and stories, primarily expressing her love for China's new socialist life. Even so, she did not escape persecution: she was labeled a chief member of two "anti-Party cliques" and was sent to labor on a farm in a remote area of northeastern China, where she remained for twelve years. During the Cultural Revolution she was imprisoned in Beijing for five years. When the Cultural Revolution ended in 1976, Ding Ling was "rehabilitated" and finally resumed writing in the form of essays, reminiscences, and reviews. The novella *Du Wanxiang* (written 1966, revised 1978) was the longest work of fiction she published during this period and her only work since Yan'an to focus on an individual woman. The story is a sketch of a model laborer whom Ding Ling had met during her stay on the farm in northeastern China. In this socialist parable, Ding Ling creates a model socialist woman: an ordinary farmer who wins the respect of others by leading a humble and yet glorious life full of traditional womanly virtues: she is hardworking, selfless, considerate, accommodating, and unassuming. Here the rebellious, restless, and inquisitive modern girl in Ding Ling's early fiction has completely given way to the traditional feminine virtues that the socialist system reaffirmed.

Ding Ling's stories, essays, and speeches are often controversial and sometimes out of tune with their times, an indication of her nonconformist attitudes and strong convictions. In 1983, at a time when many Chinese liberal intellectuals were abandoning Marxism and reevaluating their position in the global culture, Ding Ling supported the Communist Party's campaign against "spiritual pollution"—the increasing Western influence on Chinese culture. Even though her behavior puzzled many people, it was consistent with beliefs to which she had been publicly committed for decades. Given her resilient fighting spirit, it is not surprising that she remained controversial to the end. For the later Ding Ling, literature was never just pure art, it was a political vehicle by which to fulfill her deeply felt obligation to depict social changes and interpret their meaning for the community. For her, a woman's fate is always linked to that of her nation. In this sense, Ding Ling remained committed to the cause of revolution and feminism, a path on which she traveled and suffered, sometimes alone, sometimes with others, for more than sixty years, insisting to the end that in comparison with her cause, her personal sufferings were insignificant.

—*Jingyuan Zhang*

Bibliography

Anderson, Jennifer, and Theresa Munford, eds. *Chinese Women Writers: A Collection of Short Stories by Chinese Women Writers of the 1920s and '30s.* Hong Kong: Joint Publishing, 1985.

Ding, Ling. "Day." In Amy D. Dooling and Kristina M. Torgeson, trans. and eds., *Writing Women in Modern China: An Anthology of Women's Literature from the Early Twentieth Century*, 267–273. New York: Columbia University Press, 1998.

——. *I Myself Am a Woman: Selected Writings of Ding Ling.* Ed. Tani Barlow and Gary Bjorge. Boston: Beacon Press, 1989.

——. *Miss Sophie's Diary and Other Stories.* Trans. W. J. F. Jenner. Beijing: Chinese Literature, 1985.

——. *The Sun Shines over the Sanggan River.* Trans. Yang Xianyi and Gladys Yang. Beijing: Foreign Languages Press, 1984.

Feuerwerker, Yi-tsi Mei. *Ding Ling's Fiction: Ideology and Narrative in Modern Chinese Literature.* Cambridge, Mass.: Harvard University Press, 1982.

Lau, Joseph S. M., C. T. Hsia, and Leo Ou-fan Lee, eds. *Modern Chinese Stories and Novellas, 1919–1949.* New York: Columbia University Press, 1981.

70

THE DEBATE ON REVOLUTIONARY LITERATURE

Entering into a literary field in the early 1920s in which the slogan of "literary revolution" had become the principal rallying cry, young intellectuals of the time should nevertheless be excused for lacking a clear idea of what a "revolution" (*geming*) might be. At least it was clear, particularly in the wake of the events leading from the New Culture Movement in 1917 to the May Fourth Movement of 1919, that it meant the introduction of something *new* and vital and the sweeping away of the *old* forces and norms of traditional Chinese culture. However, the literary revolution—advocating the general use of a written vernacular *(baihua)* and the promotion of "new culture"—was already fading into the past, while youths shocked and tempered by the intensifying political violence of the mid-1920s were beginning to feel that it would not be enough merely to revolutionize literature: the object of revolutionary change must be society itself. Although Chinese cultural norms determined that literature would be the crucial vehicle for such revolutionary change, the passage from a "literary revolution" to a "revolutionary literature" meant reconceptualizing literature as no longer an end of a process of revolutionary change, but a means to, an instrument of, social revolution. It was in this way that the leftist writers of the 1920s, strong in impact but still a minority in literary circles, were to set themselves apart from what they were able by then to identify as a liberal humanist mainstream in modern Chinese letters.

Indications of the literary sea change that led to this debate pepper the 1920s. As early as 1923, the prominent Creation Society writer Yu Dafu published an article calling for a literature of proletarian struggle (Denton 1996:263–268), and by 1925 the Marxist critic Qu Qiubai was calling for a mass literature and a further reform of the modern written language to reach out to the working classes and vividly render their world. The violent suppression of anti-imperialist demonstrations in 1925 and 1926 made the younger generation disillusioned with older May Fourth writers, who begged their students and protégés to devote their energies to their studies and not take to the streets.

A crucial moment was the Creation Society's conversion to Marxism around 1925. Creationists such as Guo Moruo, *Yu Dafu, and Cheng Fangwu disdained the bland, pedestrian realism of the Literary Association that dominated the literary scene of the early 1920s and advocated a dynamic, vital literature that would be more in step with current world literary trends. In the early 1920s, their fiction and poetry emphasized the individualistic and romantic aspects of literary expression ("see Form and Reform"). In large part because of the influence of the contemporary Japanese literary scene, however, Guo Moruo rather ostentatiously embraced Marxism and launched the society on the path of "revolutionary literature." The rationale for this apparent reversal was vaguely evolutionary, with an emphasis on cleaving to literature's cutting edge in each succeeding era.

The Debate on Revolutionary Literature, as it was called, took place in the early spring of 1928 in the form of articles published by prominent writers in some of the leading literary magazines of the time. Cheng Fangwu's article, whose title, "From Literary Revolution to Revolutionary Literature" (Cong wenxue geming dao geming wenxue), set the terms of the debate, echoed Yu Dafu's emphasis on bringing Chinese literature up to date on the world scene. Cheng especially faults the "Threads of Talk" (*Yusi*) group of essayists, represented by Zhou Zuoren and Lin Yutang, for obstructing the current of literary progress with their apparent refusal to take burning social and political issues seriously. To the Creation Society, older May Fourth-generation writers seemed to be settling back into a quiet complacency as the world crumbled about them: if anything, the situation in China was more dire in 1928 than it had been in 1919. Cheng's article also makes the crucial point that what is required of a revolutionary literature is that it be a literature not of the individual but of the collective, of the masses.

The Sun Society (Taiyang she), which formed at about this time, also promoted revolutionary literature, but from a somewhat different perspective. In the debate on revolutionary literature, the Sun Society aimed its criticism at two of the major fiction writers of the time, Lu Xun and Mao Dun, whose works arguably manifested a revolutionary viewpoint and had inspired much of the younger generation in this very direction. Qian Xingcun launched the most vitriolic and iconoclastic of these attacks in his article "The Bygone Age of Ah Q" (Siqu le de Ah Q shidai, 1928). His main point, and one of the principal issues in the debate, was that the literature of the May Fourth movement, of which

*Lu Xun's "The True Story of Ah Q" was taken to be a paradigmatic example, was hopelessly out of date. Qian's deepest concern seems to be with the pre-May Fourth settings of almost all of Lu Xun's fiction. However, there is also the suggestion of another important point: that the *way* of writing was dated. A revolutionary literature had to differ not only in content but also in methodology (Denton 1996:276–288).

Lu Xun, for his part, maintained in speeches given in the late 1920s a strict distinction between literature and revolution; to him, writers who thought they could contribute to a revolution by writing were fooling themselves. On the other hand, Lu Xun often attacked the Crescent Moon Society (Xinyue she, whose members included Xu Zhimo, Liang Shiqiu, and *Shen Congwen) for promoting what he considered a literature of escapism—love stories and lyrical poetry—because it was too detached from contemporary social reality. Thus, though not directly engaging in the debate, Lu Xun's position was somewhere in the middle.

In another article, this time critiquing *Mao Dun, Qian Xingcun asserts another of the principal points in the debate on revolutionary literature: that writers must begin to write a forceful, positive literature that inspires readers into action. Qian complains that Mao Dun's fiction is suffused with the melancholy and angst of petit-bourgeois intellectuals who cannot realize their revolutionary dreams. In a 1929 response to Qian's attack, "On Reading *Ni Huanzhi*" (Du Ni Huanzhi), Mao Dun argues that Qian and other such radicals, in addition to misreading his works, are calling for propaganda, not literature (Denton 1996:289–306). In perhaps the only firm defensive position in the "debate" on revolutionary literature, Mao Dun affirms one of the most important tenets of May Fourth realism: that petit-bourgeois writers like himself can only write well about the life they themselves know, narrow as that experience may be on the broad social horizon. This principle would haunt Chinese fiction throughout the century and would have to be dealt with seriously by the Communist Party and its writers before a convincing revolutionary literature could emerge in actual practice.

Liang Shiqiu joined the fray with an article entitled "Literature and Revolution" (Wenxue yu geming) in *Crescent Moon* (June 1928), asserting that writers need not always write revolutionary literature and that "revolutionary," being a political term, is not a coherent category of literature. "Human nature," he says, "is the sole standard for measuring literature" (Denton 1996:310). He attacks Qu Qiubai's slogan of "mass literature," asserting that literature, revolutionary or otherwise, is always the product not of the masses but of "a few geniuses." Unlike Lu Xun and Mao Dun's defensive positions, Liang's article totally rejects the emergent, class-based view of literature that lay at the heart of the debate. Ten years later, in the early months of the war against Japan, Liang's reiteration of this extreme position on "resistance literature" got him ostracized from the literary community on the mainland.

Although it lasted only a few weeks in the spring of 1928, the issues this public debate brought to the surface remained at the center of Chinese letters throughout the century: whether literature should reflect contemporary social reality; whether it should represent a broad social horizon and be written from the point of view of the working classes (indeed, whether this was possible at all); and whether it should be obliged to be positive, forceful, and dynamic. The debate was revisited in the more protracted battle over literary freedom in the 1930s, in which the very ideological independence of the writer was at stake.

The mode of operation of these Creation and Sun Society writers, because it emerged from the same literary conditions and practices of the Literary Association and other societies of the 1920s (see "Literary Communities and the Production of Literature"), was that of a group of like-minded writers who would form an identifiable group, establish their own organs of publication, and cultivate a loyal readership, some of whom would become their protégés and hopefully successors on the literary scene. Although dominated by the bellicose voices of leftist ideologues, the debate also showed that, within the conditions of the literary arena in the 1920s, simply attacking writers and telling them what to do did not begin to address the issue. But what would ultimately characterize Chinese revolutionary literature, making it stand apart from other modes of literary practice in China, was the crucial evolution of leftist literary organizations from the late 1920s up to the early months of the outbreak of war against Japan. It was during this period that leftists came eventually to dominate the literary scene, in part by redefining literary production as an instrument of mobilization and indoctrination, even as a training ground for new writers.

—*Charles Laughlin*

Bibliography

Denton, Kirk A., ed. *Modern Chinese Literary Thought: Writings on Literature, 1893–1945*. Stanford: Stanford University Press, 1996.

Hsia, C. T. *A History of Modern Chinese Fiction*. New Haven: Yale University Press, 1971.

Hsia, Tsi-an. *The Gate of Darkness: Studies on the Leftist Literary Movement in China*. Seattle: University of Washington Press, 1968.

Pickowicz, Paul. "Qu Qiubai's Critique of the May Fourth Generation: Early Chinese Marxist Literary Criticism." In Merle Goldman, ed., *Modern Chinese Literature in the May Fourth Era*, 351–384. Cambridge, Mass.: Harvard University Press, 1977.

Wong Wang-chi. *Politics and Literature in Shanghai: The Chinese League of Left-Wing Writers, 1930–1936*. Manchester: Manchester University Press. 1991.

71

MAO DUN, THE MODERN NOVEL, AND THE REPRESENTATION OF WOMEN

Mao Dun (Shen Yanbing, 1896–1981) was a leading figure in the development of the modern Chinese novel. By the time he began to write creatively in 1927, he already had a formidable reputation as a literary editor, critic, and translator. He is best known for his reformulation of nineteenth-century European realist theory and for putting this theory into practice in a series of novellas and full-length novels. His *Rainbow* (Hong, 1929) was among the earliest full-fledged novels in modern Chinese literature, and *Midnight* (Ziye, 1933), a mature novel of nearly six hundred pages, is conventionally acknowledged as being a high point of his literary theory in practice.

Three prominent intertwining elements contribute to Mao Dun's literary vision: his realistic literary theory, his revolutionary commitment (both as a founding member of the Chinese Communist Party and as an active participant in revolutionary campaigns during the 1920s), and his stance toward women's issues. The last of these significantly illuminates our understanding of the other two.

Provoked by the extent of educational and social disadvantage of women under traditional cultural norms, male intellectuals in late-modernizing nations such as China often committed themselves to fledgling women's movements. Young, modern male intellectuals such as Mao Dun and his peers dominated the new discourses of modernity, nationalism, and cultural reconfiguration that evolved in the early decades of the twentieth century. Issues of national and individual identity, gender, women's emancipation, and so on were therefore spoken with a male voice. Mao Dun was a prolific contributor to contemporary journal-based debates on the "woman question" *(funü wenti)* where he wrote in general support of the cause of women's emancipation. For May Fourth intellectuals, issues such as the emancipation of the individual from such traditional patriarchal constraints as arranged marriage scarcely took on a gendered aspect: young men were just as much victims of such abhorrent practice as their female comrades. From this easy assumption of advocacy, it was no difficult leap for May Fourth male intellectuals not only to identify with the new woman's quest for identity and meaning but also to appropriate it.

Mao Dun's fiction offers an insightful illumination into the problematic of May Fourth male feminism, both in the light of his obsessive reconstructions and reconfigurations of the new woman and in the way these intersect with his interest in literary realism. His first short story, "Creation" (Chuangzao, 1928), a reworking of the Pygmalion myth, offers an allegory for the project of "writing woman." Junshi, a modern educated intellectual chooses a distant cousin Xianxian, "a piece of uncut jade," as a wife to "carve" into his ideal of modern womanhood. He attempts to do this by acquainting her with fashionable new books on culture and politics. But Xianxian is stirred by the radical message in these books, becomes actively involved in political work, and eventually leaves him out of frustration at his inertia and self-absorption. Although a third-person narrative, the story is recounted in flashback from the perspective of Junshi. One morning, Junshi wakes first and ponders the education and transformation of his wife who sleeps beside him. He has created her to complete his own sense of self, but she has precipitated in him a crisis. She undermines his assumption of moral ascendancy over her by developing views of her own, and, worse, she even assumes a position of sexual dominance over him by her captivating sensuality. The portrayal of Xianxian is often read as an affirmation of both the realization of feminist aspirations and, as Mao Dun suggests in his memoirs, a symbol of fulfilled revolutionary vocation (1997, 1:393). Yet, as a sexualized object and male construct, Xianxian is portrayed only through the consciousness of her creator. She has no inner identity. Any meaning her portrayal signifies has been inscribed by her creator in terms of his own crisis. All we learn of her is what she is not; that is, how she does not correspond to his ideal. Finally, Junshi, ironically the main obstacle to her own becoming, is so unaware of who Xianxian has become, he scarcely notices her final departure. A deep-seated anxiety thus reveals itself whereby serious intellectual commitment to the cause of women's emancipation, which contains significant investment on the male intellectual's own behalf, is continually threatened by a fear of the sexually independent woman. (For more on this "politics of desire," see Chung 1998.)

The conflict between sexuality and revolutionary commitment is a hallmark of May Fourth male discourses of feminism and emancipation. Mao Dun's own theorization of "writing reality" contributed to these discourses. Western nineteenth-century realism preoccupied itself with the accurate and objective depiction of reality. Mao Dun was theoretically attracted to Zola's development of this practice, in which the writer as scientist—or naturalist—observes reality objectively and then uses this data to represent and analyze the human condition. (For an erudite and readable exegesis of Mao Dun's realistic discourse, see Wang 1992:25–66.) Such an approach only further elevates the narrative authority of the male novelist, whose position as a spokesman for the discourse of modernity is already privileged. As a novelist who consistently uses the experience of women as a vehicle for his representation and analysis of contemporary Chinese social reality, Mao Dun's scientific observation creates a hierarchy of power between the subject, who inscribes meaning, and the object of scrutiny upon whom meaning is inscribed. To inscribe meaning is to assign value, implying a position of empowerment that extends beyond the literary into the social sphere in a dynamic of mutual reinforcement.

Mao Dun inscribes the female body and psyche with meaning according to his own preoccupations and ideological commitments. In *Eclipse* (Shi, 1927–28) a progression takes place through the three volumes of the trilogy: a psychological exploration of the response of modern educated bourgeois intellectuals to the failure of the Communist Party-led uprisings of 1926–27 via the female characters in the first part is superseded by use of the mutilation of the physically alluring female body to signify the horror of the right-wing backlash in the second part; in the third part the female characters, themselves objects of love pursuits, embody the quests for direction and meaning undertaken by their suitors. Throughout, there is an unstable interaction between the author's realistic and ideological impulses where the female body as an object of desire cannot readily be appropriated as a site of revolutionary signification without undermining the very process of signification. The sexual independence and empowerment of women simply undermines male discourses of revolution and emancipation by destabilizing their male-centered perspective. The only way for this process to succeed is to divest the female body of its sexuality. Thus a countercurrent of gender transvaluation also occurs in Mao Dun's fiction whereby women who assume a viable revolutionary role, or who seek to do so, become degendered.

The novel *Rainbow* gives greater play to this countercurrent. It traces the progress of Mei, an emancipated young woman, toward an allegiance to leftist politics via a series of romantic or sexual encounters. Written during 1928–29, the novel portrays the recent past, examining the growing intellectual and political awareness of the young modern Chinese intellectual. Familiar patterns of gendered appropriation are at work in this novel; it is narrated through the lens of a young woman who seems to be working her way through all the main themes of the "woman question" debate: arranged marriage, employment opportunity and economic independence, social mobility, and finally revolutionary commitment. These patterns of appropriation are highlighted by recent revelations that

Mao Dun based the novel on the experiences of his lover Qin Dejun. At every stage in her life in Sichuan, the men whom Mei encounters inscribe meaning upon her body. Her arranged husband in a graphic and quite disturbing wedding night scene inscribes her as "wife"; her teaching colleagues make allegations of sexual impropriety, for which she loses her job, and so on. Her departure from Sichuan by steamer to Shanghai marks a turning point in her development. Up to this point in Mei's life, her fate, to which she has acquiesced, has been determined by her body, and the sexually charged environment in which she has lived. But when she comes to Shanghai, her only ambition is to conquer her environment and overcome her fate. Under the political tutelage of Communist party cadre Liang Gangfu, she learns to rein in her strong feminine nature. Liang refuses her sexual advances. Indeed, when Mei dreams of Liang, he rejects her advances with physical violence, assailing her body whose fate had been determined previously by its physical allure. He inscribes new meaning upon it: a commitment to revolution that transcends gender.

Mao Dun famously identified two master exponents of the nineteenth-century novel, Zola and Tolstoy, as major sources of his creative inspiration:

> Zola explored human conditions because he wanted to be a novelist, while Tolstoy started to write novels only after experiencing the vicissitudes of life. Despite the two masters' different starting points, their works shocked the world equally. Zola's attitude toward life can be summarized as cool detachment, which is in sharp contrast to Tolstoy's warm embrace of it; but the works of both are criticisms of and reflections of reality. I like Zola, but I am also fond of Tolstoy. At one time I enthusiastically propagandized for naturalism. Yet when I tried to write novels, it was Tolstoy I came closer to. (Wang 1992:70)

The way in which Mei's existence is at first determined by her environment and later transformed by a new and all-encompassing vision illustrates the way in which Mao Dun reinterprets both Zola and Tolstoy. Zola's scientific method examines the way in which heredity and environment shape the human condition. It is founded on a pessimistic determinism that allows no transcendence. Tolstoy offers an alternative humanistic vision. Concerned at the moral degradation of society, Tolstoy believed in the morally uplifting potential of art, offering the potential for growth and change in terms of Christian enlightenment. For Mao Dun the guiding principle for change was Marxism, which offered the means to transcend both heredity and environment. Zola's existential determinism is replaced by the historical determinism of Marxism whose vision is predicated on the necessary transcendence of heredity and environment (Wang 1992:67–110). However, reminiscent of the pattern evoked in "Creation," significant tensions exist between the authoritative narrative stance and Mei's actual physical portrayal. Whereas Mei's political transformation has been achieved, the sexual power of her body still turns heads at the political meeting as Mei rushes in "like a nude mannequin" after having been caught in the rain (220). Just like Xianxian, Mei's body ultimately resists male inscription.

Anxiety at the disruptive yet irresistible potential of independent feminine sexuality remains at the heart of Mao Dun's novel *Midnight*. An epic portrait of industrial society in 1930s Shanghai, the novel explores in Zolaesque fashion the antagonistic class conditions engendered by heredity (class) and the environment of capitalism. The narrative ranges over all classes including factory owners, stock traders, decadent bourgeois youth, and politicized youth active among the urban proletariat. In *Midnight*, the chimera of rampant, predatory feminine sexuality personifies the capitalist decadence of the city. Factory owner Wu Sunfu's elderly father, decrepit symbol of traditional patriarchy, dies of shock at his first encounter with it. Socialites beguile and manipulate their millionaire patrons; sex is used as a commodity to buy stock market information upon which livelihoods depend. By contrast, the committed revolutionaries, particularly in the person of Ma Jin, who rejects the advances of her comrade Su Lun, occupy the moral high ground. However her "nice, firm little breasts" (434) are just as threatening to *his* revolutionary commitment as the jutting, swelling curves of the women associated with the decadent classes. Ma Jin may embody revolutionary sublimation for the greater cause, but her body is still the locus of anxiety for her male comrade.

Defiance against the oppression of patriarchy by the modern woman is a beguiling metaphor for revolutionary vocation. Although Mao Dun identifies with the defiance, as soon as he appropriates it, by imposing *his own* interpretation on feminine experience he colludes with the original problematic of sexual oppression. Thereafter, however much he seeks to inscribe new meanings onto her, in response to *his own* quests, beliefs, and crises, the sexual nature of metaphor disrupts and threatens his male-centered discourse.

—*Hilary Chung*

Bibliography

Chen, Yu-shih. *Realism and Allegory in the Early Fiction of Mao Tun*. Bloomington: Indiana University Press, 1986.

Chung, Hilary. "Questing the Goddess: Mao Dun and the New Woman." In Raoul D. Findeisen and Robert H. Gassmann, eds., *Autumn Floods: Essays in Honour of Marián Gálik*, 165–183. Bern: Peter Lang, 1998.

Mao, Dun. "Creation." Trans. Gladys Yang. In *The Vixen*, 5–35. Beijing: Panda Books, 1987.

——. "From Guling to Tokyo." Trans. Yu-shih Chen. *Bulletin of Concerned Asian Scholars* 1 (1976): 38–44.

———. *Midnight*. Trans. Meng-hsiung Hsu. Beijing: Foreign Languages Press, 1957.

———. *Rainbow*. Trans. Madeline Zelin. Berkeley: University of California Press, 1992.

———. *Wo zuoguo de daolu* (Roads I Have Traveled). 2 vols. Beijing: Renmin wenxue, 1997.

Wang, David Der-wei. *Fictional Realism in Twentieth Century China: Mao Dun, Lao She, Shen Congwen*. New York: Columbia University Press, 1992.

72

BA JIN'S *FAMILY:*

FICTION, REPRESENTATION, AND RELEVANCE

Ba Jin (pen name of Li Feigan, b. 1904) completed his most famous novel, *Family* (Jia), in 1931. Originally entitled *Torrent* (Jiliu), it was first published in serial form in the pages of the newspaper *Shibao*. Later in the same year, the story appeared in book form under its present title. Although his first two novels had been well received, *Family* established Ba Jin as one of the most popular of progressive Chinese writers of the 1930s and 1940s, second only to Lu Xun (Lang 1967:3). The great success of *Family* eventually inspired Ba Jin to write a sequel, which he entitled *Spring* (Chun, 1938). Two years later a third novel, *Autumn* (Qiu), was added, forming a trilogy collectively entitled *Torrent*. The trilogy received critical acclaim, but only *Family* has since been canonized as one of the great masterpieces of modern Chinese literature. It has even been compared favorably with China's great literary classic, *Dream of the Red Chamber* (Mao 1978:88–102; Lang 1967:83–84). Outside China, Ba Jin's literary output has earned him considerable recognition, especially since the 1958 English translation of *Family*. In 1975 he was nominated for the Nobel Prize. Ba Jin's writing style has been compared to that of Balzac, Dreiser, and Thomas Wolfe (Mao 1978:146).

Of course, we gain little by simply accepting such praise and favorable comparisons with famous Western novelists as unquestionable proof of *Family's* literary value. We learn more by carefully analyzing and interpreting some of its most important textual and contextual details. In other words, readers must still carefully and critically read *Family* to gain a deeper understanding of the novel and discover for themselves why it might be relevant today.

Family chronicles the breakdown of the Gao family, a large and wealthy scholar-gentry family. Three brothers, grandsons of the family patriarch, are the novel's main characters: the eldest is Gao Juexin, followed by Gao Juemin and Gao Juehui. The three struggle against their family to gain control over their own lives and develop a sense of individuality. Theirs is a traditional Chinese multigenerational, extended family living within the walls of a vast compound of residential quarters, meeting rooms, temples, kitchens, gardens, and servants' quarters. It is governed by a set of unbreakable rules that demand the subjugation of each individual in accordance with his or her predetermined role in the family and in Chinese society. The author portrays such a family structure as perfectly designed to crush exactly the type of individual aspirations and personal dreams that the three boys hold dear.

Through the portrayal of the contemptible patriarch, Master Gao, Ba Jin shows how the traditional Chinese family structure is not an impersonal, abstract system but is embodied in the conservative tyrants who uphold it. Master Gao rules the large household with an iron fist, tolerating neither debate nor dissension. The aging despot keeps an especially tight rein on Juexin, because Juexin is the eldest son of his own deceased eldest son and thus the main heir to the top post in the family hierarchy. Juexin and his brothers are being groomed for their future roles as leaders of the clan and pillars of society. As manager of their futures, their grandfather hands down decisions concerning every aspect of their private and social lives, and most of these decisions run counter to the boys' desires. The conflicts between the generations generate the dramatic events of the novel. Ba Jin focuses on the three brothers' various responses of rebellion, resistance, or acquiescence to Grandfather Gao's unwelcome dictums. In addition to this focus on the three grandsons (mainly Juexin and Juehui), there are parallel threads in the novel depicting the suffering of women under the traditional Chinese family and social systems.

The story takes place between 1919 and 1923, when outside the walls of the Gao family compound the historical events of China's warlord era were taking place, including the student-led May Fourth movement (the editor's note in the 1989 translation erroneously places the events of the story in 1931, the year it was written [1989:vi]). These larger, well-known historical events, though not described in detail, are shown to provide the brothers with the critical awareness and "enlightenment" necessary to launch an attack against their family structure. Much of their new knowledge comes directly from the many journals such as *New Tide* (Xinchao) that disseminated the values of May Fourth iconoclasm. This relationship between literature, enlightenment, and the transformation of Chinese society is reflected both in the content of the story as well as in the novel's popular reception. Just as the youthful characters in the story are inspired by the journal articles coming out of social and intellectual movements

of the early 1920s, so were 1930s and 1940s readers of *Family* moved by its indict-
ment of the traditional family system. For Chinese readers, the "family" of the
title was representative of all Chinese families, seen as the bedrock of traditional
values. The author himself claimed that in *Family* he "wanted to write … the
history of a typical feudal family," and the "inner struggles and tragedies inside
those families—how lovable youths suffer there, how they struggle and finally
do not escape destruction" (Lang 1967:71). As Ba Jin portrays it, the traditional
Chinese "family" is, ironically, a hotbed of cruelty, corruption, greed, hypocrisy,
misogyny, infighting, and other generally negative attributes.

Given Ba Jin's intentionally one-sided portrait, the traditional upper-class
Chinese family in this book is certainly an easy target for exposure and ridicule.
This sometimes leads to a partially justifiable yet oversimplified study of characterization in the novel. In this vein, Nathan Mao (1978:90–96) describes characters who are "defenders of the status quo, victims of the status quo, and those
who rebel against the status quo." Similarly, Olga Lang divides members of the
younger generations in *Family* into two main groups, either "victims" or "fighters" (1967:78). Lang, citing and supporting the author's own claim that "the root
of evil lies not in personalities but in the family system itself," tends simply to
curse the system and treat the characters as helpless victims (1967:76). But of
more importance to the author was the way that his young characters responded
to this decadent family, for their responses are seen as a measure of their moral
fortitude.

A closer look at the text reveals a more ambivalent representation of character, for some of Ba Jin's male "victims" are clearly represented as not wholly innocent and at least partially to blame for their own fates. For example, the eldest
of the three brothers, Juexin, is faulted for frequently bending to his grandfather's will. Consider the following:

> Indeed, Chueh-hsin [Juexin] found the "compliant bow" philosophy and
> the "policy of non-resistance" most useful.… They were a solace to him,
> permitting him to believe in the new theories while still conforming to
> the old feudal concepts. He saw no inconsistency. (1989:43)

> He had never disagreed with anyone in his life, no matter how unfairly
> they may have treated him. He preferred to swallow his tears, suppress his
> anger and bitterness; he would bear anything rather than oppose a person
> directly. Nor did it ever occur to him to wonder whether this forbearance
> might not be harmful to others. (1989:296–297)

The novel's attitude toward Juexin has its origins in Ba Jin's attitude toward
his eldest brother, on whom Juexin was closely modeled. Their lives are very
similar, except for the fact that Ba Jin's real brother committed suicide rather
than have his dreams crushed by his family. News of his brother's suicide

reached Ba Jin as he was finishing the sixth chapter of the novel, a chapter he had entitled "Eldest Brother" (1993:15). About a year after the novel was completed, Ba Jin wrote a short preface, entitled "Presented to a Certain Person," in which he accuses someone addressed only as "you" of "ruining your own splendid fantasies; destroying your own bright future," and becoming a "completely unnecessary sacrificial object and dying" *(bu biyaode xishengpin er sile)* (1993:376–377). Clearly aware of his brother's complicity in his own misfortunes, Ba Jin is careful to demonstrate in the novel that much of Juexin's suffering is a result of his own spinelessness. That Ba Jin takes such a critical stance toward some characters' willful ignorance or passivity helps to temper criticism that his characters are "extremely sentimental" (Mao 1978:98) and reveals that sometimes he is deliberately exaggerating a character's self-indulgent emotional sensitivity in order to contrast it with a necessary action or attitude that the character is neglecting. This is certainly the case with the character of Juexin, but less so in the case of Gao Juehui, the youngest and most rebellious of the three brothers and the main protagonist of *Family.*

Juehui cannot be discussed outside of Ba Jin's own thoughts and beliefs, for the character is somewhat an alter ego for the author. Like the youthful Ba Jin, Gao Juehui reads avant-garde journals and becomes politically aware at a young age. Combined with the events witnessed in his own home, these publications help to shape a strong determination to reject traditional vices and to believe in a vision of a better future for China's people. In this respect, Juehui and Ba Jin are almost stereotypical examples of the young (mostly male) Chinese intellectuals who came of age in the early years of the twentieth century. They saw Chinese society and culture as decrepit, poisoned by the "feudal" ways of its past, and they viewed themselves as ultimately responsible for bringing about its change and reform. However, although Juehui has been autobiographically linked to the author himself, he is more accurately described as Ba Jin's *idealized* version of the rebellious youth he might have wished he had been: "I wanted to describe a rebel, a young but courageous rebel. I wanted to personify in him my hope. I wanted him to bring fresh air to us.... In those families we do not have much fresh air" (Lang 1967:70). Ba Jin clearly felt that his imagination and creativity had to express and transmit his hope for change, for a better society. Such desires were common among Chinese writers of his time, partially inspired by literature and ideas from other cultures.

As noted earlier, the young Ba Jin (like Juehui) was an avid reader of May Fourth-era journals, and his intellectual, political, and literary development were heavily influenced by the Western ideas and literary styles promoted in those journals. Lang argues that "in the formation of his ideals three Western ideological complexes were of primary importance: international anarchism, Russian populism, and, to a lesser extent, the Great French Revolution" (1967:224–225). Among these three foreign influences, anarchism had by far the greatest impact on his beliefs and attitudes. Anarchism, as Emma Goldman said, is a belief in "a new social order based on liberty unrestricted by man-made law; the theory that all forms of government rest on violence, and are therefore wrong and harmful as well as unnecessary" (Lang 1967:46). So influential was this philosophy on Ba Jin that he created his pen name from the Chinese transliterations of the surnames of the two anarchist thinkers he most admired, Bakunin and Kropotkin. By his own account, anarchism helped to give form and structure to his feelings of sympathy for the poor and downtrodden which he had felt from an early age (his favorite childhood companions were the much-abused servants in and around his family's wealthy compound). In addition to anarchist political writers, Ba Jin was also deeply impressed by Russian and French writers such as Turgenev, Zola, Maupassant, and Romain Rolland (Lang 1989:viii). He not only emulated the content of their work in his deeply emotional, realistic, and sympathetic descriptions of the poor and dispossessed, he also tried to imitate their writing style, particularly "Europeanized sentences" (Ba Jin 1993:17).

Aside from matters of imitation and grammatical style, Ba Jin's favored technique in *Family* is the didactic description of individual characters' responses to decisive events, through which he hopes to inspire his readers to act and think. For example, when Juehui magnanimously gives some money to a poor beggar on a cold night, he is still haunted by a voice that criticizes the stopgap nature of individual acts of charity. The voice implies that only when collective, large-scale change is undertaken will Chinese society be reformed and China's people truly saved: "A voice seemed to shout at him in the silence: 'Do you think deeds like that are going to change the world? Do you think you've saved that beggar child from cold and hunger for the rest of his life? You—you hypocritical "humanitarian" what a fool you are!'" (1989:104). From a comparative perspective, as readers we must weigh the relative merits of Juehui's isolated act of kindness against our own responses to similar situations and then reflect on the need for collective change that such deeds necessarily point toward.

The character Juehui is also held up as a negative example of those who privilege purely academic approaches to changing society over immediate, practical responses to events. Although Juehui is the "courageous rebel" of the story, his devotion to changing China through intellectual means, at the expense of concrete action, is shown to be a tragic flaw. In this sense, he is responsible for some of the very same willful ignorance that Juexin frequently displays. In one of the story's most tragic events, the servant Mingfeng seeks out Juehui in desperation (she is to be married off as a concubine to a "lecherous old man"), but he is enthusiastically immersed in his editorial duties for a journal "introducing new ideas and attacking all that was unreasonable of the old" (1989:186). Absorbed in his own idealistic pursuits in the world of letters, Juehui ignores the very real crisis at hand. He is deaf to the passionate and urgently repeated pleas of Mingfeng (his secret love). With no one else to turn to, she commits suicide.

As Mingfeng's death demonstrates, although some of the young male characters in *Family* are shown to be partially responsible for the evils of the traditional patriarchal family system, the same cannot be said for the young female characters. The women and girls in the story are almost all victims, helpless to influence their own lives without the intervention of a male character (even the enlightened and outgoing Jin, the boys' cousin, needs Juemin's help in her quest for selfhood). This aspect of the novel—the one-sided and simplistic portrayal of women—has upset some critics. Rey Chow, for example, has noted that a character like Mingfeng is sympathetically portrayed as a "sacredly human" being, but the economic and gender-specific conflicts that determine her fate are not adequately explored (1991:99). In other words, the story glosses over the complicated personal, economic, social, and sexual specifics of Mingfeng's life; she becomes just another of the countless victims of the traditional patriarchal family and social system. Readers are instead encouraged to sympathize and commiserate with the man who could have saved her, Juehui. As Chow argues (1991:102), "as [Juehui] mourns her, we feel that he is mourning the destructiveness of the 'system,' not the death of the woman who has devoted her life to him." In the final analysis, Chow argues, it is the rebellious young man's fight against the male-dominated family system that takes center stage in *Family*. Women are just sympathetic grist for the mill.

Much like his attack on the traditional Chinese family, Ba Jin's portrayal of women was caught up in some of the most important issues of the day: How could Chinese women be liberated? How could male writers bring about that liberation? As Rey Chow's analysis makes clear, there was a danger that female characters in stories were just being used by male writers as weapons in their own fight against the male-oriented traditional Chinese cultural system. Women were excluded from the battle, not treated as whole, complex human beings by either side. This raises an important question of contemporary relevance: How does the way that (male) writers represent women affect their other literary goals, such as Ba Jin's goal of discrediting the traditional family system and modernizing Chinese society? In more cross-cultural terms: How are men's attitudes and behaviors toward women related to larger social projects? As can be seen in the previous discussion, a careful reading of Ba Jin's *Family* leads readers to explore the ways that this novel deals with matters of gender, self and society, social reform, individual responsibility, and many other different issues that haunted Ba Jin and other modern Chinese authors. When a writer sees unfair conditions in his life and society, how does he turn that awareness into a fictional story? Should he try to portray the situation accurately and objectively, exposing his culture's evils in a realistic fashion? Or, should he try to imagine a possible alternative to those conditions, such as characters who rebel against and change society, even if this has never actually happened in real life? Is there some third alternative that gets beyond these two choices? Why must some people (like writers) respond to their experiences by creating fictional stories? And why do so many people feel the urge to read these stories? Furthermore, a discussion of these issues reveals that the novel deals with many experiences and questions that are as alive and relevant today as they were in Ba Jin's youth. A detailed and thoughtful analysis of *Family* thus leads readers to connect the events of the novel both to the specific historical circumstances of 1920s China and to experiences and questions concerning our own lives and the society around us.

—*Nicholas A. Kaldis*

Bibliography

Ba Jin. *Ba Jin xiaoshuo quanji: disi juan: Jia* (Ba Jin's Collected Fiction, vol. 4, *Family*). Taipei: Yuanliu, 1993.

——. *Family.* Trans. Sidney Shapiro. Beijing: Foreign Languages Press, 1989.

Chow, Rey. *Women and Chinese Modernity: The Politics of Reading between West and East.* Minneapolis: University of Minnesota Press, 1989.

Lang, Olga. "Introduction." In Ba Jin, *Family*, vii–xxvi. Beijing: Foreign Languages Press, 1989.

——. *Pa Chin and His Writings: Chinese Youth between the Two Revolutions.* Cambridge, Mass.: Harvard University Press, 1967.

Larson, Wendy. "Shen Congwen and Ba Jin: Literary Authority against the 'World.'" In *Literary Authority and the Modern Chinese Writer: Ambivalence and Autobiography*, 61–85. Durham, N.C.: Duke University Press, 1991.

Mao, Nathan. *Pa Chin.* Boston: Twayne, 1978.

73

CHINESE MODERNISM: THE NEW SENSATIONISTS

The literary revolution that swept through China in the early twentieth century brought with it an openness to new modes of writing that drew on a wide variety of non-Chinese literatures. As writers cast aside old forms and language, they eagerly experimented with new approaches to creative writing found in the literatures of Asia, Europe, and America and introduced by students studying overseas or by translators working in Shanghai and Beijing. One such approach, the modernism represented by the path-breaking New Sensationists *(xin ganjue pai)*, arose in the late 1920s and flourished in the early to mid-1930s. Although initially their impact was limited, the New Sensationists' revolutionary use of language, structure, theme, and style influenced later generations of writers in China and Taiwan.

During the 1930s, the conservative literary policies of the Nationalist government on the right and the radical Marxist literary program of the League of Left-Wing Writers on the left dominated the literary scene. By encouraging innovative attempts to capture the unique urban milieu of Shanghai, modernist writers created an alternative space for literature to develop outside of the strict bounds of prescribed policies of either left or right. Although the political constraints and the exigencies of war would end the movement in the late 1930s, it would leave a legacy of experimental writing for later modernist movements to follow.

The contours of Chinese urban modernism have much to do with its point of origin, Shanghai, among the largest and most modern cities in the world in the late 1920s. A semicolonial city with foreign concessions and a cosmopolitan flavor, it provided the rich material culture that would feature so prominently in modernist fiction: the dance halls, cinemas, nightclubs, department stores, skyscrapers, and racetracks. Its abundance of Chinese and foreign bookstores and secondhand bookstalls gave writers ready access to books and periodicals from around the world. Residents of Shanghai could enjoy the latest Hollywood films at numerous movie theaters. The material trappings of modern life—cars, cigarettes, alcoholic beverages, and stylish clothes—appeared in magazines and on billboards and signs, and they would make their way into fiction. The metropolis pulsated with flashing neon lights and the rhythm of jazz music. Although the fast-paced lifestyle of the metropolis exhilarated, it also exhausted. A person could feel lonely amid the crowds (Lee 1999).

New Sensationism had its own unique characteristics. Its practitioners, unlike many European and American modernists, did not reject outright the city and the modernization and development it represented. The dynamic environment of the metropolis and its urban culture attracted them. Because many of these writers were newcomers to Shanghai, they had yet to experience the full forces of modernization and urbanization. Modernism became "a literary fashion, an ideal" rather than an "objective reality" for them (Lee 1999:147). Thus the Shanghai modernists had mixed feelings for the metropolis and viewed it with a combination of titillation and trepidation. They reveled in the sensory stimuli (the sounds, sights, smells, tastes, and feelings) it provided and sought new ways to depict them in their writing, just as a group of writers that included Yokomitsu Rîchi and *Kawabata Yasunari, known as the Shinkankakuha (New Sensationalists), had done a decade earlier in Japan. The Chinese term for New Sensationist derives from the name of the Japanese group; it signifies the common attempt by both Chinese and Japanese writers to "create a language that could account for the new sensations of modernity" (Shih 2001). Through reading Japanese and European literature, the Chinese New Sensationists were introduced to the psychological themes of repression, obsession, and the erotic, which allowed them to probe the loneliness, anxiety, and alienation of the metropolis. The impact of cinema and popular music came through in the characterization, pacing, and structure of their works. Authors modeled their depictions of modern women on Hollywood film stars and used jazz to set the tempo for their stories (Lee 1999:194–198, 220–223). The New Sensationists' simultaneous feelings of affection for and repulsion from the city set them apart from European and American high modernists who rejected outright urban life and the modernization it represented.

New Sensationism began with Liu Na'ou (1900–1939), who had studied literature in Japan and came to Shanghai in the mid-1920s to study French. With the help of classmates Shi Zhecun (b. 1905) and Dai Wangshu (1905–1950), Liu published the journal *Trackless Train* (Wugui lieche, 1928). It introduced Chinese readers to modernist fiction, including translations of the work of the Japanese Shinkankakuha and the French writer Paul Morand, whose work influenced both Japanese and Chinese New Sensationists, and featured fiction by Shi and poems by Dai. After *Trackless Train* was closed by the Nationalist government, the friends collaborated on a second journal, *La Nouvelle Littérature* (Xin wenyi, 1929–30), which included fiction by Shi and Liu, translations of French poetry by Dai Wangshu, literary news from around the world, and a story by the young writer Mu Shiying (1912–1940), who was soon to become one of the luminaries of New Sensationism.

Experience gained from working on these publications prepared Shi to edit *Les Contemporains* (Xiandai zazhi, 1932–35), the journal that showcased many of the mature New Sensationist works. It also introduced Chinese readers to the best Chinese literature of the day, offered a wide selection of foreign literature in translation, and provided news of literary developments abroad. Unlike other journals that were associated with a particular literary group and political stance, *Les Contemporains* maintained an apolitical editorial position; its neutrality attracted contributors from across the political spectrum. It enjoyed a wide circulation and introduced thousands of readers to modernist literature and modernist techniques from China and around the world.

Two examples of New Sensationist fiction, an early work by Shi Zhecun and a later story by Mu Shiying, both focus on the seductive and repellent sides of the city. Shi's "One Evening in the Rainy Season" (Meiyu zhi xi, 1929), a portrait of "urban eroticism," reveals the meandering of the narrator's imagination as he struggles with pent-up desire and the guilt that it elicits (Y. Zhang 1996:173). The story's straightforward plot (returning from work, a man encounters an attractive young woman whom he then escorts to her home before continuing on his way) is made more complex by using interior monologue to describe the narrator's thoughts in detail. The story begins with a lengthy description of the sights, sounds, smells, and sensations of Shanghai on a rainy evening. The narrator then meets a young woman stranded in the rain. He watches her for some time, imagining her thoughts and debating in his mind whether he should invite her to share his umbrella. After he issues an invitation and she accepts it, they walk along the street together. The narrator fantasizes that she is his first girlfriend, a woman he has not met in seven years and whom he believes he still loves. When she nears her destination and bids him farewell, his mind races to find a way to delay their parting. The narrator's barely concealed desire for the woman also stimulates his own guilt, which manifests itself in hallucinatory images of his wife, first in the face of a shopkeeper and then in the young woman herself. His initial attraction to and later repulsion from the woman are symbolic of the New Sensationists' attraction to and repulsion from Shanghai.

Whereas Shi explores the flights of imagination of a single character, in "Five in a Nightclub" (Yezonghuili de wuge ren, 1933), Mu Shiying focuses on a group of characters who struggle against the fast pace of city life. In Shi's story, the city retains a measure of beauty and glamour, as it appears filtered through the spring rain. In Mu's, however, the intoxicating nocturnal world of Shanghai, the "Heaven built on Hell," becomes a vortex that threatens to destroy the sybaritic urbanites who populate it (Lee 1988:177). The opening section of the story offers a series of quick vignettes describing setbacks suffered by each of the five major characters that afternoon. A tycoon loses his fortune, a student is jilted by his girlfriend, a socialite discovers she has lost her youth, a scholar questions the significance of his work, and a senior city clerk is unexpectedly terminated. A second section, set that same evening, captures the city in motion and sets the pace for the story. In this world rich in sensory images, revolving glass doors become crystal pillars, automobiles rush onward, crowds of people become schools of fish, and all is bathed in the glow of myriad neon lights.

Mu introduces the fundamental rhythm of the city and this story when he notes, "The world of Saturday night is a cartoon globe spinning on the axis of jazz" (1992:9). Jazz music, an essential part of Mu's "urban nocturnal landscape," leads the reader into and sets the pace of action for the third and longest section of the story, in which the five characters show up at a nightclub (Lee 1999:141). The narrative cuts quickly from one character to another as they enter and leave the dance floor. Characters struggle but ultimately fail to make their personal time or pace of life match up with that of the city, as symbolized through jazz. The drummer for the club's band cannot get time off to be with his wife, who is about to give birth. Through a series of phone calls, he learns that she has gone into labor, given birth to a stillborn child, fainted, and died. The role of the drummer—the setter and keeper of time in both music and in the story—is vital: he cannot leave. His attempts to cheer up the nightclub's guests, as well as himself, through frenzied dancing and fast-tempo drumming fail to dispel the gloom of the characters, who are ironically called "Five Happy People" in the title of this section of the story. Time, signified by the jazz, the drumming, and the dancing, "beats a soft but steady tread into the heart[s]" of the characters (1992:19–20). They share an inability to keep up with the city's time or gauge it correctly. The socialite is past her time, the tycoon missed the right time to sell his gold, and the student was too late to win his girl. The punctual and perfect senior clerk failed to anticipate his termination, and the scholar confronts the dilemma of the time-dependent concepts of being and existence. As the story concludes, the tycoon commits suicide in order to free himself from the fast pace of urban life and pressures of time to which the other characters are still subject. The story exemplifies the New Sensationists' ambivalent view of the city as both titillating and exhausting.

Although most often associated with experiments in fiction, the New Sensationists also included the pioneer modernist poet Dai Wangshu. Dai sought to describe sensations and depict the workings of the imagination and desire in his poetry, much as Shi did in his stories. However, he only occasionally featured the city in his works and drew frequently on his knowledge of classical Chinese literature, something the fiction writers seldom did. "Rainy Alley" (Yu xiang,

1928) describes the poet-subject's seeing and then walking past a "lilac-like" woman in a lonely alley on a rainy evening, an image reminiscent of Shi Zhecun's story. The reference to lilacs suggests sadness and reveals Dai's knowledge of French symbolism and the work of Frances Jammes, whose poetry he had translated (G. Lee 1989:144–148). It also shows his conversance with traditional Chinese poetry and the work of Li Jing (916–961) and Li Shangyin (813–858), who also referred to lilacs (G. Lee 1989:148–150). Like Shi and Mu, Dai focuses on sensory imagery, including the lilac color and fragrance of the woman. Like Shi's narrator, Dai's poet-subject offers a rich psychological description of the perceived emotions of the woman: her resentment, melancholy, uncertainty, and apathy. The depiction of the dreamlike state of the poet-subject and his scarcely suppressed desires in the latter half of the poem are typical of the psychological probing of New Sensationist fiction. That the woman shares the poet-subject's own emotions and his dreamlike state, and that he "hopes" to meet her, suggest that she may be a projection of his imagination. In light of the poem's circular structure, wherein it ends as it begins, it can be read as a meditation on poetry itself. The rainy alley "is a symbol of the poetic imagination," and the woman represents the fickle inspiration for the poet's work — his muse — whom he hopes to reencounter (Yeh 1991:98). "Rainy Alley" exemplifies Dai's ability to draw on Chinese and Western literature to create original poetry in a modernist mode.

The flow of New Sensationist literature slowed significantly in the mid-1930s. Shi Zhecun abandoned his experimental writing because of criticism from the League of Left-Wing Writers. Trapped between leftist polemics, Nationalist censorship, and the financial pressures of his publishers, he gave up his position as editor of *Les Contemporains* in 1934 (L. Lee 1999:148–149). Both Liu Na'ou and Mu Shiying turned to editing and criticism and abandoned modernist fiction by the mid-1930s. The threat of war with Japan in the mid-1930s led to calls from both the left and the right for engaged, patriotic writing known as "literature for national defense" *(guofang wenxue)*. With paper shortages and the destruction of printing plants caused by the outbreak of war in 1937, modernist periodicals closed and experimentation came to an end. By 1940 Shi had taken up researching classical Chinese literature, and both Liu and Mu were dead. Dai, who shifted his energies from poetry writing to translation in the mid-1930s, moved to Hong Kong in 1938, where he edited several literary journals and supplements, engaged in resistance work, and published nationalistic and patriotic poetry. He returned to China in 1949, where he died the following year. Leftist polemics, rightist censorship, and the exigencies of the times eroded the pocket of creative freedom that the New Sensationists had established.

In the early 1940s, modernist experimentation resumed briefly in Japanese-occupied Shanghai with the creative writing of *Zhang Ailing (Eileen Chang). Zhang's short fiction and essays, similar to those of the New Sensationists, captured the sights, sounds, and other sensations of Shanghai. Like her predecessors, Zhang depicted both the excitement and strain of urban life in her work. Yet she brought to modernist writing a probing exploration of everyday city life and its slower pace that contrasts with the glitz and fast rhythm of Mu Shiying's nightclubs and dance halls (Lee 1999:270–271). She set many of her essays and stories in homes and apartments and analyzed the development of male-female relationships in these domestic spaces. Zhang became one of the most popular and critically acclaimed exponents of urban modernist literature in China.

Just as the New Sensationists did in the 1930s, writers in Taiwan and China in the past five decades have used modernism to create space for literary experimentation. In Taiwan in the 1950s, Ji Xian, a former associate of Dai Wangshu's, helped organize a revival of modernist poetry. The founding of literary associations, journals, contests, and publishing houses gave rise to a thriving, unofficial literary scene separate from the Nationalist government's promotion of anticommunist literature. The journal *Modern Literature* (Xiandai wenxue, 1960–73) introduced the fiction of young writers such as Bai Xianyong, Chen Ruoxi, Chen Yingzhen, and Wang Wenxing and published translations of modernist literature from Europe and America (see "The Taiwan Modernists"). Available in Taiwan since the 1950s, Zhang Ailing's fiction, with its focus on everyday life, domestic settings, and male-female relations, has influenced such writers as Bai Xianyong, Wang Zhenhe, and Yuan Qiongqiong.

With political liberalization in the People's Republic of China during the 1980s, writers gained access to literature from overseas, including modernist literature from Europe, the Americas, and Japan as well as the fiction and poetry of the Taiwan modernists. Modernism contributed to the development of *Misty Poetry that emerged in the pages of *Today* (Jintian, 1978–80). *Avantgarde fiction writers including Can Xue, Mo Yan, Su Tong, and Yu Hua experimented with decadence and desire in their stories and novels. Although modernist writing expanded the bounds of literature, it was also attacked by campaigns against "spiritual pollution" and "bourgeois liberalism" for what the government deemed to be its detachment from everyday life and its non-Chinese origins.

The recent modernist literatures of Taiwan and China have surpassed the New Sensationists in their sophisticated treatment of desire and repression and in their experiments with stream of consciousness and other linguistic innovations. However, like their predecessors, contemporary writers have also captured the sights, sounds, and other sensations unique to urban locales and have created new space for writing in spite of official literary policies and campaigns. Given the centrality of the unique cultural milieu of semicolonial and cosmopolitan Shanghai in the 1930s and 1940s to the works of Shi Zhecun, Mu Shiying, and Zhang Ailing, we should not be surprised that new modernist literature produced in urban settings with unique political climates has its own distinctive characteristics. New literature from the emerging metropolitan cities of Hong Kong, Taipei, and Shanghai will bear traces of each locale's particular nexus of cultural forces and will expand the modernist tradition begun by the New Sensationists.

—Steven L. Riep

Bibliography

Lau, Joseph S. M., and Howard Goldblatt, eds. *The Columbia Anthology of Modern Chinese Literature.* New York: Columbia University Press, 1995.

Lee, Gregory. *Dai Wangshu: The Life and Poetry of a Chinese Modernist.* Hong Kong: The Chinese University Press, 1989.

Lee, Leo Ou-fan. *Shanghai Modern: The Flowering of a New Urban Culture in China, 1930–1945.* Cambridge, Mass.: Harvard University Press, 1999.

——. "Zhongguo xiandai wenxuezhong de 'tuifei' ji qi zuojia" ("Decadence" and Decadent Writers in Modern Chinese Literature). *Dangdai* 93 (1994): 22–47.

Li Oufan, ed. *Xinganjue pai xiaoshuo xuan* (Selected New Sensationist Fiction). Taipei: Yunchen, 1988.

Mu, Shiying. "Five in a Nightclub." Trans. Randolph Trumbull. *Renditions* 37 (1992): 5–22.

Shi, Zhecun. *One Rainy Evening.* Trans. Zuxin Ding. Beijing: Panda Books, 1994.

Shih, Shu-mei. *The Lure of the Modern: Writing Modernism in Semicolonial China, 1917–1937.* Berkeley: University of California Press, 2001.

Yan Jiayan, ed. *Xinganjue pai xiaoshuo xuan* (Selected New Sensationist Fiction). Beijing: Renmin wenxue, 1985.

Yeh, Michelle. *Modern Chinese Poetry: Theory and Practice since 1917.* New Haven: Yale University Press, 1991.

Zhang, Jingyuan. *Psychoanalysis in China: Literary Transformations, 1919–1949.* Ithaca, N.Y.: Cornell University Press, 1992.

Zhang, Yingjin. *The City in Modern Chinese Literature and Film: Configurations of Space, Time, and Gender.* Stanford: Stanford University Press, 1996.

74

SHEN CONGWEN

AND IMAGINED NATIVE COMMUNITIES

Shen Congwen (1902–1988), whose works open a window on modern Chinese rural idealism, was one of the great Chinese writers of the first half of the twentieth century. Proscribed by mainland China and Taiwan after 1949 until both liberalized in the 1980s and exalted him as an independent writer, he was a reminder of how much had been lost of China's earlier cultural modernity. Revisionist critics in the People's Republic recast Shen Congwen as an eminent Other of revolutionary writing: a non-*Lu Xun, neither socialist nor realist, treading his own anti-Confucian, pro-Western, yet nonurban and apolitical path. Taiwan, long open to the West but not to writers like Shen who remained on the mainland, reenvisioned him as a great modern "native" writer—rustic, noncommunist—*not* so westernized. From 1982 until his death, Shen Congwen was in the running for a Nobel Prize in literature, though he had abandoned creative writing after attempting suicide in 1949. Having studiously avoided political front groups for writers before the revolution, under Communism he found a new career in the less turbulent field of art history.

Shen Congwen as a writer favored craft, experimentation, and Western modernism, but the public loved his reimagining of China as a preindustrial moral community offering not the modern solaces of nation, race, or strength in unity, but the familiar comforts of home and local diversity of custom. Calling himself a country boy and recorder of life, Shen developed a tradition of impressionistically documenting local places and their culture that came to be conceptualized as *xiangtu* (native-soil, local, nativist, rural-native; cf. German *Heimat*). But many of his works blended that with a visionary cultural revivalism. It applied literary modernism to a far less "earthbound" Chinese tradition—of frontier exoticism, primalism, and spirit journeys.

As a documenter of his native West Hunan, Shen Congwen brought the craft of the traditional literati poet, gazetteerist, and travel writer into the twentieth century by using the colloquial language of the literary revolution. Avoiding set phrases for describing scenery and emotions and eschewing the rhythms of classical Chinese, he employed modern and often idiosyncratic grammar. Meantime he exploited the unique lexical resources of classical Chinese, whose building blocks were not words but a much vaster galaxy of morphemes (Chinese characters). The result was a very literary vernacular lyricism.

West Hunan was a mountainous internal frontier without many cities, literati, passable roads, or trappings of high culture. During the disorders of the early republic, local warlords kept it autonomous from China and even the rest of Hunan. Southwestern non-Han "tribespeople," mostly Tujia and Miao (Méo, Hmong), lived in the hills. Shen's forebears were military officers who intermarried with them. The crossing of that local equivalent of a color line was hidden from Shen Congwen in his youth, but ethnic-minority folklore, martial arts, and religion tinged the whole regional culture. He identified with his native region particularly after entering the local armies in adolescence and becoming personal clerk to Chen Quzhen, the warlord of West Hunan from 1921 to 1935. Shen started to chronicle the demise of his region in *Long River* (Chang he, 1943). Had he completed the two sequels he intended to add to the single volume he published, the work might have been China's first sectionalist epic until the advent of the Taiwan independence writers (see "The Taiwan Nativists").

When he left West Hunan in 1923, Shen adopted Beijing as his home and hoped to become a new-style intellectual dedicated to social change and the new thought from Japan and the West. Homesick and living in genteel poverty at the margins of the old capital's student subculture, he discovered a literary atmosphere that favored dialect, folklore, and cultural diversity, and in which he could satisfy national curiosity about his "barbarous" region while writing to reform, de-Confucianize, and revitalize China. The initial result was short sketches and plays rich in vignettes of local custom, such as "Snow" (Xue, 1927) and "The Celestial God" (Xiaoshen, 1925?). He wrote to show urban intellectuals the uncouthness and camaraderie of warlordism in "My Education" (Wo de jiaoyu, 1929). In "Ah Jin" (1928) and "Long Zhu" (1929), he wove tales from legends and customs of the hill tribes. Their free-loving ways at festival gatherings, where boy met girl through alternating songs like those in "Songs of the Zhen'-gan Folk" (Ganren yaoqu, 1926), fascinated Chinese urbanites enjoying their own sexual revolution.

The term *xiangtu* is said to have been first applied to *Lu Xun's work in 1926. Shen credited Lu Xun's "Village Opera" (Shexi, 1922) and Fei Ming (Feng Wenbing, 1901–1967) with teaching him how to write about country life; he also esteemed Wang Luyan (1901–1944). Lu Xun deployed the term *xiangtu* in an influential compendium of modern Chinese literature, in praise of regional works by recently urbanized writers such as Jian Xian'ai (1906–1994) of Guizhou. Peasants, rural themes, and even local color were a subsidiary concern of China's new literature until social science interest in peasants and rural reconstruction picked up in the 1930s, followed by the Communist movement to promote literature of, for, and eventually by "workers, peasants, and soldiers." Peasants made many intellectuals think solipsistically of their own elevated social status and mission.

In 1979 the newly exonerated former rightist writer Liu Shaotang (b. 1936) raised the banner of *xiangtu* literature. He admitted to inspiration from Taiwan, where the term had been hotly debated since the 1960s (on the mainland, Marxist-Leninist concepts had long overshadowed discourses of Lu Xun's era, although a textbook by Wang Yao preserved the *xiangtu* concept). Because much Communist literature was already set in the countryside, featured peasants, and used dialect (typically Northern), with Hao Ran's (b. 1932) epics as the capstone, when Liu Shaotang and his friend Sun Li (b. 1913) sought status as *xiangtu* writers, they evidently meant to be more ruralist than Mao. Many critics considered the *xiangtu* formulation an attack on Western trends, as it had been in Taiwan, and Liu's and Sun's works still to be hackneyed revolutionary "realism," however much they focused on the authors' North China homes.

But both the mainland and Taiwan went on to hail the older, "rediscovered" works of Shen Congwen, and those of Lu Xun (another nostalgic non-northerner), as model *xiangtu* literature steeped in local cultural sensitivities China had suppressed since 1949. Gu Hua (b. 1942), Sun Jianzhong (b. 1939?), He Liwei (b. 1954), Xiao Jianguo (b. 1952), Cai Cehai (b. 1954), and other Hunanese writers took inspiration from Shen. Bai Xianyong (b. 1937), a displaced mainlander living and publishing in Taiwan, also claimed past influence. Shen's pre-1949 protégés were being rediscovered too—Xiao Qian (1910–1999), Wang Zengqi (1920–1996), and many poets. Some had written of common folk and colorful local trades, even if in Beijing—but then, Shen Congwen was now hailed as dean of a 1930s "Beijing School" that favored northern academism over "Shanghai School" commercialism, trendiness, and politicization, because he had polemicized against "Shanghai Types" in the 1930s.

Shen Congwen's classic 1930s stories, rich in mood and finely wrought in plot, language, and symbolism, are mostly about city people, but his most memorable characters are common country folk he wanted to defend from encroachment by outlanders and their commercial, bureaucratic, military, and moral and ritual worldliness. The country folk of *The Frontier City* (Bian cheng, 1934), "The New and the Old" (Xin yu jiu, 1935), "Sansan" (1931), "Guisheng" (1937), and "Xiaoxiao" (1930) live quiet, "pastoral" lives amid natural beauty. They have their own rich life of the mind and seldom dwell on their poverty. Indeed, Sansan stands to inherit a mill, and Cuicui ("Green Jade," in *The Frontier City*) a ferry. Guisheng is just a hired laborer, but he has a chance to marry up;

he loses that chance only because of superstition. Even the regional backdrop acquires the density of a fictional actor. Although he mixed cultural criticism and nostalgia, often using his region as a foil for humanity's dark side like Thomas Hardy, Shen Congwen was optimistic about human nature. Xiaoxiao, the powerless child bride of an infant boy, is seduced by an adult farm hand and bears his child (a capital offense), but she survives. Shen's failure to take a class stand and his distance from conventional urban nationalism with its absorption in anti-imperialism or neotraditionalism angered political critics of the day, yet this may explain why he, more than the engagé realists and satirists Zhang Tianyi (1906–1985), *Mao Dun (1896–1981), *Xiao Hong (1911–1942), Zhao Shuli (1906–1970), Gao Xiaosheng (1928–1999), or even Wu Zuxiang (1908–1994), retrospectively won accolades as a *xiangtu* writer—for Shen seldom wrote of place for its own sake either.

The more exotic tradition Shen Congwen plumbed begins with texts associated with Daoism and the *Chu ci* (*Ch'u Tz'u, The Songs of the South*), attributed to Qu Yuan (ca. 343–277 B.C.), in which that Chu poet, misunderstood by his king, communes with shamans and female goddesses on a vision quest in the wondrous Southwest of his day (West Hunan, Shen believed). After the Han dynasty fell and the Chinese people migrated to the South, poets and essayists further celebrated its exotic biota, landscapes, and customs, as did officials exiled there, like Shen's soldier-scholar hero, Wang Yangming (1472–1529). A search for personal meaning in the Southwest animates Han Shaogong's (b. 1953) "Homecoming" (Guiqulai, 1985) and *Gao Xingjian's (b. 1940) *Soul Mountain* (Ling shan, 1990), which won that author the 2000 Nobel Prize in literature. Preceding them were "manias" for Chinese "culture," the Chinese West, ancient Chu (Hunan-Hubei), and a search for "roots" of Chinese literature; in "Pa Pa Pa" (Bababa, 1985), Han Shaogong sought "roots" in West Hunan. Shen Congwen's achievement is another way station between Qu Yuan and Gao Xingjian. He assuredly influenced "roots-seekers" Han Shaogong, Han's colleagues Ah Cheng (b. 1949) and Jia Ping'ao (b. 1952), and Wang Zengqi, said to have inspired the "roots" movement.

The modern upward revaluation of China's frontier peoples, cultures, and lore is seen in the histories of Gu Jiegang (1893–1980), who theorized that China's diverse regional cultures took their distinctiveness from border peoples, and Fan Wenlan (1891–1969), who stimulated speculation about the role of the Miao in ancient Chu culture. Shen Congwen created beautiful modern myths about Southwestern tribespeople in a similar spirit: his aboriginals bear a vital and unspoiled primal culture that the Han once possessed, but lost through Confucian bureaucratism, puritanism, and urban worldliness. If his characters look like noble savages, Shen's concern was Social Darwinist: that China, owing more to cultural than racial-national enervation, had lost the strength to survive in the modern world. Southwestern mores implicitly reprove Han high culture in "Seven Barbarians and the Last Spring Festival" (Qi ge yeren yu zui hou yi ge yingchun jie, 1929). Bai Hua's (b. 1930) *Remote Country of Women* (Yuanfang you ge nüer guo, 1988) repeats the theme.

China's spiritual and existential literary explorations in the late twentieth century recapitulated those of Shen Congwen and other modernists, much as the 1980s cult of "subjectivity" echoed the earlier generation's discovery of the "self." Shen split himself and an imaginary female companion into conscious and subconscious personalities to explore desire, memory, and illusions of reality in "Gazing at Rainbows" (Kan hong lu, 1941). In "Water and Clouds" (Shuiyun, 1943), a psychological autobiography contemplating how libido shaped his romances and works, he cleaved his soul into mutually questioning narrative voices: ego, alter ego, and superego (cf. Zhang Xianliang's [b. 1936] *Getting Used to Dying* [Xiguan siwang, 1989]. Shen's spiritual and philosophical quests converged with his southwestern regionalism in unfinished story cycles of the 1940s, which include "Qiaoxiu and Dongsheng" (1947) and the Seven-color Nightmares—generically unclassifiable autobiographical meditations beginning with *Green Nightmare* (Lü yan, 1944). By 1948 Shen Congwen felt he could not go on writing.

Noted for their style are *Recollections of West Hunan* (Xiang xing san ji, 1934) and *West Hunan* (Xiangxi, 1938). They probe the meaning of Shen's regional roots in episodic travelogue form. *The Frontier City*, which analyzes the emotional and sexual awakening of a pubescent orphan girl, is his masterpiece in fiction. The limpid prose sculpting the novella's pastoral setting is really a palimpsest for Freudian images. Regional ethos is evoked by mountain songs, but they, like the alternative futures the heroine imagines, lie subconscious until frontier fate brings on a tragedy. For all its local color, the novella sublimates *xiangtu* concreteness as fully as a timeless myth.

—Jeffrey Kinkley

Bibliography

Bai, Hua. *The Remote Country of Women*. Trans. Qingyun Wu and Thomas O. Beebee. Honolulu: University of Hawai'i Press, 1994.

Feuerwerker, Yi-tsi Mei. *Ideology, Power, Text: Self-Representation and the Peasant "Other" in Modern Chinese Literature*. Stanford: Stanford University Press, 1998.

Han, Shaogong. *Homecoming and Other Stories*. Trans. Martha Cheung. Hong Kong: Renditions, 1992.

Hsia, C.T. *A History of Modern Chinese Fiction*. Rev. ed. New Haven: Yale University Press, 1971.

Kinkley, Jeffrey C. *The Odyssey of Shen Congwen*. Stanford: Stanford University Press, 1987.

Liu Hongtao. *Hunan xiangtu wenxue yu Xiang Chu wenhua* (Hunan Nativist Literature and the Chu Culture of the Hunan Region). Changsha: Hunan jiaoyu, 1997.

Liu Shaotang. *Xiangtu wenxue sishi nian* (Forty Years of Nativist Literature). Beijing: Wenhua yishu, 1990.

Peng, Hsiao-yen. *Antithesis Overcome: Shen Congwen's Avant-Gardism and Primitivism*. Taipei: Institute of Chinese Literature and Philosophy, Academia Sinica, 1994.

Shen, Congwen. *The Chinese Earth: Stories by Shen Ts'ung-wen*. Trans. Ching Ti and Robert Payne. New York: Columbia University Press, 1982.

——. *L'Eau et les nuages* (Water and Clouds). Trans. Isabelle Rabut. Paris: Bleu de Chine, 1996.

——. *Genesis of a Revolution*. Trans. Stanley R. Munro. Singapore: Heinemann Asia, 1979.

——. *Imperfect Paradise: Stories by Shen Congwen*. Trans. Jeffrey Kinkley. Honolulu: University of Hawai'i Press, 1995.

——. *Recollections of West Hunan*. Trans. Gladys Yang. Beijing: Panda Books, 1982.

——. *Shen Congwen wen ji* (The Works of Shen Congwen). Ed. Shao Huaqiang and Ling Yu. 15 vols. Hong Kong and Guangzhou: Sanlian and Huacheng, 1982–85.

Wang, David Der-wei. *Fictional Realism in Twentieth-Century China: Mao Dun, Lao She, Shen Congwen*. New York: Columbia University Press, 1992.

Wang Runhua (Wong Yoon Wah). *Shen Congwen xiaoshuo xinlun* (New Perspectives on the Fiction of Shen Congwen). Shanghai: Xuelin, 1998.

Xiang Chengguo. *Huigui ziran yu zhuixun lishi: Shen Congwen yu Xiangxi* (Return to Nature and Quest for History: Shen Congwen and West Hunan). Changsha: Hunan Shifan Daxue, 1997.

Zhang, Xianliang. *Getting Used to Dying*. Trans. Martha Avery. New York: Harper-Collins, 1991.

75

XIAO HONG'S *FIELD OF LIFE AND DEATH*

Few twentieth-century Chinese women writers have attained the canonical stature Xiao Hong (Zhang Naiying, 1911–1942) now enjoys. Almost all her fiction, including two novels and numerous short stories, and a major autobiographical work, have been translated into English, and she is currently one of only two modern woman writers whose life and writing have been extensively examined in English-language scholarship.

The Field of Life and Death (Shengsi chang, 1934) was Xiao Hong's debut novel, written in Qingdao, where she and her lover Xiao Jun, another young soon-to-be literary celebrity, had sought refuge from the Japanese occupation of their native Manchuria before moving on to Shanghai. Originally titled *The Wheat Field* (Mai chang), two installments of the work were serialized under the penname Qiao Yin in the spring of 1934 in a Harbin newspaper. In 1935, after being rejected by the Literary Censorship Committee of the Central Propaganda Bureau, it was published in *Lu Xun's semi-underground Slave Series, the third (and last) volume in the series that had also featured works by Ye Si and Xiao Jun. Whether or not Lu Xun went so far as to personally finance the publication of Xiao Hong's novel is unknown, but there can be little doubt that his patronage was instrumental in the success the work was soon to have. Having taken both Xiaos under his wing upon their arrival in Shanghai, he had already introduced the couple to intellectual luminaries such as *Mao Dun and Hu Feng and had helped Xiao Hong place several essays in journals such as *Wenxue* and *Taibai*. He now personally endorsed her novel by writing its preface and recommending it to friends and colleagues. *Field of Life and Death*, as it was renamed at Hu Feng's suggestion, brought Xiao Hong overnight fame in Shanghai's literary world; despite Guomindang censorship, the novel underwent six consecutive printings within a year and continues to be regarded as one of the masterpieces of modern Chinese fiction today.

Set in the Manchurian countryside on the eve of the war against Japan, *Field* owed much of its initial success to its timely treatment of subject matter that weighed heavily on the minds of the 1930s cultural left—namely, rural realities and the problem of national salvation. Qu Qiubai and others affiliated with the League of Left-Wing Writers had grown disenchanted with what they now saw as the elitism of May Fourth romanticism, and they called for a revolutionary literature attuned to the plight of China's collective masses (Anderson 1990). Xiao Hong's novel resonated with these concerns, and Xiao Hong herself, recently dislocated by the war, was hailed as an exemplar of this alternative literary voice. Xiao Hong abandons classical realist conventions of a tightly woven plot driven by individual protagonists, opting for a more fractured presentation of the peasant condition. Through a series of loosely related episodic vignettes involving locals such as Two-and-a-Half Li and Mother Wang, Xiao Hong presents a montage of rural society mired in poverty, disease, and injustice. It is a profoundly unsettling vision: juxtaposed with unsentimental scenes of the desperation and drudgery of peasant life are lyrical glimpses of the regional locale that bear a certain resemblance to the "nativist" *(xiangtu)* tradition of *Shen Congwen. With these jarring narrative shifts, the author accentuates the discordant relationship between the peasants and the land upon which they labor.

If the novel dwells on the material hardships of the countryside, the subaltern figure occupying this fraught terrain cannot be understood in terms of economic oppression alone. As she does in much of her work, Xiao Hong brings a profoundly gendered consciousness to her account. Men and women alike suffer under the numbing tyranny of poverty and deprivation, but women bear the additional strain of male abuse. Over the course of the novel, for instance, we are confronted with graphic scenes that include the violent demise of an unwanted newborn daughter, a drunk who beats his wife during an agonizing childbirth, and the gruesome neglect of an invalid wife. In the final chapters, when the village is decimated by Japanese troops, the rape of Golden Bough by a Chinese is a poignant reminder that women are subject to distinct forms of domination beyond those of their exploited class or nation.

Inevitably, however, given the heightened anxieties and patriotic fervor in the wake of the Mukden Incident of 1931, it was not Xiao Hong's sensitive representation of patriarchy, but the theme of nationalist awakening as it emerges toward the end of her novel that contemporary critics privileged in their readings. Lu Xun, who stirred fresh memories of the bombing of Shanghai (1932) in his preface, promised readers that the novel would imbue them with "the strength to persevere and resist," while Hu Feng (who wrote the epilogue) lauded the work for its depiction of "a persecuted people in a pillaged land." For her part, Xiao Hong would remain aloof from the contentious literary politics of the years following the novel's publication (to the dismay of many critics), but she would never quite shake the legacy she acquired from this novel as a prescient voice of Chinese national resistance.

The nationalist significance of *Field* persists as the core issue around which contemporary commentators have focused their attention, though recent interpretations have shifted from acclaiming its patriotic spirit to analysis of how the text has been historically misread as an allegory of anti-imperialist struggle. In the view of Howard Goldblatt, the American sinologist instrumental in resuscitating Xiao Hong's oeuvre in the 1970s, the novel is "seriously impaired by its forced anti-Japanese ending," a flaw he attributes to Xiao Hong's limited grasp of the circumstances engulfing northeastern China and to Xiao Jun's (alleged) influence over her writing at this stage in her career (Goldblatt 1976:123). Lydia Liu, in a compelling feminist reading of the work, suggests that *Field* articulates an "ambivalent" nationalism through its unswerving scrutiny on the female body (Liu 1994). Repudiating its canonical label as a patriotic novel, Liu contends that the life cycle of individual women, not the rise and fall of the nation, occupies the work's central concern. Thus, whereas the Japanese invasion is shown to mobilize new forms of national identity in male characters—even in men as apathetic as Two-and-a-Half Li—Xiao Hong reveals that for women the experience of male sexual violence can complicate an affective allegiance to the "homeland."

Insofar as Xiao Hong does little to foreshadow the theme of anti-Japanese resistance early in the narrative, it is not difficult to appreciate why the final scenes have been interpreted as either contrived or ironic. The first reference to the foreign threat looming along China's borders does not occur until chapter 11, when, without warning, "a flag never before seen by the villagers was raised" (73). Taken in the context of Xiao Hong's overall representation of the rural condition, however, the novel's resolution may not be so incongruous after all. To begin with, unlike many writers of the 1930s and 1940s, Xiao Hong is clearly not interested in enshrining the peasant as savior of China's historical predicament. Whether delineating the class awakening of the peasantry amidst rural economic devastation (Mao Dun's "Spring Silkworms"), natural disaster (*Ding Ling's "Flood"), or foreign incursion (Xiao Jun's *Village in August*), new narrative paradigms of Chinese fiction of this period reflected an emerging leftist discourse on the "masses" that invested the figure of the peasant (and worker) with extraordinary historical agency. In sharp contrast, Xiao Hong evokes a grim world of seemingly unceasing misery, hardly a breeding ground for the earthy heroism and solidarity celebrated by her contemporaries. Her novel does depict historical change, change that issues not from the peasants themselves but violently from the outside.

Indeed, the bulk of the text explores the peasantry not as subjects of the national narrative but as marginal to that history, conditioned by rural realities that all but stifle a collective political consciousness and will. Most notable in this regard is Xiao Hong's extensive use of natural symbolism. Rather than evoke visually the regional landscape, animals and insects are depicted on the same narrative level as humanity itself, as if to challenge conventional distinctions between humankind and nature and to underscore the brute existence all living creatures endure. Consider, for example, the description of Mother Wang's mare:

> When there was work to be done, it worked with resignation. When ropes and chains were fastened onto its body, it obeyed its master's whip. The master's whip rarely fell on its body. But sometimes, when it was too exhausted and could not go on, its steps would slow down, and the master would beat it with a whip or with something else. Yet it would not rear wildly, because its future had already been determined by all the past generations. (16)

Like the old workhorse, the peasants who inhabit the novel have meekly surrendered to the harsh circumstances around them and evince little consciousness that things could be different. Life proceeds on the most elemental level, driven by basic physical needs (hunger, desire, and self-preservation). As the narrator comments dispassionately: "In the village, one remained forever unaware. One could never experience the spiritual side of life; only the material aspects gave these people sustenance" (37).

Contributing to Xiao Hong's vision is her skillful manipulation of cyclical imagery: recurring references to the passing seasons, agricultural routines, the movement from day to night, and biological procreation. Time in the rural village is not the progressive, linear chronology of (national) history, but a time suspended in a relentless natural rhythm. Her point is not that peasants lack the human capacity to protest their lot or to express joy or compassion, but that the continual grind of daily survival takes precedence. When Mother Wang and Fifth Sister find the former town beauty, Yueying (Yueh-ying), on the verge of death, her paralyzed body infested with maggots, they do not balk at providing her the comfort she so desperately craves. Yet in a world consumed with eking out a meager existence, the narrative does not linger on this poignant moment: "Three days later Yueh-ying's coffin was borne swiftly over the desolate hill to be buried at the foot of the slope. The dead were dead, and the living still had to plan how to stay alive. In winter the women made ready the summer clothes; the men started scheduling the next year's crops" (41).

By immersing the reader within the circumscribed world of a peasant constituency, and not simply furnishing the patronizing "cold glances from above" that Lu Xun deplored (Anderson 1991:189), the text offers a sensitive analysis of this pivotal moment in modern Chinese history. For the pressing question it poses is this: how can historically oppressed subjects surmount the material and mental circumstances that pin them down in order to break free from an entrenched cycle of poverty, sexual violence, and habitual apathy? And under what circumstances can an entity as inert and unconscious as the Chinese peasantry be transformed into a force of positive change?

One (somewhat paradoxical) answer the novel suggests is that war itself—and the destruction it spelled for the village—may provide just such a catalyst for social transformation. Whereas in the conventional revolutionary bildungsroman, peasant (or worker) resistance is shown to materialize from either an innate insurgent spirit or gradual processes of education and collectivity, here the quiet misery of the insulated rural community is initially barely shaken by the horrors of Japanese occupation. The occupation accelerates the rate of death beyond peasant expectations as the Japanese routinely massacre and torture the local population. Despite the mounting piles of corpses and incidences of atrocity, however, most of the peasants are not immediately stirred to action or revolt. Yet, the violent disruption of age-old habits eventually forces open alternative patterns of human behavior from which new forms of consciousness might emerge. For example, whereas early in the novel the past is described as "a dead tree that can never be revived" (19), by the end memory begins to serve as a source of hope and resistance. The moment of resistance, in other words, simultaneously marks the beginning of a new kind of history for peasants: the past looked back upon nostalgically. Yet at the same time, the "patriotic awakening" that occurs in the village at the end of the novel is hardly romanticized. In contrast to the brigade of heroic peasant-guerillas in novels like Xiao Jun's *Village in August*, Xiao Hong's characters possess little more than a rudimentary understanding of the broader national implications of the struggle in which they are to become involved. More important, what still moves them to action is not lofty patriotic conviction (despite their undigested political rhetoric) but more basic concerns about material survival. Indeed, the looming image of barren wheat fields—where not even a few scattered kernels of grains can be scrounged—dominating the final pages reminds us what this is really all about. National liberation in other words is imbued with a radically different meaning: it is not a noble patriotic struggle to protect native soil or to safeguard traditional Chinese life; rather for Xiao Hong it represents a historical opportunity to break the brutal cycle of contemporary existence itself.

—*Amy D. Dooling*

Bibliography

Anderson, Marston. *The Limits of Realism: Chinese Fiction in the Revolutionary Period.* Berkeley: University of California Press, 1990.

Goldblatt, Howard. *Hsiao Hong.* Boston: Twayne, 1976.

Liu, Lydia. "The Female Body and Nationalist Discourse: Manchuria in Xiao Hong's *Field of Life and Death.*" In Angela Zito and Tani Barlow, eds., *Body, Subject, and Power in China,* 157–177. Chicago: University of Chicago Press, 1994.

Meng Yue and Dai Jinhua. *Fuchu lishi dibiao: Zhongguo xiandai nüxing wenxue yan-jiu* (Emerging on the Horizons of History: Research on Modern Chinese Women's Writing). Zhengzhou: Henan renmin, 1989.

Xiao, Hong. *The Field of Life and Death and Tales of Hulan River*. Trans. Howard Goldblatt and Ellen Yeung. Bloomington: Indiana University Press, 1979.

——. *Market Street: A Chinese Woman in Harbin*. Trans. Howard Goldblatt. Seattle: University of Washington Press, 1986.

——. *Selected Short Stories of Xiao Hong*. Trans. Howard Goldblatt. Beijing: Chinese Literature Press, 1982.

——. *Xiao Hong quanji* (Stories of Xiao Hong). Harbin: Harbin, 1998.

Xiao, Si. "Loneliness among the Mountain Flowers—Xiao Hong in Hong Kong." Trans. Janice Wickeri. *Renditions* 29–30 (1988): 177–181.

76

PERFORMING THE NATION:
CHINESE DRAMA AND THEATER

Early in the twentieth century, when China struggled to emerge from its imperial past and build a new republic, "performing the nation" was a theme shared by both the traditional operatic theater *(xiqu)* and the emerging modern spoken drama *(huaju)*. The latter was promoted by May Fourth men of letters as an alternative to the former, which they saw as too constrained to express the sentiments and concerns of modern times, and as a vehicle for transforming China into a modern nation. Less known than their peers who promoted modern spoken drama, artists in operatic theaters initiated reforms to free traditional theater from its ancient rules so that opera could also play a significant role in constructing a new nation.

*Liang Qichao initiated traditional theater reform *(xiqu gailiang)* in 1902 while in exile in Japan, where he published three operatic texts in New Citizen (Xinmin congbao) to raise the spirit of the Chinese people to avenge their humiliation by foreigners. Between 1901 and 1912, as many as 150 new scripts of *chuanqi* (southern plays) and *zaju* (northern plays) emerged in different magazines and newspapers. Some of these works dramatized the deeds of ancient national heroes who became models for patriotic resistance against the Qing. Other plays, in contrast, depicted significant contemporary events, such the Hundred Days Reform in *Dreams of Reform* (Weixin meng, 1903–4), written by Mao Yuanxi Qiusheng and others. Another remarkable example is a biographical play about the life of Qiu Jin, a female revolutionary executed for her anti-Qing activities in 1907. In a similar fashion, new Peking operas exposed foreign imperialist aggressions against China: Russia's invasion of Heilongjiang Province in *An Un-Russian Dream* (Fei xiong meng), the Eight Allied Armies' invasion of China in 1900 in *Wuling Spring* (Wuling chun), and the protest against America's Chinese immigration exclusion acts in *The Spring of Overseas Chinese* (Haiqiao chun).

To help depict an ideal new nation, foreign heroes and heroines also occupied center stage in these reform dramas. The French Revolution and the execution of Louis XVI are depicted in *Guillotine* (Duantou tai), the Cuban student struggle against Spanish colonialism in *Student Wave* (Xue hai chao). *Resentment over the Lost Country* (Wang guo hen) portrays a heroic An Chung Keun, a Korean nationalist who in 1909 assassinated Itô Hirobumi, architect of the Japanese colonization of Korea. In addition to foreign paragons, Chinese heroines became popular symbols both as victims of a patriarchal society and as champions for women's rights and liberation. Such figures are found in Liu Yazi's late Qing text, *New Daughter of Songling* (Songling xin nü'er), a remarkably well written one-act play. Depicting women's resistance to arranged marriage in defense of women's rights, Liu allows his dramatic character, who is dressed in a Western suit, to speak her mind to the audience: Asians are people. Europeans are people. But why does China, the great land, trample women's rights? Chinese women are still suffering every passing day while those white and fair foreign women enjoy equal rights with men; their names are even recorded in history. Liu's female protagonist expresses her deep admiration for Madame Roland, condemned and guillotined for her revolutionary activities during the French Revolution, and Sophia Perovskaya, executed for her abortive attempt to assassinate Tsar Alexander II. Liu Yazi's championing of Chinese women's rights, although in tune with the times, is not without problems: it reflected a white supremacy attitude common among the Chinese literati, who looked up to the West as the model for China's modernization.

Although Peking opera originated in the north, the center of operatic theater reform was Shanghai, a vibrant city in the south open to Western influence and innovative in artistic experience. Wang Xiaonong, one practitioner of the "Shanghai school of Peking opera" *(haipai jingju)*, scripted new Peking operas that depicted the contemporary state of affairs. In 1908, Wang even introduced a new stage in Shanghai for producing Peking opera, using imported equipment and technology for stage designing and lighting. To promote new Peking operas with contemporary themes, Wang and his cohorts successfully adapted Harriet Beecher Stowe's *Uncle Tom's Cabin* from a "new drama" *(xinju)* version, a forerunner of modern spoken drama recently imported from the West. Influenced by the impact of modern drama at the beginning of the twentieth century, some theater reformers in the late Qing and early Republican period experimented with new Peking operas with contemporary costumes *(shizhuang xinxi)* in Shanghai.

One literary historian has recorded as many as two hundred reformed dramas tailored to the taste and concerns of contemporary audiences. Mei Lanfang performed five Peking operas with contemporary costume in Beijing after two visits to Shanghai in 1913 and 1914, where he had watched modern Western dramas. Mei's desire to reform traditional opera to reflect contemporary reality, however, found fresh expression in his new historical drama *(xinbian lishi ju)*, performed after Japan's invasion of China became imminent. His *Resisting the Jin Invaders* (Kang Jin bing) and *Hatred in Life and Death* (Shengsi hen), premiered in Shanghai in 1933 and represented the best of these dramas, which he continued to work on in the PRC period. Mei, of course, was not alone in his attempt to reform Peking opera. Tian Han also scripted in 1940 *Jiang-Han Fishermen's Song* (Jianghan yuge), a new Peking opera *(xin pingju)* that depicted a fishermen's uprising to defeat Jin aggressors in the Song dynasty. Tian also wrote *Heroic Stories of New Sons and Daughters* (Xin ernü yingxiong zhuan, 1940), which dramatizes a Ming dynasty hero fighting against foreign invaders. Similarly, Ouyang Yuqian transformed *Peach Blossom Fan* (Taohua shan, premiere 1937), originally a *chuanqi* text, into a new Peking opera, with a revised image of Li Xiangjun, the female protagonist who would rather die than see her lover turn into a traitor.

Unlike operatic theater, modern spoken drama did not have to combat a tradition of its own. Its dialogue-only form, moreover, was thought by its promoters to allow for greater freedom to express complicated ideas and plots than its traditional operatic counterpart. In spite of its marginal position in modern Chinese literary and cultural history, the development of modern spoken drama played a significant role in constructing an image of a modern Chinese nation. Advocated as a weapon to battle traditional operatic theater, early advocates such as Hu Shi introduced Western drama, such as the plays of Ibsen and Shakespeare, to create a "new drama" *(xinxi)*. Hu's *The Greatest Event in One's Life* (Zhongshen dashi, 1919) depicts a modern woman who elopes with her Japan-educated fiancé to avoid an arranged marriage. This Nora-like character heralded a series of female protagonists who leave home in search of free love and participation in public life. Female playwright Bai Wei in her *Breaking out of Ghost Pagoda* (Dachu youling ta, 1928), for instance, creates a courageous daughter who dies in the arms of her mother in her struggle against the patriarchal home, symbolized by her domineering and lustful father. The old and isolated rural village, as depicted in Tian Han's *The Night a Tiger Was Captured* (Huo hu zhi ye, 1922), however, prevents its main character, Liangu, from escaping her cruel father, who dictates that if a tiger is killed he will use its sale for her dowry to marry a rich man. The tragic ending of the play, which presents the death of her lover, signifies the hopeless fate of Chinese women, who in turn symbolize the plight of the suffering nation, also bound by Confucian doctrines of traditional society.

In contrast to these plays that foreground contemporary life, Guo Moruo's trilogy of plays about women rewrote traditional stories. His *Zhuo Wenjun* (1923), for instance, depicted the title heroine as challenging the strong will of her father by eloping with her lover, Sima Xiangru; she also confronts the Confucian ideology that expects a widow never to remarry. In a similar fashion, *Wang Zhaojun* (1923) creates its title heroine as a dignified courtesan who rejects the love of the Han emperor by willingly marrying an outsider from a "barbarous" tribe. In a way more politically relevant to the reality of 1920s China, Guo Moruo's third play, *Nie Ying* (1925), presents the title character as a martyr who stands by her patriotic brother against outside invaders. In Guo Moruo's father figures—the domestic father in *Zhuo Wenjun*, the imperial father in *Wang Zhaojun*, and the imperialist father in *Nie Ying*—we see the anti-Confucian theme in May Fourth drama.

Men traveling to Western countries and encountering foreign women is another theme taken up by spoken drama, a theme that allowed dramatists to reflect on the negative Western influence on China. Ouyang Yuqian's *Homecoming* (Huijia yihou, 1924) depicts a Chinese overseas student, torn between his homebound wife acquired through an arranged marriage, a loving and understanding woman with all the traditional virtues, and his Chinese American lover, a nagging and unpleasant woman. Such a questioning of Western values resurfaced in Xiong Foxi's *Foreign Graduate* (Yang zhuangyuan, 1926), in which the main character expects his parents to address him respectfully as "Doctor" upon his homecoming with a foreign degree and foreign wife.

Such an anti-imperialist theme assumed a higher profile with Japan's encroachment on Chinese territory in the 1930s. The 1930s was a thriving period for Chinese spoken drama, which came to maturity with Cao Yu's plays (see "Cao Yu and *Thunderstorm*"), but it also witnessed the rise of "defense drama" in 1935–36, which connected dramatic performance even more closely to the defense of the Chinese nation. With the impending Japanese invasion, the Friendly Association of the Shanghai Dramatic Circle was organized in 1936 to unite dramatists of diverse political and ideological backgrounds to create a drama of national resistance. The most popular pieces were Xia Yan's *Sai Jinhua* (1936) and *Under Shanghai Eaves* (Shanghai wuyan xia, 1937), representing respectively two distinct subgenres, the history play and the contemporary realist play. *Sai Jinhua* retells the story of the title character, a famous Qing dynasty courtesan who won over important Western men and persuaded them to lessen their demands on China during the Boxer Rebellion. According to PRC drama historians, this play's obvious allusion to the Guomindang's nonresistance policy toward the Japanese (reminiscent of the corrupt and cowardly Chinese officials' "kowtowing to Western powers" in the Qing dynasty) made the play a popular hit, with a record twenty-two full-house performances. Its immediate banning by the Guomindang and the subsequent public uproar (known as the "*Sai Jinhua* incident") seemed only to have confirmed the genius of the playwright, whose allegorical use of a patriotic prostitute to save her nation at the time of crisis was not lost on either political camp.

In contrast to *Sai Jinhua*, Xia Yan's *Under Shanghai Eaves* presents a cross-section of a typical house in Shanghai, occupied by five poor families struggling for survival. The play focuses on a single event, the "homecoming" of Kuang Fu, who upon his release from prison after eight years, finds Yang Caiyu, his wife, living with (and emotionally attached to) his friend Lin Zhicheng. The originally scheduled premiere of *Under Shanghai Eaves* in Shanghai on August 15, 1937 was canceled, because two days earlier war with Japan had broken out. Xia Yan later wrote that instead of feeling disappointed, he was excited about the dramatic turn of events: the war effort and its eventual victory should, he felt, bring an end to the sad stories presented in the play. In fact, he wished that the play would never have to be performed so that Chinese children would not be reminded of their parents' past suffering.

The time of the war against Japan has been referred to as the "golden age of Chinese theater," when drama played a more significant and direct role than any other literary genre in promoting the war effort. The best-known performances include *In Defense of Lugou Bridge* (Baowei lugou qiao, 1937), a play that represents the heroic efforts to resist the Japanese invasion. The play was written by the joint efforts of seventeen playwrights; its production was made possible with the help of six musicians, nineteen directors, and a cast of close to a hundred actors and actresses. In August 1937, twelve National Salvation Drama Troupes were organized in Shanghai to perform resistance plays in different parts of China. Their most frequently produced plays include *Put Down Your Whip* (Fangxia nide bianzi, 1936), which depicts a starving daughter being whipped by her helpless, tearful father. Actors "planted" in the audience urge him to put down his whip and join the national effort to fight Japanese invaders. The stage lines from the actors and actresses elicited responses from the audience. The play was frequently performed outdoors; it has been hailed as an important example of "street theater" (*jietou ju*).

Stage production flourished from 1938 to 1945 in the unoccupied areas of Chongqing and Guilin, where a series of drama festivals and exhibitions helped produce the most successful plays of the war period. During the "misty season" from October to May, when Chongqing was shrouded by heavy mist and sheltered from Japanese air raids, an annual Misty Season Drama Festival was held. The year 1944 witnessed a total of 118 drama performances, written by diverse playwrights and performed by a variety of drama troupes. Among the best-known pieces produced in Chongqing were Cao Yu's *Metamorphosis* (Tuibian, 1940) and *Peking Men* (Beijing ren, 1941) and Guo Moruo's six history plays, including *Qu Yuan* (1942). The last shows Qu Yuan as a tragic poet whose patriotic feelings and heroic spirit in fighting against the corrupt status quo made this drama a hit.

Whereas wartime dramas featured the common theme of defending the nation, the dramas performed after 1949, under the guiding influence of Mao's

*"Yan'an Talks," present workers, peasants, and soldiers building a new socialist life. Jin Jian's one-act play *Zhao Xiaolan* (1950), for instance, dramatizes the courage of one woman's fight for free love against the will of her parents, a fight that contrasts sharply with her sister, who suffers greatly from an arranged marriage. In PRC drama, the fate of women is usually narrated in the larger context of "building up a socialist motherland," which, according to state ideology, provided women a perfect stage for public performance. Such a feature can be found in Hu Ke's *Huaishu Village* (Huaishu zhuang, 1959), the story of Mother Guo, a prototype of the loving "earth mother" now transformed into a "revolutionary mother." The loss of her only son to the Korean war only reinforces her determination to take the lead in numerous political events in the countryside: the land-reform movement, the movement to support the Korean war effort, the collective farming movements, and finally, the Great Leap Forward, aimed at boosting agricultural and industrial productivity.

Because Communist Party ideology promoted workers as pillars of socialist society, worker plays helped to validate the new PRC state. *The Red Storm* (Hongse fengbao, 1958), for example, portrays the famous Peking-Hankou railroad workers' strikes brutally suppressed by the warlord Wu Peifu and his foreign supporters on February 7, 1923. Jin Shan wrote and directed the play, and starred in the "unforgettable" role of Shi Yang, who supports the workers' strikes. Legend has it that Jin spent only seventy-two hours rehearsing the play before its highly successful premiere by the China Youth Art Theater in 1958. In the 1960s, the worker plays changed dramatically. Plays sought to educate the younger generation of workers "never to forget" such a revolutionary history and "never to forget the class struggle," as expressed in the title of Cong Shen's play *Never to Forget* (Qianwan buyao wangji). Premiered by Ha'erbin Theater in 1964, and soon followed by numerous productions throughout the country, *Never to Forget* depicts a young worker whose desire for a better material life is criticized as an example of a worker's family being "eroded" by bourgeois ideology. Such a theme culminated during the Cultural Revolution, when eight model revolutionary theatrical pieces dominated the Chinese stage for ten years. Most rehearsed past revolutionary war experiences to remind the audience never to forget class struggle (see "The Cultural Revolution Model Theater").

Spoken drama experienced a remarkable renaissance in the post-Mao period. Much of post-Mao theater was a reaction against the politics and culture of the Cultural Revolution. The popular anti–Gang of Four plays, for instance, depicted Jiang Qing and her followers as destroyers of the country, and the post-Mao regime as builders of a new nation moving toward democracy and modernization. An example is *Winter Jasmine* (Bao chun hua, 1979), which recounts the discrimination suffered by Bai Jie, a young female worker in a textile factory, because of her "politically incorrect" family origins: her father was declared a "counterrevolutionary" because he had worked for the Guomindang before

1949, and her mother charged a "rightist" for challenging the Communist Party's radical policies in 1958. Xing Yixun's *Power Versus Law* (Quan yu fa, 1979) portrays a party secretary, assigned to his post after the overthrow of the Gang of Four, who seeks to expose corruption and crimes within the party system and protect the wife and daughter of a "rightist." Such a positive image of the party representative, however, is challenged in another highly controversial play entitled *If I Were for Real* (Jiaru wo shi zhende, premiered in 1979) written by Sha Yexin, Li Shoucheng, and Yao Mingde. In this play, a young man from a worker's family with no connection to the privileged and the powerful finds himself impersonating the son of an important party official in order to get permission to return to his home city to marry his pregnant girlfriend before the child's delivery. The play's setting in post-Mao China made it politically suspect; its critique of party corruption was obviously not limited to the Gang of Four, who were no longer in power. Anti–Gang of Four plays include what drama historians term "revolutionary leader plays," which depict the wartime stories of high-ranking party and army officials, some of whom, in real life, had been persecuted during the Cultural Revolution (or before), such as Chen Yi, He Long, and Peng Dehuai. Meanwhile, female playwrights began to emerge. The best known among them, Bai Fengxi, distinguished herself with her women's trilogy, which depicts a post–Gang of Four society that fails to protect women, especially those living in rural China, from oppression. Female intellectuals and urban dwellers, likewise, struggle in Bai's plays to find their own identities and voices in an increasingly modernized China. Once again, women occupied a central position in the drama's construction of the nation.

Parallel with these developments, experimental plays such as *Bus Stop* (Che zhan, 1983), by *Gao Xingjian, and *WM* (1985), by Wang Peigong and Wang Gui, experimented with elements of Western absurdist theater. In essence, however, these plays did not depart radically from the realist tradition of the Maoist era, although they critiqued Maoist ideology by exposing the effects of the Cultural Revolution. Wei Minglun's Sichuan opera *Pan Jinlian: The History of a Fallen Woman* (Pan Jinlian: yige nüren de chenlunshi, 1985) represents the best example of experimental theater. Wei attempted to reform the Chinese traditional theater by combining elements of absurdist theater with the realist tradition. Unlike his Western counterparts, Wei believed that the play's "absurdity" resided only in its "absurdist form," in which characters from different countries and various historical periods appear on stage to comment on the tragic story of Pan Jinlian, one of the most notorious femme fatale characters in Chinese literature. The play centers around the dramatic conflicts between Pan Jinlian and five men: the rich man, Zhang Dahu, who forces her into an arranged marriage with Wu Dalang; Wu Dalang, the short and ugly man Pan marries; Ximen Qing, the vicious playboy who sleeps with Pan and plots with her to kill Wu; Wu Song, Wu Dalang's brother who avenges his murder by killing Pan; and Shi Nai'an, the author of the *Water Margin*, the original source of the story. Shi's misogyny is challenged by various fictional and historical characters from several works, both from the East and the West. This controversial play was so warmly received that it inspired numerous productions in other genres, such as modern spoken drama and local operas popular in Shanxi Province and Shanghai. At one point, fifty theaters in twenty cities were performing the work. Articles appeared in 130 newspapers and journals, ten of which dedicated special columns to discussion of the play. Wei's play reminds one of Ouyang Yuqian's earlier *Pan Jinlian* (1928), a modern spoken drama that borrowed formal features and plots from traditional operatic theater. At the same time, it presented a daring critique against the Confucian tradition that saw women as the source of evil. Like Ouyang's text, Wei's play portrays a sympathetic Pan Jinlian trapped by patriarchal society.

Other traditions such as the Greek theater and Chinese folk dance and singing found their way into *Sangshuping Chronicles* (Shangshuping jishi, 1988), about the sorrows of the local peasants in a small, isolated village in the northwestern part of China. Despite the reforms that have happened elsewhere, ignorance, illiteracy, sexual oppression, and patriarchal structure dominate this place that has remained unchanged for thousands of year. Once again, theater productions reflected a continued tension between individuals, their efforts to seek personal happiness, and the demands of the nation-state.

If domestic concerns still ruled the Chinese stage, global perspectives in which China redefined itself became increasing popular. Guo Shixing's *Birdman* (Niaoren, premiered 1992) presents dramatic conflicts between a Chinese man, a Chinese American man, and an American-educated Chinese man. The play revolves around a group of bird-loving men who spend all of their leisure time raising, examining, and talking about birds. Fascinated by this phenomenon, Dr. Paul Ding, a Chinese American psychiatrist, establishes a Birdman Psychiatric Center in order to restore the mental health of the birdmen by retrieving their deeply buried memories of traumatic childhood experiences. Dr. Ding's experiment, however, proves frustrating and confusing. He does not always understand the literary and dramatic allusions that his patients make under hypnosis. In the end, San Ye, a retired Peking opera star, easily masters Ding's psychiatric tricks. He rewrites, directs, and acts out a familiar scene from a Peking opera that puts Ding on trial and forces him to admit that he suffered from the very psychological problems he had attributed to his patients as a result of growing up in an American Chinatown. In an effort to show Ding up, San Ye performs his "swan song" as a Peking opera actor, a performance that helps him regain something of his previous power and heroic stature. In this role, he plays the wise, incorruptible Judge Bao, a figure in traditional theater who never fails to protect the innocent and punish the criminal. He sentences Ding. He also condemns another defendant, Dr. Chen, a Chinese bird expert admired globally for his dedication to animal protection, who has killed the last surviving bird of an endangered species so as to preserve it as a specimen for public display.

This sarcastic commentary on hypocritical intellectuals reflects a fear of losing Chinese identity, which had rendered Chinese economically and culturally vulnerable to imperialist powers. The use of Peking opera in the play-within-a-play comments on the decline of the opera and lends the entire play an un-matched charm. Lin Liankun, the actor who played San Ye, displayed a great range of body movements, singing, and acting that he used to shuttle between the two dramatic genres. More than any other, this play needs to be seen on stage if one is to appreciate the beauty and depth of the diverse acting styles and local color, as well as the display of conventions from both modern spoken drama and traditional operatic theater.

— *Xiaomei Chen*

Bibliography

Bai, Fengxi. *The Women Trilogy*. Trans. Guan Yuehua. Beijing: Chinese Literature Press, 1991.

Chen, Xiaomei. *Acting the Right Part: Political Theater and Popular Drama in Contemporary China*. Honolulu: University of Hawai'i Press, 2002.

———, ed. *Reading the Right Texts: An Anthology of Contemporary Chinese Drama*. Honolulu: University of Hawai'i Press, 2003.

Cheung, Martha P. Y., and Jane C. C. Lai, eds. *An Oxford Anthology of Contemporary Chinese Drama*. Hong Kong: Oxford University Press, 1997.

Eide, Elisabeth. *China's Ibsen*. London: Curzon Press, 1987.

Gao, Xingjian. *The Other Shore: Plays*. Trans. Gilbert C. P. Fong. Hong Kong: The Chinese University Press, 1999.

Gunn, Edward, ed. *Twentieth-Century Chinese Drama: An Anthology*. Bloomington: Indiana University Press, 1983.

Guo, Moruo (Kuo Mo-jo). "Cho Wen-chün." In Harold R. Isaacs, trans. and ed., *Straw Sandal: Chinese Short Stories, 1918–1933*, 45–67. Cambridge, Mass.: MIT Press, 1974.

———. *Chu Yuan*. Trans. Yang Hsien-yi and Gladys Yang. Beijing: Foreign Languages Press, 1953.

———. *Five Historical Plays*. Beijing: Foreign Languages Press, 1984.

Mackerras, Colin. *The Chinese Theatre in Modern Times: From 1840 to the Present Day*. Amherst: University of Massachusetts Press, 1975.

Tung, Constantine, and Colin Mackerras, eds. *Drama in the People's Republic of China*, Albany: State University of New York Press, 1987.

Wagner, Rudolf G. *The Contemporary Chinese Historical Drama*. Berkeley: University of California Press, 1990.

Yan, Haiping, ed. *Theater and Society: An Anthology of Contemporary Chinese Drama*. Armonk, N.Y.: M.E. Sharpe, 1998.

Yu, Shiao-Ling S., ed. *Chinese Drama after the Cultural Revolution, 1979–1989: An Anthology*. New York: Edwin Mellen, 1996.

77

CAO YU AND *THUNDERSTORM*

Cao Yu (1910–1966) is conventionally considered by literary historians and critics, in both China and the West, to be one of the leading modern Chinese playwrights. He is credited with bringing spoken drama to its maturity in the 1930s.

Born Wan Jinbao, Cao Yu grew up in Tianjin in an aristocratic family whose wealth and prestige was declining. His youthful experiences growing up in this milieu provided the material for most of his early dramas. He received a classical education in a private family school and had access to a large family library. His mother, an aficionado of the performing arts, introduced Cao Yu to various regional dramatic forms, folk performance arts, and Western-style spoken dramas. He entered Tianjin's Nankai Middle School in 1922, joining its renowned drama troupe and acting in such plays as Ding Xilin's *Oppression* (Yapo, 1926), Ibsen's *A Doll House*, and Hauptmann's *Weavers*. Frequently playing female roles, he earned the sobriquet the "flower of the Nankai drama troupe." In 1930 he enrolled in Qinghua University's Department of Western Languages and Literatures and assiduously delved into literary works from China and the West, in particular Western classical and modern plays.

Cao Yu's first spoken drama, *Thunderstorm*, was written and published while he was still enrolled at Qinghua. It is by most accounts the most famous spoken drama of the prewar era and the most frequently performed play in the history of Chinese theater. Initially published in Zheng Zhenduo and Jin Yi's *Literary Quarterly* (Wenxue xunkan) in 1934, it was first performed later the same year at Ji'nan University. With Cao Yu playing the lead, a 1936 production was a great commercial success and established Tang Huaiqiu's Traveling Drama Troupe of China as China's first professional spoken-drama troupe. *Thunderstorm* was adapted into two different film versions in 1938 by studios in Hong Kong and Shanghai.

The commercial success of *Thunderstorm* greatly increased the prestige and popularity of the new genre of spoken drama (see "Performing the Nation") and contributed to the play's subsequent canonization in China's modern literary history. One of the major reasons for the favorable reception of *Thunderstorm* was its articulation of the main political causes and artistic practices of the May Fourth generation. *Thunderstorm* adheres to the central mission promoted by the May Fourth intellectuals: the iconoclastic destruction of the shackles of tradition for the purposes of emancipating the individual and strengthening the nation. Set in the 1920s, *Thunderstorm* is a well-constructed four-act play that explores the themes of patriarchal capitalistic oppression and female emancipation through the dramatic conventions of tragic fate, revenge, and destined retribution. The dramatic conflict revolves around the complex three-decade entanglements between two economically disparate families: the Zhou family, headed by Zhou Puyuan, a foreign-educated wealthy owner of a mine, and the Lu family, all the members of which have at one time been employed by the Zhou family.

The action is triggered when Lu Shiping arrives at the Zhou household at the behest of Zhou Fanyi, the wife of Zhou Puyuan. Shiping comes to the horrifying realization that her daughter, Sifeng, is currently employed as a maid by the man whom she served thirty years ago and with whom she had a love affair. After bearing two of his sons, due to her low station, Shiping was abandoned by Zhou Puyuan. Her first son, Zhou Ping, remained with his father, while Shiping was permitted to keep her younger son, Lu Dahai, because of his weak and sickly condition. Fearing that her daughter, Sifeng, will encounter a similar calamity, Lu Shiping willingly consents to Zhou Fanyi's request to have Sifeng discharged from the Zhou household's service. Fanyi is motivated in part by jealousy, wishing to have Zhou Ping to herself. Fanyi had previously been carrying on an affair with her stepson, but as of late, Zhou Ping has taken a fancy to Sifeng. Two triangular relationships emerge in the first act: between Zhou Puyuan, Fanyi, and Lu Shiping, on the one hand, and between Fanyi, Sifeng, and Zhou Ping, on the other.

The laying bare of these triangular relationships, both past and present, is interspersed with scenes that highlight the ruthless oppression inflicted by the Zhou patriarch upon his subordinates — his immediate family members and the workers at his mine. His past abandonment of Lu Shiping and his present actions toward his wife, Fanyi, reveal him as a cruel victimizer. Convinced of Fanyi's insanity, Puyuan orders her locked up in her room and forces her to take regular doses of medicine. Puyuan's forcing his wife to take the medicine is the most poignant illustration of his character's callousness and is symbolic of the hypocritical compassion of the Confucian patriarchy. Another example of Puyuan's lack of compassion for or exploitation of the downtrodden is exemplified by his quashing and underhanded manipulation of a strike at his mine. The leader of the strike, ironically and unbeknownst to Zhou Puyuan, is his own son, Lu Dahai. Representing the antithesis of the Confucian filial son and the hope for a proletarian revolution, Lu Dahai epitomizes the radical politics of the era.

The third act ends with the fleeing of Sifeng and Zhou Ping from the Lu's residence, pursued by Lu Dahai, who is motivated by class hatred, and Shiping, who hopes to prevent Sifeng and Ping from unwittingly committing incest. When Zhou Ping returns home near the beginning of Act Four, Fanyi begs Zhou Ping to take her with him to the mine, even if accompanied by Sifeng. At Zhou Ping's refusal, Fanyi declares that she has nothing to live for, and the stage is set for a desperate act of revenge. The denouement of the fourth act is one of the most melodramatic in the history of Chinese modern drama—composed of a sequence of revealed secrets, fated coincidences, and tragic deaths. Fully aware of her daughter's love affair with Zhou Ping, Shiping continues to demand the termination of the relationship. However, on learning that Shiping is already pregnant, she resigns herself to wishing the couple well while concealing from them the reality of their incestuous relationship. Shiping only blames herself: "What have I ever done to bring such a calamity down on our heads? ... Oh, God, if anyone has to be punished, why can't it just be me? It's my fault and no one else's: it all began when I took the first false step. They're my innocent children; they deserve a chance in life. The guilt here is in my heart, and I should be the one to suffer from it" (142).

Shiping's compassionate and self-effacing support of her children's elopement, however, is compromised by Fanyi's need for revenge upon Zhou Ping and her husband. To Fanyi's astonishment, Puyuan reveals Shiping's true identity as Zhou Ping's long-lost mother, thereby shocking everyone into realizing Zhou Ping and Sifeng's relationship as incestuous. A horror-stricken Sifeng runs outside into the pouring rain and is electrocuted by a loose electrical wire; Zhou Chong is electrocuted in the process of trying to save her. Zhou Ping shoots himself in his father's study, leaving Zhou Puyuan with only one son, Lu Dahai, who runs off, according to some interpretations, to join the Communist cause. The epilogue and prologue, which are usually not performed or published with the script, reveal that years later Shiping is immobilized by grief and Fanyi has perhaps truly gone mad.

One of the overarching themes of *Thunderstorm* is the suppression of personal freedom generated by the patriarchal structure, order, and ethics of traditional Chinese society. The Zhou household has been interpreted by most critics as a microcosm of the "old society," doomed to decline into obscurity. *Thunderstorm* can be viewed as a variation on the May Fourth trope of the decadent, male-dominated, hypocritical, and oppressive old family, a legacy of earlier May Fourth dramas, such as Chen Dabei's *Ms. Youlan* (Youlan nüshi, 1921), Bai Wei's *Breaking Out of Ghost Pagoda* (Dachu youling ta, 1928), and Ouyang Yuqian's *Behind the Screen* (Pingfeng hou, 1919). However, Cao Yu's drama has garnered its canonical status as the paragon of the doomed "feudal family" because it represents, according to many critics, a more profound and complete artistry. Zhou Puyuan, for example, could have been facilely sketched as a stereotypical archvillain, a symbol of all feudalism and patriarchal hegemony, but his sentimental musings on the past complicate this reading. Likewise, Lu Dahai's dogmatic hatred for the Zhou brothers makes it difficult to wholeheartedly sympathize with him and adopt him as a humanistic hero.

The flip side of the oppressive social structure is the emancipation of the individual. Fanyi has conventionally been read as representing the May Fourth ideal of the individual's desire for liberation from an authoritarian stronghold. As stated in his preface, Cao Yu regarded her as a personal heroine: "She has a blazing passion and a dauntless heart which pushes her through all obstacles in her life-and-death struggles" (Lau 1970: 23). Female emancipation was another prominent trope during the May Fourth period, in part propelled by the fashion of Ibsenism, as articulated in other dramas such as Hu Shi's *Greatest Event in Life* (Zhongshen dashi, 1919) and Guo Moruo's *Zhuo Wenjun* (1923) and *Wang Zhaojun* (1923).

Thunderstorm is Cao Yu's first exploration of the trope of female liberation, a theme as prominent as that of the oppressive, patriarchal family in his later plays. Fanyi's rebellion against the patriarchal institutions is both motivated by personal desire and provoked by society's oppression. Whereas Fanyi challenges the patriarchal logic, Shiping and Sifeng are portrayed more as victims of the system. This trope of female emancipation, however, is complicated within the drama. Fanyi's personal liberation is dependent upon Zhou Ping's acceptance of her. She places herself in the hands of an incipient patriarch and then is left without hope when he deserts her: "I'd resigned myself to my fate, when along came someone who must need revive me—and then tire of me and cast me aside, and leave me to wither and slowly die of thirst" (51). Despite Cao Yu's sympathetic interest in the fate of women in modern China, the convention of using the trope of female emancipation as a signifier for the emancipation of the individual may in fact have stripped women of their unique identity and subjectivity, unwittingly transferred from the rule of the old patriarch to the hands of their "enlightened saviors."

The 1936 preface to the play asserts that "cosmic cruelty" and "primitive passion," not class conflict and individual emancipation, were Cao Yu's main concerns in *Thunderstorm*, showing that Cao Yu was to some degree influenced by the Greek tragedies. However, based on the notion that personal will is a prerequisite to "tragedy," the deaths of Sifeng and the fate of Shiping are better explained by Cao Yu's interest in exploring the mystery of heaven's will. The tight threads of blood relations and ethics creates an inescapable "heaven's net" in

Thunderstorm. The deaths of Zhou Chong and Zhou Ping recall the traditional Chinese concept of "retribution" *(baoying),* inasmuch as their deaths leave Zhou Puyuan with his enemy Lu Dahai as his only descendant. According to a reading based on traditional morals, the deaths of his sons are "retribution" for his illicit affair with and subsequent abandonment of Lu Shiping. In conjunction with a Marxist reading, the "retribution" is caused by his callous feudal behavior, of which his illicit relationship is only a symptom.

Two other plays written in the same decade, *Sunrise* (Richu, 1936) and *The Wilderness* (Yuanye, 1936), continue to manifest the leftist agenda of opposing the feudal and patriarchal institutions of traditional China and capitalist exploitation. His *Metamorphosis* (Tuibian, 1940) and *Peking Man* (Beijing ren, 1940) also articulate the theme of the superfluous and oppressive traditional family, although in a comical mode and in the Chekhovian dramatic style of indirect action.

Cao Yu held many academic and government positions in the fields of drama and the arts. From 1934 to 1935 he was employed at Tianjin's Hebei Women's Normal College, before being invited to instruct the National Academy of Dramatic Arts in Nanjing. In 1946, invited by the U.S. State Department, Cao Yu, along with Lao She, stayed in America for one year giving lectures. After the founding of the PRC, Cao Yu took the positions of vice president of the Central Academy of Drama (1949), member of the board of directors of the All-China Dramatic Association (1952), president of the Beijing People's Institute of Drama and Art (1956), and deputy of the National People's Congress (1954, 1958, 1964). He also wrote several plays, including *Bright Skies* (Minglang de tian, 1954), *The Gall and the Sword* (Dan jian pian, 1961), and *The Consort of Peace* (Wang Zhaojun, 1978).

—*Jonathan Noble*

Bibliography

Cao, Yu. *Bright Skies.* Trans. Pei-chi Chang. Beijing: Foreign Languages Press, 1960.
——. *The Consort of Peace.* Trans. Monica Lai. Hong Kong: Kelly/Walsh, 1980.
——. *Peking Man.* Trans. Leslie Nai-kwai Lo et al. New York: Columbia University Press, 1986.
——. *Sunrise.* Trans. A.C. Barnes. Beijing: Foreign Languages Press, 1978.
——. *Thunderstorm.* Trans. Wang Tso-ling and A. C. Barnes. Beijing: Foreign Languages Press, 1978.
——. *The Wilderness.* Trans. Christopher Rand and Joseph Lau. Hong Kong: Hong Kong University Press, 1980.
Galik, Marian. "Ts'ao Yu's *Thunderstorm:* Creative Confrontation with Euripides, Racine, Ibsen and Galsworthy." In Marian Galik, ed., *Milestones in Sino-Western Literary Confrontation (1898–1979),* 101–122. Wiesbaden: Otto Harrassowitz, 1986.
Hu, John Y. H. *Ts'ao Yu.* New York: Twayne, 1972.

Lau, Joseph S. M. *Ts'ao Yu: The Reluctant Disciple of Chekhov and O'Neill—A Study in Literary Influence.* Hong Kong: Hong Kong University Press, 1970.

Robinson, Lewis S. "On the Sources and Motives behind Ts'ao Yu's *Thunderstorm.*" *Tamkang Review* 16 (1983): 177–192.

Wang, Aixue. *A Comparison of the Dramatic Works of Cao Yu and J. M. Synge.* Lewiston, N.Y.: Edwin Mellen, 1999.

78

THE RELUCTANT NIHILISM
OF LAO SHE'S *CAMEL XIANGZI*

Camel Xiangzi (Luotuo Xiangzi) appeared in installments in the magazine *Yuzhou feng* (Cosmic Wind) from September 1936 to October 1937 and as a book in 1939. Editions published in China from 1955 through the 1980s delete sexual references, criticism of Ruan Ming (in translation, "Yuan" is a misreading), the last half of chapter twenty-three, and all of chapter twenty-four. Author Lao She (pen name of Shu Qingchun, 1899–1966) bent with political winds and endorsed these revisions, despite the fact that he was proud of the novel as it was and was not in the habit of tinkering with completed material (Lao She 1980:69–71; 1981:231–236). Jean James's translation, *Rickshaw*, follows the original. Of Lao She's substantial output—novels, stories, plays, poems, librettos for traditional Chinese opera, drum songs, comic dialogues, criticism, and essays—*Camel Xiangzi* is the work for which he is best remembered. It continues to have influence; Liu Heng's 1988 *Black Snow* (Hei de xue) may be read as an updating of Lao She's novel.

The story is simple. Xiangzi comes to Beiping an eager young man and tries to make it as a rickshaw puller; he ends as a shuffling bum. The first cause of Xiangzi's downfall is a corrupt society. To blame are Detective Sun and other unsavory characters who represent problems of early twentieth-century China, including political thuggery and class oppression. Second, Xiangzi is unlucky; his name, literally "fortunate son," is ironic. And finally, Xiangzi is at fault; his individualism isolates him from potential allies. We have a vicious circle: poverty, injustice, and contingency bring out the worst in a good person, who then makes a bad society worse. The denouement is no surprise. We are warned at the beginning that "hopes for the most part come to nothing and Xiangzi's were no exception" (1979:10). The rest of the novel fulfills this promise, leaving it to us to explain how such pessimism translates into memorable literature.

If we assume that *Camel Xiangzi* is an imaginary investigation of the real crisis facing China in the 1930s, then Beiping, the rickshaw puller, and the rickshaw are perfect symbols of this crisis. In 1928 the Nationalist government unified China and moved its capital to Nanjing; what had been for five hundred years Beijing (northern capital) became Beiping (northern peace); internal evidence suggests that Xiangzi has been press-ganged by a warlord army in retreat from Beijing as Nationalist forces advanced in the spring of 1928 (Shi 1980:287). Each mention of Beiping connotes tumultuous change (the translation calls the city Peking, but it is Beiping in the original). China's new literature assigned itself the task of writing about the exploited, and Beiping's rickshaw pullers were highly visible members of this group; stories about them were ubiquitous in fiction and journalism. The rickshaw was a fairly modern device, but the sight of poor men pulling foreigners and rich Chinese around the city was a reminder of the costs of China's particular modernity. Rickshaw pullers, David Stand (1989:36) observes, dragged the machinery of the industrial age and their exploiters behind them.

Camel Xiangzi is often read as an allegory of Republican China. This is a valid starting point. The novel suggests that the Chinese people were bullied by imperialist powers, misled by the false promise of capitalist modernization, and betrayed by corrupt government, miscarried revolution, and their own disunity. Innumerable details in the novel contribute to the message that the poor were dehumanized by a system that only punished the virtues Xiangzi embodies. For example, Xiangzi's nickname, Camel, and his obsession with his rickshaw imply that the worker was treated as a beast of burden and a machine. Because the novel criticizes individualism, we anticipate a call for collective action, but instead we get the parable of the locusts, which suggests that mass revolution would be catastrophic (Lao She 1979:229). The iconography of the Chinese revolution typically placed the hopes of the nation on the shoulders of robust young people, but Xiangzi and Xiao Fuzi are infected with venereal disease, a conventional symbol of China's "sickness." And Mr. Cao, surrogate for the enlightened intellectual, is completely ineffectual. There is no hint as to how China might escape its predicament.

Lao She's main achievement, however, was not the encoding of social critique for decoding by the reader. We value *Camel Xiangzi* because of its pellucid language (necessarily lost in translation), elegant narrative structure, vibrant characters, and vivid descriptive passages. Attempts to reduce the novel to a single thesis lead to confusion—over how to interpret its stand on individualism, for example—because it is built around tension and contradiction. The most insightful of the dozens of critics who have written about *Camel Xiangzi* touch on ways in which the novel is divided against itself. Frederic Jameson (1984:69) sees two narrative paradigms (narrative patterns) at work and at odds in *Camel Xiangzi*. The "outer" form is associated with Xiangzi and a traditional "precapitalist view of money as hoard or treasure [think of his chamber pot piggy bank] (or of value as the possession of the unique, quasi-sacred object [the rickshaw])," while the "inner" form is linked with Hu Niu and the values of "emergent capitalism and the market [she wants to invest her capital and let their money make money]." Edward Gunn (1991) looks at language and shows that in writing *Camel Xiangzi*, Lao She's talent for and enjoyment of stylistic wordplay ran up against his felt obligation to write something socially progressive. David Der-wei Wang (1992:119) names the tension in *Camel Xiangzi* as that between melodrama and farce; the former contains "a longing for the return of a certain order" while the latter "ventures to laugh away such efforts." Marston Anderson's (1990) argument that many Chinese novels of the 1930s contain an allegory by which authors explore fiction's inability to mirror or change reality applies to Lao She's novel.

Lydia Liu (1995) finds contradiction embedded in the novel's language and mode of narration. Liu demonstrates that the term *geren zhuyi* (individualism)—used in *Camel Xiangzi*—was important in late Qing and Republican China but did not refer to a fixed concept. Progressive thinkers defined *geren zhuyi* as a positive aspect of tradition, then promoted it as antithetical to tradition, and finally attacked it as an obstacle to socialist revolution (Liu 1995:88–99). All along they struggled to reconcile individual liberation with patriotic self-sacrifice. To Liu's exegesis, we may add that in an essay published in 1936, the same year he wrote *Camel Xiangzi*, Lao She explained how this contradiction was worked out in literature: "social consciousness" (*shehui zijue*) unfortunately led authors to renounce the creation of character as the "dregs of individualism" (*geren zhuyi de yunie*) (Lao She 1936:219). Lao She wanted it both ways. *Camel Xiangzi* is a novel of profound social consciousness built around a memorable character: exploration of Xiangzi's interior life is the literary endorsement of the same "individualism" the narrator condemns. Liu argues that Lao She's narrative method forestalls any conclusion about the meaning of his novel. The narration moves from the narrator's voice to Xiangzi's voice and back without marking the transitions (this less evident in translation), and it is occasionally impossible to tell if a sentence is the narrator's thought, indirect representation of Xiangzi's thought, or direct quotation of what Xiangzi says to himself (Liu 1995:111–113). We cannot trust Xiangzi's interpretation of his story, but there is no reason to accept uncritically the narrator's judgment, especially given that five times Xiangzi tells his story but five times the narrator turns away or interrupts with an indirect summary of what Xiangzi says (Lao She 1979:36, 118, 141, 221–222, 228). All this encourages us to consider "alternative ways of looking at [Xiangzi's] situation" (Liu 1995:124).

The novel contains a final, fundamental tension. Lao She believed that fully realized characters emerge through the writing of their psychology (Lao She 1936:219). Among the aspects of Xiangzi's psychological makeup that Lao She was out to explore was sexual desire *(xing yu)*, which as much or more than romantic love engaged his interests as a novelist (Lao She 1985:541–542; 1980:68). To think through what sex means in *Camel Xiangzi*, we have to think about Hu Niu. For most commentators, Hu Niu is nothing more than a wanton woman who ruins a good man. Perhaps so; perhaps Lao She's novel simply reflects gender ideologies of its time. Xiao Fuzi is a prostitute with a heart of gold; Mrs. Xia is a slattern; and Hu Niu fits what publications of the period offered as the profile of the spinster who suffers from sexual frustration and a need for "invigorating male secretions" (Xiangzi is convinced that sex with Hu Niu saps his energy—a myth about the danger of female sexuality that circulated in the 1930s) (Dikötter 1995:47, 56). However, Hu Niu is too interesting to be so easily dismissed; she is also puzzling; we do not know, for example, why she has three wine cups prepared the night Xiangzi visits (for mysteries surrounding Hu Niu, see Wong 1995).

In the prodigality of her language, sex, and eating, Hu Niu is Xiangzi's opposite. He denies himself debilitating pleasures; she takes what sensual gratification she can. But neither Xiangzi's sober asceticism nor Hu Niu's exuberant licentiousness budges them from the course poverty dictates. The novel does not offer the irony that vice succeeds while virtue fails. He becomes degenerate; she dies. Readings of *Camel Xiangzi* that reproach Hu Niu for her behavior or ask whether Xiangzi can be forgiven for his theft of the camels fail to notice the novel disallows the comfort of such moralizing. The fictional world of *Camel Xiangzi* is amoral; there is no ground from which to rebuke Xiangzi and Hu Niu for their transgressions. Honesty, hard work, and chaste living get one nowhere, and appeal to a transcendent code of ethics is precluded: poverty and elemental desires render irrelevant such abstractions as love and honesty. Xiangzi learns this lesson from Hu Niu and sex. He does not want to want Hu Niu, but he does, which undermines his dream of success through self-discipline (Liu 1995:121). Xiangzi's desire for Hu Niu scares him because it is beyond his control, and his fear becomes loathing: "Hu Niu relied on her stinking X—to humiliate him!" (85). (Lao She unhappily deleted language that would offend censors [Lao She 1951:108]; James's translation restores it [Lao She 1979:85]). Xiangzi hates Hu Niu *because* he desires her. Hu Niu is deceitful, mean, foulmouthed, gluttonous, promiscuous, and a voyeur. On the other hand, by the logic of the novel, if virtue is its own reward, then virtue is meaningless, and Hu Niu is smart for realizing it. If we cannot judge Hu Niu, we can judge no one. Hu Niu functions to make as uncomfortable and therefore as powerful as possible *Camel Xiangzi's* despairing recognition that the conventional morality shared by author and reader—any reader, anywhere, anytime—

is precisely that: conventional, made up out of thin air. The moral indignation the narrator rouses is canceled by reluctant nihilism. This is the final tension.

Lao She was not typical of his generation of writers: he was from Beijing; he was Manchu; he was comfortable with the working class and popular art forms; his literary instinct was comic rather than Romantic; and until the war with Japan he was largely uninvolved with the left-wing artistic vanguard and its feuds. From 1924 to 1929, Lao She lived in London, taught Chinese at the School of Oriental Studies at the University of London, read Dickens, Conrad, and Hardy, helped Clemont Egerton translate *The Golden Lotus*, and wrote his first three novels. In the 1930s he taught literature at Cheeloo (Qilu) and Shandong Universities and wrote prolifically. From 1937 to 1945 he directed the All China League of Resistance Writers. After 1949 he continued to write and held posts in the cultural bureaucracy of the PRC. Lao She was attacked during the Cultural Revolution and, in circumstances that remain unclear, committed suicide by drowning during the night or early morning of August 24–25, 1966.

— Thomas Moran

Bibliography

Anderson, Marston. *The Limits of Realism: Chinese Fiction in the Revolutionary Period.* Berkeley: University of California Press, 1990.

Dikötter, Frank. *Sex, Culture and Modernity: Medical Science and the Construction of Sexual Identities in the Early Republican Period.* Honolulu: University of Hawai'i Press, 1995.

Gunn, Edward. *Rewriting Chinese: Style and Innovation in Twentieth-Century Chinese Prose.* Stanford: Stanford University Press, 1991.

Jameson, Fredric. "Literary Innovation and Modes of Production: A Commentary." *Modern Chinese Literature* 1, no. 1 (September 1984): 67–77.

Lao, She. "How I Came to Write the Novel *Camel Xiangzi*." *Camel Xiangzi*, 231–236. Trans. Xiaoqing Shi. Bloomington: Indiana University Press, 1981.

———. "Wo zenyang xie *Luotuo Xiangzi*" (How I Wrote *Camel Xiangzi*). *Lao She shenghuo yu chuangzuo zishu* (Lao She's Essays on His Life and Work), 65–71. Ed. Hu Jieqing. Hong Kong: Sanlian shudian, 1980.

———. *Luotuo Xiangzi* (Camel Xiangzi). Shanghai: Chenguang chuban gongsi, 1951.

———. "Renwu de miaoxie" (On the Description of Character). *Yuzhou feng* 28 (November 1936): 219–222.

———. *Rickshaw: The Novel Lo-t'o Hsiang Tzu.* Trans. Jean M. James. Honolulu: University of Hawai'i Press, 1979.

———. "Wo zenyang xie *Da ming hu*" (How I Wrote *Da Ming Lake*). *Lao She yanjiu ziliao* (Research Materials on Lao She), 1:541–543. Ed. Zeng Guangcan and Wu Huaibin. Beijing: Shiyue wenyi, 1985.

Liu, Heng. *Black Snow.* Trans. Howard Goldblatt. New York: Grove Press, 1993.

Liu, Lydia H. *Translingual Practice: Literature, National Culture, and Translated Modernity—China, 1900–1937.* Stanford: Stanford University Press, 1995.

Shi Chengjun. "Shilun jiefang hou Lao She dui *Luotuo Xiangzi* de xiugai" (Lao She's Revisions of *Camel Xiangzi* since Liberation). *Zhongguo xiandai wenxue yanjiu congkan* 4 (1980): 278–288.

Strand, David. *Rickshaw Beijing: City People and Politics in the 1920s.* Berkeley: University of California Press, 1989.

Wang, David Der-wei. *Fictional Realism in Twentieth-Century China: Mao Dun, Lao She, Shen Congwen.* New York: Columbia University Press, 1992.

Wang Runhua (Wong Yoon Wah). *Lao She xiaoshuo xinlun* (New Views on Lao She's Fiction). Taipei: Dongda tushu gongsi, 1995.

79

EILEEN CHANG

AND ALTERNATIVE WARTIME NARRATIVE

Eileen Chang (Zhang Ailing, 1920–1995) began her writing career in the early 1940s in the Japanese-occupied city of Shanghai and went on to become the most prominent author and public intellectual in the besieged city. Chang's reputation waned significantly after the war ended in 1945. Postwar cultural politics repeatedly scrutinized her connections with the collaborationist forces in the occupied territory. It became increasingly difficult for her to continue pursuing her writing career, a situation that only worsened after the Communist takeover in 1949. Chang eventually left the mainland for Hong Kong in 1952. Official literary histories produced in the following decades in the People's Republic of China made no mention of Chang and her work, mainly owing to the anticommunist stance of her early 1950s fiction, written in Hong Kong. In the late 1960s and early 1970s, literary scholars such as C.T. Hsia and Shui Jing reclaimed her significance and assigned her an unparalleled position in the canon of modern Chinese literature. Her works became popular again among readers in Taiwan, Hong Kong, and the Chinese diaspora communities. Only with the reexamination of literary history in the post-Mao era did a renewed Eileen Chang "fever" sweep through cities on the mainland. Pirated editions of her early fiction and essays flooded street vendors' stalls, a phenomenon that went hand in hand with a collective effort to uncover a cultural history of Shanghai from the prerevolutionary era and to redefine the city as a major metropolis on a new global map.

The rediscovery of Chang's fiction had an important impact on a host of writers in both Taiwan—where a group of young women writers formed an "Eileen Chang school" in the 1970s—and in the PRC in the 1980s and 1990s. The solitude of the latter half of Chang's life (after immigrating to the United States in the fall of 1955, she lived a reclusive life) forms a sharp contrast to the glory of the war years in Shanghai, when she was perhaps more famous than the most acclaimed movie actresses and popular singers. Like Greta Garbo, her reclusion only contributed to her being repeatedly fashioned into a mythical figure. The last decade of the twentieth century saw yet another wave of media coverage on both sides of the Pacific after Chang's quiet death in a West Los Angeles apartment in 1995.

Eileen Chang's writing is deeply imprinted with marks of her own time. Her best work was published during the first few years of her career—that is, between 1941 and 1945—and much of it was collected in two volumes, a collection of short stories and novellas entitled *Romances* (Chuanqi, 1944) and a book of prose entitled *Written on Water* (Liuyan, 1945). Her best-known short stories and novellas include *Romance from the Ruins* (Qingcheng zhi lian), *The Golden Cangue* (Jin suo ji), "Traces of Love" (Liu qing), "Blockade" (Fengsuo), "Red Rose and White Rose" (Hong meigui yu bai meigui), "Aloewood Ashes: The First Incense Brazier" (Chen xiang xie: di yi lu xiang), and "Aloewood Ashes: The Second Incense Brazier" (Chen xiang xie: di er lu xiang). By naming the story collection *Romances* (the Chinese title, *Chuanqi*, was used as a generic designation for short "accounts of marvels" during the Tang dynasty), Chang seems to suggest one way of reading her fiction: that is, as a modern appropriation and invocation of themes from China's literary past, themes that also recur in the urban popular fiction prominent in the 1920s and 1930s known as the *Mandarin Ducks and Butterflies school (yuanyang hudie pai).

Chang's most important literary legacy is the construction of an alternative wartime narrative, one that contradicted the grand narratives of national salvation and revolution that dominated the wartime literary scene. This narrative embraces a unique vision of modern history and depicts the shifting borders of a metropolis set against a backdrop of turmoil and ruins. In both her fiction and essays, Chang often turns history into a stage production, with her characters dressed in "costumes" embedded with symbolic meanings. Her impressionistic view of modern history highlights colors, lines, shapes, textures, and moods, which are often crystallized in the drastically changing styles of women's clothes. In the midst of an orchestra of city sounds and myriad colors and shapes, the reader observes a social gallery of figures roaming between the territory of historical reality (war, turbulence, blockade, hunger, death, and scarcity) and the domain of domesticity and private life (love, loss, fantasy, emotional yearning, and artistic creativity). Chang's choice of narrative style demonstrates her self-positioning—an entanglement between a personalized inward journey and a persistent, although not always explicit, attempt to come to terms with the immediate experience of the war.

"Blockade," a story written in August 1943, illustrates this unique sense of history and is typical of her wartime romances. The story depicts a brief encounter between a man (an office worker) and a woman (a college teacher) on a streetcar during an air raid, when the city comes to a standstill. The story concludes with an ironic twist: the brief "romance" draws to an abrupt end when the blockade ends and the streetcar moves again; both protagonists resume their original positions, and "everything that had happened while the city was sealed was a non-occurrence. The whole of Shanghai had dozed off, had dreamed an unreasonable dream" (1995:197).

Here the concept of "blockade" is a metaphor for a kind of confined time and space that is particular to the besieged city during wartime occupation; the story is therefore an allegory of life in wartime. As in other works by Chang, one senses the omnipresent threat of war—in the air raid and in other manifestations of modern warfare—but is also reminded that life goes on, like the two streetcar tracks "never ending, never ending" (188). The threat of massive destruction lurks in the background, but what is foregrounded is a preoccupation with the immediate present and the everyday. The interior of a streetcar caught in the middle of a citywide blockade conveniently provides the spatial and temporal frame for the reader to imagine what it is like to live in a war-torn city. But the story depicts war only in a metaphorical sense, functioning more as a literary device to create a sense of temporal and spatial isolation. Various borders and divisions that already cut across the cityscape are further sharpened because of the intrusion of war. Chang's narrative depicts individual experiences of war as an integral part of urban sensibilities.

In Chang's widely acclaimed novella *Romance from the Ruins*, written just one month after "Blockade," modern warfare intrudes into the central romance in a different fashion—it ironically completes the narrative. The protagonists travel back and forth between Hong Kong and Shanghai around the outbreak of the Pacific War and in the end conclude their romance in happy matrimony. *Romance from the Ruins* is Chang's most skillful and elaborate attempt at constructing an alternative wartime narrative. The title alludes to an ancient tale, in which the beauty of a woman is blamed for the collapse of a kingdom. Chang's modern tale shares with the ancient legend a sense that war and turbulence are always lurking in the background and will eventually emerge as a substantial force that transforms the individuals in question.

In the beginning of the novella, the female protagonist, Bai Liusu, a young widow who has returned to her parents' home, is at odds with her environment: "Liusu feels that she herself has become a character in a rhymed couplet, floating in the air. The Bai residence is somewhat like a cave dwelling of a supernatural being: one day in the house is equal to one thousand years in the outside world. But even if one thousand years did finally elapse inside the house, it would not be any different from the passing of one single day, for every day is as lusterless and gloomy as ever" (my translation). In Chang's descriptions, the Bai residence appears to be a mythical construction capable of endlessly reproducing itself. Generation after generation of women are subsequently absorbed into the background of this ghostly realm and doomed to repeat the same tragic fate over and over.

In *Romance from the Ruins* the mythical construction eventually falls apart, and it is Liusu, the female protagonist, who manages to turn the contemporary war and turbulence into a new stage for the enactment of a different kind of romance. As the story unfolds, Liusu encounters the male protagonist, Fan Liuyuan, a wealthy dandy from an overseas aristocratic family, decisively leaves the decaying Bai residence, and travels to Hong Kong according to Liuyuan's master plan. In Hong Kong, a city depicted as an exotic mirror image of Shanghai, Liusu gradually falls under the spell of Liuyuan's strategies of seduction. She would have continued to be Liuyuan's mistress if not for the outbreak of the war, which destroys the city but brings the two protagonists closer to each other: "As if in a dream, she arrives at the foot of the broken wall; toward her approaches Liuyuan. She finally meets Liuyuan.... In this turbulent world, nothing is reliable, money, property, or talk about everlasting love. The only dependable things are her own breath from inside her chest, and the man sleeping next to her" (my translation). The novella ends with another ironic twist: "The demise of Hong Kong completes her. In this inexplicable world, who can say for sure what is the cause and what is the effect? Who knows.... Perhaps a metropolis is toppled precisely for the sake of fulfilling her romance" (my translation).

In Chang's portrayal, the dark and gloomy city in ruins sets off the beauty and brilliance of the face, gestures, and voices of the female protagonist. In other words, it is only in the most tumultuous moments that women such as Bai Liusu are able to demonstrate their talents and personalities, something they would not be able to do during a peaceful era. In one of her essays from the same period, Chang states that "the more turbulent our era becomes, the more outstanding one's personality appears" and "distinctions between individuals are magnified" at these extraordinary moments. What makes Chang's textual strategies particularly important is the fact that this process of destabilizing the conventional mythical construction and recreating a new urban legend is located precisely in the very center of the social and political strictures resulting from the wartime occupation.

Through her fictional writing, Eileen Chang pieces together a unique aesthetic vision of life. Wartime chaos is turned into an extraordinary opportunity for the woman writer to initiate a new kind of cultural reconstruction. While turbulence on the social and political scale is accompanied by a constant negotiation between different cultural and intellectual forces, new forms of literature and arts could emerge from a shattered system of thoughts, beliefs, and aesthetic principles. The urgency to construct a new cultural realm goes hand in hand with a sheer sense of the impending destruction on a massive scale. Like her female characters, Chang's agency and creativity are highlighted against a historical moment that is conventionally characterized by themes of disruption, agitation, and transience. But unlike fellow writers of her time, Chang demonstrates no interest in composing a comprehensive account of war, resistance, or the awakening of individual consciousness. In her own words, "Liusu escapes from a corrupt family, yet the baptism by war in Hong Kong does not change her into a revolutionary woman" ("My Writing," 1944). Her wartime narrative tells how individuals go on living and resuming their daily routines despite the intrusion of war. Chang's alternative wartime narrative actively responds to the immediate reality and, more important, challenges the way that war, history, and individual lives have always been represented in the master narrative of her time.

—*Nicole Huang*

Bibliography

Chang, Eileen. *Chuanqi* (Romances). Shanghai: Zazhishe, 1944.
——. *The Golden Cangue.* Trans. Nathan Mao. In Joseph S. M. Lau, C. T. Hsia and Leo Ou-Fan, eds., *Modern Chinese Stories and Novellas, 1919–1949,* 530–559. New York: Columbia University Press, 1981.
——. *Liuyan* (Written on Water). Shanghai: Zhongguo kexue gongsi, 1945.
——. *Love in a Fallen City.* Trans. Karen Kingsbury. *Renditions* 45 (Spring 1996): 61–92.
——. "My Writing." Trans. Wendy Larson. In Kirk A. Denton, ed., *Modern Chinese Literary Thought: Writings on Literature, 1893–1945,* 436–442. Stanford: Stanford University Press, 1996.
——. "Sealed Off." Trans. Karen Kingsbury. In Joseph S. M. Lau and Howard Goldblatt, eds., *Columbia Anthology of Modern Chinese Literature,* 188–197. New York: Columbia University Press, 1995.
——. "Traces of Love." Trans. Eva Hung. *Renditions* 45 (Spring 1996): 112–127.
——. "Wo kan Su Qing" (The Way I See Su Qing). In *Yuyun* (Lingering Tunes), 75–96. Taipei: Crown Publishers, 1991.
Chow, Rey. "Modernity and Narration—in Feminine Detail." In *Woman and Chinese Modernity: The Politics of Reading between West and East,* 84–120. Minneapolis: University of Minnesota Press, 1991.
Lee, Leo Ou-fan. *Shanghai Modern: The Flowering of a New Urban Culture in China, 1930–1945.* Cambridge, Mass.: Harvard University Press, 1999.

80

LITERATURE AND POLITICS:
MAO ZEDONG'S "TALKS AT THE YAN'AN FORUM ON ART AND LITERATURE"

It may seem odd that Mao Zedong (1893–1976), head of the Chinese Communist Party (CCP), would give lectures on art and culture to cultural workers in Yan'an in the midst of the War of Resistance against Japan (1937–45) and an ongoing conflict with their erstwhile allies, the Nationalists or Guomindang (GMD). But just as Mao developed during the war major ideological writings that would become known as "Mao Zedong thought," he also felt a need to forge a cultural policy. The "Talks at the Yan'an Forum on Art and Literature (Yan'an wenyi zuotanhui de jianghua)," given in the spring of 1942, although not original or sophisticated literary theory, would become the theoretical basis for the rigid cultural policy implemented by the CCP after the revolution. It is as such among the most important texts in the cultural history of the People's Republic of China (PRC). Even today, in the freewheeling atmosphere of the PRC cultural market, their presence as a reminder of more oppressive times is keenly felt.

To understand the "Talks" it is important to know something of the history of their conception and dissemination. The early 1940s was a critical moment in CCP history. Party membership had increased dramatically since the war began, and most of these new recruits had little knowledge of Marxism. Although Mao had by this time begun to consolidate his control over the party leadership, he was not without opposition. Wang Ming and his supporters, who favored a more classically Marxist proletarian revolution over Mao's peasant focus and took a relatively conciliatory stance to the GMD, were still in Mao's way. Moreover, partly with Mao's encouragement, writers had begun to turn their pens to exposing problems in Yan'an. Ai Qing, Luo Feng, *Ding Ling, Wang Shiwei, and Xiao Jun wrote essays and stories that cast the CCP paradise in a negative light, depicting it as a place of darkness in which women were unequal to men, party members had special privileges, and intellectuals were given little creative freedom. Ding Ling's "Thoughts on March Eighth," for example, criticizes CCP patriarchal attitudes that existed beneath their rhetoric of official feminism; Wang Shiwei's "Statesmen and Artists" called for an independent and vital role for the intellectual, and his "Wild Lilies" attacked CCP privilege and its alienation from the people.

In this atmosphere, Mao saw a pressing need for ideological and political uniformity among party ranks and so, in early 1942, launched the Rectification Campaign, which set the pattern for most subsequent PRC campaigns against intellectuals: Mao calls for a liberalization in cultural matters, encouraging writers to voice their dissent; writers respond; the party-led media attacks the dissenting writers, who are then punished, typically by being sent to the countryside to engage in labor reform. Dissenting writers in particular had to be reined in with a clear party policy on art and literature. The "Talks" were thus part of the larger CCP program to "rectify" (*zhengfeng*) wayward intellectuals, to offer them guidelines for accepting the authority of the party and their subservient roles in the revolution. Those writers who had spoken up were criticized and punished by being sent to the countryside to engage in labor reform. Wang Shiwei, the focus of the campaign, was tried and kept under house arrest until 1947, when he was executed (Dai 1994).

The "Talks" were presented in two lectures as part of a larger conference on literature and art. The more dogmatic tenor of the conclusion, as compared with the introduction, may indicate that there was oppositional debate at the conference and that Mao saw a need to deepen his rationale for a political role for culture (McDougall 1980:14). Most scholars agree that the ideas expressed in the "Talks" are not original but rather are the crystallization of ideas that date back at least to the *Revolutionary Literature debate of the late 1920s. Mao's debt to Qu Qiubai, one of the first Chinese translators of Soviet literary theory and a former secretary of the CCP, is particularly strong. Through Qu, Mao was introduced to Soviet theory, particularly that of the Prolekult movement (formed after the 1917 revolution to create a purely proletarian culture void of bourgeois influence) and RAPP (All Russia Association of Proletarian Writers), founded in the 1920s to combat liberalism and absorb all cultural organizations under the banner of socialist realism.

The "Talks" were not published until October 1943. According to one scholar, the long delay in publication (more than a year) was a reflection of political debate within the party leadership about how far to take the Rectification Campaign (Kondo 1997:87). The "Talks" were republished in Chongqing (1944) as the Rectification Campaign extended into the Nationalist-controlled areas, becoming the textual authority in the attack on such independent leftists as Hu Feng and his ideas on literary subjectivity. In the postrevolutionary period the "Talks" quickly assumed a leading role in CCP cultural policy. They were referred to, for example, by Zhou Enlai in a July 1949 conference of representatives in literature and art. They were republished, with some revisions, in the 1953 four-volume *Selected Works of Mao Zedong* and thus became an essential part of the canonical Maoist corpus, required reading for all party officials and intellectuals. (See McDougall 1980 for a discussion of the differences between the two versions.) All the cultural campaigns of the 1950s and 1960s were accompanied by calls for writers and intellectuals to accept the absolute authority of the "Talks." As one of the signals of the launching of the Cultural Revolution, *Hongqi*, the official party organ, republished the "Talks" in its pages on July 1, 1966.

In the cultural liberalization of the post-Mao period, the "Talks" were the focus of heated debate. Many denounced them and saw an imperative for writers to get out from under the shackles of the politicized role for literature enshrined in them. Conservatives continued to appeal to the authority of the "Talks" even as they recognized that their dogmatic imposition on writers, especially during the Cultural Revolution, had seriously hindered literary creativity (Xia 1989). The "Talks" were blamed for a vacuous culture that eschewed the portrayal of complex characters, the themes of love and sexuality, difficult moral issues, and the depiction of real social problems in favor of a bright world of ideological simplicity. During the cultural crackdown of the early 1990s, following the violent suppression of the 1989 movement, the "Talks" were again invoked as conservative cultural figures attempted to restore socialist culture (Barmé 1999:27–28).

Mao's ideas are not nearly as dogmatic as they were later interpreted by CCP cultural czars who, often with Mao's blessing, implemented and enforced them. Although the subservient role for literature is clearly expressed, one is struck by Mao's balanced approach to, for example, the use of both Chinese and Western literary models, and to the question of literature's role as satirical exposure or ideological extolling; he never unequivocally denounces Western literary models, nor does he completely erase a critical role for literature. This tension in Mao's ideas on literature is reflected in the schizophrenic cultural policy implemented by the CCP after 1949, which wavered from relative freedom to strict control, shifts that were invariably justified by calling on the authority of Mao's "Talks."

In the introduction Mao tackles the central question of the class stand (*lichang*) of intellectuals. To write a literature in the interest of the laboring classes, writers, most of whom Mao recognized as coming from gentry or bourgeois families, had to embrace the class stand of the masses. This means, says Mao in an elitist leap that is typical of Leninists, accepting the will of the party that represents the masses. To embrace the class stand of the laboring masses, "the thoughts and feelings of our writers and artists should be fused with those of the masses of workers, peasants, and soldiers. To achieve this fusion, they should conscientiously learn the language of the masses.... If you want the masses to understand you, if you want to be one with the masses, you must make up your mind to undergo a long and even painful process of tempering" (Denton 1996:461–462). Mao then goes on to present a personal anecdote, describing how in his youth his elitist disdain for the dirty peasant class was gradually transformed into deep respect: "I came to feel that compared with the workers and the peasants the un-remolded intellectuals were not clean and that, in the final analysis, the workers and peasants were the cleanest people, and, even though their hands were soiled and their feet smeared with cow dung, they were really cleaner than the bourgeois and petit-bourgeois intellectuals" (462). In accepting that the bourgeois writer needed to change consciousness in order to create a revolutionary literature, Mao is very much in line with mainstream leftist literary criticism of the late 1920s and 1930s, which sought a union of intellectuals with the masses, a union that would gave voice to the unconscious desires of the masses and empower intellectuals with a historical dynamism.

In the conclusion Mao points to several negative examples of intellectuals who failed to accept the stand of the masses: Zhou Zuoren (*Lu Xun's younger brother, who at this time was working in the Ministry of Education in Japanese-occupied Beiping), Zhang Ziping (a leftist writer also seen as a traitor for accepting a post in the Japanese government in Shanghai), and Liang Shiqiu (a humanist essayist and translator who rejected the radicalism of his day and had often been criticized by Lu Xun). Liang in particular is shown to represent the humanist fallacy of a classless literature: in promoting a literature that depicts human nature, humanists like Liang actually contribute to the interests of the ruling minority over those of the oppressed majority. Instead, Mao urges, writers should self-consciously write for that majority, composed of workers, peasants, and soldiers.

Mao then looks at the question of literary form. On the one hand, he advises writers to raise literary standards and, on the other hand, to popularize their language and style so that it is accessible to the masses. He qualifies his remarks on raising artistic standards, which might be interpreted as favoring aesthetic formalism, to mean raising artistic standards "in the direction in which the masses are moving." He maintains the usefulness of traditional Chinese and progressive foreign models of literature (which are connected to the will of the people), but urges writers not to blindly adhere to form, but to "unreservedly and wholeheartedly go among the masses of workers, peasants, and soldiers, go into the heat of the struggle, go to the only source, the broadest and richest source, in order to observe, experience, study, and analyze all the different kinds of people, all the classes, all the masses, all the vivid patterns of life and struggle, all the raw materials of literature and art" (Denton 1996:470). But Mao is no empiricist favoring a "critical realist" literature; he also sees art in a highly romantic and revolutionary mode: "Life as reflected in works of literature and art can and ought to be on a higher plane, more intense, more concentrated, more typical, nearer the ideal and therefore more universal than actual everyday life." As such, art can and should "help the masses propel history forward" (470). Again, this synthesis of the empiricist with the subjectivist is typical of Mao, but was also something many literary critics who preceded him had attempted to do (Denton 1996:51–53).

In the next section Mao treats the essential question of the relationship between the Communist Party and the cultural worker. He shares Lenin's view that art is the "cogs and wheels" in the revolutionary machine: "Party work in literature and art occupies a definite and assigned position in Party revolutionary work as a whole and is subordinated to the revolutionary tasks set by the Party in a given revolutionary period" (474). Perhaps reflecting a traditional Chinese propensity for seeing culture's centrality to political life, but also trying pragmatically to enlist intellectuals' support for the revolution by assigning them an important role, Mao sees art "as an indispensable part of the entire revolutionary cause" (474).

Finally, after discussing the role of literary criticism in fusing political and aesthetic standards, Mao dissects and attacks views of literature commonly associated (although not explicitly by Mao) with the May Fourth literary tradition, particularly humanism and the role of literature in exposing the darkness of society. Mao is clearly trying to undermine the very notion of intellectual autonomy that the May Fourth generation of intellectuals, particularly Lu Xun, sought to uphold. Ironically, just as he attacks much of what Lu Xun held dear, at the very end of the "Talks" Mao raises him as a literary ideal in what is perhaps a willful misreading of Lu Xun's famous classical couplet: "Fierce-browed, I coolly defy a thousand pointing fingers, / Head-bowed, like a willing ox I serve the people." Mao interprets "pointing fingers" as the enemy and the children (*ruzi*) as the proletariat and the masses, while the ox are the revolutionary vanguard. In Mao's hands, the line demonstrates Lu Xun's willingness as a writer to serve the masses, whereas Lu Xun's intention was perhaps more along the lines of a defiance of the status quo.

The "Talks" are as much a legacy of the Chinese literary tradition as they are a product of Leninist influence or the CCP/Maoist desire for political and ideological hegemony. When seen in the context of Confucian literary didacticism (from the "Great Preface" of the *Book of Odes* to *Liang Qichao), Mao's view of a political/moral role for literature seems almost natural and normal. What is most obviously different between Confucian literary didacticism and Maoist literary politics is that Mao's ideas were implemented by a state apparatus far more powerful and interventionist than any seen before in Chinese history. Mao's ideas are also not as at odds with the May Fourth tradition as they have been made out to be. The May Fourth liberal-humanist mode has often been pitted against the Yan'an legacy of cultural dogmatism and the imposition of literary models, a struggle between May Fourth enlightenment values and those of national salvation and collectivism, the former succumbing inevitably to the latter. The importance Mao placed on culture as a tool in political transformation is also a legacy of traditional and May Fourth views of writing's power to transform values. *Wen* (culture) was traditionally viewed as the fabric of society, inseparable from moral-political values. The Song neo-Confucian philosopher Zhu Xi, for example, saw *wen* as arising out of the Dao, leaving no distinction between the two. In contrast to Zhou Dunyi's slogan "literature conveys the Way," which saw *wen* as a vehicle for the propagation of the Dao, Zhu wrote that "Dao is the root of culture, culture is the limbs and leaves of the Dao" (*Zhu Zi yulei*, vol. 139). Literary critics in the May Fourth movement sought to create for literature, now termed *wenxue*, an autonomous field separate from morality and politics. Yet even as they did this, they continued to ascribe to literature a key moral-political function. Mao inherited this traditional view via the May Fourth movement. In seeing literature as a "tool" of politics, Mao seems to share Zhou Dunyi's view that literature is a "vehicle" for the Way; yet Mao's view of the organic interrelationship of art and politics is more in line with Zhu Xi's position. Given this traditional legacy and the extreme exigencies of the war period, it is not particularly surprising that Mao would adhere to a rigidly political role for literature.

—Kirk A. Denton

Bibliography

Ai Ke'en. *Yanan wenyi yundong jisheng* (Record of the Rise of the Yan'an Literary Movement). Beijing: Wenhua yishu, 1987.

Apter, David, and Tony Saich. *Revolutionary Discourse in Mao's Republic*. Cambridge, Mass.: Harvard University Press, 1994.

Barmé, Geremie. *In the Red: On Contemporary Chinese Culture*. New York: Columbia University Press, 1999.

Cai Qingfu. "Zai Yan'an wenyi zuotanhui de jianghua zai Guomindang tongzhiqu de chuanbo" (The Dissemination of the Yan'an Talks in the Nationalist Areas). *Zhongguo xiandai wenxue yanjiu congkan* 1 (1980): 306–311.

Dai, Qing. *Wang Shiwei and "Wild Lilies": Rectification and Purges in the Chinese Communist Party, 1942–1944*. Armonk, N.Y.: M. E. Sharpe, 1994.

Denton, Kirk A., ed. *Modern Chinese Literary Thought: Writings on Literature, 1893–1945*. Stanford: Stanford University Press, 1996.

Kondo, Tatsuya. "The Transmission of the Yenan Talks to Chungking and Hu Feng: Caught between the Struggle for Democracy in the Great Rear Area and Maoism." *Acta Asiatica* 72 (1997): 81–105.

Li Xin. "Guanyu 'Yan'an wenyi zuotanhui' de zhaokai, 'Jianghua' de xiezuo, fabiao he canjia huiyi de ren" (On the Convening of the Yan'an Forum on Art and Literature, the Writing and Publication of the Talks, and the Participants of the Meeting). *Xin wenxue shiliao* 2 (1995): 203–210.

McDougall, Bonnie. *Mao Zedong's "Talks at the Yan'an Conference on Literature and Art": A Translation of the 1943 Text with Commentary.* Ann Arbor: University of Michigan Center for Chinese Studies, 1980.

Xia Zhongyi. "Lishi buke bihui" (History Cannot Be Evaded). *Wenxue pinglun* 4 (1989): 5–20.

81

REVOLUTIONARY REALISM AND REVOLUTIONARY ROMANTICISM: *THE SONG OF YOUTH*

To generalize a style of fiction from the period between the founding of the People's Republic of China (1949) and the beginning of the Cultural Revolution (1966–76), one may resort to the phrase "revolutionary romanticism combined with revolutionary realism," a phrase sometimes deemed equivalent to "socialist realism." The slogan was instituted in 1958 by Mao Zedong (1893–1976) during the 8th Party Congress as the guiding principle for artistic work (Wang Geding 1992:170). In that year, China was poised to make a "great leap forward," striving to catch up overnight with Great Britain and the United States in industrial, technological, and military power. The call for romanticism in literary production conforms to the utopian fervor of the time, but the combination of realism and romanticism was also the result of an extended controversy over the meaning of "socialist realism." Since 1949, writers, critics, and literary bureaucrats had argued back and forth about its "real" significance. One camp advocated an honest, down-to-earth immersion in everyday life and free depiction of any aspect of social and psychic realities. Hu Feng was one of the most important champions of this earthy realism (Denton 1998:153–154). The other side, mostly Communist Party bureaucrats and ideologues, asserted that only party policy and socialist ideology could inform and shape literary images of reality. After Hu Feng was persecuted for his views in 1955, the doctrinaire camp got the upper hand. But with the advent of the *Hundred Flowers campaign (1956–57) to promote more imaginative and critical works, the issue was reopened. Unorthodox views, such as those of Qin Zhaoyang, reappeared, only to be smothered with the consolidation of doctrinaire views in the Anti-Rightist Campaign (1957) and the elevation of romanticism in the Great Leap Forward (1958).

To understand what revolutionary romanticism and revolutionary realism mean, we need to know what they are not in light of the usual range of meanings conventionally associated with romanticism and realism. Revolutionary realism names a style of writing very different from the nineteenth-century realism of Balzac, Eliot, or Flaubert; it is not keen on depicting the vicissitudes of quotidian life lived out by average, individual men and women. Whereas the Balzac-influenced realist gives the illusion that fictional scenes mirror the contemporary life of common readers (Abrams 1981:153), revolutionary realism aims at something much "higher." This leads us to the other side of the coin: revolutionary romanticism. Unlike European romanticism, Chinese revolutionary romanticism does not favor individual originality, unbounded creativity, and the spontaneous overflow of feelings and emotion. It may deploy these elements, surely, but it does not give them a central place; nor does it set the life of the imagination and poetry against rationality and convention. Indeed, this literary mode should be understood in terms of the interaction of its two component parts.

Revolutionary realism becomes intelligible in terms of a Marxist interpretation of history and its related notion of reality. This interpretation sees history as obeying a preconceived motive that propels society from the lower stages of feudalism and capitalism to the higher stages of socialism and communism. The driving force of this social advance is class struggle, and the final victor is the emergent class. The Chinese revolution is but a local case of this universal goal-directed historical movement. As shown, *The Song of Youth* (Qingchun zhi ge, 1958), a novel by Yang Mo (b. 1914), history with real substance means the crisis of the Chinese nation: the struggle against the Japanese occupation and the constant political realliances along class lines. These are the specified contents of China's reality grounded in Marxist historical materialism. Whoever participates in this historical current comes in touch with reality; whoever deviates from it will be swept into the dustbin of history. Coupled with this view of reality is the imperative to transform older modes of ideas and feelings in order to fashion members of a new society. Understanding the law of history, on one hand, and constantly transforming traditional mentality and habits *(ziwo gaizao)*, on the other hand, become the hallmark of fictional realism (Zhang 1997:52).

Revolutionary realism therefore has more to do with an abstract worldview than with literary techniques for representing nitty-gritty details of human experience. This worldview is an ideal, and revolutionary romanticism is a literary and fictional idealization of that ideal. At the bidding of this Marxist telos of history, revolutionary romanticism aims to transcend empirical reality in the very act of representing it. One of Mao's remarks in the *"Yanan Talks" best illustrates this paradox. Literature and art, Mao says, should draw on revolutionary practice and be realistic, but at the same time they should be "more intense, more concentrated, more typical, nearer the ideal and therefore more universal than actual everyday life" (Mao 1967:266). Revolutionary romanticism is not marked by the whims of authorial imagination, but it does possess an imaginative license that allows it to keep pace with goal-oriented history. It can exaggerate, elevate, emotionalize, and intensify; it creates mythical, heroic, and larger-than-life characters.

The Song of Youth may be regarded as the exemplar of fictional works in the mode of revolutionary realism and romanticism. By no accident, the novel was published in 1958, when revolutionary realism and romanticism became the official guideline for artistic creation. Other novels of this period, such as *Red Crag* (Hong yan), *The Saga of Red Flag* (Hongqi pu), or *Three Family Alley* (San jia xiang), also belong to this mode, but *The Song of Youth* more clearly traces the individual's coming of age in the revolutionary movement, thus illustrating the dual themes of history and of self-transformation.

The Song of Youth follows the growth of the main protagonist Lin Daojing from a lonely and romantic young woman into a mature revolutionary. The narrative of her personal growth in the bildungsroman mode (Meng 1993:126) can be read as an allegory of the nationalist project of saving an endangered China and transforming it into a strong, modern nation. The story is set from 1930 to 1935, a time of deepening national crisis that saw Japan's gradual occupation of northeastern China, concessions made by the Nationalist government, and the constant irruption of patriotic protests among the urban population. Like many of her generation, Lin's urgent problem is to find a way out of both personal and national desperation. That way out is found in being guided into the revolutionary ranks and becoming a participant in history.

In the first part of the novel, Lin is out of touch with this "real" history in the making. She escapes her stepmother's scheme to sell her as a mistress to a powerful official, but this spontaneous act of rebellion only lands her in further trouble. She finds herself stranded in a seashore village, with no human relation to turn to. Yu Yongze, a student at Beijing University who becomes her first lover, saves her from a suicide attempt. Between them they form an emotional haven, spending their time in romantic musings nourished by the poetry of Heine and Goethe. Their romance exemplifies the individualistic desire for self-fulfillment characteristic of the May Fourth generation, which favored Western romantic literature. This desire turns out to be far too individualistic, trivial, and "petit bourgeois" when Lin Daojing later comes into contact with Lu Jiachuan, a student leader and underground party member. Lu, and later Lin Hong and Jiang Hua, are "true" characters at the vanguard of history. With their heroic deeds and self-sacrifice, they envision, write, and act out the real "romance" of Chinese revolution. In contrast, Lin's lover Yu Yongze is a self-centered, mediocre, trivial individual who preoccupies himself only with personal survival and is totally unconcerned with the nation's destiny. History and politics—the stark re-

ality of national salvation—become a dividing line that demarcates good characters from the bad, the progressive from the retrogressive, the youthful from
the prematurely aged. In her life trajectory, Lin Daojing encounters a spectrum
of these characters and values. Her bildungsroman is an ascent from a weak and
wavering "bourgeois" individual into a firm revolutionary fighter. In the beginning of the novel, Lin is both physically and mentally homeless and fragile. She
is helpless, and abandoned in the wilderness. In utter despair, she contemplates
suicide. In the closing scenes, by contrast, she emerges as a leader in the 1935
student protest against government pacifism in the face of Japanese encroachment. She is now a powerful figure that "merges into many other selves, forming a gigantic collective, which grants her identity, gives her life and meaning,
and secures her emotional attachment and fulfillment. The collective seems to
enable her to exercise to the full her energy and to fulfill her desire" (Wang Ban
1997:130).

Lin's story shows how crucial it is to get involved in history and how one can,
in the process, transform oneself into the "subject of history." This is what is
meant by realism in the Chinese socialist context. The romantic component of
revolutionary realism is much less obvious. In spite of the stark and painful reality of class and national struggle, one is struck by the exuberance of emotion
and passion that the positive characters display. A character like Lu Jiachuan is
passionate as well as charming, youthful, and energetic. He falls in love with
Lin Daojing at first sight. His bombastic slogans and histrionic gestures may
make for bad art, but this theatricality only shows how important it is to elevate
and dramatize, and to inject transcendence and romance into a sordid reality
and a dogmatic character.

The romantic impulse—love, affection, poetry, passion, and imagination—
is not opposed to national or class politics; it gets intertwined with them. We
may characterize this process as sublimation, a psychic and literary process of
rechanneling one's desire, impulse, and affection into politically acceptable
outlets. To put it more plainly, in revolutionary romanticism an individual can
love politics as passionately and intensely as she loves another human being,
sometimes even more fanatically.

The Song of Youth is a textbook case of this romantic sublimation. Lin
Daojing's life starts like those of many female characters in May Fourth fiction:
she breaks away from the patriarchal family, seeks personal freedom, and falls in
love, only to find herself economically dependent and psychologically disori-
ented when she finally marries and becomes a housewife. Lin's predicament is
that diagnosed by *Lu Xun (1881–1936) in his celebrated essay "What Is Nora to
Do after She Leaves Home," which makes reference to Ibsen's play *A Doll's
House* and the fate of many self-emancipated Chinese Noras. As Lin lives with
Yu Yongzhe and busies herself with household chores, her romantic fervor
lapses into domestic trivia. On New Year's Eve, when she joins the patriotic students and hears Lu Jiachuan's inspiring talk, the encounter is nothing less than

a turning point in her life: not just a political awakening, but also a rekindling of romantic love for a really lovable person. A jealous Yu rightly senses in her sparkling eyes a person newly in love (Yang 1964:115). Lin is in love with the revolution as much as she is with the gallant, inspirational, and devoted revolutionary, Lu Jiachuan.

From this point on, Lin encounters other exemplary figures—including Jiang Hua, a sober-minded underground party member, and Lin Hong, a female party member and Lin's prison cellmate—who serve as signposts on her life's journey. Her growth is thus one of education, of political involvement and experience, and of consciousness-raising; it culminates in her joining the party and becoming a political activist. This political growth should not obscure the romantic undercurrent that is always present in her relationship with male revolutionaries. She not only identifies with these political figures but also becomes emotionally attached to them. In other words, her libidinal impulse is gradually purified of its private and primal stratum and becomes "sublimated" into "higher" objects of affection.

It is important to remember this libidinal stratum is not sublimated out of existence. It is not repressed for the sake of revolution, but appears in a different form. Lin's attachment to male revolutionary figures is still couched in the name of love, even romantic love. Her love for Lu Jiachuan illustrates this "purer" form of love. When Lu is arrested and Lin is unsure if he has been executed, she writes a love poem to him (424), gazing imaginatively at his image and awaiting him with heartfelt passion. Political identification and love become one. This sublimated desire can sustain itself without the presence of a real person; it readily dotes on a distant and abstract object, including a dead person, allowing it to be easily transferred. How she comes to love Jiang Hua illustrates this point. Jiang Hua is clearly a "substitute" for Lu Jiachuan. At first, Jiang is just a comrade and friend (although he is secretly in love with her), but Lin gradually discovers that he and Lu have the same admirable qualities. This political affinity increases Jiang's lovability. Toward the end of the novel, Jiang Hua asks if they could be "more to each other than comrades" (548). Lin is overwhelmed by his expression of love, but the image of Lu intervenes and makes her hesitate. Yet this momentary hesitation quickly gives way to a new thought and new love for Jiang, because she realizes how alike they all are—Lu Jiachuan, Lin Hong, and Jiang Hua.

Lin Daojing's "love affair" with revolutionary male figures may be seen as an allegory of romanticism married with realism. Revolutionary realism signifies the direction of history, the destiny of the nation, and the political and class identity of positive characters. Yet realistic portrayal of history can have emotional appeal, even sensual attraction, only when it is written as a "romantic" love story of a pretty young woman. If the reader believes that one can love one's nation and comrades as one loves one's beloved, then he or she is well prepared to accept and appreciate the marriage between revolutionary realism and revolutionary romanticism.

—*Ban Wang*

Bibliography

Abrams, M.H. *A Glossary of Literary Terms.* 4th ed. New York: Holt, Rinehart and Winston, 1981.

Denton, Kirk A. *The Problematic of Self in Modern Chinese Literature: Hu Feng and Lu Ling.* Stanford: Stanford University Press, 1998.

Mao Zedong. *Selected Readings from the Works of Mao Tse-tung.* Beijing: Foreign Language Press, 1967.

Meng, Yue. "Female Images and National Myth." In Tani E. Barlow, ed., *Gender Politics in Modern China: Writing and Feminism,* 118–136. Durham, N.C.: Duke University Press, 1993.

Wang, Ban. *The Sublime Figure of History: Aesthetics and Politics in Twentieth-Century China.* Stanford: Stanford University Press, 1997.

Wang Geding and Chen Shijing, eds. *Lishi yu meixue de xuanzhe* (Judgments of History and Aesthetics). Nanjing: Guangxi jiaoyu, 1992.

Yang Mo. *Qinchun zhi ge* (Song of Youth). Beijing: Shiyue wenyi, 1992.

———. *The Song of Youth.* Beijing: Foreign Language Press, 1964.

Zhang Dexiang. *Xianshi zhuyi dangdai liubian shi* (Contemporary History of the Changing Faces of Realism). Beijing: Shehui kexue wenxian, 1997.

82

THE HUNDRED FLOWERS

The twin slogans "let a hundred flowers bloom, let a hundred schools of thought contend" *(bai hua qi fang, bai jia zhengming)* were introduced by Communist Party chairman Mao Zedong in May 1956. The call for a "hundred flowers" was designed to inspire greater variety in the arts, and the "hundred schools" to encourage initiative and expertise, particularly on the part of scientists. This appeal by Mao to the nation's intellectuals, articulated on his behalf by propaganda minister Lu Dingyi, prompted vigorous debates over Communist Party policies in the arts and led to a brief outburst of literary works portraying a system of government that was autocratic and inefficient. The party's tolerance of such criticism was short-lived: following publication in June 1957 of a revised edition of Mao's "On the Correct Handling of Contradictions among the People" (Guanyu zhengque chuli renmin neibu maodun de wenti), a speech given in February of that year, the dissenting intellectuals were condemned as "anti-Party," "revisionists," and "rightists" in the subsequent Anti-Rightist Campaign.

The decision to call for the blooming of a hundred flowers (a slogan that referred back to the Warring States period more than two thousand years earlier) was motivated by a combination of domestic realities and developments elsewhere in the Communist bloc, most notably the Soviet Union. At home, the transformation of agriculture and industry from private to public ownership was virtually complete, and the leadership was contemplating a second five-year plan and looking to the intellectuals, hitherto often reluctant partners in building socialism, for technical support and cultural enrichment. In the Soviet Union, the death of Stalin in 1953 was followed by an ideological "thaw" (a term borrowed from the title of a novella by Ilya Ehrenberg) characterized by condemnation of the personality cult that had surrounded Stalin, and by a relaxation of the party's demand for absolute adherence on the part of artists to the whims of their political masters. Russian writers in the "thaw" years who influenced the Chinese Hundred Flowers included Valentin Ovechkin, creator of investigative reports on official malfeasance, and Galina Nikolaeva, author of *The Director of the MTS and the Chief Agronomist.* In Nikolaeva's novella, the newly appointed young female agronomist is an inspirational model, working with local activists to achieve higher production in a poor collective, despite technical and organizational obstacles. Elsewhere in Eastern Europe, worker unrest in Poland and a Hungarian leadership proposing to secede from the Warsaw Pact showed the cracks that existed in post-Stalin international Communist solidarity.

In China, much of the liveliest debate on the role of the arts in society, and many of the reports and stories most critical of officialdom, appeared in the pages of the journal *People's Literature* (Renmin wenxue), where they were published by the newly appointed associate editor Qin Zhaoyang. Qin, who was forty in 1956, had impeccable revolutionary credentials: he came from an impoverished intellectual background, studied at the Lu Xun Academy in Yan'an, and began his career as editor and writer of fiction in the Communist-liberated areas. After 1949, in addition to holding editorial posts, he published short stories and a novel. Qin was no liberal dissident: his mission was to cultivate the hundred flowers required by the Party leadership, and in pursuit of this goal he argued for greater scope for authors to write truthfully about problems in society rather than being bound by party-imposed idealism. In the September 1956 issue of *People's Literature*, Qin Zhaoyang published what may be regarded as the manifesto of the Hundred Flowers literary reformers, his own article "The Broad Road of Realism" (Xianshizhuyi—guangkuo de daolu). In it he argued that the doctrine of socialist realism inherited from Stalin's Russia mandated slavish adherence to ephemeral party policies and stifled artistic creativity, resulting in formulaic and mediocre works. Qin advocated instead a new "realism of the socialist age" that would better reflect the complexities of society in transition.

Literary works published in *People's Literature* took Qin's "broad road" of critical realism; they included stories of young and energetic intellectuals frustrated in their attempts to bring about much-needed change by their craven and bureaucratic superiors. Most celebrated at the time, and most notorious in the antirightist backlash, were the works of the young writers Liu Binyan and Wang Meng; despite later accusations that they had formed a clique with Qin Zhaoyang, these were young authors whose connection to Qin was intellectual rather than personal. Liu Binyan, an admirer of Ovechkin who had met and interviewed the Russian author, contributed the investigative report "At the

Bridge Construction Site" (Zai qiaoliang gongdi shang) to the April 1956 issue of *People's Literature*, prefaced by an editorial note from Qin Zhaoyang calling for more such "pointed, critical, and satirical" works. In this report, an engineer attempts to speed up the construction of a bridge before rising water levels on the Yellow River halt work for the season. His plan is in the national interest, and the workers support him, but an incompetent local management denounces him for rashness, prevents his proposal from reaching the higher leadership, and waits for directives from above before making even the most trivial decisions; the journalist reporting the case can only lament such conservatism and the effect it will have on the achievement of state goals.

A frustrated journalist is also the focus of Liu Binyan's short story "Our Paper's Inside News" (Benbao neibu xiaoxi), published in the June 1956 issue of *People's Literature*, with a sequel appearing in the October issue. The story's young heroine is on assignment at a mine where skilled personnel are underemployed by a management unwilling to share them with other units. She supports the mineworkers' protests against insufficient work and excessive meetings, only to be summoned back to her paper, where her report is suppressed and she is told that her application for party membership will be successful only if she is compliant and makes no trouble for her superiors. The heroine is idealistic about the power of journalism to agitate for change; the editors are content merely to publish official pronouncements of no interest to the readership, consoling themselves that they are following the party's lead. Liu Binyan satirizes the working of the bureaucratic mind in the thoughts of the heroine's boy friend and colleague: "Leadership, organization, and discipline are the main things ... even if you overdo them a bit, you can't go too far wrong."

Wang Meng's story "The Young Newcomer in the Organization Department" (Zuzhibu xin lai de qingnian ren), which was published in the same issue of *People's Literature* as Qin's "broad road" essay, repeats the theme of youthful idealism suppressed. Here the young newcomer, inspired by Galina Nikolaeva's novella (a copy of which he carries in his pocket), seeks to clean up the party organization at a mismanaged factory. He is supported by a female colleague with whom he listens to Russian music and enjoys an innocent friendship, but his superiors, men made jaded and cynical by their years in the system, invent facts and couch them in officialese to assure the authorities that nothing drastic needs to be done. Wang Meng's conclusion is more optimistic than Liu Binyan's—even though his initiatives are stifled, the young newcomer remains determined to bring about change for the better.

To these stories, Qin Zhaoyang added a short one of his own in January 1957. "Silence" (Chenmo) tells of the wife of an official who objects when a line of carts is led by the slowest, with carts behind forbidden by the local district head to pass; she encourages the other carters to pull ahead. The district head is tyrannical toward the carters, shouting at those who have disobeyed his orders, and is abusive toward the woman when she protests. He changes his tune only when he finds that her husband outranks him; then he too is silenced. Qin's allegory is clear: Chinese society will develop at a snail's pace as long as officials jealous of their power thwart the initiative of those who want to bring about improvement.

The authors of these works were exercising an autonomy that had not been evident under the rule of the Communist Party since the writings of the novelist *Ding Ling, the poet Ai Qing, and others in Yan'an in the early 1940s. Rather than accept Lenin's formulation (repeated by Mao in his *"Yan'an Talks") that literature was "a cog and a screw," a small component in the machinery of revolution, Qin Zhaoyang and the writers he published were giving themselves a less subservient role, characterized by Liu Binyan in his writing about Ovechkin as that of an army scout, acting independently to inform his commanders of the real situation in the field.

Complaints about the system in literary works were echoed in articles by academic, scientific, and professional intellectuals, especially after the party launched the brief Rectification Campaign to correct the bureaucratic practices of officials. The criticism was clearly more virulent than the party had expected, and the backlash was not long in coming. Those who had responded to Mao's appeal and voiced their objections found themselves denounced in the Anti-Rightist Campaign that began in the summer of 1957; by the time the campaign ended, half a million had been condemned. Many of China's most prominent scholars were denounced, along with well-known writers such as Ding Ling and Ai Qing—in the latter cases, as much for their writings at Yan'an fifteen years before as for any offences committed during the Hundred Flowers period.

In the June 1957 revised version of his "Correct Handling" speech, Mao gave his ruling on the distinction between the "fragrant flowers" of socialist art and "poisonous weeds" of the kind Qin Zhaoyang had cultivated, emphasizing that the arts should benefit socialism and strengthen the leadership of the Communist Party. Mao left the final word on the Hundred Flowers to Zhou Yang, the official charged with overseeing culture: in February 1958, Zhou likened the "rightists" to those who had incited the Hungarian uprising against the Soviet Union (the suppression of which the Chinese government approved); Zhou also confirmed the party's commitment to the loyalist optimism of socialist realism.

Qin Zhaoyang was denounced at a meeting in the offices of *People's Literature*, and dismissed from his editorial post; his Communist Party membership was also revoked. Qin, Liu Binyan, Wang Meng, and many other condemned "rightists" were ostracized and banished to the countryside for two decades. They were to return to Beijing in the post-Mao rehabilitations, vindicated and remarkably unreconstructed by two decades of ideological remolding, to play their part in the second "Hundred Flowers" in the late 1970s.

—*Richard King*

Bibliography

Barmé, Geremie, and Bennett Lee, eds. *Fragrant Weeds: Chinese Short Stories Once Labelled As "Poisonous Weeds."* Hong Kong: Joint Publishing, 1983.

Børdhal, Vibeke. *Along the Broad Path of Realism: Qin Zhaoyang's World of Fiction.* London: Curzon Press, 1990.

Fokkema, D. W. *Literary Doctrine in China and Soviet Influence, 1956–1960.* The Hague: Mouton, 1965.

Goldman, Merle. *Literary Dissent in Communist China.* Cambridge, Mass.: Harvard University Press, 1967.

Nieh, Hua-ling, ed. *Literature of the Hundred Flowers.* 2 vols. New York: Columbia University Press, 1981.

Wagner, Rudolf G. "The Cog and the Scout: Functional Concepts of Literature in Socialist Political Culture—The Chinese Debate in the Mid-Fifties." In Wolfgang Kubin and Rudolf G. Wagner, eds., *Essays in Modern Chinese Literature and Literary Criticism*, 334–400. Bochum: Brockmeyer, 1982.

83

THE TAIWAN MODERNISTS

Owing to translations, close relationships with the American academy, and the high quality of their work, the fiction of the Taiwan Modernists is some of the best known of modern Chinese literature to English-speaking audiences. The Modernists emerged through a critical engagement with more ideologically motivated literature, for fiction writing in the immediate postwar period in Taiwan was dominated by lengthy historical romances laden with anticommunist political rhetoric. Wang Lan's (b. 1922) popular novel *The Blue and the Black* (Lan yu hei, 1958) typifies this period, while Peng Ge's (b. 1926) *Setting Moon* (Luo yue, 1956) functions as a transition to modernism in Taiwan. Superficially, *The Blue and the Black* is pulp romance. It features Zhang Xingya, whose affections waver between a patriotic young nurse and the temperamental daughter of a Sichuan warlord. The predicament of a youth torn between two women of different temperaments is at least as old as *The Dream of the Red Chamber* and was replayed again in *Mandarin Ducks and Butterflies fiction and the "love and revolution" model of leftist writers such as *Mao Dun. Wang Lan follows this latter model, but for him there is no dispute as to the hero's alliance—he is firmly entrenched in the Nationalist camp. Thus, more profoundly, *The Blue and the Black* is a politically charged narrative, first depicting the Japanese invasion and then the Communist takeover, seeking to legitimate the Nationalist position along the way. From Tianjin, the novel wends its way to Chongqing and eventually Taiwan, recounting the story of the mainlanders' flight to Taiwan in 1949. Xingya engages in armed combat with both the Japanese and the

Eighth Route Army. Staunchly anticommunist, this work occasionally even paints the Japanese soldiers somewhat sympathetically, while the Communists are portrayed as sinister, soulless traitors to the Nationalist cause.

The slightly less ideological *Setting Moon* shares this loose narrative style. Although it also involves idealistic youths dedicated to the Resistance, it is foremost a romantic story of the heroine, Yu Xinmei. In his mainly stylistic analysis of the novel, T.A. Hsia (1916–1965) almost single-handedly shifted the intellectual discourse in Taiwan from political ideology to literary form. *Literary Review* (Wenxue zazhi), where the article was published, served as a transitional venue between the two poles of ideologically informed historical romanticism and the more intricately wrought, less tendentious works of the *Modern Literature* (Xiandai wenxue) group, established in 1960.

Modern Literature was founded by Hsia's Taiwan University undergraduates, the most notable fiction writers of whom were Bai Xianyong (b. 1937), Wang Wenxing (b. 1939), and Chen Ruoxi (b. 1938). They self-consciously adopted modernism from the dominant literary trends of Western Europe and the United States. Stylistically, they experimented with allegory, stream of consciousness, allusion, and alliterative description; thematically, with the emergence of individualism and breakdown in relational forms of subjectivity, such as traditional filiality and the collective identity of Communism. The emphasis on style over ideology is evident even in the juvenilia of these three writers.

In his early works, Bai Xianyong used stream of consciousness in short stories such as "Hong Kong—1960" (Xianggang—1960; 1963), and often depicted inexplicable suicides, such as that of a dejected youth in "Death in Chicago" (Zhijiage zhi si, 1964). His "New Yorker" series focuses on Chinese suffering from alienation after relocating to the United States. *Wandering in the Garden, Waking from a Dream* (Taibei ren, 1973), perhaps his most beloved work, is a collection of short stories, each portraying a different member of the "lost generation" of mainlanders who fled to Taiwan after the revolution. In contrast to the 1950s generation, whose fiction consists of reciting their mainland experiences, the characters in *Wandering* are haunted by apparitions of the past. The stories are not structured as historical romance but as vignettes that highlight exquisitely mellifluous language and delicate yet complex psychological portraits. Though sympathetically rendered, the characters are seldom viewed as exemplars of the Nationalist cause.

Wandering begins with "The Eternal Snow Beauty" (Yongyuande yin xueyan, 1965), in which mainland exiles attempt to reconstruct their lives in Taipei, even if only in an imaginary way. The use of interior space to evoke claustrophobia reminds one of *Eileen Chang's style, without the contemptuous tone. The protagonists of *Wandering* appear as small islands disconnected from each other, yet when connected in the mind of the reader their stories form a larger narrative of exile among these mainland refugees. Another one of the small islands is Taipan Jin, formerly a taxi dancer on the mainland. "The

Last Night of Taipan Jin" (Jin Daban de zuihou yiye, 1967) commingles moments from the present with recollections of the past. However, unlike the historical narratives of the 1950s, Bai Xianyong's more modernist approach avoids direct narrative, instead blending in recollections by way of interior monologue. He deploys supporting characters that enhance these reminiscences, as the two men, Jin's Shanghai lover Moon Boy and Phoenix's Cantonese fling, serve as foils that illustrate the changes in Taipan Jin's attitude toward life with the passage of time. The predicament of the isolated émigré seeking refuge in historical imagination also gives rise to moments of poetic commentary. The reminiscence affords Taipan Jin's otherwise hardened character a soft pathos, contrasting her present unromantic view of men with her youthful naiveté. Such a pathos is found in "Winter Nights" (Dongye, 1970) as well, wherein two original members of the May Fourth movement, one a specialist on Byron, the other an ancient Chinese history professor at Berkeley, find themselves marginalized fifty years later. Mixed in with the story are lyrical descriptions of the decrepit home, the ailing physical condition of the characters, and the incessant rain of the Taipei winter—each a memento of Wasteland imagery, echoing the disillusioned tone of Bai's modernist master T.S. Eliot.

The most sophisticated work in *Wandering* is the title story, "Wandering in the Garden, Waking from a Dream" (Youyuan jingmeng, 1965). The heroine, Madame Qian, has come to a party from southern Taiwan, a double exile, first from her home in mainland China and second from her fellow mainlanders in Taipei. The story's drama hinges on the reemergence of her repressed memory during the course of the party in the form of one of the finest examples of stream-of-consciousness in Chinese. Madame Qian's reverie is quilted together with allusions to *The Dream of the Red Chamber*, *The Peony Pavilion*, Cao Zhi's "The Goddess of Lo River," and Li Shangyin's "Brocade Zither." The intended effect cannot be appreciated without conversance with the literary tradition, which suggests that Bai is inscribing his work into that tradition as a means to resolve textually his political and cultural marginality. Bai Xianyong's later fiction includes the long novel *Crystal Boys* (Niezi, 1983), which extends the theme of exile to the social issue of homosexuality in Taiwan (see "Same-Sex Love in Recent Chinese Literature").

Wang Wenxing's novels *Family Catastrophe* (Jiabian, 1973) and *Backed against the Sea* (Beihaide ren, 1981 and 1999) are more concerned with cultural critique than Bai Xianyong's fiction; a cacophony of subversive linguistic experimentation, his works challenge the reader much more than Bai's relatively euphonic style. Wang Wenxing embraces and even accentuates his marginal status. His iconoclasm and avant-garde sensibility is demonstrated by his enthusiastic efforts to publish translations of many European modernists in *Modern Literature*, which he edited with Bai Xianyong, Chen Ruoxi, and others. Wang's early stories are often accounts of eccentric young boys. In "Flaw" (Qianque, 1964), the young first-person narrator falls for a beautiful neighbor woman and is able to temper it only by focusing on her flaws. The story ends ironically when she swindles all the neighbors, absconds with their money, and turns out indeed to be tragically flawed.

Family Catastrophe, Wang Wenxing's first novel, is one of the most uniquely structured novels in any language, composed of a bifurcated narrative with one part ordered alphabetically from A to O and the other numerically from 1 to 157. Focusing on the Fan family, the novel begins in the alphabetical narrative, with the flight of the family patriarch Fan Minxian from the home and the discovery that he is missing by his wife and the main character, son Fan Ye, who then spends the rest of the alphabetical narrative searching for his father. The alternating numerical narrative recounts the family history from when the toddler Fan Ye begins reading to the present. The narratives converge at the end of the book when Fan Ye abandons his search and concedes that his father is gone for good. The two narrative modes are characterized by antithetical tones: the numerical one a rejection of filiality; the alphabetical one conciliatory and contrite. Together, the two narratives form a "split" psyche, a subjectivity divided against itself. The unfolding of the narrative seems like a futile attempt to suture the insurmountable fissure between a Western individual subject position on one hand and the more relational, respectful, and submissive subject position of filiality on the other. The double narrative also undermines any attempt to establish a stable, univocal reading of *Family Catastrophe*. It neither positions itself against the tradition nor endorses the resurgence of filiality. Although the family saga parallels the postwar flight from mainland China, the incorporation of history is effected obliquely. Direct references to history, such as the family's voyage to Taiwan in the bottom of a fishing vessel, are inserted almost parenthetically.

Backed against the Sea, Wang's subsequent novel, extends the linguistic and structural experimentation of *Family Catastrophe*, heightening the ambivalent tone exhibited in the earlier work. However, in contrast to the first novel, *Backed against the Sea* is a narrative of near pure isolation, featuring Lone Star, the one-eyed, blathering soothsayer, on the lam from the police and in hiding from Taipei gangsters. His comical persona makes this work more playful and humorous, and while the themes dredged up—fate and fortune telling, the Chinese political bureaucracy, and prostitution—are all standard themes in Chinese literature, the bantering tone of the narrator foils attempts to discern whether Wang Wenxing employs Lone Star to satirize these institutions and rituals or whether Lone Star's participation in them is the principle object of ridicule. The language is a tour de force of linguistic play—everything from double entendre and mixed metaphor to more visual escapades such as the insertion of phonetic symbols, inverted characters, stuttering, gaps in the text, and so on.

Bai Xianyong and Wang Wenxing deal with the inexorable weight of history elliptically, but in her mature work Chen Ruoxi directly addresses political and historical issues. Her early works were case studies combined with formal experimentation. "The Last Performance" (Zuihoude yanxi, 1961), for example, is a psychological portrait of Jin Xizi, a drug-addicted opera singer, on her last professional legs. It dramatizes the diminished life of the heroine, hopelessly smitten with a lover and left to raise his child. Chen uses symbolism in the description of the child's face, which resembles her lost love, along with clipped, economical dialogue, to articulate Xizi's predicament and achieve the literary ideals advanced by T.A. Hsia: to show rather than tell. Although somewhat similar to Bai Xianyong's depiction of the unseemly life of female singers, Chen's work contains more social commentary, foreshadowing her movement toward political concerns. Xizi initially admires the beauty of her own child, but his physical similarity to her lover gives the work an ironic twist.

Chen Ruoxi's best-known work is the collection *The Execution of Mayor Yin* (Yin xianzhang, 1976), which germinated from an ill-fated "return" to China on the eve of the Cultural Revolution. For many years, the stories in this collection were considered the literary word on the Cultural Revolution. Her ambiguous status as a returned overseas Chinese enabled her to carry out the project; such an account would have been unimaginable had she grown up in the PRC. *Mayor Yin* subjected the Cultural Revolution to a critique honed according to the methods she developed as a student of modernism. Her Taiwanese background was effaced, at least to English-speaking audiences, adding power to her voice. But her unique status was precisely what afforded her a position to speak out, even as it determined the form in which the critique would be delivered.

In the title piece, Chen Ruoxi's depiction of Mayor Yin, the former Nationalist commander turned Communist exemplar, who faces persecution during the Cultural Revolution with demure yet dignified resignation, represents a further development of her ability to project political and social commentary onto the description of individual characters. In his initial fervor to be absolved of all feudal sins, Mayor Yin proffers a false confession that he originated from the landlord class. His yearning for absolution could only be satisfied through confession, which eventually results in the confusion over his class background being exploited by Red Guards. The narrator is a first person observer of the situation, not unlike that found in *Ding Ling's "When I Was in Xia Village." She relates the story in a tone of understated disbelief. Her own implicit biases are undercut by Mayor Yin's unwittingly poignant questioning of her political stance. Chen Ruoxi wages the critique not by frontal assault but by shaping the events of the narrative into dramatic irony. These stories solidify Chen's stature as a writer whose art emerges from the mixture of personal lives with cataclysmic political events.

"Chairman Mao Is a Rotten Egg" (Jingjingde shengri, 1976) uses humor to illustrate the absurdity of the Cultural Revolution. Here, Teacher Wen, the first person narrator, is pregnant and finds herself implicated in a political situation: her toddler son allegedly has called Chairman Mao a rotten egg. Chen uses dialogue to achieve ironic effect, for the embattled condition of the individual, pitted against state-sanctioned selflessness, is underscored by the little boy who, rather than anticipating his birthday, asks his mother, "Mommy, what's a birthday?" The claustrophobia and domestic paranoia of Teacher Wen forced into tight living quarters with suspicious neighbors reveals a debt to the work of *Eileen Chang.

Chen Ruoxi also has continued to compose social satire, as the story "The Tunnel" (Didao, 1978) indicates. The story opens with the widower Master Hong, who seeks a relationship with a middle-aged divorcee named Li Mei, whom he admires for her diligence as a model worker. Their relationship is discouraged by friends and family, so they seek privacy in an air raid tunnel, only to be locked inside and left to die. After settling in the United States in the late 1970s, Chen began exploring the contradictions overseas Chinese and China experts encounter in dealing with the PRC. The story "The Crossroads" (Lu kou, 1980), for example, involves Yu Wenxiu, a divorcee from Taiwan who lives near a busy intersection in Washington, D.C. The crossroads becomes a leitmotif in the story as she debates whether to embark on a new relationship with a Chinese economist also from Taiwan but now much more tilted toward China. Wenxiu's daughter Ading illustrates the generational differences among Chinese in the diaspora. The political subtext for "The Crossroads" is the imprisonment of Wei Jingsheng during the Democracy Wall incident, an issue as timely today as it was twenty years ago. Her ultimate decision not to pursue the relationship has personal as well as political implications and exemplifies how inextricably related these levels are.

Whether crafting lyrical descriptions of tragically marginalized characters (as in the case of Bai Xianyong), or rendering characters tormented by social conflict (with the formal experiments of Wang Wenxing), or confronting the historical problems of contemporary China (as in the psychological profiles of Chen Ruoxi), the Taiwan Modernists share a devotion to individualism and respect for literary perfectionism, as well as antipathy toward more broad historical narrative, making their work unique in Chinese literature during the time they flourished and affording them a prominent place in the history of modern Chinese literature.

—*Christopher Lupke*

Bibliography

Bai, Xianyong (Pai Hsien-yung). *Crystal Boys*. Trans. Howard Goldblatt. San Francisco: Gay Sunshine Press, 1990.

———. "Death in Chicago." Trans. Susan McFadden. *Tamkang Review* 9, no. 3 (1979): 344–358.

———. *Wandering in the Garden, Waking from a Dream*. Trans. Bai Xianyong and Patia Yasin. Bloomington: Indiana University Press, 1982.

———. "Xianggang—1960" (Hong Kong—1960). *Xiandai wenxue* 21 (1964): 14–20.

Chang, Yvonne. *Modernism and the Nativist Resistance: Contemporary Fiction from Taiwan.* Durham, N.C.: Duke University Press, 1993.

Chen, Ruoxi. "The Crossroads." Trans. Hsin-sheng Kao. In *The Short Stories of Chen Ruoxi*, 16–75. Lewiston, N.Y.: Edwin Mellen Press, 1992.

——. *The Execution of Mayor Yin and Other Stories of the Great Proletarian Cultural Revolution.* Trans. Nancy Ing and Howard Goldblatt. Bloomington: Indiana University Press, 1978.

——. "The Last Performance." Trans. Timothy Ross and Joseph Lau. In Joseph Lau, ed., *Chinese Stories from Taiwan: 1960–1970*, 3–12. Columbia University Press, 1976.

——. "The Tunnel." Trans. C.C. Wang. In Joseph S.M. Lau and Howard Goldblatt, eds., *The Columbia Anthology of Modern Chinese Literature*, 301–314. New York: Columbia University Press, 1995.

Faurot, Jeannette, ed. *Chinese Fiction from Taiwan.* Bloomington: Indiana University Press, 1980.

Lee, Leo Ou-fan. "Dissent Literature from the Cultural Revolution." *Chinese Literature: Essays, Articles, Reviews* 1, no. 1 (1979): 59–80.

Lupke, Christopher. "(En)gendering the Nation in Pai Hsien-yung's (Bai Xianyong) 'Wandering in the Garden, Waking from a Dream.'" *Modern Chinese Literature* 6, no. 1–2 (1992): 157–177.

——. "Wang Wenxing and the 'Loss' of China." *boundary 2* 25, no. 3 (1998): 97–128.

Peng Ge. *Luoyue* (Setting Moon). Taipei: Yuanjing, 1977.

Wang, Lan. *The Blue and the Black.* Trans. Michael Steelman. Taipei: Chinese Materials Center, 1987.

Wang, Wenxing. *Backed against the Sea.* Trans. Edward Gunn. Ithaca, N.Y.: Cornell University Press, 1993.

——. *Family Catastrophe.* Trans. Susan Wan Dooling. Honolulu: University of Hawai'i Press, 1995.

——. "Flaw." Trans. Chen Zhuyun. In Joseph Lau, ed., *Chinese Stories from Taiwan: 1960–1970*, 15–27. New York: Columbia University Press, 1976.

84

SAME-SEX LOVE
IN RECENT CHINESE LITERATURE

Queer criticism, which aims to show how literature influences and reflects our ideas about homosexuality, can provide surprising insights (for an overview of lesbian, gay, and queer criticism, see Tyson 1999:317–361). For example, a queer reading of A Cheng's "The Chess King" (Qi wang, 1984) would begin by emphasizing the novella's theme of male-male friendship: there are no women in the story, and the emotional ties that matter are between the male narrator and his male friends. Chinese culture is accepting of open expressions of friendship between men, and it is unremarkable when a Chinese story foregrounds male homosocial bonding. Things get interesting if we argue there is something subtly homoerotic about "The Chess King." In the story the narrator shows a consistent interest in male bodies. More specifically, the painter sketches the narrator and his friends bathing nude together in a river, but this is perhaps too stereotypical a marker of the homoerotic to mean much. When one of the young men remarks that the "private parts [don't] look nice" and the painter blots out the "privates" (xiuchu) with his pencil, we recognize this as the symbolic assertion that the story's interest in men is not sexual. However, this is also a tacit admission that homoeroticism is present; otherwise, it would not need to be denied. When we identify homoerotic tension in the story, some will insist that Western theory is distorting our understanding of Chinese fiction. This should give us pause, but because there was until very recently no room in Chinese literature for the explicit discussion of homosexuality, it is probable that Chinese homoeroticism here and there finds implicit expression in works that are apparently heterosexual, and we should be ready to interpret it when it does. A model of how to proceed is the 1996 documentary film *Yang ± Yin: Gender in Chinese Film* by Stanley Kwan (Guan Jinpeng). Kwan, too, finds homoeroticism where one least expects it—for example, in films such as John Woo's *The Killer* (1989).

*Wang Anyi's "Brothers" (Dixiongmen, 1989) is about intense friendship among three married college students. While at school away from their husbands, the women think, talk, and behave in ways that are conventionally male. Only in this way are they free to develop their intellectual, artistic, and emotional selves. This female bonding, they understand, is incompatible with traditional gender roles. In the end, social norms cannot be overcome—"women were still women, and men were still men" (161). The youngest is the first "traitor" to the group; she leaves to be with her husband and disappears from the story. The eldest, Lao Li, and the second eldest, Lao Wang, also return to their husbands, but they attempt to maintain their relationship. However, Lao Li's strongest loyalty is now to her baby, and in the story's emotional climax, she rejects Lao Wang's attempt to take over some of the duties of her (Lao Li's) husband. In "Brothers," biology is destiny for mature women; female-female friendship is at odds with female-male sexual love and the maternal instinct. Or, as the narrator puts it, "There are some things women can't do together. Like sex" (180). In "The Chess King" the denial of homoeroticism is indirect; in "Brothers" it is direct (and repeated three times): the women, the narrator declares, share "a pure, innocent friendship unfettered by sexual desire" (189). "Brothers" recognizes the existence of a same-sex bond that is more than friendship, but it is unable or unwilling to imagine a world in which women can do all things together, including sex. Female same-sex desire threatens the patriarchal, heterosexual order by rendering men irrelevant (Sang 1996). In fiction, this problem is solved when lesbian characters die, as in the Taiwan film *Twin Bracelets* (Shuang zhuo, dir. Huang Yushan, 1990) for example, or when women choose men for lovers and homoeroticism is shifted to the realm of nonsexual, spiritual companionship, as in "Brothers."

Queer criticism helps us understand works such as "The Chess King" and "Brothers" as texts that deny their homoerotic undertones while celebrating homosocial bonding. Queer criticism also helps us notice flat out homophobia in literature. To choose just one example, the narrator of *Gao Xingjian's *Soul Mountain* (Ling shan, 1990) is nauseated by a lesbian character, whom he finds "hateful" for not wanting children and for ruining her lover's chances for a "normal marriage" (514–515). But the main concern of queer criticism is the way in which homosexual experience is treated in works that intend to deal with it, which—uniquely for modern Chinese literature—is true of a body of work that emerged together with a gay rights movement in Taiwan in the 1990s. Lin Huaimin's story "Cicada" (Chan, 1969) and Bai Xianyong's novel *Crystal Boys* (Niezi, 1983) are early works of what became Taiwan queer literature. "Cicada" follows a group of college students over a long weekend as they drift from a smoky Taipei café to a mountain resort. Fey, neurasthenic Fan Chuoxiong reminds protagonist Zhuang Shihuan of his gay roommate, Wu Zhe, who has recently left for military service. Tao Zhiqing, a bohemian coed, hints that Zhuang should admit his love for Wu Zhe, but Zhuang cannot shed, like a cicada, his heterosexual skin. Fan Chuoxiong kills himself. The story skips ahead six years and closes with bittersweet correspondence between Zhuang and Tao, who have gone their separate ways and are happy, if unfulfilled.

If in "Cicada" homosexual desire is faint and elusive, in *Crystal Boys*—still the best-known Chinese novel on a gay theme—it takes center stage. The title, *Niezi*, means "unfilial son"; "crystal boys" refers to the *boli quan* (glass crowd), Taiwan slang for the gay community. The narrator is A-Qing, an eighteen-year-old from the slums who is expelled from school and banished from home for having sex with a man. A-Qing goes to Taipei's New Park—a real place with a real history as a gay oasis—and joins the young men who flock around protector, father figure, and pimp, Chief Yang. Estranged from his father and in mourning for his mother and beloved younger brother, A-Qing looks for friends and mentors with whom he can build a new family (family is important in many Taiwanese works on homosexual themes; see, for example, Ang Lee's film *Wedding Banquet* [Xiyan, 1992] and Chen Junzhi's documentary *Beautiful Boys* [Meili shaonian, 1998]). A-Qing and his fellows move in a world of sadomasochism, rape, alcoholism, suicide, adultery, drug abuse, and poverty, but they dream of the sort of grand operatic romance played out in the story of A-Feng (Phoenix Boy) and Wang Kuilong (Dragon Prince). Until the late 1980s, critics read *Crystal Boys* as a study of the "causes" of homosexuality (for example, poverty, a broken home, a weak father) or as an allegory of something else (for example, the conflict between the mainland and Taiwan). Bai Xianyong's typical themes of exile and nostalgia do suffuse *Crystal Boys* (see "The Taiwan Modernists"), but homosexuality is central to the novel, not incidental. *Crystal Boys* neither defends nor explains homosexuality; it assumes that male same-sex love is common and natural, that gay men in Taiwan are the targets of prurient curiosity, ridicule, and oppression, and that gay men epitomize masculinity. The novel's insistence on these three points is why Taiwan's gay rights movement has for the most part embraced *Crystal Boys*, even though it links homosexuality with prostitution, violence, and pederasty. Bai Xianyong first introduced some of the characters from *Crystal Boys* in "A Sky Full of Bright, Twinkling Stars" (Man tian li liangjingjing de xingxing, 1969) and wrote about lesbian love in "Love's Lone Flower" (Gulianhua, 1970).

Du Xiulan's melodramatic *Unfilial Daughter* (Ni nü, 1993) is worth mention as a lesbian counterpart to *Crystal Boys*. The narrator, Ding Tianshi, is a smart, wild tomboy growing up in the Taipei suburbs in the 1970s and 1980s; she is ashamed of her dysfunctional family and its poverty and uneasy about her homosexuality until she falls in love with high school classmate Zhan Qingqing.

Zhan commits suicide when the affair is discovered. After college, Tianshi stumbles upon Taipei's semisecret lesbian world and manages to build something of a life with her companion, Zhuang Meiqi (Maggie), and friends Xu Jiazhen and Xu's lover, Lin Zhongwei (Angela). Tianshi insists her homosexuality is innate, but she cruises bars for older women in search of the love her mother refused to give her. She complains that the straight world stereotypes gays and lesbians as promiscuous, but she blots out psychic pain with anonymous sexual encounters.

Exemplary of Taiwan *ku'er* (queer) or *tongzhi* (comrade) literature are the novels *Notes of a Desolate Man* (Huang ren shouji, 1994) by Zhu Tianwen and *Crocodile's Journal* (Eyu shouji, 1994) by Qiu Miaojin. In *Crocodile's Journal*, an unnamed narrator tells the story of her years at National Taiwan University from 1987 until 1991. The narrator falls in love with the conventionally feminine Shuiling. The narrator fears that Shuiling will eventually leave her for a man. To inoculate herself against abandonment and, she claims, spare Shuiling the pain that transgressive love can bring, the narrator pushes Shuiling away. Ironically, the spurned Shuiling falls in love with another woman, while the narrator struggles with guilt and self-hatred. The narrator also tells the stories of four classmates. She is fascinated by the iconoclast Mengsheng and his morose male lover, Chukuang; she delights in Zhirou and Tuntun and commiserates with them when their nascent lesbian love is smothered by the "compulsory" heterosexuality of the college environment. The crocodile of the title is introduced after the narrator represses her desire for Shuiling. Having internalized society's homophobia, the narrator refers to herself as a *guaiwu* (monster); the crocodile, we understand, is this *guaiwu* made manifest. The narrator reads about Taiwan's "crocodiles" in the newspaper; they are reported to disguise themselves as human but are somehow different from humans—no one knows exactly how. The narrator meets a crocodile—the *only* crocodile apparently—hides it in a basement apartment, and gives it a chance to tell its story. The crocodile is eager to make friends but shy about coming out. As Tze-lan Deborah Sang (1996:234) observes, the crocodile's experience is an allegory for the lesbian experience in Taiwan: "Rumors about 'crocodiles' in the text mimic and parody the phobic and voyeuristic conjectures about lesbians and gay men in the Taiwan media." (Qiu Miaojin committed suicide in 1995. Other Taiwan "queer writers" are Hong Ling, Chen Xue, and Ji Dawei; for an annotated bibliography of gay, lesbian, and queer literature from Taiwan, see Ji 1997; on lesbian literature from Taiwan, see Sang 1996:190–245 and Martin 1999; for a full study of Taiwan queer literature, see Martin 2000. Martin has also published translations of stories by Chen and Ji.)

The title *Crocodile's Journal* is a reference to *Journal du voleur* (The Thief's Journal), Jean Genet's 1949 account of his life as a thief and male prostitute. From Genet, Qiu borrows the notion of homosexuality as a crime. Zhu Tianwen's *Notes of a Desolate Man* does not mention Genet, but it echoes his idea that art offers escape from the "sterility of homosexuality" (White 1993:390). *Notes of a Desolate Man* is, like Wang Wenxing's *Backed against the Sea* (Bei hai de ren, 1981) (see "The Taiwan Modernists"), a fictional monologue that tests the ability of language to express and define the self. The narrator, Shao, is forty and gay. He lives in Taipei and is a well-off, well-traveled sophisticate. Shao tells the story of his life and loves and contrasts himself with his childhood friend Ah Yao, who has died of AIDS. Ah Yao was a political activist and sexual adventurer confident in his identity as queer; Shao is a reluctant epicurean tormented by efforts to figure out who he is. Shao makes reference to the high, popular, and mass cultures of East and West, as he goes back and forth between philosophical inquiry and camp digression (right after Ah Yao dies, Shao gives us several pages on his pet fish). Shao's erudite ramblings and his appeal to the transcendence of art constitute his attempt to understand, accept, and deny death, in particular death from AIDS, which seems to Shao a particular injustice when it kills gay men, because gay men do not find their existence validated by family or extended by children. This is where Zhu Tianwen echoes Genet.

Notes of a Desolate Man is as much about a particular conception of the feminine as it is about homosexual men—Shao conceives of the straight world as *yang* (male) and the homosexual world as *yin* (female). The extravagant, discursive language of the novel represents *yin* as style: *yin* is an indulgent, sensual aestheticism that opposes the restrictive, ordered world of *yang* society. Male homosexuality in *Notes of a Desolate Man* also stands for the "postcolonial" situation of middle-class intellectuals in late twentieth-century Taiwan: a struggle to define themselves as authentically "Chinese" when Taiwan is cut off from China and as authentically "modern" when "modernity" would seem to require surrender to Western forms of political, economic, and cultural life (the issues of homosexuality and postcoloniality do come together: the gay community in Taiwan faces the question of how a *ku'er* identity can be fashioned using language and concepts from the West without being a repetition of the West). In the novel, the implicit allegory is that homosexuality is to heterosexuality as Taiwan is to China, on the one hand, and the West, on the other hand. The heterosexual majority defines homosexuality as inauthentic human sexuality; China defines Taiwan as inauthentically Chinese, and the West defines Taiwan as inauthentically modern. Shao is gay and lives in Taipei and therefore is doubly "inauthentic." His solution is to use language to make something beautiful and define himself through beauty: "The place I'd longed to visit, the place I'd dreamed about, does not, cannot actually exist. It is an unattainable place that has always existed only in the written word" (151).

In China, there is no body of fiction equivalent to Taiwan queer literature. Male homosexuality is the subject of Zhang Yuan's film *East Palace, West Palace* (Dong gong xi gong, 1997) and of *Their World* (Tamen de shijie, 1993), a work of reportage by Li Yinhe and the late Wang Xiaobo, who together wrote the screenplay for *East Palace, West Palace* (for an overview of journalism on homosexuality in China, see Zhou 1996:23–37). *Peach-Colored Lips* (Taose zuichun, 1997), by Beijing-based Cui Zi'en, is marketed by its Hong Kong publisher as China's first homosexual novel (its publisher has also put out *His His Her Her Stories* [Ta ta ta ta de gushi], an anthology of short fiction on homosexual themes by writers from Taiwan, Hong Kong, and mainland China). In *Peach-Colored Lips*, there are four narrators: the director of a hospice for the terminally ill; Ye Hongju, who spends his dying days under the director's care; Xiaomao, the director's thirty-year-old son; and a man named Chunyu Xianfeng. The director listens and reacts as Ye, Xiaomao, and Chunyu tell their stories, challenging the heterosexual director with their different understandings of homosexuality. Before Ye dies, he narrates his experiences as a young man in the late 1920s or early 1930s. The director is appalled by Ye's homosexuality but moved by his capacity for love and reassured that Ye had tried to change his sexual orientation. Twenty-five years later, Xiaomao confronts his father with his homosexuality. Xiaomao has built a philosophy upon sex, centered around the term *kong*, which is both his "emptiness, void" and his "hole/s." Xiaomao is the passive, penetrated partner in sex; sex fills him both physically and existentially. Xiaomao rebels against the authority of the heterosexual male and the binary opposition of male and female. His father punishes him by castrating him. For this, the director is sent to prison. In prison, the director's cellmate is Chunyu Xianfeng, who turns out to be the son of a man Ye Hongju loved and one of Xiaomao's lovers. For Ye, sex is romance; for Xiaomao, it is philosophy; for the bisexual Chunyu Xianfeng, it is physical pleasure. In contrast to Xiaomao, with men Chunyu takes the active, penetrating role. The message to the director is that male homosexuality is not lack or inversion and that male sexuality exceeds conventional categories. The director is left in a symbolic psychological prison; the voices of his homosexual informants reverberate in his head, mock his conventional morality, and suggest that his biases have destroyed his life and left him to face the existential void his son combated. *East Palace, West Palace*, one of the only other mainland works on homosexuality, is also constructed around the testimony of a gay man given to a straight man. Beijing's gay scene was the inspiration for the film, but the story is not a straightforward treatment of this scene. A policeman arrests and interrogates a young gay man named A-lan, who has been cruising for sex in a park. Over the course of one night, the policeman asks questions and A-lan answers. Eventually, the policeman must interrogate and question his own sexuality.

The work of studying the representation of homosexuality in Republican-era fiction has barely begun (Sang 1996). More work has been done on homosexuality in traditional literature (Hinsch 1990). Twentieth-century Chinese writers who deal with homosexuality have largely ignored traditional Chinese attitudes toward homosexuality and representations of it in literature.

—*Thomas Moran*

Bibliography

Ah, Cheng. *Three Kings: Three Stories from Today's China*. Trans. Bonnie S. McDougall. London: Collins Harvill, 1990.

Bai, Xianyong. *Crystal Boys*. Trans. Howard Goldblatt. San Francisco: Gay Sunshine Press, 1990.

——. *Wandering in the Garden, Waking from a Dream*. Trans. Bai Xianyong and Patia Yasin. Bloomington: Indiana University Press, 1982.

Chen, Xue. "Searching for the Lost Wings of the Angel." Trans. Fran Martin. *positions* 7, no. 1 (1999): 51–69.

Cui Zi'en. *Taose zuichun* (Peach-Colored Lips). Hong Kong: Huasheng shudian, 1997.

Du Xiulan. *Ni nü* (Rebel Girl). Taipei: Huangguan, 1993.

Gao Xingjian. *Ling shan* (Spirit Mountain). Taipei: Lianjing, 1990.

Hinsch, Bret. *Passions of the Cut Sleeve: The Male Homosexual Tradition in China*. Berkeley: University of California Press, 1990.

Ji Dawei. *Ku'er kuanghuanjie: Taiwan dangdai Queer wenxue duben* (Queer Carnival: A Reader of Contemporary Queer Literature from Taiwan). Taipei: Yuanzun wenhua qiye gufen youxian gongsi, 1997.

——. "The Scent of HIV" and "I'm Not Stupid." Trans. Fran Martin. *antiThesis* 9, no. 1 (1998): 141–151.

Li Yinhe and Wang Xiaobo. *Tamen de shijie* (Their World). Hong Kong: Tiandi tushu youxian gongsi, 1993.

Lin, Huaimin. "Cicada." Trans. Timothy A. Ross and Lorraine S.Y. Lieu. In Joseph Lau, ed., *Chinese Stories from Taiwan: 1960–1970*, 243–319. New York: Columbia University Press, 1976.

Lu Jianxiong, ed. *Ta ta ta ta de gushi* (His His Her Her Stories). Hong Kong: Huasheng shudian, 1996.

Martin, Fran. "Chen Xue's Queer Tactics." *positions* 7, no. 1 (1999): 71–94.

——. "Situating Sexualities: Queer Narratives in 1990s Taiwanese Fiction and Film." Ph.D. diss., University of Melbourne, 2000.

Qiu Miaojin. *Eyu shouji* (Crocodile's Journal). Taipei: Shibao wenhua chuban qiye gongsi, 1994.

Sang, Tze-lan Deborah. "The Emerging Lesbian: Female Same-Sex Desire in Modern Chinese Literature and Culture." Ph.D. diss., University of California, Berkeley, 1996.

Sieber, Patricia, ed. *Red Is Not the Only Color: Contemporary Fiction on Love and Sex between Women*. Lanham, Md.: Rowman and Littlefield, 2001.

Tyson, Louis. *Critical Theory Today: A User-Friendly Guide*. New York: Garland, 1999.

Wang Anyi. "Brothers." In Diana B. Kingsbury, ed., *I Wish I Were a Wolf: The New Voice in Chinese Women's Literature*, 158–212. Beijing: New World Press, 1994.

Wang Wenxing. *Backed against the Sea*. Trans. Edward Gunn. Ithaca, N.Y.: Cornell University East Asia Program, 1993.

Wang Xiaobo. "Dong gong xi gong: dianying juben" (East Palace, West Palace: Film Script). In *Di jiu tian chang: Wang Xiaobo xiaoshuo juben ji* (Everlasting and Unchanging: An Anthology of Fiction and Scripts by Wang Xiaobo). Changchun: Shidai wenyi, 1998.

White, Edmund. *Genet: A Biography.* New York: Alfred A. Knopf, 1993.

Zhou Huashan. *Beijing tongzhi gushi* (Stories of Beijing Comrades). Hong Kong: Xianggang tongzhi yanjiushe, 1996.

Zhu, Tianwen. *Notes of a Desolate Man.* Trans. Howard Goldblatt and Sylvia Li-chun Lin. New York: Columbia University Press, 1999.

85

THE CULTURAL REVOLUTION MODEL THEATER

Revolutionary model theater *(geming yangbanxi)* first appeared in the Chinese cultural scene in 1966, the year the Great Proletarian Cultural Revolution started. The term *model theater* was coined to describe, loosely, a collection of revised performing arts productions guided by Mao Zedong's wife Jiang Qing (1914–1992). The earliest official source proclaiming the existence of the model theater was a special news report entitled "Carrying Out Chairman Mao's Line on Literature and Art: Brilliant Models." A short editorial on the same page celebrated the birth and significance of these works:

> Since 1964, under the brilliant radiance of Chairman Mao's line on literature and art, the high-tide of revolutionary reform in the fields of Beijing opera, of ballet drama, and of symphonic music has swelled. The revolutionary model theater has been created, which consists of five Beijing operas: *Shajiabang, The Red Lantern, Taking Tiger Mountain by Strategy, On the Docks, Raid on the White Tiger Regiment;* two ballet dramas: *The White-Haired Girl, The Red Detachment of Women,* and the symphony *Shajiabang.* (*Renmin ribao,* December 6, 1966)

In the process of the development of the Cultural Revolution, the term *model theater* became a common designation for any Beijing opera or ballet production that had the exemplary qualities shown by the original eight. As the fame of the symphony *Shajiabang* faded (it was not a theatrical piece in the first place, but it was adapted from the Beijing opera of the same name and equipped with costumed soloists and chorus), more popular newcomers, such as the Beijing operas *Azalea Mountain* (Dujuan shan, 1973) and *The Song of the Dragon River* (Long jiang song, 1972), took its place as models. (The model dramas underwent many revisions and productions; the dates given here indicate their official publication as "models" in the journal *Hongqi*.)

The model theater dominated the Chinese cultural stage from 1966 to 1976. During these ten years it was praised for its revolutionary reformation of the ideals for literature and art advocated by Mao Zedong in his 1942 *"Yan'an Talks."* Mao had established two criteria for literature and art: political content and artistic form, with the former of primary importance. Because the overall purpose of literature and art, according to Mao, is to educate the people politically and ideologically, the content should carry the message while the form should be an effective means to help spread the message. The making of the model theater was a process of revising and reforming existing popular literary works that had not quite met the standard of Mao's ideals, but nevertheless showed a potential for reaching that standard.

In terms of its content, model theater follows a central theme, which is to eulogize the victories of the Communist Party-led revolution and socialist construction. A group of idealized characters—the Communist Party members—and a series of idealized situations—the party-led victories—are created so as to trumpet the virtues of Chinese Communist ideology. The selection of Beijing opera and ballet as the model forms was not accidental. One indigenous, one foreign, both forms require highly symbolic and suggestive performance, scant verbal exchanges, and exaggerated postures and choreography. They accommodate fittingly the contents, characterized by rigid structures of plots, dogmatic language, and larger-than-life heroes and heroines. Model theater, thus, became a powerful weapon to educate the people, indoctrinating them into a standardized view of Chinese revolutionary history and class struggle.

Many of the model dramas are set during the revolutionary struggles. The model opera *The Red Lantern* (Hong deng ji, 1970), for example, takes place during the war against Japan (1937–45). Li Yuhe, a seasoned underground party member, receives a mission to deliver a secret code to the guerrillas. Before he can fulfill his mission, however, he is betrayed and gets arrested by the chief of the Japanese gendarme, Hatoyama. Li meets the enemy with unflinching courage. At his wit's end, Hatoyama executes Li and his mother. Li's daughter, Tiemei, takes over the mission for her martyred father. Led by the party and helped by her neighbors, she succeeds in delivering the secret code to the guerrillas. *Taking Tiger Mountain by Strategy* (Zhiqu Weihushan, 1970) centers on the shrewdness, skill, and nerve of Yang Zirong, a People's Liberation Army scout during the War of Liberation (1946–1949). Disguised as a bandit and with a convincing cover story, Yang infiltrates the enemy headquarters on Tiger Mountain and wins its occupants' trust. When the Nationalist soldiers celebrate the chief's fiftieth birthday, Yang manages to get them all drunk. He has also managed to persuade them to light up the mountain with torches for the celebration of the birthday, a signal for the PLA to overrun the headquarters, which they do, of course, successfully. *Raid on the White-Tiger Regiment* (Qixi baihutuan, 1972) is a celebration of internationalism and the self-sacrifice of Chinese Communists during the Korean War (1950–53). Yan Weicai, leader of a scout platoon of the Chinese People's Volunteer Army, successfully defeats the so-called indestructible White-Tiger Regiment of the South Korean army, advised by American military personnel.

Model theater is well known for its heroic female characters. These women resemble their male counterparts in always representing political and ideological correctness and serving as deus ex machina in critical situations. But these women are not women at all. They are stripped of most, if not all, feminine traces; they do not have families, are not wives and mothers, and more than anything else they are not sexual. In *Shajiabang* (1970), for example, Sister Aqing is a splendid, dynamic party secretary during the war against Japan. She works underground to protect the wounded soldiers of the New Fourth Army, providing them with food and medicine under extremely complicated political circumstances in which the Japanese aggressors, puppet troops, and Guomindang diehards conspire together to capture the wounded. In the end, she outwits these enemies and fulfils the task given her by the party. *Azalea Mountain* portrays another heroic woman. Party member Ke Xiang is sent by the Central Committee to provide much-needed leadership for a peasant self-defense corps in the 1920s. She has gone through many tests and difficulties. Eventually she wins the trust of the peasants and leads them in victory over a reactionary armed force; more important, she has transformed the undisciplined peasants into an able fighting force with a proletarian worldview. *Azalea Mountain* and *Shajiabang* are also dramas about the relationship between a gendered identity and political identity. Sister Aqing parades as a "woman," shielding her true political identity from the enemy behind a masquerade of femininity. Ke Xiang has to prove to the peasant corps she oversees that she is not a "woman," and that her being a biological woman will not prevent her from being a worthy political and military leader.

On the Docks (Hai gang, 1972) and *The Song of Dragon River* are sister dramas; both are set after the revolution and both deal with the issue of class struggle. In the former, a Shanghai Communist Party secretary, Fang Haizhen, is in charge of the important operation of shipping rice seeds to Africa. She successfully fights back the class enemy's attempt to spoil this internationalist activity and succeeds in shipping out the seeds in time for the sowing season. *The Song of the Dragon River* is set in rural China. Jiang Shuiying, secretary of a Dragon River production brigade, sacrifices the interests of her own collective by encouraging the construction of a dam to divert the water of Dragon River. This action will save a nearby and much larger drought-stricken area. A former landlord intervenes by convincing the brigade leader to breach the dam at the critical moment. The timely entry of Jiang Shuiying saves the situation. She gives the order to open the gate and exposes the dark scheme of the class enemy.

The two plays are similar in many ways. Both dramas present ideological disputes between two contradictory classes. The nature of the class struggle is less about economical divisions than moral conflicts. In their characterization, the proletarian class, represented by women, is dedicated to serving the public without any thought of self. On the other hand, the class enemy of the proletariat seeks nothing but to destroy the great cause of communism and internationalism. In between these two polarized positions is a more human group composed mostly of men; they are susceptible to the class enemy because they always put their own interest or their small group's interest before that of the larger public. When they fall into the enemy's scheme, the proletarian women come to their rescue, rectifying their ideological positions and exposing the evil intentions of the class enemies (also usually male).

Model ballet dramas *The White-Haired Girl* (Bai mao nü) and *The Red Detachment of Women* (Hongse niangzi jun, 1970) are stories about poor peasant girls becoming staunch Communists. Two themes overlap with each other in both plays: class struggle and women's liberation. *The Red Detachment of Women* is about poor bondmaid Wu Qinghua's political maturation in the 1930s, when the Communists were fighting Nationalist rule. Wu manages to escape her abusive landlord's house and join a fighting force of "Red Women." Nurtured by the party and tested by the severe armed struggle, Wu finally transforms from a rash, naive girl into a conscious proletarian fighter.

The White-Haired Girl is arguably the most popular of the model dramas and can be looked at as the masterpiece of Jiang Qing's radical feminism. This feminism is best illustrated by comparing the model ballet with the original opera on which it is based. The opera was first produced as a collective effort in 1945, and it immediately gained an unparalleled popularity in the Communist controlled areas. Set in the latter half of the 1930s, it relates the tragic story of a poor peasant girl, Xi'er. Her father, Yang Bailao, works for the vicious landlord Huang Shiren. Unable to pay his rent and an accumulated cash debt, Yang is forced in his confusion and bewilderment to sign a contract that promises his daughter to the Huang family as payment. Yang, in desperation, commits suicide, whereupon Xi'er is forcibly taken away by the Huang family. Wang Dachun, Xi'er's betrothed, runs away and joins the Eighth Route Army. Xi'er is treated cruelly in the Huang family and is raped by Huang Shiren. Seven months later, after Xi'er has become pregnant, Huang decides to sell her to a brothel—to the surprise of Xi'er, who expects that Huang will marry her. On learning of Huang's scheme, she escapes from the landlord's household and flees to the wild mountains, where she gives birth to Huang's child, who later dies. For more than two years, Xi'er exists like an animal in a mountain cave, hiding from humanity. This hard life, and especially the lack of salt in her diet, turns her hair completely white. The villagers who encounter her take her to be an apparition. Finally, a detachment of the Eighth Route Army led by Wang Dachun comes to her rescue. The village is liberated, the landlord Huang is executed. Liberated Xi'er marries Dachun, and they live happily ever after.

The model ballet version keeps close to the original story line, but the plot is much thinner and the characters more abstract. The most obvious change is that Yang Bailao, the father, does not commit suicide, but in the spirit of revolt fights against his oppressors and is beaten to death. Similarly, Xi'er is changed into an embodiment of hatred, the spirit of revenge. She is treated cruelly in the ballet version of the story, but is not sexually assaulted by Huang Shiren. Wang Dachun's significance fades and he becomes just another of Xi'er's class brothers, with no special romantic relationship. In the epilogue, Xi'er picks up a gun and joins the ranks of the Eighth Route Army to carry on the revolution. As such, she becomes a symbol of that class.

The simplification of the story, the politicization of the theme, and particularly the abstraction of characters reveal the centrality of the class dynamic concept in the model theater. Class is the only social category within which characters function. Traditional kinship relations are eliminated. The relations between Yang Bailao and Xi'er and between Xi'er and Wang Dachun take on a class character. Most important, the model theater excludes the sexual. Huang Shiren's sexual assault of Xi'er in the original opera is deleted in the ballet. They are only class enemies. Xi'er's previous vulnerability as a woman, a female body, disappears. Her rape and pregnancy are excised. Xi'er is no longer a betrothed daughter to be raped, nor a mother giving birth to a dead child, nor a ghost waiting to be liberated. Structurally speaking, the elimination of the female body enables Xi'er to gain equality with the members of her class.

In the West, model theater has been generally regarded as the dead end of the Communist Party's political and ideological appropriation of art that began with Mao's "Yan'an Talks." Its critics have dismissed it as "artless, sterile, without depth, without truth, and without reality" (Meserve 1970). Another kind of scholarship analyzes the literary-artistic value in model theater and largely restricts its focus to form. This approach is interested in how the work is constructed as popular art and how it is a product of the party's manipulation of mass performing art and popular culture. Even its obvious feminism looks suspicious. The nongendered women in the model theater can be easily explained away as a mere parodying of masculinity. In China, model theater is seen by literary critics not only as the evil products of a political and cultural disaster, but also as being partially responsible for that turmoil. What's more, anti-Jiang Qing sentiment runs high when the model theater is mentioned. The sole reason for the existence of model theater, some critics argue, was to simply serve and satisfy Jiang Qing's personal ambition (Yan 1996).

Surprisingly, the 1990s saw a renewed popular interest in the model theater in China. New productions of *The Red Lantern, The Red Detachment of*

Women, Shajiabang, and *The White-Haired Girl* were instant commercial successes, in spite of their obviously outdated political messages. The images of revolutionary heroes and heroines once again entered ordinary people's homes by videotapes and DVDs, and Ke Xiang's famous aria could be heard blasting in busy department stores. Model theater requires an in-depth study so as to reach a fresh understanding of its complex cultural meaning, its position in PRC political history, its artistic achievement, and to explain its undying popularity.

—*Di Bai*

Bibliography

"Azalea Mountain." *Chinese Literature* 1 (1974): 3–69.

Chen, Xiaomei. *Acting the Right Part: Political Theater and Contemporary Chinese Drama (1966–1996).* Honolulu: University of Hawai'i Press, 2002.

Denton, Kirk A. "Model Drama As Myth: A Semiotic Analysis of *Taking Tiger Mountain By Strategy.*" In Constantine Tung, ed., *Drama in the People's Republic of China,* 119–136. Albany: State University of New York Press, 1987.

Mackerras, Colin. *The Chinese Theatre in Modern Times from 1840 to the Present Day.* London: Thames & Hudson, 1975.

Meserve, Walter J., ed. *Modern Drama from Communist China.* New York: New York University Press, 1970.

"On the Docks." *Chinese Literature* 5 (1973): 22–48.

"Raid on the White-Tiger Regiment." *Chinese Literature* 3 (1973): 3–54.

"Red Detachment of Women." In Martin Ebon, ed., *Five Chinese Communist Plays,* 119–151. New York: John Day, 1975.

"The Red Lantern." *Chinese Literature* 8 (1970): 8–52.

"Shajiabang." *Chinese Literature* 11 (1970): 3–62.

"Song of the Dragon River." *Chinese Literature* 7 (1972): 3–57.

"Taking the Tiger Mountain by Strategy." *Chinese Literature* 1 (1970): 58–74.

"The White-Haired Girl." In Martin Ebon, ed., *Five Chinese Communist Plays,* 27–117. New York: John Day, 1975.

Yan, Jiaqi, and Gao Gao. *Turbulent Decade: A History of the Cultural Revolution.* Trans. D. W. Y. Kwok. Honolulu: University of Hawai'i Press, 1996.

86

THE TAIWAN NATIVISTS

*Lu Xun and *Mao Dun introduced the term *xiangtu wenxue,* or "nativist literature," to Chinese literary circles in the 1920s. Interest in the term, a loose translation of the German *Heimat Roman* (homeland novel), stemmed from a desire
for writers from the provinces to express the local color of the places from which
they originated (see "Shen Congwen and Imagined Native Communities"). In
Japan, anthropologists adopted the term *kyôdo bungaku,* or "nativist art," to describe works that epitomize the national character of Japan by crystallizing the
essence of particular localities. *Nativism* is a term of layered ironies, for what
has come to stand for the intrinsic features of a culture has in fact been imported twice over, from Europe via Japan. In addition, what was once a term
employed to express national characteristics, eventually, in its most notable in-
carnation, has come to stand for the depiction of regional elements in Taiwan
society in contrast to Taiwan modernism and literature from mainland China.

Nativist literature movements and debates occurred in Taiwan during the period of Japanese occupation (1895–1945) and in the late 1940s, but the best-
known writers associated with the term "nativist" are those who flourished in the
1960s and 1970s. Of them, three of the most prominent fiction writers are Huang
Chunming (b. 1935), Wang Zhenhe (1940–1990), and Chen Yingzhen (b. 1937).
Huang Chunming embarked on his writing career in 1962 by submitting short
stories to the *United Daily News* (Lianhe bao) literary supplement, edited by Lin
Haiyin (1918–2001), a native Taiwanese of Hakka descent. As he developed confidence as a writer, Huang branched out and submitted works to numerous publi-

cations, including *The Literary Quarterly* (Wenxue jikan), the most important venue for the nativist writers during the 1960s and 1970s. "The Fish" (Yu, 1968), a haunting work that evokes the poverty of Taiwanese in the countryside, begins with adolescent A Zang pedaling furiously on an oversized bicycle toward home, a fresh fish dangling precariously from the handlebars. The narrative shifts between the boy's eagerness to demonstrate to his grandfather his accomplishment and flashbacks detailing his bitter childhood as an apprentice. "The Fish" is filled with suspense over what will happen when the boy meets up with his grandfather without the fish, which fell off the bike en route. The suspense turns to pathos as the grandfather, taunted by the boy's insistence that he did indeed bring home the fish, beats him. The dramatic tension hinges upon the discrepancy between what each views as important: A Zang values the gesture of bringing home the fish, while the old man considers the act irrelevant if one fails to produce the fish. Poverty drives people to relinquish their sense of propriety.

For Huang, propriety is a combination of mutual respect and filial behavior, both of which have been undermined by global capitalism. In "His Son's Big Doll" (Erzi de da wan'ou, 1967), for example, Kunshu makes his living wearing a sandwich board and clown makeup, transforming himself into a human advertisement. The torment Kunshu feels is enacted structurally by mixing a distanced third-person narrative voice with first-person comments made through the use of interior monologue and with depictions and dialogue from supporting characters that have no access to this interiority. This reinforces the vividness of Kunshu's isolation from others and his own self-loathing. His facial makeup masks his identity, yet is necessary for the job and thus for his economic survival. In a futile effort to escape humiliation, Kunshu secures the more "dignified" position of pedicab driver, which means he can shed the makeup. But his son, crying out in fright, ironically mistakes his true face for a stranger. His feelings are assuaged only by his father's reapplication of the clown makeup. Although a stirring critique of emergent capitalism in a client state to the Cold War–era United States, the most remarkable feature of Huang's descriptive technique rests in his ability to penetrate the thoughts and feelings of lower-class, marginal figures such as the Sandwich Man. Revealing the interiority of characters that appear to mainstream society to be opaque and inaccessible is one of the hallmarks of Huang's craft.

This is equally true of "A Flower in the Rainy Night" (Kan hai de rizi, 1967), which remains oddly ambivalent about traditional Chinese values. Huang walks a tightrope between a maudlin rendering of the prostitute heroine Amei that celebrates traditional notions of nature, reproductivity, and filiality, and a feminist critique that repudiates the patriarchal system. Amei, a foster daughter bonded into prostitution, abhors her lot. She paradoxically seeks deliverance from her fate through the birth of a son. Indeed, when she returns to her impoverished natal family in the mountains, the villagers all feel that the apportionment of government-owned potato fields to them is a result of her auspiciousness. Her reward is the birth of a son. However, Amei's conceiving with an inexperienced man and then leaving the trade to raise her child alone is a mark of agency seldom depicted in Chinese literature. Huang Chunming's work is distinguished by probing the bewildering middle ground between resignation and hope.

Huang's "Young Widow" (Xiao guafu) builds on this ambivalence. Beginning as a critique, the narrative voice ultimately cannot help but render the young American GIs in a sympathetic light, leaving war itself the ultimate villain. The story begins with Ma Shanxing recasting a typical nightclub into something Confucian. His new creation, Young Widow, is predicated upon fetishizing traditional Chinese feminine virtue, particularly chaste widowhood, as it plays libidinally on the psyches of American troops on furlough from Vietnam. The transgression of this Confucian virtue is supposed to forge a sense of the erotic and illicit. The ideal "young widow" would be "like an iceberg on the outside, but inside she is a seething volcano." The erotics of transgression is too subtle for the young GIs, who are more preoccupied with the trauma of fighting a war they do not understand. Huang's inclusion of the sexually impotent Louie, for example, haunted by grotesque battle images that mix violence, sex, and guilt over the war effort, anticipates subsequent American literary and filmic psychodramas of the Vietnam War.

While Wang Zhenhe shares some concerns with Huang Chunming, such as the tensions between urban and rural, native Taiwanese and mainlanders, and the prostitution of women in both the war effort and global capitalist economy, the tone of his work is quite different and very individualistic. Wang's early work was first published in *Modern Literature* and later in *The Literary Quarterly*. Wang Zhenhe is fascinated with exploring the grotesque and unseemly side of the human character, in particular marginal figures who by nature transgress the social norms of cultured society. By flouting social etiquette, Wang's carefully etched incendiaries perform for the reader the clash between high culture, that is, the literary apparatus, and the low culture of the *laobaixing* (common people). His first story, "Ghost, North Wind, Man" (Gui, beifeng, ren, 1961), is just such an exploration, for long before he acquired a penchant for social commentary, Wang was writing about bizarre figures. "Ghost" depicts Qin Guifu, the alcoholic, gambling indigent who desires to sleep with his sister Li Yue. There is no silent dignity in the face of social pressures for Wang Zhenhe's literary cast. A modernist piece that exposes perversion, "Ghost" is a vignette that discloses human putrefaction through interior monologue and variable points of view, as well as flashbacks.

Wang's first mature work is the short story "An Oxcart for Dowry" (Jiazhuang yi niuche, 1967), a scandalous, comical portrait of destitution. Exhibiting neither sympathy nor contempt, the narrator presents Wanfa, a deaf peasant who farms an infertile plot of land with his wife. The remarkable feature of this story is not the subject matter; peasants abound in modern Chinese fiction. What is astounding is the manner in which the characters are subjected to ridicule by the narrator and the subtle juxtaposition of elements requiring great erudition, such as the Henry James quote at the beginning (decrying in English the limitations of Schubert), with the profanity of Wanfa and his ilk. Wang Zhenhe's clever intellect even mocks the reader, for in the end we cannot discern a stable moral tone but are left with an indelible image of the abjectly impoverished, forced to perform the unthinkable in order to survive. Rather than an opportunity for sympathy, Wanfa's deafness allows the narrator carefully to maneuver the narrative point of view in various directions.

"Xiao Lin Comes to Taipei" (Xiao Lin lai Taibei, 1973) represents a new stage for Wang. Though one of his finest social satires, the work is decidedly monologic in tone. The comic elements tend to serve the very serious goal of exposing the exploitative effects of capitalism on the daily lives of Taipei's urban workers. The theme of the Taiwanese rustic coming to the city to seek his fortune only to be disaffected by its commodified culture has since become pervasive in Taiwan literature and film. Wang is far more sympathetic to the protagonist in this story than he is in his previous work. Additionally, he has developed his use of wordplay by inserting English words for humorous effect. The character's names are homophonous with words for "Rotten Corpse," "Throw out the Garbage," and the like. The work focuses on the compradore class in Taiwan, with Xiao Lin playing the role of observer. It takes place in a travel agency, describing the sycophantic way that Taiwanese workers toady to foreign clientele and sacrifice the well-being of others for material gain.

Wang extends his satiric voice in the campy burlesque *Rose, Rose, I Love You* (Meigui, meigui, wo ai ni, 1984). Though it shares the theme of Huang's "Young Widow," both involving pimps who hawk their prostitutes to U.S. military personnel on leave from the Vietnam War, the tone of *Rose* could not be more different. Wang uses the theme of war and prostitution to exercise his boundless affinity for linguistic play. The characters all possess humorous or ironic names, with that of the main character, the pimp Dong Siwen, meaning "to understand high culture." The novel centers on a few key scenes that feature Dong's scatological performance judging bar girls, goading a politician into striptease for votes, and beholding a medical doctor's homosexual advances on a patient. Deft use of transliteration and double entendre for satirical effect turns this work into a cultural battleground, for it is reminiscent of a ribald Broadway musical comedy whose carefully choreographed theatricality forces the reader to contemplate what in Taiwanese society is the limitation of kitsch.

One does not associate humor with Chen Yingzhen. He is the most politicized of the nativist group, and he spent years as a prisoner of conscience in Taiwan. His work has evolved greatly, given what he has encountered in life, but some themes have nevertheless remained constant. Chen Yingzhen always has been interested in the power of literature to conjoin seemingly unbridgeable experiences and relationships. The structure of his works is often self-consciously disjunct, compelling one to piece together the "mysteries" of the characters within them. In "A Race of Generals" (Jiangjun zu, 1964), for example, one must ask why the two main characters are referred to as generals. What is the cause of their inexplicable deaths at the end? Triangle Face and Skinny Little Maid are musicians in a funeral troupe thrown together by predicament—he a mainlander who has escaped to Taiwan during the Civil War and left his wife behind, she a Taiwanese sold into prostitution, several years his junior. While fundamentally different in background, the two seem naturally drawn to each other. This unique bond combined with the jarring shift back and forth between past and present undermines the reader's attempt to make complete sense of the story. The oblique references to Taiwan's infamous Green Island political prison testifies to Chen's courage. A work, no matter how elliptical, that mixes images of dead generals, metaphorical or not, with references to Green Island could incite the ire of censors and thus contribute to Chen's eventual incarceration.

The difficulty of Taiwanese and mainlanders to fathom each other's identity resurfaces in Chen's existentialist classic "My First Case" (Di yi jian chaishi, 1967). In this story, a young Taiwanese police detective must figure out why a middle-aged mainlander has committed suicide. Detective Du notes that the deceased Hu Xinbao has been pondering life's meaning, a story line that could be read as the plight of the human condition. However, the references to his ethnic dislocation highlight the specificity to Taiwan and militate against a universalist reading. The story consists of splicing together Du's interviews with various characters. This paratactic narrative reveals as much about those characters as it does the mystery of Hu's untimely expiration.

Following his release from prison in 1975, Chen Yingzhen turned to exposing problems of Taiwan's economic dependency on the United States and Japan. "Night Freight" (Ye xing huoche, 1978) is an intriguing accumulation of characters who all work in the Taipei office of a large American multinational firm. How they deal with their situation is very interesting: J. P., a Taiwanese executive, placates his American boss while biding his time until he can take over the office when Morgenthau retires. Morgenthau seems more preoccupied with his lust for Chinese women and derision of their culture than for maintaining a profit margin. Linda—Liu Xiaoling, born to mainlander parents—is hoping to find a husband someday but has given up on her longtime affair with J. P. in favor of the tempestuous "James" Zhan Yihong, who loathes the American company and eventually takes umbrage at an off-color remark from Morgenthau. Linda is attracted to Zhan's anti-imperialistic fury but fears it too. She contemplates "escaping" to America, which functions as an imaginary promised land. The notion of cultural ventriloquism, where one assumes the voice of the economic dominant and adopts a "slave" mentality, exhibiting no allegiances, no convictions, but only fetishes for "classy" automobiles and women is counterposed by the deep baritone of the freight train, Taiwan's bloodline running from the countryside to the city.

With the tacit relaxation of political censorship in the 1980s, Chen Yingzhen began to write stories detailing the political history of Taiwan. "Zhao Nandong" (1987), about the way in which family and friends are rent asunder by the February 28 Incident of 1947, is the most important. It contains explicit reference to the Nationalist pacification campaign in which thousands of leftists were executed. Ye Chunmei, a Taiwanese woman sentenced to life imprisonment (commuted after twenty-five years), seeks closure on her past by finding Zhao Nandong. Zhao is the son of two political prisoners. His mother, Song Rongxuan, was executed after giving birth to him in prison. His father Zhao Qingyun served twenty-five years. Each section of the narrative is told from the perspective of one of the major characters. For Chen, the insurmountable cultural fissure created by political terror is healed only through literature.

Strictly speaking, *Nativism* is a misnomer; all three writers under discussion have at one time or another disavowed the term. Moreover, it would be an injustice not to mention at least some other major postwar nativists—Zhong Lihe (1915–1960), the most important Taiwanese (Hakka) writer of the 1950s, whose tragic death cut short a prolific career; Ye Shitao (b. 1925) and Zhong Zhaozheng (b. 1925), who, in addition to their literary writings, have been stalwarts in the publication of major journals devoted to nativist literature such as *Taiwan Wenyi*; Li Qiao (b. 1934), whose long fiction is perhaps the most important expression of nativist consciousness; and Zheng Qingwen (b. 1932), whose short works are also greatly admired. The breadth of their works scarcely allows one to consider them as part of single movement.

—*Christopher Lupke*

Bibliography

Chang, Yvonne. *Modernism and the Nativist Resistance: Contemporary Fiction from Taiwan.* Durham, N.C.: Duke University Press, 1993.

Chen, Yingzhen. "My First Case." Trans. Cheung Chi-yiu and Dennis T. Hu. In Joseph S. M. Lau and Timothy Ross, eds., *Chinese Stories from Taiwan: 1960–1970*, 26–61. New York: Columbia University Press, 1976.

——. "Night Freight." Trans. James C.T. Shu. In Joseph Lau, ed., *The Unbroken Chain: An Anthology of Taiwan Fiction from 1926*, 103–132. Bloomington: Indiana University Press, 1983.

——. "A Race of Generals." Trans. Lucien Miller. In *Exiles at Home: Short Stories of Ch'en Ying-chen*, 69–82. Ann Arbor: University of Michigan Center for Chinese Studies, 1986.

——. "Zhao Nandong." Trans. Duncan Hewitt. *Renditions* 35–36 (1991): 65–86.

Faurot, Jeannette, ed. *Chinese Fiction from Taiwan.* Bloomington: Indiana University Press, 1980.

Goldblatt, Howard. "The Rural Stories of Huang Ch'un-ming." In Jeannette Faurot, ed., *Chinese Fiction from Taiwan*, 110–133. Bloomington: Indiana University Press, 1980.

Huang, Chunming. "The Fish." Trans. Howard Goldblatt. In *The Drowning of an Old Cat and Other Stories*, 1–11. Bloomington: Indiana University Press, 1982.

——. "Flowers in the Rainy Night." Trans. Earl Wieman. In Joseph S. M. Lau and Timothy Ross, eds., *Chinese Stories from Taiwan: 1960–1970*, 195–241. New York: Columbia University Press, 1976.

——. "His Son's Big Doll." Trans. Howard Goldblatt. In *The Drowning of an Old Cat and Other Stories*, 37–60. Bloomington: Indiana University Press, 1980.

——. "Young Widow." In Rosemary Haddon, trans. and ed., *Oxcart: Nativist Stories from Taiwan, 1934–1977*, 221–304. Dortmund: Projekt Verlag, 1996.

Kinkley, Jeffrey. "From Oppression to Dependency: Two Stages in the Fiction of Chen Yingzhen." *Modern China* 16, no. 3 (1991): 243–268.

——. "Mandarin Kitsch and Taiwanese Kitsch in the Fiction of Wang Chen-ho." *Modern Chinese Literature* 6, nos. 1–2 (1992): 85–113.

Lau, Joseph. "Death in the Void: Three Tales of Spiritual Atrophy in Ch'en Ying-chen's Post-Incarceration Fiction." *Modern Chinese Literature* 2, no. 1 (1986): 21–29.

——. "'How Much Truth Can a Blade of Grass Carry?': Ch'en Ying-chen and the Emergence of Native Taiwan Writers." *Journal of Asian Studies* 32, no. 4 (1973): 623–638.

Miller, Lucien. "A Break in the Chain: The Short Stories of Ch'en Ying-chen." In Jeannette Faurot, ed., *Chinese Fiction from Taiwan*, 86–109. Bloomington: Indiana University Press, 1980.

Wang, Zhenhe. "Ghost, Northwind, Person." In Nancy Ing, ed., *Winter Plum*, 413–436. Taipei: Chinese Materials Press, 1982.

——. "An Oxcart for Dowry." Trans. Joseph S. M. Lau and Jon Jackson. In Joseph S. M. Lau and Timothy Ross, eds., *Chinese Stories from Taiwan: 1960–1970*, 75–99. New York: Columbia University Press, 1976.

——. *Rose, Rose, I Love You*. Trans. Howard Goldblatt. New York: Columbia University Press, 1997.

87

MARTIAL-ARTS FICTION AND JIN YONG

Wuxia xiaoshuo, here loosely translated as "martial-arts fiction," more literally means fiction *(xiaoshuo)* whose subject matter is the intersection of the martial arts *(wu)* with altruistic ideals and the figure of the "Chinese knight-errant" *(xia)*. Martial-arts fiction refers specifically to extended prose narratives on these themes written in vernacular Chinese during the twentieth century. Histories and "encyclopedias" of martial-arts fiction generally trace the genre's roots to the classical tales of the Tang dynasty or even the historical records of the Han period (Liu 1967), and martial-arts novels themselves often draw on such texts or cite them as predecessors.

There is good reason, nonetheless, to consider martial-arts fiction a uniquely twentieth-century literary genre. The compound *wuxia xiaoshuo* did not appear in the Chinese vocabulary until the first decade of this century, apparently borrowed from the Japanese designation for a genre of contemporary adventure novels. Both the newness of the term and its transmission from the hands of China's forward-looking neighbor make it a fitting designation for a genre that, whatever its thematic and formal links with an ancient literary tradition, owes its modern form and popularity to the particular conditions of early twentieth-century China. Urbanization, changes in education and social structure, and the growth of commercial publishing all supported martial-arts fiction as one element within the rising medium of mass-distributed entertainment literature; the fundamental nostalgia and nativism of the genre—its setting in a premodern rural past, a moment of historical crisis, or a mythic antiquity, and its celebration of the martial arts as a uniquely Chinese cultural practice—reflect the social disruptions of modernization and a self-consciousness nourished by cultural plurality and imperialist menace.

The Republican vogue for martial-arts fiction is generally credited to Pingjiang Buxiaosheng (pen name of Xiang Kairan, 1890–1957), who first won a place in the Shanghai fiction scene through satires of overseas student life based upon his own experiences in Japan. His *Marvelous Knights of the Rivers and Lakes* (Jianghu qixia zhuan, 1923), which interweaves local legends with a saga of warring sects of preternaturally powerful martial artists, both established some of the genre's key themes and narrative techniques and heralded its potential as a mass-culture phenomenon; the novel not only sustained the journal in which it was serialized but also gave birth to China's first martial-arts film, *The Burning of the Red Lotus Monastery* (Huoshao Hongliansi, 1928), and its seventeen sequels. *Righteous Heroes of the Modern Age* (Jindai xiayi yingxiong zhuan, 1923) strings together tales of the historical figure Huo Yuanjia and other martial artists of the late Qing and early Republic. Its comparatively realistic depiction of martial-arts practice and of actual martial lineages and its celebration of Chinese national spirit through fighters' triumphs over foreign challengers reflect Xiang Kairan's own involvement in the institutionalization and nationalistic reimagining of the martial arts during the Republican decades, and initiated a strain of martial-arts fiction that was to attain periodic prominence in later decades—influencing, for instance, Bruce Lee and the "kung fu" films of the 1970s as well as the patriotic martial-arts fiction that emerged in the mainland in the early 1980s.

A number of Buxiaosheng's contemporaries and successors developed distinctive fictional voices. Bai Yu (pen name of Gong Zhuxin, 1899–1966) is often noted for his strong characters and supple prose, and Wang Dulu (pen name of Wang Baoxiang, 1909–1977) for the wedding of martial themes with tragic romance and for the emotional intensity of his narration. Perhaps the most popular and influential (after Buxiaosheng) of the prewar authors was Huanzhulouzhu (pen name of Li Shoumin, 1902–1961), whose most famous work, the mammoth *Swordsmen of the Mountains of Shu* (Shushan jianxia zhuan, 1932), remained unfinished when its serialization came to an end in 1948. Some of its essential components are replicated in the shorter *Blades from the Willows* (Liuhu xiayin, 1946): the protagonists, taking refuge from a conquering foreign dynasty in remote mountain realms, become involved in the quests and feuds of warring sects of flying swordsmen, eccentric immortals, and supernatural monsters. Huanzhulouzhu's rich prose, labyrinthine (at times trackless) narratives, evocative descriptions of landscape, and incorporation of imagery and concepts from the Daoist and Buddhist heritages all contribute to his elaboration of what is sometimes described as a "Peach Blossom Spring" mode of martial-arts fiction—the creation of a fantastic never-never land of martial adventure.

For literary and political reformers of the Republican era, martial-arts novels represented the worst of "old-style" fiction, their alleged superstition, violence, and encouragement of the passive desire for an all-powerful savior exacerbating the faults (ideological backwardness, artistic inflexibility, and an unshakeable monopoly on the general population's affections) imputed to popular fiction and commercial entertainment culture more generally. Critics including Zheng Zhenduo, Qu Qiubai, and *Mao Dun penned bitter attacks on the genre during the 1930s, and after 1949 the writing and publication of this "poisonous weed" were prohibited. The emergence of what is sometimes called New School martial-arts fiction in Hong Kong and Taiwan beginning in the latter half of the 1950s can be understood negatively, as simply the corollary of the banning of this form on the mainland; but it can also be interpreted more positively as a reinvigoration of the genre through its responses to the recent and continuing crises of civil war, change of regime, and exile from the ancestral homeland. In Hong Kong, the Communist victory, the experience of colonial rule, and the geopolitics of the Cold War era gave new resonance to such conventional plot elements as Ming loyalist resistance to the foreign Manchu dynasty. Writers in Taiwan, cautious under the Guomindang government's tight controls over cultural expression, avoided direct historical references but joined their Hong Kong colleagues in exploiting the genre's timely mix of violence, altruism, and romantic evocation of China's geography and cultural heritage.

Martial-arts fiction gained momentum simultaneously and to some extent independently in Taiwan and Hong Kong during the 1950s, but it was developments in the British colony that have had the greatest impact upon the genre. In 1954 Liang Yusheng (pen name of Chen Wentong, b. 1922) took advantage of the excitement generated by a match between local martial artists to begin serializing *Lion and Tiger Vie in the Capital* (Longhu dou jinghua, 1954). This successful effort was followed by more than thirty patriotically themed martial-arts novels published in Hong Kong's left-leaning newspapers over the following decades. But Liang Yusheng's reputation was soon overtaken by that of one of his many successors and imitators—his colleague Jin Yong (pen name of Zha Liangyong, or Louis Cha, b. 1924), who by the end of the century emerged as not merely the most successful author of martial arts fiction but perhaps the most widely read of all twentieth-century Chinese novelists.

Like most of Jin Yong's works, his first novel, *The Book and the Sword* (Shujian enchou lu, 1955, rev. 1975), is set at a historical moment of China's conquest by a foreign power. Here Jin Yong employs the legend that the Qianlong emperor (r. 1736–95) of the Manchu Qing dynasty was actually a Han Chinese by birth, and makes him the brother of the leader of the anti-Qing resistance, Chen Jialuo. The resistance's political failure thus acquires the aspect of personal tragedy, which is further given a romantic dimension by the sacrifice of Chen Jialuo's Muslim lover, Princess Fragrance. These political and personal tragedies are offset, however, by the first expressions of what will emerge in later novels as one of Jin Yong's hallmarks—the celebration of the martial arts as an epitome of the Chinese cultural tradition. The "culturalization" of the martial arts, a deepening exploration of characters' moral, psychological, and romantic lives, and a corresponding attenuation of the purely political aspects of the chosen historical settings can be traced (with variations and exceptions) through the course of the author's subsequent works. The epic *Legend of the Eagle-Shooting Heroes* (Shediao yingxiong zhuan, 1957, rev. 1978), which solidified the author's reputation, is set against the Mongol conquest. Its protagonist, the slow-witted but indomitable Guo Jing, represents the acme of ingenuous patriotism; at the same time, however, the novel's "Dispute of the Swords upon Mount Hua" and the fantastic characters associated with this episode create a milieu that is far more mythic than historical. *Fox Volant of the Snowy Mountain* (Xueshan feihu, 1959, rev. 1976) employs the Qing conquest primarily as a distant motivation for a tale whose primary focus is the conflict of personal loyalties. This novel also features a formal intricacy, which testifies to the author's ambitions for expanding the aesthetic possibilities of the genre. In several late novels, the historical references disappear. The achievement of martial enlightenment through a classical poem encountered on an island in *Song of the Swordsman* (Xiake xing, 1966, rev. 1977) epitomizes the identification of the martial arts with a timeless and geographically decentered (diasporic?) essence of Chinese culture; the absence of a dynastic setting in *The Proud and Gallant Wanderer* (Xiaoao jianghu, 1967, rev. 1978) allows the tale's venomously warring sects to mirror the contemporary politics of the Cultural Revolution, or the nature of political life in the abstract. *The Deer and the Cauldron* (Luding ji, 1969, rev. 1981), Jin Yong's last novel to date, returns to a concrete historical setting. It brings both culturalism and political cynicism to bear on the problem of the Qing conquest, justifying the reign of the Kangxi emperor (1662–1722) through his "sinicization" or mastery of the Chinese cultural heritage. This reversal of the earlier novels' (and the majority of martial-arts fiction's) historical vision is accompanied by the jettisoning of many of the genre's conventions; its protagonist, the Yangzhou brothel urchin Wei Xiaobao, masters no martial arts at all but wins wealth, glory, and a harem of seven wives by devoting his skills in deceit, flattery, and invention to the service of his beloved alter-ego, the Qing emperor.

Wei Xiaobao is Jin Yong's most famous and controversial creation, and it is tempting to read this worldly southerner's conquest of and service to the Manchu court as an allegory or omen of the author's career. Jin Yong's earliest works were serialized in Hong Kong papers sympathetic to the left, but most of his later novels in his own *Ming Pao*, established in 1959. The 1960s saw the mutual growth of the popularity of his fiction, his influence as a publishing magnate, and his reputation as a political commentator—the last forged in particular by his scathing reports on the Cultural Revolution. In the 1970s, Jin Yong devoted ten years to the revision of his novels and the production of the thirty-six-volume *Collected Works*. Entering Taiwan (where they had been banned because of the author's early ties with the left) and the mainland (where Deng Xiaoping's economic and cultural policies fostered exchange with the outside world and a boom in entertainment culture) in the 1980s, his works won both immense readerships and increasing critical and scholarly attention. Zha Liangyong (Jin Yong) himself, meanwhile, became an influential supporter of Deng's pragmatic policies and a facilitator of Hong Kong's return to Chinese sovereignty. The success of Jin Yong's novels spurred debate and resistance on the mainland, to some extent echoing earlier critiques of martial-arts fiction but more directly expressing intellectuals' distress at the commercialization of culture and the avant-garde's dismay at the lack of an audience for their own writing. Although debate continues, the awarding of an honorary degree by Beijing University in 1994 consecrated Jin Yong's status as a master of the art of fiction and a spokesman for the glories of the Chinese cultural heritage. Jin Yong's elevation reflects popular culture's domination of the cultural sphere in the 1990s, but at the same time it reveals some critics' inclination to reinterpret his work as "high" culture and divorce it from its roots as genre fiction.

Prominent among Jin Yong's successors have been Gu Long (pen name of Xiong Yaohua, 1936–1985) and Wen Ruian (b. 1954); and martial-arts fiction continues to be written to this day. As a literary form, the genre has felt the effects of the waning of full-length fiction as a primary medium of popular culture, but through the media of films, television serials, comic books, and videogames its themes, conventions, and imagery circulate more widely than ever. Despite, or thanks to, its emphatic "Chineseness," martial-arts fiction has proved popular throughout East Asia, and in translation and adaptation it can be found from Japan and Korea to Indonesia and Vietnam.

—*John Christopher Hamm*

Bibliography

Cha, Louis (Jin Yong). *The Book and the Sword.* Trans. Graham Earnshaw. Hong Kong: Oxford University Press. 2000.

——. *The Deer and the Cauldron.* Trans. John Minford. Hong Kong: Oxford University Press, 1997–2000.

Chen Pingyuan. *Qiangu wenren xiake meng: wuxia xiaoshuo leixing yanjiu* (The Literati's Age-Old Dream of the Knight-Errant: A Genre Study of Martial Arts Fiction). Beijing: Renmin wenxue, 1993.

Danjiang daxue Zhongwen xi (Chinese Department, Tamkang University), ed. *Xia yu Zhongguo wenhua* (The Knight-Errant and Chinese Culture). Taipei: Xuesheng shuju, 1993.

Hamm, John Christopher. "The Marshes of Mount Liang beyond the Sea: Jin Yong's Early Martial Arts Fiction and Postwar Hong Kong." *Modern Chinese Literature and Culture* 11, no. 1 (Spring 1999): 93–123.

Huanzhulouzhu. *Blades from the Willows*. Trans. Robert Chard. London: Wellsweep Press, 1991.

Jin, Yong. *Fox Volant of the Snowy Mountain*. Trans. Olivia Mok. Hong Kong: Chinese University Press, 1993.

Liu, James J.Y. *The Chinese Knight-Errant*. London: Routledge and Kegan Paul, 1967.

Wang Hailin. *Zhongguo wuxia xiaoshuo shi lüe* (A General History of Chinese Martial-Arts Fiction). Taiyuan: Beiyue wenyi, 1988.

88

TAIWANESE ROMANCE: SAN MAO AND QIONG YAO

From 1949 until the late 1980s, Chinese-language romantic fiction (like other popular-entertainment literary genres, such as *martial-arts fiction) was dominated by writers from outside mainland China. The most famous of these, the Taiwanese romantic novelist Qiong Yao, whose novels have sold steadily for more than three decades, is one of the most widely read authors in the Chinese-speaking world. Her contemporary, San Mao, had a similar measure of fame. Although San Mao's classification as a romance writer is not unproblematic, and although there are substantial differences in the kinds of literature produced by these two writers, Qiong Yao and San Mao have generally been placed together as the two major female stars of popular Taiwanese literature, particularly in the 1970s and 1980s when their success ("Qiong Yao fever" and "San Mao fever") was at its height. Because romantic fiction has been little valued by translators, academics, and other arbiters of literary canons, translations of this genre into English are few and secondary literature is relatively scarce. Thus, the names of Qiong Yao and San Mao have not been accepted into prevailing Chinese literary canons, though the twin effects of time and the weakening of boundaries between genres may yet bring this about.

Qiong Yao (Chen Zhe, b. 1938) made her mark on the Taiwanese literary scene in 1963 with her first novel *Outside the Window* (Chuang wai). The story (ostensibly based on her own experience) concerns a high school student who is lonely and struggling to cope with the pressures of schoolwork and high familial expectations. A romantic liaison develops between her and her teacher, a lonely middle-aged man whose family was left behind on the mainland when he fled to Taiwan after the Communist revolution. After her mother breaks up the relationship, believing it to be destructive, she fails the all-important university entrance exams that would have ensured a secure career. The story was variously interpreted by critics as a case of true and freely chosen adolescent love thwarted by an interfering mother and as a destructive relationship to which a wise mother rightly put an end. The fact that the novel attracted critical and scholarly discussion at all suggests that, initially at least, Qiong Yao was considered to be a serious author dealing with important social issues (Lin 1992).

In terms of productivity (sixty-one novels to date) and romantic subject matter (all of her novels have romantic relationships as their central focus), Qiong Yao has often been likened to Barbara Cartland; yet the scope of her work, issues underlying her stories, and various structural aspects of her novels differentiate her markedly from the queen of the English-language romance. The plot construction of Qiong Yao's novels does not necessarily follow the axiomatic "boy-meets-girl, obstacle arises, obstacle is overcome, couple are united" pattern that tends to prevail in English-language romantic fiction. "Obstacles" do arise (often on a large scale—wars, deaths, illnesses, and suicides), but they are generally significant elements in the plot rather than pretexts for delaying the expected romantic reunion. Indeed, romantic union does not always take place; many of Qiong Yao's novels conclude with the couple's being parted, either by death or by renouncing their relationship.

Comparing narrative structures of the novels of Qiong Yao with Janice Radway's (1984) paradigms of American romance fiction, the Taiwanese literary sociologist Lin Fangmei has noted the following features of Qiong Yao's writing: (1) the romantic encounter between hero and heroine tends to occur early in the narrative, with the realization and declaration of true love being immediate (the plot action never hinges on the difficulties of recognizing true love); (2) obstacles to romance tend to be external (for example, parental opposition) rather than internal psychological and emotional dilemmas; (3) love scenes typically include some ritual (occurring in generally predictable contexts) in which the couple commemorate their love (with poetry, letters, gifts, or items from nature such as flowers or leaves), and these tokens become significant to the subsequent action; (4) members of the romantic couple's family are usually vital to the plot; and (5) stories do not always end with the couple's being happily united.

All of these features can be traced back to earlier forms of romantic writing in Chinese, such as the *Mandarin Ducks and Butterflies fiction of the Republican period and Cao Xueqin's mid-Qing classic vernacular romance novel *The Dream of the Red Chamber* (Honglou meng). Indeed, Qiong Yao has self-consciously drawn on the Chinese literary tradition in her novels through frequent poetic and classical allusions.

Changes over time in the settings and plot constructions of Qiong Yao's novels may reflect trends or preoccupations in Taiwan society in general. Her nov-

els of the 1960s are mostly set in the period of civil war and the flight of the Nationalists to Taiwan, and they often feature dislocated families, straitened circumstances, and loneliness. Her 1970s novels tend to portray secure and stable
family lives and end happily. In the 1980s and 1990s, more historical themes and
settings emerged and happy endings were fewer.

Qiong Yao's writings have often been called "morbid" *(you bingtai)*, perhaps
because in many of her novels the central romantic liaison is socially questionable (relationships between teacher and student, guardian and ward, brother-in-
law and sister-in-law). She has been praised by some, however, for the quality of
her prose, for her poetry (chiefly in her earlier works), and the literary allusions
in her book titles. Most of her books are novels; three are collections of short stories, and she has also written an autobiography and an account of a trip to
China. Her biggest selling, most reprinted novels are *Outside the Window* and
Deep Is the Courtyard (Tingyuan shenshen, 1969), the story of a couple parted
by a cruel mother-in-law and reunited a decade later by the self-sacrifice of the
man's second wife who, recognizing their superior fated love, divorces him so
that they may be together.

From the beginning of her career, Qiong Yao has had strong links with the
mass media. Her novels have been serialized in *Crown* (Huangguan) magazine
(owned by her husband, Ping Xintao) before being published as monographs by
Ping's Crown publishing house. Many of her stories have been adapted as
movies and television series, often with either Qiong Yao herself or Ping Xintao
writing the screenplays and supervising production. These activities have contributed to her enormous fame, not only in Taiwan and in mainland China
(where pirated editions of her novels started to appear in the mid-1980s) but all
over the Chinese-speaking world.

San Mao (Chen Ping, 1943–1991) is often paired with Qiong Yao in terms of
fame, popularity, and influence. She, too, was made famous by Ping's publishing house, Crown Press; indeed, stories by San Mao and Qiong Yao alternated
for some years as a prime selling point of *Crown* magazine.

Her writing contains features of autobiography and travelogue, as well as romance, and takes short-story rather than novel form. Whereas Qiong Yao wrote
romantic stories, it could be said that San Mao lived one, or narrated her life as
one: she opted out of high school and was educated at home; traveled to Europe
and Africa at a time when few in Taiwan had the means to do so; married a
Spanish man (supposedly after he had waited faithfully for her for six years); was
caught up in the drama of Spanish decolonization in the Western Sahara; was
widowed after six years of marriage; returned to Taiwan a celebrity; and spread
her philosophy of happiness, beauty, love, and human concern wherever she
went.

San Mao consistently claimed that everything she wrote was based on her
own life, and almost all of her stories are narrated in the first person by a character named "San Mao." This has led to a blurring of the identities of and

boundaries between the person Chen Ping and the pen name and literary persona San Mao; this tendency has been exacerbated by biographers, who have reproduced events described in San Mao's own stories as "facts" of her life.

San Mao's fame began with "The Restaurant in the Desert" (Shamo zhong de fandian), a story about cooking Chinese food in Western Sahara, published in Taiwan's *United Daily News* (Lianhe bao) in 1974. Further stories of the Sahara and of Europe followed, published in *Crown*; later stories dealt with her childhood, her return to Taiwan after the death of her Spanish husband, her attitudes to and relations with family and work, her philosophies of life, her studies in the United States and her trip to China. In addition to short stories, she wrote the screenplay for the award-winning film *Red Dust* (1990); her list of "complete works" also contains cassette tapes of her public storytelling, translations, and two collections of readers' letters to her and her replies as an "agony aunt" in magazine columns.

It is for her Saharan stories, however, that San Mao is best known. Collected in *Stories of the Sahara* (Sahala de gushi), *Crying Camels* (Kuqi de luotuo), and *The Tender Night* (Wenrou de ye), the tales intersperse playful and ironic accounts of commonplace events, such as cooking, furnishing her home, or taking a driving test, with stories of the "exotic" (Sahrawi bathing customs), the "barbaric" (Sahrawi marriage customs, or the keeping of slaves), the supernatural (a mysterious illness caused by a necklace that carries a curse), the adventurous (evading assailants and saving her husband from drowning in a freezing swamp), and the politically significant (friendship with Sahrawi independence activists). Several stories present San Mao as a therapeutic presence, bringing medicines, basic education, and hygiene to Sahrawi people; narratives of Europe present a similar scenario as San Mao assists friends and neighbors in need and manifests a persona of caring and goodness.

Although romantic relationships are not the main focus of her work, biographers have paid particular attention to this aspect of her writing, depicting her relationship with the Spaniard José as an ideal romantic union of two exceptional characters brought about by fate, in the manner of a Qiong Yao story. Indeed the Taiwan critic Li Ao famously suggested that the only difference between San Mao's writing and Qiong Yao's was "a handful of sand"—in other words, San Mao wrote romantic stories in which she herself was the heroine, then added the exotic setting of the Sahara Desert.

Both San Mao and Qiong Yao created worlds in which emotion was paramount, along with an emphasis on the beauty and sincerity of that emotion. San Mao's writing about foreign countries provided readers with visions of exotic places, and Qiong Yao's historical settings provided exotica of time; and although Qiong Yao's chief subject is the heterosexual romantic bond and San Mao's the romantic individual in a world of wider connections (romantic, familial, community, and international), both embody a romantic sensibility and maintain a focus on the individual and the individual's emotions.

At the end of the 1990s, Qiong Yao was still publishing and her work continued to be adapted into television serial format. Many new romantic writers had
emerged—for example, Zhang Manjuan with her stories of ill-fated love. Responding to changes in Taiwan society through the 1970s, 1980s, and 1990s, romance writers increasingly incorporated such subjects as premarital sex and co-
habitation, extramarital affairs, and divorce into their fiction; in addition, plots
became more likely to emphasize the heroines' working lives, to explore the
conflicting obligations of work and family, and to present heroines as self-
sufficient beings for whom heterosexual love and romance is just one aspect of
life and not, as in Qiong Yao's novels, women's prime goal and ultimate fulfillment.

—*Miriam Lang*

Bibliography

Gu Jitang. *Pingshuo San Mao* (Evaluating San Mao). Beijing: Zhishi, 1991.

Lin, Fangmei. "Social Change and Romantic Ideology: The Impact of the Publishing
Industry, Family Organization and Gender Roles on the Reception and Interpretation of Romance Fiction in Taiwan, 1960–1990." Ph.D. diss., University of Pennsyl-
vania, 1992.

Lu Shiqing, Yang Youli, and Sun Yongchao. *San Mao zhuan* (San Mao: A Biography).
Taipei: Chenxing, 1993.

Qiong Yao. *Chuang wai* (Outside the Window). Taipei: Huangguan, 1963.

——. *Tingyuan shenshen* (Deep Is the Courtyard). Taipei: Huangguan, 1969.

Radway, Janice. *Reading the Romance: Women, Patriarchy, and Popular Literature.*
Chapel Hill: University of North Carolina Press, 1984.

San Mao. *Kuqi de luotuo* (Crying Camels). Taipei: Huangguan, 1977.

——. *Sahala de gushi* (Stories of the Sahara). Taipei: Huangguan, 1976.

——. *San Mao zuori, jinri, mingri* (San Mao—Yesterday, Today, and Tomorrow).
Hong Kong: Wenxue yanjiushe, 1983.

89

MISTY POETRY

Menglong shi, also known as Obscure Poetry and translated here as Misty Poetry, was originally used in a derogatory sense to describe the poetry that emerged in 1979–80 during the period of "thaw" following Mao Zedong's (1893–1976) death and the arrest of the Gang of Four. First appearing in August 1980 in a short essay published in *Poetry Monthly* (Shi kan), the largest official poetry journal in China, "misty" *(menglong)* was defined by the critic Zhang Ming as a poetic style of opaqueness (Bi 1984:151–153). The term quickly caught on and was—and still is—commonly used to refer to the work by a new generation of poets published from 1979 to the mid-1980s. "Misty" also took on positive meanings as it attracted national attention: a fresh new poetry distinguished from the formulaic, didactic poetry endorsed by the cultural establishment. Among the best-known Misty Poets were Bei Dao (b. 1949), Shu Ting (b. 1952), Gu Cheng (1956–1993), Jiang He (b. 1949), Yang Lian (b. 1955), Liang Xiaobin (b. 1954), Wang Xiaoni (b. 1955), and Mang Ke (b. 1951), although not every one of them was singled out for criticism.

The controversy over Misty Poetry first erupted in 1980–81, then again in 1983–84 during the Anti-Spiritual Pollution Campaign (Larson 1989; Yeh 1992). In both cases, the main charges against Misty Poetry mounted by the establishment can be summarized as follows. First, by indulging in obscurantism and individualism, Misty Poetry separated itself from the people and deviated from the realist tradition, the officially espoused norm in PRC literature. Second, the critical tone of much Misty Poetry revealed a skeptical, pessimistic outlook that ran counter to the spirit of the Four Modernizations, the regime's new national economic plan. Finally, obscurity, individualism, and skepticism were deemed the result of Western influences, especially that of modernism; because China did not "face a crisis, either spiritual or material, that would produce modernism in literature" (Larson 1989:51), Misty Poetry was an anachronistic imitation of the West and suggested a loss of the Chinese national character. Although most establishment critics and veteran poets, such as Ai Qing (1910–1998) and Zang Kejia (b. 1905), were vehement in their attacks, a few, including Xie Mian, Sun Shaozhen, Xu Chi, and Du Yunxie (b. 1918)—the last a poet whose "Autumn" in 1979 was among the first poems to be criticized as "misty"—defended Misty Poetry and advised tolerance.

The establishment's charges against Misty Poetry are essentially political. According to the official ideology, poetry, like all cultural forms, should serve the people by being politically correct in content and easily comprehensible in language and form. Shu Ting's "Assembly Line" (Liushui xian) and Gu Cheng's "The End" (Jieshu), for example, were deemed unacceptable because of their contents. Based on the poet's personal experience as a worker in a light-bulb factory, "Assembly Line" depicts the erasure of individuality in an unnatural, dehumanizing environment of mechanized mass production. It was criticized for expressing discontent with modernization. "The End" compared the Jialing River to a soiled shroud and was accused of disrespect for the beloved motherland.

Even when a poem is devoid of political implications, obscure imagery constitutes another reason for criticism. The most notorious examples are Gu Cheng's "Arcs" (Huxian) and "Far and Near" (Yuan he jin). The second reads:

> You
> Sometimes look at me,
> Sometimes look at the clouds.
>
> I feel
> You're so far away when you look at me
> You're so close when you look at the clouds.

To most readers outside China, this poem would not come across as obscure, although it might lend itself to different interpretations. Ambiguity and polysemy, however, were alien to Chinese readers who had grown accustomed to the transparent, message-oriented poetry dictated by the Communist Party propaganda machine throughout Mao's era. The initial reaction of bewilderment and shock at poems like "Far and Near" is indicative of the bleak literary scene in the aftermath of the Cultural Revolution (1966–76).

To trace the origins of Misty Poetry, one must go back to the Cultural Revolution, when underground poetry was widely circulated among dislocated youths in rural and urban areas. Because it was typically short and relatively easy to commit to memory, underground poetry exerted an immense influence on the generation growing up during the Cultural Revolution. Although the complete story has not been told, and probably never will be owing to the loss of original material, some of the underground poetry has survived (Yang 1993). The one poet who was to have a lasting impact on the Misty Poets is Shizhi ("index finger," the pen name of Guo Lusheng, b. 1948). Shizhi's early association with a group of underground poets in Beijing, which called itself the Sun Column (Van Crevel 1996:25–29), inspired his signature poems: "Believe in the Future" (Xiangxin weilai) and "This Is Beijing at 4:08" (Zhe shi sidian ling ba fen de Beijing), both written in 1968. With the title memorializing the parting words of fellow poet Zhang Langlang (b. 1943), whose underground literary activities in the Sun Column led to his imprisonment from 1968 to 1977, "Believe in the Future" expresses hope in the face of hopelessness. The second poem was written when the poet was aboard the 4:08 train taking him away from home toward an uncertain future. "Believe in the Future" reportedly displeased Jiang Qing, Mao's wife and spokesperson. Political persecution contributed to the poet's mental breakdown in the early 1970s and intermittent hospitalization ever since (Van Crevel 1996:28–34).

Although written mostly in a regular form with rhymes, Shizhi's early work is refreshingly different from the officially sanctioned "political lyric" for its natural cadence and introspective, personal tone. The first stanza of "Believe in the Future" is a fine example:

> When cobwebs ruthlessly seal my cooking stove,
> When smoldering smoke mumbles the grief of poverty,
> I stubbornly spread out the ashes of disappointment on the floor
> And write these words with beautiful snowflakes: Believe in the future.

Much of Shizhi's early poetry was published in *Today* (Jintian, 1978–80), an underground literary journal founded and edited by two Beijing poets, Bei Dao and Mang Ke. Besides Shizhi and the two editors, *Today* also published such poets as Shu Ting, Fang Han (b. 1947), Yi Qun (b. 1947), Jiang He, Gu Cheng, Yan Li (b. 1954), Yang Lian, Tian Xiaoqing (b. 1953), and others, many of whom were to become leading Misty Poets.

Today played an instrumental role not only in the rise of Misty Poetry but also in post-Mao literature and art in general. Its founding members included the painter Huang Rui, joined by four more painters (Lu Huanxing, Shen Liling, Zhang Pengzhi, and Sun Junshi), all of whom left in early 1979 over disagreement on how much political involvement the journal should have. The popularity of *Today* signaled a transition to what came to be called post-Mao China. The first sign of "thaw" in the social and cultural sphere was visible in late 1978, two years after the fall of the Gang of Four, when underground journals like *Explorations* (Tansuo) emerged for the first time in the history of the PRC (Xu 1981). Consisting mostly of fiction that depicted and critiqued the horrendous injustices suffered during the Cultural Revolution, *scar literature appeared at the same time. Many of the underground publications, in mimeographs, found their way onto big-character posters in Beijing. Among them was *Today*. In its inaugural preface, the editors of *Today* rejected the "cultural dictatorship" of the Gang of Four and identified the April Fifth populist demonstrations of 1976 as the beginning of a new era. In tune with the time, they sought to explore "the meaning of individual existence" and deepen "people's understanding of the spirit of freedom." The preface also advocated a "horizontal" perspective that would reassert China's place among other nations in the world (*Today* 1:1–2).

Today was representative of the time in many ways. First, it embodied the pervasive mood of disillusionment in China. Quite appropriately, the first short story published in the journal was entitled "On the Ruins." Mang Ke compared the rising sun—an unmistakable symbol of Chairman Mao—to a blood-dripping shield in his poem sequence "Sky," and Shu Ting referred to the "crown of thorns" on her head. In a short essay on the early issues of the journal, Jiu Min (pen name of A Cheng) said: "A salient characteristic of the younger generation is its disbelief in 'God.' This is a most profound change, as reflected in the fiction authors of *Today*; in their works there is no 'human being' who is 'tall, great, perfect'" (*Today* 9:59). Second, disillusionment led to defiance of existing norms and conventions. Bei Dao's "I—don't—believe!" (a line from his poem "Reply") became the battle cry of his generation; its categorical rejection of the orthodoxy alarmed the establishment and invited harsh criticism. Gu Cheng's "A Generation" (Yidairen) transforms the legacy of evil into hope: "Black night gave me black eyes, / But I use them to look for light." Yang Lian's "From Our Own Footprints ... " (Women cong ziji de jiaoyin shang) begins with these lines:

> From our own footprints
> We understand history
> From the age of ravished poetry
> From the age of guilty doves and flowers
> From the age of quietly weeping children
> From the age of unexpressed friendship and love ...

Third, defiance also meant new approaches to literature and art. After decades of subordination to political contingencies, poetry now asserted its independence and freedom. Yang Lian hailed the poet as Prometheus and declared: "Poetry is first of all *poésie*"; it "cleanses and purifies all" and "is above all" (*Today* 9:62). Romantic love, nature from a childlike perspective, personal memories and aspirations, tributes to the victims and martyrs of the Cultural

Revolution—themes that would have been taboo in Mao's era—now appeared in abundance, and political correctness gave way to individual expression in both form and content.

During the two years of its existence, *Today* published nine issues of the journal and four books: collections of poetry by Mang Ke, Bei Dao, and Jiang He, and a novella by Ai Shan (pen name of Bei Dao). It also sponsored two poetry readings (on April 8 and October 21, 1979, respectively) and cosponsored two exhibits of the Stars Group, the first nonofficial painters in the PRC. On September 12, 1980, *Today* was suspended by the authorities for having failed to register, but it went on to publish three more issues of "literary data" of the Today Literary Research Society, edited by Wan Zhi (pen name of Chen Maiping, b. 1952), in October–December 1980 before it finally folded (Pan and Pan 1985). By then, however, publication outlets were no longer limited to underground journals. In the more open climate of post-Mao China, many new official literary journals were established all over the country, some more liberal than others. The *Today* poets, along with many other new poets, published in official journals at all levels, including the nationwide *Poetry Monthly*, and were especially popular on college campuses.

The *Today* group overlapped significantly with Misty Poets, although the latter designates a much larger number of poets, many of whom never published in *Today*. The aforementioned characteristics identified in *Today* poetry are for the most part applicable to Misty Poetry in general and suggest both its accomplishments and limitations. Although Misty Poetry represented a promising start of a new, vital poetic movement and helped usher in a literary renaissance, it had to overcome many disadvantages that were not so much political and social as educational and cultural. Because the Cultural Revolution deprived most Misty Poets of a high school education, their exposure to both traditional Chinese and world literature was severely limited. Not unaware of this poor foundation, Misty poets eagerly looked to translations of foreign, predominantly European and Anglo-American, literature for resources (Van Crevel 1996:35–41). Most Misty Poets acknowledged having been directly influenced by Western poets and writers, but their access to translations (none of the poets was proficient in a Western language) was haphazard, and they ingested the foreign works with haste and often without an adequate understanding of the cultural context in which those works were written.

Furthermore, despite the intention of separating literature from politics, much of Misty Poetry remained firmly grounded in a political framework. The collective self, against whom the individual self struggled to find meaning, never really disappeared from Misty Poetry, as amply seen in the early work of Jiang He, Bei Dao, Shu Ting, Yang Lian, and Duo Duo, and, with few exceptions, their poetic language was unable to walk out of the shadow of Maospeak. In addition, some of the Misty Poets' attempts "to change the inert components in the Chinese national character … also placed excessive stress on the role of literature" (Pan and Pan 1985:215), which ironically undermined its stated ideal of pure literature.

In retrospect, Misty Poetry should be seen as transitional. By 1986 a second wave of new poetry had appeared on the scene. The generational differences were striking. Commonly referred to as the Third Generation or the Newborn Generation, these poets were born in the late 1950s through the mid-1960s. Unlike the Misty generation, they were too young to be permanently imprinted with the scars of the Cultural Revolution. They also received complete formal schooling and were generally better educated, most having college degrees and some proficient in one or more foreign languages. Finally, in an economically more developed and socially more open environment, they had extensive exposure to foreign literatures and cultures, including those from other Chinese domains.

Misty Poetry was an important chapter in the literary history of the People's Republic of China. It was also the first Chinese poetry since that of the May Fourth period in the 1920s to receive wide international recognition. Some Misty Poets went on in new directions, whereas others simply stopped writing and left the literary scene.

—Michelle Yeh

Bibliography

Barnstone, Tony, ed. *Out of the Howling Storm: The New Chinese Poetry*. Middletown, Conn.: Wesleyan University Press, 1993.

Bi Hua and Yang Ling, eds. *Jueqi de shiqun—Zhongguo dangdai menglongshi yu shilun xuanji* (The Rising Poetry Group: A Collection of Chinese Misty Poetry and Poetic Criticism). Hong Kong: Dangdai wenxue yanjiushe, 1984.

Finkel, Donald, ed. *A Splintered Mirror: Chinese Poetry from the Democracy Movement*. San Francisco: North Point Press, 1991.

Larson, Wendy. "Realism, Modernism, and the Anti-'Spiritual Pollution' Campaign in China." *Modern China* 15, no. 1 (January 1989): 37–71.

Morin, Edward, ed. *The Red Azalea: Chinese Poetry since the Cultural Revolution*. Honolulu: University of Hawai'i Press, 1990.

Pan, Yuan and Jie Pan. "The Non-Official Magazine *Today* and the Younger Generation's Ideals for a New Generation." In Jeffrey Kinkley, ed., *After Mao: Chinese Literature and Society, 1978–1981*, 193–219. Cambridge, Mass.: Harvard University Press, 1985.

Tay, William. "'Obscure Poetry': A Controversy in Post-Mao China." In Jeffrey C. Kinkley, ed., *After Mao: Chinese Literature and Society, 1978–1981*, 133–157. Cambridge, Mass.: Harvard University Press, 1985.

Van Crevel, Maghiel. *Language Shattered: Contemporary Chinese Poetry and Duoduo*. Leiden: Research School CNWS, 1996.

Xie Mian and Tang Xiaodu, eds. *Zai liming de tongjing zhong: menglongshi juan* (In Dawn's Bronze Mirror: An Anthology of Misty Poetry). Beijing: Beijing shifan daxue, 1993.

Xu, Xing. "The Rise and Struggle for Survival of the Unofficial Press in China." In *Documents on the Chinese Democratic Movement 1978–1980*, 33–45. Paris and Hong Kong: Écoles des Hautes Études en Sciences Sociales and Observer Publishers, 1981.

Yang Jian. *Wenhua dageming zhong de dixia wenxue* (Underground Literature during the Cultural Revolution). Ji'nan: Zhaohua, 1993.

Yeh, Michelle. "Light a Lamp in a Rock: Experimental Poetry in Contemporary China." *Modern China* 18, no. 4 (October 1992): 379–409.

Yeh, Michelle, ed. *Anthology of Modern Chinese Poetry*. New Haven: Yale University Press, 1994.

Zhuang Rouyu. *Zhongguo dangdai menglongshi yanjiu—cong kunjing dao qiusuo* (A Study of Contemporary Chinese Misty Poetry: From Quandary to Quest). Taipei: Da'an, 1993.

90

SCAR LITERATURE AND THE MEMORY OF TRAUMA

In November 1977, the official literary journal *People's Literature* (Renmin wenxue) published the first of a series of stories about suffering during the Cultural Revolution and about the spiritual state of the Chinese people who had survived it. In Liu Xinwu's "Class Counselor" (Ban zhuren, 1977), a devoted teacher, Zhang Junshi, chooses to help a youth whose delinquency he sees as a casualty of his upbringing during the reign of the ultraleftist Gang of Four. As Zhang confronts his students' resistance to accepting the boy, he realizes the harm that "fascist cultural tyranny" (157) has done to even the exemplary youth, most notably the well-intentioned Youth League Branch Secretary. Though tendentious passages condemn the Gang of Four and lecture on the need to cure the body politic, the story expresses impassioned faith in a teacher's ability to open his students' eyes to the wider achievements of human civilization. In this way, the story confronts the nation's "spiritual impoverishment" (161) while still proclaiming deep devotion to the cause of national salvation.

Liu's story was immediately followed by an outpouring of similar works testifying to the immeasurable trauma and dislocation of Mao's massive national campaign to create unending revolution. After the publication the following August of Lu Xinhua's story "The Wounded" (Shanghen, 1978), such works became known collectively as "scar literature" or "literature of the wounded" *(shanghen wenxue)*. By portraying the suffering endured by unjustly persecuted artists, intellectuals, common people, cadres, and educated youth "sent down" to the countryside, these stories explicitly criticized the unrestrained implementation of political orthodoxy. Although scar literature did not yet question the revolutionary cause or challenge culture's instrumental subservience to it, it did reintroduce such humanist subjects as the importance of individual autonomy, the exercise of individual conscience, complex moral dilemmas, and literature's role in exposing the dark aspects of society. Its appearance, within two years of the death of Chairman Mao Zedong and the fall of the Gang of Four, testifies to the authors' courage in reviving Chinese writers' traditional duty to expose injustice and corruption.

Scar literature thus holds great historical significance as the first stage in the liberalization of Communist Party literary policy in the post-Mao era. For the preceding three and a half decades, ever since Mao's *"Yan'an Talks" (1942), literature had been more in the service of politics than at any other time in China's long literary history. With the "Yan'an Talks" as textual authority, the PRC cultural bureaucracy implemented a rigid program centered around *"revolutionary realism and revolutionary romanticism," making use of "rectification" campaigns *(zhengfeng yundong)* to silence alternative voices. In 1953, Mao's cultural czar Zhou Yang (1908–1989) solidified the rules for literary production by reiterating the tenets of socialist realism first developed in the Soviet Union. Thereafter, Communist Party literary doctrines lay an ever more hazardous minefield of taboos against "middle characters," psychological analysis, critical realism, or accounts of autonomous actions not dictated by party ideology. The persecution of writers in the Anti-Rightist Campaign (1957–58) (see "The Hundred Flowers") and the Cultural Revolution taught writers the often fatal consequences they could face for unflattering portrayals of socialist society, or for depictions of humanist principles or romantic love that might transcend class lines or overshadow social issues (Pollard 1978:100–102).

By reaffirming the value of individuals and their inner struggles, scar literature broke decisively with the cultural paradigm of the Mao period. At the same time, the inclusion of an obligatory "bright tail" *(guangming weiba)* ending in these stories affirmed faith in the new regime under Deng Xiaoping (1904–1997) and thus limited these stories' censure to the wrongdoings of the past. By demonizing the Cultural Revolution and the Gang of Four, moreover, these works served a conservative ideological and political function: they reinforced the Deng regime's efforts to consolidate its power by distancing itself from Maoist ideology through its campaign of intellectual liberation *(sixiang jiefang)* and its creation of a "new era" *(xin shiqi)* through the Four Modernizations economic program. In its implicit reassertion of individualism, scar literature might even have reinforced the Communist Party's new leniency toward the pursuit of profit and Deng's program of promoting a rational, progressive, and affluent society. By classifying recent literary production into categories such as "literature of the wounded" and its heirs the "literature of reflection" *(fansi wenxue)* and "literature of reform" *(gaige wenxue)*, critics encouraged writers to repeat formulas. Official Party endorsement of these new genres soon followed as the

leadership announced the relaxation of thought control in late 1978 and ushered in the "Beijing Spring" of 1979. At the fall 1979 Fourth Congress of Writers
and Artists, Deng Xiaoping and Zhou Yang relaxed literary policy and sanctioned all works helpful to the realization of the Four Modernizations.

The literary significance of scar literature lies primarily in its potential to
serve as a forum for moral reflection. Although many of the early stories de-
nounce the Gang of Four for the country's ills and thus avoid issues of personal
responsibility, soon bolder stories broached characters' guilt over their participation in the persecution of their loved ones. The epithet "literature of the
wounded" draws attention to the suffering of the victims, but these works increasingly hinted at their characters' roles as victimizers as well.

Such new attention to personal responsibility is evident in the story from
which scar literature derives its name. One of the saddest stories of modern Chinese fiction, Lu Xinhua's "The Wounded," describes a former Red Guard's
gradual coming to terms with her earlier disavowal of her mother after the latter
is branded a "renegade." The story opens nine years after Xiaohua's departure
from Shanghai as she travels back from Liaoning Province in the hopes of seeing her now-rehabilitated mother. Arriving only after her mother has passed
away, Xiaohua finds a note in which her mother not only refuses to blame her
daughter but also expresses concern for the ordeal she has lived through.
"While she hasn't been as physically mistreated as I was by the Gang of Four,"
the note says, "the wound in her heart will be much worse than all the wounds
on my body" (Barmé and Lee 1979:23). This assertion of Xiaohua's position as a
victim does not put to rest the issues raised by her earlier recollections and by
her pain upon seeing a mother and child together on the train. Xiaohua's remorse leads the reader to question how she came to believe official accusations
against her mother in the first place. How would a daughter resolve to repudiate
her mother and perceive her act as a matter of choice? "She had no choice but
to criticize her own petite-bourgeois instincts and draw a line of demarcation
between herself and her mother" (11).

Loath to identify with a criminal, had the sixteen-year-old Xiaohua abandoned her mother to pursue her own dreams and plans or in order to follow the
party's program for what a good revolutionary's plans and dreams should be? In
returning her mother's care packages, had she not become an instrument of the
party's persecution of her mother? The barriers Xiaohua has erected to sever her
love for her mother are further demonstrated when she doubts what her mother
writes in her letter about her rehabilitation, illness, and concern that she may
not live long enough to see her daughter. The possibility that Xiaohua could
have acted otherwise, at least in not delaying her return, is implied by her
boyfriend's suggestions that she inquire about her mother's status after the fall of
the Gang of Four and by his own visit to Xiaohua's mother in her stead. The
story's hopeful ending suggests Xiaohua's control over her emotions, but it
leaves the reader to imagine the remorse left unexplored: "Dear mother, rest in

peace. I will never forget who was responsible for your wounds and mine. I shall never forget Chairman Hua's kindness and closely follow the Party's Central Committee headed by him and dedicate my life to the cause of the Party" (23–24). Xiaohua's faith in her nation's progress toward a just and affluent society does not placate the deep sense of collective grievance brought out in other parts of the story.

The concrete depictions of trauma in much scar literature dispel some of the mystery surrounding the Cultural Revolution and testify to the peril that results when people are made into instruments of political movements. The senseless chaos that resulted from Mao's headlong pursuit of ideological purity and utopian ends is clearly depicted in such stories as Zheng Yi's "Maple" (Feng, 1979) about a young couple who find themselves on opposite sides of warring Red Guard factions. Such works may have helped renew readers' concerns for their own lives, souls, and families. For example, Chen Guokai's "What Should I Do" (Wo yinggai zenme ban, 1979) tells of the heartache, suffering, and near death of a woman after her husband suddenly disappears; one evening years later, having remarried, she answers the door to find her first husband freed from a labor camp. Kong Jiesheng's "On the Other Side of the Stream" (Zai xiaohe neibian, 1979) also treats the trauma of a family's separation during the Cultural Revolution. Brought back together by coincidence, a brother and sister fail to recognize each other and fall in love. "Neither wanted to open the other's wounds" (185), and so they never ask about each other's families until they decide to marry and are thus forced to discover their original relationship.

If works of *revolutionary romanticism had endorsed a Maoist version of history, scar literature often undermined Mao's faith in collective voluntarism. These stories revived the May Fourth tradition of critical realism in exposing China's social and economic problems, political corruption, and the disillusionment and utter exhaustion of a people still reeling from the anguish of the immediate past. Some authors used parody, as in Gao Xiaosheng's story about how shifts in official policy continually frustrate a peasant's attempts to build his family a home in "Li Shunda Builds a House" (Li Shunda zao wu, 1979). Others portrayed the immorality of the bureaucracy, fraud and opportunism, as in Liu Ke's depiction of the rape of a young army recruit in "Feitian" (1979), or of influence peddling, as in Xu Mingxu's "Transfer" (Diaodong, 1979).

The most intense moments in these stories occur when a character is caught between two conflicting sets of norms, such as humanist and socialist. In Chen Rong's novella *At Middle Age* (Ren dao zhongnian, 1980), for example, cramped quarters, exhaustion, and finally failing health reduce a self-sacrificing ophthalmologist from a model cadre who can perform seventeen operations in a morning to a woman debilitated by depression. Such "literature of reflection" condemned not only particular events and individuals, but questioned the ideological foundations of China's socialist system. Some such works even explored traumas of the seventeen years between 1949 and the onset of the Cultural Revolution in 1966.

Although much scar literature seems to imply that honest analysis and individual responsibility will lead to reform, it often presents the injustices of the political system as ineluctable. In this way, it paved the way for the inward turn of the psychological fiction that emerged around 1980 and the "sketch" *(texie)* or "reportage" *(baogao wenxue)* that began with "People or Monsters" (Renyao zhi jian, 1979) by journalist Liu Binyan (b. 1925).

In terms of its function as cultural memory, scar literature may also be seen as a predecessor to later testimonial literature about the Cultural Revolution, some of which first appeared in English, such as Nieh Cheng's *Life and Death in Shanghai* (1986) and Gao Yuan's *Born Red: A Chronicle of the Cultural Revolution* (1987). More probing Chinese works also followed in the tradition of scar literature, most notably, "prison literature" *(daqiang wenxue*, literally "literature of the big wall") such as Cong Weixi's novella *Red Magnolias beneath the Wall* (Daqiang xia de hong yulan, 1979) and Ma Bo's *Blood Red Sunset* (Xuese huanghun, 1987). Ma's harrowing novel, which sold 400,000 copies in China, describes how a Red Guard ransacks his family home and denounces his mother and how he himself suffers persecution as a counterrevolutionary.

Literature of the wounded is often criticized for formulaic and didactic content, but it is difficult to write about suffering and not deliver a message. Its great significance deserves further consideration through comparison with other trauma literature, such as works about the European Holocaust or the repression of intellectuals under Stalin.

—Deirdre Sabina Knight

Bibliography

Barmé, Geremie, and Bennett Lee, eds. *The Wounded: New Stories of the Cultural Revolution*. Hong Kong: Joint Publishing Company, 1979.

Duke, Michael, ed. *Contemporary Chinese Literature: An Anthology of Post-Mao Fiction and Poetry*. Armonk, N.Y.: M. E. Sharpe, 1985.

Jenner, W.J.F. "A New Start for Literature in China?" *China Quarterly* 80 (June 1981): 274–303.

King, Richard. "'Wounds' and 'Exposure': Chinese Literature after the Gang of Four." *Pacific Affairs* 54, no. 1 (1981): 82–99.

Kinkley, Jeffrey, ed. *After Mao: Chinese Literature and Society, 1978–1981*. Cambridge, Mass.: Harvard University Press, 1985.

Lau, Joseph S.M. "The Wounded and the Fatigued: Reflections on Post-1976 Chinese Fiction." *Journal of Oriental Studies* 20, no. 2 (1982): 28–42.

Lee, Yee, ed. *The New Realism: Writings from China after the Cultural Revolution*. New York: Hippocrene, 1983.

Link, Perry. *The Uses of Literature: Life in the Socialist Chinese Literary System.* Princeton: Princeton University Press, 2000.

——, ed. *Roses and Thorns: The Second Blooming of the Hundred Flowers in Chinese Fiction, 1979–1980.* Berkeley: University of California Press, 1984.

——, ed. *Stubborn Weeds: Popular and Controversial Chinese Literature after the Cultural Revolution.* Bloomington: Indian University Press, 1983.

Liu, Binyan. *People or Monsters and Other Stories and Reportage from China after Mao.* Trans. Perry Link. Bloomington: Indiana University Press, 1983.

Ma, Bo. *Blood Red Sunset: A Memoir of the Chinese Cultural Revolution.* Trans. Howard Goldblatt. New York: Viking, 1995.

Pollard, David E. "The Short Story in the Cultural Revolution." *China Quarterly* 73 (March 1978): 99–121.

91

CULTURE AGAINST POLITICS:
ROOTS-SEEKING LITERATURE

The current of "roots-seeking literature" *(xungen wenxue)* dominated China's literary scene between 1985 and 1988. Although it is sometimes referred to as a literary movement guided by a manifesto, "roots-seeking" *(xungen)* is perhaps better seen as a pervasive theme that has preoccupied writers during a certain period of time—a theme that stirred up lively debates in literary circles of the time. The main characteristic shared by these writers is that they have all in some manner stressed the importance of their cultural identity for their creative work; in other words, they considered their Chinese or ethnic minority identity as a relevant or even decisive element of a successful Chinese literature.

The roots-seeking phenomenon was initially a theoretical affair that started with an essay, "Literary 'Roots'" (Wenxue de gen, 1985), by the fiction writer Han Shaogong (b. 1953). Han's essay immediately provoked a flood of articles that did not subside until the spring of 1988. The central issue raised by Han and many of the other participants in this debate was this: How can writers renovate Chinese literature when they find themselves so cut off from their cultural tradition? In this call for revitalization, roots-seeking literature was clearly a reaction against, on one hand, politically controlled or socially engaged literature (for example, *"scar literature" and "reform literature," respectively, of the early 1980s), and, on the other hand, the "pseudomodernists" *(wei xiandai pai)* who, in the eyes of the roots-seeking authors, ran the risk of being a shallow imitation of Western literature. In the latter, they discerned a superficial focus on formal techniques borrowed from Chinese translations of Western literature. In reacting against these

Western imitators, the roots proponents called for a return to China's indigenous cultures as the fountainhead for literary creativity.

Almost all theorists of roots-seeking literature mention May Fourth iconoclasm—and its culmination in the Cultural Revolution—as the main cause for their sense of cultural uprootedness. They oppose the May Fourth not only for its radical break with tradition in favor of the appropriation of Western literary techniques, but also for its tendency to use literature for moral and sociopolitical engagement, to the detriment of art. The roots writers' stress on "culture" *(wenhua)* can also be seen as an alternative to, or a weapon against, "politics," which Mao had put in command of the arts. This can also be seen from the issue of language raised by the critic Li Tuo, a promoter of roots literature. Li opposed the westernized May Fourth language and the so-called Mao style *(mao wenti)*, language colored by political ideology. These views of language were shared by writers not directly associated with roots literature. *Gao Xingjian, for example, proposed that writers should return to basic characteristics of the traditional Chinese language to produce "modern literature imbued with an Asian spirit." The call for a "stronger national literature" (as some writers put it) was thus based as much on artistic and aesthetic motives as nationalist ones.

It was to the countryside, either in the writer's own home region or among the many minority cultures that lived there, that writers were to turn in search of their roots. It is perhaps not surprising that these writers looked to the countryside for their inspiration, for almost all of them had been sent there as educated youth *(zhiqing)* in the 1960s and 1970s and had spend a great part of their formative years living among the rural population. Roots writers and theorists saw the remote rural and minority areas as preserves of cultures somehow untouched by the homogenizing influence of modernization, westernization, and even the Chinese revolution on one hand and the Confucian or dominant Han-Chinese culture on the other.

Because of its subject matter, roots-seeking literature is often equated with, or treated as a subdivision of, "native soil literature" *(xiangtu wenxue)* (see "Shen Congwen and Imagined Native Communities" and "The Taiwan Nativists"). Apart from the fact that both draw material or inspiration from the countryside, they have little in common. The nostalgic mood of the native soil literature of the Republican period and the more ideological nature of Taiwanese nativist literature of the 1960s and 1970s, for example, cannot be called the main motives of roots-seeking literature. An exception is the native-soil literature of *Shen Congwen, who was an example to many roots writers by virtue of his shunning of politics in favor of aesthetics and his blending of modern (Western) and traditional (Chinese) literary influences.

In the aforementioned essay, Han Shaogong points to Jia Pingwa's (b. 1953) series of short stories *Records of Shangzhou* (Shangzhou chu lu, 1982) and A Cheng's (b. 1949) novella *The King of Chess* (Qi wang, 1984) as early manifestations of roots literature. These works, along with Han's own work and Mo Yan's (b. 1956) internationally acclaimed *Red Sorghum* (Hong gaoliang jiazu, 1987), have since been labeled standard works of the roots-seeking current. The well-known film by Zhang Yimou based on Mo Yan's novel (*Red Sorghum*, 1988), as well as Chen Kaige's *Yellow Earth* (Huang tudi, 1984) and *King of the Children* (Haizi wang, 1987), based on a novella by A Cheng, represent a roots-seeking current in cinema around the same period. This current is further marked by films such as *Horse Thief* (Dao ma zei, dir. Tian Zhuangzhuang, 1986) and *Old Well* (Laojing, dir. Wu Tianming, 1987), based on novels by the roots writers Zhang Chengzhi (b. 1948) and Zheng Yi (b. 1947), respectively. Interestingly, a current of roots-seeking in poetry has also been discerned in the work of Yang Lian and Jiang He, among others, whose poetry employs imagery drawn from Chinese history, myth, and legends.

Jia Pingwa has declared that depicting the local customs of everyday people, as he does for his home district in rural Shanxi in his *Records of Shangzhou*, is the only way to revitalize Chinese literature, and he thereby explicitly agrees with the roots-seeking theory. Whereas his subject matter is contemporary (namely, the Cultural Revolution), Jia's style is said to hark back to the traditional prose sketch (*biji*) (see, for example, "How Much Can a Man Bear" [Renji, 1985]). The paradoxical and alienating effect of a traditional style combined with a modern content is a typical feature of roots literature.

A Cheng's *The King of Chess* has been noted for a linguistic style that is reminiscent of China's premodern novels. But more important is the story's attempt to link traditional Daoist spirituality with modern, everyday life. Set in the Cultural Revolution, it tells of a young man who is obsessed with food and chess. The protagonist's emphasis on eating marks his status as a poor commoner, whereas his craze for chess is enshrouded in Daoist philosophy. The story can be read as an attempt to show how the Daoist tradition is alive among the common folk, paradoxically even during the Cultural Revolution. "The Tree Stump" (Shu zhuang, 1984) also attempts to bring tradition and modernity together; the plot recounts an aged folksinger participating in a modern singing contest. In his essays, A Cheng has explicitly stated that literature, just like humanity, is conditioned by culture, as revealed in secular customs and language.

Han Shaogong shows great interest in marginal worldviews and local beliefs of the Hunanese countryside, which he traces back to the ancient Chu culture. Another inspiration drawn from China's southern cultures is a spirit of Zhuangzi's relativity and ambivalence, which can be seen as a central governing aspect of Han's work; it is manifest in the questioning of the validity of all kinds of pairs of opposites. His best-known story, "Pa Pa Pa" (Ba ba ba, 1985), set in a remote mountain hamlet, is a social satire in which primitive "nonrationality" (instinctive thought and superstition) is set off against the rationality (modern logic and scientific values) of the implied modern reader. If "Pa Pa Pa" focuses on social history, "Woman Woman Woman" (Nü nü nü, 1986) reflects the other side of the coin: individual action. The protagonist's love-hate relationships with his traditional, self-effacing, austere aunt and her hypermodern, emancipated, hedonist goddaughter, reveal his ambivalent attitude toward both modern and traditional values, in particular the questions of individual freedom and compliance to social norms. In the short story "Homecoming" (Guiqu lai, 1985), the first-person narrator comes to an unknown remote village where everyone takes him for someone else, an experience so haunting that he starts to question his own identity. The story's dreamlike atmosphere alludes to Zhuangzi's "butterfly dream" and the issue of the relativity of identity. The abundant depictions of strange local customs are not used for exotic effect or nationalistic identification; they can be seen as imagery in the service of the identity theme: they accentuate the alienating contrast between the individual and the outside world, the Self and the Other. In addition, Han's interest in Hunan's local dialects has led him to a preoccupation with the use of language, even in his later work of the 1990s.

Besides the attention to regional customs, which all writers discussed here share, other related aspects of literary roots-seeking include the conflict between tradition and modernity, marginal cultures, magic realism, ethnic minorities, and nature. The conflict between tradition and modernity is a major theme in the work of Li Rui (b. 1950), Li Hangyu (b. 1957), and Zheng Yi. Li Rui has been noted for his series of short stories *The Solid Earth* (Houtu, 1986), of which the title already speaks volumes, and his novel *Silver City* (Jiuzhi, 1992), a family saga set in a fictitious Chinese town in which modernity challenges traditional culture. Li Hangyu, besides having been an active theorist of the current, has written a series of short stories set by the Ge River, in the Yangtze delta south of Shanghai. Both Li Hangyu's best-known story, "The Last Angler" (Zuihou yige yulaor, 1982), and Zheng Yi's novel *Old Well* (Lao jing, 1985) portray men who are reluctant to give up their humble, traditional professions or to leave the rural place where they have their roots, even if that means forfeiting a chance to be with the modern or urban woman they love.

Another pervasive aspect of roots-seeking fiction is its interest in marginal cultures as alternatives to the mainstream. In their essays Han Shaogong, Gu Hua (b. 1942), and Li Hangyu all explicitly claim that orthodox culture is less conducive to artistic production than the unorthodox. The Confucian tradition is seen as more practical and less spiritual than, for example, Daoism, the *Songs of Chu*, Song lyric meters, and Ming-Qing fiction, influence of which can be seen in most roots-seeking works: for example, Daoism and Ming-Qing fiction in A Cheng, or the *Zhuangzi* and Chu culture in Han Shaogong.

A conspicuous feature of roots-seeking fiction is magic realism, either influenced by its Latin American counterpart or derived from indigenous roots. Authors such as Han Shaogong and Mo Yan prefer to point to China's rich, persistent tradition of tales of the supernatural and the fantastic, the *zhiguai* (records of anomalies) and the *chuanqi* (accounts of the extraordinary); this influence is clear in Han Shaogong's short story "Embers" (Yujin, 1994). Others such as Jia Pingwa and Zhaxi Dawa (b. 1959) have acknowledged that Nobel Prize-winner Gabriel García Márquez, after his *Hundred Years of Solitude* was translated into Chinese in 1982, had a great influence on them, both in terms of literary techniques—specifically, his blending of local traditional culture with Western modernity—and in offering a positive example of a writer from an economically backward nation who has gained global recognition. Traits of magic realism can be detected in the work of the Han-Tibetan writer Zhaxi Dawa, among others. In stories such as "A Soul in Bondage" (Xi zai pisheng kou shang de linghun, 1985), traditional Tibetan values and modern Western culture exist side by side. He and others also use notions of cyclical time in a subversive— call it postmodern—narrative. Han Shaogong often presents odd local customs, superstition, and violent primitivism in a way intended to convince us of their internal logic, and maybe to hold up a mirror to modern culture; in this sense, it can be superficially likened to García Márquez's writing.

Minority cultures provide material for many roots works. For some writers, Zhaxi Dawa for instance, this is a case of drawing from their own ethnic origins. But Han writers have also often written about minority cultures. Experimental writer Ma Yuan (b. 1953), for example, has often written about Tibetan culture (although his treatment of it is too casual to allow him to be included in the roots-seeking current). Zheng Wanlong (b. 1944) is inspired by the Oroqen minority group of northeastern China among whom he spent his youth. The title of his series of stories *Strange Tales from Strange Lands* (Yixiang yiwen, 1985) already evokes the sense of estrangement the writer apparently feels toward the culture of his home region, which he consciously portrays as exotic. This alienation of intellectuals in rural areas is a typical theme in the literary works and theoretical essays of most roots-seeking writers, who have more than once acknowledged that ethnic identity can be used as a metaphor through which to pursue personal identity.

Nature is another important theme in roots-seeking literature. Many roots-seeking writers reveal a certain nostalgic longing for the authentic, natural life embodied in their rural characters and from which they feel alienated. A clear example of this is Mo Yan's work. Second, there is a tendency to see ethnic or personal identities as determined by regional environment and natural conditions. Zhang Chengzhi, a member of the Hui Muslim minority, has written extensively about the regional cultures of Inner Mongolia, Ningxia, and Xinjiang, the homelands of the Hui. The identity theme is apparent in his novella *Rivers of the North* (Beifang de he, 1984), for instance, where the protagonist likens the Yellow River to his father, just as in several short stories the grassy plains are likened to the protagonist's mother. Zhang's well-known novella *The Black Steed* (Hei junma, 1982; adapted for the screen by Xie Fei in *A Mongolian Tale*,

1997) is a pastoral love story that combines the typical oppositions of root-seeking fiction: that between local and central (Han) culture, city and country-side, and intellectual and peasant.

Other writers can be seen as belonging somewhat more loosely to root-seeking literature than the writers discussed earlier. Wang Zengqi (b. 1920), for example, is an older writer who had published in the 1940s and made a come-back in the post-Mao era, when he was hailed as the inheritor of the legacy of Shen Congwen, whose pupil he had been. Younger generations of writers ap-preciated his stories, such as "Ordination" (Shoujie, 1980), for the language and the cultural atmosphere that hark back to the pre-Communist period. Wang Anyi's (b. 1954) *Baotown* (Xiao Bao zhuang, 1984) is often referred to as a roots-seeking work. Finally, Gu Hua's *A Small Town Called Hibiscus* (Furong zhen, 1981) clearly also has a rural community as its subject, but it has been mostly ap-preciated for its political views.

Roots-seeking literature has been criticized for its hostility to foreign influ-ence and its "inward turn" to its own culture. Critics have also disapproved of its "turning backward" to tradition, even glorifying tradition, while neglecting the issues of modernity and progress. Other critics, on the contrary, highlight the open-mindedness of the current: its treatment of Chinese culture from a mod-ern point of view, absorbing Western culture as a frame of reference from which to understand Chinese culture better and more critically. They also agree with some of the writers involved in the movement that only a literature that is firmly rooted in its national soil can enter the stage of world literature.

The attention given to culture in this literary current can be seen as a part of the larger debates on culture in the sociopolitical sphere in the mid-1980s, known as a time of "culture fever" *(wenhua re)*. In political as well as intellec-tual fields, Chinese felt the need to reestablish their national identity in the modern world after years of isolation. It can be argued that roots-seeking litera-ture presents an alternative to the shallow nationalism of Communist Party or-thodoxy; thanks to its aesthetic ambitions, the literary search for roots resulted in a much more subtle and even ambivalent attitude toward questions of cultural identity.

Although it may be justified to criticize roots theory for its fixation on Chi-nese culture, in literary practice, as we have seen, many writers go beyond that theme and delve into deeper questions of subjectivity and modernity. Root-seeking literature should be seen as an important phase in the development of contemporary Chinese literature. One could say that it moved literature away from its narrow sociopolitical engagement by stressing much broader cultural aspects of literature. By drawing attention to aesthetic dimensions of literature and delving into questions of identity and subjectivity, moreover, it paved the way for the *avant-garde literature of the later 1980s and 1990s.

—*Mark Leenhouts*

Bibliography

Ah, Cheng. *Three Kings: Three Stories from Today's China.* Trans. Bonnie S. McDougall. London: Collins Harvill, 1990.

——. "The Tree Stump." In Jeanne Tai, trans. and ed., *Spring Bamboo: A Collection of Contemporary Chinese Short Stories*, 25–33. New York: Random House, 1989.

Feuerwerker, Yi-tsi Mei. "The Post-Modern 'Search for Roots' in Han Shaogong, Mo Yan, and Wang Anyi." In *Ideology, Power, Text: Self-Representation and the Peasant "Other" in Modern Chinese Literature*, 188–238. Stanford: Stanford University Press, 1998.

Gu, Hua. *A Small Town Called Hibiscus.* Trans. Gladys Yang. Beijing: Panda Books, 1983.

Han, Shaogong. "Embers." Trans. Thomas Moran. In Henry Zhao, John Rosenwald, and Yanbing Chen, eds., *Fissures: Chinese Writing Today*, 263–279. Brookline, Mass.: Zephyr Press, 2000.

——. "The Homecoming." In Jeanne Tai, trans. and ed., *Spring Bamboo: A Collection of Contemporary Chinese Short Stories*, 19–40. New York: Random House, 1989.

——. *Homecoming? and Other Stories.* Trans. Martha Cheung. Hong Kong: Renditions, 1992.

——. "The Leader's Demise." Trans. Thomas Moran. In Joseph Lau and Howard Goldblatt, eds., *The Columbia Anthology of Modern Chinese Literature*, 387–398. New York: Columbia University Press, 1995.

Jia, Pingwa. *The Heavenly Hound.* Beijing: Panda Books, 1991.

——. "How Much Can a Man Bear?" and "Family Chronicle of a Wooden Bowl Maker." In Zhu Hong, trans. and ed., *The Chinese Western*, 1–52, 100–117. New York: Ballantine, 1988.

Li, Hangyu. "In a Little Corner of the World." Trans. Sally Vernon. In Henry Zhao, ed., *The Lost Boat: Avant-garde Fiction from China*, 59–74. London: Wellsweep, 1993.

——. "The Last Angler." Trans. Yu Fanqin. *Chinese Literature* (Autumn 1984): 40–51.

——. "The Old Customs of Brick Stove Beach." Trans. Kuang Wendong. *Chinese Literature* 12 (1983): 19–40.

Li, Rui. "Electing A Thief." Trans. Jeffrey C. Kinkley. In Helen F. Siu, ed., *Furrows: Peasants, Intellectuals, and the State: Stories and Histories from Modern China*, 201–211. Stanford: Stanford University Press, 1990.

——. "Sham Marriage." Trans. William Schaefer and Fenghua Wang. In Howard Goldblatt, ed., *Chairman Mao Would Not Be Amused: Fiction from Today's China*, 90–98. New York: Grove Press, 1995.

——. *Silver City.* Trans. Howard Goldblatt. New York: Henry Holt, 1997.

Mo, Yan. "Dry River." In Jeanne Tai, trans. and ed., *Spring Bamboo: A Collection of Contemporary Chinese Short Stories*, 207–227. New York: Random House, 1989.

——. *Explosions and Other Stories.* Trans. Janice Wickeri. Hong Kong: Renditions, 1991.

——. *Red Sorghum.* Trans. Howard Goldblatt. New York: Viking, 1993.

Wang, Anyi. *Baotown.* Trans. Martha Avery. New York: Viking Penguin, 1985.

——. "Lao Kang Came Back." In Jeanne Tai, trans. and ed., *Spring Bamboo: A Collection of Contemporary Chinese Short Stories*, 41–55. New York: Random House, 1989.

Wang, Zengqi. "The Love Story of a Young Monk" and "Story after Supper." Trans. Hu Zhihui and Shen Zhen. *Chinese Literature* 1 (1982): 58–96.

——. *Story after Supper*. Beijing: Chinese Literature Press, 1990.

Zhang, Chengzhi. *The Black Steed*. Trans. Stephen Fleming. Beijing: Chinese Literature Press, 1989.

——. "The Nine Palaces." In Jeanne Tai, trans. and ed., *Spring Bamboo: A Collection of Contemporary Chinese Short Stories*, 245–279. New York: Random House, 1989.

Zhaxi, Dawa (Tashi Dawa). *A Soul in Bondage: Stories from Tibet*. Beijing: Panda Books, 1992.

——. "Souls Tied to the Knots on a Leather Cord." In Jeanne Tai, ed., *Spring Bamboo: A Collection of Contemporary Chinese Short Stories*, 135–169. New York: Random House, 1989.

Zheng, Wanlong. "Clock." In Jeanne Tai, ed., *Spring Bamboo: A Collection of Contemporary Chinese Short Stories*, 3–18. New York: Random House, 1989.

——. *Strange Tales from Strange Lands*. Ithaca, N.Y.: Cornell University Press, 1993.

Zheng, Yi. *Old Well*. Trans. David Kwan. San Francisco: China Books and Periodicals, 1989.

Zhong, Xueping. "Manhood, Cultural Roots, and National Identity." In *Masculinity Besieged? Issues of Modernity and Male Subjectivity in Chinese Literature of the Late Twentieth Century*, 150–170. Durham, N.C.: Duke University Press, 2000.

92

MO YAN AND *RED SORGHUM*

Mo Yan, born Guan Moye in 1955, has often been mentioned as a candidate for the Nobel Prize, and his prolific output and innovative style have earned him nearly every national award in the People's Republic of China since he started publishing in 1981. He has also won international fame, notably for the film script *Red Sorghum* (Hong gaoliang, 1987), and many of his works have been masterfully translated into English by Howard Goldblatt, in a close collaboration that has at times influenced Mo Yan's writing.

Mo Yan has contributed to shaping the course of Chinese fiction by introducing a mixture of reality and the supernatural, akin to the magic realism of Gabriel García Márquez. He acknowledges that García Márquez's *One Hundred Years of Solitude* triggered in him a "shock of recognition" (1991:ix), although he did not read the novel until after writing his best-known work, *Red Sorghum* (Hong gaoliang jiazu, 1986). His first major work, the novella *A Transparent Carrot* (Touming de hongluobo, 1984), won Mo Yan immediate renown for its crisp descriptions that blur into surreal fantasy. The novella contains themes and stylistic features that would become central to Mo Yan's writing, such as life in a backwater village and an outcast's point of view. Because the plot is set in a rural area during the Cultural Revolution, Mo Yan's work was identified as part of the contemporary *"roots-seeking literature" *(xungen wenxue)* movement. Yet, unlike many other writers associated with the trend, Mo Yan was not a "sent-down" urban youth unfamiliar with the countryside. In fact, he was born to a peasant family, and some of his works—notably *Explosions* (Baozha, 1985)—depict life in his native Gaomi County in Shandong Province. Mo Yan's work sets itself apart from fiction in the mid-1980s by emphasizing the surreal, a trait that would become popular only later in the decade with the rise of *"avant-garde literature."

During the Cultural Revolution, Mo Yan's schooling was interrupted and he was sent back to help in his family's field work. In 1976 he joined the People's Liberation Army and served as political commissar and propaganda officer. While continuing his formal education (B.A. in literature from the PLA Academy of Art, 1984–86; M.A. from Beijing Normal University's Lu Xun Literary Institute, 1988–91), Mo Yan developed a distinctive voice. His work reached an important landmark in 1986, with the publication of a series of novellas later compiled into *Red Sorghum*. What caught the eye of readers was the work's deviation from the accepted practice for the historical novel. The story takes place in 1939, in the heat of the anti-Japanese war. Since the late 1940s many novels have focused on the theme of resistance during the war, portraying Chinese fighters in heroic colors. Mo Yan's protagonists, too, win the narrator's admiration, yet they are as superhuman in their desires and faults as they are in their zeal to fight the Japanese. Yu Zhan'ao, a sedan-bearer, falls for a woman he carries in a wedding sedan. Having killed the bride's husband and father-in-law, he takes over the woman and her new property, including a sorghum-wine brewery. A boisterous, fearless man, he becomes a bandit leader and later the commander of a militia. After his two women—he has meanwhile established a second household—are murdered by the Japanese, he takes his fifteen-year-old son and continues to fight. In the same narrative breath one is told of Yu's valiant killing, his looting, and his defense of the country.

Red Sorghum reclaims historiography from the party-line version of heroic nationalism. For example, the third chapter, "Dog Ways" (Gou dao), recounts an epic military battle, yet a battle that is ironically fought not with the Japanese but against a pack of wild dogs. There is little bravery in slaughtering dogs with hand grenades, and the dogs' strategizing against the humans is equally inglorious. The novel's rich imagery also seems to undermine official nationalist narratives. The color red that pervades the story—from the red sorghum and the red dog leader to the blinding red light and the generous splashes of blood—is far different from the glorious red flag of the PRC, the color of which is thought to have come from the blood of revolutionary martyrs. If Mo Yan's sensuous colors lend themselves to symbolic interpretation, it is one that goes against the grain of official PRC ideology.

In fact, as the text progresses it leaves behind all claim to redemption. The most heroic scene in the novel comes at the very beginning, when Yu Zhan'ao's company attacks a Japanese convoy; yet the attack is unsuccessful, and the Chinese troops, along with Yu's wife, perish. Later battles are described as senseless skirmishes and are suffused with brutality. Yu's servant, Uncle Arhat, is skinned alive—few graphic details are spared—for fleeing from the Japanese; yet he brings the calamity upon himself as he is caught taking revenge on an innocent mule. Characters' motives are often reduced to basic needs and base desires that give rise to an all-encompassing violence, which is in turn depicted with disturbing indifference as a delicate ballet.

Mo Yan departs from the *revolutionary realism that characterizes the literature of the 1960s and 1970s. *Red Sorghum* shuttles back and forth, in fuguelike form, between different points in time. Narrators and viewpoints are changed without warning until reality and fantasy fuse. As David Wang (1993:125) notes, "where facts and memory are incomplete, fantasy fills in." The novel satirizes what Li Tuo (1993:274) has mockingly called "the Mao style" *(Mao wenti)*. Tonglin Lu (1993:193) notices how frequent use of the superlative, which in Mao's jargon dictated the only course of action, serves in *Red Sorghum* to underline irony and contradiction.

The shunning of the heroic historical narrative is especially discernible in Mo Yan's use of narrative voice. The narrator, Yu Zhan'ao's grandson, returns to his ancestral village to compile a family chronicle. Yet instead of a genealogical epic, the result is an often unflattering account, one that identifies the narrator's father as "a bandit's offspring" (3) and his village as "that sinful spot known as Northeast Gaomi Township" (327). Moreover, this is not the history of great national deeds but rather of individual actions in a private time and space. By describing in detail the sexual appetites of his ancestors, the narrator writes a history of desire. Rather than use an individual story as metonym for collective history, national events serve as metaphors for personal experience.

The narrator plays an important role in pointing to the troubled relation between fact and fiction. Like Mo Yan, the narrator was born in Gaomi County in 1956, thereby bearing a slippery affinity with the author. Yet the authorial voice is misleadingly self-referential. It gives the lie to any attempt to reconstruct the past or establish a trusting relation between author and readers. Mo Yan's fictional voice addresses the reader in an inscription before the novel begins: "I am prepared to carve out my heart, marinate it in soy sauce ... and lay it out as an offering.... Partake of it in good health!" The passage implies that the relationship between Mo Yan and his readership is cannibalistic; readers consume the literary work, and the writer willingly provides them with gore. At the same time, both author and readers must accept the playfulness of such statements. The novel presents evidence contrary to the narrator's doubts toward the end of the novel: "Have I no voice of my own?"

The novel was popularized by Zhang Yimou's award-winning film, which retains the basic plot of the first two chapters. The movie loses, however, the original work's epic proportions and alternative historical view. Upholding a clearer sense of patriotic heroism and narrating the story in a linear chronology, the film nevertheless echoes the modernist drive of the novel, and Mo Yan must share credit for the rise of "fifth-generation" Chinese cinema to world fame.

Mo Yan's immediate success did not prevent him from continuing to develop his style, invoking popular premodern romance and folk verse to create his particular modern myths. The novel *The Garlic Ballads* (Tiantang suantai zhi ge, 1988) targets the social unrest that accompanied the rural reform of the late 1980s. Representing the revolt of discontented villagers whose livelihood is threatened by a slump in garlic prices, the work contains Mo Yan's signature emphasis on the senseless violence that suffuses all realms of life, including family brutality and savage injustice by the legal and punitive systems. His next novel, *The Thirteen Steps* (Shisan bu, 1988), reaches a new level of complexity as it presents multiple narrators who come to listen to a storyteller locked up in an insane asylum. As he weaves his own narrative, the storyteller devours chalk, which sticks to his lips.

The Republic of Wine (Jiu guo, 1992), arguably Mo Yan's most accomplished work, tells of a detective who travels to the town of Liquorland to investigate accusations that local officials have been eating human babies. The protagonist soon finds himself embroiled in the villagers' sexual vice and shares their culinary customs, including eating human "babies," allegedly made of pork and vegetables. The bout of ritual cannibalism and profuse drinking ends in murder and in the detective's drowning to death in a manure pit. The gory emphasis on infanticide and cannibalism may be attributed to the historical context of the novel's composition. As Xiaobin Yang (1998:7) argues, *The Republic of Wine*, written soon after the Tiananmen Square massacre of June 4, 1989, designates the "historical destiny" of the text to "demonstrate the sanguinary ruins of national history."

The Republic of Wine owes its intricacy to a particular meshing of fiction and metafiction. The detective story is disrupted from time to time by correspondence between an author by the name Mo Yan, who is in the process of writing the detective plot, and another author, Li Yidou. The correspondence shows the detective story to be the fruits of the two authors' collaboration, taking its material from Li Yidou's life. The reader who tries to trace the relation between the fictitious author and his real-life namesake, Mo Yan, is bound to end up in drunken vertigo. One may conclude that the desire to distinguish fact from fiction, history from its representation, is a dangerous form of desire.

Mo Yan's concern with creating an alternative history and with the role of the narrator is evident also in his later works, notably the novels *The Herbivorous Family* (Shicao jiazu, 1993) and *Big Breasts and Wide Hips* (Fengru feitun, 1995). Mo Yan continues to publish essays, short stories, scripts, and novels, including the essay collection *The Wall That Could Sing* (Hui changge de qiang, 1998) and the novel *The Red Forest* (Hong shulin, 1999).

Mo Yan's work has drawn much critical attention for its direct, even sensationalist presentation of sexuality, as well as for its alternate version of historical writing. Some do not believe that Mo Yan's satire of party ideology goes far enough. They regard him as "pseudomodern" (*wei xiandai*), claiming that he privileges the consciousness of the whole nation at the expense of the individual. On the other end of the ideological spectrum, some see his emphasis on aesthetics as a sign of excessive individualism and accuse him of following trendy "imported" literary styles (J. Wang 1996:186–189). These assessments may reflect the critics' agenda no less than the author's concerns. One cannot deny that Mo Yan has invented a unique literary idiom. He has brought to the fore the rupture between the claims of modernity and conditions in the Chinese countryside, especially the plight of misfits and women. The metafictional devices and self-mockery that make Mo Yan's texts seem insensitive might at times obscure the author's genuine humane concern. His bawdy language, humorous presentation, and riveting storytelling have created one of the most eloquent voices in contemporary Chinese fiction, regardless of the fact that the author uses the pen name Mo Yan, literally "don't speak."

—*Yomi Braester*

Bibliography

Li, Tuo. "Resisting Writing." In Liu Kang and Xiaobing Tang, eds., *Politics, Ideology, and Literary Discourse in Modern China*, 273–277. Durham, N.C.: Duke University Press, 1993.

Liu, Kang, and Xiaobing Tang, eds. *Politics, Ideology, and Literary Discourse in Modern China*. Durham, N.C.: Duke University Press, 1993.

Lu, Tonglin. "Red Sorghum: Limits of Transgression." In Liu Kang and Xiaobing Tang, eds., *Politics, Ideology, and Literary Discourse in Modern China*, 188–208. Durham, N.C.: Duke University Press, 1993.

Mo, Yan. *Big Breasts and Wide Hips*. Trans. Howard Goldblatt. New York: Arcade, 2002.

——. *Explosions and Other Stories*. Trans. Janice Wickeri. Hong Kong: Renditions, 1991.

——. *The Garlic Ballads*. Trans. Howard Goldblatt. New York: Viking, 1995.

——. *Red Sorghum*. Trans. Howard Goldblatt. New York: Penguin, 1993.

——. *The Republic of Wine*. Trans. Howard Goldblatt. New York: Arcade, 2000.

Wang, David Der-wei. "Imaginary Nostalgia: Shen Congwen, Song Zelai, Mo Yan, and Li Yongping." In Ellen Widmer and David Der-wei Wang, eds., *From May Fourth to June Fourth: Fiction and Film in Twentieth-Century China*, 107–132. Cambridge, Mass.: Harvard University Press, 1993.

Wang, Jing. *High Culture Fever: Politics, Aesthetics, and Ideology in Deng's China*. Berkeley: University of California Press, 1996.

Yang, Xiaobin. "The Republic of Wine: An Extravaganza of Decline." *positions* 6, no. 1 (1988): 7–31.

93

DIASPORA LITERATURE

Diaspora, literally meaning "the scattering of seeds," is a term that originally referred to the exile of the Jews from the Holy Land thousands of years ago. However, the recent boom in studies of various kinds of diasporas has broadened the use of this term to include the modern condition and experience of transnational and intercultural dispersal. This may be externally enforced or self-imposed and may involve people of any race or nation.

It is in this broader sense that I use the term *diaspora literature* to refer to modern Chinese literature written by Chinese overseas about their experience of living far away from their native country. These works are written in Chinese, mostly published in the Chinese world (including Taiwan, Hong Kong, and the People's Republic of China), and consequently are aimed at Chinese readers. Generally speaking, the writers discussed in this essay were born, grew up, and received at least their formative education in China. So even if they were living abroad when they wrote, the experience and reality they represent often straddle two worlds and cultures. I exclude works in English by writers of Chinese descent and those by expatriate writers whose writing hardly touches on the diaspora experience. Previous scholars have given alternative names and definitions to Chinese diaspora literature, depending on their emphasis and subject matter, such as "literature of exile *(liuwang wenxue)*, "literature of students abroad" *(liuxuesheng wenxue)*, and "Chinese overseas literature" *(haiwai huawen wenxue)*.

The experience of diaspora is an important phenomenon in modern Chinese history. Since the late nineteenth century, constant social and political upheavals have sent waves of Chinese intellectuals and writers abroad, fired up with the ideal of saving a nation in crisis. And though it is true that most Chinese diaspora have been voluntary exiles, the historical traumas of their homeland have certainly overshadowed their personal journeys.

The earliest diaspora literature can be traced back to the writings of a group of Chinese students in Japan between the 1910s and 1920s, who were also among the enthusiastic advocates of "new literature" in the May Fourth era. Representative of this group is *Yu Dafu (1896–1945) and his "notorious" short story "Sinking" (Chenlun, 1921). A largely autobiographical piece emulating the Japanese "I-novel" tradition, "Sinking" is one of the first works of modern Chinese fiction to present an alienated and troubled soul wandering in a foreign land. The protagonist, coming to Japan to study medicine, finds himself in a state of "hypochondria" due to sexual frustrations that are linked inextricably with his racial sensitivities. He tries to escape into solitude, severing relationships with his family and fellow Chinese students, reading the Western Romantics, and returning to nature. However, these attempts to escape prove futile, and after a night of sexual misadventures in a Japanese brothel, he becomes filled with such self-loathing that he decides to drown himself.

Although seldom read from a diasporic angle, this story introduces a character who reappears in many subsequent works: a wanderer whose pained self desperately seeks to resolve contradictory impulses toward individualism and nationalism. And even if the struggle of the protagonist appears at first sight more like a "libidinous crisis," there are powerful racial sensitivities and nationalist emotions seething beneath the surface. As Goldblatt (1981:12) points out, the "individual inadequacy" of the protagonist is closely tied up with the problem of "national impotence." On one hand, Yu blames China for her weakness and the shame and humiliation associated with her that individual Chinese people must suffer: "O China, my China, you are the cause of my death.... I wish you could become rich and strong soon.... Many, many of your children are still suffering" (141). On the other hand, he cannot help turning to her for protection and love, even his imaginary homeland is on the "distant shore." This problematic cultural identity and tenuous relation with China reappears again and again in Chinese diasporic writing.

The 1920s and 1930s saw many writers travel to the West, including poets Li Jinfa, Xu Zhimo, and Wen Yiduo and novelists *Ba Jin, *Lao She, and Qian Zhongshu. In fact, Lao She (1899–1966) started writing novels while he taught at London University. His *Ma and Son* (Er Ma, 1929) is a comedy of manners heavily influenced by the English literary tradition. Set in a hostile London, the novel depicts a troubled father-son relationship as it plays out in a restricting environment of cultural difference and racial prejudice. Few subsequent writers have been able to emulate the unsentimental and sardonic way in which Lao She treats this "expatriate Chinese syndrome" and the problematic patriotism of Chinese abroad.

Wars, revolution, and the split between China and Taiwan in 1949 shattered many Chinese lives, divided up countless families, and drove thousands into exile. One of the most ambitious and powerful works to explore this traumatic experience against the turbulent backdrop of modern Chinese history is Nie Hualing's (b. 1925) *Mulberry and Peach: Two Women of China* (Sangqing yu Taohong, 1976). After losing her father and home during the period of the anti-Japanese and civil wars, Nie went to Taiwan in 1949, but she soon became disillusioned with the Nationalist government's terrorist tactics and totalitarian regime. She fled again to Iowa in the early 1960s, becoming one of the founders and organizers of the International Writing Program at the University of Iowa. *Mulberry and Peach* largely resembles Nie's personal journey. It is a scattered history of a woman whose life has become a never-ending flight. Highly symbolic and psychological, the novel nonetheless has a realistic framework and contains many historical references. It is divided into four parts, each with two sections. The first sections of each part consist of letters sent by the protagonist Peach to U.S. immigration officials during her flight across America. They are arranged in chronological order, dating from January to March of 1970. The other sections are notebooks that Mulberry/Peach offers to immigration officials, which record different periods of her life from 1945 to the 1960s. The notebooks occupy the main body of the book and reveal a gradual transformation of the protagonist from Mulberry, a timid, terrified, traditional Chinese girl, to Peach, a fierce, vigorous, sexually liberated woman of "nowhere." First, we see Mulberry in a refugee boat stranded in the Yangtze Gorges during the war against Japan; then she is stranded again, this time in the besieged Guomindang capital of Beiping, right before the Communist takeover; the third time we see them, Mulberry and her family are trapped in an attic as a result of her husband's embezzlement in 1950s Taipei; last, the protagonist, by now a middle-aged woman, has fled to America, leaving her old self behind and wandering from one man to another.

Nie's use of the forms of diary and letter and her symbolic treatment of the theme of exile gives psychological and historical depth to the metamorphosis of the protagonist. As one critic has put it: "The author succeeds in integrating the individual's fate with the nation's destiny" (Yu 1993:138). Although one can view the tragic tale of Mulberry/Peach as a "national allegory" of disorder and fragmentation, Nie's dynamic structure offers a more reflective take on the diasporic situation. By placing the bitter memories of Mulberry's past back to back with Peach's narrative of her adventures through America, Nie displays an ambivalent attitude toward exile. It is not just a painful, negative experience of escape, but it can also be an opportunity to unleash liberating forces in the quest for personal identity. Mulberry's repeated entrapments in China contrasts with Peach's voluntary journey across America. This journey begins with an intense inner struggle between her two selves; finally, Mulberry is killed and a new self (Peach), independent of society and history, is born: "You are dead, Mulberry. I have come to life. I've been alive all along. But now I have broken free" (223). In order to gain this new identity, her traumatic memories must be shrugged off (as Peach's letters to the immigration officer make clear). Thus when Peach joins a group of drifters "on the road," she embraces the spirit of adventure at the heart of American culture and shows her determination to escape her "fate" and survive: "I am a stranger wherever I go, but I'm happy, and there are lots of interesting things to see and do" (4).

Since the 1950s there has been a constant flow of Taiwanese and Hong Kong people migrating all over the world, either to escape political uncertainty or attracted by the global economic market, or both. Many of these have been writers or budding writers. This has helped diaspora literature to flourish, no doubt encouraged by the enthusiastic support of Taiwanese and Hong Kong literary magazines and newspaper literary supplements. "Literature of students abroad" and "Chinese overseas literature" have also become fashionable topics for scholarly study and publication in Hong Kong and Taiwan.

Yu Lihua (b. 1931) is a prolific novelist whose many works depict the sentimental journey of Taiwan students abroad trying to return to a home that will not receive them. Yu became a de facto spokesperson for this "rootless generation" after her well-received novel *Again the Palm Tree, Again the Palm Tree* (You jian zhonglu, you jian zhonglu, 1967). In a realistic style full of lyricism, *Again the Palm Tree* presents another wanderer drifting between the United States and Taiwan, between a nostalgic past and an alienated present reality—and this alienation pervades both the American society where he has settled and the Taiwanese society that he visits. The uprootedness and "cultural vulnerability" (Pai 1976:208) that the protagonist experiences is sentimentally explored against the backdrop of an organic image: the tree, an age-old overseas Chinese symbol of one's relation with homeland. The huge gap between the imagined homeland and an alienated reality becomes the core of the protagonist's tragedy.

The "astronaut" characters of *Again the Palm Tree* and their anxiety over their rootlessness reappear in much Taiwanese literature of this period. And in fact, not only do modern Taiwanese writers share the tension between tradition and modernity of all Chinese intellectuals, but this tension has also been intensified by a "Taiwanese complex": a sense of being cut off from home and roots. Seen in this light, it is no coincidence that the overseas Chinese characters in Bai Xianyong's (b. 1937) *New Yorkers* (Niuyue ke, 1974) share the same fate and similar sentiments to those Taiwan mainlanders in his *Wandering in the Garden, Waking from a Dream* (Taibei ren, 1971), in spite of their different environments: "Deprived of his cultural heritage, the wandering Chinese has become a spiritual exile: Taiwan and the motherland are incommensurable.... The Rootless Man, therefore, is destined to become a perpetual Wanderer ... sad because he has been driven out of Eden, dispossessed, disinherited, a spiritual orphan, burdened with a memory that carries the weight of 5,000 years" (Pai 1976:208–209).

The other side of this desperate search for roots and homeland can be seen in the many diaspora writers who have become "nativist overseas." In the fiction of Zhang Xiguo, Liu Daren, and Chen Ruoxi, political engagement and nationalist sentiment abound, and an "obsession with China" becomes both a moral strength and a burden in their writing. Chen Ruoxi (b. 1938) is representative of these "nativist overseas" writers who are committed to writing about major social and political issues. Born in Taiwan, Chen lived in mainland China during the Cultural Revolution, then in North America for more than twenty years, before returning to Taiwan in the mid-1990s. Although best known for her stories about the Cultural Revolution (see "The Taiwan Modernists"), after 1979 she shifted her focus to the lives of Chinese intellectuals in the United States. Often her characters are depicted as sojourners whose return home is delayed by historical circumstances. Although not as dark and melancholy as Bai and Yu's characters, the overseas Chinese in Chen's works are nonetheless anxious to find stability in their floating lives by establishing a new relationship with China—be it Taiwan or the PRC—and they are all concerned with the current state and future direction of their motherland. Likewise, Chen often uses characters and their relationships to represent the various cultural and political identities and commitments of Chinese overseas.

A rare exception to Taiwanese writers' nostalgic or nationalist mode is Ma Sen (b. 1932). Heavily influenced by 1960s Western culture, especially existentialism, Ma Sen distinguishes himself from his compatriots by treating the isolation and alienation of the Chinese diaspora as part of a universal modern predicament. This approach is especially evident in the stories collected in *Isolation* (Gujue, 1979). And in his novel *Night Wandering* (Yeyou, 1984), Ma describes a Chinese immigrant experiencing a unique kind of self-imposed exile. The protagonist, Wang Peishan, chooses to leave home and befriend a group of wandering hippies as a protest against both the middle-class life style that her "white" professor husband leads and the Chinese cultural conventions and ethics of her parents. Her adventures in the underground world of Vancouver during the 1970s resemble very much the search of American youth for an alternative life and identity. With Ma Sen, the universal existential quest has replaced ethnic and cultural differences.

The "opening up" of the PRC under Deng Xiaoping led to another Chinese emigrant tide, especially after 1989, when many writers and intellectuals were forced into exile. Studies of "literature of students abroad" and "overseas Chinese literature" gained a new following in the PRC. *Today* (Jintian), a poetry magazine banned in the early 1980s (see "Misty Poetry"), then revived as a general literary journal in 1990 by the exiled poet Bei Dao, has acted as an important literary venue for mainland writers overseas.

The stories collected in Zha Jianying's (b. 1959) *Going to America, Going to America* (Dao Meiguo qu, dao Meiguo qu, 1990) are some of the earliest yet most promising works of mainland Chinese émigrés. Zha's world, although still

dominated by Chinese students and their peripheral community, often juxtaposes them with other marginal Americans, be they southerners, Jews, or South
Asians. Thus, as in the work of Ma Sen, the diasporic experience is depicted not
as uniquely Chinese but as a universal condition of the modern age, "the age of
anxiety and estrangement" (Said 1994:137). In Zha's "Ice River in the Jungle"
(Conglin xia de binghe, 1988), which describes a female student's journey to the
New World and subsequent return visit to China, both Chinese and Western
worlds play equally important roles in her search for the meaning of life, and
both cultures are given equal space in her reflections. Unlike other stories of return, which tend to be permeated with a nostalgic tone and focus on the negative aspects of marginality, this story is filled with the adventurous spirit of being
"on the road." The journey the protagonist takes to discover her destiny of living
on the periphery is an exciting and open-ended one, even if occasionally confusing and full of sadness. In Zha's work, the moral dilemmas and identity crises
of Chinese overseas are treated with a subtlety and complexity that is reminiscent of Henry James.

Before embarking on her journey to the West, Liu Suola (b. 1955), an avant-
garde novelist and musician, published a travel journal, "Rocking-and-Rolling
on the Road" (Yaoyaogungun de daolu, 1987), in which her visit to the United
States is presented as an exciting, eye-opening experience in a present-tense narrative of immediacy. However, in *Chaos and All That* (Hundun jia ligelong,
1991), written during her stay in the United Kingdom, Liu Suola presents a divided narrative whose memory-haunted narrator-character resembles much
more a creation of Salman Rushdie than one of her previous J. D. Salinger-type
protagonists. Shifting constantly between late 1980s London and Beijing of the
1950s to 1980s, this novel is like a collective autobiography of a generation growing up in the Maoist era and then drifting into the global village. The hybridity
and tension in which this diasporic subject lives are revealed by the incongruous gulf that separates her memories from her reality. To heighten this contrast,
Liu chooses two different narrative modes to indicate the difference in the character's commitment to these two worlds: while a first-person monologue presents the past in Beijing as an intimate, vigorous, and complete life, despite its
inherent absurdities, a third-person narrative depicts her London life as a bored,
nostalgic, and isolated émigré. Ultimately, recollection of the past overwhelms
the present reality. Yet having said this, we cannot help noticing that the internal exile of this generation started long before their external exile, as they grew
up in a confused "revolutionary era," feeling alienated from both tradition and
revolution. What makes this chaotic, hybrid life truly fresh and vivid is Liu's
playful but innovative use of "disparate elements" (Liu 1994:132) in her language. Emulating both literary and documentary sources of her times, Liu's narrative itself is a rich display of multiple and conflicting realities.

In Chinese, the concept of exile often connotes a negative and undesirable
"banishment as a form of punishment by government" from one's homeland and

people (Lee 1994:226). The exiled intellectual Liu Zaifu (b. 1941) was placed in that situation when he left China after the Tiananmen Square massacre of 1989. During the following decade, while traveling across different continents, Liu composed three collections of travel journals that record his pilgrimage in search of a real homeland, a spiritual space that transcends cultural and geographical boundaries and that he can share with Western intellectuals. His journey starts with pain, loneliness, and anxiety in *Notes from Drifting* (Piaoliu shouji, 1992), goes through a stage of wandering and searching for freedom and new perspectives in *The Days of Traveling Afar* (Yuanyou suiyue, 1995), and finally reaches a new understanding of the concept of homeland in *Searching for Homeland Westward* (Xi xun guxiang, 1997). He writes of the last work: "This collection is my discovery of a homeland. Rootless wandering has forced me to deconstruct and alter my ideas about my homeland.... In my questioning, I have bade farewell to the 'nostalgic' mode and the tribal concept of land ... and I have now given birth to a homeland within my heart" (Liu 1997:11, 14). In these lyrical prose works, Liu manages to combine an incisive cultural critique and scholarly breadth of knowledge with a poetic style, and is especially successful in using concrete imagery to present profound philosophical reflection.

In sum, the experience of diaspora has opened up the cultural space for being Chinese. Although it has brought with it constant anxiety regarding home and roots, it has also given a sense of liberation and the opportunity to develop a dual perspective on identity. Chinese diasporic narratives of the twentieth century began to explore this new cultural space, which transcends any single nation, and vividly described the experience of living in it. Written within a cultural tradition where roots, home, the land, and social grouping have played a decisive role in identity-formation, and under the historical shadow of a nation torn apart by war, revolution, and foreign interference, much Chinese diaspora literature depicts marginal living as emotionally traumatic, spiritually depressing, and culturally threatening. We still see in many of these works a desperate obsession with China and Chineseness. But at the same time, some diaspora writing also investigates a new kind of hybrid sensibility, which celebrates the new possibilities that travel and marginal living open up, and manages to view self, identity, and homeland from a broader, more positive perspective.

—*Shuyu Kong*

Bibliography

Goldblatt, Howard. "Modern Chinese Fiction: 1917–1949." In Winston L. Y. Yang and Nathan K. Mao, eds., *Modern Chinese Fiction: A Guide to Its Study and Appreciation*, 3–27. Boston: G. K. Hall, 1981.
Lao, She. *Ma and Son: A Novel by Lao She.* Trans. Jean M. James. San Francisco: Chinese Materials Center, 1980.

Lee, Leo Ou-fan. "On the Margins of the Chinese Discourse: Some Personal Thoughts on the Cultural Meaning of the Periphery." In Wei-ming Tu, ed., *The Living Tree: The Changing Meaning of Being Chinese Today*, 221–228. Stanford: Stanford University Press, 1994.

Liu, Suola. *Chaos and All That*. Trans. Richard King. Honolulu: University of Hawai'i Press, 1994.

Liu Zaifu. *Xi xun guxiang* (Searching for Homeland Westward). Hong Kong: Tiandi tushu, 1997.

Nieh, Hualing. *Two Women of China: Mulberry and Peach*. Trans. Jane Parish Yang and Linda Lappin. Beijing: New World Press, 1981.

Pai, Hsien-yung. "The Wandering Chinese: The Theme of Exile in Taiwan Fiction." *Iowa Review* 7, nos. 2–3 (Spring–Summer 1976): 208–209.

Said, Edward. "Reflections on Exile." In March Robinson, ed., *Altogether Elsewhere: Writers on Exile*, 137–150. New York: Harcourt Brace, 1994.

Tucker, Martin, ed. *Literary Exile in the Twentieth Century: An Analysis and Biographical Dictionary*. New York: Greenwood Press, 1991.

Yu, Dafu. "Sinking." In Joseph S.M. Lau, C.T. Hsia, and Leo Lee Ou-fan, eds., *Modern Chinese Stories and Novellas, 1919–1949*, 125–141. New York: Columbia University Press, 1981.

Yu, Shiao-ling. "The Theme of Exile and Identity Crisis in Nie Hualing's Fiction." In Hsin-sheng Kao, ed., *Nativism Overseas: Contemporary Chinese Women Writers*, 127–156. Albany: State University of New York Press, 1993.

94

AVANT-GARDE FICTION IN CHINA

▾

Perhaps no other fictional moment epitomizes the sheer audacity and self-consciously provocative spirit of the literary avant-garde that transfigured the Chinese literary scene between 1987 and 1992 so well as the final scene of Yu Hua's "One Kind of Reality" (Xianshi yizhong, 1989). The story depicts a shocking and seemingly inexplicable spiral of domestic violence between two brothers, Shanfeng and Shangang, in a nameless provincial town. When Shangang's son Pipi accidentally kills Shanfeng's infant son, Shanfeng retaliates by killing Pipi. Shangang, in turn, ties his brother to a tree, coats him with stew, and allows him to be tickled to death by a voracious dog. Finally, in a scene reminiscent of *Lu Xun's classic allegorical treatment of the Chinese national character, "The True Story of Ah Q" (Ah Q zhengzhuan), a witless and somewhat bedraggled Shangang is apprehended and publicly executed by the local authorities.

Had Yu Hua's story ended simply with Shangang's execution, "One Kind of Reality" could well be understood as heir to the tradition of critical realism in modern Chinese letters, of which Lu Xun is the foremost representative, a tradition in which the writer shoulders the heroic task of exposing social and cultural ills, and in so doing, attempts to underwrite the making of a brighter world. But the conclusion of Yu Hua's tale veers off on an entirely different tack. Rather than provide the reader with an epitaph or an explanation (be it political, social, cultural, or psychological) for the brutality they have just witnessed, Yu Hua places Shangang's lifeless body on an operating table and proceeds to narrate, in excruciating and sometimes excruciatingly funny detail, the process by which his body is strip-mined by a team of doctors for transplantable parts. The self-reflexive virtuosity of this passage—in which Yu Hua's language deftly slides between the clinical, the lyrical, and the ribald, sometimes within the space of a single sentence—signals a watershed in modern Chinese fiction. Social and political engagement is replaced by a subversive comment on the nature of fiction itself. At the same time that he dissects Shangang, in other words, Yu Hua also rather gleefully skewers the humanist pretensions and procedures of realist fiction, as well as the progressivist and nationalist ideals that have informed its use by Chinese writers since the 1920s.

Yu Hua (b. 1960) was only one of a talented group of young avant-garde writers who first burst onto the Chinese literary scene in the years directly preceding the Tiananmen Square massacre of 1989, and whose work came to be collectively referred to as "experimental fiction" *(shiyan xiaoshuo)*. United by a spirit of restless experimentation with fictional forms and cultural norms, as well as a common generational and geographical provenance (almost all of these writers were less than thirty years old and hailed from the prosperous and culturally sophisticated cities of China's southeastern seaboard), the emergence of writers such as Ge Fei (b. 1964), Su Tong (b. 1963), Sun Ganlu (b. 1959), and Bei Cun (b. 1965) was representative of a short-lived, highly significant, and somewhat anomalous cultural moment. Suspended between the "utopian fever and fascination with cultural roots" (J. Wang 1998:4) of the 1980s and the massive globalization and commodification that has characterized Chinese cultural production in the 1990s, their appropriation of a host of techniques of international modernism, their deliberate subversion of the expectations (be they ethical, ideological, or formal in nature) of their readers, and their penchant for convoluted narrative labyrinths and thematic cul-de-sacs, were enabled in part by the government subsidized literary journals in which they published much of their work, and spurred on by the enthusiastic support of a number of prominent literary critics such as Chen Xiaoming and Li Tuo.

As Jing Wang points out, however, the story of the avant-garde begins with the pivotal contributions of two maverick figures not usually associated with the youthful demographic of the avant-garde (1998:5). The first of these was Ma Yuan (b. 1953), a Han Chinese writer whose intricately constructed and sometimes enigmatic tales about an eponymous narrator's travels in Tibet insistently foregrounded the artificiality of storytelling itself. Ma Yuan's narrative innovations took place soon after the translation into Chinese of a number of works of Euro-American modernist fiction (including volumes by Jorge Luis Borges and William Faulkner), and his writings reflected their influence. His work was not, however, merely derivative in nature. It represented a deliberate use of modernism as a means of unseating the heretofore unquestioned authority of the omniscient narrator of socialist realism. Ma Yuan's efforts, moreover, signaled a desire for parity with the literary West, for a place at the world literary table: in a characteristically self-referential gesture, Ma Yuan begins his "Fabrication"

(Xugou, 1986), the tale of a Han Chinese writer's affair with a leprous Tibetan girl, with the assertion that "I am the person known as Ma Yuan.... I take some satisfaction in being able to write in Chinese characters. None of the great figures of world literature were able to do this. I am the exception" (101). This drive for formal innovation and recognition on the world stage reflected a revolt against the constraints of the Maoist period and would be central to the concerns of the nascent avant-garde.

Can Xue (b. 1953) is a second formative figure in the development of the avant-garde whose work is haunted by the Maoist legacy. A self-tutored former seamstress from Hunan Province, Can Xue emerged in 1986 as one of the most distinctive voices in post-Mao fiction with the publication of the short story "The Hut on the Mountain" (Shanshang de xiaowu, 1986) and a longer novella entitled *Yellow Mud Street* (Huangni jie, 1986). In both works, Maoist language and everyday life under socialism are refracted though a lens both scabrously grotesque—Can Xue is fond of insects, rats, dirt, disease, and rot—and relentlessly Kafkaesque. Populated by a cast of characters who speak to each other in non sequiturs that communicate little more than their own obsessive paranoia, Can Xue's claustrophobic fictional world represents a determined attack on the norms of realist fiction. And although it is clear that her work can be read as an attempt to grapple with the political violence and spiritual privation of the Maoist years, it is by no means a direct commentary on that experience. In Can Xue's work, recent history is oblique, fractured, seen only through the eyes of protagonists whose vision is both irrational and partial. They are, indeed, little more than the sum of the physical decay and psychological delusions by which they are afflicted.

A similar disdain for conventional ways of writing history and representing humanity characterizes the work of the avant-garde writers who followed in Ma Yuan and Can Xue's footsteps. They were, however, separated from these two older writers by a highly significant generational divide. Both Ma Yuan and Can Xue were born in 1953; as such, they were members of the first generation to grow up entirely under Communist rule. Schooled in revolutionary ideals and unquestioning devotion to Chairman Mao, these urban "educated youth" (as they are still referred to in Chinese) served as the shock troops of the Cultural Revolution before ultimately being sacrificed by Chairman Mao at the altar of political expediency: when Red Guard factionalism escalated into armed conflict in 1968 and 1969, an entire generation was deported en masse to rural hinterlands for reeducation. And when these disenchanted revolutionaries finally began to filter back into the cities in the late 1970s, after nearly ten years of internal exile, they rapidly took leading roles in a wide range of literary and artistic efforts to dismantle the legacy of Maoist politics and culture.

The avant-garde writers, however, came of age in an era in which that legacy had already begun to crumble under the combined pressure of economic reforms, political liberalization, and the intense cultural ferment of the 1980s.

Born too late to have participated in the Cultural Revolution and too young to have suffered the consequences of that participation, they began to attend high school (a luxury many of the previous generation had been denied) after Chairman Mao had already died. Significantly, they also grew up on a substantially different literary and intellectual diet. Whereas the educational staples of "educated youth" had consisted largely of socialist realism, translated Russian fiction, and other works of prose cast from the Maoist mold, the writers of the avant-garde were privy to a wealth of new literary translations that began to flow into Chinese book markets in the mid-1980s. Yu Hua, Ge Fei, Su Tong, and their contemporaries were well versed not only in the modernist fiction of *Kawabata, Kafka, and Borges, but also in Latin American magical realism, the French *nouveau roman,* and American postmodernist fiction.

Just as important, they were heirs of the deconstructive labors of the generation of "educated youth" that had preceded them. Beginning in the late 1970s, these returnees had launched movement after movement aimed at questioning the underlying causes of the tragic excesses of the revolutionary past, while at the same time freeing themselves from the shackles of Maoist language and literary form. Among the many accomplishments of this generation number the *Misty Poetry of Bei Dao and other writers who initially coalesced around the Beijing Democracy Wall in 1979, the Fifth Generation cinema of directors such as Chen Kaige and Zhang Yimou, and the *roots-seeking fiction of Han Shaogong and *Mo Yan. All of these authors and auteurs drew on the idiom of international modernism in order to create a new cultural space from which they could launch critiques of Maoism. And all of them shared a common, humanistic faith in the redemptive power of art in the face of the ravages of a national history gone awry. In this sense, their work represented an attempt to revive the enlightened and exploratory spirit that they saw as characterizing the May Fourth era of the late 1910s and early 1920s.

The work of the avant-garde, then, can be understood in part as an extension of this critical project, and also as a generational revolt against it. In undermining the generic conventions of not only socialist realism, but also critical realism itself, the avant-garde sought to knock down not just Maoist idols, but those of the educated youth as well. Chief among these idols was the progressivist sense of patriotic mission embodied by intellectuals such as *Lu Xun (or at least by the heroic image of Lu Xun erected by the socialist state and its literary establishment in the wake of the Communist Party's ascendancy in 1949). It is this sense of mission—one that profoundly informs the work of the roots-seekers whose fiction had electrified intellectual circles in China just two years before the emergence of the avant-garde—that is missing from the pages of these authors. Instead, they present their readers with a relentless (and sometimes playful) attack on history and humanist ideals. In practice this meant a fiction in which psychological depth is conspicuous by its absence and notions of progress are shattered by narratives that are anything but neatly linear.

This historical irreverence is a hallmark of avant-garde fiction. In the earliest short stories of perhaps the most popular and accessible of these writers, Su Tong, mythical family histories from the Republican era (his "Flying over Maple Village" [Feiyue wode fengyangshu guxiang, 1987] is one salient example) function as fractured mirrors that unevenly reflect, and thus call into radical question, official socialist historiography. In Ge Fei's fiction, historical episodes as disparate as the Nationalist Party's (GMD) Northern Expedition of 1928 ("The Lost Boat" [Mi zhou, 1989]), the turn-of-the-century "Great Game" of imperial diplomacy in Tibet ("Meetings" [Xiangyu, 1993]), and the life of the Six Dynasties poet Ruan Ji ("Whistling" [Hushao, 1990]), are deliberately rendered enigmatic, even unintelligible, by way of narratives that loop back on themselves or omit crucial pieces of information. In Yu Hua's fiction, the past is conceived of as a site overflowing with extreme cruelty and seemingly gratuitous violence. Though readers of his "The Past and the Punishments" (Wangshi yu xingfa, 1989) and "1986" (Yijiubaliu nian, 1986)—both of which touch on recent Chinese political history—may be tempted to read his work as a comment on the depredations of Maoism and the excesses of the Cultural Revolution, Yu Hua takes care to deflect just such an interpretation by pointedly deflating the reader's desire for an unambiguous, neatly resolved political allegory.

Yu Hua is also the avant-garde author most explicitly interested in collapsing the humanistic emphasis on character depiction in realist fiction, an interest partly informed by the French new novelist Alain Robbe-Grillet's critiques of the European novelistic tradition. For Yu Hua (as well as several of his contemporaries), characters represent nothing more than "props" (1996:274) or pawns to be guided by the author across a complex literary chessboard. Yu Hua's earliest and most provocative fiction thus lingers clinically over the surface of things, denying readers even the illusion of realistic, psychologically well-rounded characters.

The dense and often dreamlike mental landscapes that characterize the fiction of Sun Ganlu (for instance, "I Am a Young Drunkard" [Wo shi yige shaonian jiu tanzi, 1987]) similarly dissolve any expectation of narrative coherence. Instead, Sun's fiction presents readers with a series of fragmentary images, oblique philosophical musings, and self-reflexive linguistic conceits. The work of Bei Cun is another case in point: his labyrinthine plotting and insistent repetition of scenarios within the same story (see, for example, "The Big Drugstore" [Da yaofang, 1992]) play havoc with the conventions of realist fiction. And as with the fiction of Yu Hua, his is a fictional fabric prone to sudden and unexplained irruptions of the supernatural and the sordid.

It is these characteristics of avant-garde fiction—its refusal of historical causality and humanism, its determined avoidance of overtly politicized ways of writing and reading, its deadpan depictions of transgressive violence, its playful and self-referential experimentation with narrative form, and its preference for surfaces over psychological depths—that have led many critics, both in China and abroad, to view the movement as heralding the advent of literary post-modernity in China. Although this contention remains a matter of debate, and cultural and literary developments of a more local nature have clearly been just as important as global cultural currents in the formation of the avant-garde, the claim itself is symptomatic of a desire for contemporaneity and literary parity with the developed world.

Ironically, the brief flowering of the avant-garde may also be remembered as the last unitary literary movement in twentieth-century Chinese history. The rapid commodification and consequent market segmentation that have transfigured the Chinese cultural scene in the 1990s seems to have spelled the end of an era in which any one literary trend is able to occupy cultural center stage (see "Wang Shuo and the Commercialization of Literature"). With the escalation of economic reforms in 1992, many of the luminaries of the movement turned their attention to more conventional sorts of narrative fiction (particularly Su Tong, many of whose novels have enjoyed great popular success throughout the Chinese-speaking world), to journalism, and to collaborations with film and television directors. Indeed, the avant-garde as a viable and ideologically coherent movement ultimately fell victim not to censorship or official disapproval but to the vagaries of the market and the changing artistic agendas of its constituent members. Its artistic legacy, however—as well as the continuing creative efforts of authors such as Yu Hua and Ge Fei—remains vital to the ongoing articulation of contemporary Chinese literature and culture.

—*Andrew F. Jones*

Bibliography

Can, Xue. *Dialogues in Paradise*. Trans. Ronald R. Janssen and Jian Zhang. Evanston, Ill.: Northwestern University Press, 1989.

——. *Old Floating Cloud*. Trans. Ronald R. Janssen and Jian Zhang. Evanston, Ill.: Northwestern University Press, 1991.

——. *The Embroidered Shoes*. Trans. Ronald R. Janssen and Jian Zhang. New York: Henry Holt, 1997.

Goldblatt, Howard, ed. *Chairman Mao Would Not Be Amused*. New York: Grove Press, 1995.

——, and Joseph S. M. Lau, eds. *The Columbia Anthology of Modern Chinese Literature*. New York: Columbia University Press, 1995.

Lu, Tonglin. *Misogyny, Cultural Nihilism, and Oppositional Politics: Contemporary Chinese Experimental Fiction*. Stanford: Stanford University Press, 1995.

Su, Tong. *Raise the Red Lantern: Three Novellas*. Trans. Michael S. Duke. New York: William Morrow, 1993.

——. *Rice*. Trans. Howard Goldblatt. New York: William Morrow, 1995.

Tang, Xiaobing. *Chinese Modern: The Heroic and the Quotidian*. Durham, N.C.: Duke University Press, 2000.

Wang, Jing. *High Culture Fever: Politics, Aesthetics, and Ideology in Deng's China.* Berkeley: University of California Press, 1996.

——, ed. *China's Avant-Garde Fiction: An Anthology.* Durham, N.C.: Duke University Press, 1998.

Yu, Hua. "One Kind of Reality." Trans. Jeanne Tai. In David Der-wei Wang and Jeanne Tai, eds., *Running Wild: New Chinese Writers,* 21–68. New York: Columbia University Press, 1994.

——. *The Past and the Punishments.* Trans. Andrew F. Jones. Honolulu: University of Hawai'i Press, 1996.

Zhang, Xudong. *Chinese Modernism in the Era of Reforms: Culture Fever, Avant-Garde Fiction, and the New Chinese Cinema.* Durham, N.C.: Duke University Press, 1997.

Zhao, Henry, ed. *The Lost Boat: Avant-Garde Fiction from China.* London: Wellsweep, 1993.

——, and John Cayley, eds. *Abandoned Wine: Chinese Writing Today, Number Two.* London: Wellsweep, 1996.

——. *Under Sky Under Ground: Chinese Writing Today, Number One.* London: Wellsweep, 1994.

95

MODERN POETRY OF TAIWAN

An island is a paradox: it is simultaneously isolated and open, with the surrounding sea serving as both a protective barrier and a vital passage to other lands and cultures. Situated off the southeast coast of China, with Japan and Korea to the north and the Philippines to the south, halfway between Shanghai and Hong Kong, Taiwan is the nexus of diverse linguistic, economic, social, and cultural crosscurrents from Asia and other parts of the world. If its small size—comparable to Switzerland or Holland—has historically been a cause of Taiwan's marginalization, this is compensated for by openness and an ability to adapt to the new. Over a period of four centuries, Taiwan has evolved dramatically from a little-known island to an entrepôt, an outpost of the Qing empire, a colony first of Holland (1624–62), then of Japan (1895–1945), and, today, a nation-state with 22 million people and one of the largest economies in the world. Taiwan has garnered international acclaim for its economic miracle and hard-won democracy. Equally deserving of worldwide recognition is that some of the best modern poetry written in Chinese comes from Taiwan. The history of modern Taiwanese poetry tells the story of how the periphery has transformed itself into the frontier.

Despite linguistic and historical connections, there are significant differences between Taiwan's modern poetry and that of post-1949 mainland China. The most obvious difference has to do with the relationship between poetry and politics: whereas politics has been the determining force in the People's Republic of China, it has never played a central role in Taiwan. Although modern poetry in its formative period in May Fourth China was diverse and cosmopolitan, the dominance of Communist ideology from the 1940s on reduced it to political slogans in the sanctioned formula of "classical + folk"—a hybrid of classical Chinese poetry and folksongs—leaving little room for free expression of the literary imagination. The situation has only begun to change in the past two decades, during which poets have slowly and painstakingly tried to walk out of the shadow of Maospeak.

Despite censorship during the Japanese colonial period and the Nationalist government's martial law era (1950–87), Taiwan has had a relatively more open society and more cosmopolitan culture than that of the mainland. Even under the most repressive circumstances, political control was never complete; poetry managed to carve out a space of its own outside the official discourse and to take advantage of being on the periphery. If "political poetry"—poetry written to critique a political situation or advance a political ideal—constitutes one category among many in Taiwan, this category is simply inapplicable to mainland poetry written before the late 1970s, since all of it is, by definition and in a quite direct way, political.

The second significant difference between Taiwan and the People's Republic of China is their cultural makeup. Historically, Taiwan has been exposed to and has assimilated elements of Chinese, European, Japanese, and American cultures, in addition to having a rich aboriginal culture. The first modern poetry in Taiwan was written in two languages, Chinese and Japanese. Many poets are fluent in two or more languages, and Chinese, Japanese, and English are the most commonly used languages in Taiwan today. With close to universal literacy, contemporary Taiwan boasts a level of education that is among the highest in the world. Most poets have college degrees, and quite a few hold master's degrees and doctorates from domestic or foreign universities. These highly educated, bilingual or multilingual poets move across national and linguistic boundaries with ease and confidence, tapping into their multicultural experience and knowledge—whether literature, music, art, philosophy, or religion—of other traditions as a resource for their poetry. Taiwan's poetry is a product of cultural hybridity in the best, fullest sense of the word.

Modern poetry in Taiwan has a dual origin. The earliest modern poems published in Taiwan were written in Japanese: authored by Zhui Feng ("chasing the wind"; pen name of Xie Chunmu, 1902–1967), the sequence of four poems under the title "Imitations of Poetry" (Shi de mofang) was written in 1923 and published in *Taiwan* on April 10, 1924. At the same time, a young man from Taiwan named Zhang Qingrong (1902–1955) was studying at Beijing Normal College. Inspired by the literary revolution that had swept the mainland a few years earlier, he published "A Letter to the Youth of Taiwan," under the pen name Zhang Wojun ("my army"), in *Taiwanese People's Journal* (Taiwan minbao, April 21, 1924). In the letter he attacked classical poetry as decorative and dead, and those who wrote it as slaves to archaic conventions. After returning to Taiwan in October of that year, Zhang wrote more critiques that triggered a heated debate between the old school of poets and the new. As editor of the *Taiwanese People's Journal* from 1924 to 1926, he also introduced poetic theory and creative practice from the mainland. Finally, Zhang published a slim book of modern poetry in Chinese entitled *Love in a Chaotic City* (Luandu zhi lian, 1925), which records his romantic relationship while living in Beijing. It is the first book of modern poetry published in Taiwan.

From the very beginning, then, modern poetry in Taiwan has drawn on two traditions: Japanese and mainland Chinese. These traditions should not be seen as diametrically opposed, but as complementary and mutually reinforcing because they were often inspired by the same sources: romanticism, symbolism, and surrealism, to name but a few. If Yang Hua's (1906–1936) *petits poèmes* were influenced by those of Bing Xin (1900–1999) on the mainland, the immense popularity of the genre in China in the 1920s was itself the result of multicultural influences, including at least the Greek epigrams, Rabindranath Tagore's (1861–1941) short lyrics, the Japanese haiku, and classical Chinese poetry. Though surrealism received only cursory mentions in the Shanghai avant-garde magazine *Les Contemporains* (Xiandai, 1932–35), it exerted a major influence on the Le Moulin Poetry Society (Fengchi shi she), founded in 1933–34 by seven Taiwanese and Japanese poets in Tainan (Ye 1996).

When the island was returned to China in 1945 at the end of World War II, the cultural difference between mainland China and Taiwan, especially in terms of linguistic background and practices, was significant. Ironically, although Taiwan had identified with the Chinese motherland throughout the Japanese colonial period, the mother with whom she was finally reunited after fifty years was more or less a stranger whose language she could hardly comprehend. The February 28 Incident—when Nationalist troops violently suppressed a local uprising—aggravated the already difficult transition from Japanese colonialism to Nationalist rule. The new regime stepped up its control and, as the civil war on the mainland worsened and retreat to Taiwan seemed imminent, it tightened its grip even more, ushering in the era of White Terror, which lasted from the 1950s to the 1970s. The intensely complicated history of modern Taiwan presents an unusual case of postcolonial culture. Whereas many other countries in Asia, Latin America, and Africa that achieved independence had to—or still have to—wrestle with the issue of using the colonizer's language, postwar Taiwan's situation was reversed. Taiwanese writers in 1949 were caught between two languages, neither of which they could identify with: Japanese, the colonizer's language that they were no longer allowed to speak, and Mandarin Chinese, the language that was rightfully their mother tongue but that they could not speak. In short, Taiwanese writers were in the unique quandary of having no language of their own. This condition of "cultural aphasia" was to have a significant impact on modern Chinese poetry.

The generation of Taiwanese writers who were in their twenties and thirties when the war ended was severely handicapped linguistically: they were unable to continue to write and publish either in Japanese, which was banned, or in Chinese, of which they had yet to achieve full command. For this reason, and perhaps also out of disenchantment with the Nationalist regime, some simply gave up writing, while a few would continue to write in Japanese for the drawer or publish their work in Japan. Most of those who persisted would need fully ten years to acquire enough proficiency in Chinese to write and publish in that language. This last group of writers constitutes "the translingual generation" (*kuayue yuyan de yidai*)—a term coined by the Taiwanese poet-critic Lin Hengtai (b. 1924) in 1967, whereas the group that chose to stop writing may well be called "the silenced generation."

The lacuna thus created in the poetry scene was filled mainly by poets who had recently sought refuge in Taiwan from the mainland. Although a few native Taiwanese poets made a smooth transition from Japanese to Chinese, most of the poets active in the 1950s, notably Ji Xian (who previously used the pen name Luyishi, b. 1913) and Qin Zihao (1912–1963), had published on the mainland and had established substantial reputations there. With their credentials, some of them were able to obtain editorial positions in state-run print media, become teachers of writing workshops and state-sponsored correspondence courses, and found their own poetry societies and publish journals. Among the most important societies and magazines were *Modern Poetry Quarterly* (Xiandai shi jikan, 1953–64) and the Modernist School founded by Ji Xian in 1956, Blue Star Poetry Society (Lanxing shi she) by Qin Zihao in 1954, and Epoch Poetry Society (Chuang shiji shi she) by Luo Fu (b. 1928), Zhang Mo (b. 1931), and Ya Xian (b. 1932), also in 1954. Although these poetry journals and societies by no means excluded native Taiwanese poets, clearly the émigrés' linguistic skills provided a valuable form of cultural capital, which put them in an advantageous position.

In the nationalistic, conservative society of postwar Taiwan (Winckler 1994; Lee 1996), poets faced a dual challenge: the official anticommunist discourse (which hindered the free development of poetic art) and classical Chinese poetry (which enjoyed a much higher social and cultural status than modern poetry). It was against these two forces that poets tried to carve out a new space in which they could engage in literary experimentation relatively free from the intervention of the political and cultural establishment. The Modernist School, above all, led in this pioneering effort. Ji Xian, Lin Hengtai, and Fang Si (b. 1925), for example, defended modern poetry by decoupling poetry from song and by defining poetry as an individual, spiritually oriented endeavor. The decoupling of poetry from song suggested that the proper medium of modern poetry is prose, not rhymed verse; it further led to the view that content should determine form, rather than the other way around. The emphasis on poetry as a personal calling transcending worldly concerns sought to free the poet from political pressures and to affirm the autonomy and dignity of the poet, who was more often than not low in the economic and social structure.

If the new movement was direct in its criticism of the conservatives who up-held classical poetry as the only legitimate form, it took a more subtle approach in its dealing with the dominant discourse of anticommunism. Many avant-garde poets participated in state-sponsored poetry competitions and garnered hand-some prizes, which in turn provided the necessary resources for sustaining their privately run journals, which in turn gradually transformed the literary scene. Drawing on Pierre Bourdieu's theory of the literary field, we may describe the poets of postwar Taiwan as having created a position for themselves by two prin-cipal means: challenging the venerated position of classical verse by redefining the nature of poetry and participating in the official discourse of anticommunism in order to appropriate its abundant cultural capital to advance their own goals. As its following among the younger generation grew, the new poetic movement was able to create new forms of symbolic capital, with which it remapped the lit-erary field and further consolidated its own position (Yeh 2001).

As a result of these pioneering efforts, modern poetry flourished from the mid-1950s to the first half of the 1960s. An impressive range of styles and a large number of original poets appeared, including the modernist lyric of Ye Shan (later under the pen name Yang Mu, b. 1940), Zheng Chouyu (b. 1932), Lin Ling (b. 1938), and Xiong Hong (b. 1940); the surrealist prose poetry of Shang Qin (b. 1930) and Guan Guan (b. 1929); the existentialist musings of Bai Qiu (b. 1937), Ya Xian, and Luo Fu. They were at once intensely interested in avant-garde poetry, whether from Europe, North America, or Latin America, drawn to the lyricism of classical Chinese, and sensitive to the historical circumstances into which they were born. Ya Xian's "Colonel" (Shangxiao) provides a good ex-ample of the diverse and complex genealogy of postwar Taiwanese poetry:

> That was another kind of rose,
> Born of flames.
> In the buckwheat field they fought the biggest battle of the campaign,
> And his leg bade farewell in 1943.
>
> He has heard history and laughter.
>
> What is immortality?
> Cough syrup, razor blade, last month's rent, et cetera, et cetera
> His wife's sewing machine skirmishes
> While he feels that only the sun
> Can capture him.

With a few simple but forceful strokes, the poem reveals the pathos of war that few pay attention to: what happens to a veteran—even a war hero—after the war? For the disabled colonel, war continues (his wife's sewing machine resem-bles machine-gun shots), yet there is no glory to it. In contrast to "history" and "immortality" associated with (the rhetoric) of war, he struggles against poverty and illness—the petty but inescapable reality of daily life (with the razor blade a much diminished stand-in for the soldier's bayonet). The adroit use of irony, understatement, ambiguity, allusions both Chinese and Western, and succinct language shows a mature poet, although Ya Xian was only twenty-eight when he wrote the poem. "Colonel" and other memorable poems of Taiwan's postwar generation have rightly come to be seen as classics of modern Chinese poetry. Although some have stopped writing (Ya Xian) or developed in new directions (for example, Luo Fu and Yang Mu), their work from the 1950s and 1960s has exerted profound influences on younger generations.

The mid-1960s saw a hiatus in modern poetry in Taiwan, a result of the demise of leading poetry journals and the departures, whether temporary or permanent, of many major players, including Qin Zihao, Ya Xian, Fang Si, Zheng Chouyu, Lin Ling, and Ye Shan. In a positive vein, native Taiwanese poets who had not had the linguistic facility or confidence in Chinese were now ready to publish. In June 1964, a group of native Taiwanese poets founded a society named Bamboo Hat (Li) and a journal under the same name—which, continuing to this day, is the longest-running journal in the history of Taiwanese poetry. The contributions of *Bamboo Hat* can be summarized as follows. First, continuing the tradition of the 1950s, it defended the legitimacy and importance of modern poetry as a genre. Like its predecessors, *Bamboo Hat* encouraged individual expression and bold experiments. Second, like *Modern Poetry Quarterly*, it lamented the absence of sound literary criticism in Taiwan and sought to improve the situation by publishing detailed analyses and fair-minded critiques of poems. To achieve this goal, *Bamboo Hat* also introduced a wide range of literary movements and theories from Europe, the United States, and Japan, and it published extensively translations of creative and theoretical writings. In short, in the second half of the 1960s *Bamboo Hat* broadened the horizon and furthered the poetic movement of the 1950s. Composed almost entirely of native Taiwanese poets, *Bamboo Hat* included such established poets as Wu Yingtao (1916–1971), Zhan Bing (b. 1921), Huan Fu (b. 1922), Lin Hengtai, and Bai Qiu, as well as novices. Their styles varied, but in the 1960s displayed a generally modernist orientation. This was to change in the 1980s, when "Taiwan consciousness" emerged.

The Taiwanese poetry scene underwent a fundamental transformation in the 1970s. The forces of change came from two quarters: the 1972–73 debate on modern poetry and the nativist literature movement of 1977–79. The debate was in many ways a literary response to nonliterary circumstances. From 1970 to 1972, Taiwan suffered a series of major diplomatic setbacks, including its loss of membership in the United Nations, territorial disputes with Japan, the severance of formal ties with the United States and Japan, and President Richard M. Nixon's visit to Beijing. The loss of political legitimacy in the international community and the economic boom, which depended heavily on American and

Japanese capital, led to an explosion of nationalist sentiment. In the literary sphere, reflections on national identity triggered a series of harsh criticisms of the modernist poetry of the 1950s and 1960s as having lost its Chinese identity and become overly westernized. The experimental spirit of the earlier poetry was now condemned as shamelessly colonial and non-Chinese, its modernist orientation as decadent, irresponsible, and severed from local reality. The binary oppositions between China and the West, tradition and modernity, and the local and the cosmopolitan that had played a major role in previous cultural discussions, whether in the May Fourth period or earlier in Taiwan, once again reared their heads. Chinese identity was defined as an embracing of the Chinese tradition and local reality, a criterion to which all poetry was held (Yeh 1998).

In fact, there was little debate to speak of, with an overwhelming majority of views against modernist poetry. In the face of Taiwan's crisis in international politics and deep-rooted cultural conservatism, few poets or critics put forth an effective rebuttal. Insofar as it rejected cultural westernization and emphasized local reality, the debate was a precursor to the nativist literature movement, in which modern poetry played a negligible role (Wang 1980). However, there is an important difference between the two. With the surfacing of the underground democracy movement in Taiwan, which culminated in the demonstrations known as the Formosa Incident of December 1979, the identity of Taiwan was no longer unequivocal. "Taiwanese" identity, albeit still couched in the language of "the rural" or "native land," emerged in contradistinction to "Chinese" identity. The long-unspoken tension between native Taiwanese, most of whose ancestors came from southern China, and post-1949 mainland immigrants now regarded as outsiders erupted in the open and was to become a highly politicized issue in the next two decades.

Nationalism, democratization, nativization—two decades of social, cultural, and political movements have left indelible marks on Taiwan's poetry. The debate on modern poetry in the early 1970s led to much reflection on the relationship between the Chinese tradition and modern poetry. In the best cases it inspired poets to reevaluate tradition as a vital resource and led to a broad spectrum of neoclassicist experimentation. Poets sought to incorporate and transform traditional poetic language, imagery, and form with varying degrees of success. Similarly, the nativist emphasis ushered in a new range of themes that revolve around rural Taiwan or the native land, from the plight and perseverance of the farmer to positive depictions of folk traditions. Further, as democratization progressed in the 1980s, such political taboos as the February 28 Incident, the White Terror, or subethnic tension became common subjects, as seen in the popular "political poetry." Once the orthodoxy fell, challenge to the center from the periphery multiplied. Since the late 1980s, poetry has addressed a host of long-existing concerns, ranging from discrimination against women and homosexuals, exploitation of and injustice to aborigines, and neglect of

Guomindang veterans to environmental destruction. The rise of socially oriented poetry—whether feminist, gay, aboriginal, or ecological/naturalist—along with sci-fi poetry, computer poetry, video poetry, poetry written in Hokkien (Taiwanese) and Hakka, has enlivened Taiwan's poetry scene.

However, the impressive variety of poetry does not automatically translate into substance and accomplishment. In fact, one wonders if the topical interest of much recent poetry masquerades a lack of depth in thought and vision. The ascendancy of mass and electronic culture has severely marginalized literary culture in general. Free speech and free press have rendered the role of poetry as social criticism obsolete. Although poetry has made some inroads in popular culture, such as providing lyrics to popular songs or being quoted and displayed in public spaces, its audience is small. Poetry societies and poetry journals no longer serve as the significant public forum they once did—even in the literary sphere. Whether or not the Internet will improve the situation remains to be seen.

This does not mean that powerful, original poetry no longer exists in Taiwan. The best poetry tends to shy away from the explicitly public and political orientation of much of the poetry in the 1980s and 1990s. Instead, many poets insist on writing as a personal, even idiosyncratic, act, and they continue to contemplate what art is through their language. Poetry, after all, is one person's love affair with language, nothing more, nothing less.

—Michelle Yeh

Bibliography

Chen Shaoting. *Taiwan xin wenxue yundong jianshi* (A Short History of the New Taiwanese Literature Movement). Taipei: Lianjing, 1977.

Cheung, Dominic, ed. *The Isle Full of Noises: Modern Chinese Poetry from Taiwan.* New York: Columbia University Press, 1987.

Gold, Thomas B. "Civil Society and Taiwan's Quest for Identity." In Stevan Harrell and Huang Chün-chieh, eds., *Cultural Change in Postwar Taiwan*, 47–68. Boulder, Colo.: Westview Press, 1994.

Lee, Thomas H. C. "Chinese Education and Intellectuals in Postwar Taiwan." In Chun-chieh Huang and Feng-fu Tsao, eds., *Postwar Taiwan in Historical Perspective*, 135–157. College Park: University of Maryland, 1996.

Wang, Jing. "Taiwan Hsiang-t'u Literature: Perspectives in the Evolution of a Literary Movement." In Jeannette L. Faurot, ed., *Chinese Fiction from Taiwan: Critical Perspectives*, 43–71. Bloomington: Indiana University Press, 1980.

Winckler, Edwin A. "Cultural Policy on Postwar Taiwan." In Stevan Harrel and Chün-chieh Huang, eds., *Cultural Changes in Postwar Taiwan*, 22–46. Boulder, Colo.: Westview Press, 1994.

Ye Di. "Riju shidai Taiwan shitan de chaoxianshi zhuyi yundong—fengche shishe de shi yundong" (The Surrealist Movement on Taiwan's Poetry Scene during the Japanese Occupation: The Le Moulin Poetry Society Movement). In *Taiwan xi-*

andaishi shilun (Essays on the History of Taiwan's Modern Poetry), 21–34. Taipei: Wenxue zazhishe, 1998.

Yeh, Michelle (Xi Mi). "Taiwan xiandaishi lunzhan: zai lun 'Yi chang weiwancheng de geming'" (The Debate on Modern Poetry in Taiwan: On "An Incomplete Revolution"). *Guowen tiandi* 13, no. 10 (March 1998): 72–81.

——. "Zai women pinji de canzhuo shang: wushi niandai de *Xiandaishi jikan*" (On Our Destitute Dinner Table: *Modern Poetry Quarterly* in the 1950s). In Zhou Yingxiong and Joyce Chi-hui Liu, eds., *Shuxie Taiwan: hou zhimin, houxiandai yu wenxueshi* (Writing Taiwan: Postcolonialism, Postmodernism, and Literary History), 197–232. Taipei: Maitian, 2000.

——, ed. *Anthology of Modern Chinese Poetry*. New Haven: Yale University Press, 1994.

Yeh, Michelle, and Goran Malmqvist, eds. *Frontier Taiwan: An Anthology of Modern Chinese Poetry*. New York: Columbia University Press, 2001.

Yip, Wai-lim, ed. *Modern Chinese Poetry: Twenty Poets from the Republic of China, 1955–1965*. Iowa City: University of Iowa Press, 1970.

96

POST-MAO URBAN FICTION

In the late 1980s, writers in mainland China once again began writing on urban motifs that had been suppressed or used to promote Communist Party policy during the Maoist period. Mao Zedong's 1942 *"Yan'an Talks on Literature and the Arts," which attacked foreign-influenced genres and advocated "national forms" based on "folk customs," became official party policy in the 1950s. This formalized the primacy of rural literature until Deng Xiaoping's official statement on the arts in 1979, which effectively loosened strict party control over literary production. Unlike the rural-based *roots-seeking literature of the mid-1980s, the *avant-garde (xianfeng) writers of the late 1980s introduced urban themes as a critique of the Maoist privileging of the countryside as a progressive space. Other writers began describing the city on its own terms, without reference to the dialectical values associated with urban and rural space that dominated twentieth-century cultural production.

Su Tong (b. 1964), a Nanjing-based avant-garde writer acclaimed for his 1980s experimental fiction, uses a realistic narrative style in his first full-length novel, Rice (Mi, 1991), which contrasts urban and rural themes in depicting a peasant's coming of age in a southern town. Consistent with the avant-garde's attempt to subvert traditional connotations of city and countryside, Su Tong devalues both the impoverished village from which Five Dragons had fled and the decadent town in which he makes his fortune and meets his demise. The benefit that the urban space promises the rural immigrant to the city is demonstrably depleted, yet the rural space remains an equally ineffectual—indeed, inaccessible—grounding for modern identity. By draining both landscapes of their appeal, Su Tong displaces the familiar urban/rural terms in which the cultural debates over modernity have so often been waged. Though set in the 1930s, *Rice* speaks to the spiritual emptiness of modern Chinese life in the post-Mao era.

The neorealism *(xin xieshi)* employed by Su Tong in *Rice* first appeared in works by writers such as Wuhan-based Chi Li (b. 1957) and Fang Fang (b. 1955), and Beijing-based Liu Heng (b. 1954) and Liu Zhenyun (b. 1958). These neorealist works depict struggles of everyday urban life rather than create model characters and settings as prescribed for works of socialist realism. Liu Heng's *Black Snow* (Hei de xue, 1988) is an early example of a post-Mao novel that reflects on urban estrangement. The first-person narrative expresses the most intimate thoughts of Li Huiquan, a young man trying to negotiate the subtle complexities of modern urban life in 1980s Beijing after being released from incarceration in a labor-reform camp. The question of personal worth is foregrounded as it was in Su Tong's *Rice*, but whereas Five Dragons attempts to gain self-respect in the city by possessing women and wealth, Li Huiquan is moderate in his financial pursuits and morbidly introspective about life. He goes through the motions of rehabilitating himself as an upright modern urbanite, peddling clothes in the new market economy, jogging to maintain his health, frequenting art museums and classical music concerts, and reading the daily papers to stay abreast of current events. Yet Li is primarily fixated on acquiring an unobtainable woman, an obsession that takes on morbid dimensions due to his extreme degree of social and psychological disaffection. As he wanders through the city, he is terrified by the aimlessness of the crowd and its implications for his own insignificance, recalling classic motifs of urban alienation. Liu Heng depicts 1980s alley *(hutong)* life from the perspective of "urban youth awaiting employment" *(chengshi daiye qingnian)* who must work as street peddlers *(getihu)*, and like *Lao She's portrayal of the underclass rickshaw pullers decades earlier, he invokes empathy for these marginalized city dwellers.

The Beijing-based writer *Wang Shuo (b. 1958) also emerged as a literary force in the late 1980s, pioneering a movement labeled "hooligan literature" *(pizi wenxue)*. With his literary influence on pop culture, most critics single out "the Wang Shuo phenomenon" as the most salient epochal marker of the shift from the 1980s to the 1990s. Unlike the high-minded cynicism of avant-garde writers or the dark, neorealistic portrayal of everyday urban life, Wang Shuo writes about disenfranchised youth "playing" in the city to dispel their boredom, capitalizing on their ability to dupe members of the establishment. Wang Shuo has written more than twenty novels, selling more than ten million copies, and his joint venture into television miniseries and film scriptwriting extended "the Wang Shuo phenomenon" nationwide. *Masters of Mischief* (Wanzhu, 1987) and *Playing for Thrills* (Wande jiushi xintiao, 1988), two of his best-known works, portray unconventional characters that create elaborate games, such as the establishment of the Three T Company, specializing in "troubleshooting, tedium relief, and taking the blame." Many of his other works depict the ineffectuality of the intellectual class, instead valorizing "punks" *(liumang)* who are free from roots, bonds, and identities. Wang Shuo's works capitalize on the collapse of the utopian ideals of the 1980s, presaging the 1990s siege of consumer culture and the resulting marginalization of intellectuals.

Jia Pingwa's (b. 1952) novel *City in Ruins* (Feidu, 1993) was the best-selling novel in 1993, ending the "Wang Shuo fever" and giving rise to a series of heated cultural debates by intellectuals on the loss of "humanitarian spirit" *(renwen jingshen)* in works such as Wang's and Jia's. Jia first emerged in the 1980s as a major *roots-seeking author, best known for stories of his rural hometown in Shaanxi Province. He has lived in the ancient capital of Xi'an for years, yet was inspired to write on his urban home after a trip to the United States in order to rectify misperceptions of "authentic China" as solely situated in the countryside. *City in Ruins,* which is set in Xijing (western capital), a transparent reference to Xi'an, graphically recounts the sexual exploits of its famous author, Zhuang Zhidie, drawing upon many conventions of the traditional Ming and Qing novel. Jia's "deletion" of words in the midst of intense erotic scenes (replicating cleaned up versions of erotic Chinese classics and mimicking socialist censorship) increased its commercial value. An important subplot of the novel is a libel lawsuit by one of Zhuang's lovers, who sues Zhuang and the author of an article that recounts their love affair. The lawsuit forces Zhuang to confront his own identity through the words of others, and the notion of "authorial authenticity" is increasingly called into question throughout the novel as the classical literary allusion to the author's name (literally, "Zhuang's Butterfly") suggests. The ancient city wall also figures prominently in the novel as a symbolic demarcation between rural and urban space, locales that in turn figure the authentic self and the constructed self. Whereas some critics decry the novel as nothing more than pornography reflective of (and contributing to) the decadence of the 1990s, the novel remains a well-crafted commentary on the impotency of intellectuals in late twentieth-century society.

Song of Everlasting Regret (Chang hen ge, 1995), by the Shanghai-based writer *Wang Anyi (b. 1954), resembles *City in Ruins* in its depiction of a city in the shadow of the past. Wang, a prolific writer who gained critical acclaim with her rural-based "Three Loves" series from the mid-1980s, portrays Shanghai's historical vicissitudes by following the life of Wang Qiyao from beauty queen to empty nester. *Regret* is evenly divided into three parts, which correspond to Shanghai's Republican era in the 1930s and 1940s, the Maoist era through the 1970s, and the post-Mao 1980s. In *Regret* Shanghai's "feminine" qualities of superficiality, excess, decadence, and artificiality are dignified. As if defending Shanghai's secondary cultural status relative to Beijing in the post-Mao era, its qualities are portrayed as a necessary component in China's cultural configuration—the gossip of the alleys a counter to orthodox ideology, the charm of everyday life offsetting the weight of politics, the feminine excesses of the south balancing masculine northern starkness. Wang Qiyao is portrayed as a blend of the qualities of elegance and banality, and thus is emblematic of the true "essence" of Shanghai, a nostalgic acknowledgement that its legacy as the Paris of the East is fading and destined to die, as Wang does, a fateful death. Her charm lies in her ability to be in the city but not fully of it, her ability to be as commonplace as her times while ultimately transcending them as social and political conditions change. Yet by framing her life between the murder scene she witnesses as a girl in a movie studio and her flashback to that scene during her own murder, Wang Anyi portrays Shanghai as a superrealistic photograph. The elements are captured in minute detail, yet the net effect is stilted as Shanghai's historical identity is collapsed into a spatial identity with defined boundaries, oddly distanced from Shanghai's urban dynamism in the 1990s. This effect is consistent with Wang's preference for writing about the country-side, and her belief that urban fiction, lacking organic form, requires an analytical style.

In the mid-1990s several new forms of urban literature emerged in mainland China. Variously labeled "new urbanite fiction" *(xin shimin xiaoshuo)*, "new state of affairs fiction" *(xin zhuangtai xiaoshuo)*, or literature by a "belated generation" *(wansheng dai)* who have come of age in the 1990s, these works portray contemporary urban life in a market economy. Although the new economic configuration leaves some intellectuals at a loss, in search of a new position in society, others relish their freedom to explore previously taboo topics. Further, as the Communist Party increasingly absolves itself of its previous role as moral standard-bearer and meaning-giver for the individual, these writers often explore themes of individual ethics and purpose in life.

He Dun (b. 1958) is one of the best-known representatives of the "belated generation" of writers. He graduated from art school in the 1980s and taught art in a Changsha middle school for several years before quitting his job to do business in interior design. His lifestyle change from idealistic academic to practical businessman followed the pattern of many in the early 1990s who chose to "take the plunge [into business]" *(xiahai)*. With his changed lifestyle came an evolution of values and worldview, and he began to write about the attitudinal changes accompanying the "new state of affairs" of the 1990s, where individual choices abound and personal ethics are redefined and reexamined. He writes realistic accounts of Changsha closely based on personal experience, and first gained critical acclaim for his novellas *Hello, Younger Brother* (Didi ni hao, 1993), *Life Is Not a Crime* (Shenghuo wu zui, 1993), and *I Don't Care* (Wo bu xiang shi, 1993).

Hello, Younger Brother depicts a young man who is a "loser" by most standards, disillusioned after failing to get into Beijing University and unmotivated by his subsequent job as an elementary school teacher. After impregnating his girlfriend, Deng Heping is kicked out of his parents' house, quits his job, and joins a classmate selling cigarettes on the open market. He falls in love with the man's wife, whose contacts lead him to a job managing a nightclub. After his classmate is executed for dealing heroin and Heping divorces his wife, he marries his love and the couple starts an extremely profitable business supplying decorating materials. However, the story ends on a shocking note: just as the protagonist has "found" himself in a profitable job with a lovely wife, fate intervenes and his wife and unborn child are killed in a motorcycle accident. The value of material success in the 1990s is shown to be as ephemeral as political or academic success proved in the 1980s.

He Dun's stories are peppered with references to fate, something striking to readers in the wake of twentieth-century campaigns to eradicate superstition in mainland China. The rise of superstitious practices in the 1990s is often directly related to the market economy. He Dun elaborates on this fact in one of his more ideologically explicit novels, *The Himalayas* (Ximalaya shan, 1998). His teacher-turned-businessman protagonist claims, "The majority of Chinese businessmen in the 1990s aren't controlled by faith or ideology, they don't talk about beliefs or politics or ideas, and they certainly don't talk about movies or art, what they talk about is superstition. That's what they believe!" (358). In many of his later works, He Dun's protagonists search unsuccessfully for meaningful spiritual ideals, at odds with the decadent business environment of the city.

The Nanjing-based writer Zhu Wen (b. 1967), like He Dun, writes new-state-of-affairs fiction based on his urban experiences in contemporary urban settings. Zhu Wen's comic story "I Love American Dollars" (Wo ai meiyuan, 1995) shook the literary establishment with the carefree manner in which the young male protagonist, a Nanjing author in his early twenties, has casual sex with prostitutes and even arranges for his father to join him in his escapades. This attempt to turn 1980s sexual conservatism on its head (while adding a twist to the notion of filial piety) is one of the hallmarks of 1990s urban literature—a celebration of individuality and social freedom often expressed through sexual licentiousness.

Zhu's novel *What's Trash, What's Love?* (Shenme shi laji, shenme shi ai, 1998) is a more penetrating reworking of similar themes. Xiao Ding is in his late twenties, a struggling Nanjing writer whose father brags about his son's nonexistent success and whose mother prays for her son to get a wife (to prevent him from contracting venereal disease). Zhu Wen depicts the angst and confusion plaguing Xiao Ding and his circle of friends that are not easily remedied by lucrative jobs, free love, drugs, or even self-sacrificing volunteer work. Rather than write about such aimlessness in a didactic, moralizing manner, new-state-of-affairs literature provides a plethora of realistic details, leaving it to the readers to draw their own conclusions. Xiao Ding is frequently *fan* (fed up, disgusted) with his life, and in the manner of Jiangnan stylists, Zhu Wen details the smallest aspects of Xiao Ding's troubles, right down to his lack of toilet paper after using a filthy public toilet. Xiao Ding refuses to assist a friend in his search for his missing daughter (who has been kidnapped and gang-raped, an increasingly common occurrence in the Chinese metropolis), but stumbles into volunteer work in a futile attempt to find purpose. The novel closes with Xiao Ding, who is recovering from venereal disease, having sex with an old flame whose boyfriend died of a drug overdose, leaving him feeling more "disgusted" than ever. The novel ends as it opens, with the protagonist alone in a bar, his mouth gaping wide in a ludicrous silent scream, an appropriate coda for a literary mode that depicts existence as cyclical and meaningless.

The Beijing native Chen Ran (b. 1962) first gained critical acclaim with her short story "Sunshine between the Lips" (Zuichunli de yangguang, 1992), an experimental piece where dental work functions as a euphemism for childhood sexual abuse. Her controversial first novel, *Private Life* (Siren shenghuo, 1996), is Ni Niuniu's interior monologue reflecting on her life in Beijing from her school days in the mid-1970s until her psychological breakdown at age thirty in the mid-1990s. *Private Life* explores the usual topics of home life, school, friendship, romance, and sexuality, but in an avant-garde style that blends philosophical statements and poetic asides with idiosyncratic perspectives on events (or nonevents). The urban environment is described in a muted, understated fashion, and detailed descriptions of interior, psychic space serve to highlight the city's relative absence in the narrative. The claustrophobic, introspective tone of the novel is only temporarily alleviated by descriptions of walking in the city or an occasional drive to the rural suburbs. Niuniu repeatedly alludes to her ever-present sense of unease in the exterior space of the city, often coded as male: dominant, suffocating, time-bound, unfeeling. This is in contrast to inner spaces, which she associates with tropes of the female: obscure, eternal, sensitive, and sensuous. She augments her feminist analogies with pastoral sentiments—not unlike those of the 1930s Beijing school of literature *(jingpai)* that promoted rural values—by launching into diatribes of the rape of the pristine countryside by the colonizing city.

Niuniu's reclusion is a direct result of the city's encroachment upon her private space. The ever-expanding boulevards of Beijing invade previously enclosed spaces, just as Haussman's boulevards of the nineteenth century broke down the hermetically sealed world of the old medieval enclaves of Paris. Beijing's ancient alley culture is being overrun with major roadways as commercial construction and residential developments systematically destroy the secluded alley communities and the traditional courtyard houses *(sihe yuan)*. The intrusion of the city on Niuniu's already disjointed internal space results in her breakdown. Niuniu's bathroom, which she narcissistically decorates with mirrors so she can gaze at herself in the bathtub, is seen as an ordered, hygienic place of wholeness and sanctity where she can integrate herself to offset the chaotic fragmentation she experiences within herself and outside in the city.

In a 1997 interview, Chen Ran noted that *Private Life* had been criticized because it is *geren*—about an individual—"which is devalued by default since most value writing about larger state issues. The first 'mistake' according to Chinese cultural values is to write about something private, something individual. But my perspective is exactly the opposite—I think the more individual something is, the more universal it is." Chen Ran's writing on the city privileges female over male, local culture over global culture, and the private over the public sphere, as a means of speaking to collective issues in the postmodern metropolis.

Qiu Huadong (b. 1969) is one of the most ambitious writers of urban fiction in his self-proclaimed attempt to become "the Balzac of China" through rich descriptions invoking the ethos of the capital. According to an interview with the author, his day job as a journalist for a Beijing economic journal affords him unique opportunities to explore a wide variety of Beijing lifestyles. As a new resident of Beijing, schooled in Wuhan and raised in Urumqi, many of his works, such as *City Tank* (Chengshi zhanche, 1997), express the shock of trying to survive as an artist in an alienating commercial metropolis.

Fly Eyes (Ying yan, 1998) is one of Qiu's most successful works. In it he recounts five stories of Beijing residents whose lives are related by "six degrees of separation," and, in the tradition of Dos Passos, he depicts the complexity of the city through individual lives. Qiu's characters acknowledge that they are "two-dimensional people" *(pingmian ren)* who resist plumbing the depths of existence. Yet while they indulge in every possibility urban life offers, they also admit they are bored and disgusted with it. What distinguishes this generation is their very awareness of the "flattening" process they have gone through. As in most new-state-of-affairs novels, Qiu's characters make abrupt lifestyle changes, often from idealist artists, poets, or scholars to businesspersons in every conceivable line of work. In recollecting the idealism of their pasts, some who are satiated with the get-rich materialistic lifestyle of the 1990s even attempt to return to a slower, simpler way of living. However, it soon becomes obvious that the thinkers and closet idealists in his stories are unable to survive, not only in the metropolis but also outside it. As one of his characters from *Fly Eyes* puts it, "We won't be able to escape the city. As soon as we leave this place we'll want to return, because this is a dance floor, it is the place that nourishes dreams, and we depend on it for our very breath" (250). Those characters who attempt to find a deeper sense of meaning and value in the city perish in the attempt, whereas the "survivors" live materialistic and banal middle-class lives.

Some critics attempting to come to terms with the historical significance of the new urban fiction celebrate its absence of interiority, its unreflective representation of the raw, vulgar reality of contemporary urban culture. However, cultural reflection continues, albeit not didactically, as these writers portray the contrasting social mores that have emerged in the new market economy. The ambiguity and confusion in the lives of their characters is reflective of the times, but the provocative and often humorous manner in which these writers explore their era strongly suggests an ongoing inquiry into urban cultural values.

—*Robin Visser*

Bibliography

Chen Ran. *Siren shenghuo* (Private Life). *Chen Ran wenji* (Collected Works of Chen Ran), vol. 4. Yangzhou: Jiangsu wenyi, 1996.

———. "Sunshine between the Lips." Trans. Shelley Wing Chan. In Howard Goldblatt, ed., *Chairman Mao Would Not Be Amused: Fiction from Today's China*, 112–129. New York: Grove Press, 1995.

He Dun. *Shenghuo wuzui* (Life Is Not a Crime). Beijing: Huayi, 1995.

———. *Ximalaya Shan* (The Himalayas). Nanjing: Jiangsu wenyi, 1998.

Jia Pingwa. *Feidu* (City in Ruins). Beijing: Beijing, 1993.

Liu, Heng. *Black Snow*. Trans. Howard Goldblatt. New York: Grove Press, 1990.

Qiu Huadong. *Chengshi zhanche* (City Tank). Beijing: Zuojia, 1997.

———. *Ying yan* (Fly Eyes). Changchun: Changchun, 1998.

Su Tong. *Changhen ge* (Song of Everlasting Sorrow). Beijing: Zuojia, 1996.

———. *Rice*. Trans. Howard Goldblatt. New York: William Morrow. 1995.

Tang, Xiaobing. *Chinese Modern: The Heroic and the Quotidian*. Durham, N.C.: Duke University Press, 2000.

Visser, Robin. "Displacement of the Urban-Rural Confrontation in Su Tong's Fiction." *Modern Chinese Literature* 9, no. 1 (1995): 113–138.

———. "Privacy and Its Ill Effects in Post-Mao Urban Fiction." In Bonnie McDougall, ed., *Chinese Concepts of Privacy*, 229–256. Leiden: E. J. Brill, 2002.

———. "The Urban Subject in the Literary Imagination of Modern China." Ph.D. diss., Columbia University, 2000.

Wang, Jing. *High Culture Fever: Politics, Aesthetics, and Ideology in Deng's China*. Berkeley: University of California Press, 1996.

Wang, Shuo. *Playing for Thrills: A Mystery*. Trans. Howard Goldblatt. New York: Penguin, 1997.

———. *Wanzhu* (Masters of Mischief). *Wang Shuo wenji* (Collected Works of Wang Shuo), 2:106–167. Beijing: Huayi, 1995.

Zhang, Yingjin. *The City in Modern Chinese Literature and Film: Configurations of Space, Time, and Gender*. Stanford: Stanford University Press, 1996.

Zhang, Yiwu. "Postmodernism and Chinese Novels of the Nineties." Trans. Michael Berry. *Boundary 2* 24, no. 3 (1997): 247–259.

Zhu Wen. *Shenme shi laji, shenme shi ai* (What's Trash, What's Love?). Nanjing: Jiangsu wenyi, 1998.

———. *Wo ai meiyuan* (I Love American Dollars). Beijing: Zuojia, 1995.

97

XI XI AND TALES OF HONG KONG

Xi Xi is the pseudonym of Zhang Yan, foremost among the first generation of writers to have grown up in Hong Kong. Xi Xi was born in Shanghai in 1938 to Cantonese parents. Shortly after the Communist takeover, at the age of twelve, she moved with her family to Hong Kong. Xi Xi graduated from the Grantham College of Education in 1958 and became a primary school teacher until she gave up her teaching career to become a full-time writer at age thirty-nine. Although Xi Xi won a number of literary prizes in Hong Kong in the 1960s and 1970s, her name only became widely known after she was awarded Taiwan's prestigious *United Daily* prize for fiction in 1983. In the last three decades, Xi Xi has been one of Hong Kong's most prolific writers. Best known for her fiction, Xi Xi is equally at home in poetry, scriptwriting, the occasional essay, translation, film review, and art criticism. She was also editor of two major Hong Kong literary journals.

Throughout her writing career Xi Xi has used numerous pen names. From the mid-1970s onward, however, she has published most of her fiction, including her collected works, under the name Xi Xi. The character *xi* means "west," but Zhang Yan chooses to use this pen name not because of its literal meaning but because of its graphic quality. She explains:

When I was young I used to love playing a game similar to hopscotch, which we called "Building a House" or "Aeroplane Hopping." First you draw a series of squares on the ground. Then you tie a string of paper clips into a knot and toss it into one of the squares and start hopping from one square to the next until you reach the square with the knot in it. Then you pick it up and hop your way back to where you started.... The Chinese character "xi" looks like a girl in a skirt, her two feet planted in a square. Put two of them side by side, and they are like two frames of a film, a girl in a skirt playing hopscotch in two squares. (1986:84)

Stephen Soong suggests that this pseudonym reveals the childlike vision of the author, and other critics attribute Xi Xi's extraordinary use of narrative point of view in her fictional work, such as *My City: A Hong Kong Story* (Wo cheng, 1979), to the freshness of her childlike perception. Even more interesting is how Xi Xi wrenches the conventional and impersonal definition ("west") from the pictograph and reinvests it with a new visual quality and a personal meaning. Moreover, by reduplicating the character, she makes the linguistic sign come alive with movement: a girl playing hopscotch. This semiotic creativity is indicative of a literary imagination that is not constrained by narrative conventions.

Xi Xi's playful reinvention of the character *xi* is exemplary of the creative spirit behind her incessant exploration of new ways of storytelling. Her fiction is very often a reinterpretation of history, myth, legend, art, and literary works. She always strives to tell new stories through old ones, as suggested by the title of a recent collection, *Stories within Stories* (Gushili de gushi, 1998). In this collection Xi Xi rewrites well-known episodes from famous novels, making the reader see the familiar event with different eyes. For instance, in "Banana Fan" (Bajiao shan, 1987), by relating the incident in which Monkey King forces Princess Iron Fan to lend him the magical banana fan in *Journey to the West* (Xiyou ji, 1570s) from the perspective of Princess Iron Fan's cat, Xi Xi brings to light the injustice others suffered because of the self-righteousness of the hero. In this story, Xi Xi uses the first-person point of view to rupture the illusion of transparency and objectivity of the omniscient narrator in traditional Chinese novels. The first-person narrative voice of the cat allows the reader to see Princess Iron Fan as a woman who is mistreated by both her husband and the Monkey King, whereas in the original text she is simply cast as an unreasonable shrew whose refusal to lend them her precious fan constitutes another barrier that the main protagonists must overcome in their pilgrimage.

Xi Xi breaks down the monolithic discourse of heroism by using multiple first-person narrations in "Family Matters in the Chentang Pass Commander's Household" (Chentang guan zongbingfu jiashi, 1987). This story retells the legend of Nazha in *Creation of the Gods* (Fengshen bang), a reputed Ming novel built on folktales about the transition from the Shang dynasty (16–11 c. B.C.) to the Zhou (11 c.–770 B.C.). Nazha is the third son of Li Jing, the garrison commander of Chentang Pass, and is said to be the reincarnation of the Pearl Spirit. He is sent down by a decree from the Jade Emptiness Palace to assist King Wu of the future Zhou dynasty in launching an attack on King Zhou, a notorious tyrant fated to become the last ruler of the Shang. Nazha's birth hour predestines him to break the commandment against killing; when Nazha is only seven years old, he stirs up trouble by killing the Yaksha Sea Patrolman and the third son of the East Sea Dragon King in a quarrel, and later by beating up the Dragon King. He also accidentally kills one of Lady Rock's disciples and assaults another. However, his master considers these deaths "a minor matter," for fate has dictated that Nazha is to lead the war against the Shang, and so he helps Nazha avoid persecution from the Dragon King and Lady Rock. Nazha's killings nonetheless cause an irreparable rift in his relationship with his father, Li Jing, and he mutilates himself in front of his parents to cut ties with his family. After his death, on his master's advice, his spirit appears to his mother and begs her to build a temple for him in order that he may be reincarnated into human form (which will happen after three years' worship by the people). When Li Jing finds out that Nazha has been worshipped as a god, he smashes Nazha's image and destroys the temple. Nazha's master, however, reincarnates Nazha, who then relentlessly seeks revenge against Li Jing until the immortals give the latter a magical pagoda to subdue Nazha and force the two to reconcile.

Against this mythical background of dynastic change, the title of Xi Xi's story is ironic. By calling Nazha's legend "family matters," Xi Xi relocates Nazha within a human and familial context. His actions are judged according to his roles as son and brother, not excused because of his predetermined role in the war against the Shang. By giving the first-person narrative voice to Nazha himself and to the numerous people involved with him, such as his parents, brother, servant, and especially innocent victims and witnesses of his whimsical violence, Xi Xi unveils the absurdity of the divinities' arbitrary indulgence in Nazha's egotistical and irresponsible behavior. The multiple narrative angles raise questions about the definition of heroism as well as the meaning of fate, and challenge the reader to reflect on his or her conditioned response to the original text, which centers on Nazha and justifies his every act as simply predestined.

Through the use of first-person narration, Xi Xi gives voice to "minor" characters and puts on center stage "trivial" matters. Her fiction is never about the exceptional deeds of well-sung heroes but the ordinary life of common people. For instance, in her fiction about Hong Kong Xi Xi is not interested in weaving a grand narrative but in representing a polyphony of personal voices. She is not content with presenting things from a single perspective and a fixed position; instead, her narrative is volatile and diverse. The most acclaimed example is her first novel, *My City*. This novel does not have a conventional linear narrative that relies on emplotment. Rather, it consists of independent scenes, each with its own narrative style. Critics have compared the narrative technique in *My City* to the "scattered perspective" of traditional Chinese "long scroll" painting such as the famous Song-dynasty "Trip Upstream on Qingming Festival": instead of one focal point and a stationary position of the observer, here the angles of perception are multiple and the viewer's position is mobile. In fact, Xi Xi herself also makes explicit her use of "scattered perspective" and mobile viewpoint in the short story "Hand Scroll" (Shoujuan, 1987).

It is not coincidental that Xi Xi's narrative techniques in many of her fictional works have been compared to visual media such as painting and film. When *My City* was serialized in the literary supplement of *Hong Kong Express* in 1975, Xi Xi herself drew the illustrations for her novel. She also wrote a weekly column of essays on painting from 1974 to 1975, some of which are collected in *Jiantie ce* (Scrapbook, 1991). Xi Xi is also well versed in film, having been a film critic, scriptwriter, and an independent filmmaker in the 1960s. Her interest in experimenting with the film medium is most notable in her first novella, *Story of the Eastern City* (Dongcheng gushi, 1966). The novella is divided into sections, each like a scene within a film. The narrative includes instructions such as "fade-in," "fade-out," "cut," "dissolve," "track," "span," "close-up," "medium shot," "background music," and "subtitle." The reader not only reads but must also visualize the scenes.

Xi Xi continues to explore textual relations between different media in her later work. The short story "Drinking with General Li Among the Flowers (Pei Li Jinwu huaxia yin, 1997) is a sophisticated attempt at connecting the poetry of Du Fu to the modern film medium. Another brilliant exercise not only in interdisciplinary but also cross-cultural reading is "Marvels of a Floating City" (Fucheng zhiyi, 1988), one of Xi Xi's best-known fables about Hong Kong. This story can be seen as a creative interpretation of the paintings of the Belgian artist René Magritte. The text is based on visual images but is not contained by them. The synergetic cross-references of Western painting and the Chinese text create what the translator, Eva Hung, calls "a sense of indivisible heterogeneity which is representative of Hong Kong culture at its best" (Hung 1997:xii).

The most successful example of intertextuality in Xi Xi's work is "The Fertile Town Chalk Circle" (Feituzhen huilan ji, 1988), another of her allegories on Hong Kong. The story is based on a Yuan-dynasty drama by Li Xingdao about a court case of the legendary judge, Bao Zheng (999–1062). Judge Bao was a real official in the Northern Song dynasty, but he is elevated to a mythical stature in folklore and operas as the representative of justice in both the human world and the netherworld. The Yuan play is about two women fighting for a five-year-old child, Ma Shoulang, the heir of his murdered father's fortune; both claim to be the biological mother. Judge Bao orders the son placed in the center of a chalk circle, with each claimant holding one of his hands; whoever succeeds in pulling the child to her side, declares the judge, will win parental rights. Judge Bao discovers the true mother, of course, as the one without the heart to pull her son apart.

Li Xingdao's play was the inspiration for "The Caucasian Chalk Circle" by the German dramatist, Bertolt Brecht (1898–1956), who adapted the narrative form of traditional Chinese drama in his renowned Epic Theater. Brecht's idea of "alienation effect" in theater in turn informs Xi Xi's "The Fertile Town Chalk Circle." Critics have pointed out that although Xi Xi's story is based on the Yuan play, it is closer in form and spirit to Brecht's drama. The story is retold from the point of view of the child, who is at once the child in the play and the actor playing the child on stage. However, the narrator's voice is constrained by neither the role of the child character nor that of the actor. The narrator speaks not only in the voice of an unusually precocious child who has witnessed and understood the premeditated crimes against his parents, but also as a commentator on issues in traditional Chinese society, such as widespread corruption of government officials, legal injustice, forced prostitution of poor women, and the psychological and practical constraints for scholars. Moreover, he undermines the authority of Judge Bao by questioning the wisdom and effectiveness of using the chalk circle to settle the dispute. He even contests the way his future is decided for him without his testimony and freedom of choice. Unlike both Li Xingdao's opera and Brecht's play, Xi Xi's story ends with not a resolved case but a protest from the narrator: "I am standing here, in the court, at center stage. I ask you all, members of the audience, to listen, I have something to say. After six hundred years, are you still not going to let me grow up?" (*Marvels*, 106).

"The Fertile Town Chalk Circle" has been widely read as an allegory about Hong Kong's lack of representation in the 1980s Sino-British talks over its future. Other works of the "Fertile Town" series—the short stories "The Story of Fertile Town" (Feitu zhen de gushi, 1982), "Apple" (Pingguo, 1982), "Town Mantra (Zhen zhou, 1984), and "An Addendum to *Cosmicomics* (Yuzhou qiqu buyi, 1988) and the novel *Flying Carpet* (Fei zhan, 1996)—have also been read as parables of Hong Kong. Though an allegorical interpretation can be readily supported by textual evidence, Xi Xi's fiction is never simply realism and always more than allegory. Whether using a fable to reconstruct the history of Hong Kong, as in "The Story of Fertile Town" and *Flying Carpet*, or describing facets of Hong Kong urban life, as in *My City* and *Beautiful Building* (Meili dasha, 1990), Xi Xi persists in representing the voices of common people who are at the margins of the grand historical discourse on Hong Kong. Her work poses an artistic challenge to preconceived notions of Hong Kong not only by presenting alternative voices but also by problematizing the relationship of the reader to the text in the way the audience is questioned in "The Fertile Town Chalk Circle":

> What have you really come to see? Have you come to see costumes, make-up, movement, set, and plot, to see a classical play, an epic, a narrative or a dialectical play? Or have you come to see me, just an insignificant little child on the stage, and to see how I must struggle along life's road to gain some measure of dignity? Or did you come to see the *Chalk Circle*, to see Judge Bao once again act the part of the clever and just official? (*Marvels*, 105)

Whatever the reader comes to see, Xi Xi rejoins in the final words of *Flying Carpet*: "You want me to tell you about the story of Fertile Town. I believe I have already told you all that I know and all that you want to know" (513). Just like her pseudonym, the story of Hong Kong told by Xi Xi rejects a literal definition. It is through imaginative use of language that she represents the vibrant struggle of Hong Kong in fashioning a self-identity neither simply constrained by British colonialism nor purely impelled by Chinese nationalism.

—*Daisy S.Y. Ng*

Bibliography

Chen Jieyi. *Yuedu Feituzhen: Lun Xi Xi de xiaoshuo xushi* (Reading *Fertile Town*: A Discussion of Xi Xi's Fictional Narrative). Hong Kong: Oxford University Press, 1998.

Chen Qingqiu. "Lun dushi de wenhua xiangxiang: bing du Xi Xi shuo Xianggang" (The Cultural Imagination of the City: Reading How Xi Xi Speaks of Hong Kong). *Guodu* 1 (1995): 6–14.

Chen Yanxia. "Shuxie Xianggang: Wang Anyi, Shi Shuqing, Xi Xi de Xianggang gushi" (Writing Hong Kong: The Hong Kong Stories of Wang Anyi, Shi Shuqing, and Xi Xi). *Journal of Modern Literature in Chinese* 2, no. 2 (1999): 91–117.

Dong Qizhang. "Chengshi de xianshi jingyan yu wenben jingyan: yuedu 'Jiutu,' 'Wo cheng' he 'Jian ji'" (Urban Reality Experience and Textual Experience: Reading *The Drunkard*, *My City*, and *Paper Cut*). *Guodu* 2 (1995): 15–22.

Hung, Eva. *Marvels of a Floating City and Other Stories*. Hong Kong: The Chinese University of Hong Kong, 1997.

Huang Jichi. "Xi Xi lianzai xiaoshuo: yidu zaidu" (Xi Xi's Serialized Fiction: Remembering, Reading, and Rereading). *Bafang wenyi congkan* 12 (1990): 68–80.

Soong, Stephen C. "Building a House: Introducing Xi Xi." In Xi Xi, *A Girl Like Me and Other Stories*, 127–134. Hong Kong: The Chinese University of Hong Kong, 1986.

Xi Xi. *Dongcheng gushi* (Story of the Eastern City). Hong Kong: Mingming, 1966.

——. *Fei zhan* (Flying Carpet). Hong Kong: Suye, 1996.

——. *A Girl Like Me and Other Stories*. Hong Kong: The Chinese University of Hong Kong, 1986.

——. *Gushili de gushi* (Stories within Stories). Taipei: Hongfan, 1998.

——. *Jiantie ce* (Scrapbook). Taipei: Hongfan, 1997.

——. *Marvels of a Floating City and Other Stories*. Ed. Eva Hung. Hong Kong: The Chinese University of Hong Kong, 1997.

——. *Meili dasha* (Beautiful Building). Taipei: Hongfan, 1990.

——. *My City: A Hong Kong Story*. Trans. Eva Hung. Hong Kong: The Chinese University of Hong Kong, 1993.

Yu Fei. *Changduan zhang: yuedu Xi Xi ji qita* (Long and Short Movements: Reading Xi Xi and Others). Hong Kong: Suye, 1997.

98

WRITING TAIWAN'S FIN-DE-SIÈCLE SPLENDOR:
ZHU TIANWEN AND ZHU TIANXIN

Like the Brontës of England, the Zhu family of Taiwan produced three girls who would grow up to become writers. Like the Brontës, too, only two of the Zhu sisters became productive and successful writers: Zhu Tianwen (b. 1956), the eldest, and Zhu Tianxin (b. 1958), the second daughter. The Zhu sisters come from a prominent literary family; their father, Zhu Xining (1926–1998), was a celebrated military writer and an important participant in the development of Taiwan's literature in the 1950s and 1960s, while their mother, Liu Musha (b. 1935), a Hakka Taiwanese, is a translator of many modern Japanese literary works.

Both Zhu Tianwen and Zhu Tianxin began their writing careers when they were only sixteen and were immediately best-selling authors in Taiwan. Their early works, produced in the 1970s and early 1980s, are mainly nostalgic short stories of childhood and sentimental essays about longings for "the motherland," China. The Zhu sisters' deep roots in the Chinese literary tradition and their patriotic passion for China (which to them was mostly an imaginary homeland, inasmuch as traveling to China was at that time prohibited) are influences from their father, who followed Chiang Kai-shek's retreat from China to Taiwan in 1949, and mentor Hu Lancheng, who was an accomplished scholar and philosopher of Chinese literature and thought. The Zhu sisters' early works are consistent with the official, mainstream ideology and the sentiment that Taiwan was the defender and torchbearer of China's long cultural tradition, which was being destroyed on the mainland. Their later writings (since the mid-1980s) resonate with the political, social, and cultural changes Taiwan society underwent right before and since the annulment of martial law in 1987. What their later works reflect are remarkable changes in the literary development in Taiwan and shared concerns about Taiwan's cultural identity. The collective mentality of people in Taiwan has arrived at a point of political and cultural self-awareness about Taiwan's relation to China, as well as how Taiwan should position itself in the era of globalization. As participants in and observers of this dynamic society, the Zhu sisters have concerned themselves with the multiple cultural impacts on Taiwan society and with the question of how to conceive an authentic cultural identity in such circumstances.

Zhu Tianwen began her writing career with a series of short stories, the first collection of which, *New Stories of Minister Qiao* (Qiao taishou xinji), was published in 1977. In the following years, she continued to write short stories and published four more books: *Legends* (Chuanshuo, 1981), *Most Memorable Season* (Zui xiangnian de jijie, 1984), *City of High Summer* (Yanxia zhi du, 1987), and *Fin-de-siècle Splendor* (Shijimo de huali, 1990). Aside from fiction, she also wrote a large body of essays that are collected in *Notes of Tamkang* (Danjiang ji, 1979), *Stories of Xiao Bi* (Xiao Bi de gushi, 1983), *Three Sisters* (San jiemei, 1985), and *Afternoon Tea Conversations* (Xiawu cha huati, 1992). But Zhu Tianwen is probably best known for her collaboration with Taiwan's internationally renowned film director Hou Hsiao-hsien, for whom she wrote several major film scripts. In 1994 she finally wrote her first full-fledged novel, *Notes of a Desolate Man* (Huangren shouji, 1994).

Most scholars and critics regard the short story "Fin-de-siècle Splendor" as marking a turning point in Zhu Tianwen's style, a forerunner of a new style of writing that comes to dominate *Notes of a Desolate Man*. It is a style remarkably more sophisticated than the sentimental, nostalgic style of her earlier writing; it is, as the critic Zhang Hongzhi characterizes it, a style reflected through "an aging voice." This new style is more linguistically experimental, sharper, colder, and more nihilistic in portraying urban existence. In "Fin-de-siècle Splendor" and other stories collected under the same title, Zhu Tianwen's primary interest is to depict Taiwan's complex cultural scene, especially in Taipei. She draws attention to the dominant presence of foreign cultural elements in her narrative as a tool to critique Taiwan people's tendency to idolize as well as commercialize foreign popular culture, embracing such things as Hollywood movies and stars, popular singers from both Japan and the West (mainly the United States), and European fashions. The foreign cultural presence in Taiwan is the direct product of Japanese colonization (1895–1945) and Taiwan's fast-paced economic expansion. Taiwan's culture today is a hybrid of Chinese, native Taiwanese, and various foreign cultural imprints. How one makes sense of such a cultural hybrid is a question central to Taiwan society, and one that is pursued in Zhu Tianwen's writing. Her use of exoticized language, such as inserting English or Japanese words in the Chinese text or using translated foreign terms and phrases (which are not easy to read), is intended to reflect Taiwan culture's highly hybridized condition.

"Fin-de-siècle Splendor" is set in 1992 Taipei. It tells the story of a professional model, Mia, who, at the age of twenty-five, already feels "old" and is ready for a life of retirement. She is the mistress of a much older man, Lao Duan, and enjoys being outside the marriage institution. She and her model friends live only for the present, chasing the glamour and fun of big city life. Narcissism dominates their lives, which is reflected in the story's endless description of clothes and the young models' obsession with self-image. The language of "Fin-de-siècle Splendor" is laden with fashionable designer brand names, scents, perfumes, the intricate texture and colors of fabric, and exotic plants and herbs. Mia centers her life on experiences and memories of colors and fragrances from the ever-changing world of fashion and from the dried plants she collects. It seems as though the function of such concrete objects as her dried flowers and colorful fabrics is to define the meaning of her existence. What prevails in Zhu Tianwen's later works is a sense of individuality that manifests itself in a flair for exotic linguistic practices. Zhu's characters, male and female alike, are narcissistic. Her fashion models, for example, are always conscious of the image they convey to others. They are individualistic in the ways they live their lives, the self-image they project to others, and the performative nature of their behavior. The particular narcissistic practice of these characters is to affirm the importance of the body through fetishization of exotic objects. But the celebration of narcissism is not without irony. Mia's obsession with sensuous exotic objects, such as high fashions, fabrics, plants, herbs, as well as scents and colors, reflects a culture that is saturated with commodities and in which the individual is subsumed in commercialism.

In such a milieu, time and history are reduced to fashion. The history of Taipei is marked by each emerging new fashion: 1986, frankincense; 1987, irises; the summer of 1990, pale seaside colors. To Mia and her model friends, time does not become history; it simply flows through life, neither treasured nor lamented over. As Mia and her fashionable gang gaze at Taipei at dawn from the top of Mount Yangming, the city appears like a rising mirage, its image reflecting in the water vapor. The ephemerality of Taiwan's social and historical existence cannot be described better than in this powerful and chilling image.

Mia intends to create a sense of eternity through collecting dried flowers and herbs, and by learning how to make paper. With her first two pieces of handmade paper, she believes that this skill will sustain her until the day when the world built by men collapses. She will rebuild it with her memories of scents and colors; the record of her rebuilding the world will be written on her own rose paper. In this new vision, her individual subjectivity can become complete and independent from all institutions. This is a new brand of existentialism conceived at the end of the millennium, in the late capitalist metropolis, and at the juncture of Taiwan's cultural self-awareness. On an allegorical level, Zhu Tianwen also calls attention to the politics of the center (China) versus the marginal (Taiwan), the material versus the spiritual, and woman versus man.

Although the characteristics of exoticism and narcissism have been consistently present in Zhu Tianwen's fiction since the late 1980s, it is in *Notes of a Desolate Man* that these two characteristics come to pervade the narrative and become significant elements in the formation of a coherent sense of the self for the novel's gay protagonist, whose sexual identity is not yet accepted by society (see "Same-Sex Love in Recent Chinese Literature"). Before this novel, Zhu Tianwen's employment of exoticism and her characters' narcissism emerge only in a more performative and deliberate fashion: in these works, although exoticism serves as a mirror to reflect the image of the narcissistic self, it is mainly a tool of cultural critique. In *Notes of a Desolate Man* the coalition of narcissism and linguistic exoticism is the means by which the gay protagonist's sexual and cultural identities are explored. The novel's provocative subject matter (male homosexual eroticism), unusual authorial perspective (a female writer assuming the voice of a gay man), excessively exoticized and floral language (mixed with Buddhist scriptural language, English words, transcribed foreign names, and borrowed texts), and the indeterminacy of its genre (prose? fiction? allegory? theoretical monograph?), all add to the intrigue and complexity of the protagonist's encyclopedic exploration on the subject of identity.

The novel is about a middle-aged gay man searching for true love and his struggle to come to terms with his sexuality. This journey takes him to the great books of East and West, to many far corners of the world, and to all kinds of cultural venues. Along his soulful search for his gender and cultural identities, he discovers that defining oneself is often a game of naming; it is only by being in touch with one's self that one can establish a clear sense of one's subjectivity and an unambiguous sense of identity.

By bringing so many cultures into the protagonist's search for identity, Zhu Tianwen also places us in the multicultural world and challenges us to think and imagine what our cultural identity is. This novel is about the experience of cultural identity in a globalized world. At the center of this globalized world is the self; cultural identity is not defined by one's connection to a place or determined by a collective. With linguistic exoticism, Zhu Tianwen is able to conceive of a new kind of individual subjectivity that is not only in alliance with capitalist materialism but is born of cultural globalism.

Zhu Tianxin began her writing career in high school in 1974. Her first publication of collected short stories was *Days on the Boat* (Fangzhou shang de rizi, 1977). Subsequent publications include *Yesterday When I Was Young* (Zuori dang wo nianqing shi, 1980), *Unfinished Affairs* (Wei liao, 1982), *Passages of Things Past* (Shiyi shiwang, 1984), *Remembering My Brothers in Military Housing Compounds* (Xiang wo juanchun de xiongdimen, 1992), and *The Ancient Capital* (Gudu, 1997).

From her first works she has exhibited an unusual sensitivity to and passionate concern for history and her Chinese heritage. Like her sister in her earlier works, Zhu Tianxin also uses an imaginary China as a necessary anchor for her sense of cultural heritage and identity. But as Taiwanese identity grew in the mid-1980s, Zhu Tianxin began to turn her attention toward social critique and politics. Discussions on the issue of national, cultural, and ethnic identities dominated the mass media, the arts, and academia during these formative years of Taiwan's democratization. A few years before the annulment of martial laws in 1987, the Taiwan government finally allowed limited contacts and communication with China, and activities between people on both sides of the Taiwan Straits accelerated. In the cultural sphere, such intensive contacts with the "motherland" have prompted Taiwan writers to reevaluate their place in the "greater Chinese" literary tradition. Zhu Tianxin's fiction published in the 1990s reveals a serious attempt to articulate the cultural identity crisis that has surfaced in this milieu. As Taiwan moves into a new century, reflections on its past and present will certainly affect how it builds its future. Like many writers who are her contemporaries, Zhu Tianxin seeks to understand the impact of many political, social, and cultural changes and to find ways of articulating a coherent and independent cultural identity for people in Taiwan.

In her 1997 collection of stories *Ancient Capital*, the general impression one gets is Zhu Tianxin's obsession with the prevalence of foreign cultural influences in Taiwan. The collection is filled with references to foreign cities and countries, world literature, mythology, religion, the latest (thus most fashionable) theoretical jargon from many academic disciplines, and more popular artifacts such as pop music, fashion, and movies. Her choices of such materials share two characteristics: they represent "high culture," and they are held as cultural icons signifying nostalgic sentiments shared by her generation in Taiwan who grew up during the 1960s and the 1970s when Taiwan was culturally dominated by the United States. Zhu Tianxin appropriates bits and pieces of foreign cultures by freely making them a potent part of her narrative strategy. She imitates and appropriates Western literary works, films, and aesthetic ideas to help her articulate the cultural identity crisis facing people in Taiwan.

The first short story in the collection *Ancient Capital*, "Death in Venice" (Weinisi zhi si, 1992), recalls Thomas Mann's highly celebrated story of the same title. Zhu Tianxin's "Death in Venice" is about a writer who is unable to resist the impact his environment has on his creative process. For example, a café filled with the sounds of cell phones beeping and conversations buzzing influences him to change the main character of the novel he is writing from a simple villager into a reporter who decides to throw himself into the life of urban Taipei.

In our information age, Zhu Tianxin is interested in exploring how transient information, including cultural imports from around the world, has possessed the psyche of the people in Taiwan, or at least of those who live in Taipei. In "Death in Venice," Zhu Tianxin makes evident that it is not just the incidental information we are barraged with on a daily basis that tends to lose its value by the minute; even the more endurable sort of information, such as philosophy, psychology, or sociology, faces the danger of being "out of fashion" faster than before. Because both types of information change so rapidly, they are treated as everyday cultural products. This is exactly how Zhu Tianxin treats borrowed foreign cultural material in "Death of Venice."

In this story, Zhu Tianxin portrays an unusual writer who sees writing as both a passive activity and a manifestation of his nearly involuntary interaction with his environment. Writing is also a process of collecting and recalling minute experiences and observations from the past and the present. In this strange relationship between the writer, his surroundings, and the fiction he produces, Zhu Tianxin exposes the postcolonial predicament of a writer facing a hybridized literary heritage. Unable to find something in the past from which to draw authenticity, the postcolonial writer can only find a meaningful identity in the presently occupied space, manifested, for example, in exotically decorated cafés. Here, Zhu Tianxin uses her protagonist's penchant for processing his thoughts and ideas through Western high culture formulations to expose the predicament of lacking one's own cultural voice.

In the next story, "Ancient Capital," Zhu Tianxin moves into history to find ways to resolve the problem of constructing cultural identity in an essentially hybrid culture. In this story, she goes into a space between past and present, the historical real and the imaginary, ideality and disillusionment, to find a balance between cultural hybridity and identity. To lay claim to a cultural identity, one must believe that this identity will give one uniqueness, that it is inherently original and authentic. "Ancient Capital" digs deeply into the very core of what cultural identity means and what reconciliations one must make before the construction of this identity can even begin.

Zhu Tianxin borrowed the title "Ancient Capital" from Japan's Nobel Prize winner *Kawabata Yasunari's canonical novel *The Old Capital* (Koto). The plot of "Ancient Capital" is linear, and the story parallels Kawabata's novel thematically. It begins with the narrator's remembering her high school years, spent with her best friend, A. But gradually, as they move into their adult years, they grow apart, until one day the narrator receives a fax from A inviting her to meet in Kyoto. The narrator thus begins her journey to Kawabata's old capital. While she awaits A's arrival, she takes a walk through streets and alleys in the city, remembering her residence there with her daughter some years before. After waiting for a day, she realizes that A will not show up, and thus she decides to return to Taipei earlier than scheduled. At the Taipei airport she is approached by a cab driver who mistakes her for a Japanese tourist; without attempting to correct the driver, she gets into the cab and drives into the city. As soon as she decides to return to her home city as a foreigner, everything begins to look different. She finds in her bag a Japanese tourist map of colonial Taipei and is inspired to follow it and revisit the city as it was half a century ago. This map lays out Taipei the way it was designed by the Japanese, with streets, governmental buildings, and landmarks appearing under their previous colonial names. She thus experiences present-day Taipei through the filter of its colonial past. What makes this switch of perspective most intriguing is that she is pretending to be someone other than herself—a Japanese tourist. With this disguise she can remove herself psychologically from the immediacy of her surroundings and allow the map to guide her to see the city anew. The narrator begins a journey back to the past, only to realize at the end that she no longer knows where she is.

"Ancient Capital" is also a story of remembering the history of Taiwan as a Japanese colony. References to foreign cultures constitute the narrative's cultural setting. In the first section of the story, before the narrator's trip to Kyoto, the cultural milieu is depicted through references to American popular music and movies. In this section, the narrator recalls her adolescent years and the way Taipei was at the time. Conflicts between the native and the foreign are apparent. As the narrator goes to Kyoto, anticipating a reunion with A, the scene turns to Kyoto and Kawabata's *Old Capital* provides the narrator guidance in revisiting the city. In the next section, where she pretends to be a foreign tourist back in Taipei, the narrative is dominated by historical and cultural references alluding to the colonial period, thus calling attention to the contrast between the historical and the contemporary. For each section, space and time are constituted by different sets of cultural references and structured by different principles.

This desire to see similarity between Taipei and Kyoto is itself a symptom of the very issue Zhu Tianxin wants to explore in her narrative, namely, discontinuity in the historical record of Taiwan and the disruption of the collective memory of the people of Taiwan. Zhu Tianxin's recuperation of Kawabata's old capital thus is not a sign of her naiveté about history or mere romanticism for an ancient city, but rather, it is her own sense of the lack of a coherent and continuous historical and cultural heritage. It is understandable that Zhu Tianxin's narrator finds in Japan and Kyoto material necessary for constructing Taiwan's (via Taipei's) past. The historicity that Kyoto represents is authentic; the previous colonial connection between Japan and Taiwan provides Zhu Tianxin a reference to retrace the city of Taipei as it was built during the colonial period.

From dealing with culture in "Death in Venice" to investigating history in "Ancient Capital," Zhu Tianxin recognizes that the essence of Taiwan's culture is a product of colonialism and capitalism. Although rooted in Chinese culture, Taiwan culture has also absorbed tremendous Japanese and Western (mainly American) cultural influences. Therefore, maintaining cohesion between history, memory, and place becomes a crucial way to establish an independent cultural identity.

—*Lingchei Letty Chen*

Bibliography

Chang, Yvonne Song-sheng. "Chu T'ien-wen and Taiwan's Recent Cultural and Literary Trends." *Modern Chinese Literature* 6, nos. 1–2 (1992): 61–84.

———. *Modernism and the Nativist Resistance: Contemporary Chinese Fiction from Taiwan.* Durham, N.C.: Duke University Press, 1993.

———. "Beyond Cultural and National Identities: Current Re-evaluation of the *Kominka* Literature from Taiwan's Japanese Period." *Journal of Modern Literature in Chinese* 1, no. 1 (July 1997): 75–107.

Chen, Lingchei Letty. "Rising from the Ashes: Identity and the Aesthetics of Hybridity in Zhu Tianwen's *Notes of a Desolate Man.*" *Journal of Modern Literature in Chinese* 4, no. 1 (July 2000): 101–138.

Gold, Thomas B. "Civil Society and Taiwan's Quest for Identity." In Steven Harrell and Chün-chieh Huang, eds., *Cultural Change in Postwar Taiwan*, 47–68. Boulder, Colo.: Westview Press, 1994.

Kawabata Yasunari. *The Old Capital.* Trans. J. Martin Holman. San Francisco: North Point Press, 1987.

Wang, David Der-wei. "Fin-de-siècle Splendor: Contemporary Women Writers' Vision of Taiwan." *Modern Chinese Literature* 6, nos. 1–2 (Spring–Fall 1992): 39–59.

———. *Fin-de-siècle Splendor: Repressed Modernities of Late Qing Fiction, 1849–1911.* Stanford: Stanford University Press, 1997.

Zhan Hongji. "Yizhong laoqi de shengyin" (A Kind of Aging Voice). In Zhu Tianwen, ed., *Shijimo de huali* (Fin-de-siècle Splendor), 7–9. Taipei: Yuanliu, 1990.

Zhu, Tianwen (Chu T'ien-wen). "Fin-de-siècle Splendor." Trans. Eva Hung. In Joseph Lau and Howard Goldblatt, eds., *The Columbia Anthology of Modern Chinese Literature*, 444–459. New York: Columbia University Press, 1995.

———. *Notes of a Desolate Man.* Trans. Howard Goldblatt and Sylvia Li-chun Lin. New York: Columbia University Press, 1999.

Zhu, Tianxin (Chu T'ien-hsin). "The Last Train to Tamshui." Trans. Michelle Yeh. *The Chinese Pen* (Spring 1988): 41–71.

———. "Nineteen Days of the New Party." Trans. Martha Cheung. *Renditions* 35–36 (1991): 144–170.

99

WANG ANYI

Born in 1954 in Nanjing and brought up in Shanghai, the daughter of the noted writer Ru Zhijuan, Wang Anyi had only just graduated from junior high school in 1969 when she volunteered to go down to a commune in northern Anhui Province. Disappointed by her peasant's life there, she left Anhui in 1972 and was admitted to a local performing arts troupe in Xuzhou, Jiangsu, where she began writing and publishing short stories. She returned to Shanghai in 1978 to serve as an editor of a literary journal and began her career as a professional writer in 1980. Since then she has won many national literary prizes and become one of the most prominent and prolific writers in China.

The work that established Wang Anyi's reputation as a promising writer is "And the Rain Patters On" (Yu, sha sha sha, 1980). Influenced by other women writers in the early post-Mao era such as Zhang Jie and Zhang Xinxin, Wang Anyi emphasized subjective perspectives, personal ideals, and daily experience that were not directly in line with the grand narrative advocated by the state and consequently challenged the dominant literary style that centered on collectively validated and politically oriented topics (Wang Lingzhen 1998:403). In "And the Rain Patters On," Wang tells the story of a young and innocent woman, Wenwen, who falls in love with a young male bicycle rider when he helps her on a rainy night. Although her mother pressures her to accept a conventional view of love and consider an arranged marriage, Wenwen refuses to compromise or to relinquish the memory of the young man, who stands in her mind for hope, courage, and ideal love. Though Wang's exploration of love shares much with that of her contemporaries in its pursuit of the poetic, personal, and idealistic, it is also distinguished by its unusual emphasis on the ordinary and nonheroic and on daily urban experience.

In the early 1980s, Wang Anyi also wrote many stories about people from a variety of social groups and their attendant concerns, among which "The Destination" (Benci lieche zhongdian, 1981) and *Lapse of Time* (Liu shi, 1982) were awarded national literary prizes. It was not until *Baotown* (Xiao Bao zhuang, 1985) was published, however, that Wang was recognized as a self-transforming, mature, and successful writer. *Baotown* was written after Wang had paid a four-month visit to the United States to attend an international writers' workshop; she was shocked by the dramatic difference in cultural values between the United States and China, and this "led to the profound discovery that she was indeed Chinese and to the decision to 'write on China' when she returned" (Feuerwerker 1998:227).

Drawing on historical material, legendary stories, personal imagination, and her own past experience in the countryside, *Baotown* creates a world that both represents a mythical and timeless China and that depicts in detail the crisis, heterogeneous voices, and fragmented state of life that contradict any claim of a homogeneous and stable Chinese tradition. Although the Confucian ideal of *renyi* (benevolence and righteousness) is presented as the defining characteristic of Bao village, the village is, at the same time, poverty-stricken, conservative, passive, and fatalistic. Furthermore, coexisting with the ideal of *renyi*, embodied by Laozha (Dregs), a young child who sacrifices his own life to save an old man in a catastrophic flood, are the ordinary lives of rural folk full of prejudice, selfishness, and cruelty, to which most women and outsiders fall victim. The death of Dregs, therefore, both symbolizes the traditional ideal of *renyi* and announces its demise; after all, the village benefits from Dregs's death and its inhabitants live completely different lives afterward.

Wang's ambivalent attitude toward the death of Dregs parallels ambivalence toward her ambitions to represent China in her works: she is at once sanguine and suspicious about the validity of such a project. Her conscious problematization of the reliability of writing itself through the figure of Bao Renwen, the peasant writer in *Baotown*, further destabilizes the act of representation and thus resists "the rationalized interpretations of society promoted by modern ideologies defining nation-state" (Gunn 1991:176). If *renyi* is set up at the beginning of the story as the ideal origin of Chinese civilization, this ideal is challenged by the lives of marginalized groups of people in the village and breaks down toward the end of the story, when different narratives compete with each other to appropriate the death of Dregs. Claimed as one of the most representative works of *roots-seeking literature, *Baotown* also questions the value of traditional origin and challenges the political and cultural significations of the literary movement.

Wang Anyi returned to the subjective mode of writing in her famous "romance trilogy" (*sanlian*): *Love On a Barren Mountain* (Huangshan zhi lian,

1986), *Love in a Small Town* (Xiaocheng zhi lian, 1986), and *Brocade Valley* (Jinxiugu zhi lian, 1987). *Love on a Barren Mountain* tells the story of how two people who grow up in different regions and with different backgrounds and experience fall into a transgressive extramarital relationship and end their lives with tragic suicide; *Love in a Small Town* depicts two adolescents' awakening to libidinal desire that is too powerful for them to control and becomes the sole basis of their relationship for years, until the girl becomes a mother and suddenly transcends the restlessness of her sexual drive; *Brocade Valley* represents a narcissistic young married woman who is suffocated by her uneventful marriage and her indifferent and boring husband and seeks to recreate a new self through a brief romantic liaison with a famous male writer at a conference held on Lu Mountain. Although Wang's romance trilogy is claimed as having successfully broken socialist taboos on carnal love and sexuality, the three novels, with their foregrounded psychological activity and subjective perspectives, center on the role of sex and desire in the formation of subjectivity and consequently the trilogy "tackles the problematic of sexual difference as an immediate reality rather than as a signifier of social and ideological entities" (Chen 1998:93).

Wang Anyi's popular story "Brothers" (Dixiongmen, 1989) explores the tenuousness of a same-sex love relationship (see "Same-Sex Love in Recent Chinese Literature") built without sexual, material, and institutional grounds. After years of separation, two married women, Lao Li and Lao Wang, resume an intimate relationship developed during their years in an art college. In order to help Lao Li to give birth to her son, Lao Wang moves from Nanjing into Lao Li and her husband's apartment in Shanghai. Just as their relationship develops and demands new terms, an unexpected incident—Lao Li's son's fall from the stroller—tears them apart. Their relationship ends in frustration for want of a new set of terms for understanding and defining it. "The fragility and rupture of the female bond testify to the difficulty a woman encounters in sorting out her desire in a society that privileges patriarchal heterosexuality" (Liu 1993:56) and institutionalized marriage and motherhood.

In *Love in Brocade Valley*, Wang Anyi begins her experimentation in metafiction, a trend that is further developed in *The Story of Uncle* (Shushu de gushi, 1990), a critically acclaimed novel that "ushers in a new logic of literary creation, the premise of which is no longer referential experience or reality but the independent technique of crafting fiction" (Tang 1997:181). *The Story of Uncle* is told by a narrator whose own recent personal experience prompts his desire to tell a story. But unwilling to disclose his own story, he decides to tell a story about Uncle, an established writer from the older generation of rehabilitated rightists, whose recent insight into his own unhappy fate corresponds to that of the narrator's. With Uncle at the center of his story, the narrator not only maximizes the effect of the emotion he just experienced from an incident of his own life but also sets out to undermine the romantic, optimistic, idealized, and heroic narrative about Uncle's generation. In order to reconcile the story with the views of the narrator's generation, which is depicted as embracing a cynical, pragmatic, and nihilistic attitude toward history and life, the narrator shows how he fabricates the story of Uncle by piecing together multiple and conflicting threads and fragments of information (including his own pure speculation). If the process of fabricating and narrating Uncle's story serves to debunk the cultural myths of his generation, it simultaneously undermines the validity of the narrator's generation; when all is said and done, youths like the narrator share with Uncle's generation a profound sense of despair over their unhappy fates.

In her writing of the early 1990s, Wang Anyi probes into questions regarding the intrinsic logic and technique of storytelling, as well as the nature and status of literature in contemporary China. She endorses the idea that literature, fiction in particular, is an autonomous field independent of historical reference and utilitarian function. At the same time, however, she also insists on a personal angle that links individual minds, emotions, moods, temperaments, experiences, and desires to the act of writing. Literature is, from another perspective, a purely personalized activity for Wang. Indeed, in her more than twenty-year writing career, she has constantly returned to a personal mode of writing that centers on its characters' internal worlds and produced many autobiographically stories and novels.

Documentation and Fabrication: One Method of Creating the World (Jishi yu xugou: chuangzao shijie fangfa zhiyi, 1993) manifests the two major principles of Wang's writing. The novel consists of two interwoven parts: one part investigates how the narrator reconstructs her lost maternal genealogy with well-researched public and historical materials that may or may not have anything to do with the narrator's mother; the other part concerns how the narrator connects her own isolated life with its immediate physical environment, the city of Shanghai in socialist China. The latter part contains many references to the author's life and is also a rewriting of earlier autobiographical stories. Searching for maternal family roots and self-identity, Wang Anyi employs the most accurate and concrete materials, both historical and personal, only to construct imagined entities, thus bearing testimony to the irretrievability of the past and instability of the self. The novel dispenses with the literary conventions that differentiate fiction from autobiography and creates its own distinctive world and logic that are both independent from and dependent on history and reality.

Wang Anyi originally planned to name the novel *The Shanghai Story* (Shanghai gushi), a title that reveals both the binding relationship between place and narrative invention and Wang's desire to recreate the city of Shanghai through narration. Her novel *The Song of Everlasting Sorrow* (Chang hen ge, 1995) paints a portrait of the city through its historical and social changes of the past forty years. Different from her other Shanghai stories, which are set in post-1949 Communist China, this novel goes back to the early 1940s and thus connects itself with other fiction about Shanghai composed at that time by such writers as *Eileen Chang and Su Qing. (See "Post-Mao Urban Fiction.")

Shanghai is the primary subject of this novel; Wang Anyi uses much textual space to depict the city, its alleys, the gossip (or street talk), the girl's inner chambers, the doves, and the vicissitudes of the common city dwellers, of whom Wang Qiyao, the female protagonist, is but one. Shanghai is defined through its *shimin* (common city inhabitants) and their daily lives, and the story of Wang Qiyao is in fact the story of Shanghai. Born into a *shimin* family in the alleys, Wang Qiyao grows up to become Miss Shanghai of 1946, after which she gets involved with different men at different stages of her life. She survives all the turmoil of modern and contemporary Chinese history only to be murdered in a fight with a thief over a box of gold bars in the 1980s. Despite her quite eventful life, Wang Qiyao is represented as the quintessence of the Shanghai *shimin* class; she embodies the down-to-earth, prudent, shrewd, pragmatic, and flexible lifestyle of the Shanghai people, who with a *shimin* spirit and practicality found a world of their own that both indulges in and resists dominant ideological impositions that Shanghai has been made to embody. The novel, therefore, illustrates Wang Anyi's view of the city of Shanghai in the history of modern China.

—*Lingzhen Wang*

Bibliography

Chen, Helen H. "Gender, Subjectivity, Sexuality: Defining a Subversive Discourse in Wang Anyi's Four Tales of Sexual Transgression." In Yingjing Zhang, ed.. *China in a Polycentric World: Essays in Chinese Comparative Literature*, 90–109. Stanford: Stanford University Press, 1998.

Feuerwerker, Yi-tsi Mei. *Ideology, Power, Text: Self-Representation and the Peasant "Other" in Modern Chinese Literature*. Stanford: Stanford University Press, 1998.

Gunn, Edward. *Rewriting Chinese: Style and Innovation in Twentieth-Century Chinese Prose*. Stanford: Stanford University Press, 1991.

Liu, Lydia H. "Invention and Intervention: The Female Tradition in Modern Chinese Literature." In Tani Barlow, ed., *Gender Politics in Modern China: Writing and Feminism*, 33–57. Durham, N.C.: Duke University Press, 1993.

Tang, Xiaobing. "Melancholy against the Grain: Approaching Postmodernity in Wang Anyi's Tales of Sorrow." *boundary 2* 24, no. 3 (Fall 1997): 177–200.

Wang, Anyi. *Baotown*. Trans. Martha Avery. London: Viking, 1989.

——. *Brocade Valley*. Trans. Bonnie S. McDougall and Chen Maiping. New York: New Directions, 1992.

——. "Brothers." Trans. Diana B. Kingsbury. In Diana B. Kingsbury, ed., *I Wish I Were a Wolf: The New Voice in Chinese Women's Literature*, 158–212. London: New World Press, 1994.

——. *Chang hen ge* (The Song of Everlasting Regret). Beijing: Zuojia, 1996.

——. *Jishi yu xugou: chuangzao shijie fangfa zhiyi* (Documentation and Fabrication: One Method of Creating the World). Beijing: Renmin wenxue, 1993.

——. *Lapse of Time*. San Francisco: China Books, 1988.

———. *Love in a Small Town.* Trans. Eva Huang. Hong Kong: Renditions, 1988.

———. *Love on a Barren Mountain.* Trans. Eva Hung. Hong Kong: Renditions, 1991.

———. *Shushu de gushi* (The Story of Uncle). In *Xianggang de qing yu ai* (Love and Sentiment in Hong Kong), 1–77. Beijing: Zuojia, 1996.

Wang, Lingzhen. "Retheorizing the Personal: Identity, Writing, and Gender in Yu Luojin's Autobiographical Act." *Positions* 6, no. 2 (Fall 1998): 394–438.

100

WANG SHUO AND THE COMMERCIALIZATION
OF LITERATURE

Although disparaged by many literary critics as a profiteering purveyor of insipid tales about the sordid urban underworld, few deny that Wang Shuo (b. 1958) poignantly represents the transformation that Chinese culture experienced during the late 1980s and early 1990s. Wang Shuo has become a household name referring to an epochal "cultural attitude" associated with his status as one of China's best-selling authors and media savvy writers of television series and films. The emergence of his widespread yet controversial popularity, known as the Wang Shuo "phenomenon" *(xianxiang)*, reveals the contradictions between a "brave new world" generated by market reforms and China's gradual opening to outside capital, ideas, technology, and images.

When Wang Shuo began writing in the early 1980s, China was experiencing tremendous social and economic reforms. The casting away of the "iron rice bowl" system, which guaranteed life-long tenure of employment, in tandem with the introduction of profit as a key economic and social logic, created new economic possibilities as well as social unrest, alienation, and uncertainties. On the streets and in literature, new social roles emerged, such as the "sugar daddies" *(da kuan)* who successfully navigated the new market and emerged as emblems of a new era of materialism and money worship. Slipping through the cracks of the new market, however, were the *liumang,* a multifaceted cultural term referring to a spectrum of lowlifes, riffraff, vagrants, hooligans, and slackers, who negotiated the market terrain by designing cunning scams and running at least marginally criminal operations.

Depending on one's point of view, Wang Shuo can be seen as *liumang* culture's self-appointed advocate and spokesperson, the lucky commercial benefactor of a topsy-turvy world, or an insincere hack parasitic on those alienated and morally adrift in the brave new world. Regardless, Wang Shuo's works and pop image are best understood in relation to this *liumang* culture. Wang Shuo himself shares much in common with the *liumang* featured in his works. As by-products of the rapidly changing economy, most *liumang* were dismissed or resigned from their government-allocated jobs—in particular, the military—before sinking into a life of drifting, slumming, conniving, or scamming.

Although the market reforms are central to the psychological and social formation of the *liumang*, the violence and chaos of the Cultural Revolution played an equally influential role. As part of the Red Guard generation, the *liumang* were trained at an early age in street violence and inculcated in the attitude of collective rebellion. Wang Shuo, as a prototypical *liumang*, entered the People's Liberation Army as a sailor after finishing middle school at the end of the Cultural Revolution. The submission of his first story, "Waiting" (Dengdai, 1978), to *Liberation Army Literature and Art* (Jiefang jun wenyi) earned him a job as editor with the magazine, but this failed to stave off his *liumang* proclivities; he started a smuggling operation in the south. After being demobilized and fined for illegal trade, he loafed about working for a pharmaceutical company for three years and continued writing while living off his female companions, many of whom became celebrated characters in his works. Even after he made it big in the late 1980s, Wang Shuo was unable and unwilling to shed his reputation as a *liumang*. In fact, it became one of his great selling points.

The Wang Shuo phenomenon is, in part, the story of the commercialization of culture in post-Mao China. From one perspective, Wang Shuo is just one of the many profit-minded entrepreneurs engendered by the market reforms. Wang supports the role of the market in cultural production and candidly admits that he strives to appeal to a large audience: "What I am most interested in and pay the closest attention to is popular lifestyles. This includes violence, sex, mockery, and shamelessness. I just reproduce these in my works" (Zhang and Jin 1993:67). He is accused of promoting a "bestseller consciousness" (Wang 1997:262) or condemned as a panderer to vulgar, popular tastes. But Wang is unrepentant: "I'm not interested in dreams that are painted all rosy, thought by all as so wonderful. By the time you snap out of it, wouldn't you have already wasted your time? The reality is that people already have it tough and are tired. They would just get even more tired if forced to think on a deeper level. I tell people the way things really are to make them laugh and relieve their tedium, to let them live a bit more relaxed and more true to themselves and life itself. Is this really so irresponsible?" (Zhang 1993:76).

Wang Shuo also worked with his publishers to devise marketing schemes to increase sales. When his four-volume collected works was published in 1992, Wang gained the reputation of being the first author to have glossy poster-sized advertisements pushing his works. Always consumer-oriented, his latest novel, *Seemingly Beautiful* (Kanshangqu hen mei, 1998), was accompanied by a CD-ROM of his selected works. Most of his wealth, however, has been earned from writing scripts for miniseries and films. Wang said that the purpose of his first miniseries, *The Editorial Office* (Bianji bu de gushi, 1992), was "giving the commoners a dream to play with" (Wang 1992:47). He unabashedly derives pleasure from flaunting, or even mocking, his market promiscuity. Television miniseries scriptwriters, he states, are "goods for sale … no different from prostitutes" (Wang 1992:65). Wang's Seahorse Company, a writing salon established with a group of friends and with a sideline into the karaoke restaurant business, most poignantly indicates his role in fusing culture with the market.

What is the commercial appeal of Wang Shuo's works? Certainly, Wang's unfettered pursuit of making a buck in catering to the public's taste for profane cynicism and voyeuristic pleasure contributed to his commercial success. His works portray the vagrancies of the *liumang* in a pseudo-realist style, similar to the more serious reportage literature that was gaining prestige and widespread popularity during the 1980s. However, Wang Shuo clearly rejects the heroic models—intellectuals, students, rustic peasants, and so on—offered in some post–Cultural Revolution literature. His characters, as the dregs of society, pursue unethical and illegal activities, such as racketeering and pimping, or more innocuous activities, such as slacking off, shooting the breeze *(da kanr)*, swindling, seducing women, and living aimlessly *(hunr)*. The merging of author, narrator, and protagonist in Wang's fiction, moreover, heightens readers' sense of peering into the life of a *liumang*, vicariously experiencing their self-indulgent idleness and the urban underworld they inhabit.

The neorealist first-person mode combined with such popular genres as the love story, detective story, and comical satire contributed enormously to Wang Shuo's commercial success. Love was the major theme of his early stories. His first story to gain notoriety, "The Stewardess" (Kongzhong xiaojie, 1984), which is semi-autobiographical, tells of a young girl who irrationally falls for the romantic image of the story's protagonist. After the protagonist is relieved from his duties with the navy some years later, adopting a rootless lifestyle, he attempts to carry on a relationship with his former idolater, Ah Mei, who is now a flight attendant. The relationship fails, with Ah Mei becoming disillusioned by the protagonist's slothfulness and social indifference, including his inability to express affection for her. After Ah Mei dies in a plane crash, the protagonist searches to find out what she truly thought of him before she tragically died. Although a callow work, "The Stewardess" foreshadows Wang Shuo's focus on irreconcilable and usually tragic love relationships, the emergence of the *liumang* type, and a nostalgic, albeit implied or tacit, intellectual pursuit of a system of values or morality, partially signified by the image of an innocent girl.

His later fiction includes similarly sentimental love stories. In "Lost Love Forever" (Yongshi wo ai, 1989), for example, the protagonist is unwilling to disclose his terminal illness to his fiancée, leading her to marry another. However, in general, the male protagonists in his stories become increasingly misogynistic as the innocent and pure women are symbolically deflowered by the *liumang*'s decadent and immoral lifestyles, emotional indifference, and licentious womanizing. For example, in *Half Hot, Half Cold* (Yiban shi huoyan, yiban shi haishui, 1986), Wu Di, originally a wholesome college student with a bright future, is led to join the cold-shouldering protagonist's racketeering scam as a prostitute, leading to her eventual suicide.

Another major genre in Wang's oeuvre is comical satires, of which *Masters of Mischief* (Wanzhu, 1987) is a masterpiece. It tells the story of enterprising *liumang* who start a shady business called "Three T Company," providing three services: "troubleshooting, tedium relief, and taking the blame." The company's employees are hired as surrogates, standing in for a client's date or providing a target for a housewife's frustrated harangues. The appeal of this story lies not only in the slapstick and irreverent antics but also in the mockery of official culture. Serious official functions are subject to absurd parodies in much of Wang Shuo's fiction. In the film adaptation of *Masters of Mischief*, a phony literary award ceremony hosted by the Three T Company concludes with a performance in the style of a fashion show accompanied by a disco beat. This farcical yet highly symbolic performance juxtaposes sacred images, such as that of the People's Liberation Army (PLA) soldier, with the popular and vulgar, as embodied by the scantily clad female weightlifter. One of Wang Shuo's trademarks is his subversion of political rhetoric. In "An Attitude" (Yidianr zhengjing meiyou, 1989) the protagonist, Fang Yan, provides a mocking rendition of Deng Xiaoping: "I have repeatedly said with all sincerity and concern that under no circumstances should we ever forget the masses, 99 percent of the population. So long as the 800 million peasants and 3 million PLA members are at peace, the empire will be stable" (Barmé 1999:78). It is no exaggeration to say that Wang Shuo's mockery of official slogans and speeches has infiltrated the Chinese popular imagination, making it virtually impossible not to snicker at hackneyed official rhetoric and jargon. However, as Dai Jinhua (1995:52) points out, although Wang Shuo mocks and deconstructs the sacrosanct official discourse, he at the same time promotes the government's official agenda of pursuing material wealth.

In the history of contemporary Chinese literature, Wang Shuo represents the arrival of a commercialized cultural cynicism and the ebbing of serious cultural questioning of identity and a sanguine view of literature's role in shaping society. This displacement of elite literature can in part be attributed to the commercialization of culture or the market's new key role in cultural production and consumption. Despite Wang Shuo's popular appeal and his condemnation by academics and supporters of elite culture as pandering to vulgar tastes, he can not be entirely disassociated from elite culture. Not only do intellectuals make up a large part of his readership, but there are also important elements of an elite literary discourse in his fiction. In fact, in his controversial collection of essays published for the new century, Wang Shuo diffidently owns up to the trend toward intellectualization in his fiction while maintaining his trademark sardonic repartee: "What I would like to say is that over the years I have become an intellectual through my works…. In my view, the course of intellectualization is one of abstraction, in which the living is made machine-like…. I don't know how to free myself from the shackles of abstraction and whether this direction can be reversed. I feel repulsed by my tendency toward intellectualization in my writing's train of thought and style" (Wang 2000:107–109).

Most literary historians divide Wang Shuo's works into three periods, within which we see an elite literary discourse gaining greater prominence. Throughout Wang Shuo's literary career, his "literature of escape and sublimation" (Barmé 1999:63) is gradually tainted by the very elitist discourse and intellectuality previously scoffed and subjected to derisive ridicule in his fiction and public statements. The shameless pursuit of making a buck through lawless, semi-criminal, or unethical endeavors is gradually obscured by a proclivity for waxing witticisms and falling prey to the pursuit of meaning. *Playing for Thrills* (Wande jiu shi xin tiao, 1989) is a transitional work displaying both the vivid lifelike portrayal of *liumang* culture of his earlier works and his later interest in language games and philosophical musings, not so different from those of the school of *avant-garde experimental writers. *Playing for Thrills* narrates the concoction of a fictitious murder by idle, spent *liumang* for the purpose of relieving their tedium. Mockery of intellectuality gives way to a mental pursuit of solving a whodunit puzzle. *Wanr* ("fooling around") serves as a bridge between Wang Shuo's earlier fiction, in which the *liumang* irreverently mess about town, and his later works, in which *wanr wenxue* ("to play at writing literature") is created through garrulous banter *(kan)* verging on existential or absurdist language games. Wang Shuo's more recent works, such as *Vicious Beasts* (Dongwu xiongmen, 1991) and *Seemingly Beautiful*, attempt a greater balance between a realist style and the play of cynicism, wit, and language games. Moreover, as both of these works explore the childhood environment of the *liumang*, they search for the root causes of China's current historical predicament in its recent socialist past.

A discussion of Wang Shuo would not be complete without placing him within the greater tradition of Chinese literature. Because his works are replete with Beijing colloquialisms and slang, Wang Shuo can be considered a major force in exploring a Beijing indigenous style in the tradition of the dramatist and author *Lao She. The *liumang* adhere to an unofficial pact of collective camaraderie and adhere to a common ideology, even if that ideology amounts to lackadaisical lethargy, sedition, seduction, and sardonic banter. The disintegration of the work unit *(danwei)* as the basic structure of society in the 1980s provided the impetus for new solidarities to form based on shared values or lifestyles. The emergence of clans of "buddies," who referred to each other as *gemen'r*, is a symptom of these social changes, even as it draws on cultural memory and shared values of community and loyalty. The clans of *liumang* in Wang Shuo's works are not so far removed from the bands of lawless heroes in the tradition of *wuxia* (*martial arts) fiction (Barmé 1999:85). It is perhaps not coincidental that at the time of Wang Shuo's commercial success, *Jin Yong's martial-arts novels were becoming bestsellers in China. Both are essentially entertainment genres that provide a myth of individual emancipation, either through heroic feats or subversive behavior, and that appealed to readers in a era of new economic anxieties, angst, and alienation.

—Jonathan Noble

Bibliography

Barmé, Geremie. *In the Red: On Contemporary Chinese Culture*. New York: Columbia University Press, 1999.

Dai Jinhua. *Jingcheng tuwei: nuxing, dianying, wenxue* (Breaking out of the Mirrored City: Woman, Film, Literature). Beijing: Zuojia, 1995.

Wang, Jing. *High Culture Fever: Politics, Aesthetics, and Ideology in Deng's China*. Berkeley: University of California Press, 1997.

Wang Shuo. *Kanshangqu hen mei* (Seemingly Beautiful). Beijing: Huayi, 1999.

——. *Playing for Thrills*. Trans. Howard Goldblatt. New York: William Morrow, 1998.

——. *Please Don't Call Me Human*. Trans. Howard Goldblatt. New York: Hyperion, 2000.

——. *Wang Shuo wenji* (Collected Works of Wang Shuo). Beijing: Huayi, 1996.

——. *Wo shi Wang Shuo* (I Am Wang Shuo). Beijing: Guoji wenhua, 1992.

——. *Wuzhizhe wu wei* (The Ignorant Have Nothing to Fear). Beijing: Chunfeng wenyi, 2000.

Zhang Dexiang and Jin Huimin. *Wang Shuo pipan* (Critique of Wang Shuo). Beijing: Zhongguo shehui kexue, 1993.

101

VOICES OF NEGOTIATION
IN LATE TWENTIETH-CENTURY
HONG KONG LITERATURE

Hong Kong literary critic Wong Wai-leung claims that Hong Kong literature integrated with modern Chinese literature during World War II, when Hong Kong became the stopover for refugee writers from the mainland. It is true that for a few decades Hong Kong literature was mainly produced by writers either passing through or residing temporarily in Hong Kong. However, this mainland-based view of Hong Kong literature has been altered by the emergence of the generation of writers born and raised in Hong Kong, whose voices are distinguishable from those in earlier times and those from mainland China and Taiwan. There are some among them who, with the benefit of a Western-style education and opportunities of traveling or studying abroad, have started to translate or "co-translate" their own work. The cases of Dung Kai-cheung and Leung Ping-kwan demonstrate internationalization in recent Hong Kong literary production. Unlike earlier writers who either ignore its existence or simply denigrate it as an uninteresting commercial enclave, these younger writers turned to Hong Kong as their major subject matter. Partly triggered by the looming 1997 turnover, this new literary attention to Hong Kong was more than an uncritical celebration of Hong Kong; it marked a generation of voices aiming to negotiate with cliché images, to rediscover the colonial process, and to rewrite local history. These writers are preoccupied with the need to consider the paradoxical nature of the Hong Kong urban space through which the notion of home is addressed, and they are interested in forging a postcolonial identity for Hong Kong through the process of writing and rewriting Hong Kong history.

To discuss the Hong Kong urban space, it is important to start with Liu Yichang (b. 1918), an older émigré writer who came to Hong Kong from the mainland before the Communist takeover in 1949 and whose dedication to Hong Kong literature—as both author and editor—has earned him the status of "institution" (Liu Yichang 1995:vii). Unlike other émigré writers who fled to Hong Kong in 1949, Liu demonstrates genuine interest in writing about the Hong Kong experience. Although Liu is a prolific writer, not many of his works are available in English translation. *Intersection* (Duidao), a novella, is representative of his perspective of Hong Kong. Originally serialized in a Hong Kong newspaper in 1972 and then translated into English in 1988, the story traces the crisscrossing paths of a middle-aged man and a young woman who have never known or spoken to each other. Their brief encounter in the cinema is only a natural prelude to their final divergence—something all passers-by in the city experience. Readers also familiar with Gogol's "Nevsky Prospect" may immediately discover that Liu's Hong Kong urban space is not merely a paradoxical modern space where desires, hopes, and fantasy are juxtaposed with disappointment and misrecognition; it is also a site of divergent cultural routes. The man, an immigrant from Shanghai, heads north while the woman, a Hong Kong-born youngster, heads south. These directional markers figuratively signify different kinds of cultural identities in Hong Kong. The older man's memories of the "north," Shanghai, often flit by, creating some sense of cultural displacement of living in Hong Kong. In contrast, the woman's emotional engagement is with her here and now in Hong Kong. Whereas the man considers Hong Kong a stopover, the woman's sense of belonging to Hong Kong is naturally assumed. The author subtly implies a sense of impossibility for such identities to converge, as the story ends with two birds taking off in different directions, one toward the east, the other the west. To Liu, such cultural identities, intertwined with personal and gendered desires and dreams, maintain an uneasy coexistence in Hong Kong.

Liu's recognition of the paradoxical nature of the Hong Kong urban space finds echoes in Leung Ping-kwan (pen name of Ye Si, b. 1949). Leung's verse and prose bring readers to almost every corner of Hong Kong: from the most representative, such as Victoria Harbor and Lan Kwai Fong, to the most mundane, such as Ap-liu Street and Ladder Street; from the historical, such as the main building at the University of Hong Kong, to the seemingly exotic Walled City in Kowloon. Born in China but educated in Hong Kong, Leung is particularly interested in exploring the tactics of negotiating with this contradictory space—a space he calls "home." In an analysis of "North Point Car Ferry," collected in *City at the End of Time* (1992), a book of forty poems, critic Ackbar Abbas (1997:131) describes Leung's urban images as "surreal," turning "the familiar sights of Hong Kong into a post-apocalyptic landscape." His poems vigorously work against clichés, particularly clichéd images of Hong Kong. In his poetic world, there is a strong sense of urgency about the end of time, an urgency that is not a mere lamentation of the destructiveness of modernity, but that is fueled by an earnest determination to find fresh images for Hong Kong as the city contemplated its "end," its reintegration with China in 1997. In another poem, "Images of Hong Kong," he urges for "a new angle / for strictly visual matters," because in this "sign" city "history" has diminished into "a montage of images, / of paper, collectibles, plastic, fibers, laserdiscs, buttons" (33), erasing contradictions and differences. Similarly, "In Fabric Alley," which weaves a world of colorful and yet trite patterns and fabrics, Leung expresses a strong desire for "tailoring something new, / to make it so it wears the body well" (29). Driven by a sense of belonging to Hong Kong, Leung constantly urges for new angles and new patterns to negotiate with hackneyed stories of Hong Kong imposed mainly from the outside. Paradoxically, as he himself describes in "The Sorrows of Lan Kwai Fong," his poems about Hong Kong are "homeless" at home, with no opportunities for publication in Chinese. It is only through translation and the English language that they find a temporary home, an alternative cultural space in which to speak. To him, Hong Kong is a paradoxical site; while he intends to regard Hong Kong as home, he inevitably feels a sense of displacement, driving him to "drift from place to place" (Leung 1998:95).

Wong Bik-wan (b. 1961) is less interested in dealing with cultural images than Leung, but she is also concerned with the condition of homelessness. As the title of her second collection of short stories, *Tenderness and Violence* (Wenruo yu baolie, 1994), indicates, homelessness is experienced through contradictions that are an existential and cultural condition. "Losing the City" offers a good example of this treatment of homelessness. Written in the thriller mode, the story is set on the eve of the 1997 turnover, invoking home as an uncanny trope with a strong sense of displacement and desperation. The story is about a middle-class Hong Kong Chinese who, feeling an immense threat to his capitalist way of life because of the turnover, resorts to emigration with his wife. However, the sense of homelessness is felt everywhere: he ends up "tenderly" killing his family when they return to their birthplace, Hong Kong, after years of bitter isolation in America. Another character, an Irish inspector in Hong Kong, cannot but sense his uprootedness with the approaching end of colonial Hong Kong. Apart from this historical background, Wong seems to suggest that this contradictory experience is also partly an existential crisis as both characters demonstrate their lack of ability to negotiate with fear, pain, and despair. It is only through two other characters, an ambulance driver and his wife (a funeral agent), who witness the bloody aftermath of the murder, that we realize how people can cope with trauma with "the principle of hope." The story ends with an ironic actualization of this principle. By pouring red wine into the bathtub and turning the water into blood, the two make love in the "blood pool," trying to reenact violence "tenderly" and to "exorcize" their fear and despair.

The 1997 turnover triggered various kinds of voices of negotiation with such an important historical change. Dung Kai-cheung (b. 1967), a young Hong Kong writer, chose to rewrite the history of colonial Hong Kong, which he calls "the city of Victoria," in his *The Atlas: Archeology of an Imaginary City* (Ditu ji: Yige xiangxiang de chengshi de kaoguxue, 1997). As the work is set in the future when the city no longer exists, Dung demonstrates that history is a matter of interpretation; instead of writing history as a grand narrative, he resorts to a fragmented microhistory of Hong Kong local streets. Taking the readers through a spatial and temporal journey through Possession Street, Aldrich Street, and so on, he writes the histories of the streets through a blending of fact and fiction. In his "atlas" of this imaginary city, the local streets are less like static remains of the past than dynamic processes of cultural translations and of domination and resistance. The story of Possession Street is a case in point. Named by the British as a sign of their military achievements in Hong Kong, the street holds a story about how fear of the colonizers gives rise to an imaginary local resistance in the form of ghostly vengeance. The British ultimately restore the original Chinese name Shui Hang Hau to "exorcise" evils and avoid being "possessed."

Many other writers who similarly write the history of Hong Kong through the stories of the common people and the mundane practices of everyday life share Dung's preoccupation with the past. *Xi Xi (b. 1938) is perhaps the writer most dedicated to this project. She makes use of microhistorical details (legends, myths, oral narratives, and local social customs) to weave a collection of stories that critics call the "Fertile Town" series, among which is the novel *The Flying Carpet* (Fei zhan, 1996). To turn to the past, Leung Ping-kwan also seeks to demythologize the Walled City as a common place, "the place in which we live, the space which we all share" ("Walled City," 39). Hong Kong citizens have known the Walled City in Kowloon, now demolished and turned into a park, as a dirty, dangerous no man's land without law and jurisdiction, a place of prostitution, drug trafficking, illegal dental and medical services, and so on. Without denying the above, Leung describes the place as "messy, complicated, intriguing" and "frightening" but it is where "most people continued to lead normal lives. Just like Hong Kong" (37).

Unlike Leung and others who demythologize dominant cultural representations of Hong Kong, Xin Qishi (b. 1950) is less interested in aggressive challenge than the rendering of stories of common people. Her major work, *The Red Chequers Pub* (Hong gezi jiupu, 1994) depicts the experience of some Hong Kong activists who participate in social and nationalistic movements—namely, the Protect Diaoyu Islands Campaign and the pro-democracy movement of 1989. By setting the story against this kind of historical backdrop, Xin demonstrates how the collective experience of living in Hong Kong is inextricably and inevitably bound up with a sense of Chineseness. In "The Ghost Story," Xin's interest in the Chinese roots of Hong Kong culture is also evident. This story of a garbage collector depicts life in the public housing estates and the local custom of the Ghost Festival, expressing the writer's preoccupation with the past. But similar to other writers, fact blends with gossip and legends in Xin's writing of the past.

The ambitious Hong Kong trilogy by Shi Shuqing (b. 1945), a Taiwanese who lived in Hong Kong from the 1970s to 1997, is a sustained effort to reconfigure Hong Kong as a prostitute, but not in the trite way imposed by some earlier mainland Chinese and foreign writers. Working with a huge reservoir of anthropological details of local culture (for example, the breed of yellow butterfly and bauhinia flowers), she composes a series of rich microhistorical texts of a "promiscuous" place called Hong Kong (Wang 1996:85) where modernity mixes paradoxically with colonialism (Li 1997:201). Shi uses the prostitute, her "bastard" son, the butterfly, and bauhinia to represent Hong Kong not only as promiscuous and impure but also as a potent figure threatening and surpassing her colonizer.

William Tay notices that the ideological struggles between Taiwan and mainland China during the Cold War era has turned Hong Kong into a space for literature to flourish (Tay 1996:147); Hong Kong speaks from the margins. In the past two decades, partly due to historical events such as the Tiananmen Square massacre in 1989 and the 1997 turnover, and partly due to institutional support such as the establishment of the Hong Kong Arts Development Council, more and more literary voices are heard. Some are gentle, some humorous, some indignant. They all share an urgent need to represent Hong Kong when the city was undergoing drastic political and cultural transformations. The notion of home was central to their representations because the city was contemplating its inevitable reentry into the political reality of the Chinese nation-state. Rewriting Hong Kong history can be seen as attempts "to seize hold of a memory as it flashes up at a moment of danger," "at an instant when it can be recognized and is never seen again" (Benjamin 1969:255).

The future of Hong Kong literature remains to be seen. Perhaps one direction, the signs of which are already visible, is Hong Kong's interface with the larger world outside and with new technology. Some writers working in English, for example, have established a web journal called *Dim Sum* and have begun writing hypertextually. Others writing in Chinese have set up their own websites. What lies ahead may be the production of new voices writing about new concerns through various kinds of media and languages, spreading across visible and invisible boundaries.

—*Esther M.K. Cheung*

Bibliography

Abbas, Ackbar. *Hong Kong: Culture and the Politics of Disappearance*. Hong Kong: Hong Kong University Press, 1997.

Benjamin, Walter. "Theses on the Philosophy of History." In *Illuminations*, 253–264. New York: Schocken, 1969.

Cheung, Martha P.Y., ed. *Hong Kong Collage: Contemporary Stories and Writing*. Hong Kong: Oxford University Press, 1998.

Dung Kai-cheung (Dong Qizhang). *Ditu ji: Yige xiangxiang de chengshi de kaoguxue* (The Atlas: Archeology of an Imaginary City). Taipei: Lianhe wenxue, 1997.

Leung, Ping-kwan (Liang Bingjun). *City at the End of Time.* Trans. Gordon Osing. Hong Kong: Twilight Books, 1992.

——. "The Walled City in Kowloon: A Space We All Shared." Trans. Janice Wickeri. In Martha P.Y. Cheung, ed., *Hong Kong Collage: Contemporary Stories and Writing,* 34–39. Hong Kong: Oxford University Press, 1998.

——. "The Sorrows of Lan Kwai Fong." Trans. Martha Cheung and P. K. Leung. In Martha P.Y. Cheung, ed., *Hong Kong Collage: Contemporary Stories and Writing,* 85–95. Hong Kong: Oxford University Press, 1998.

Li Siu-leung. "Wo de Xianggang: Shi Shuqing de Xianggang zhimin lishi" (My Hong Kong: Shi Shuqing's History of Colonial Hong Kong). In Wong Wang-chi, Li Siu-leung, and Chan Ching-kiu Stephen, eds., *Fou xiang Xianggang: Lishi, wenhua, weilai* (Hong Kong Unimagined: History, Culture and the Future), 181–208. Taipei: Maitian, 1997.

Liu, Yichang. *The Cockroach and Other Stories.* Hong Kong: The Chinese University of Hong Kong, 1995.

——. "Intersection." Trans. Nancy Li. *Renditions* 29–30 (1988): 84–101.

Shi Shuqing. *Bian shan yang zijing* (Bauhinia Are Everywhere). Taipei: Hongfan, 1995.

——. *Jimo yunyuan* (The Lonely Garden). Taipei: Hongfan, 1997.

——. *Ta ming jiao Hudie* (Her Name Is Butterfly). Taipei: Hongfan, 1993.

Tay, William. "Colonialism, the Cold War Era, and Marginal Space: The Existential Conditions of Four Decades of Hong Kong Literature." *Literature East and West* 28 (1995): 141–147.

Wang, David Der-wei. "Late Twentieth-Century Chinese Fiction: Four Discourses." *Literature East and West* 28 (1995): 63–88.

Wong Bik Wan (Huang Biyun). *Wenrou yu baolie* (Tenderness and Violence). Hong Kong: Cosmos Books, 1994.

Wong, Wai-leung. *Hong Kong Literature in the Context of Modern Chinese Literature.* Hong Kong: Centre for Hong Kong Studies, Chinese University of Hong Kong, 1987.

Xi Xi. *The Flying Carpet.* Hong Kong: Hong Kong University Press, 2000.

Xin, Qishi. "Excerpts of *The Red Chequers Pub.*" Trans. Cathy Poon. *Renditions* 47–48 (1997): 73–82.

——. "The Ghost Festival." Trans. Cathy Poon. In Martha P.Y. Cheung, ed., *Hong Kong Collage: Contemporary Stories and Writing,* 107–121. Hong Kong: Oxford University Press, 1998.

102

RETURNING TO RECLUSE LITERATURE:
GAO XINGJIAN

On October 12, 2000, a Swedish Academy press release announced that the Nobel Prize in literature had been awarded to Gao Xingjian for a body of writings that "opened new paths for the Chinese novel and drama." Significantly, this was the first time the prize had been given for literature in the Chinese language, and it affirmed the potential of the Chinese language to meet the challenges of contemporary literature in a world context. Literary historian and writer Liu Zaifu points to the singular praise of the French Ministry of Culture in its statement that Gao Xingjian had by his writings in Chinese "enriched French literature." Liu adds that French literature is the creation of geniuses such as Balzac, Flaubert, Zola, Baudelaire, Proust, and Camus, and he jubilantly declares Gao's win as "a victory for literature in the Chinese language" (Liu 2000:2–3).

At the time of the Nobel announcement, virtually all of Gao's major works of fiction and drama had been published in Chinese, French, Swedish, and English. During the 1980s his plays *Absolute Signal* (Juedui xinhao, 1982), *Bus Stop* (Chezhan, 1983), and *Wild Man* (Yeren, 1985) had been performed to enthusiastic audiences in China, although *Bus Stop* was banned after a few performances. In 1987 Gao left China and took up residence in Paris. His plays relocated to the stages of various French theaters as well as theaters throughout the world, and his prolific writings found new publishers in Taiwan and Hong Kong. His contribution to literature and the arts was acknowledged by the

French government as early as 1992, when he was honored as Chevalier de l'Ordre des Arts et des Lettres. In 1997 he became a French citizen.

On December 7, 2000, Gao delivered his Nobel lecture, "The Case for Literature" (Wenxue de liyou, 2000), in Chinese at the Swedish Academy in Stockholm. Printed copies were available for the audience in Chinese, Swedish, French, and English, and by the time he had finished speaking it was available on the Swedish Academy web site in those languages: Gao Xingjian was addressing a world audience. His Nobel lecture represents the essence of a lifetime of voracious reading in Chinese and French literature as well as much critical and creative thinking about literature itself. His thirst for the creative expression of a self that had been endowed with rich artistic sensibilities is driven by an intense curiosity about the human psyche and behavior, and this forms the kernel of all of his writings. For him the basic prerequisite for literature is freedom of artistic expression. Literature is the solitary act of the individual and such literature has its own rationale for existence: "Literature can only be the voice of the individual and this has always been so." Gao Xingjian writes for himself and he is his own reader and critic. He began writing his epic novel *Soul Mountain* (Lingshan, 1990) in 1982 in China when it was futile and even dangerous to try to submit it for publication. But he maintains that literary creation is essentially for the writer's own aesthetic fulfillment and there is no compulsion for the reader to read it. However, as he said in his Nobel lecture, "Once literature is contrived as the hymn of the nation, the flag of the race, the mouthpiece of a political party, or the voice of a class or group, it can be employed as a mighty all-engulfing tool of propaganda. However, such literature loses what is inherent in literature, ceases to be literature, and becomes a substitute for power and profit."

The extreme repression of individual autonomy during the Cultural Revolution (1966–76) in China had given Gao unique insights into the substance and intrinsic value of literature. Speaking to the world with the authority of a Nobel laureate, he argues for a form of writing akin to Chinese recluse writings of the past. It was a common practice for scholars to isolate themselves from time to time on remote mountains, far away from their family concerns, the political arena, and bureaucratic restraints. However, more often writers would "recluse" themselves in a metaphorical sense while living in the midst of the hustle and bustle of society; the Daoist of the Green Vines, alias Xu Wei (1521–1593), who feigned madness, attempted suicide several times, and then finally killed his wife, is an extreme example. However, it was Xu Wei who wrote perceptively on the corrosive effect of politics on literature and the absurd outcome of politicians acting as the arbiters of literary worth. Xu Wei also derided those of his contemporaries who slavishly followed fashionable trends and produced works lacking in originality that filled the literary world with "poets but no poetry" (Lee 1998:405–408).

Gao refutes the imposition of the collective will on the individual and the writer. Although he suggested in his Nobel lecture that Friedrich Nietzsche's influence had led to instances of destructive megalomania during the twentieth century, it should be noted that the foundations of China's modern literature had internalized elements from Nietzsche's *Thus Spake Zarathustra* and that Gao's conception of literature coincides with Nietzsche's. In Gao's view, to preserve the integrity and autonomy of the self against the inroads of political authority, public opinion, ethical preaching, and party or group advantage, the only option for the writer is to flee. To flee is Gao's formula for physical and metaphorical "recluse" literature, and there are striking similarities to Nietzsche's *Zarathustra*: Gao Xingjian, like Zarathustra, chooses to live in human society and must therefore address the eternal existential issues of being in his writings.

The ancient Daoist text *Zhuangzi*, long revered as a literary masterpiece, has inspired generations of Chinese writers for its notion of the untrammeled self, and beauty of thought and language. Various fragments of the work in translation presumably traveled along the maritime routes with missionaries and sailors to Europe but its substantial influence on European intellectuals came with the publication of scholarly French translations in the early half of the nineteenth century. At the time, French culture represented the epitome of European culture, and this was the intellectual matrix that nurtured Nietzsche (1844–1900), that exponent of the untrammeled self and the Superman. Following his death, Nietzsche's works both spawned unbridled individualism and were used to support totalitarian regimes and the Nazi movement in Europe. However, Chinese intellectuals, notably the writer *Lu Xun (1881–1936), in the early years of the twentieth century were attracted to *Zarathustra*'s language and message for the individual that resonated strongly with the *Zhuangzi* and Chinese literature inspired by that early Daoist text (Lee 1999).

Nietzsche's *Zarathustra*, through the writings of Lu Xun and others, formed the intellectual core of China's modern literature alongside a fervent and deeply entrenched patriotism that had begun to take root during the late nineteenth century. China's modern literature emerged in the cultural movement that later came to be known as the May Fourth movement, a period of intellectual liberation when the autonomy of the self was eulogized and traditional culture was castigated as failing to meet the needs of modern times. However, as Japanese imperialist designs on China intensified, Chinese patriotism escalated so that demands for individual autonomy gradually gave way to the collective demand for national survival. Lu Xun, like Gao Xingjian, began to read widely in European literatures as a student and played a leading role in establishing China's modern literature. However, for patriotic reasons he chose to allow his creative self to atrophy so that he could devote himself to polemical writings: he chose politics although he was painfully aware that without literature he would be like a corpse with its heart gouged out. Fifty years later, Gao chose to flee so that he could devote himself to literature (Lee 1998, 1999).

Gao Xingjian was born in Ganzhou, Zhejiang Province, on January 4, 1940, during the war against Japan. He was a voracious reader and as a child began to work his way through the substantial family library while receiving his formal education in the newly established People's Republic of China. As China's literary heritage was progressively vilified as "old," out of keeping with the "new" socialist society, and finally banned, Gao found that he could gain access to literature in French at the library of the Foreign Languages Institute, from which he graduated with a major in French in 1962. When he was assigned work as a translator and editor for the French version of *China Reconstructs*, he continued to read French literature until all foreign books were banned during the Cultural Revolution. Gao had been addicted to writing since he was a teenager, and over the years he had written many manuscripts that he knew could not be offered for publication. At the height of the Cultural Revolution he burned several kilos of manuscripts: ten plays, a novella, short stories, essays, and poems. During the Cultural Revolution Mao Zedong's directive to serve the masses was carried to extremes, and individuals were exhorted to offer themselves as sacrifices to the masses and the nation. Because writers were the most articulate group in society and persisted in voicing their views, they were persecuted and cowed into silence, so that the human in the individual was virtually annihilated in literature.

In *A Preliminary Discussion on the Art of Modern Fiction* (Xiandai xiaoshuo jiqiao chutan, 1981), Gao Xingjian was the first to argue cogently on the importance of the value of the individual in the literary process. His introductory essays on modern European writers, his translations of modern writers (Ionesco and Prévert), and his experimental plays and fiction were avidly read and established his credentials as a prominent leader of the new literature and theater of the post-Mao era. His reputation was further "enhanced" by the reaction of the authorities to his writings. In 1982, *A Preliminary Discussion on the Art of Modern Fiction* was banned and he was subjected to public criticism for promoting the modernism of decadent Western bourgeois literature. In 1983, the performance of his play *Bus Stop* was banned, and he was singled out again for criticism and barred from publication.

The ban on Gao Xingjian's publications was lifted in 1984, and he went on to publish the plays *Soliloquy* (Dubai, 1985), *Wild Man* (Yeren, 1985), and *Other Shore* (Bi'an, 1986). Of these plays only *Wild Man* went to stage in China, and although there was no public criticism of it, the performers were intimidated. Gao Xingjian's major publications in this period are *Collected Plays of Gao Xingjian* (Gao Xingjian xiju ji, 1985), the novella *A Pigeon Called Red Beak* (You zhi gezi jiao Hong chunr, 1985), and *In Search of a Modern Form of Dramatic Representation* (Dui yizhong xiandai xiju de zhuiqiu, 1987).

Gao's unrelenting quest for freedom of creative expression led to his leaving the stifling literary environment of China in 1987. In Paris he has found an environment where he has the freedom to write as a metaphorical recluse. His winning the Nobel Prize suddenly turned his books into best-sellers in Chinese, French, Swedish, and English, but until then he was not a conspicuous figure on the Chinese literary scene. His uncompromising apolitical stance in literature was a major factor in his being relegated to a position out of the spotlight. He was not daunted by the experience of being "frozen out" of the Chinese literary scene, and throughout this period he retained a small but staunch Chinese-language readership as well as a substantial readership for his works in French, Swedish, and later English.

Gao is uncompromising in both his political and literary stances. On French radio and in the Italian daily *La Stampa*, he vehemently denounced the June 1989 Chinese government crackdown on student protestors in Beijing. Soon afterward he submitted his play *Fleeing* (Taowang, 1990) to an American theater group, but there was a request for changes because there were no student heroes. He declined to make any changes and withdrew his manuscript. The play is set in the early hours of June 4, just after the tanks have rolled in. However, *Fleeing* is not a morality play in support of either political side but, like all of Gao's works, an exploration of the human psyche and behavior. Even in those times of high emotions Gao rigidly adhered to his "recluse" stance and failed to please either the Chinese authorities or the various Chinese democracy groups. To please others is not Gao Xingjian's rationale for writing.

Fleeing examines instinctual behavior arising from the fear of death, and the tribal instincts and mass hysteria induced by frenzied dancing, ghetto-blasters, and the worship of totems (even those as noble as nation, freedom, and democracy). *Fleeing* was published in 1990 in the Chinese literary journal *Today* (Jintian). Two years later, labeled a "reactionary" work, it was reprinted in *Collected Reactionary Works by the Diaspora "Elite"* (Taowang "jingying" fandong yanlun ji, 1992). Gao was expelled from the Chinese Communist Party and his apartment in Beijing was confiscated. The publication of Gao's works in China since then has been problematic. When the Nobel award was announced few of Gao's works were available in China, but within days various enterprising Chinese Internet sites changed this.

Literature is Gao's primary commitment in life, but he has also won acclaim for his Chinese ink paintings, and for many years he supported himself and his literary activities by selling his artwork.

—Mabel Lee

Bibliography

Chen, Xiaomei. "A Wildman between Two Cultures: Some Paradigmatic Remarks on 'Influence Studies.'" *Comparative Literature Studies* 29, no. 4 (1992): 397–416.

Gao, Xingjian. "*Bus Stop*: A Lyrical Comedy on Life in One Act." Trans. Kimberly Besio. In Haiping Yan, ed., *Theater and Society: An Anthology of Contemporary Chinese Drama*, 3–59. Armonk, N.Y.: M.E. Sharpe, 1998.

——. "Contemporary Technique and National Character in Fiction." Trans. Ng Mau-sang. *Renditions* 19–20 (1983): 55–58.

——. "*Fugitives:* Translation of a Play by Gao Xingjian." Trans. Gregory B. Lee. In Gregory B. Lee, ed., *Chinese Writing and Exile*, 89–138. Chicago: University of Chicago Center for East Asian Studies, 1993.

——. "Literature As Testimony: The Search for Truth." Trans. Mabel Lee. Stockholm: Swedish Academy, 2001.

——. "Nobel Lecture: The Case for Literature." Trans. Mabel Lee. Stockholm: Swedish Academy, 2000.

——. *One Man's Bible.* Trans. Mabel Lee. New York: HarperCollins, 2002.

——. *The Other Shore: Plays by Gao Xingjian.* Trans. Gilbert C. F. Fong. Hong Kong: The Chinese University Press, 1999.

——. "The Other Side: A Contemporary Drama Without Acts." Trans. Jo Riley. In Martha P.Y. Cheung and Jane C.C. Lai, eds., *Oxford Anthology of Contemporary Chinese Drama*, 149–183. New York: Oxford University Press, 1997.

——. *Soul Mountain.* Trans. Mabel Lee. New York: HarperCollins, 2000.

——. "The Voice of the Individual." Trans. Lena Aspfors and Torbjörn Lodén. *The Stockholm Journal of East Asian Studies* 6 (1995): 71–81.

——. "*Wild Man:* A Contemporary Chinese Spoken Drama." Trans. Bruno Roubicek. *Asian Theater Journal* 7, no. 2 (1990): 184–249.

——. "Without Isms." Trans. Winnie Lau, Deborah Sauviat, and Martin Williams. *Journal of the Oriental Society of Australia* 27–28 (1995–96): 105–114.

Lee, Mabel. "Gao Xingjian's Dialogue with Two Dead Poets from Shaoxing: Xu Wei and Lu Xun." In R.D. Findeisen and R.H. Gassman, eds., *Autumn Floods: Essays in Honour of Márian Gálik*, 401–414. Bern: Lang, 1998.

——. "Gao Xingjian on the Issue of Literary Creation for the Modern Writer." *Journal of Asian Pacific Communication* 9, nos. 1–2 (1999): 83–96.

——. "Walking out of Other People's Prisons: Liu Zaifu and Gao Xingjian on Chinese Literature in the 1990s." *Asian & African Studies* 5, no. 1 (1996): 98–112.

——. "Without Politics: Gao Xingjian on Literary Creation." *The Stockholm Journal of East Asian Studies* 6 (1995): 82–101.

Liu Zaifu. "Lun Gao Xingjian zhuangtai (On the Gao Xingjian situation)." In *Lun Gao Xingjian zhuangtai*, 2–32. Hong Kong: Mingbao, 2000.

Lodén, Torbjörn. "World Literature with Chinese Characteristics: On a Novel by Gao Xingjian." *The Stockholm Journal of East Asian Studies* 4 (1993): 17–40.

Ma, Sen. "The Theatre of the Absurd in Mainland China: Gao Xingjian's *The Bus Stop.*" *Issues and Studies* 25, no. 8 (1989): 138–148.

Quah, Sy Ren. "Searching for Alternative Aesthetics in the Chinese Theatre: The Odyssey of Huang Zuolin and Gao Xingjian." *Asian Culture* 24 (2000): 44–66.

Special issue on Gao Xingjian. *Modern Chinese Literature and Culture* 14, no. 2 (Fall 2002).

Tam, Kwok-kan. "Drama of Dilemma: Waiting As Form and Motif in *The Bus Stop* and *Waiting for Godot.*" In Yun-Tong Luk, ed., *Studies in Chinese–Western Comparative Drama Hong Kong*, 23–35. Hong Kong: The Chinese University Press, 1990.

——, ed. *Soul of Chaos: Critical Perspectives on Gao Xingjian.* Hong Kong: The Chinese University Press, 2001.

Tay, William. "Avant-Garde Theatre in Post-Mao China: *The Bus Stop* by Gao Xingjian." In Howard Goldblatt, ed., *Worlds Apart: Recent Chinese Writing and Its Audiences*, 111–118. Armonk, N.Y.: M.E. Sharpe, 1990.

Zhao, Henry Y.H. *Towards a Modern Zen Theatre: Gao Xingjian and Chinese Theatre Experimentalism.* London: SOAS Publications, 2000.

PART IV

Korea

BRUCE FULTON, ASSOCIATE EDITOR

Thematic Essays

103

HISTORICAL OVERVIEW

Modern Korean literature is best viewed as a combination of the modern and the traditional. It is modern in form, structure, technique, and language. It is traditional in its need, as perceived by Korean literary scholars and many writers, to be relevant: to enlighten readers in issues of contemporary importance, to bear witness to the turbulent currents of the nation's history, to engage in a quest for identity both personal and national. It is traditional in its lyricism, which informs the very earliest of extant Korean songs. Finally, it is traditional in terms of its cultural context, which in turn is much influenced by the hierarchical nature of Korean society. Modern Korean literature, heir to a written tradition extending back well over a millennium and an oral tradition much older, is a distinctly conservative form of artistic expression, especially in contrast with art forms such as film.

Scholars tend to view the development of modern Korean literature in one of two ways. Some see it as the continuation of a native tradition dating back to later Chosŏn times (1592–1910) and drawing on Korea's rich oral tradition as well as a substantial body of fictional narratives in Chinese or Korean. Others see a sharp break between premodern fiction and modern fiction, viewing the latter as a product of foreign, mostly Western, literary influences imported into Korea in the early decades of the twentieth century by way of Japan. As in other areas of Korean studies in Korea, nationalism complicates the debate, with Korean literature specialists tending to emphasize the importance of the native tradition in modern Korean literature, and specialists in Western literatures often emphasizing external literary influences. But if we read, for example, the stories produced before 1945, we see that they reflect both kinds of influences. That is, although the psychological realism, plot and character development, and narrative technique of these stories, and indeed the short-fiction form itself, may be Western-inspired, the mood of the stories, their subject matter, their worldview, and in many cases the voices are distinctly Korean. This melding of influences should come as no surprise. For Korean literature, from its earliest surviving examples, has reflected a blend of foreign (mostly Chinese) and native influences, a tension between intellectual rigor and native emotion, a merging of written and oral traditions, a combination of head and heart. These dualities survive in modern Korean literature.

The careers of early modern writers (those active from the 1910s through 1945) bear out this duality of native and foreign influences. Almost all of these writers took their primary and secondary education at the new Western-style schools in the metropolises of Pyongyang and Seoul, many studied for a time in Japan, and a few were home-schooled at an early age in the traditional way, studying the Chinese classics. Some writers experienced all three kinds of learning. As part of their education these writers read a variety of texts, whether in classical Chinese, *hangŭl* (Korean), or Japanese. At the same time, a variety of foreign works had begun to appear in translation in Korea, typically by way of Japan. There was thus a heady mix of influences on the new writers, "not only historical influences (Confucian didactic materials in Korean, vernacular written fiction, Buddhist narratives, and oral literature) but also contemporary experiments in Korean composition (Bible translation; reports, editorials, sketches, and anecdotes in early newspapers; and textbooks for modernized education)" (Pihl 1991:3).

Especially significant in the exposure of young Korean writers to the literary scene in Japan is that they saw, in the person of Natsume Sōseki, what was still a rarity in Korea: the professional writer of fiction. To be sure, a writer class had begun to develop in Korea among those hired by vernacular newspapers in the first decade of the twentieth century to write serial novels (Kwon 1994). But the notion of a fiction writer not only making a living from his writing but also gaining critical as well as popular recognition for it—this was new.

THE TRANSITIONAL PERIOD

The development of a modern literature in Korea was conditioned by two watershed events: the modernization movement that swept East Asia at the turn of the twentieth century and the Japanese annexation of Korea in 1910. The modernization movement gave young Koreans exposure to enlightenment ideals such as literacy, education, equality, and women's rights. Annexation inspired a wave of nationalism that finally legitimized *hangŭl* as the literary language of all Koreans (the scholar-bureaucrat elite had in spite of the promulgation of *hangŭl* in 1446 continued to favor classical Chinese for centuries thereafter), and it forced Korean writers to come to grips with the necessity of preserving their own language and literature in an increasingly repressive colonial environment.

Modern Korean literature is dated by some scholars to 1908, the year in which Ch'oe Namsŏn's poem "From the Sea to the Youth" (Hae egesŏ sonyŏn ege) appeared, but by most others to 1917, the date of publication of *Yi Kwangsu's novel *Heartlessness* (Mujŏng). But whereas *Heartlessness* is considered distinctly modern in its use of language and its psychological description, Ch'oe's poem was of a transitional genre known as *shinch'e shi* ("new-style poetry"), which resembled traditional poetry in its use of a rhyme scheme but was new in its optimistic enlightenment outlook. Corresponding to the "new-style poetry" as a transitional genre was the *shin sosŏl* ("new fiction"), which flourished from 1906 to the early 1910s. Designed to appeal to the masses and distinguished from staid "old fiction," the "new fiction" dealt with contemporary history, addressed real-life social problems, depicted intrafamily intrigues, or inspired patriotism through portraits of national heroes both in Korea and abroad. Yi Injik (1862–1916) is the best-known writer of the *shin sosŏl*, and the novel *Tears of Blood* (Hyŏl ŭi nu, 1906) his best-known work.

THE EARLY MODERN PERIOD

The first generation of writers of modern Korean literature were for the most part young men born around the turn of the century who had received their higher education in Japan and had there been introduced, in Japanese translation, to literature from the West. There resulted an influx of Western literary models into Korea, primarily realism in fiction and symbolism, imagism, and romanticism in poetry. These writers tended to gravitate toward new, mostly short-lived, literary journals in which they published poetry, short fiction, and essays (both critical and personal, the latter form termed *sup'il*). Novels maintained the mass readership they had enjoyed since late Chosŏn times and continued to be serialized in newspapers, but the literary elite considered them lowbrow entertainment. Important among the first generation of fiction writers were Yi Kwangsu (1892–1950?) for his enlightenment and nationalist agenda, as exemplified in *Heartlessness* and other novels; Yŏm Sangsŏp (1897–1963) for his psychological realism; Kim Tongin (1900–1951) for his modernization of the Korean language and his art-for-art's-sake views; and Hyŏn Chingŏn (1900–1943) for his fictional slices of life of colonial Korea (see "Realism in Early Modern Fiction").

Kim Tongin is important as well for initiating a debate that continues to this day in the Korean literary world: Should literature be written as an artistic end in itself, or should it engage itself with the nation, the people, and contemporary societal and political realities? Kim fell squarely on the side of literature as art, and, with like-minded fellow students in Japan, he founded the journal *Ch'angjo* (Creation) in 1919 in direct opposition to the enlightenment propensity of Yi Kwangsu's novels. (See "Pure Literature versus the Literature of Engagement.")

Early modern poetry is best represented by Kim Sowŏl (1902–1934), Chŏng Chiyong (1903–?), and Han Yongun (1879–1944). Kim (known better by his pen name, Sowŏl, than by his given name, Chŏngshik) used traditional Korean folk-song rhythms to produce lyrics of exceptional melody. His "Azaleas" (Chindal-lae kkot, 1922) remains the best-loved poem of modern Korea. Chŏng was a master technician, drawing on both native and foreign sources for a rich bank of images in poems that often combine solitude, nostalgia, and nature. Han was a man of action, actively opposing the Japanese occupation, working to reform Buddhism, and attempting to instill in his readers a sense of their cultural identity. His best-known poem, "The Silence of My Love" (Nim ŭi ch'immuk, 1926), resounds on a number of levels.

*Sŏ Chŏngju (1915–2000), the consensus choice as modern Korea's most accomplished poet, debuted in the 1930s; but, unlike the poets just mentioned, he was active beyond the post-1945 era. His early poetry is both modern to Western eyes accustomed to the striking images of the French symbolists and traditional to Korean ears accustomed to songs flowing from the heart rather than the head.

Proletarian literature was tolerated by the Japanese colonial authorities from the mid-1920s to 1935. This literature is cited today more for its historical interest than its literary value. After the Japanese put an end to the Korean proletarian literature movement in 1935, Korean fiction writers began looking to the past or the countryside for their inspiration. A variety of new voices appeared: *Hwang Sunwŏn (1915–2000), modern Korea's most accomplished short-fiction writer; *Kim Tongni (1913–1995), considered by many Koreans the fiction writer who best exemplifies a distinctly Korean ethos; Ch'ae Manshik (1902–1950), a writer of wit and irony who employed a direct, conversational style; Yi T'aejun (1904–?), a polished stylist; Kim Yujŏng (1908–1937), possessor of an earthy, colloquial style rooted in the oral tradition; and *Yi Sang (1910–1937), an avant-garde poet as well as a modernist fiction writer. Their combined efforts led in the mid- to late 1930s to an early flowering of fiction, featuring stories such as Yi Sang's "Wings" (Nalgae, 1936), Kim Tongni's "The Shaman Painting" (Munyŏdo, 1936), Kim Yujŏng's "The Camellias" (Tongbaek kkot, 1936), Yi Hyosŏk's "When the Buckwheat Blooms" (Memil kkot p'il muryŏp, 1936), and Chu Yosŏp's "Mama and the Boarder" (Sarang sonnim kwa ŏmŏni, 1935). What are the reasons for this concentration of achievement?

For one thing, the forced dissolution by Japanese authorities of the proletarian literature movement in 1935 drastically limited the opportunities for Korean writers to use fiction in the service of ideology and class struggle. The consensus of literary historians such as Cho Tongil is that the proletarian writers produced little of lasting literary merit—although they did, as in the case of hardliner Im Hwa, produce important literary criticism. From 1935 on, then, fiction writers were more or less compelled to focus in their works on other elements of fiction—setting, characterization, structure, and language. Free of the need to write fiction that ideologues considered relevant, writers were able to produce stories such as "When the Buckwheat Blooms," with its faultless structure, memorable characters (including a donkey!), and vivid evocation of the Korean countryside, and "Mama and the Boarder," with its poignant narrative, told by a six-year-old girl, and its tension, embodied in a young widow, between traditional and modern mores.

By the mid-1930s young Korean intellectuals in particular were realizing to their dismay that life in colonial Seoul offered few jobs commensurate with their education. And with the outbreak of the Pacific War, colonial Japan tightened the screws of its colonial overlordship of the Korean peninsula. In the last years of the occupation, the *amhok shidae* ("dark age"), Koreans were forbidden to publish in Korean or even to speak their own language in public. Pressure on Korean writers to publish in Japanese and publicly support the Japanese war effort intensified, and many succumbed.

THE CONTEMPORARY PERIOD

Korean literature after 1945, termed *hyŏndae* ("contemporary") by Korean literary critics, has been conditioned largely by the realities of modern Korean history. Korean literati from premodern times to the present have often felt obligated to bear witness to the times, and authors from 1945 on have been no exception. The literature of the 1950s and 1960s is a good example. Reacting to the devastation inflicted on the peninsula by the Korean War (1950–53), writers produced poems and stories portraying not just a shattered landscape but also traumatized psyches and corrupted values (see "Postwar Fiction"). The stories of Son Ch'angsŏp (b. 1922) and the poems of *Kim Suyŏng (1921–1967) are excellent illustrations.

In the late 1960s and early 1970s there appeared a new generation of writers, a group educated in their own language (their parents' generation had been educated in Japanese, and the literary language of their grandparents' generation was more often than not Chinese). With little or no memory of the occupation period and a sardonic attitude toward the authoritarian rule that had marked South Korean politics since 1948, they produced fiction and poetry that display a more freewheeling use of language and a powerful imagination. Fiction writers Kim Sŭngok (b. 1943) and Ch'oe Inho (b. 1945) are representative. Their contemporaries *Ch'oe Inhun (b. 1936) and *Yi Ch'ŏngjun (b. 1939) are known for the intellectual rigor of their fiction. The former has mined traditional Korean literature for some of his material and is also an accomplished playwright.

The 1970s brought to the fore a collection of powerful voices that exposed the social ills attending the rapid industrialization pushed by President Park Chung Hee. There is no better fictional treatment of this subject than *Cho Sehŭi's (b. 1942) *The Dwarf* (Nanjangi ka ssoaollin chagŭn kong, 1978), perhaps the most important one-volume novel of the post-1945 period. *Yun Hŭnggil (b. 1942) wrote of the scars left by the civil war and of citizens coerced into supervising "subversive" neighbors. *Hwang Sŏgyŏng (b. 1943) portrayed the masses—itinerant construction workers, urban squatters, and refugees from

North Korea. Cho Chŏngnae (b. 1943), in his ten-volume novel *The T'aebaek Mountains* (T'aebaek sanmaek, 1989), took a revisionist approach to modern Korean history. The 1970s also marked the debut of *Yi Munyŏl (b. 1948), perhaps the most important Korean novelist at the century's end. Yi is concerned with the retrieval of Korean tradition in an age of rampant materialism, the territorial division of the peninsula, the legacy of colonialism, and the challenges posed by modernization and urbanization.

Among the most important works of modern Korean fiction are the multi-volume novels called *taeha sosŏl* ("great-river fiction"). These romans-fleuves have precedents in the family sagas of premodern times and usually feature a historical background and several generations of family life. In addition to Cho Chŏngnae's *T'aebaek Mountains*, the most important examples are Hong Myŏnghŭi's (1888–?) *Im Kkŏkchŏng* (1939), about a Chosŏn-period bandit chief of that name; *Pak Kyŏngni's (b. 1927) *Land* (1994); Hwang Sŏgyŏng's *Chang Kilsan* (1984), also about a Chosŏn bandit leader thus named; and Ch'oe Myŏnghŭi's (1947–1999) *Spirit Fire* (Honpul, 1996).

Sŏ Chŏngju, *Shin Kyŏngnim, Kim Chiha, and *Ko Ŭn stand out among poets of the post-1945 era. Sŏ is Korea's most important modern poet, a master of the Korean language who mines Korean history and culture and the Buddhist worldview to produce short, revelatory lyrics and longer prose poems, all of them characterized by a sensuousness derived from the Korean soil and, earlier in his career, from French symbolism. Ko, Kim, and Shin have all exhibited a populist streak and have incorporated the spirit of political activism in their poetry. Ko (b. 1933), a former Buddhist monk, is a passionate witness of the powerless. Shin (b. 1936) sings of farmers and workers in a verse enlivened by folk rhythms. Kim's (b. 1941) "Five Bandits" (Ojŏk, 1970) is a courageous satire of dictatorship that, along with other works, earned the poet a jail term.

Modern Korean drama, like fiction and poetry, was subject to considerable Western influence early in the 1900s. Among the earliest examples of modern drama is Kim Ujin's (1897–1926) *Boar* (San twaeji, 1926). Yu Ch'ijin's (1904–1973) *Piece* (T'omak, 1932) marked the advent of a new realist drama. *O T'aesŏk, the most important contemporary playwright, blends an innovative, Western-influenced style with texts drawn from Korean history and folklore recent and past. A good example is *Why Did Shim Ch'ŏng Plunge into the Sea Twice?* (Shim Ch'ŏng-i nŭn oe Indangsu e tu pŏn man ŭl tŏnjŏnnŭnga, 1991).

RECENT DEVELOPMENTS

The most noteworthy trend in Korean literature at the dawn of the new millennium is the prominence achieved by women writers (see "Women's Literature"). Long marginalized by the overwhelmingly male literary establishment, Korean women writers, building on the pioneering efforts of writers such as Ch'oe Chŏnghŭi (1912–1990), have since the 1970s gained both critical and commercial success through the technical and thematic innovations of *Pak Wansŏ (b. 1931), *O Chŏnghŭi (b. 1947), *Ch'oe Yun (b. 1953), and others. They, along with Yi Munyŏl, Hwang Sŏgyŏng, Yun Hŭnggil, Cho Chŏngnae, and Yi Ch'ŏngjun and poet Ko Ŭn, are among the most important living Korean authors.

The situation with respect to women's poetry is more problematic. No genre reflects the patriarchal nature of the Korean literary world more than poetry. In premodern times poetry was the measure of an educated man, professionally and personally. A mastery of poetry, both its traditions and its craft, was essential for government office and hence was tested on the civil service exam that granted entrance (to men only) to the bureaucracy. The composition of poetry was in addition an omnipresent recreational activity among men, "something practiced by most members of the educated class ... with about as much frequency as we talk on the telephone" (McCarthy 1994:9). Countless were the occasions when literati challenged one another to impromptu poetic displays and took up the brush. Even in modern times women have rarely been admitted to this bastion of literary privilege. They have been more successful with short fiction, widely considered a Western import, and as such do not constitute a risk of penetrating the venerable native genre that is poetry. Long fiction is also an option for women so long as it reflects the realities of Korean history, society, and culture.

This is not to say that women poets in Korea have not developed distinct and powerful voices. Rather, those voices are not acknowledged by the literary establishment to the extent that those of women fiction writers are. Nevertheless, corresponding in importance to fiction writers Pak Wansŏ, O Chŏnghŭi, and Ch'oe Yun are poets such as Kang Ŭngyo (b. 1945), Mun Chŏnghŭi (b. 1947), Kim Sŭnghŭi (b. 1952), and Kim Hyesun (b. 1955).

Korean literature in translation has gained modest international visibility in recent decades. In the English-speaking world poetry is better represented than fiction, and modern literature more than premodern. The short fiction of Hwang Sunwŏn and the poetry of Sŏ Chŏngju are especially well represented in the West, and Yi Munyŏl's novels are commanding increasing attention abroad.

Diaspora literature — works by ethnic Koreans outside of Korea — is flourishing. Yi Mirok's German-language memoir *Der Yalu Fliesst* (The Yalu Flows, 1946) and Richard Kim's English-language novel *The Martyred* (1964) are well known. In Japan, several writers of Korean descent, such as Yi Yangji and Yu Miri, have captured the Akutagawa Award, that nation's most prestigious short-fiction prize. Young Korean American novelists such as Chang-rae Lee, Heinz Insu Fenkl, and Nora Okja Keller have achieved commercial and critical success in the United States. In contrast with these authors, who write in the language of their adopted land, ethnic Koreans in China's Yanbian region continue to publish in Korean.

Little is known of literature produced in the Democratic People's Republic of Korea (North Korea), either by native northerners or by the *wŏlbuk chakka* — those writers, some one hundred of them, who migrated from southern Korea to what is now North Korea following liberation from Japanese colonial rule in 1945 (see "The *Wŏlbuk* Writers"). The works of both groups were unavailable in the Republic of Korea (South Korea) until that state's democratization movement of the late 1980s. A full account of literature in North Korea must await reunification of the Korean peninsula. In the meantime, fiction writers in South Korea have already begun to chronicle the experiences of Northern defectors in the South.

THE LITERARY CULTURE

Korean writers constitute a culture that, if not close knit, places them in close proximity with one another and with the critics and scholars (often one and the same) who wield the most power in the Korean literary establishment. In premodern times most Korean writers belonged to an educated scholar-official elite that competed for a limited number of positions in the bureaucracy. This competition, and a master-disciple tradition deriving from Confucianism, helped spawn factions in which worthies rallied around venerable seniors. This tradition carried over into modern times, with the faction replaced by the literary circle and its doctrine expressed not in memorials to the throne but in literary and cultural journals. Younger writers typically debuted under the tutelage of seniors who occupied editorial positions at literary journals or vernacular dailies. Kim Tongni, for example, when he debuted as a fiction writer in 1935, chose to do so not in the *Tonga ilbo* but in a less prestigious daily, the *Chungang chosŏn ilbo*, out of respect for the latter's editor, Yi T'aejun. As recently as the 1970s it was still possible for an aspiring writer to debut by means of sponsorship by an established author.

Today writers tend to debut either through publication in a literary journal or through participation in one of the annual new year's literary-arts competitions sponsored by various literary journals and dailies. Writers often become associated with one or another of the some two dozen literary journals (mostly quarterlies) published in South Korea at any point in time. Some journals sponsor annual literary awards, with the candidates tending to be drawn from authors published therein and the panel of judges consisting of senior scholar-critics and (increasingly) authors who are former prizewinners. The two most prestigious of the annual awards for short fiction are the Tongin Literature Prize, named for the early modern writer Kim Tongin, established in 1956 and currently sponsored by the *Chosŏn ilbo*, a powerful conservative daily; and the Yi Sang Literature Prize, named for that innovator of the 1930s and awarded yearly since 1977 by the publishers of the quarterly *Munhak sasang* (Literature and Thought).

Censorship, whether imposed from outside or from within, is another legacy of tradition, but one that has been reinforced by Korea's modern history. Just as premodern writers exercised self-censorship, learning early on to couch their political concerns in stylized metaphors, so did early modern writers express anti-Japanese sentiment allegorically if at all. Government censorship in modern times begins with the Japanese thought police, who routinely censored any reference to socialism, and continued during the succession of dictatorships in South Korea in the period 1948–87. During that time the writings of, or research on, the hundred-odd writers who migrated from southern Korea to northern Korea between 1945 and 1950 were banned. Antigovernment writing resulted in jail terms for several established writers. Pornographic writing is seldom published through the customary network of journals, dailies, and books, but at least two writers—Ma Kwangsu and Chang Chŏngil—have been imprisoned in recent years for writing novels deemed injurious to public morals. In North Korea socialist realism as a literary ideology has been used to purge writers who have fallen out of favor with the leadership.

Whether because of the premodern inclination to couch personal vendettas in veiled language, the close quarters at which Korean writers and scholar-critics exist, or the traditionally didactic posture of the Korean man of letters, essays on authors and works tend to be interpretive rather than judgmental. Established authors may be awarded prizes on the basis of their seniority rather than the quality of their recent work. The subjects of theses, dissertations, and scholarly books are limited primarily to deceased authors or elderly writers no longer active.

CRITICAL READINGS
OF MODERN KOREAN LITERATURE

Critical writing on modern Korean literature is a relatively recent development. Men and (rarely) women of letters from the early modern period often assumed the multiple roles of writer, editor, critic, and occasionally translator. After liberation from Japan, departments of Korean language and literature in Korean universities began to produce a growing number of specialists in the nation's modern literature, a development that led in turn to a growing separation between the roles of scholar-critic and creative writer. Perhaps as much as in any other area of Korean scholarship, the field of Korean literature in Korea is conditioned by the nation's modern history, and especially by its subordinate position to Japan and subsequently the superpowers. One result of this history is that it is not always easy to distinguish foreign influence on modern Korean history from foreign influence on modern Korean literature. Another result is a tendency in certain quarters of the Korean literary establishment to make value-laden critiques of modern Korean literature, with the Western-influenced literature of the early modern period often seen in a negative light and the socially committed and issue-driven works of the contemporary period viewed more favorably. Because Korean literature has always had a didactic element, social engagement is often seen as a reflection of an ages-old native literary tradition.

Modern Korean literature cannot be understood apart from its sociopolitical context. From at least Shilla times (57 B.C.–A.D. 935) Korea has been a highly stratified society. Class relations have long been a rich source of thematic materials, especially in the Korean oral tradition, which is never as popular as it is when lampooning the peccadilloes of the aristocratic scholar-gentry class known as *yangban*. In modern literature, class relations received their most impassioned critiques during the heyday of the proletarian writers (1925–35). These works are the forebears of a sizable body of powerful literature dating from the 1970s that combines incisive social commentary with increasingly sophisticated technique. In the category of fiction the pinnacle of this work is Cho Sehŭi's linked-story novel *The Dwarf*.

One way to understand the sociopolitical context of modern Korean literature is in terms of confinement, whether physical (the fate of authors who ran afoul of a repressive politics), spiritual (the legacy of a nation having continually to safeguard its cultural and political independence in a period of colonial and then superpower rivalries), or psychological (the mindset of individuals living in a highly structured society). The list of authors imprisoned for political offenses under colonial or domestic regimes is sobering: Yi Kwangsu, Kim Chiha, Yi Hoch'ŏl, Ku Sang, Ko Ûn. Not all writers survived their prison terms: Yi Sang died in large part as the result of imprisonment in Japan, as did the poet Yun Tongju. Confined spaces (rooms, caves, cells) and stifling interpersonal relationships (arranged marriages, reciprocal obligations with extended family, coworkers, and fellow alumni) loom large in the background scenery and metaphoric vocabulary of Korean writers. The importance attributed by many scholar-critics to historical consciousness, moreover, may help to explain why so many contemporary Korean stories take place within the confines of the interior landscape of memory rather than in the exterior landscape of the here and now.

—*Bruce Fulton*

Bibliography

Fulton, Bruce, ed. *Modern Korean Fiction: An Anthology*. New York: Columbia University Press, forthcoming.

Kim Chŏngnan. "The Achievements and Prospects of Modern Korean Women's Poetry: On the Formation of the Female Identity." Trans. Mickey Hong. Paper presented at the Korean Literature and World Literature Conference, University of California at Los Angeles, 1996.

Kim Chong-un and Bruce Fulton, trans. and eds. *A Ready-Made Life: Early Masters of Modern Korean Fiction*. Honolulu: University of Hawai'i Press, 1998.

Kwon Youngmin. "Enlightenment Period Fiction and the Development of a Writer Class." Trans. Bruce Fulton. *Korean Studies* 18 (1994): 23–29.

McCarthy, Kathleen. "*Kisaeng* and Poetry in the Koryŏ Period." *Korean Culture* (Summer 1994): 4–13.

O'Rourke, Kevin, trans. and ed. *Looking for the Cow: Modern Korean Poems*. Dublin: Daedalus, 1999.

Pihl, Marshall R. "Narrative Technique in Korean Fiction, 1860–1940." Paper presented at the Association for Asian Studies Annual Conference, New Orleans, 1991.

Shin Jeong-Hyun. *The Trap of History*. Berkeley: University of California Institute of East Asian Studies, 1998.

Yi Injik. *Tears of Blood*. Trans. William Skillend. In Chung Chong-wha, ed., *Classical Korean Literature*, 159–220. London: Kegan Paul International, 1989.

104

PURE LITERATURE VERSUS THE LITERATURE
OF ENGAGEMENT

Should literature be an artistic end in itself, or should it be a means to an end? This question has loomed large in the cultural history of modern Korea. In premodern Korea there was little dispute over the issue. Literature—in particular poetry—was a skill, mastery of which was a necessary condition for admission to the ranks of the scholar-bureaucrat literati who administered the nation. To be sure, poetry was also an art, composed in private for self-expression, but more important in the minds of the literati it was the mark of a cultivated man, a skill to be displayed in public when a poem might be required in impromptu poetry-creating gatherings or even in stylized poetic "dialogs" with the monarch.

In modern Korea, literature-as-art has supplanted literature-as-skill, but the question remains: Literature as art-for-art's-sake or literature as art-for-the-people's-sake? Debate over this question goes back to the beginnings of modern Korean literature. When *Yi Kwangsu's novel *Mujŏng* (Heartlessness) was published in 1917, Korea had already experienced seven years of the anomaly that was Japanese colonial occupation. At once demoralized by the loss of national sovereignty but inspired by the possibilities held out by the enlightenment movement then sweeping East Asia, intellectuals such as Yi Kwangsu saw in literature a tool for empowering the Korean people. In Yi's case, he proceeded in a series of novels to emphasize individual self-determination—to be achieved through literacy, education, women's rights, and a loosening of the traditional class-based social structure—as a means for restoring national self-determination.

Enter Kim Tongin. Kim, like Yi, had studied in Japan. Unlike Yi, Kim, along with colleagues such as Yŏm Sangsŏp and Hyŏn Chingŏn, decided to write not of life as it could or should be but of life as it was. Thus was born realism in modern Korean fiction (see "Realism in Early Modern Fiction") as well as a call for the artistic independence of literature. In the early 1920s, while Yi Kwangsu was writing a series of reform-minded essays and a novel, *The Pioneer* (Kaech'ŏkcha, 1923), Kim, Yŏm, and Hyŏn were concentrating on short fiction that was in Yŏm's case increasingly sophisticated in psychological terms and in Hyŏn's case increasingly bleak and deterministic, culminating in 1926 with the publication of the latter's story collection *The Faces of Korea* (Chosŏn ŭi ŏlgul).

It was at this time, with the formation of the Korean Artist Proletarian Federation (KAPF) in 1925, that engaged literature made a comeback. KAPF writers focused in their literature on class conflict and engaged in a recurring debate on the direction that literature should take. The hardliners among them were silenced by the forced dissolution of KAPF by the Japanese in 1935, but only temporarily: in 1945, upon the occupation of northern Korea by the Soviet army, there began a migration of Koreans from South to North that would eventually include a hundred-odd established writers, the *wŏlbuk* ("gone-north") writers (see "The *Wŏlbuk* Writers"). Under Kim Il Sung, literati in North Korea adopted a policy of socialist realism that was designed to place literature in the service of the Communist party.

Whether by coincidence or as a result of the muting of KAPF voices, the mid-1930s witnessed an early high point of modern Korean fiction. Most remarkable is the wealth of quality short fiction by such diverse voices as *Hwang Sunwŏn, *Kim Tongni, *Ch'ae Manshik, *Yi Sang, Kim Yujŏng, and Yi Hyosŏk. The stories of these writers are memorable in terms of structure, narrative technique, character, mood, description, and dialog. Novels of note also appeared: Yŏm Sangsŏp's *Three Generations* (Samdae, 1931), a family chronicle with echoes of the premodern Korean family saga; Ch'ae Manshik's *Peace under Heaven* (T'aep'yŏng ch'ŏnha, 1938); and Pak T'aewŏn's modernist *Streamside Sketches* (Ch'ŏnbyŏn p'unggyŏng, 1938). That Ch'ae's novel contains a good helping of satire should remind us that the contest between pure and engaged literature should be viewed not as a campaign between polar opposites but as a continuum ranging from direct commentary at one extreme through indirect commentary and "literature with a conscience" to art-for-art's-sake literature at the other extreme.

The contest resumed, as did debate in most every other realm of Korean society, in the chaotic period from liberation in 1945 to the establishment in 1948 of the Democratic People's Republic of Korea and the Republic of Korea. That the *wŏlbuk* authors were willing to abandon their ancestral homes in the South for what they expected to be a freer environment in the North for the literary expression of their ideologies attests to the tenacity of the contest. Their departure left writers in South Korea to cope with the harsh legacy of the Korean War primarily through aesthetics rather than ideology (see "Postwar Fiction"). Writers such as Chang Yonghak and O Sangwŏn found in existentialism a congenial philosophical framework for their response to the absurdities of the civil war. The stories of Son Ch'angsŏp tended toward nihilism, but with a defiant, darkly humorous edge. The antiheroes in such stories culminated in Ch'ŏrho, the protagonist of Yi Pŏmsŏn's "A Stray Bullet" (Obalt'an, 1960), which outraged an increasingly Christian society in South Korea with its suggestion of an uncaring Supreme Being. As a consequence, author Yi was removed from his middle-school teaching post.

With the rare exception of stories such as Sŏnu Hwi's "Flowers of Fire" (Pulkkot, 1957), which offered voluntarism as an antidote to the prevailing tendency among authors toward a deterministic and fatalistic worldview, literature of the 1950s and 1960s was marked by dismal portraits of the human wreckage of the Korean War and a young intelligentsia disillusioned by the military coup of May 1961. True, immense social, political, and cultural problems loomed in the background, but these stories tended to focus on the individual and only by extension the larger society. Though the 1950s writers and the newer generation of authors who debuted in the 1960s shared a pessimism toward their society and a preference for aesthetic rather than ideological expression in their art, they differed in outlook. The previous generation had grown up during the Japanese occupation and had been educated in Japanese; the newer generation had grown to maturity during the postwar years, had been educated in Korean, and often majored in Western literatures in college. The result is a more freewheeling aesthetics in which narratives are liberated from strict adherence to realism. Kim Sŭngok's "Seoul: 1964, Winter" (Sŏul, 1964, nyŏn kyŏul, 1965) and Ch'oe Inho's "The Poplar Tree" (P'op'ŭlla namu, 1981) are good examples.

By the 1970s South Koreans had endured more than two decades of authoritarian leadership. More onerous to the populace was the program of economic modernization instituted by President Park Chung Hee (ruled 1961–79), who had assumed power after the 1961 coup. Park's New Village Movement in the countryside and his program of export-led industrialization centered in the cities left few Koreans unaffected. There began a massive movement of population from rural areas to metropolises such as Seoul, a migration that has continued into the new millennium. Ongoing political problems were joined by a host of social problems as a traditional social structure rooted in the extended family began to break down. It was only a matter of time before literature began to address these various problems, and in the early 1970s the balance of power in the pure-versus-engaged-literature debate swung back to the side of engagement. Poets aligned with fiction writers in a campaign to restore to their works a historical consciousness and a sensitivity to *hyŏnshil*, or contemporary realities. The result was a literature as powerful and outspoken as anything in twentieth-century Korean letters. Poets *Kim Suyŏng and *Shin Kyŏngnim, two of the earliest champions of this literature, reflected an urban and a rural sensibility, respectively. Kim Chi-ha stretched the limits of government censorship with his "Five bandits" (Ojŏk, 1970) and was duly imprisoned. *Ko Ûn has increasingly broadened his worldview in massive works such as *Ten Thousand Faces* (Maninbo, 1986–) and the historical epic *Mt. Paektu* (Paektusan, 1991–93), with its impassioned declaration and graphic descriptions of the violence perpetrated on the Korean land and its people. Of note in his works and those of Kim Chiha are their affinities with the Korean oral tradition.

Engaged fiction flourished in the 1970s and 1980s in the hands of *Hwang Sŏgyŏng, Cho Chŏngnae, *Yun Hŭnggil, and *Cho Sehŭi. The works of the first two are more overtly issue-driven, and Cho has tended toward historical epics with works such as *The T'aebaek Mountains* (T'aebaek sanmaek, 1989). Those of Yun and Cho are more symbolic. All are richly peopled.

With the democratization of the political process in South Korea in 1987 came an easing of the political issues that had concerned writers for much of the previous two decades. An increasingly affluent society, moreover, reduced the potential audience for authors concerned with labor and other economic problems. Regrettably, but not surprisingly, Cho Sehŭi, author of *The Dwarf*, the outstanding single-volume novel of post-1945 Korean literature, fell silent (but continued in his social activism).

By the early 1990s, Korean fiction reflected uncertainty. Hwang Sunwŏn and Kim Tongni, the two surviving patriarchs of Korean fiction, had retired. Hwang Sŏgyŏng languished in self-imposed exile. Cho Sehŭi rarely published. Kim Chi-ha resumed writing but seemed shattered by his prison experience. Engagement literature was weakened by a perceived lack of issues. Emerging in this state of flux was a new generation of women writers (see "Women's Literature"). Inspired by the earlier successes of *O Chŏnghŭi and *Pak Wansŏ, and like the former increasingly the product of university creative writing programs, they breathed new life into both pure and engaged literature. *Ch'oe Yun is closer to the pure literature side, Kong Chiyŏng nearer the engaged stance.

—*Bruce Fulton*

Bibliography

Ch'ae Manshik. *Peace under Heaven*. Trans. Chun Kyung-Ja. Armonk, N.Y.: M. E. Sharpe, 1993.

Cho Sehŭi. "A Little Ball Launched by a Dwarf." Trans. Bruce and Ju-Chan Fulton. *Korean Literature Today* (Fall 1998): 126–169.

Ch'oe Inho. "The Poplar Tree." In Bruce and Ju-Chan Fulton, trans. and eds., *Deep Blue Night*, 73–83. Seoul: Jimoondang, 2002.

Ch'oe Yun. "The Last of Hanak'o." In Bruce and Ju-Chan Fulton, trans. and eds., *Wayfarer: New Fiction by Korean Women*, 11–41. Seattle: Women in Translation, 1997.

Kim Sŭngok. "Seoul: 1964, Winter." Trans. Marshall R. Pihl. In Marshall R. Pihl and Bruce and Ju-Chan Fulton, eds., *Land of Exile: Contemporary Korean Fiction*, 84–101. Armonk, N.Y.: M. E. Sharpe, 1993.

Kong Chiyŏng. "Human Decency." In Bruce and Ju-Chan Fulton, trans. and eds., *Wayfarer: New Fiction by Korean Women*, 42–78. Seattle: Women in Translation, 1997.

Myers, Brian. *Han Sŏrya and North Korean Literature: The Failure of Socialist Realism in the DPRK*. Ithaca, N.Y.: Cornell University East Asia Program, 1994.

O'Rourke, Kevin. "The Korean Short Story of the 1920s and Naturalism." *Korea Journal* (March 1977): 48–63.

O Sangwon. "A Respite." Trans. Kim Chongun. In Peter H. Lee, ed., *Modern Korean Literature: An Anthology*, 96–104. Honolulu: University of Hawai'i Press, 1990.

Sŏnu Hwi. "Flowers of Fire." (Excerpt.) Trans. Peter H. Lee. In Peter H. Lee, ed., *Flowers of Fire: Twentieth-Century Korean Stories*, 184–245. Honolulu: University Press of Hawai'i, 1974.

Yi Pŏmsŏn. "A Stray Bullet." Trans. Marshall R. Pihl. In Marshall R. Pihl, ed., *Listening to Korea: A Korean Anthology*, 127–154. New York: Praeger, 1973.

105

THE LITERATURE OF TERRITORIAL DIVISION

In 1945, near the end of World War II, the United States and the Soviet Union agreed to divide Korea at the thirty-eighth parallel for the purpose of accepting the surrender of Japanese troops on the Korean peninsula. The Soviet and American forces occupied their respective spheres north and south of that line until 1948, when separate regimes, the Democratic People's Republic of Korea (North Korea) and the Republic of Korea (South Korea), were established. The border between these two states hardened at the conclusion of the Korean War in 1953 with the establishment of a cease-fire line that roughly followed the thirty-eighth parallel. That line, expanded into a five-kilometer-wide demilitarized zone (DMZ), has separated the Korean people ever since; a formal peace treaty has yet to be signed, and technically the two Koreas are still in a state of war. The DMZ marked an end to virtually all communication and transportation between the two sides.

The division of the peninsula has occasioned such a wealth of literature that it can be considered the central motif of post-1945 literature in South Korea. The impact of the division on the daily lives of all Koreans is such that even writers with no firsthand experience of the events leading to the division have drawn on it for inspiration in their works. The literature of territorial division— or division literature, for short—comprises a great variety of works. There is the literature authored by the *yibuk* writers—those who migrated from North Korea to South Korea, such as *Hwang Sunwŏn (1915–2000), Sŏnu Hwi (1922–1986), and Yi Hoch'ŏl (b. 1932). These works tend to focus on the uprooting of northerners—some 800,000 from 1945 to 1947 alone (Lee 1984:375)—from their centuries-old ancestral homes and their relocation in the South. Second are the works dealing with soldiers and partisans trapped on the enemy side of the 1953 cease-fire line. Third are the accounts of some of the millions of family members separated by the DMZ. Fourth, much of postwar fiction (that produced in the 1950s after the Korean War; see "Postwar Fiction") concerns the psychological scars left by the war. Fifth are the *kijich'on* (military camptown) stories dealing with the impact of the American military presence in South Korea. Last are the "sins of the fathers" stories, which portray the effects of an older generation's political transgressions on the subsequent generation.

Characteristic of the *yibuk* writers' work is Yi Hoch'ŏl's "Leaving Home" (T'arhyang, 1955). It concerns the attempt of three young men to resettle in the South when their ostensibly temporary departure from their ancestral home in the North begins to seem permanent. Hwang Sunwŏn's *The Descendants of Cain* (K'ain ŭi huye, 1954) is valuable for its account of the land reform undertaken in 1946 in North Korea, the immediate reason for the departure of the author's own family for the South in that year.

An example of stories of the second type is Sŏnu Hwi's "One Way" (1956). Communist partisans in South Korea are described at length in Cho Chŏngnae's roman-fleuve *The T'aebaek Mountains* (T'aebaek sanmaek, 1989), which broke new ground in South Korea by drawing on recently declassified documentation of Communist activities in the South.

Accounts of families separated by the war range from those focusing on permanent separation to stories of problematic reunions of long-divided family members. *Hwang Sŏgyŏng's "The Chronicle of a Man Named Han" (Han sshi yŏndaegi, 1972) is characteristic of the former; *Ch'oe Yun's "His Father's Keeper" (Abŏji kamshi, 1990) is an example of the latter.

Many works vividly depict the psychological scars of the war. *Ch'oe Inhun's *The Square* (Kwangjang, 1961) portrays a prisoner of war (POW) who elects to migrate to a third country rather than settle in either North or South Korea. Chang Yonghak's existential "Poems of John the Baptist" (Yohan shijip, 1955) describes the absurdities of the horrific and ideologically inspired violence among North Korean soldiers confined in a South Korean POW camp. The protagonists of both stories ultimately commit suicide.

Kijich'on stories often describe divisions among Koreans, or the exacerbation of longstanding class conflicts, occasioned by the foreign military presence on their soil. Kang Sŏkkyŏng's "Days and Dreams" (Nat kwa kkum, 1983) illuminates the ambivalence toward Korean men felt by bargirls who cater to the GIs at an American military base, as well as the emotional strain on family members who deplore a camptown bargirl's job yet depend on the money she earns from the foreigners.

The sins-of-the-fathers literature emphasizes the lingering effects of South Korea's use of anticommunism as a state policy to control the populace and thereby safeguard its strategy of export-led development aimed at securing a place among the world's advanced nations. Kim Minsuk's "Scarlet Fingernails" (Pongsunga kkommul, 1987), for example, in addition to depicting a problematic reunion between a woman in the South and her father, jailed as a Communist spy, whom she has never met, describes the political restrictions imposed by ROK law not only on the father's children but on his nieces and nephews as well.

— Bruce Fulton

Bibliography

Chang Yonghak. "Poems of John the Baptist." In Kim Chong-un, trans. and ed., *Postwar Korean Short Stories*, 2d ed., 19–46. Seoul: Seoul National University Press, 1983.

Ch'oe Inhun. *The Square*. Trans. Kevin O'Rourke. Devon: Spindlewood, 1985.

Ch'oe Yun. "His Father's Keeper." In Suh Ji-moon, trans. and ed., *The Rainy Spell and Other Korean Stories*, rev. ed., 248–270. Armonk, N.Y.: M. E. Sharpe, 1998.

Hwang Sŏgyŏng. "The Chronicle of a Man Named Han." Trans. Yu Young-nan. *Korean Literature Today* (Summer 1998): 7–76.

Hwang Sunwŏn. *The Descendants of Cain*. Trans. Suh Ji-moon and Julie Pickering. Armonk, N.Y.: M. E. Sharpe, 1997.

Kang Sŏkkyŏng. "Days and Dreams." In Bruce and Ju-Chan Fulton, trans. and eds., *Words of Farewell: Stories by Korean Women Writers*, 1–27. Seattle: Seal Press, 1989.

Kim Minsuk. "Scarlet Fingernails." In Bruce and Ju-Chan Fulton, trans. and eds., *Wayfarer: New Writing by Korean Women*, 79–114. Seattle: Women in Translation, 1997.

Kwon Youngmin. "Contemporary Korean Literature as Division Literature." Trans. Marshall R. Pihl. *Korea Journal* (July 1987): 34–40.

Lee Ki-baik. *A New History of Korea*. Trans. Edward W. Wagner and Edward J. Shultz. Cambridge, Mass.: Harvard University Press, 1984.

Sŏnu Hwi. "One Way." In Kim Chong-un, trans. and ed., *Postwar Korean Short Stories*, 2d ed., 62–71. Seoul: Seoul National University Press, 1983.

Yi Hoch'ŏl. "Leaving Home." Trans. Theodore Hughes. In Bruce Fulton, ed., *Modern Korean Fiction: An Anthology*. New York: Columbia University Press, forthcoming.

106

WOMEN'S LITERATURE

Scholars commonly date modern Korean fiction to the year 1917, when *Yi Kwangsu's novel *Heartlessness* (Mujŏng) was published. Lesser known, but significant in its own way, is another fictional work published that year, Kim Myŏngsun's story "A Suspicious Girl" (Ŭishim ŭi sonyŏ). In terms of its characterization, plot, and psychological insight, this story is among the very first modern Korean short stories, and it is likely the first published story by a woman (So 1994:35).

The comparatively obscure status of this work, and of Korean women's literature in general until recent decades, is explained in large part by traditional Korean social structure. Any discussion of women's writing in Korea must begin by acknowledging the longstanding compartmentalization of women's literature by the overwhelmingly male literary establishment. That phenomenon is conditioned by traditional Korean gender-role expectations, which militated against education—and, by extension, literacy and letters—for women. Education in premodern Korea was a privilege extended almost exclusively to men, for education prepared one for a position in the government bureaucracy, which was open to men only. Thus, women who learned to read and write were rare indeed; rarer still were those who attached their names to literary works. Korean men of letters often refer to the modern descendants of this select group as *yŏryu chakka* ("female writers"), a term deriving from the Japanese *joryū sakka*. (Male writers are referred to simply as *chakka*.)

There is a considerable irony in this categorization of women writers in modern Korea, one that is centered in the history of the native script, *hangŭl*. Though it was promulgated in 1446 and has been admired by linguists at home and abroad for its logic and simplicity in representing spoken Korean, the great majority of literati in premodern times disdained it as something fit for women and commoners—*amgŭl* ("female letters"), they called it. Instead the literati maintained their centuries-old preference for classical Chinese as a literary language. In premodern Korea most women who wrote did so in the native script; the male literati continued to produce works in Chinese, primarily poetry, until the twentieth century, when annexation by Japan made the use of *hangŭl* by Koreans a matter of cultural life and death. The irony, then, is that Korean women, traditionally marginalized in the literary realm, had remained steadfast throughout the centuries in their use of what became the literary language of Korea in the twentieth century.

Kim Myŏngsun and a small group of cohorts began publishing during a promising time. Women's issues—not surprisingly, discussed at first only by men—were by the 1920s being debated by members of both sexes (Kim Yung-Hee 1994:28). Though Korea's March 1, 1919, independence movement had been crushed by imperial Japan, it was followed by an easing of colonial control over matters cultural, allowing a ferment in literary activity as young Korean intellectuals returned from schooling in Japan armed with Japanese translations of Western literary and critical works and set about rendering them into Korean as well as composing their own stories, verse, and essays. Women such as Kim Wŏnju and Na Hyesŏk spoke out on women's issues (Kim Yung-Hee 1994) and, like Kim Myŏngsun, published literature. Other women, less inclined toward activism than these three, also launched writing careers: Pak Hwasŏng and Ch'oe Chŏnghŭi were the longest-lived, but Kang Kyŏngae, Paek Shinae, and Yi Sŏnhŭi produced noteworthy fiction as well.

Between the early burst of women's writing in the 1920s and the 1930s and the breakthrough achieved by *O Chŏnghŭi and *Pak Wansŏ in the 1970s, the best-known women fiction writers included Han Musuk, Kang Shinjae, and Han Malsuk, in addition to Pak Hwasŏng and Ch'oe Chŏnghŭi. The sisters Han were a rarity, encouraged from an early age to cultivate themselves in the arts and enjoying the wherewithal to create at a time when many Koreans were struggling to survive postwar deprivations. Another member of that generation is *Pak Kyŏngni, whose sixteen-volume family saga *Land* (T'oji, 1994) is one of the great achievements of modern Korean literature.

The very different voices of O Chŏnghŭi and Pak Wansŏ established Korean women's fiction on its own terms. O's contribution was to strip her fiction of the sentiment that had been both a blessing and a curse to her predecessors, a quality that brought acceptance from the literary establishment but at the same time undercut the integrity of the works, and to transfer darkness and gloom, perpetual metaphors of the tragedies of modern Korean history, from the level of historical consciousness to that of the individual psyche. Her "Wayfarer" (Sullyeja ŭi norae, 1983) is a good example. Pak, on the other hand, has enjoyed great commercial success with empathic, even cathartic stories that attract readers to a cozy and neighborly narrative persona, as well as critical praise by responding amply to the scholar-critics' felt need for issue-driven works. Her "Winter Outing" (Kyŏul nadŭri, 1975), for instance, is a sensitive portrayal of a middle-aged woman emotionally distanced from her husband and stepdaughter, refugees from North Korea. Readers identify with the family situation, which is not unusual in the divided land that is Korea, while critics applaud the author for her "historical consciousness."

Although Pak Wansŏ's appeal held steady in the 1990s and the often-cited lyricism of a younger writer, Shin Kyŏngsuk, probably had the greatest impact among a new generation of women writers emerging in that decade, it is most likely *Ch'oe Yun whose reputation will flourish in the new millennium. A scholar (her first published works were criticism), a prolific translator, and an essayist, Ch'oe has served the rigorous literary apprenticeship lacking in many contemporary Korean writers, debuting as a fiction writer only in her midthirties with the ambitious novella *There a Petal Silently Falls* (Chŏgi sori ŏpshi han chŏm kkonnip i chigo, 1988). In terms of technique, imagination, and polish, she has few equals, male or female, among contemporary writers.

At the turn of the millennium, writers such as Ŭn Hŭigyŏng, Cho Kyŏngnan, and Kong Chiyŏng were spearheading a new wave of fiction that reflected a technologically advanced urban society and career women working within it. Kong's "Dreams" (Kkum, 1993) is representative.

Critical and commercial success in poetry has proved more elusive for Korean women. Poetry's long pedigree in traditional Korea, when it was primarily a pursuit of men, has made it a bastion of male privilege more than is the case with the short story, which in Korea is widely seen as a Western import. Perhaps the two best-known women poets of an earlier generation, Mo Yunsuk and No Ch'ŏnmyŏng, exist in the critical imagination in no small part as personality types, with Mo considered the producer of flamboyant, passionate lyrics and No the creator of elegant, subdued verse. Not until the 1970s did women poets secure both an independent female identity and a high standard of poetic achievement (Kim Chŏngnan 1996:2). Their predecessors in earlier decades were considered deficient initially in technical sophistication and then in female self-consciousness. Poets since the 1970s who have met this double test include Kang Ŭngyo, Mun Chŏnghŭi, Kim Hyesun, and Kim Sŭnghŭi, but only the last has gained widespread critical recognition. She and Kim Hyesun have also written perceptively on poetry.

Not surprisingly, given Korean poetry's traditional connection with the male scholar-bureaucrat elite, it has proved to be a symbolic tool for challenging the ongoing weight of patriarchy. Here is Kim Sŭnghŭi on gender-role expectations (Suh Ji-moon 1987:38):

> Darling, Darling,
> Please be a saint,
> Look after me like a nurse,
> Give me pleasures like a whore,
> And be a sturdy servant as well.

Other poets, such as Ch'oe Sŭngja, have targeted dictatorship as an extension of patriarchal authority. The voices of these and other women are in turn ironic, sardonic, resigned, and defiant. Their voices ring clearer, for unlike many of their counterparts among contemporary fiction writers, they do not always feel compelled to measure up to the yardstick of historical or ideological relevance that has sealed so many literary reputations in Korea.

Until recently women have also been underrepresented among Korean playwrights. The iconoclastic Kim Charim, South Korea's first professional woman playwright (Shim Jung Soon 1990:32), explores the sexual double standard and other issues tempered by traditional gender-role expectations. The one-act play *Prostitute Pig* (Hwadon, 1970), for example, portrays a married woman numbed by her cloistered domestic life.

Critical readings of contemporary Korean women's literature often focus on representations of the body. By making the female body the subject of a poem or story, the writer symbolically reclaims what has traditionally been the possession of men, as Kim Hyesun so wryly describes (Suh Ji-moon 1987:37):

> You are a superb taxidermist.
> You disembowel us with dexterous hands....
>
> I take off my clothes when I see you,
> Because I have no bowels to hide.
>
> I bloom under your touch,
> Thanks to the paint you put on me....
>
> I have been your faithful puppet,
> Opening and closing my arms and my mouth
> Just as you pulled the strings.

O Chŏnghŭi's coming-of-age story "Chinatown" (Chunggugin kŏri, 1979), for example, includes a protagonist who experiences her first menstrual cycle, a fecund mother, and a neighborhood woman who provides sexual favors to an

African American soldier from a nearby army base. The military-camptown element of this story links the individual female body to the female body politic of Korea, in that military prostitution has been sanctioned in Korea, at least unofficially, since the dictatorship of Park Chung Hee (1961–79). Pak Wansŏ's "Three Days in That Autumn" (Kŭ kaŭl ŭi sahŭl tongan, 1980) features a woman who makes her living from the female body—an abortionist who reckons that the number of lives she has terminated would equal the population of a large town. Her choice of livelihood is in large part the result of the violation of her own body by an American soldier during the Korean War. To suggest the extent to which the female body continues to be held hostage, if only by the male imagination, Ch'oe Yun's "The Last of Hanak'o" (Hanak'o nŭn ŏpta, 1994) is about an accomplished woman who is known to her male friends by her nickname Hanak'o, which refers to her shapely nose. The men fantasize about Hanak'o as an ideal girlfriend but remain oblivious not only to her real name but also to her professional successes and her apparently lesbian orientation.

By the year 2000 women fiction writers in Korea had gained widespread acceptance in the Korean literary world—but not without occasional speculation as to the supposed feminization of Korean literature. They thus face a continuation of the dilemma that has confronted Korean women writers since the previous century: how to meet the expectations of a readership that appears to be increasingly young and female, and the demands of a critical audience that has always been overwhelmingly male. If the 1990s—a decade of signal advances for women writers—were any indication, the vitality of Korean literature in the near future will depend to a significant degree on whether women writers can prosper in this challenging environment.

—Bruce Fulton

Bibliography

Ch'oe Yun. "The Last of Hanak'o." In Bruce and Ju-Chan Fulton, trans. and eds., *Wayfarer: New Fiction by Korean Women*, 11–41. Seattle: Women in Translation, 1997.

———. *There a Petal Silently Falls*. Trans. Bruce and Ju-Chan Fulton. *Korea Journal* (Winter 1997): 221–239; (Spring 1998): 357–392.

Kim Chŏngnan. "The Achievements and Prospects of Modern Korean Women's Poetry: On the Formation of the Female Identity." Trans. Mickey Hong. Paper presented at the Korean Literature and World Literature Conference, University of California at Los Angeles, 1996.

Kim Yung-Hee. "Women's Issues in 1920s Korea." *Korean Culture* (Summer 1994): 27–33.

Kong Chiyŏng. "Dreams." Trans. Kim Miza and Suzanne Crowder Han. *Manoa* 8, no. 2 (1996): 184–202.

O Chŏnghŭi. "Chinatown." In Bruce and Ju-Chan Fulton, trans. and eds., *Words of Farewell: Stories by Korean Women Writers*, 202–230. Seattle: Seal Press, 1989.

——. "Wayfarer." In Bruce and Ju-Chan Fulton, trans. and eds., *Wayfarer: New Fiction by Korean Women*, 184–205. Seattle: Women in Translation, 1997.

Pak Kyŏngni. *Land.* vol. 1 Trans. Agnita Tennant. London: Kegan Paul International/ UNESCO Publishing, 1996.

Pak Wansŏ. "Three Days in That Autumn." Trans. Ryu Sukhee. In Chun Kyung-Ja, ed., *My Very Last Possession and Other Stories by Pak Wansŏ*, 156–197. Armonk, N.Y.: M. E. Sharpe, 1999.

——. "Winter Outing." Trans. Marshall R. Pihl. In Marshall R. Pihl and Bruce and Ju-Chan Fulton, eds., *Land of Exile: Contemporary Korean Fiction*, 150–164. Armonk, N.Y.: M. E. Sharpe, 1993.

Shim Jung Soon. "Torn between Self and Tradition: The Image of Women in the Plays of Kim Cha-rim." *Korean Culture* (Summer 1990): 32–37.

So, Carolyn P. "Seeing the Silent Pen: Kim Myŏngsun (1896–c. 1951), a Pioneering Woman Writer." *Korean Culture* (Summer 1994): 34–40.

Suh Ji-moon, trans. "Seven Feminist Poems." *Korea Journal* (September 1987): 34–42.

107

THE *SŎNGJANG SOSŎL*

Though not a clearly defined genre, the *sŏngjang sosŏl* is a fictional narrative generally involving an individual's internal development in relation to social changes. There is in Korean literary criticism a tradition of comparing the *sŏngjang sosŏl* to the bildungsroman, or novel of formation, as a genre that can expose cultural ideology within a period of great change. This comparison has some limitations, but its value lies in the fact that, as Franco Moretti (1987) writes, the novel of formation takes the experience of modernity as its originating principle. Korean narratives of formation date back to the colonial period, but only comparatively recently has the term *sŏngjang sosŏl* become the most widely accepted designation of this genre. Other common terms for the Korean narrative of formation are *palchŏn* (development) *sosŏl*, *kyoyang* (education) *sosŏl*, *kyŏnghŏm* (experience) *sosŏl*, *hyŏngsŏng* (formation) *sosŏl*, and *kaksŏng* (awakening) *sosŏl*. These various terms indicate the breadth of concerns of the genre.

The Korean narrative of formation offers a distinct perspective through which the writer or protagonist questions particular values and ways of life as they are undergoing transformation. The protagonist's development is part of the larger historical moment, and he or she serves as a witness to the period that is unfolding. In contrast with the Western novel of formation, the *sŏngjang sosŏl* frequently uses the first-person point of view and its narrator often looks back to childhood or youth. The reader is given a perspective that is both intimate and immediate, inasmuch as first-person narration tends to privilege interiority, and yet that is distanced enough (due to the temporal disjuncture between the events narrated and the time of the narration) to be able to assess the social structures and values embedded in the work.

Research on the formal structure and thematics of the *sŏngjang sosŏl* began in the late 1970s with Yi Chaesŏn's examination of the childhood narratives of *Hwang Sunwŏn, one of the masters of Korean short fiction. In Hwang's stories, the immature protagonist's process of formation upon encountering the harsh realities of life is a rite of passage, as in the Western initiation story. Yi focuses on childhood narratives to discern two dominant themes of the *sŏngjang sosŏl* that are specific to Korean modernization since liberation from Japanese rule in 1945: the child's experience of the Korean War and of relocation from the countryside to the city.

Critical interest in the *sŏngjang sosŏl* began with a 1982 essay in which Kim Pyŏngik suggested that it is a literary form that can expose cultural ideology — those values and customs that are embedded within a society. Kim applied the eighteenth-century bildungsroman to the Korean cultural context and found it useful to consider the *sŏngjang sosŏl* its Korean equivalent. According to Kim, the *sŏngjang sosŏl* reveals the limits and possibilities of self-formation within Korean society, which had not permitted the growth of the "individual self" due to the Confucian emphasis on the "social self." Kim's pioneering essay offers a way to explore the possibilities of individual consciousness specific to Korean society, a problem that became especially acute during the 1970s and 1980s under the social and ethical conditions created by an authoritarian state.

Although the *sŏngjang sosŏl* shares characteristics of the bildungsroman and the initiation story, it is also a successor to traditional oral tales. It is heir to Korean heroic legends, folktales, and myths and retains the didactic function of educating the reader through the trials and tribulations of an individual. In the modern version of these tales, however, the protagonist's search is for abstract ideals rather than concrete objects or individuals. Other important characteristics of the *sŏngjang sosŏl* relative to its antecedent forms are the youth of the protagonist (children or youth under the age of twenty), the family-centered focus of the plot, the predominance of first-person narratives, and the retrospective viewpoint of the narrator.

The 1970s *sŏngjang sosŏl* was predominantly a narrative of childhood. South Korean writers turned to their own childhoods to recall the history of the Korean War and employed a retrospective viewpoint to connect the chaos of the postliberation period to their own present-day circumstances. Their narratives showed how the war affected the lives of ordinary Koreans and continued to have traumatic repercussions for families that had lost members, and particularly fathers, as a result of the national division. Using a child's point of view, *Yun Hŭnggil's "The Rainy Spell" (Changma, 1973) examines how each individual within an extended family is forced to choose between left-wing and right-wing forces. In Kim Wŏnil's "The Soul of Darkness" (Ŏdum ŭi hon, 1973), the child protagonist tries to comprehend why Communists are being killed as he awaits the execution of his leftist father. In both stories, the perspective is split between the child's point of view, which serves as naive witness to the social and political upheaval of the Korean War, and an adult consciousness that attempts to decipher the meaning of these events for the present.

In the 1980s and 1990s, short stories and novels exploring questions of individual development increased. Correspondingly, the background of the *sŏngjang sosŏl* broadened beyond familial relationships to focus increasingly on the formation of an individual self not limited to familial obligation or the fulfillment of expected social roles. Along with this proliferation of the *sŏngjang sosŏl* came an effort to establish guidelines for defining the genre. Literary critics emphasized that the *sŏngjang sosŏl* not only described childhood but also depicted the process of formation as a psychic crisis that causes both self-awakening and the binding of relations between the self and the world. The question of whether the individual can achieve a mature self-formation, and under what conditions, was increasingly foregrounded in the *sŏngjang sosŏl*. *Yi Munyŏl's *A Portrait of My Youth* (Chŏlmŭn nal ŭi ch'osang, 1981), a trio of linked stories, heralded the search for an individuated identity outside the structure of the family. "That Winter of My Youth" (Kŭ hae kyŏul), the first part of the trilogy, portrays a disillusioned college student who quits school and roams the countryside in an existential search for meaning in his life.

An important development in the *sŏngjang sosŏl* occurred with the sharp increase in prominence of women writers in the 1980s. Whereas in the 1970s the depiction of individual development had been limited largely to male subjects, from the 1980s on the narrative of formation increasingly portrayed the development of girls and young women as female writers sought to recall their own pasts. *Pak Wansŏ is well known for serial autobiographical fiction that explores the relationship between mother and daughter as the primary site for the formation of identity. Good examples are her debut work, *The Naked Tree* (Namok, 1970), and the "Mother's Hitching Post" trilogy (Ŏmma ŭi malttuk, 1979, 1981, 1991). Short-fiction writer *O Chŏnghŭi's "Chinatown" (Chunggugin kŏri, 1979) and "The Garden of Childhood" (Yunyŏn ŭi ttul, 1980) are based on childhood memories of the Korean War. Other women writers, such as Kang Sŏkkyŏng in the novella *A Room in the Woods* (Sup sog ŭi pang, 1985), have joined O and Pak in portraying the growth of female protagonists to examine how individuals are formed as gendered subjects.

—*Helen H. Koh*

Bibliography

Kang Sŏkkyŏng. "A Room in the Woods." In Bruce and Ju-Chan Fulton, trans. and eds., *Words of Farewell: Stories by Korean Women Writers*, 28–147. Seattle: Seal Press, 1989.

Kim Pyŏngik. "Sŏngjang sosŏl ŭi munhwajŏk ŭimi" (The Cultural Significance of the *Sŏngjang Sosŏl*). In *Chisŏng kwa munhak* (Intellect and Literature), 144–160. Seoul: Munhak kwa chisŏng sa, 1982.

Kim Wŏnil. "The Soul of Darkness." Trans. Lee Sang-sup. In Shin Dong-wook, Cho Nam-hyun, and Kim Seong-kon, eds., *Journey to Mujin: Anthology of Korean Short Fiction*, 112–136. Seoul: Korean Culture and Arts Foundation, 1988.

Moretti, Franco. *The Way of the World: The Bildungsroman in European Culture*. New York: Verso, 1987.

O Chŏnghŭi. "Chinatown." In Bruce and Ju-Chan Fulton, trans. and eds., *Words of Farewell: Stories by Korean Women Writers*, 202–230. Seattle: Seal Press, 1989.

Pak Wansŏ. *The Naked Tree*. Trans. Yu Youngnan. Ithaca, N.Y.: Cornell University East Asia Program, 1995.

Yi Chaesŏn. *Hanguk hyŏndae sosŏl sa* (A History of Modern Korean Fiction). Seoul: Hongsŏng sa, 1979.

——. *Hyŏndae Hanguk sosŏl sa, 1945–1990* (A History of Modern Korean Fiction, 1945–1990). Seoul: Minŭm sa, 1991.

Yi Munyŏl. "That Winter of My Youth." In Suh Ji-moon, trans. and ed., *The Rainy Spell and Other Korean Short Stories*, rev. ed., 213–247. Armonk, N.Y.: M. E. Sharpe, 1998.

Yun Hŭnggil. "The Rainy Spell." Trans. Suh Ji-moon. In J. Martin Holman, ed., *The House of Twilight*, 1–77. London: Readers International, 1989.

Authors, Works, Schools

108

YI KWANGSU

Yi Kwangsu (1892–1950?) was born in the Chŏngju area of present-day North P'yŏngan Province in North Korea. Orphaned at ten, he went to Japan at thirteen to study, graduating with a degree in philosophy from Waseda University in 1918. A prolific author, Yi wrote in a variety of genres and was also a prominent journalist. He may well have enjoyed the largest readership of any early modern Korean author (Pihl 1991:20). Yi was abducted to North Korea after the outbreak of the Korean War in 1950; sometime thereafter he died in custody.

Any attempt to assess Yi as a writer is complicated by his lifetime of activism, first as a nationalist and then as a collaborator with imperial Japan late in the colonial period; by the didactic nature of his writing, which owes not only to the traditional Korean writer's need to enlighten the people but also to Yi's own intellectual and spiritual debt to Tolstoyan humanism and Mahayana Buddhism; and by his insistence that he considered writing to be merely a pastime. Indeed, it may be that history will most usefully judge him as more a humanist than a writer. In any event, his literary reputation has not thrived in recent decades, with attention still tending to focus on his debut novel, *Heartlessness* (Mujŏng, 1917), at the expense of his many later works. Nevertheless, his contribution as a writer to the evolution of modern Korean culture and society remains substantial. In his writing he pioneered in at least three respects: as a reformer, as a modernizer of Korean literary language, and as an architect of modern Korean literary theory.

First of all, in a variety of literary forums he attacked the repressive Korean political tradition and Confucian social structure, championed the rights of women, and pressed for a vernacular literature that would address contemporary themes. He was the first important modern Korean novelist at a time when many of his contemporaries in fiction writing disdained the novel as hackwork and instead embraced the short story, and he unabashedly used his novels to promote the enlightenment agenda that he viewed as the means to strengthen Korea during the colonial period. Important too in Korean literary history is the contest between socially engaged literature and art-for-art's-sake literature initiated by Yi's programmatic novels and by the pure literature–based response that they elicited from Kim Tongin and his followers.

Yi's efforts to modernize Korean literary language are evident in *Heartlessness*. After an apprenticeship with the short story in the 1910s, for which he wrote in a mixed script of native *hangŭl* as well as Chinese, he used the native script exclusively in this path-breaking novel. The language of the work is more akin to modern spoken Korean than is that of the transitional *shin sosŏl* (new fiction), which flourished in the decade preceding the publication of *Heartlessness*. The novel is also modern in its diction, its relatively terse sentence structure, its criticism of traditional mores, its physical description, and its use of irony. Moreover, introspection and internal conflict replace the traditional pattern of conflict between a virtuous character and hostile external forces. Finally, Yi introduced a distinction between what in Korean would correspond to English past and present tense. His other major works of fiction include the novel *Soil* (Hŭk, 1932) and the story "The Unenlightened" (Mumyŏng, 1938).

Yi's contribution to the evolution of literary theory in modern Korea was to divest the Sino-Korean term *munhak* of its connotations of scholarship and science and instead to equate it with the English word *literature*, in its modern sense of imaginative and creative writing. This marked a fundamental rupture with the traditional understanding of literature among Korean literati. Moreover, by understanding literature as an independent art form, Yi may be said to have aestheticized the traditional Korean concept of literature.

—*Bruce Fulton*

Bibliography

Hwang Jong-yon. "The Emergence of Aesthetic Ideology in Modern Korean Literary Criticism: An Essay on Yi Kwang-su." Trans. Janet Poole. *Korea Journal* (Winter 1999): 5–35.

Kim Kichung. "The Question of Betrayal." *Korea Journal* (Winter 1991): 40–53.

Lee, Ann Sung-hi. "The Early Writings of Yi Kwang-su." *Korea Journal* (Summer 2002): 241–278.

——. "Yi Kwangsu and Korean Literature: The Novel *Mujong*." *Journal of Korean Studies* 8 (1992): 81–137.

Pihl, Marshall R. "Narrative Technique in Korean Fiction, 1860–1940." Paper presented at the Association for Asian Studies Annual Conference, New Orleans, 1991.

Yi Kwangsu. "The Unenlightened." Trans. Chang Wang-rok. *Korea Journal* (March 1970): 23–31; (April 1970): 26–33; (May 1970): 31–36.

Yu Beongcheon. *Han Yong-un and Yi Kwang-su: Two Pioneers of Modern Korean Literature*. Detroit: Wayne State University Press, 1992.

109

REALISM IN EARLY MODERN FICTION

In 1908 Ch'oe Namsŏn, a young poet-nationalist, produced a magazine called *Sonyŏn* (Youth). Korea's first literary magazine, it provided a forum for the ideas of young intellectuals lately returned from Japanese universities. In *Sonyŏn* and similar magazines, these young intellectuals set about writing what was in effect a propaganda literature of nationalism, modernization, and enlightenment. All the hopes of these young nationalists were shattered by the failure of the March First independence movement in 1919. A period of intense disillusion ensued that proved very important for the development of literature in that it limited the possibilities open to intellectuals: they could be escapist like the symbolist poets; they could be propagandist like the nationalists; or they could be Marxist.

*Yi Kwangsu (1892–1950?) was one of the most prominent of the nationalist leaders. Up to 1919 he had been a radical idealist, preaching independence through education, modernization, and popular demonstrations. Now he became a political realist, thinking in terms of what was feasible here and now, with independence as a long-range goal. He used novels such as *Heartlessness* (Mujŏng, 1917) to propagate his ideas on morality, education, and the improvement of social life. Naturally there was a reaction against this doctrinaire literature. It came in 1919 in the form of *Ch'angjo* (Creation), a literary magazine written by a group of young writers inspired and led by the eccentric Kim Tongin (1900–1951), who liked to parade up Chongno in Seoul wearing a tailcoat, striped trousers, spats, and a carnation. *Ch'angjo* was a manifesto of literary realism. The purpose of literature, the new magazine announced, lay not in political propaganda but in the depiction of life as it was.

Young writers such as Kim Tongin, Hyŏn Chingŏn (1900–1943), and Yŏm Sangsŏp (1897–1963), publishing in a variety of coterie magazines, notably *Ch'angjo, Paekcho* (White Tide), and *P'yehŏ* (Ruins), began to write about Korean life as they found it. Reality was their slogan, and under the Japanese, Korea was a very grim reality indeed. These young writers had been introduced to Zola and Maupassant, to Dostoevsky, Tolstoy, and Turgenev. The Europeans had a tremendous appeal for the young Koreans, mainly because of shared pessimism: the political pessimism of France after the Franco-Prussian War; the pessimism in Russia because of the corrupt tsarist government; and the pessimism generated in Korea by the oppression of the colonial regime and the failure of the independence movement in 1919. Such was the pessimism prevailing in Korea that the young generation of writers developed a form of hyperrealism, what is called Korean naturalism, and this became the dominant mode of fiction in Korea in the 1920s.

Korean naturalism and European naturalism had very little in common apart from the pessimism generated by the background of political defeat and a certain bond of connectedness forged by determinism as a philosophy in the West and the notion of *unmyŏng* (fate) in the Korean tradition. European naturalism sought to apply scientific principles to literature. For Zola the novel was a laboratory where the forces working on man in society could be analyzed clinically. Korean writers had no such scientific brief; they were just trying to paint reality as it was. Yŏm Sangsŏp, the only Korean writer of the period who set out consciously to write in the naturalist mode, seems to have misunderstood the nature of European naturalism (Ch'ŏn 1969:46). Yŏm thought of naturalism in terms of self-realization and iconoclasm, slogans at the time in Korea; self-realization, he said, grew from the negation of authority, while iconoclasm produced an organic disillusion. "Naturalism," he tells us, "is no more than a literary tool, in reaction to romanticism and idealism, to show that this is the reality of life" (quoted in Paek 1968:158).

European naturalism was radically different. It relied heavily on determinism. Korea had no awareness of determinism as a Western philosophy, but it had a deterministic philosophy of its own: *unmyŏng*. Zola saw man as an animal, reacting to internal and external forces—hereditary, environmental, sexual, political, economic, and religious—that he could neither control nor understand; man was helpless, determined to act in predictable ways. Korean naturalist writers saw man as living in an oppressive society, a prey to forces such as sex, anger, poverty, the marriage system, and the political system. These forces led to inevitable defeat and destruction. They represented fate, which the individual was helpless to change.

The great unifying theme of Kim Tongin's work is the pursuit of happiness, vitiated by forces inside and outside man. In each of his stories, the protagonist walks an inevitable path toward defeat. In "Potatoes" (Kamja, 1925) the defeating principle is a combination of poverty and cupidity, in "The Seaman's Chant" (Paettaragi, 1921) it is blind unreason, and in "The Frenzied Sonata" (Kwangyŏm sonat'a, 1929) it is abnormal psychology.

Hyŏn Chingŏn's story collection *The Faces of Korea* (Chosŏn ŭi ŏlgul) was published in 1926. These stories are slices of Korean life showing how the Japanese occupation affected various representative figures in society: intellectuals ("A Society That Drives You to Drink" [Sul kwŏnhanŭn sahoe], "The Depraved" [Tarakcha]); a working man ("A Lucky Day" [Unsu choŭn nal]); the unmarried ("The Dormitory Mistress and the Love Letter" [B sagam kwa lŏbu let'a]); the father of a family ("The Director of the Private Mental Hospital" [Sarip chŏngshin pyŏngwŏn chang]); a young girl ("Fire" [Pul]). Hyŏn superimposes on his realist "life as it is" technique a vision of fate as controlling force—Korean naturalism. Circumstances always contrive to lead the hero to inevitable destruction. In terms of storytelling skills, Hyŏn was perhaps the most talented writer of his generation. "A Lucky Day" recounts the tragedy of a rickshaw man with all the pathos of Chekhov.

Yŏm Sangsŏp's early work—"The Tree Frog in the Specimen Room" (P'yobonshil ŭi ch'ŏng kaeguri, 1921) is a representative story—has the same morbid sense of oppression by society, the same pessimistic view of life, the same preoccupation with fate as a force that destroys and cannot be changed. However, subsequent work, notably "Death and the Shadow" (Chugŭm kwa kŭ kŭrimja, 1923), "Unforgettable People" (Ijŭl su ŏmnŭn saram tŭl, 1924), and *Three Generations* (Samdae, 1931), the last commonly regarded by Korean critics as one of the best modern Korean novels, reveal a much more objective approach to reality.

—*Kevin O'Rourke*

Bibliography

Ch'ŏn Idu. *Hanguk hyŏndae sosŏl lon* (The Modern Korean Novel). Seoul: Hyŏngsŏl ch'ulp'ansa, 1969.

Hyŏn Chingŏn. "Fire." In Peter H. Lee, trans. and ed., *Flowers of Fire: Twentieth-Century Korean Stories*, 1–9. Honolulu: University Press of Hawai'i, 1974.

——. "A Lucky Day." In Kevin O'Rourke, trans. and ed., *Ten Korean Short Stories*, 211–224. Seoul: Yonsei University Press, 1997.

——. "A Society That Drives You to Drink." In Kim Chong-un and Bruce Fulton, trans. and eds., *A Ready-Made Life: Early Masters of Modern Korean Fiction*, 7–16. Honolulu: University of Hawai'i Press, 1998.

Kim Tongin. "Potatoes." In Kevin O'Rourke, trans. and ed., *A Washed-Out Dream*, 272–285. New York: Larchwood, 1980.

——. "The Seaman's Chant." In Suh Ji-moon, trans. and ed., *The Rainy Spell and Other Korean Stories*, rev. ed., 10–24. Armonk, N.Y.: M. E. Sharpe, 1998.

Paek Ch'ŏl. *Pip'yŏng ŭi ihae* (Understanding Criticism). Seoul: Minjung sŏgwan, 1968.

110

CHŎNG CHIYONG

Chŏng Chiyong was born to a Catholic family in Ch'ungch'ŏng Province in 1902. He was married when he was twelve and attended Hwimun Secondary School in Seoul. In 1922 he went to Japan for university studies in English literature, writing a thesis on William Blake. He began publishing poetry in earnest in 1926, and upon returning to Korea in 1929 he taught English at his high school alma mater. In 1950 he was apparently kidnapped to North Korea. Until 1987, publishers in South Korea were forbidden to publish his poems.

Chŏng's poems express attitudes that Koreans have long treasured as their own: a loving closeness to nature and other human beings; an appreciation of truths implicit in the heart's longing; a fondness for playful humor and childlike wonder; a tendency toward indirectness and ambiguity; and a predilection for drawing beauty out of the ordinary. Chŏng draws the reader into a particular locale whose horizons, nonetheless, are universal. The affection, longing, humor, and wonder that characterize his work are rooted in commonplaces of the human heart.

The poems fall into four periods. The first (1922–28), his student years, is represented by fifty-four poems; the second (1929–35), his early teaching years, by forty-seven poems; the third (1936–42), his later teaching years, by twenty-nine poems; and the fourth (1945–50), the years after liberation, by only nine poems. The poems of the first period express a fond attachment to one's home village and loved ones. Personal feeling finds embodiment in scenes blended from realistic description, metaphors, and evocative symbolist details, all of which are reinforced by graceful rhythmic cadences. The highly treasured "Nostalgia" (Hyangsu, 1927) fondly recalls

> The place where a rill, babbling old tales,
> Meanders on eastward toward the end of a broad plain
> And a mottled bull ox lows
> In dusk's plaintive tones of golden indolence—

In poems such as "Little Sister and the Setting Sun" (Chinŭn hae, 1926), child-like voices give utterance to the warmth of family ties and the poignancy of loss in a series of naive Blakean poems. In the symbolist "A Pomegranate" (Sŏngnyu, 1927), bonds of affection glow with sensuality and latent sexuality.

Many poems of the first and second periods express a strong attraction for nature, especially the sea, which often provides a setting for solitary musing. In "A Dream of Windblown Waves 1" (P'ungnang mong, 1927), the poet marshals a series of long rhythmic cadences fashioned from evocative images of solitude and longing that are alive with wonder. In the haiku-like "Winter" (Kyŏul, 1930) and other short poems, he likewise presents the sea as a focus of solitude, longing, and mystery, but in much simpler fashion. In "The Sea 6" (Pada 6, 1930), he uses imagist techniques to give a taste of the physicality of the sea:

> Amid rock crannies fragrant with sea weed,
> Azalea-colored clams bask in the sun,
> While gliding blue terns wheel on their wings
> In the glasslike sky.

In the second period, ties of human affection give center stage to solitude, and the sea yields to the night sky as the most common backdrop for nostalgic solitude. Pride of place belongs to a series of night poems in which the sinuous realist-symbolist cadences of the best early poems become more compact and chiseled in the imagist manner. The silken dream monologue of "A Reed Flute" (P'iri, 1930) evokes the magic and nostalgia of a lone moonlit night. The compact, tangled night cry of "Window 1" (Yurich'ang 1, 1930) expresses the poet's turmoil at the death of his child. The solitary speaker of this poem appears many times over the next twelve years, peering from a window up at the night sky. The dreamy lullaby lyric "Stars 2" (Pyŏl 2, 1941) presents the speaker as filled with a longing that finds fulfillment in the utter wonder of the night stars:

> Washed in cold water
> Spilling gold dust—
> the silver currents of the Milky Way!

"Window" (Ch'ang, 1942), the epitome of the lean, evocative style of the third period, expresses a longing for darkness itself, a nocturnal darkness "lovely like vapor."

In the third and last of Chŏng's main periods, the mountains that hover in the background of earlier poems advance to the fore. The poet sets aside the mask of a child, but still speaks with a child's fond fancy and loving wonder. We find whimsical verse vignettes of nature in the mountain sun and prose poems of life in the rugged solitude and mystery of the mountains at night.

Less rich in emotional warmth than earlier poems, but charged with sudden sparks of wonder, the verse poems are gemlike imagist mosaics of nature under the mountain sun that demonstrate the poet's skill with vivid, concise, evocative language at his best. A few of these poems are more picturesque than profound, but in poems such as "Piro Peak 1" (Pirobong 1, 1933), eye-catching description, inventive fancy, and enigmatic symbols crystallize in moments of mystical awe.

The mountain prose poems that appeared between 1938 and 1941 are the crown of Chŏng's achievement. Their compact, rustic style transmutes a vivid naturalism, playful fancy, and symbolist evocativeness into a world of mountain magic. Western readers will be taken aback if they expect to find in these prose poems the stylized grace of a Tang dynasty poem or a Korean *shijo*. They are the equal of his most graceful poems in freshness of fancy and depth of feeling, but they represent a Korean aesthetic that seeks beauty not in refinement and elegance but in things commonplace and rough. Poems such as "Hot Springs" (Onjŏng, 1938) project an ambiguously nuanced world in which feelings of solitude, fellowship, and warmth inside are cradled in the forbidding cold and soothing wonder of a winter night outside.

Though Chŏng's poetry was long banned in South Korea on the grounds of his supposedly leftist ideas, his poems are remarkably free of the burden of conceptual thought. They are also free of sentimentality and "poetic" diction. Termed a "modernist" and "the first modern Korean poet," he showed fellow poets the way to mold the language of the common people into vibrant, well-crafted lyrics. He was a leading figure in the Shimunhak (Poetry) school, which fostered pure poetry in the early 1930s, and he later promoted the Ch'ŏngnok (Green) poets—Pak Tujin, Pak Mogwŏl, and Cho Chihun.

—Daniel Kister

Bibliography

Chŏng Chiyong. *Chŏng Chiyong chŏnjip* (Collected Works of Chŏng Chiyong). Seoul: Minŭm sa, 1988.

——. *Distant Valleys: Poems of Chŏng Chiyong.* Trans. Daniel A. Kister. Berkeley: Asian Humanities Press, 1994.

111

YI SANG

The startling poetry, short stories, and anecdotal essays that earned Yi Sang (1910–1937) a reputation as the most daring experimentalist of Korean literary modernism were all published during the last few years of his brief life. The popularity of his work among university students, the rapidly growing body of scholarship on his work since the 1960s, and the frequency with which Yi Sang is depicted in South Korean artistic and popular culture attest to the recurring value of his work as a rebellion against lifeless social conventions and commodification, an endlessly intriguing conundrum, and a source of ironically romantic renewal in a culture that has undergone tremendous tumult during most of the preceding century.

Yi Sang (one of the pen names of Kim Haegyŏng) was also an award-winning visual artist with a degree in architecture from the most demanding polytechnic institute in Kyŏngsŏng (Seoul). His first literary publications were maddeningly recursive and abstract poems written in Japanese that incorporated diagrams, number charts, and mathematical equations that showed the influence of Dada, the special theory of relativity, Bauhaus treatments of space, and the poetics of Japanese modernists such as Haruyama Yukio. These initial experiments laid the foundation for much of Yi Sang's later poetry and appeared in the official journal of the colonial government-general's department of public works, where he was employed as an architectural engineer. After poor health forced him to leave this post, Yi Sang published in such Korean-language periodicals as *Morning Light (Chogwang)*, *Catholic Youth (K'at'ollik ch'ŏngnyŏn)*, *Woman*

(Yŏsŏng), and *The Korea Daily News* (*Chosŏn ilbo*), making brilliant contributions to each genre in which he wrote. His travel essays, for instance, with their alternation between erudite irony and sentimentality, convoluted self-reference and sharp social observation, both parodied and reinvigorated the form. They include such works as "Lingering Thoughts from a Mountain Village" (Sanch'on yŏjŏng, 1935), "Boredom" (Kwŏnt'ae, 1937), and "Tokyo" (Tonggyŏng, 1939). Yi Sang's most widely read work is a short story, "Wings" (Nalgae, 1936), that was both praised and ostracized by critics of the time for its extensive use of stream-of-consciousness technique and ironic depiction of the desperate relationship between a listless, willfully ignorant intellectual and his prostitute wife.

It is the poems of "Crow's-Eye Views" (Ogamdo, 1934), however, that provoked the most controversy when they began to appear in the *Chosŏn ilbo*. Their rejection of lyricism, consistency of viewpoint, and conventional symbolism, grammar, and punctuation caused so much bewilderment and indignation that the series had to be canceled lest the newspaper lose too many subscribers and editors. Such reactions did not prevent Yi Sang from building a distinctive body of work that continually challenged literary assumptions, constraints on sexuality and psychological association, and various discursive pieties, including his own societal role as debauched genius. It is in his work that radical forms of modernism and its associated lifestyles under Japanese colonial rule attain their utmost audacity and alienation. (These qualities are also strikingly conveyed in Yi Sang's illustrations of urban life for both his own writing and that of authors such as Pak T'aewŏn, a close friend and fellow member of the Kuinhoe [Circle of Nine] literary coterie.) Writing during a time when political resistance was being ruthlessly extirpated in both Japan and its Korean colony, Yi Sang explored alternative means of being unruly. He cleverly exploited channels that colonial modernization had, in fact, stimulated through translation, new mass media, and an emerging cosmopolitan commodity culture's aesthetics of speed, collage, mechanization, ephemerality, and Western fashion and eroticism. The prose poem "Paper Memorial Stone" (Chibi, 1936) is typical of Yi Sang's combination of difficult grammatical structure, odd imagery, and a romantic defiance that questions visions of rational progress, even as the poem makes strident use of new form:

> because i'm tall my legs are long my left leg's lame and my wife is small so her legs are short and her right leg's lame and so my right leg with my wife's left leg if that pair of sound legs goes walking like one person ahhh this Husband and Wife end up a cripple that no one can help the whole Problem Free World is a Hospital and its Cure-awaiting Absence of Illness will definitely persist right up to the end.

Thus, it is important to remember that Yi Sang, though commemorated as an iconoclast, often described himself as existing *between* modernity and tradition, between the future and an older "solemn morality ... flowing like menacing blood in [his] veins"; in a letter to the poet and critic Kim Kirim, Yi Sang deemed himself a "vagrant who slipped into a crack between the centuries with the sole intent of collapsing there." "Poem No. II" of "Crow's-Eye Views" expresses a similar fatalism in a style that reflects his poetry's deep engagement with mechanistic replication and breakdown, whether linguistic, intergenerational, or psychological:

> when my father dozes off beside me i become my father and also i become my father's father and even so while my father like my father is just my father why do i repeatedly my father's father's father's ... when i become a father why must i lopingly leap over my father and why am i that which while finally playing all at once my and my father's and my father's father's and my father's father's father's roles must live?

Two other frequently anthologized poems are "Mirror" (Kŏul, 1933) and "Flowering Tree" (Kkot namu, 1933). As interpretations influenced by the psychoanalytic theories of Jacques Lacan and Julia Kristeva have shown (Kim Sŭnghŭi 1998; Lew 1995), the mirror symbolism and acts of doubling in these and other poems trenchantly depict how the self's "reflection"—which, in Lacanian terms, is a formative misrecognition in or across a supposedly mirroring Other—can unify subjectivity only by alienating it; as the narrator of "Mirror" asserts: "Because of the mirror I can't touch the mirror's I but if it were not a mirror / How could I've ever done something like meet myself in a mirror?"

Several lesser-known groups of poems are as bizarre and quizzical as "Crow's-Eye Views." These include three groups published in 1936: the "Chibi" series, "Fortune Telling" (Yŏktan), and "Critical Condition" (Widok). Many of these poems explore the particular recursive possibilities of Korean grammar and its compendious, richly nuanced lexicon, as in the twisting, syncopated sentences of "Soyŏng Problems" (Soyŏng wije, 1934). For all their pranks and absurdist humor, the poems' use of modulated repetition, highly hypothetical or abstract situations, and scientific and mathematical terminology constitute a rigorous probing and performance of how identity and separation, imitation and divergence, and knowing and repression are produced at many levels. In doing so they reveal the frailness of conventional distinctions between emotion and pose, signified and signifier, original and copy, masculine and feminine, and even person and person.

Yi Sang's most widely read stories relate narratives of mistrust, idleness, and urban anomie, typically through characters betrayed by their lovers, exhausted by disease or debilitating labor, or susceptible to thoughts of suicide. This group includes the canonical "Wings," "Record of a Consummation" (Pongbyŏlgi, 1936), "Children" (or "Child Skeletons"; Tonghae, 1937), "Summation of a Life" (Chongsaenggi, 1937), "Phantom Illusion" (Hwanshigi, 1938), and "Lost

Flower" (Shilhwa, 1939), among others. They use clipped language, an often farcical wit, nimble segueing of scenes, and sudden confusions of the narrator's identity with that of other characters or "Yi Sang" himself. Allusions range from classical Chinese poetry and philosophy to Hollywood films, phonograph recordings of Korean and foreign music, and both Eastern and Western modern literatures. The memorable opening paragraphs of "Wings" raise the hope of a new life (here equated with new writing and new love) regardless of the deceit, decay, and derangement already suffered by the speaker and his lover:

> Have you heard about "the genius who ended up a stuffed specimen"? I'm thrilled. At moments like this, even love is thrilling.
>
> Only when the body crumples in exhaustion is the mind bright as a silver coin. Whenever nicotine sinks into the worm-ridden coil of my intestines, a clean sheet of paper is ready in my head. On it I line up wit and paradox like *paduk* stones. Sick with despicable common sense.
>
> Once again I draw up plans for life with a woman. One who's become clumsy at love-making, who's peeked at the peak of knowledge, that is, a kind of schizophrenic. To be in receipt of just half—which would be half of everything—of such a woman, that's the life for which I'm drawing up plans. I'll dip but one foot in that life and like two suns we'll stare away at each other, giggling and giggling. Maybe everything in life was so bland I couldn't put up with it anymore and just quit. *Goodbye.*

As the story progresses, however, the narrator's wife, pretending to give him aspirin for his cold, drugs him with sleeping pills so that she can carry on her activities as a prostitute in the adjoining room—work of a nature that, along with the fact that it provides for the narrator's own survival, he only gradually comes to understand. In a final epiphany that has influenced much subsequent Korean literature and film, the narrator stands alone on the roof of a Japanese department store in downtown Seoul after fleeing yet again his wife's cruel insults; he suddenly imagines new wings sprouting from his armpits that might lift him beyond the hellish world of commerce below:

> At that point, the noon siren cried out: *Duu-u—!* People looked like chickens unfolding their four wings and flapping around and in that instant, when all sorts of glass, steel, marble, money, ink seemed to bubble and whirl up, the noon attained the zenith of its dazzling splendor.
>
> All of a sudden, I feel an itch under my arms. Aha! The itching is a trace of where my artificial wings once sprouted. The vanished wings, pages from which my hopes and ambition have been erased, flash in my mind like a leafed-through dictionary.
>
> I want to halt the steps I've taken and just once shout out somewhere: "Wings! Rise up again!"

Thematically continuous with the depiction in "Wings" of betrayal and jealousy between a male narrator and his prostitute lover, "Record of a Consummation" is a marvel of narrative compression and elision that ends surprisingly with a tearful exchange of verses from ardent Korean folk songs. The underappreciated achievements of "Lost Flower" include image-linked cross-cutting between scenes in Seoul and Tokyo, perhaps related to Yi Sang's interest at one point in writing film scenarios.

Yi Sang's most famous essays are ruminations on trips he took to rural P'yŏngan Province, either as temporary respites from Seoul or in hopes of alleviating his consumptive condition. The droll "Boredom" and erudite yet anxiety-ridden "Lingering Thoughts from a Mountain Village" bring attention to the particular nature of the confrontation between the urban and agrarian and between the metropole and colony that was taking place at that point in Korea's history. In both cases, the initial confidence and condescending attitude toward village life of the bohemian narrator sojourning in the countryside are shaken by his sense of the vulnerability of all Koreans to political and economic transformations emerging in the landscape, as personified in a detective and representatives of the colonial government's agrarian reform programs. In "Tokyo," the narrator performs an inverse act: the colonized subject travels to the metropole only to find it vulgar, miasmic, and pathetically anxious to emulate Western development.

Born in Seoul the year of Japan's annexation of Korea, Yi Sang was arrested as a *futei Senjin* (Japanese for "unlawful Korean") during his one sojourn in Tokyo. He died there at the age of twenty-six soon after his release from prison. This severe framing makes it important to interpret dimensions of his work as political allegory (Choi 1999; Em 1995). Most of the copious criticism produced to date, however, follows diverse other paths. These include attempts to establish accurate texts and track down allusions; psychoanalytic interpretations of the works' relations to the author's childhood; explanations of the scientific, formal logical, and mathematical concepts used in the poetry; studies of Yi Sang's orthography and his pioneering manipulation of typefaces and graphic design; illumination of certain poems as homoerotic palimpsests; applications of Walter Benjamin's concept of the *flâneur* and modern shock to Yi Sang's descriptions of streets and other urban spaces; utilization of Pierre Bourdieu's theory of fields of cultural production to help understand both Yi Sang's relation to the Circle of Nine and that coterie's function within the larger system of modern Korean literature; use of Mikhail Bakhtin's and Kristeva's theories of intertextuality to decode subtexts; and the reframing of works not only as Korean national literature but also as part of a new Japanese literature that emerged across the empire. (For an introduction to the variety of work that has been done by Korean, Japanese, and American critics, see the essay collections edited by Kim Yunshik [1995, 2001] and the *Yi Sang Review*, an annual journal founded in 2001.)

Amid all this scholarly activity, however, one should keep in mind that Yi Sang's renunciation of unified lyricism and his relations to Dada, Chuang-tzu, and mathematical abstraction make it inappropriate to reduce his work to any single message or ideology. As implied in the title, Yi Sang's architectonically precise "Crow's-Eye Views" may have been drawn from the perspective of a shunned omen who looked coldly askance at any hope for complete answers. The opening section of "Lost Flower" succinctly states that "for someone to have no secrets is to be as destitute and miserable as having no possessions." If so, then Yi Sang's cryptic writing has proven to be prosperous indeed: a richly intriguing mirror that never allows thieves complete entry into its other side.

—Walter K. Lew

Bibliography

Choi Won-shik. "Seoul, Tokyo, New York: Modern Korean Literature Seen through Yi Sang's 'Lost Flowers.'" *Korea Journal* 39, no. 4 (1999): 118–143.

Em, Henry H. "Yi Sang's 'Wings' Read As an Anti-Colonial Allegory." *Muae* 1 (1995): 104–111.

Kim Sŭnghŭi. *Yi Sang shi yŏngu* (A Study of the Poems of Yi Sang). Seoul: Pogo sa, 1998.

Kim Yunshik, ed. *Purok: Yi Sang yŏngu e kwanhan taep'yojŏk nonmun moŭm* (Major Critical Essays on Yi Sang Research), vols. 4 and 5. Seoul: Munhak sasang sa, 1995, 2001.

Lew, Walter K. "A Crow's-Eye View: Selections from the Poetry of Yi Sang." *Korean Culture* 13, no. 4 (1992): 33–40.

———. "Jean Cocteau in the Looking Glass: A Homotextual Reading of Yi Sang's Mirror Poems." *Muae* 1 (1995): 118–149.

Yi Sang. "Crow's-Eye Views: Poem No. I." Trans. Kathleen L. McCarthy. *Muae* 1 (1995): 112.

———. "Crow's-Eye Views: Poems No. II, IV, V, VII, X, XIII, XV." Trans. Walter K. Lew. *Muae* 1 (1995): 78–89, 132, 137–138.

———. "Flowering Tree," "I Wed a Toy Bride," "Crow's-Eye Views: Poems No. I, VI, XI–XII." Trans. Walter K. Lew. *Korean Literature Today* 4, no. 2 (1999): 8–10.

———. "Paper Memorial Stone," "Soyŏng Problems," "Precipice," "Crow's-Eye Views: Poems No. II, III, V, X, XV." Trans. Walter K. Lew. In Jerome Rothenberg and Pierre Joris, eds., *Poems for the Millennium: The University of California Book of Modern & Postmodern Poetry*, vol. 1, 718–723. Berkeley: University of California Press, 1995.

———. "Phantom Illusion." In Kim Chong-un and Bruce Fulton, trans. and eds., *A Ready-Made Life: Early Masters of Modern Korean Fiction*, 172–178. Honolulu: University of Hawai'i Press, 1998.

———. "Record of a Consummation." Trans. Heinz Insu Fenkl and Walter K. Lew. *Koreana* 14, no. 4 (2000): 94–99.

———. "Tokyo." Trans. Michael D. Shin. *Muae* 1 (1995): 96–101.

———. "Wings." Trans. Walter K. Lew and Youngju Ryu. In Bruce Fulton, ed., *Modern Korean Fiction: An Anthology.* New York: Columbia University Press, forthcoming.

———. *Yi Sang munhak chŏnjip* (Complete Literary Works of Yi Sang), vol. 1, *Shi* (Poems). Ed. Yi Sŭnghun. Seoul: Munhak sasang sa, 1989.

———. *Yi Sang munhak chŏnjip* (Complete Literary Works of Yi Sang), vol. 2, *Sosŏl* (Fiction). Ed. Kim Yunshik. Seoul: Munhak sasang sa, 1993.

———. *Yi Sang munhak chŏnjip* (Complete Literary Works of Yi Sang), vol. 3, *Sup'il* (Essays). Ed. Kim Yunshik. Seoul: Munhak sasang sa, 1993.

112

KIM SOWŎL

Kim Sowŏl was born Kim Chŏngshik in 1902 in Kwaksan, a town near Pyong-yang. He attended Osan Middle School, then went to Paejae Academy in Seoul, graduating in 1923. The same year he traveled to Japan to enter Tokyo Commercial College. But perhaps because of a failure in his family's business, he returned to spend the next two years in Seoul living the writer's life. His career failed to develop as he had hoped, so he left Seoul and took up the post of manager of the branch office of the *Tonga ilbo*, a daily newspaper, in Namshi, near his ancestral home. He died in 1934, an apparent suicide.

Sowŏl's one book of poems, *Azaleas* (Chindallae kkot), was published in 1925 to no major notice. His teacher and literary mentor, Kim Ŏk, recalled that he had few friends in the literary world and that he had pursued Korean forms of expression in his poetry at a time when other writers were excitedly trying every new foreign fashion that appeared. The social and literary critic Kim Kijin, re-viewing the year 1926 in poetry in *Kaebyŏk* (Genesis) magazine—where many of Sowŏl's poems had appeared before book publication in 1925—opined that apart from a certain prettiness of expression in the folksong style, there was not much to recommend in Sowŏl's work.

What Kim Kijin missed was the whole point of Sowŏl's poetry, its remarkable expressiveness in the Korean language, and its realization of a lyrical voice—one adapting traditional diction, form, images, and rhythm—that simply had no equal in the twentieth century. The complex mix of open and closed vowels and syllables in the poem "Azaleas," shifting from the *a, o, i,* and *a* sounds of the first phrase to the regurgitative noise of *yŏkkyŏwŏ* in the second, cannot be duplicated in translation but deepens and enriches the effect of the poem. The story of the cuckoo crying for her lost brothers, and the plaintive sound of her call, in the poem "Cuckoo Bird" (Chŏptongsae, 1923) likewise embodies in Korean something that would be challenging to capture in English, but that resonates strongly with the Korean reader. Kim Ŏk in his remembrance also noted in Sowŏl's poems such technical innovations as the separation of the traditional folksong verse line into its components in the poem "The Road Away" (Kanŭn kil, 1923) and their deployment down across the page in a strikingly new typographical rendering of the verse line:

> Missing you;
> should I say it, I
> would only miss you more.

How did Sowŏl's reputation grow from one of almost complete obscurity to his present position as one of modern Korea's finest poets? For one thing, Kim Ŏk continued to promote his former student's work, publishing a newly edited collection of his poems in 1939. And in the 1960s and 1970s Sowŏl became part of the official literary canon—that is, those writers and literary works taught in the South Korean public schools, incorporated in the annual university entrance examinations, and then studied again in university literature classes. At that time Sowŏl and his poetry were described as having expressed the sad voice of the Korean people during the Japanese colonial occupation. In the 1980s there was some criticism of Sowŏl for his failure to become more directly engaged in the social and political struggle of the Korean people for liberation, an opinion somewhat reminiscent of Kim Kijin's unfriendly comments in 1926. Later in the 1980s writers on Sowŏl began to take notice of his work as an expression of what is called *han*, a term that entered broad usage in Korea only in the 1980s and 1990s, but that is described in at least one Korean-English dictionary as a deeply Korean sentiment of "discontent, regret ... [and] unsatisfied desire."

More significantly, the poems themselves have continued to capture readers with their melancholy, exquisitely apt expression and elegantly simple formal structure. Many have sought to translate the better known of Sowŏl's works; still one of the best efforts is Kim Dong Sung's *Selected Poems of Kim So-wol*, first published in 1956 and still in print, the book that inspired my own interest in the poet. His rendering of Sowŏl's "Azaleas" follows:

> If you would go,
> Tiring of me,
> Nothing will I say.
> I shall pick azaleas
> At the Yaksan, Yungbyun,

And deck the path you tread.
Tread gently
on my azaleas
Where the path is decked.
If you would go,
Tiring of me,
No cry shall you hear of mine.

I offer the following version as a token of thanks and appreciation to Kim Dong Sung, and by way of suggesting that a poem that provokes such various readings is precisely the kind that will survive our efforts to put it into English.

When you're sick of it
and want to get out of it
Go ahead, I won't say anything about it.
I'll go to Yaksan in Yŏngbyŏn,
for those azaleas,
and pick a bunch to scatter on your path.
Every step you take
on those flowers, lying there:
Step on them, press on them, just go ahead and do it.
When you're sick of it
and want to get out of it,
I won't let it kill me, and I won't shed a tear.

—*David R. McCann*

Bibliography

Kim Sowŏl. *Selected Poems of Kim So-wol.* Ed. Kim Dong Sung. Seoul: Sung Moon Gak, 1956.

113

CH'AE MANSHIK

Ch'ae Manshik—fiction writer, playwright, essayist, critic—was born in a coastal village in North Chŏlla Province in 1902. Like many of the intellectuals of his generation, he studied for a time in Japan, then returned to Korea to work at a succession of writing and editorial jobs. He died of tuberculosis in 1950.

Ch'ae is one of the great talents of modern Korean literature. His penetrating mind, command of idiom, utterly realistic dialogue, and keen wit produced a fictional style all his own. The immediacy of some of his narratives produces a strong sense of a storyteller speaking to his readers.

Often pigeonholed as a satirist, Ch'ae was much more. Long before such satirical sketches as "My Innocent Uncle" (Ch'isuk, 1938), about a political misfit during the Japanese occupation, and "Mister Pang" (Misŭt'ŏ Pang, 1946), set during the American military occupation, Ch'ae had written *Age of Transition* (Kwadogi, 1923), an autobiographical novella about Korean students in Japan testing the currents of modernization that swept urban East Asia early in the twentieth century. In other early works, such as "In Three Directions" (Segillo, 1924) and "Sandungi" (1930), he dealt with the class differences that are so distinct in Korean society past and present. In these earlier stories, and especially in "A Ready-Made Life" (Redimeidŭ insaeng, 1934), Ch'ae is concerned as well with the plight of the unemployed young intellectuals turned out by the modernization movement—young men who perpetually make the rounds of publishing houses, pawnshops, and cheap bars. Ch'ae was also at home depicting the rural underclass, so long suppressed as to be almost incapable of autonomous action, in stories such as "On a Train" (Ch'ajung esŏ, 1941). *Peace under Heaven* (T'aep'yŏng ch'ŏnha, 1938), on the other hand, is a pointed treatment of traditional Korean etiquette in the person of one who thrived materially but wasted spiritually during the Japanese occupation. It has been acclaimed one of the great Korean novels.

Ch'ae's later works are somewhat more muted and introspective. In these stories the author's wit is tempered by the spiritual turmoil of having to come to grips with the role of the artist in a colonized society. "Public Offender" (Minjok ŭi choein, 1948–49), for example, is a semiautobiographical apologia for those branded as collaborators for their failure to actively oppose Japanese colonial rule. "Constable Maeng" (Maeng sunsa, 1946) satirizes Koreans who served as police officers during the Japanese occupation. "Once upon a Paddy" (Non iyagi, 1940), ostensibly about changes in landholding patterns during the colonial period, asks if the situation of Korean peasants under Japanese rule was any worse than their lot during the last decades of the Chosŏn kingdom (1392–1910). "The Wife and Children" (Ch'ŏja, 1948) portrays a man who finds himself out of political favor after the liberation. The man's exile from his family echoes not only premodern Korean history, in which victims of factional infighting in the capital were frequently banished to the countryside, but also contemporary history, with its record of house arrests of dissident politicians. In this and other works Ch'ae also offers keen insights into the long-standing oppression of Korean women.

—Bruce Fulton

Bibliography

Ch'ae Manshik. "Constable Maeng." Trans. Joel Stevenson. *Acta Koreana* 2 (1999): 145–152.
——. "Mister Pang." Trans. Bruce and Ju-Chan Fulton. *Asian Pacific Quarterly* (Winter 1994): 80–87.
——. "My Innocent Uncle." Trans. Bruce and Ju-Chan Fulton. In Bruce Fulton, ed., *Modern Korean Fiction: An Anthology*. New York: Columbia University Press, forthcoming.
——. "Once upon a Paddy." Trans. Robert Armstrong. In Bruce Fulton, ed., *My Innocent Uncle*, 83–117. Seoul: Jimoondang, 2003.
——. *Peace under Heaven*. Trans. Chun Kyung-Ja. Armonk, N.Y.: M. E. Sharpe, 1993.
——. "A Ready-Made Life." In Kim Chong-un and Bruce Fulton, trans. and eds., *A Ready-Made Life: Early Masters of Modern Korean Fiction*, 55–80. Honolulu: University of Hawai'i Press, 1998.
——. "The Wife and Children." Trans. Bruce and Ju-Chan Fulton. In Marshall R. Pihl and Bruce and Ju-Chan Fulton, eds., *Land of Exile: Contemporary Korean Fiction*, 3–14. Armonk, N.Y.: M. E. Sharpe, 1993.

114

THE UNENCUMBERED IN SŎ CHŎNGJU

There is general agreement in the Korean world of letters that Sŏ Chŏngju (1915–2000) is the most important Korean poet of the twentieth century. The appeal of his work rests first in his use of language, so distinctively that of his native Chŏlla Province; second in the sensuality apparent particularly in his earlier work, which has evoked comparisons with Baudelaire and Yeats; and third in his return to the spirit of the Shilla kingdom (?57 b.c.–a.d. 935) in the later work for the values he believes should inform contemporary Korea.

Sŏ Chŏngju has defined his stance as poet very clearly. He insists on poetry as discourse that records the movements of the heart rather than the head: an account of feelings in moments of great intensity, illustrations rather than definitions of how the wise man lives life at its most intense. Human nature is his major concern, not language or Western artistic ideas. He sees man as in danger of losing his humanity, and he sees the poet as driven by the need to get back to his original nature.

In the early poems Sŏ Chŏngju is cultivating sensation for its own sake, seeking therein a heightened human awareness, in the tradition of Baudelaire, Oscar Wilde, and the decadent movement at the end of the last century in Europe. Life itself is the supreme art form; good and bad are irrelevant. Sŏ Chŏngju sees man as at his most quintessentially human in the sensual, experiencing life at its deepest. In the later poems the focus changes from the purely sensual to a broader concentration on exquisite Zen moments of insight—golden moments of experience when the poet sees deeply into himself and into the heart of things. Much of the early modern poetry tradition in Korea filtered in through Japanese translations of Arthur Symons's ideas on symbolism, and his preoccupation with "moods." Sŏ Chŏngju, however, shows no overt awareness of this, presumably because the insights achieved by the French symbolists into the nature of poetic discourse were commonplace in Tang and Song China and in Korea's Koryŏ kingdom. Sŏ Chŏngju comes at his material from another direction. His approach is Buddhist, based on the Korean *hanshi* (poems in Chinese by Korean poets) tradition. He presents an ideal, illustrates this ideal with flamboyant examples, and suggests that many men have zenlike transcendent moments of experience when they are enabled to approach this ideal. He shows no awareness of the English tradition of a poetry of golden moments that runs through Wordsworth, Hardy, Symons, Yeats, and some of the best English-language poets of the twentieth century, notably Larkin and Heaney. In modern terms, Sŏ Chŏngju's ideal is the spirit of the "unencumbered," a sort of emotional and intellectual flexibility or largesse that allows a person to experience life to the full. Being unencumbered demands a complete emptying of the self. There is no question here of moral categories: the central thrust is on experience and emotional response. "A Flower Blooming" explains the notion:

> You must rinse even the water
> from the bowl: just leave
> the empty bowl.
> And with the most gossamer cloud you must part.
> Bright red flowers bloom in the sunlight,
> mere optical illusions,
> illusions folded twice, thrice:
> tiny shadowed figments of the mind.

This sort of inner cleansing is Buddhist as Sŏ Chŏngju conceives it, but adepts of mystical practices East and West will recognize common ground here.

"The Old Man's Flower Song," an imaginative reworking and expansion of a famous Shilla *hyangga* poem, illustrates what it means to be unencumbered. Sŏ Chŏngju tells the story of the beautiful Lady Suro, how she was captivated by a bunch of azaleas perched perilously on top of a sheer cliff, how her insensitive husband shows no reaction to her need, and how an old man, "utterly unconnected," who happens to pass by, gallantly plucks the azaleas for her. Sŏ Chŏngju's version emphasizes the inadequacies of Lady Suro's husband and retinue, the failure of their emotional response, and the sharply contrasting generous free spirit of the old man:

> The woman rode
> with her horseman husband and company.

> " ... those flowers are so beautiful,
> I wish I.... "
> She seemed to speak to the flowers,
> to the company, to the air.
> Thus the wife,
> angled slightly on her horse.
> The husband, fool that he was, made no response,
> while the company reacted as if her words
> had rolled from their ears.
> The old man, passing by,
> utterly unconnected,
> cocked his ears
> and acceded to her request.

The transcendence of the old man is presented not as the norm but as an ideal in a nonideal world:

> His was the heart of a flower
> that laughs when it sees a flower,
> the heart of the unencumbered.

Husband and retinue are encumbered, and the implication is that most men are encumbered. They fail in their humanity, as most men fail, because they are encumbered. "The Old Man's Flower Song" has a special emotional complexity in that the old man is not the only representative of the ideal: Lady Suro, whom the old man recognizes as a "flower," is herself an example of the "unencumbered." Being unencumbered is a spiritual quality, an opening of the heart to emotional response, which enables one to be above life while experiencing life's full intensity.

What is the typical Sŏ Chŏngju methodology? He takes a vignette from the thirteenth-century *Memorabilia of the Three Kingdoms* (Samguk yusa), an anecdote from Old Chosŏn (trad. 2333 B.C.–?), an old legend or custom from his home in Chilmajae, and lets his imagination play around with it in the way Yeats lets imagination work in "Lapis Lazuli" or Keats plays with imagination in "Ode to a Grecian Urn." Always he is looking for the "unencumbered" or transcendent, or the lack of these qualities, not so much to establish the claims of a transcendent "other" world, as to demonstrate models of how to cope with the real world. If one were asked to name one quality all Sŏ Chŏngju's "unencumbered" have, it would have to be an extraordinary courage. Sŏ Chŏngju's poems are illustrations of the courage to drink life to the full and the courage to meet death when it comes with the same equanimity. Sŏ Chŏngju is an extraordinary poet; the tragedy is that he died without the West's being aware of his genius.

—*Kevin O'Rourke*

Bibliography

O'Rourke, Kevin, trans. and ed. *Looking for the Cow: Modern Korean Poems.* Dublin: Dedalus, 1999.

Sŏ Chŏngju. *Midang So Chong Ju: The Early Lyrics, 1941–1960.* Trans. Brother Anthony of Taizé. London: Forest Books, 1993.

——. *Poems of a Wanderer: Selected Poems of Midang So Chong-ju.* Trans. Kevin O'Rourke. Dublin: Dedalus, 1995.

——. "Sŏ Chŏngju: Winter Sky." Trans. David McCann. *Quarterly Review of Literature* (1981): 82–83.

——. *Unforgettable Things: Poems by Sŏ Chŏngju.* Trans. David McCann. Seoul: Sisa-yong-o-sa, 1986.

115

HWANG SUNWŎN

Hwang Sunwŏn was born in 1915 near Pyongyang in present-day North Korea and was educated there and at Waseda University in Tokyo, where he read widely in world literature. He was barely in his twenties when he produced two volumes of poetry, and in 1940 his first volume of stories was published. He subsequently concentrated on fiction, turning out seven novels and more than one hundred stories. In his later years he came full circle: his last published works (1992) were poems. He died in 2000.

In 1946, in the midst of the radical land reform instituted in the Soviet-occupied northern sector of Korea—the backdrop for his 1954 novel *The Descendants of Cain* (K'ain ŭi huye)—Hwang, a member of a landed family, left with his parents, wife, and children for the American-occupied South. There, in September of that year, he began teaching at Seoul High School. Like millions of other Koreans, the Hwang family was displaced by the civil war of 1950–53. Returning to Seoul, Hwang resumed teaching, and from 1957 to 1993 he taught creative writing at Kyung Hee University.

Hwang is the author of some of the best-known stories of modern Korea: "The Stars" (Pyŏl, 1940), "An Old Man's Birthday" (Hwang noin, 1942), "The Old Potter" (Tok chinnŭn nŭlgŭni, 1944), "Cranes" (Hak, 1953), and "The Cloudburst" (Sonagi, 1952), among others. In a creative burst in the mid-1950s he produced the story collection *Lost Souls* (Irŏbŏrin saram tŭl). This volume, a series of variations on the theme of the outcast in a highly structured society, is unique among Hwang's story collections for its thematic unity.

In the 1950s Hwang also began publishing novels. During the next two decades he produced his most important work in this genre. *Trees on a Slope* (Namu tŭl pit'al e sŏda, 1960), perhaps his most successful novel, deals with the effects of the civil war on three young soldiers. *The Sun and the Moon* (Irwŏl, 1965) is a portrait of a young intellectual coming to terms with the belated realization that he is a *paekchŏng* (untouchable). *The Moving Castle* (Umjiginŭn sŏng, 1972) is an ambitious effort to synthesize Western influence and native tradition in modern Korea.

In the 1960s and 1970s Hwang's short fiction became more experimental. Some of his most memorable and challenging stories date from this period: "Conversation in June about Mothers" (Ŏmŏni ka innŭn yuwŏl ŭi taehwa, 1965), "The Curtain Fell, but Then ... " (Mak ŭn naeryŏnnŭnde, 1968), "A Numerical Enigma" (Sutcha p'uri, 1974). Hwang's creative powers were undiminished as late as the 1980s, as the highly original "A Shadow Solution" (Kŭrimja p'uri, 1984) demonstrates.

The length of Hwang's literary career, spanning seven decades, is virtually unparalleled in Korean letters. But it is his craftsmanship that sets Hwang apart from his peers. It is safe to say that Hwang is *the* consummate short story writer of twentieth-century Korea. His command of dialect, his facility with both rural and urban settings, his variety of narrative techniques, his vivid artistic imagination, his diverse constellation of characters, and his insights into human personality make Hwang at once a complete writer and one who is almost impossible to categorize. Modern Korea has produced a number of short story masters, indeed prides itself on its accomplishments in that genre, but Hwang stands above them all. There are a number of reasons for this.

First of all, Hwang is one of the great storytellers of modern Korea. As such, he has gone against the grain of much of modern Korean fiction, especially post-1945 fiction, which is to a large extent an issue-driven literature (see "Pure Literature versus the Literature of Engagement"). That is, many writers select an issue or problem, then develop a story around it. A prominent example of this in post–Korean War fiction is *pundan munhak*—the literature inspired by the territorial division of the peninsula (see "The Literature of Territorial Division"). Hwang's tendency, however, is to start with a story and allow issues, such as they are, to unfold from it.

Second, Hwang's command of the Korean language is enviable. Whether he is using Sino-Korean or native vocabulary, the standard speech of Seoul or one of several dialects (including his own, that of P'yŏngan Province), whether he is phrasing dialogue in direct or indirect speech, he has a knack of finding the right word or expression. His style, moreover, is for the most part economical; he wastes few words and, except when he uses repetition to establish a narrative rhythm or parallelism, rarely repeats himself. This approach stands in sharp contrast with the discursive, rambling style employed by many Korean writers of more recent times.

Not surprisingly, Hwang's mastery of Korean and his precision of style make his stories more amenable to English translation. This is not to say that they are easy to translate. Although the lexical problems are comparatively few, Hwang's stories resonate on several levels. They are rich in symbols, dreams, implications, and other subtleties. Word choices in English are therefore crucial. The translator who fails to capture these subtleties risks producing a skeletal translation, one that, though accurate, lacks depth.

Also appealing is the great variety of Hwang's hundred-plus stories. They range from the naturalistic to the surreal. Their settings are rural or urban, mountain or seaside, sometimes specifically Korean and, more often in his early stories, sometimes culturally nonspecific. Some stories are autobiographical but the majority are told in the third person. Among the latter, the protagonists range from children to the elderly to animals, from the educated to the uneducated. Hwang is attentive to local customs and dialect and knowledgeable about Korean folktales and occasionally incorporates these to good effect.

Finally, Hwang was a perfectionist. He observed a regular writing schedule, working on one story at a time and then returning to revise and edit before first publication. He was known even to revised published versions of his stories for subsequent editions. During the late years of the Japanese occupation, when Koreans were forbidden to publish in their own language, Hwang would gather his friends at his rural home and read aloud to them drafts of his stories—a practice that may help account for the pitch-perfect dialogue of many of those early stories.

Hwang Sunwŏn is the Korean short-fiction writer of transcendence. He was solidly rooted in Korean tradition, but instead of being bound by it, he was able to incorporate that tradition into a broader creative vision, such that his artistic imagination continued to develop throughout his long career. More than any other modern Korean fiction writer, Hwang elevated the Korean short story to the world stage.

—Bruce Fulton

Bibliography

Epstein, Stephen J. "Elusive Narrators in Hwang Sun-wŏn." *Korean Studies* 19 (1995): 104–111.

Fulton, Bruce. "Lost Souls." *The World & I* (March 1990): 381–389.

Holman, J. Martin. "A Visit with Hwang Sun-wŏn." *The World & I* (March 1990): 365–369.

Hwang Sunwŏn. "The Cloudburst." In Edward W. Poitras, trans. and ed., *The Stars and Other Korean Short Stories*, 133–148. Hong Kong: Heinemann Asia, 1980.

——. "Conversation in June about Mothers." Trans. Suh Ji-moon. In J. Martin Holman, ed., *The Book of Masks*, 1–5. London: Readers International, 1989.

——. "Cranes." In Kevin O'Rourke, trans. and ed., *A Washed-Out Dream*, 126–135. New York: Larchwood, 1980.

——. "The Curtain Fell, but Then … " Trans. Bruce and Ju-Chan Fulton. In J. Martin Holman, ed., *The Book of Masks*, 141–153. London: Readers International, 1989.

——. *The Descendants of Cain.* Trans. Suh Ji-moon and Julie Pickering. Armonk, N.Y.: M. E. Sharpe, 1997.

——. *The Moving Castle.* Trans. Bruce and Ju-Chan Fulton. Seoul: Si-sa-yong-o-sa, 1985.

——. "A Numerical Enigma." In Edward W. Poitras, trans. and ed., *The Stars and Other Korean Short Stories*, 213–227. Hong Kong: Heinemann Asia, 1980.

——. "An Old Man's Birthday." In Edward W. Poitras, trans. and ed., *The Stars and Other Korean Short Stories*, 100–117. Hong Kong: Heinemann Asia, 1980.

——. "The Old Potter." In Edward W. Poitras, trans. and ed., *The Stars and Other Korean Short Stories*, 118–132. Hong Kong: Heinemann Asia, 1980.

——. "A Shadow Solution." In J. Martin Holman, ed., *Shadows of a Sound*, 203–215. San Francisco: Mercury House, 1990.

——. "The Stars." In Edward W. Poitras, trans. and ed., *The Stars and Other Korean Short Stories*, 81–99. Hong Kong: Heinemann Asia, 1980.

——. *Trees on a Slope.* Trans. Bruce and Ju-Chan Fulton. Honolulu: University of Hawai'i Press, in press.

Kim Chong-un et al., trans. *The Drizzle and Other Korean Short Stories.* Seoul: Si-sa-yong-o-sa, 1983.

Pihl, Marshall R. "Anatomy of a Story." *The World & I* (March 1990): 371–379.

Poitras, Edward W. "Finding the Epic in the Ordinary: Hwang Sun-won and His World." In Edward W. Poitras, trans. and ed., *The Stars and Other Korean Short Stories*, 6–43. Hong Kong: Heinemann Asia, 1980.

116

THE SHORT FICTION OF KIM TONGNI

Known best for his short stories, Kim Tongni (1913–1995) was also recognized for his poetry, and through his writing on literary theory and his participation in literary organizations he played a major role in the formation of Korean literature as we know it today. No other Korean author, with the possible exception of Hwang Sunwŏn, has been translated as much. The settings of his stories are quintessentially Korean and a treasure chest for ethnological study, but his themes are of universal significance.

Kim began his career in literature at a comparatively early age. Already puzzling over immediate and metaphysical questions on the ways that humans dealt with fate, in 1929 he dropped out of his last year at normal school to immerse himself in four years of study of Eastern and Western literature, history, and philosophy to get some answers. In 1934 he debuted as a poet in the *Chosŏn ilbo*, a Seoul daily. The following year saw the publication of his first story, "A Descendant of the Hwarang" (Hwarang ŭi huye). He spent the next couple of years at various Buddhist temples, devoting himself to the continued study and writing of both prose and poetry, coincidentally establishing himself quickly in literary society. During those years he also taught in small academies in the countryside and finally established one himself, but this was closed three years later by the Japanese occupation government because of his anti-occupation activities. By the time of Korea's liberation in 1945, he had become an active and prominent figure in Korea's literary world; with other colleagues he established and led literary organizations and also participated in the turbulent postliberation struggle against leftist writers. Over the next few years he served in senior editorial positions at major nationwide newspapers, and then, despite having never graduated from high school, he began to teach creative writing at universities in the early 1950s and rose in academia to the position of dean of the College of Arts at Seoul's Chungang University. His public life ended with his last lecture at Chungang University in 1989.

The plots of almost all of Kim's stories originate in two historical events: Korea's painful transition from a closed agricultural society to an open industrial one (the process began in the last quarter of the nineteenth century), and the Japanese occupation (1910–45). However, there is no direct mention of the country's transition or of the Japanese in Kim's stories, most of which depict traditional Korea and are populated by commoners in rural settings far from the seats of power in the city.

These denizens of Kim's fictional world live their difficult lives in extremis, and they cross the border from story to epic. Most of his early and much of his later fiction depicts extreme circumstances that intensify and magnify personal events, the first step of a plot's elevation to a universal philosophical theme. An event, though, is epical not in itself but in the questions it raises about humankind. An incident of suicide in a tiny hamlet, for example, becomes a universal theme when its cause is nihilistic rejection of value in life. Kim's tortured characters do crazy, almost implausible things. A husband tries to poison his leper wife ("The Rock" [Pawi, 1936]); two close friends fight for no apparent reason to an apparently senseless end ("Loess Valley" [Hwangt'ogi, 1939]); a mother kills her son and then herself ("The Shaman Painting" [Munyŏdo, 1936]). But Kim's stories are as believable as they are fantastical when we read them in the context of the grueling afflictions that lower-class Koreans experienced in those times, and they take on universal significance by transfixing us with their mythical, epic qualities.

In the first half of his life Kim used his stories to study how humans confront the cruelties that fate dishes out. He pondered over what, if any, value could be found in such a painful existence. He thought, like Camus, that there was one substantial question for us to answer: If this life, which has no value, torments us so, why do we keep on? Why not end it with suicide? His early stories wonder at the possibility and even the sense of living in the face of the nihilistic abyss.

As Kim matured, though, he came to think that life is, after all, worth living. The value that he eventually discovered is to be found in a person's growth into a worthy human being, a participant in "the third humanism." The first humanism was Hellenism, with its focus on reason, and Judaism, with its focus on the God-reflecting nature of the human soul; the second humanism was the Renaissance's reinstatement of the human being in the scheme of things. Kim's third humanism is a dialectical synthesis of the negative demeaning oppression of industrialization with the positive ennobling powers of the West's conscious rationality and the East's unconscious intuition. This synthesis produced Kim's "new human."

Particularly rich literature stimulates volumes of discussion among the critics. Like the plots and story elements of other great writers, Kim's have produced endless debate. One plot will elicit five different identifications of theme, one element in a story will stimulate ten conflicting interpretations of symbolic value. Some critics identify the clash between Christianity and shamanism as the basic theme of "The Shaman Painting," others see a clash between modernity and tradition, others see the inscrutable silence of a supreme being, and yet others perceive a struggle between lust and spirituality. Some interpret Mohwa's death as Christianity's victory over shamanism, others see it as the martyr's salvation of Korea's imperiled identity, still others see it as the consequence of her children's incest. Some insist that good comes of Mohwa's suicide, others see a continued confrontation, and others read it as the author's attempt to have us comprehend it as life's absurd waste of life.

In writing that is so abundant in all sorts of possibilities it is understandable that Kim's readers see so much in so many different ways. "The Shaman Painting" begins:

> Low hills slumbering on night's distant horizon. Broad river winding black across the plain. Sky spangled with stars about to rain down on hills, river and plain as this night approaches its climax. On the broad sandy river bank under a large canopy a crowd of village women held in thrall by a shaman's magic song for a lost soul, sadness and hope in their faces and a weariness that tells of coming dawn. In their midst the shaman caught up in the ecstatic throes of her dance, spinning weightless in her swirling mantle, pure spirit freed of flesh and bone.

At one extreme of scholarly interpretation the night sky, river, stars, climax, the sadness and hope that greet the coming dawn: all of these are symbols conveying one meaning or another bearing on one theme or another. At the other extreme these elements are regarded simply as tools used in describing the painting.

Translators embark on a work of Kim Tongni with eager trepidation. To achieve a true Korean milieu, Kim uses mostly native Korean vocabulary, eschewing the more easily translated Chinese loanwords (and, in effect, limiting the English translator to Anglo-Saxon). He combines consummate skill with spare use of psychological, emotional, and physical description to produce powerful impressions that are very difficult to fully convey with equally spare use of the target language. His plots and symbols so pregnant with meaning, while giving scholars the luxury of endless debate, provide translators a confusing extravagance of possibilities on which to base decisions.

Considering each of his stories' intriguing blend of the local and the universal, and the impossibly rich language he uses to accomplish this blend, it is no wonder that Kim Tongni is venerated by many as the father of modern Korean literature and is one of the most widely read Korean authors outside of Korea.

—*John Holstein*

Bibliography

Kim Tongni. "A Descendant of the *Hwarang*." In Kim Chong-un and Bruce Fulton, trans. and eds., *A Ready-Made Life: Early Masters of Modern Korean Fiction*, 107–120. Honolulu: University of Hawai'i Press, 1998.

——. "Father and Son." In Kim Chong-un, trans. and ed., *Postwar Korean Short Stories*, 2d ed., 1–8. Seoul: Seoul National University Press, 1983.

——. "Loess Valley." Trans. John Holstein. *Korea Journal* (December 1977): 45–57.

——. "The Post Horse Curse." Trans. Marshall R. Pihl. In Marshall R. Pihl and Bruce and Ju-Chan Fulton, eds., *Land of Exile: Contemporary Korean Fiction*, 15–33. Armonk, N.Y.: M. E. Sharpe, 1993.

——. "The Rock." In Kevin O'Rourke, trans. and ed., *A Washed-Out Dream*, 286–300. New York: Larchwood, 1980.

——. "The Shaman Painting." Trans. John Holstein. In Bruce Fulton, ed., *Modern Korean Fiction: An Anthology*. New York: Columbia University Press, forthcoming.

117

THE *WŎLBUK* WRITERS

The term *wŏlbuk* ("gone-north") designates those writers native to what is now South Korea who migrated—or, less commonly, were taken involuntarily—north of the thirty-eighth parallel to present-day North Korea after the liberation of the nation in 1945 from Japanese colonial rule. Among these writers were hardline socialists as well as those who merely sympathized with socialist ideals. Many migrated shortly after liberation in August 1945. A second group left in 1947 and 1948 as separate regimes were established north and south of the thirty-eighth parallel. A few went north with the retreating People's Army in September 1950, during the Korean War, when North Korean military forces were forced to evacuate South Korea in the aftermath of the landing of United Nations forces at the port city of Inchon. And a few others, including such well-known literary figures as prose writer *Yi Kwangsu and poet *Chŏng Chiyong, were taken north against their will.

Consistent with the anticommunist posture of a succession of regimes in postwar South Korea, the works of these authors were banned in that nation until the democratization movement of 1987. Only then were readers in South Korea granted access to the works of fiction writers such as Yi T'aejun, a distinctive stylist; Pak T'aewŏn, one of the few fiction writers to experiment with literary modernism; and Yi Kiyŏng, perhaps the most critically and commercially successful socialist writer in the pre-1945 period; and poets such as Chŏng Chiyong, perhaps the first successful poet of modern Korea.

As in other fields of intellectual activity in the period immediately following liberation, schisms between the ideological left and right opened in literary circles. Leftist writers were themselves divided over the strength of their commitment to socialism, and when in December 1945 the two main leftist writer organizations formed a united front, hardline writer Yi Kiyŏng migrated to the north in protest. He was one of the first to go north. The widening of left–right divisions led to an increasing exodus of writers to the north from late 1946 to mid-1947, and a few remaining writers followed suit around the time of the establishment in 1948 of separate regimes in the north and south.

Yi T'aejun, Pak T'aewŏn, and Yi Kiyŏng are three of the most distinctive voices among the *wŏlbuk* writers. Yi T'aejun (1904–?) wrote essays and children's stories, held editorial positions with literary journals and daily newspapers, and was a member of the influential Kuinhoe (Circle of Nine), but he is best known for his short fiction, written primarily in the 1930s. The protagonist of "Crows" (Kkamagwi, 1936) is an idiosyncratic writer and a throwback to the premodern, self-exiled, rustic man of letters. Crows, snow, and tubercular blood form a stark palette against which a neighbor woman's death is played out. Yi went north in June 1946 and is thought to have been purged by the North Korean leadership in the mid-1950s.

Pak T'aewŏn (1909–?), also a member of the Kuinhoe, was first a poet and then a writer of experimental fiction. He is remembered today for his camera-eye accounts of his native Seoul during the Japanese occupation, especially those in the novella *A Day in the Life of Kubo the Writer* (Sosŏlga Kubo sshi ŭi iril, 1934) and *Streamside Sketches* (Ch'ŏnbyŏn p'unggyŏng, 1937–38). Representative of his experimentation in the latter is "The Barbershop Boy" (Ibalso ŭi sonyŏn), a good example of Korean modernist fiction with its bustling urban backdrop, narrative disjunctures, and jump-cut glimpses of life along a stream cutting through central Seoul. Pak went north in 1948 and published at least two historical novels there in the 1960s.

In terms of ideological commitment Yi Kiyŏng (1896–1984), a hardline socialist since the 1920s, provides a sharp contrast with Yi T'aejun and Pak T'aewŏn. He produced a great deal of criticism as well as fiction. Many of his works have a rural setting, and early stories such as "A Tale of Rats" (Chwi iyagi, 1926) reveal a familiar socialist line. But Yi has also left us with one of the most accomplished novels of the colonial period, *The Ancestral Home* (Kohyang, 1933–34). After migrating to the north in 1945 Yi lived a long and apparently productive life.

—*Bruce Fulton*

Bibliography

Kwon Youngmin. *Wŏlbuk munin yŏngu* (Studies of the *Wŏlbuk* Writers). Seoul: Munhak sasang sa, 1989.

Pak T'aewŏn. "The Barbershop Boy." In Kim Chong-un and Bruce Fulton, trans. and eds., *A Ready-Made Life: Early Masters of Modern Korean Fiction*, 161–171. Honolulu: University of Hawai'i Press, 1998.

Stevenson, Joel. "Korean Short Fiction from the Liberation Period, 1945–1948." M.A. thesis, University of British Columbia, 1999.

Yi Kiyŏng. "A Tale of Rats." In Kim Chong-un and Bruce Fulton, trans. and eds., *A Ready-Made Life: Early Masters of Modern Korean Fiction*, 23–31. Honolulu: University of Hawai'i Press, 1998.

Yi T'aejun. "Crows." Trans. Bruce and Ju-Chan Fulton. *Korea Journal* (Winter 1991): 97–107.

118

SHORT FICTION FROM THE LIBERATION PERIOD

The liberation period *(haebang konggan)* is usually defined in South Korea as lasting from the Japanese surrender on August 15, 1945, until August 15, 1948, when the Republic of Korea was formed south of the thirty-eighth parallel. To date fewer than a dozen works of Korean short fiction from that period have been translated into English and published. These include four works by *Ch'ae Manshik (1902–1950), two by Ch'oe Chŏnghŭi (1912–1990), two by *Kim Tongni (1913–1995), and one by *Hwang Sunwŏn (1915–2000). An Hoenam's "Fire" (Pul, 1946), Chi Hayŏn's "Milestones" (Tojŏng, 1946), and Yi T'aejun's "Liberation, Before and After" (Haebang chŏnhu, 1946) have been translated but not published.

With liberation, Korea's writers clamored to restore the literary activity that had been snuffed out in the last years of Japanese rule. Writers active during the colonial period who resumed writing after liberation include Yŏm Sangsŏp (1897–1963), Yi Kiyŏng (1896–1984), An Hoenam (b. 1910), and Yi T'aejun (b. 1904), to name but a few. These were tumultuous and confusing years in Korea, but a time in which writers were free to write as they pleased. This confusion and freedom are reflected in the short fiction produced in the liberation period. Some of the themes common to these stories are the return of Koreans from overseas, whether from exile, forced labor, or conscription; collaboration; "self-criticism"; hope for a bright new future; and the realization that nothing was going to change.

During the colonial period many Koreans left for a better life in Manchuria and Russia. During the Japanese military buildup in the late 1930s, many other Koreans were taken to Japan to work. Those who fled Korea for a better life seldom found it. By the same token, those laboring in the mines of Japan or toiling for the Japanese war effort elsewhere led a deplorable existence at best. Upon liberation, many of these agricultural refugees and overseas laborers streamed home. Hŏ Chun's (b. 1910) "Last Glimmering" (Chandŭng, 1946) tells of two such agricultural refugees and what they find when they return to Korea. An Hoenam's "Fire" is the story of a writer who befriends a returnee from the horrors of laboring for the Japanese on Truk Island in the South Pacific.

With liberation came the return of Korea to the Korean people, and with it high expectations for the future. But these dreams, articulated by Mr. Lee in "Fire," were soon dashed, as first the Soviets occupied the north and later the Americans occupied the south. Liberation for Korea did not mean independence. There was a sense that with liberation, the tyranny of the Japanese was simply replaced by the tyranny of fellow Koreans. This can be seen in Ch'ae Manshik's "Constable Maeng" (Maeng sunsa, 1946) and "Once upon a Paddy" (Non iyagi, 1946).

Collaboration was very much a part of Korea under Japanese domination. With liberation there was a call to cleanse society of collaborators and traitors. In the realm of literature, these efforts consisted mainly of self- and group criticism by members of the literary groups that sprang up after liberation. This effort to come to terms with the societal problems resulting from collaboration was reflected in some of the short fiction from the liberation period. "Constable Maeng" deals with this issue in a satirical way.

Immediately following liberation, the opposing political camps of the left and right began to vie for control of Korea. At the same time, the debate that had raged in the 1920s and 1930s between the pure literature camp and the socially driven KAPF was rekindled. Yi T'aejun's "Liberation, Before and After" brings this debate down to the individual level. The main character is a writer of the art-for-art's-sake camp who searches within himself for direction and ultimately joins the left. Self-criticism as well as group criticism were encouraged by leftists at this time. "Milestones" by Chi Hayŏn is the story of a leftist who takes a critical look at himself in order to come to terms with his own ideology and convictions upon liberation. Ch'ae Manshik's "Public Offender" (Minjok ŭi choein, 1948–49) is the author's autobiographical self-examination and self-criticism.

With the formation of the Republic of Korea and the Democratic People's Republic of Korea late in the summer of 1948, Korea was politically polarized for the remainder of the twentieth century. Already by the time of this division, left-leaning writers had migrated north, while those in the rightist camp moved or remained south.

—Joel Stevenson

Bibliography

Ch'ae Manshik. "Constable Maeng." Trans. Joel Stevenson. *Acta Koreana* 2 (1999): 145–152.

——. "Once upon a Paddy." Trans. Robert Armstrong. In Bruce Fulton, ed., *My Innocent Uncle*, 83–117. Seoul: Jimoondang, 2003.

Stevenson, Joel. "Korean Short Fiction from the Liberation Period." M.A. thesis, University of British Columbia, 1999.

——. "Literature of the Liberation Period: Ch'ae Manshik and 'Constable Maeng.'" *Acta Koreana* 2 (1999): 125–144.

119

POSTWAR FICTION

Postwar fiction is the term generally applied to stories and novels published between the 1953 armistice that brought an end to the Korean War and the April 19, 1960, student revolution that toppled the regime of President Yi Sŭngman (Syngman Rhee) in South Korea. The war that broke out in June 1950 between the Republic of Korea and the Democratic People's Republic of Korea ravaged the entire land, cities and countryside alike, leaving indelible marks on the consciousness of the people. It was the omnipresent core, the shadow as well as the substance, the protagonist as well as the antagonist, of virtually all the novels and stories produced during the 1950s. The legacy of the war—the vast dehumanizing aspects of the conflict and the alienation from self, society, and nature—rather than the war efforts and activities themselves loomed large in fiction. The huddled and uprooted figure dumbfounded by the sense of universal and irrevocable loss; the small people wandering among the ravaged ruins wondering where the next meal would come from; individuals perplexed by the sudden shift and cleavage in moral ground; the intellectual groping for an adequate response to the condition of humanity in the face of metaphysical anguish and despair brought about by the war—these are the images of humanity that populate the fictional works of the period. They are the people maimed by the legacy of the war, the wounded people, physically or spiritually, or both, and the general tone is largely despairing and apocalyptic.

This sense of painful loss is caught in *Kim Tongni's story "Father and Son" (Puja, 1951), in which an ill and decrepit father decides to visit his son, who has not written home since his enlistment. The journey will cost money, which the father does not have, and so he borrows heavily and sets out. Father finally meets son after a long and arduous journey, but neither really has anything to say to the other, and they part after a brief and inarticulate meeting, the son going back to his post, the father going on the long trudge home. The sense of acute pain and loss is poignantly captured without recourse to sentimentality.

The horrors and nightmares of the war were replaced in the postwar period by dire economic conditions and moral confusion. The disintegration of the moral order is another recurring theme of postwar fiction. Despair bred new mores that challenged established behavioral norms. Son Ch'angsŏp's "Walking in the Snow" (Sŏlchunghaeng, 1956) is a good example. In this story a young man and his girlfriend move in with the man's former teacher and proceed to sponge off him shamelessly. The young woman, an aspiring playwright, asks the teacher rhetorically, "Is not life itself a play? ... You pretend to yourself that others are sincere but it takes a real actor to make others believe he is sincere." The young man, for his part, asks, "What are any of us but merchandise? As long as we are to be sold, we should make sure we are sold into wealth." Infuriated by this assault on his cherished standards of personal integrity, the teacher leaves to walk aimlessly in the snow.

A story dealing with essentially the same problem is Sŏ Kiwŏn's "The Uncharted Map" (Amsa chido, 1956). But whereas Son's story concentrates on revealing the emerging pattern and on presenting the perplexity and ambivalence that grip the older generation, Sŏ's story not only delimits the new pattern but also suggests its viability as a norm of existence in the changed landscape. Two war veterans set up housekeeping with a young woman who has been disowned by her family, and they eventually share sexual ownership of her. But they run into a crisis when the woman announces she is pregnant. Taken aback, the two men suggest abortion, but she laughs in their faces and leaves the house for good, declaring almost cheerfully that the baby will be hers and hers alone. The awakening in the woman of a primitive affirmation of life strikes a note of hopefulness despite the smothering atmosphere of the setting. The moral climate of the postwar landscape is aptly an uncharted map that must be completed by each individual with proper landmarks and contours.

In the mid-1950s a group of writers tried to link the postwar Korean situation to that of world literature, or more particularly, European literature. In their opinion, the common ground was an existential approach to the predicament of man in this age and space. Chang Yonghak's "Poems of John the Baptist" (Yohan shijip, 1957) is a case in point. Almost plotless and indebted spiritually to Sartre's *Nausée*, the story is largely a tract of existential philosophy interspersed with an allegory-packed parable of a fabulous cave rabbit that seeks freedom; the description of an inhuman ideological war that spreads into a prisoner-of-war camp on a southern island; the suicide of Nuhye, a North Korean prisoner of war; and the recollection of Nuhye's life in the camp by Tongho, a fellow prisoner, after the latter's release from the prison. The story is about an effort to recapture the root of existence upturned by the cruel and meaningless ideological war. The cave rabbit of the parable, lured by the resplendent rainbow-colored light that seeps into the cave from the outside world, forsakes the peace and comfort of the inner cave and is stricken blind and dead the moment he reaches the crack that opens to the outer world. This unfortunate rabbit is a metaphor for humanity in general in this time and place, and more particularly for Nuhye and Tongho. Indifferent to the acrimonious hatred and bloodshed between the opposing ideological factions within the camp, Nuhye commits suicide at the barbed-wire fence of the camp. This ultimate existential act is for Nuhye an expression of a will to freedom in the face of the cruel hate machine called ideology.

These images of humanity, which we might characterize as the walking wounded, can take on still another guise: that of the maimed figure in the social-environmental nexus, suffering from economic indigence, sociopolitical injustices, and other absurdities of postwar society.

The approach is broadly realistic, but the dominant image of humanity is still that of the walking wounded. For instance, Ha Kŭnch'an's "The Suffering of Two Generations" (Sunan idae, 1957) and "The White Paper Beard" (Hŭin chongi suyŏm, 1959) portray moods and lifestyles native to rural Korea. Caught in his poised and genial style are authentic rural men, women, and children: inarticulate, destitute, yet patient. They are the sufferers of the war's deprivation. What Ha does for rural people, Son Ch'angsŏp does for city dwellers. What the war-veteran protagonist of Son's "A Washed-Out Dream" (Yushilmong, 1956) finds in Seoul is a suffocating poverty, material and spiritual. Some suffer more than others in the cutthroat game that is the main business of postwar society, and the worst is usually received by gullible men and women of good faith. That is what Son's satirical "Superfluous Men" (Ingyŏ ingan, 1959) is about—misfit and forsaken individuals doomed to a life of misery and failure. The men and women who are unable to "function" in this society must become superfluous human beings.

In this connection let us also consider Yi Pŏmsŏn's "A Stray Bullet" (Obalt'an, 1959). Here an erratically fired bullet aimed at nothing becomes a metaphor for the image of humans as walking wounded. Ch'ŏrho, a lowly clerk in a downtown accountant's office, wants to lead a righteous life in spite of poverty. His deranged mother, who continually cries out, "Let's go back!" (meaning back to North Korea, where the family formerly enjoyed a decent life), is a permanent fixture of the cardboard shack that they call his "house." His pregnant wife, who "does not even remember that she was once beautiful," patiently performs household chores even when the expected date of confinement draws near. His sister, a prostitute who caters to foreign soldiers, and his brother, a war veteran with no prospects for a job, are two off-and-on dwellers of his cardboard "house."

One evening the younger brother comes home drunk and boldly challenges the elder's outlook on life—that a man must never succumb to the degradation of conscience no matter how he suffers from other degradations. Ch'ŏrho is so poor that he no longer has any zest for life, but he can never adopt his brother's attitude. The following day he learns that his younger brother has been apprehended while committing a robbery. Going home from the police station, he is met by his sister, who tells him that his wife is having trouble giving birth at the hospital. Reaching the hospital, he finds that his wife has died. Sinking into a daze, Ch'ŏrho muses, "Perhaps I am a stray bullet accidentally fired by God."

A new pattern slowly evolved in response to the image of the walking wounded. A new image was presented—that of a positive hero with wisdom and courage who defies the encroaching surroundings. Sŏnu Hwi's "Flowers of Fire" (Pulkkot, 1957) is generally considered the story that started to turn the tide in favor of a positive hero. In this work, the author seems to criticize the easy, resigned attitude of Koreans toward the force of history. The story concerns three generations of a family (Hyŏn, the protagonist, and his father and grandfather), using as a backdrop the turbulent period from the March 1, 1919, independence movement to the June 1950 civil conflict. Hyŏn's father lost his life in the fight against the Japanese in the March 1 movement, and Hyŏn is brought up by his mother and grandfather. Having no personal knowledge of his own father, Hyŏn grows up under the influence of his grandfather's passive individualism, and that attitude becomes part of his consciousness. But once in a while a contrary, innate urge challenges this indifference. And when the civil war breaks out in June 1950 his indifference cannot last long. He is forced to participate in a so-called people's trial in which innocent people are summarily sentenced to death in the name of people's democracy. The absurdity and atrocity of the proceedings suddenly awaken in him the will to resist, and he launches a lone but hope-laden fight against the Communists, just as his father had against the Japanese army thirty years earlier. He receives a fatal wound in the fighting, and in his dying moment he sees the flowers of fire, the sign of his liberated life force.

Important as a source of inspiration for this and similar works of fiction was the Korean people's search for cultural identity. The shabbiness of Korean culture of that day—epitomized in the epithet "the chewing-gum culture"—does not adequately describe the hollowness and confusion caused by the wholesale influx of foreign ideas and lifestyles in which many intellectuals saw the cause of the national plight. This naturally led to a heightened historical consciousness, which in turn was linked to a sociopolitical consciousness. Thus came a flood of fiction that attempted to see the present in a clearer light. The history of the Korean people under Japanese colonial rule, the heroic fight against the oppressor in the March 1 independence movement, the tragic division of the country, and other such historical events became favorite subjects, as evidenced by the works of such writers as Yu Chuhyŏn (1921–1982), An Sugil (1911–1977), *Ch'oe Inhun (b. 1936), Yi Hoch'ŏi (b. 1932), and Sŏnu Hwi (1922–1986).

—*Kim Chong-un*

Bibliography

Chang Yonghak. "Poems of John the Baptist." In Kim Chong-un, trans. and ed., *Postwar Korean Short Stories*, 2d ed., 19–46. Seoul: Seoul National University Press, 1983.

Ha Kŭnch'an. "The Suffering of Two Generations." In Kevin O'Rourke, trans. and ed., *A Washed-Out Dream*, 171–190. New York: Larchwood, 1980.

——. "The White Paper Beard." In Kevin O'Rourke, trans. and ed., *A Washed-Out Dream*, 301–324. New York: Larchwood, 1980.

Kim Tongni. "Father and Son." In Kim Chong-un, trans. and ed., *Postwar Korean Short Stories*, 2d ed., 1–8. Seoul: Seoul National University Press, 1983.

Sŏ Kiwŏn. "The Uncharted Map." In Kim Chong-un, trans. and ed., *Postwar Korean Short Stories*, 2d ed., 72–91. Seoul: Seoul National University Press, 1983.

Son Ch'angsŏp. "Superfluous Men." Trans. Chang Young-hee. *Korean Literature Today* (Spring 1998): 35–65.

——. "Walking in the Snow." In Kim Chong-un, trans. and ed., *Postwar Korean Short Stories*, 2d ed., 47–61. Seoul: Seoul National University Press, 1983.

——. "A Washed-Out Dream." In Kevin O'Rourke, trans. and ed., *A Washed-Out Dream*, 210–248. New York: Larchwood, 1980.

Sŏnu Hwi. "Flowers of Fire." (Excerpt.) Trans. Peter H. Lee. In Peter H. Lee, ed., *Flowers of Fire: Twentieth-Century Korean Stories*, 184–243. Honolulu: University Press of Hawai'i, 1974.

Yi Pŏmsŏn. "A Stray Bullet." In Marshall R. Pihl, ed., *Listening to Korea: A Korean Anthology*, 127–154. New York: Praeger, 1973.

120

O YŎNGSU AND *THE GOOD PEOPLE*

South Koreans sometimes see their nation as a dichotomy: there is Seoul, and there is the rest of Korea. To an extent this observation holds true even at the advent of the new millennium as Korea continues its rapid technological advance. And it is "the rest of Korea" — the rural farming and seafaring villages with their traditional patterns of work, play, and family — that forms the landscape of O Yŏngsu's fiction.

O Yŏngsu (1914–1979) is one of the second generation of twentieth-century Korean writers — those who by and large received their higher education in Japan and became active forces in the Korean literary world after liberation from Japanese colonial rule in 1945. Like *Hwang Sunwŏn and *Kim Tongni — two other representatives of that generation — O is well known for his portraits of country people. Not quite as versatile, powerful, or imaginative as those two giants of modern Korean fiction, O nevertheless offers much that is worthwhile in his stories.

The title of the 1985 story collection *The Good People* captures both O Yŏngsu's abiding faith in human decency and his admittedly lyrical approach to writing. "Mine is an extremely pure and simple affirmation of humanity," O once wrote. "If I lost my faith in humanity I could no longer write." O flourished in the 1950s and early 1960s, and his concern with the timeless values of human existence was atypical of the Korean fiction of this period (see "Postwar Fiction"), when writers such as Yi Pŏmsŏn, O Sangwŏn, and especially Son Ch'angsŏp portrayed a society ravaged by political violence and civil war, by hunger and homelessness, a society bereft of moral signposts.

A recurring theme in his stories is the quest for security and permanence. In "Uncle" (Atchiya, 1952), set during the Korean War, a sentry befriends a young boy whose neighborhood playground has been taken over by the army. In "Migratory Birds" (Hujo, 1958) a shoeshine boy leaves his stepmother and his brutish father and attaches himself to a schoolteacher. "Seaside Village" (Kaenmaŭl, 1953) tells of a young widow who remarries and moves inland, only to be drawn back to her seaside home when her new husband is drafted during the war. And the central figure of "The Girl from an Island" (Sŏm esŏ on shingmo, 1965), who has journeyed to the capital to work as a maid, returns to her home on a south-coast island when she sees her long-lost lover in a dream. As if to underscore the nature of the times, a relationship is cut short in each of these stories—albeit somewhat arbitrarily in the case of "Uncle." Even so, we are left with the impression that the juncture, though temporary, has helped make the participants resilient enough to survive a very uncertain period of their country's history.

This is not to say that O Yŏngsu is merely a naive optimist. Indeed, his works contain their share of unsavory moments. In "The Woman from Hwasan" (Hwasan taegi, 1952), one of O's stronger stories, a young man who has married and left home rebuffs his ignorant mother's attempts to keep him in the family web. Illness robs the protagonist of "A Death at the Mill" (Ŏttŏn chugŭm, 1955) of his parents, and after years of abuse by his brother and sister-in-law he becomes a miser. A father's insistence on an arranged marriage promises to end a budding romance in "Nami and the Taffyman" (Nami wa yŏtchangsu, 1949). "Wine" (Sul, 1978) ends with a penniless sot flattering a homely tavern keeper to obtain a drink. And in "Spring's Awakening" (Taech'ungi, 1956), a kitchen maid manipulates a young boy in order to safeguard her sexual liaison with a village youth.

Such stories reveal a mature grasp of human nature, and they illustrate O's gift for characterization. Moreover, they are not without humor. As such, they offer a pleasant contrast with the constricted focus and the earnest soul searching that characterize some of his younger colleagues. A rare exception is "Afterglow" (Noŭl)—a memoir more than a story, a snapshot rather than a character study.

O's critical reputation has not flourished in recent years. Like Hwang Sunwŏn, he has sometimes been labeled an outdated, escapist writer who lacks "historical consciousness." True, O has written escapist fiction. "Echoes" (Meari, 1959) is a well-known example. Still, the recurring themes of human dignity and social propriety in his stories, far from being old-fashioned, are among the benchmarks of Korean culture. Moreover, O's stories, like much Korean literature of the twentieth century, succeed in reflecting the stressful realities of contemporary Korean history. The civil war figures prominently in "Uncle," "Seaside Village," and "Migratory Birds." The status of outcasts in Korea's tightly structured society is depicted unsparingly in "A Death at the Mill." The traditionally subordinate position of women in Korea is reflected in

"Nami and the Taffyman." Such subject matter, combined with the author's proclivity for the affective rather than the intellectual, suggests that history will likely remember O Yŏngsu as a writer solidly grounded in Korean tradition.

—*Bruce Fulton*

Bibliography

O Yŏngsu. "Echoes." Trans. W.E. Skillend. In Chung Chong-wha, ed., *Meetings and Farewells: Modern Korean Stories*, 67–107. New York: St. Martin's Press, 1980.
——. *The Good People: Korean Stories by Oh Yong-su*. Trans. Marshall R. Pihl. Singapore: Heinemann Asia, 1985.

121

CH'OE INHUN'S *THE SQUARE*

Two seagulls follow the *Tagore* on its voyage from Korea. The time is immediately after the Korean War. On board are a group of Korean prisoners of war who choose to go to a neutral country rather than live in South or North Korea. For Yi Myŏngjun the birds symbolize two lost loves, a girl from the south and a girl from the north. They also symbolize the elusive nature of his dreams—the failure of democratic institutions in the south and the failure of the totalitarian value system in the north. Although Yi Myŏngjun is a sort of spokesman for the POWs on board, he has little in common with them. In fact, he is so disillusioned with things Korean that he avoids the company of his compatriots insofar as he can, preferring to share with the captain of the boat the little human warmth he allows himself. Thus begins Ch'oe Inhun's novel *The Square* (Kwangjang, 1961).

The story unfolds in a series of flashbacks. Myŏngjun recalls his life as a young, introspective philosophy major in prewar Seoul. Politically and socially unaware, he searches for an understanding of life. His quest is to find the square, a symbol of space, light, meaning, and understanding, the place where we meet destiny. While forming an uneasy relationship with his first girl, Yunae, he is taken in for questioning by the police because his father is an active, ranking member of the Communist Party in the north. Beaten up in the course of the interrogation, he becomes disillusioned and alienated. Subsequently, he takes up a chance offer of smuggled passage to the north, where in his encounters with his father and the party he again finds nothing but disillusion and alienation.

In the north, Myŏngjun meets the second girl in his life, Ŭnhye, a dancer and a free spirit, who is quite untouched by political posturing. Ŭnhye loves Myŏngjun but does not share his intellectual melancholia. Myŏngjun becomes dependent on her and demands that she refuse a chance to dance in Moscow. She initially agrees but in the end fails to keep her promise. Myŏngjun is left once again with a sense of ultimate betrayal.

Myŏngjun returns to Seoul as an intelligence officer during the Communist occupation of the city during the war. He meets Yunae again only to discover that she has married his old friend Taeshik. Taeshik is in trouble with the occupying authorities, and Yunae pleads with Myŏngjun for his old friend's life. Myŏngjun humiliates Yunae. However, he relents, stopping short of subjecting her to the ultimate degradation of rape. In the end he arranges the escape of both Yunae and Taeshik.

Back at the battlefront Myŏngjun is reunited with Ŭnhye, who in the meantime has become a nurse. They snatch whatever human warmth fate decrees them within the harsh reality of life at the front, until finally Ŭnhye is killed. Myŏngjun is left once again in complete disillusion. He has nothing to live for, south or north. He is taken prisoner. When offered the choice of South Korea, North Korea, or a neutral place of residence, he chooses the third. However, he disappears overboard before the boat reaches its destination. He chooses the ultimate disillusion.

The Square reflected the existential mood that was dominant in European literature in the 1950s. It was a towering best-seller in Korea at the time of its publication, and, interestingly enough, it returned to the best-seller charts during the democratization crisis of the late 1980s. As a depiction of a young Korean intellectual under stress, it is second to none. *The Square* combines the best qualities of Camus and Hemingway. It features an intellectual hero, intent on finding meaning in life but ultimately failing in his quest; Yi Myŏngjun is aloof, detached, even cruel, yet always vulnerable in his humanity. In telling the story, Ch'oe Inhun uses all the ingredients of the thriller: love, intrigue, betrayal, violence, brutality.

Though it has all the ingredients of a successful novel, *The Square* is a difficult book for the Western reader. Why? Critics point out that the philosophical content of the novel is distracting, that it is not fully integrated into the text, but this is not enough to account for the book's difficulty. The theme is extremely dark and pessimistic—but pessimism did not stop Graham Greene from writing very successful novels. The problem the Western reader experiences with *The Square* has to do with the character of the hero. Yi Myŏngjun seems never to be able to get outside himself; he never attains any sort of vision of a world that does not turn within the confines of his own private experience. Yi Myŏngjun is unabashedly self-centered. His quest for meaning is totally personal and selfish.

When he is also revealed to be diabolically cruel, the Western reader, unfamiliar with Korea, finds it virtually impossible to empathize with him in his dilemma.

None of this is a problem for a Korean audience. Yi Myŏngjun is the quintessential dark, introspective Korean hero. Every Korean reader shares his pain. The sheer magnitude of his pain seems to excuse his human failings. We are dealing here with different visions of the world. The Korean vision is always abstract, conceptual, always directed toward the general, the universal. It takes little account of family, friends or social context. The Korean reader does not demand social realism, he does not ask the same questions as the average Western reader, nor is he nearly as judgmental as his Western counterpart is. The tradition of Korean poetry has always been confessional; Korea's fictional heroes are also fundamentally poetical constructs.

Ch'oe Inhun was born in North Korea in 1936. He came to the south during the Korean War and studied law at Seoul National University. Having lived through the political decadence of the 1950s and the early 1960s, he shared the characteristic disillusion of the intelligentsia of the time (see "Postwar Fiction"). What distinguishes his work is the broad sweep of his mind, his familiarity not only with the Eastern tradition but also with the tradition of Western philosophy, and his ability to analyze the deformity of current societal structures in both Eastern and Western terms.

—*Kevin O'Rourke*

Bibliography

Ch'oe Inhun. *A Grey Man.* Trans. Chun Kyung-Ja. Seoul: Si-sa-yong-o-sa, 1988.
——. *The Square.* Trans. Kevin O'Rourke. Devon: Spindlewood, 1985.

122

PAK KYŎNGNI AND *LAND*

Pak Kyŏngni was born in 1926 in the port city of Ch'ungmu, South Kyŏngsang Province. She attended Chinju Girls' High School under Japanese colonial rule. A keen student of history with an insatiable appetite for literature, she read many major works of nineteenth-century European writers in Japanese translation. These works may have had a lasting influence on her writing. She also attempted writing poems. She married in 1946, a year after Korea's liberation from Japan. Four years later, when the Korean War broke out, she became a widow and suddenly found herself the breadwinner of a family that included her mother and her four-year old daughter. It was a desperate need to support them that turned her to writing. She made her literary debut in 1955 with the short story "Calculation" (Kyesan), which was followed in 1956 by "Black Is Black, White Is White" (Hŭkhŭk paekpaek). She has since devoted herself to writing and has established herself as one of the greatest living writers. By 1969, the year she started to write *Land* (T'oji), her magnum opus that was to take up all her soul and energy for the next twenty-five years, she had published more than twenty novels and forty stories.

We can examine the development of Pak Kyŏngni as writer and the bulk of her work in three stages: the 1950s, the 1960s, and the 1970s on. In the postwar years of the late 1950s Pak mostly wrote short stories based on her own experience as a widow undergoing harsh times in a war-ravaged country. These stories were variations on a basic pattern involving a trio of characters—an elderly mother, a child, and the breadwinner, a young woman. This phase in her writing career ended with the publication of "A Time of Disbelief" (Pulshin shidae, 1957), a vivid portrayal of the anguish of an educated young widow as she tries to sustain her family and struggles to remain a decent human being amidst the shameful irregularities of a corrupt society. It was the culmination of what she had been writing over the previous few years and became an instant success, earning her a New Writers' Award from the publishers of *Hyŏndae munhak* (Contemporary Literature), a prestigious literary journal.

With new confidence she now launched into her second phase. Starting with *Floating Islands* (Py'oryudo, 1961) she published a series of major novels through the 1960s: *The Daughters of Apothecary Kim* (Kim Yakkuk ŭi ttal tŭl, 1962), *The Fish Market* (P'ashi, 1964–65), and *Marketplace and Battlefield* (Shijang kwa chŏnjang, 1964). "Illusion" (Hwansang) is a chapter from *Marketplace and Battlefield*; it deals with the painful struggles of two intellectuals caught in ideological strife.

The third phase in Pak's writing commenced in 1969 with the publication of part 1 of *Land*, a roman-fleuve of some seven thousand pages in five parts and sixteen volumes. It has been acclaimed the most significant work of contemporary Korean literature and has attracted unprecedented popularity. The initial volume has been translated into English. It covers only one-tenth of the entire work but gives insight into the scale of the work, Pak's genius, and her descriptive power, and it stands on its own.

Set in the agrarian community of P'yŏngsa-ri during the years 1897–1905, at the very end of the Chosŏn kingdom (1392–1910), the novel revolves around the decline of the Ch'oe house, a family of landlords that has reigned over the district for five generations. The author uses different techniques in different parts of this epic work. In part 1 the story moves quickly and dramatically. The main plot includes an elopement of a servant with the young mistress, the wife of the present master of the house; treachery by individuals who covet the Ch'oe property; and the assassination of the master, Ch'isu. Subplots involving the lives of villagers, peasants, and servants of the Ch'oe household weave a rich texture. Readers familiar with Thomas Hardy may find affinities in Pak's writing style and in the lyricism, tragic romance, and humor exhibited by the colorful rustics who inhabit the novel.

Pak's underlying themes in all her stories and novels are women's sorrows and human dignity and decency. These are fully explored and developed in *Land*. More than thirty characters appear in part 1 alone. They are so vividly drawn and memorable that reading the book is like seeing a gallery of archetypal Korean characters. Pak's works continue to be a popular subject for research and literary criticism. At least two articles have appeared in English (Zeong 1990; Kim 1991).

—*Agnita Tennant*

Bibliography

Kim Hyung-kook. "The Literature and Dreams of Pak Kyong-ni." *Koreana* (Summer 1996): 38–40.

Pak Kyŏngni. "Illusion." In Hong Myoung-Hee [Agnita Tennant], trans. and ed., *Korean Short Stories*, 174–189. Seoul: Ilji-sa, 1975.

———. *Land*. vol. 1 Trans. Agnita Tennant. London: Kegan Paul International/UNESCO Publishing, 1996.

———. "A Time of Disbelief." Trans. Kim Ki-chung. *Korea Journal* (September 1975): 22–33.

Zeong Hyon-kee. "Park Kyung-ree: Looking Back As She Completes *The Earth*." *Koreana* (Spring 1995): 47–50.

123

O CHŎNGHŬI

More than any other author, O Chŏnghŭi (b. 1947) has contributed to the success of women fiction writers in Korea today. One of the most accomplished writers of short fiction in modern Korea, she is one of the few authors to have captured both the Yi Sang and the Tongin awards—Korea's two most prestigious prizes for short fiction—and translations of her works into Japanese, English, French, and other languages have begun to garner her an international reputation. English translations of her works have won her comparisons with such writers as America's Joyce Carol Oates, Canada's Alice Munro, and England's Virginia Woolf.

O was just out of her teens when she burst onto the literary scene by winning a competition for aspiring writers sponsored by the *Chungang ilbo*, a Seoul daily, in 1968. The prizewinning story, "The Toyshop Woman" (Wangujŏm yŏin), concerns a high school girl's descent into madness punctuated by kleptomania and an obsession with the crippled owner of a toyshop. That this highly original debut story was begun while the author herself was still in high school suggested the arrival of a gifted literary talent. There is very little like it among previous Korean fiction writers, male or female.

O has since published some four dozen stories and novellas. This is a comparatively meager output for a writer whose career spans four decades. But it is also an oeuvre of consistently high quality, comprising provocative, densely textured stories, many of them infused with a restrained intensity that is unsettling, sometimes shocking. Not until 1977 did O publish her first collection of fiction,

River of Fire (Pul ŭi kang). There followed an especially productive period in which many of her most memorable stories were composed—"Evening Game" (Chŏnyŏk ŭi keim, 1979), "Chinatown" (Chunggugin kŏri, 1979), "Words of Farewell" (Pyŏlsa, 1981), "The Bronze Mirror" (Tonggyŏng, 1982), and "Wayfarer" (Sullyeja ŭi norae, 1983). The first three stories appeared in her second volume of fiction, *The Garden of Childhood* (Yunyŏn ŭi ttŭl), the last two in her third collection, *Spirit on the Wind* (Param ŭi nŏk, 1986). O's production has since been more sporadic, but works such as "Lake P'aro" (P'aroho, 1989), "The Old Well" (Yet umul, 1994), and *Birds* (Sae, 1996) suggest that the author has maintained the high standards she set for herself at the very beginning of her career.

Technically, O has few peers among contemporary Korean fiction writers. Her command of language is formidable—her vocabulary impressive, her word choices deliberate and suggestive. Stories such as "The Cookout" (Yahoe, 1981) and "Morning Star" (Saebyŏk pyŏl, 1984) reveal a good ear for dialog, an attribute many Korean fiction writers neglect in favor of narrative. Flashbacks, stream-of-consciousness technique, and interior monologues constitute much of her narratives. Long paragraphs juxtaposing images and points of view of family members past and present are not uncommon. "Words of Farewell," which depicts separate but parallel spiritual journeys by a woman and her lost husband, is a striking example. This concern with the interior landscape of the characters is for O a means for dealing with her characteristic themes of abandonment and loneliness. Heightening the impact of these themes is the author's typically dispassionate narrative tone, which in her earlier stories takes the form of a nameless first-person narrator (every story in *River of Fire* is told in this manner). These nameless narrators become Everywoman and Everyman (some of her narrators are male), struggling in an emotionally parched landscape that is sometimes specifically Korean, as in "A Portrait of Magnolias" (Mongnyŏnch'o, 1975), sometimes not, as in "The Toyshop Woman." That is, without ignoring the upheavals that have attended Korea's rapid modernization, O's stories transcend cultural boundaries to speak to universal themes of emotional rootlessness and a yearning for permanence, whether in the immediate context of the family or in the larger society.

O, in fact, has been fascinated with family relationships ever since her literary debut. Her best stories are powerful yet sensitive portraits of families strained to the breaking point by suppressed emotions and invisible external forces. In these works, O penetrates the surface of seemingly pedestrian lives to reveal nightmarish family constellations warped by divorce, insanity, abandonment, and death. Darkness is prominent in these stories, representing among other things these family nightmares. In "The Toyshop Woman," "The Cookout," "The Bronze Mirror," and elsewhere, darkness creeps upon the scene like a sinister beast, unleashing black memories among the characters.

O is by no means a writer of historical fiction, and yet her stories reflect, albeit obliquely, the familial and emotional costs of Korea's headlong industrialization since the 1960s. In most of her stories the support network traditionally offered by the extended family is absent, leaving the characters to struggle on their own for emotional sustenance. The loneliness of the aged couple in "The Bronze Mirror" and their torment by the kindergarten girl who lives next door to them are as vivid as almost anything in contemporary Korean fiction. In "Fireworks" (Pullori, 1986) and "Lake P'aro," O touches on the theme of younger people suffering for the political misadventures of their elders — a theme mined with success in recent years by many of her male contemporaries. In the case of "Lake P'aro," an American setting provides added interest in the form of the cultural and linguistic dislocations suffered by Korean immigrants and graduate students. The story also provides glimpses of the author's own two-year sojourn with her family near Albany, New York, in the mid-1980s.

— *Bruce Fulton*

Bibliography

O Chŏnghŭi. "The Bronze Mirror." Trans. Bruce and Ju-Chan Fulton. In Marshall R. Pihl and Bruce and Ju-Chan Fulton, eds., *Land of Exile: Contemporary Korean Fiction*, 244–263. Armonk, N.Y.: M. E. Sharpe, 1993.

——. "Evening Game," "Chinatown," and "Words of Farewell." In Bruce and Ju-Chan Fulton, trans. and eds., *Words of Farewell: Stories by Korean Women Writers*, 181–274. Seattle: Seal Press, 1989.

——. "Fireworks." Trans. Bruce and Ju-Chan Fulton. *Asian Pacific Quarterly* (Winter 1993): 53–76.

——. "Lake P'aro." Trans. Bruce and Ju-Chan Fulton. *Korean Literature Today* (Winter 1998): 90–125.

——. "Morning Star." Trans. Bruce and Ju-Chan Fulton. *Manoa* 8, no. 2 (1996): 103–115.

——. "A Portrait of Magnolias." Trans. Bruce and Ju-Chan Fulton. *Koreana* (Summer 1992): 56–61.

——. "The Toyshop Woman." Trans. Bruce and Ju-Chan Fulton. *Korea Times*, November 5, 7, and 8, 1989.

——. "Wayfarer." In Bruce and Ju-Chan Fulton, trans. and eds., *Wayfarer: New Fiction by Korean Women*, 184–205. Seattle: Women in Translation, 1997.

Yi Hyangsoon, "The Journey as Meditation: A Buddhist Reading of O Chŏng-hŭi's 'Words of Farewell,'" *Religion and Literature* 34, no. 3 (2002):57–73.

124

PAK WANSŎ

Pak Wansŏ (b. 1931) touched off a prolific career in 1970 with the publication of her novel *The Naked Tree* (Namok). She lived in Seoul throughout the Korean War, then married and raised five children before rendering her experiences on paper with wit and blunt, earthy language. This award-winning author has produced several novels, short story collections, and essays. A number of her works, albeit disappointingly small compared with her overall output, have been translated into English.

Pak does not identify her style with any one school of criticism. She professes that her stories simply raise a mirror to the realities of her life, yet it takes a masterful storyteller to transfer the everyday into a tale of universal meaning. She achieves this universality by exposing the profundity of human emotion. Meanwhile, her gift for insightfully probing the minds of her fellow Koreans imparts a distinctly local flavor to her stories.

Pak's protagonists are often women, though the men are rarely far off, and some even play leading roles. "Mr. Hong's Medals" (Ajŏsshi ŭi hunjang, 1983), for example, depicts the sad existence of a man whose sense of filial piety is distorted when he takes in an orphaned nephew to raise. He becomes obsessed with promoting his act of charity as the quintessential Confucian ideal, to the point of neglecting his biological son.

The Naked Tree and the first story in the "Mother's Hitching Post" trilogy (Ŏmma ŭi malttuk, 1979, 1981, 1991) focus on struggles arising from mother–daughter relationships. The former paints a stark picture of a young woman living alone with her ghostlike mother. The Korean War takes the lives of her two broth-ers when a bomb rips through the roof of their home. The girl, already bereaved of her father, loses her brothers during her impressionable adolescence. Her mis-ery is compounded when her mother loses the will to live, cursing fate for having left "only the girl." This attitude is based on a traditional Confucian tenet that ex-alts men and demeans women except in relation to their husbands and sons.

In "Mother's Hitching Post," the mother–daughter relationship plays against other bipolar conflicts such as city versus country and modernity versus tradi-tion. The girl in this story has a brother and neighborhood friends, which allows for broader reflections on life than are found in *The Naked Tree*. The title is in-dicative of the roots the mother figure plants in Seoul in order to give her chil-dren a better chance of succeeding economically and making good lives for themselves in the "real" world—that is, in the modern city.

Most of Pak's stories treat social maladies such as alienation, boredom, hypocrisy, and the bitter aftertaste of neo-Confucian reliance on empty formal-ity. In "Three Days in That Autumn" (Kŭ kaŭl e sahŭl tongan, 1980), the pro-tagonist is raped and impregnated by an American soldier during the Korean War. Telling no one of this tragedy, she secretly has an abortion. Her fate casts her to the periphery of society, at first perhaps only in her mind. She actualizes her position as an outcast by becoming an obstetrician and gynecologist—later performing only abortions—in an era when women's clinics were shunned. In the end this woman recognizes her inner desire to be a mother and raise a living child, a dream fueled by the same societal forces that had prevented her from living within the safety net of the accepted majority.

"A Certain Barbarity" (Ŏttŏn yaman, 1976) and "Thus Ended My Days of Watching over the House" (Chip pogi nŭn kŭrŏke kkŭnnaetta, 1978) open to the reader the inner minds of their middle-class protagonists. "A Certain Bar-barity" satirizes the dislike and distrust, mixed with envy, of all things Japanese, particularly Japanese wealth, amid the industrialization of South Korea in the 1960s. The obsequious demeanor of the protagonist's wife and neighbors in the face of wealth keeps the man literally constipated until the denouement of the story. "Thus Ended My Days of Watching over the House" finds the color drained from the life of its female protagonist. Her daily routine is disrupted when her husband is taken away by the police for questioning during the politi-cal purges of the 1970s. Her husband's absence helps her realize that his grip on household operations has stripped their lives of true familial interactions. He demands a "respectable household" according to the Confucian dictate that nothing must disturb the appearance of calm. She likens his painstaking atten-tion in sculpting bonsai trees to the way he subtly contorts the family; symboli-cally emerging from her husband's insistence on empty formality, she allows the trees to wither and tosses them out the window.

Pak's imagery is sharp and vibrant as she relays the inner workings of the Ko-rean mind and the middle-class experience. Her narrative voice is one of intimate familiarity, like that of an all-knowing aunt who lives down the street, and is praised and enjoyed by readers throughout South Korea. Her direct language unapologetically gives voice to taboo issues in Korean society. Her attitude is raw, her diction unassuming, and her tone colloquial—often steeped in regional dialect—making her accessible to readers of every ilk. Her comfortable language and typically uncomplicated plots make page-turners of Pak's works; yet as she plumbs the inner clockwork of her characters, a vast and deeply historical collective unconscious is revealed.

—*Diana Hinds*

Bibliography

Pak Wansŏ. *My Very Last Possession and Other Stories*. Trans. Chun Kyung-Ja et al. Armonk, N.Y.: M. E. Sharpe, 1999.

——. *The Naked Tree*. Trans. Yu Young-nan. Ithaca, N.Y.: Cornell University East Asia Program, 1995.

——. *A Sketch of the Fading Sun: Stories by Wan-suh Park*. Trans. Hyun-jae Yee Sallee. Buffalo, N.Y.: White Pine Press, 1999.

125

KIM SUYŎNG

Kim Suyŏng was born in Seoul in 1921. His death in a traffic accident in 1968 robbed Korea of a major poetic and critical voice. During his lifetime he did not enjoy the reputation he deserved, but in the years following his death critics and writers began to pay much more attention to him, and his importance in the development of contemporary Korean poetry is now widely recognized.

He studied for a time in Japan and at what is now Yonsei University in Seoul. His early poems, some of which were published in 1949 in the important anthology *The New City and the Chorus of Citizens* (Seroun toshi wa shimin tŭl ŭi hapch'ang), were marked by the modernism so popular at that time, with complex imagery and a far from simple system of references. During the Korean War he was forcibly conscripted into the North Korean army and as a result was interned by the South for a time in the prisoner-of-war camp on Kŏje Island. These harsh experiences confirmed him in the conviction that Korean poetry needed to seek a deeper relationship with reality. He later worked as a journalist and lectured part-time.

Kim had initially followed the modernist model enthusiastically. His early work is as difficult as any, and at least on the surface far removed from the suffering of ordinary people. However, the April 1960 student-led revolution that deposed strongman Syngman Rhee gave him immense hopes, coupled with apprehension. His hopes were soon dashed when the military took power in May 1961, but even before then he had felt betrayed by the way in which society was evolving away from the ideals of April 1960. In his poems, the words *love* and *freedom* are virtually synonymous, and both are shown to be hard to find.

His April 1968 lecture "Spit, Poetry" (Shi yŏ, ch'im ŭl paet'ŏra) and his essay of the same year "Theory of Anti-Poetics" (Panshiron) were particularly important manifestoes arguing for a renewal of Korean poetry, which seemed to him to have become far too mannered and artificial, bogged down in sterile aesthetic conventions. In "Experimental Literature and Political Freedom" (Shirhŏmjŏgin munhak kwa chŏngch'ijŏk chayu), an essay published in early 1968 in the *Chosŏn ilbo*, a Seoul daily, he took issue with two articles by the critic and writer Yi Ŏryŏng:

> Michel Butor, the French originator of the *anti-roman*, who recently visited Korea, has said that any work of experimental literature is necessarily bound to stand on the side of progress, which has as its goal the realization of a perfect world. All avant-garde literature is subversive. All living culture is essentially subversive. Quite simply because the essence of culture is the pursuit of dreams, the pursuit of the impossible. Yet according to [Yi Ŏryŏng], if we propose to set out in those directions, experimentation limited to the formal aspects of literature is good, but investigations of political and social ideology are wrong.

Conservative critics such as Yi Ŏryŏng and the novelist Sŏnu Hwi (originally from North Korea) denounced Kim Suyŏng and his like as dangerous radicals, while for others these ideas represented a rallying cry. Out of this debate there arose in the troubled years ahead a tendency, one that found expression in the pages of *Ch'angjak kwa pip'yŏng* (Writing and Criticism), a quarterly founded in late 1966, to promote the literary and social values Kim Suyŏng had advocated.

The vision of these writers, who were long denigrated by the conservative establishment as "dissidents," is now largely vindicated. The vast majority of younger writers active in Korea today follow Kim Suyŏng's assumptions quite naturally. It is clear to them that literature must necessarily be subversive, for the ruling classes in society are corrupt and the dominant ideology not so much discredited as morally bankrupt (see "Pure Literature versus the Literature of Engagement"). In taking this stance Kim made a conscious departure from the path laid down by *Sŏ Chŏngju, Pak Mogwŏl, and their followers among the older generation of poets. His support and recognition were important to younger poets such as *Shin Kyŏngnim, who were writing in ways and on topics not likely to be approved by that generation.

Kim Suyŏng remained to the end an intellectual poet, but at a crucial moment he rejected the idea that certain lofty topics alone are worthy to be the subjects of a poetry written in a corresponding style. Instead he began to focus on the most ordinary events of daily life, often pathetic or bathetic, domestic and social. He equally rejected the idea of "decorum" (by which he meant a special poetic language and tone) and introduced ordinary speech, vulgarity, and slang into his works. The tone of his later poems is frequently colloquial, satiric, or self-mocking. Yet in poems addressing social realities and human suffering and hope, he can rise to rhetoric of heroic style. His poetry is at times prosaic, for he consciously rejected artificial techniques of rhythm. Yet he is capable of great intensity because his poems, even at their most iconoclastic, always reflect his own intense emotion.

—*Brother Anthony of Taizé*

Bibliography

Kim Su-Young, Shin Kyong-Nim, and Lee Si-Young. *Variations: Three Korean Poets.* Trans. Brother Anthony of Taizé and Young-Moo Kim. Ithaca, N.Y.: Cornell University East Asia Program, 2001.

126

KO ŬN

Ko Ŭn has published more than 120 volumes of poetry, drama, fiction, essays, translations, and manifestos, and at the dawn of the new millennium he continues to write prolifically in a great variety of genres. Born in 1933 in Kunsan, North Chŏlla Province, he showed early signs of talent by mastering the introductory primers for the Chinese classics by the time he was eight. He dates his poetic vocation to the day in 1945 when he discovered a book of poems by the leper-poet Han Haun by the roadside and was deeply impressed by them.

During the Korean War (1950–53) he was appalled by the atrocities tearing his country apart, and after a suicide attempt he decided to become a Buddhist monk. He was quickly noticed, became the disciple of a great monk, the Venerable Hyobong, and served for a time as acting head of Haein Temple; he helped found the *Pulgyo shinmun*, a Buddhist newspaper, and published his first collection of poems, *Other-World Sensitivity* (P'ian kamsŏng) in 1960. This was followed by his first novel, *Other-World Cherry* (P'ian aeng). In 1962 he quit the monastic life, dissatisfied with its formalism.

He spent several years teaching on Cheju Island, where he published his second poetry collection, *Seaside Poems* (Haebyŏn ŭi unmunjip), in 1964. Those were years of deep anguish and he barely survived a suicide attempt in 1970. Finally, in 1973, he found a mission—that of a leading spokesman in the campaign against President Park Chung Hee's Yushin policies—that delivered him from excessive nihilism. He spoke as an ardent nationalist and quickly became known as one of the country's leading dissident writers and speakers, a man whose voice could be heard at every important demonstration and protest. He became the first secretary general of the Association of Artists for Practical Freedom when it was founded in 1974. He was frequently arrested. He continued to write and publish poetry, including the volumes *On the Way to Munŭi Village* (Munŭi Maŭl e kasŏ, 1974), *Going into Mountain Seclusion* (Ipsan, 1977), and *Early Morning Road* (Saebyŏk kil, 1978). In the 1970s he also published a series of poetic biographies of artist Yi Chungsŏp, modernist writer *Yi Sang, and poet Han Yongun, as well as travel documentaries and several novels, including *Young Traveler* (Ŏrin nagŭne, 1974) which was later republished as the first half of *The Garland Sutra* (Hwaŏmgyŏng, 1991).

He was among those incarcerated in May 1980 following the Kwangju Uprising, and he thought he might be executed. In prison, he recalled all the people whose paths had crossed his own since childhood and vowed to write about each of them, if he survived. This was the beginning of his *Ten Thousand Lives* (Maninbo) project, the first part of which appeared in 1986. As of 1999 the series numbered fifteen volumes with another fifteen promised, each poem devoted to one person or group of people.

His earlier poetry is often marked by a sense that life is essentially futile. Poems in his 1980s collections, though, begin to celebrate life as something beautiful, sublime, and precious, precisely because of each moment's impermanence. This celebratory tone begins with *Homeland Stars* (Choguk ŭi pyŏl, 1984), his first collection since 1978, and continues in such volumes as *Fly High, Poem!* (Shi yŏ, naragara, 1986).

In 1983 Ko Ŭn married and moved to Ansŏng, Kyŏnggi Province. This did not mean a withdrawal from his social involvement, which continued; he became president of the Federation of Korean Nationalist Artists in 1989 and served into the 1990s as president of the Association of Writers for National Literature. With the long-awaited return of his passport in the early 1990s, he has made many journeys to give readings all over the world, including Germany, Holland, France, the United States, Australia, Canada, and Mexico. In addition, he has made expeditions to India and Tibet and was able to visit North Korea in 1997. In 2000 he was a member of the delegation that accompanied President Kim Dae-jung on his visit to Pyongyang.

The 1990s saw an intensification of his creative activities. In 1991–93 he published the seven-volume *Mt. Paektu* (Paektusan), an epic poem evoking the history of the Korean struggle for independence from Japan. After a decade without any novels, he finally completed the task he had begun while still a monk, of retelling the story of the travels of the child Sudhana, found at the end of the Avatamsaka Sutra, by publishing *The Garland Sutra* in its entirety (1991). His return to specifically Buddhist subjects was also marked by the publication in 1995 of *Zen* (Sŏn), a novel in which he tells the story of the first Zen patriarchs in China, and by a collection of Zen poems, *Beyond Self* (Muonya, 1991). *The Garland Sutra* is particularly interesting because it reflects so clearly the evolution of its author's concerns. The first chapters, written while he was still a monk, are in a highly lyrical style, and the child Sudhana begins his journey with some strange encounters. Central chapters reflect a growing concern with life in society and with the possibility of a Buddhist social ethic. The second half of the novel, written in the late 1980s, continues to reflect the author's own life-itinerary as it enters far more deeply into abstruse Buddhist doctrine and the mystical world of the Avatamsaka Sutra.

It is impossible to evaluate Ko Ŭn's work in a few lines, and very little has been published on him in English. Ko Ŭn himself wrote in the introduction to the collection *Sea Diamond Mountain* (Haegŭmgang, 1991): "If someone opens my grave a few years after my death, they will find it full, not of my bones, but of poems written in that tomb's darkness." His work arises not from any personal ambition but from a deeply felt need to give voice to the pains and hopes of the still divided Korean people. His writing is deeply nationalistic, yet is increasingly being read and admired far beyond the limits of the Korean Peninsula.

— Brother Anthony of Taizé

Bibliography

Ko Ŭn. *Beyond Self: 108 Korean Zen Poems*. Trans. Young-Moo Kim and Brother Anthony of Taizé. Berkeley: Parallax Press, 1997.
———. *The Sound of My Waves: Selected Poems*. Trans. Brother Anthony of Taizé and Young-Moo Kim. Ithaca, N.Y.: Cornell University East Asia Program, 1993.

127

HWANG SŎGYŎNG

More has been expected of Hwang Sŏgyŏng than of almost any other Korean writer of the past quarter-century. Since the early 1970s, when Hwang began to write stories about the nameless millions on whose backs the Korean "economic miracle" was realized, he has been regarded as a champion of the people. This reputation took shape with his 1971 novella *Far from Home* (Kaekchi), was buttressed by such stories as "The Chronicle of a Man Named Han" (Han sshi yŏndaegi, 1972), "A Dream of Good Fortune" (Twaeji kkum, 1973), and "The Road to Samp'o" (Samp'o kanŭn kil, 1974), and was solidified by the roman-fleuve *Chang Kilsan* (1984), about a bandit leader of that name who lived in Chosŏn times.

A useful point of departure for an appreciation of this body of fiction is the life of the author himself. Hwang was born in 1943 in Manchuria and lost his father at an early age. His family moved in 1945 to Hwanghae Province in what is now North Korea, and then in 1949 to the Yŏngdŭngp'o district of Seoul. In 1950 the family fled to the city of Taegu after the outbreak of the Korean War. Hwang's interest in writing developed early, and in 1954 he was selected for a nationwide children's literary contest. Also during that year he briefly ran away from home—the first in a series of pilgrimages that has marked his life ever since. Though an honor student at Seoul's prestigious Kyŏngbok High School, he was not satisfied with school life and in 1962 was expelled. The same year, his story "Near the Rock Marker" (Ipsok pugŭn) was entered in a new-writers' contest sponsored by the journal *Sasanggye* (The World of Thought) and published therein. In 1964 he enrolled in Sungshil University; he eventually graduated from Tongguk University with a degree in philosophy. Also in 1964 he was jailed for political reasons. In prison he met labor activists, and upon his release he worked at a cigarette factory and at several construction sites around the country. In 1966 he enlisted in Korea's Blue Dragon marine unit and served in the Vietnam War; he was discharged in 1969. He gained renewed attention for his writing when in 1970 his story "Pagoda" (T'ap), based on his experiences in Vietnam, captured a prize in a literary arts competition sponsored by the *Chosŏn ilbo*, a Seoul daily. The Vietnam War is also the setting of his novel *The Shadow of Arms* (Mugi ŭi kŭnŭl, 1992). A series of unauthorized visits to North Korea beginning in 1989 resulted in political exile in Japan, Germany, and the United States. Returning to South Korea in 1993, he was jailed for violating the National Security Law. He was released in 1998 as part of a group amnesty granted by President Kim Dae-jung. From 1989 until that time little was published by or about him.

Hwang's varied life experiences and his constant fictional concern with the lives of common people have given him unquestioned legitimacy among a group of fiction writers including *Yun Hŭnggil, Yi Mungu, *Cho Sehŭi, Cho Chŏngnae, *Yi Munyŏl, and Kim Wŏnil, who came to prominence in the 1970s with a body of work marked by a strong awareness of social, political, historical, and cultural issues. Such is the status accruing to Hwang over his years of literary witness to the cause of laborers and other disadvantaged members of Korean society that the 1985 report on the Kwangju massacre of 1980, *Beyond Death, Beyond the Darkness of the Times* (Chugŭm ŭl nŏmŏ, shidae ŭi ŏdum ŭl nŏmŏ), written by Yi Chaeŭi, was initially credited to Hwang.

With his very first published story, "Near the Rock Marker," written when he was a high school student, Hwang began to establish a brand of realism that has roots in some of the earliest of modern Korean stories—those of Kim Tongin, Hyŏn Chingŏn, and Yŏm Sangsŏp (see "Realism in Early Modern Fiction")— but that also exhibits a strength of character and power of will rarely seen in Korean fiction before the publication in 1957 of Sŏnu Hwi's novella *Flowers of Fire* (Pulkkot). In "Near the Rock Marker," young friends survive a dangerous rock climb by risking their lives for one another and rejecting the temptation to hammer out handholds to make the climbing easier. Their success suggests to us that a group—here, the team linked by the rope—is greater than the sum of its individual members. In his subsequent fiction Hwang would turn to marginal or outcast figures in Korean society to illustrate this same capacity for integrity and strength of character amid difficult circumstances.

"The Chronicle of a Man Named Han" is a poignant example. This long story begins with the death of the protagonist, Han, then backtracks to cover a life of astonishing vicissitudes that initially shows great promise in northern Korea but ends in dismal solitude in the south. Han's separation from his ancestral home in the north justifies the inclusion of this story in the broad category of *pundan munhak* (see "The Literature of Territorial Division"). Even among the tragedies spoken of by this literature, what is especially noteworthy about this story is the fundamental integrity of a man subjected to the ideologies, cruelty, self-interest, and, eventually, indifference of others. Unlike fictional characters who commit moral lapses that return to haunt them, Han remains true to himself and to his calling when as a young doctor in the newly established North Korea he chooses to save the life of girl rather than tend to the less serious wounds of a party member—a decision, however, that starts Han's life unraveling. That the outrages visited upon this man are related with calm objectivity in the third-person narrative testifies to the maturity of Hwang's fictional style at that early stage.

That style blends an idealistic vision with forceful, often gritty language and realistic depictions of those who, like Hwang himself, have found themselves "far from home." *Far from Home* and "The Road to Samp'o" deal with the lives of itinerant construction workers. The former deals specifically with a group of laborers involved in a land reclamation project defending themselves from exploitation by unscrupulous foremen. Here, as in "Near the Rock Marker," Hwang hints at the effectiveness of group action. The timeliness of such stories lies in their depiction of the human costs of President Park Chung Hee's economic strategy of export-led development coupled with his New Village Movement, which in the 1970s fostered a building boom in the provinces. Many of the construction projects depended for manpower on day labor, and once a project was finished the workers had to journey elsewhere for work. The insecurity of this lifestyle and the rapidly changing face of the countryside are reflected vividly at the end of "The Road to Samp'o," when one of the protagonists, returning to his ancestral home after a ten-year sojourn among construction sites scattered about the nation, finds that the Samp'o he once knew no longer exists. This scene is echoed in "A Dream of Good Fortune" (Twaeji kkum, 1973) when a squatter neighborhood is razed and vanishes within a day.

"The Road to Samp'o" is also interesting for its three-dimensional portrait of Paekhwa, a bargirl and prostitute with a fondness for young soldiers who have recently been released from a military prison. Realistic, fully developed female characters who, like Paekhwa, are social outcasts are somewhat rare in Korean fiction before the 1970s. More to the point, Hwang's treatment of Paekhwa speaks to his recognition, reinforced in "A Dream of Good Fortune," that Korean women, once confined to the domestic sphere, have become an important and necessary presence in the work force. Significantly, at the end of "The Road to Samp'o," when Paekhwa bids farewell to her two male traveling companions and departs for home and family and a return to a life of farming, she discards her "work name" of Paekhwa and reveals her real name—an acknowledgment of her abiding self-respect, which in turn has gained her the respect of the men.

Women are also a strong force, within and outside the home, in "A Dream of Good Fortune." The Korean title, "Twaeji kkum" (literally, "pig dream"), refers to a folk belief that a dream in which pigs appear heralds a windfall. The story has three parts, each featuring an unexpected windfall of sorts: a feast for a squatter neighborhood, a henpecked husband's sexual liaison with a young factory woman, and much-needed money to finance a shotgun wedding. The irony is that the third of these windfalls—thirty thousand wŏn in compensation awarded to Kŭnho, a young factory hand—comes at the expense of Kŭnho's disfigurement in a workplace accident. More generally the story concerns one of the most visible social problems attending the industrialization of South Korea in the 1970s: the mass influx of rural immigrants to urban areas and their establishment of squatter neighborhoods. Distinguishing the residents of these areas—who in some cases emigrated more or less en masse from the same countryside location—is a sense of traditional group solidarity within the neighborhood but a breakdown of traditional values in the commercial areas and factories outside it. The "evil-looking smokestack," "denuded hillside," "great heaps of rubbish," and "grayish waste water" mentioned at the beginning of the story are pointed references to the baggage of unbridled industrialization.

Whereas the protagonists of these stories are nonheroic, even antiheroic, Chang Kilsan, the subject of Hwang's magnum opus of the same name, is a figure larger than life. Chang is considered one of the three great bandit leaders of Chosŏn times. Significantly, the other two, Hong Kiltong and Im Kkŏkchŏng, had earlier received exemplary fictional treatments. "The Tale of Hong Kiltong" (Hong Kiltong chŏn, c. 1610), attributed to Hŏ Kyun (1569–1618), is thought to be the first fictional narrative written in *hangŭl*, the vernacular script. Im, a brigand leader active in the mid-1500s in and around Hwanghae Province, is the subject of splendid storytelling by Hong Myŏnghŭi (1888–1968) in his lengthy *Im Kkŏkchŏng* (1939). That Hwang sought in *Chang Kilsan* to follow upon these hallowed literary precedents with a long work on the third great bandit leader testifies to his links with Korean tradition and suggests that he meant to encapsulate the humble protagonists of his early works in a historical figure noted for his rebellious and independent ways.

In *The Shadow of Arms*, Hwang's last major work before his exile and imprisonment, he turned his attention abroad. This novel, Ahn Junghyo's *White Badge* (Hayan chŏnjaeng, 1989), and Yi Sangmun's *The Yellow People* (Hwangsaegin, 1987), are perhaps the three best-known Korean novels about the Vietnam War. In contrast with the psychological emphasis of *White Badge*, Hwang's focus in *The Shadow of Arms* is primarily economic. Specifically, he describes the black marketeering that emanated from the American military presence in South Vietnam in the 1960s and 1970s. In this respect, the parallel with Korea, which itself continues to experience an American military presence, is obvious. Another emphasis of this novel, one that links it to Hwang's stories about workers, is the mercenary nature of South Korea's involvement in the Vietnam War. The hard cash earned by the Republic of Korea for its role in Vietnam was channeled in large part toward Park Chung Hee's industrialization program. Here, as in his earlier stories, Hwang implicitly asks us to consider whether the ends (South Korea's economic progress) justify the means (exploitation of workers at home and soldiers abroad).

Upon his release from jail in 1998 Hwang declared his intention to write half a dozen novels based on outlines composed during his confinement. The first was to be based in Hwanghae Province, the author's short-lived childhood home in North Korea, but would take place during the Japanese occupation. It remains to be seen if a subsequent novel will focus on the North Korea of more recent years, based on the author's personal observation. Such a work would provide a fitting capstone to Hwang's tenacious concern with the destiny of the 70 million Koreans now inhabiting the peninsula.

—Bruce Fulton

Bibliography

Ahn Junghyo. *White Badge*. New York: Soho Press, 1989.

Hǒ Kyun (att.). "The Tale of Hong Kiltong." Trans. Marshall R. Pihl. In Peter H. Lee, ed., *Anthology of Korean Literature: From Early Times to 1900*, 119–147. Honolulu: University Press of Hawai'i, 1981.

Hwang Sǒgyǒng. "The Chronicle of a Man Named Han." Trans. Yu Young-nan. *Korean Literature Today* (Summer 1998): 7–76.

——. "A Dream of Good Fortune." Trans. Bruce and Ju-Chan Fulton. In Marshall R. Pihl and Bruce and Ju-Chan Fulton, eds., *Land of Exile: Contemporary Korean Fiction*, 115–149. Armonk, N.Y.: M. E. Sharpe, 1993.

——. "The Road to Samp'o." Trans. Agnita Tennant. *Acta Koreana* 3 (2000): 145–159.

——. *The Shadow of Arms*. Trans. Chun Kyung-Ja. Ithaca, N.Y.: Cornell University East Asia Program, 1994.

Lee Taedong. "History and Humanism: The Early Work of Hwang Sǒg-yǒng." Trans. Yu Young-nan. *Korean Literature Today* (Summer 1998): 77–90.

Sǒnu Hwi. "Flowers of Fire." (Excerpt.) Trans. Peter H. Lee. In Peter H. Lee, ed., *Flowers of Fire: Twentieth-Century Korean Stories*, 184–243. Honolulu: University Press of Hawai'i, 1974.

128

YUN HŬNGGIL

Yun Hŭnggil was born in 1942 in Chŏngŭp, North Chŏlla Province, and graduated from Chŏnju Teachers School and Wŏngwang University. Originally a schoolteacher, he has made a living from writing since 1976. He made his literary debut in 1968, receiving the annual Newcomers Literary Award given by the *Hanguk ilbo,* a Seoul daily. He has since published more than a dozen volumes of fiction. Yun's works have been translated into French, German, English, and especially Japanese, as a result of which he is one of the best-known Korean authors in Japan.

Yun is one of the exceptionally influential group of South Korean writers who came to prominence in the 1960s and 1970s. Like his contemporaries, he has addressed a variety of social and historical issues, such as the scars left by the Korean War and the plight of country people transplanted to Seoul to augment the urban labor pool. In the process he has maintained a distinct voice characterized by gentle humor and an evenhanded treatment of his many flawed characters—no mean feat considering the volatility of some of his themes, such as police pressure on neighbors to inform on one another. So delicate did he consider the subject matter of his novel *Sickle* (Nat, 1989), for example, which takes place in the chaotic period extending from the last years of the colonial period (1910–45) to the outbreak of the Korean War (1950), that he published it in Japanese translation before bringing it out in Korean.

Among Yun's important works are the stories "The House of Twilight" (Hwanghon ŭi chip, 1970), "Gang Beating" (Molmae, 1975), "The Rainy Spell"

(Changma, 1973), and "The Man Who Was Left As Nine Pairs of Shoes" (Ahop k'yŏlle ŭi kudu ro namŭn sanae, 1977). The impact of these works is strengthened by the images they employ. The titles, for example, are deeply resonant. "The House of Twilight" recalls the countless families whose fortunes have faded into the gloom of historical calamity and presages the dreariness of a new urban, industrial economic order. "Gang Beating" points to the power of the group in Korean society and hints ominously at the authoritarianism of 1970s South Korea. "The Rainy Spell" (perhaps more accurately "The Rainy Season" or "The Long Season of Rain") encapsulates the oppressiveness felt by the millions of families that to this day remain separated by the ideological and territorial division of the Korean Peninsula. "The Man Who Was Left As Nine Pairs of Shoes" follows an educated man's desperate attempt to retain some semblance of dignity after a political transgression reduces his employment options to day labor and leaves him with virtually no material possessions other than an immaculately maintained collection of footwear.

Particularly effective among Yun's stories are those portraying recent Korean history as seen through the eyes of children (Kim 1997:76; see also "The Sŏng-jang Sosŏl"). In "Fuel" (Ttaelkam, 1978) a boy witnesses his poverty-stricken father reduced to pilfering firewood from a forest preserve, then himself joins friends in stealing coal briquettes from a railroad car. The aforementioned "House of Twilight" and "The Rainy Spell" are also told from a child's point of view.

—*Bruce Fulton*

Bibliography

Kim Chie-sou. "Old Wounds and the Anguish of Reality: Yun Heung-gil's 'The Rainy Season.'" *Koreana* (Autumn 1997): 76–77.

Yun Hŭnggil. *The House of Twilight*. Ed. J. Martin Holman. London: Readers International, 1989.

——. "The Man Who Was Left As Nine Pairs of Shoes." Trans. Bruce and Ju-Chan Fulton. In Marshall R. Pihl and Bruce and Ju-Chan Fulton, eds., *Land of Exile: Contemporary Korean Fiction*, 165–199. Armonk, N.Y.: M. E. Sharpe, 1993.

129

CHO SEHŬI AND *THE DWARF*

If Cho Sehŭi (b. 1942) had written nothing else besides his linked-story novel *The Dwarf* (Nanjangi ka sosaollin chagŭn kong [literally, "a little ball launched by a dwarf"], 1978), he would remain one of modern Korea's most important writers. Such is the significance of that work in the history of modern Korean letters. After making his literary debut in the *Kyŏnghyang shinmun*, a Seoul daily, in 1965, Cho published but a single story during the next ten years. But then in short order, from 1975 to 1978, he published the twelve stories that would form *The Dwarf*. Two books have appeared since: *Time Travel* (Shigan yŏhaeng, 1983) and *The Roots of Silence* (Ch'immuk ŭi ppuri, 1985).

Industrialization in South Korea during the Park Chung Hee regime (1961–1979) was gained at the cost of civil, labor, and environmental abuses of the sort that attracted the attention of American muckrakers early in the 1900s. The cast of characters included a large number of laborers, many of them recent immigrants to Seoul from the countryside; a small urban middle class suddenly faced with civil and social issues larger than those encountered in the hometown village; and the crony capitalists who headed a few powerful conglomerates. Cho Sehŭi's daunting task in *The Dwarf* was to describe the dark side of this industrialization without running afoul of dictator Park's strict national security laws. His solution was to use subtle irony in his narratives and at the same time, in order to reach the widest possible audience, to write in syntax simple enough to be understood by any Korean with a rudimentary education. The result is a book whose basic message—the social costs of reckless industrialization—is evident but whose deeper meanings—the spiritual malaise of the newly rich and powerful and of a working class subject to forces beyond its control—await discovery by the careful and deliberate reader. Cho Sehŭi succeeded admirably in his undertaking: in his native Korea the book has appeared in more than 150 printings since its publication in 1978.

The Dwarf is set in turn among a laboring family, a family of the newly emerging middle class, and a wealthy industrialist's family that looks for inspiration to German big business. The twelve stories are written in a lean, clipped style that features rapid shifts of scene and viewpoint. Long paragraphs alternate with stretches of terse dialogue. A demolition notice reproduced in "A Little Ball Launched by a Dwarf" (1976) and an extract from a laboring family's budget book in "The Cost of Living for a Family of Ŭngang Laborers" (Ŭngang nodong kajok ŭi saenggyebi, 1977) give us a taste of the realities of a dwarf's life—the dwarf epitomizing the "little people" on whose backs the Korean economic miracle took place, and his tiny ball suggesting the eternal legacy of the laboring masses. These particularities of life in South Korea in the 1970s are juxtaposed with snippets of information on science past and present and allusions to the workings of the universe. Two stories, "The Möbius Strip" (Moebiusŭ ŭi tti, 1976) and "The Klein Bottle" (K'ŭllain sshi ŭi pyŏng, 1978), are built on the concept of spatial form, their titles referring to objects whose inner and outer surfaces are actually one. This seeming contradiction and the references to the history of science and space exploration suggest to us that the dualities, contradictions, and anomalies of industrialization described in *The Dwarf* are not unique to Korea but result in large part from global economic forces that have accumulated over the centuries.

Abuse of power is a vivid presence in *The Dwarf*. Typically power is exercised through intimidation and violence, as in "Knifeblade" (K'allal, 1975) and "A Little Ball Launched by a Dwarf," and through sexual domination, evident also in the latter story. Violence begets violence, as when in the penultimate story in *The Dwarf*, "The Bony-Fish That Came into My Net" (Nae kŭmul lo onŭn kashigogi, 1978), a captain of industry is assassinated. Here the author is obliquely critiquing the authoritarian leadership that has plagued much of modern Korean history, as well as questioning Korea's traditionally patriarchal social structure. "City of Machines" (Kigye toshi, 1978) vividly portrays the new mechanized industrial society and its impact on the natural world.

South Korea's recent spate of industrial accidents and economic troubles as well as the more desperate environmental degradation and food shortages in North Korea have served to reinforce the contemporaneity of *The Dwarf* and its status as the most important postwar Korean novel.

—*Bruce Fulton*

Bibliography

Cho Sehŭi. "The Bony-Fish That Came into My Net." Trans. Sol Sun-bong. *Korea Journal* (November 1978): 19–36.

———. "City of Machines." Trans. Marshall R. Pihl. *Korea Journal* (March 1990): 68–74.

———. "The Cost of Living," Trans. Bruce and Ju-Chan Fulton. *Kyoto Journal*, no. 53 (2003): 79–83.

———. "Knifeblade." Trans. Bruce and Ju-Chan Fulton. *Korean Literature Today* (Fall 1998): 107–125.

———. "A Little Ball Launched by a Dwarf." Trans. Bruce and Ju-Chan Fulton. *Korean Literature Today* (Fall 1998): 126–169.

———. "The Möbius Strip." Trans. Bruce and Ju-Chan Fulton. *Korean Literature Today* (Fall 1998): 170–181.

Pihl, Marshall R. "The Nation, the People, and a Small Ball: Literary Nationalism and Literary Populism in Contemporary Korea." *Korea Journal* (March 1990): 16–25.

130

THE INTELLECTUAL REALM OF YI CH'ŎNGJUN

Yi Ch'ŏngjun is one of South Korea's most distinguished and prolific writers. His literary career spans the postwar decades of political upheaval and social unrest from the April 19 student uprising (1960) to the Kwangju Massacre (1980). Many of his important works were produced during Park Chung Hee's authoritarian regime (1961–79), providing important sociopolitical commentary and pointed criticism of the military government. His works provide critical insights into a turbulent era when the state suppressed cultural and political expression. Since his literary debut in 1965, he has produced a number of highly acclaimed works, winning numerous awards and attracting public and critical attention. He has written more than 120 stories and novellas and fourteen novels, and his works have been translated into English, French, German, Japanese, and Spanish. Yi Ch'ŏngjun's corpus encompasses a wide range of genres and styles: plays, *p'ansori* (a traditional oral narrative, part sung and part spoken), and children's stories, as well as prose fiction.

Yi is known as a *chijŏgin chakka* (intellectual writer) and as a writer of *kwallyŏm* (concepts); he writes with a language of reason and intellect, rather than of sensibility. His writing style is often considered difficult and abstruse as he grapples with the relationship between the real and the ideal, the meaning of language and structure, and representations of the intellectual and symbolic realms.

Born in Changhŭng, South Chŏlla Province, in 1939, Yi experienced the loss of his father, older and younger brothers, and a sister-in-law before he turned ten. Yi also experienced the trauma of the Korean War (1950–53), physical and psychological wounds that reappear as literary themes in his work. After leaving his mother and hometown in his teens to live with relatives in Kwangju, he entered Seoul National University to study German literature in 1960. Before graduation he made his literary debut with a story entitled "Discharge from the Hospital" (T'oewŏn, 1965), illustrating an oppressive relationship between a father and son. In the story, the protagonist is hospitalized for a stomach ailment, but his illness originates in a childhood trauma resulting from his father's having locked him in a storage room for two days with no food. The repressive apparatus of institution, embodied in the father figure, mirrors the Park military regime in the early 1960s.

Upon graduation Yi published "The Wounded" (Pyŏngshin kwa mŏjŏri, 1966) in the literary journal *Ch'angjak kwa pip'yŏng* (Writing and Criticism), problematizing the issues of trauma, violence, guilt, and responsibility. "The Wounded" underscores the trauma of experiencing violence and death during the Korean War and the impossibility of expressing that experience. Yi structures the story in a frame style, where multiple voices emerge from the narrative-within-narrative framework. The conflation of real and phantasm in "The Wounded" creates ambivalence and uncertainty, with Yi attempting to represent experienced reality in both symbolic and intellectual terms. Situated in the context of modern Korean history, this story brings forth questions of historical responsibility and unresolved issues, such as the territorial division of the peninsula, the separation of family members, and the legitimacy of the two states, North and South. In a later story, "An Assailant's Face" (Kahaeja ŭi ŏlgul, 1992), Yi returns to this theme of responsibility, but frames it in a victim/aggressor binary. The impossibility of defining the victim/victimizer positions in the story raises the issue of who really are the victims of the national tragedy, challenging the South Korean state's perpetuation of the idea that South Korea is the victim of North Korea.

At the height of the political oppression of the 1970s Yi wrote works such as "Wall of Rumor" (Somun ŭi pyŏk, 1971), "Floating Words" (Ttŏdonŭn mal tŭl, 1973), *Your Paradise* (Tangshin tŭl ŭi ch'ŏnguk, 1976), "The Prophet" (Yeŏnja, 1977), and "The Cruel City" (Chaninhan toshi, 1978). In these works he illustrates the power relations between the state/institution and the individual, and how people confront and resist such oppression. The characters in the stories are deeply wounded by traumatic events, whether national or individual. Both *Your Paradise* and "The Cruel City" portray a closed society and grapple with the notion of freedom and power. *Your Paradise* in particular is regarded as one of the most important literary challenges to political hegemony. Through its exploration of various dichotomies (ruler/ruled, healthy/sick, love/hatred) the novel delineates the complex and intense psychological struggles of its characters to make meaning for themselves in a circumscribed society. Throughout the novel, Yi questions what a "true paradise" is and for whom it is created.

In works such as "Time's Gate" (Shigan ŭi mun, 1982), "The Fire Worshipers" (Pihwa milgyo, 1985), and "Tale of an Insect" (Pŏlle iyagi, 1985), Yi explores the meaning of human existence and the themes of revenge and forgiveness. He often introduces craftsmen who attempt to draw meaning from the uncertainties of urban modernization. Examples are "The Target" (Kwanyŏk, 1967), "The Falconer" (Maejabi, 1968), "The Western Style" (Sŏp'yŏnje, 1976), and "The Resplendence of Sound" (Sori ŭi pit, 1978). Yi often treats the loss of tradition in Korean modernity, giving voice to the artisan who struggles to maintain what was once deemed significant. In "The Western Style," which was adapted into the blockbuster film *Sŏp'yŏnje*, a father struggles to carry on the *p'ansori* tradition, despite his son's rejection of it. To continue the tradition, the father goes to the extreme of blinding his daughter, whom he is training as a performer. Similarly, in "The Falconer" the protagonist starves himself to death when he is forbidden to continue falconry. Both physical (corporeal) and symbolic (blindness) deaths signify the fate of those who are alienated, who are driven to the margins of society, or who fail to adapt to rapid modernization.

Several other stories, such as "Homecoming Practice" (Kwihyang yŏnsŭp, 1972), "Footprints in the Snow" (Nunkil, 1977), and "The Living Marshland" (Sarainnŭn nŭp, 1980) center on sentiments evoked by the *kohyang* (ancestral home or hometown) and the mother-son relationship. The author's own traumatic separation from his mother and hometown is projected onto these stories, yet "homecoming" becomes impossible. "Footprints in the Snow" concerns the ambivalent relationship between a mother and son, a guilt-ridden urban intellectual who struggles with his abandonment of his elderly mother and hometown. The mother's deep affection toward her son is beautifully portrayed, yet subtle. The story critically examines the plight of people who leave the poverty-stricken countryside for the wealthy city, deserting their ancestral homes.

One of the prominent roles of intellectuals in Korean society is to oppose institutions that reject intellectual activities, and Yi Ch'ŏngjun through his writings has endlessly voiced his resistance to authoritarian regimes. His keen critiques of the political situation, using allegorical images, are often compared to those of Thomas Mann and Franz Kafka. Yi searches endlessly for ways to express the notions of freedom and truth through writing (language), whether in a confessional mode or through storytelling. He firmly believes in the power of artistic creation and will continue to wield the power of writing to examine society's contradictions.

—*Jennifer M. Lee*

Bibliography

Yi Ch'ŏngjun. "An Assailant's Face." Trans. Jennifer M. Lee. *Manoa* 11, no. 2 (Winter 1999): 181–198.

———. *The Prophet and Other Stories*. Trans. Julie Pickering. Ithaca, N.Y.: Cornell University East Asia Program, 1999.

———. "The Target." Trans. Kim Chongch'ŏl. In Peter H. Lee, ed., *Modern Korean Literature: An Anthology*, 233–251. Honolulu: University of Hawai'i Press, 1990.

———. "The Wounded." Trans. Jennifer M. Lee. *Manoa* 11, no. 2 (Winter 1999): 128–147.

YI MUNYŎL

Fate was as kind to Yi Munyŏl in his thirties and forties as it was cruel to him in the first two decades of his life. Yi was born in 1948 in Yŏngyang, North Kyŏngsang Province, to an affluent family of the local aristocracy, but his luck plummeted when his socialist father defected to North Korea at the outbreak of the Korean War. Bereft of its breadwinner, his family had to struggle not only with poverty but also with the stigma of being the blood kin of a Communist, which in turn resulted in their subjection to police surveillance. These and other factors led Yi to drop out of high school and college and drove him to the brink of suicide. Throughout it all, however, he read omnivorously, which has served him well in his writing career.

Yi turned the unhappiness of his childhood and early youth superbly to account when he became a writer at age thirty. And luck seemed bent on making amends to him, too: even though almost all his works are serious even to a fault and are conspicuously lacking in sensational or erotic interest, he won an enthusiastic popular following as well as high critical acclaim. He has been a reigning figure in the Korean literary world since the 1980s, winning every prestigious literary award in Korea, including This Year's Writer Award (1979), the Tongin Literature Prize (1982), the Republic of Korea Literature Award (1983), the Yi Sang Literature Prize (1987), and the Hoam Award (1999). In his late thirties he began to receive attention and praise from renowned European critics for his translated works. In 1992 the French government awarded him L'Ordre des Arts et des Lettres for enriching the literary landscape of France. He has yet to conquer the American literary market but seems well poised to do so with his novella *Our Twisted Hero* (Uri tŭl ŭi ilgŭrŏjin yŏngung, 1987), published in translation by a major American commercial press in 2001, an American edition of *The Poet* (Shiin, 1992) in preparation, and a translation of *You Can't Go Home Again* (Kŭdae tashi nŭn kohyang e kaji mot'ari, 1980) forthcoming.

Yi has proved himself a master of all fictional forms—short story, novella, and novel. At the outset of his career he wrote solidly realistic stories dealing with social problems, but he quickly went on to reveal his protean faces one by one. In *The Son of Man* (Saram ŭi adŭl, 1979, rev. 1987), he explored numerous Western and Asian theologies in the course of tracing a young man's determined quest for spiritual transcendence. *A Portrait of My Youth* (Chŏlmŭn nal ŭi ch'osang, 1981), a trilogy of novellas, is a record of a young man's Herculean efforts to overcome his romantic nihilism and suicidal wishes (see "The Sŏngjang Sosŏl"). These and other early works exerted a powerful appeal on Korean young men who felt, in the late 1970s and early 1980s, that they were living in a world barren of spiritual values and devoid of nurturing human relationships.

Hail to the Emperor (Hwangje rŭl wihayŏ, 1983) showed that Yi has a robust sense of humor as well. This rambunctious satire on a deluded young man's imperial dreams also showcases the author's amazing erudition. In *An Age of Heroes* (Yŏngung shidae, 1984), Yi imaginatively reconstructs what his father's career among the ruthless Communists might have been after his defection to North Korea. Writing the novel was no doubt an attempt to lay to rest the ghost of his (living) father, who has haunted him in so many ways.

Along with the legacy of his father's politics and the sociohistorical factors that made him a Communist, Yi has been obsessed with the conflict created in Korean society and its citizens by the influx of an alien culture—that is, Western ways of life and thought. He grapples with the problem repeatedly in his important works. In each of the sixteen stories making up *You Can't Go Home Again*, Yi examines, with nostalgia, fury, or pained amusement, an aspect of a Korean's relationship to his hometown, a psychological and spiritual space that has vanished beyond recall. In "The Golden Phoenix" (Kŭmshijo, 1985), a calligraphy master is torn between Asian aesthetics, which evaluate a work of art as visual evidence of the integrity and loftiness of the artist's character, and Western aesthetics, which accord value to a work of art as an object of beauty on the basis of its formal perfection. In *The Poet*, a nineteenth-century vagabond poet is torn between his political commitments to the people and the pursuit of his artistic ideals, and he suffers from the distrust of his own motives as well.

Odyssey Seoul (Odisseia Sŏul, 1992) proves that Yi not only meditates on lofty world-historical subjects but also is thoroughly familiar with the seamy side of contemporary Seoul. In this two-volume novel the author takes his readers through all the mazes of Seoul's underworld, turning up evil and corruption every step of the way. *The Afternoon of Adulthood* (Sŏngnyŏn ŭi ohu, 1994) is a midlife-crisis novel with strong autobiographical elements. His frank portrayal of the frustrations and inner conflicts of an eminently successful literary man stirred a responsive chord in many adult males. The novella "An Appointment with My Brother" (Au wa ŭi mannam, 1994) is a fictional projection of the author's meeting with his younger half-brother (an offspring of his father's second marriage, after his defection to North Korea) and is an eloquent testimony to the human cost of Korea's territorial and ideological division.

In 1996 Yi had the daring (or foolhardiness) to publish *A Choice* (Sŏnt'aek), a short novel delineating the admirable life of an ancestor of his who seemingly embodied the highest ideals of Confucian womanhood. In this book he argued that this virtuous forebear deliberately "chose" to be a dedicated wife and wise mother (rather than be lazy, selfish, or rebellious) and extolled women to seek self-fulfillment in their homes. Thanks to the controversy it raised, the work sold more than 300,000 copies and made Yi the most prominent antifeminist in the land. He seemed staggered by the vehemence of the feminists' response to what he insists was a modest suggestion to women reluctant to embrace feminist rhetoric. Nevertheless, he mustered his willpower to complete what he said was the most difficult undertaking of his life: *Borderland* (Pyŏngyŏng, 1998), a ten-volume portrait of the times of his own boyhood and young manhood, which he wrote over a dozen years. He then wrote *Song of Songs* (Aga, 1999), which takes a nostalgic look at the old days when even halfwits were humored and given a haven and a role.

In addition to more than twenty novels and five collections of short stories and novellas, Yi has written a tremendous amount of weighty social commentary and essays on topical subjects. Moreover, his ten-volume translations of the great Chinese classics *Sankuoji* (1988) and *Shuheji* (1994) sold more than one million sets. In 1995 he tried his hand at playwriting and produced an operatic script on the life and death of the much-misunderstood and maligned penultimate empress of Korea. The resulting operetta, *The Last Empress*, was a big hit on Broadway and in Los Angeles as well as on the Korean stage.

In many of his works Yi shows himself to be nostalgic for old ways and old values. It could well be that he feels himself born out of his time. Still, he has exerted a powerful hold on his contemporaries, and even the controversies surrounding him have served to enhance or confirm his stature. Luck must have had a hand in it, but he has certainly deserved his success because of his dedication to his vocation, his unremitting labors, and the dignity with which he has worn his laurels.

—*Suh Ji-moon*

Bibliography

Yi Munyŏl. "An Appointment with My Brother." Trans. Suh Ji-moon. *Korean Literature Today* (Winter 1999): 94–153.

———. "Early Spring, Mid-Summer." Trans. Suh Ji-moon. *Korea Journal* (October 1982): 52–62.

———. "The Golden Phoenix." In Suh Ji-moon, trans. and ed., *The Golden Phoenix: Seven Contemporary Korean Short Stories*, 11–45. Boulder, Colo.: Lynne Rienner, 1998.

———. *Hail to the Emperor!* Trans. Sol Sun-bong. Seoul: Si-sa-yong-o-sa, 1986.

———. "The Idiot and the Water Snake." Trans. Suh Ji-moon. *Korean Literature Today* (Fall 2000): 99–114.

———. "The Old Hatter." Trans. Suh Ji-moon. *Korean Literature Today* (Spring 1999): 139–160.

———. *Our Twisted Hero.* Trans. Kevin O'Rourke. New York: Hyperion, 2001.

———. *The Poet.* Trans. Brother Anthony and Chung Chong-wha. London: Harvill Press, 1995.

———. "That Winter of My Youth." In Suh Ji-moon, trans. and ed., *The Rainy Spell and Other Korean Stories*, rev. ed., 213–247. Armonk, N.Y.: M. E. Sharpe, 1998.

———. "The Vagabond Guest: My Cousin's Story." Trans. Suh Ji-moon. *Manoa* 2, no. 2 (Fall 1990): 14–20.

132

SHIN KYŎNGNIM

Shin Kyŏngnim was born in 1935 in Chungwŏn, North Ch'ungch'ŏng Province. In his youth he frequented Korea's rural villages and collected the traditional songs he heard sung there. Much of his poetry reflects rhythms he heard then. His poems often express the pain and hurt of Korea's poor, not only those in the remote villages but also the urban poor and those marginalized in society. He uses easily accessible, rhythmic language to compose lyrical narratives that in some cases resemble shamanistic incantation and in other cases recall popular songs still sung in bars.

His literary career dates from 1955, but after the publication of a mere seven poems, including "The Reed" (Kaltae, 1956), between that year and 1957, he published only a single poem before 1969, immersing himself instead in the world of the working classes and working as a farmer, miner, and merchant. The experience of those years underlies his work as a poet. His fame dates mainly from his collection *Farmers' Dance* (Nongmu, 1973). It would be difficult to exaggerate the significance of this volume in the development of modern Korean poetry. It earned Shin the first Manhae Literary Award (named after the early modern poet-activist Han Yongun) in 1974, bringing his work unexpected publicity and critical attention. Shin thus helped open the way for public acceptance of a poetry rooted in harsh social realities, a militant literature that was to grow into the workers' poetry of the 1980s. The first edition of *Farmers' Dance* contained just over forty poems, some written years earlier and full of echoes of rural life. A second edition, published in 1975, added two sections containing nearly twenty poems written after 1973, reflecting life in a more urban context. Some critics regret this expansion, feeling that the newer poems are less powerful, but the fuller version represents the poet's final option.

Many of the poems in this collection are spoken by an undefined plural voice, a "we" encompassing the collective identity of the *minjung*—the poor farmers, laborers, and miners among whom the poet had lived. He makes himself their spokesman on the basis of no mere sympathy; he has truly lived as one of them, sharing their poverty and pains, their simple joys and often disappointed hopes.

The leading recognized Korean poets in the 1960s and 1970s were writing in a highly aesthetic style inspired by certain aspects of French symbolism. Many poets and critics of that time insisted that literature should have no direct concern with political or social issues. This assertion, however, had already been challenged in the earlier 1960s by a number of younger writers and critics, including the poet and essayist *Kim Suyŏng. In particular, Kim's advocacy of a poetic style reflecting everyday spoken language, with its colloquialisms and pithiness, is reflected in Shin's poems.

Appearing in a literary culture accustomed to the individual "I" speaker of the Western Romantic tradition or the unspecified voice of traditional Korean lyrics, the "we" employed in *Farmers' Dance* was shocking, almost offensive to some. This usage became an element in the critical debate sparked by Kim Suyŏng's dictum, "All avant-garde literature is subversive." The "we" gave rise to a critical controversy out of which emerged a major poetic movement of social involvement, in which Shin has continued to play a leading role. He has served as president of the Association of Writers of People's Literature and of the Federated Union of Korean Nationalist Artists. Subsequent volumes of poetry have appeared from 1979 through 1998. He has also published several collections of literary and personal essays.

Many of Shin's poems take on increased power by suppressing explanatory background; readers are invited to supply from their own memories or imaginations an explanation for the scene recorded. Many report what at first sight appears to be a happy scene of conviviality, but we are soon made to feel very strongly an underlying contradiction between the festive appearance and harsh social realities, with an accompanying sense of helplessness. In a number of poems unspoken memories of past events cast dark shadows. Other poems seem an evocation of almost nothing happening. There is a feeling of absurdity in a lot of his work; people spend whole lifetimes waiting for sense to come, but in vain, it seems. The celebrations that tradition imposes serve only to highlight the lack of any will to rejoice, while any preparation for resolute action, or even protest, turns quickly into a whimper or a drunken riot. The dance of the farmers announced in the title barely rises above a shuffle except when it turns into a rowdy, drunken shambles, and never takes off into the carefree mirth that the simple peasants are expected to enjoy in the lighter forms of pastoral and georgic. The reader in search of charm and aesthetic pleasure is bound to be frustrated.

Instead, we see that the poet has brought us into direct contact with people whose lives could scarcely be more remote from that of the poetry-reading milieu of 1970s Seoul. Not that those lives were totally unfamiliar, for many of the people living in Seoul had arrived there from precisely such remote villages; but it was the first time that anyone had ventured to make such realities the subject of lyric verse that clearly had no other purpose. This is not activist poetry in the sense that it seeks to provoke outrage and social change. It is much closer to memorial verse, a commemoration of lost generations, an expression of "Lest we forget."

No poet has expressed so well, and so humbly, the characteristic voice of Korea's masses, both rural and urban. Shin never sentimentalizes his subjects but rather takes the reader beyond the physical and cultural exterior to reveal them as intensely sensitive, suffering human beings.

—*Brother Anthony of Taizé*

Bibliography

Kim Su-Young, Shin Kyong-Nim, and Lee Si-Young. *Variations: Three Korean Poets.* Trans. Brother Anthony of Taizé and Young-Moo Kim. Ithaca, N.Y.: Cornell University East Asia Program, 2001.

Shin Kyong-Nim. *Farmers' Dance.* Trans. Brother Anthony of Taizé and Young-Moo Kim. Ithaca, N.Y.: Cornell University East Asia Program, 1999.

133

THE THEATER OF O T'AESŎK

Playwright O T'aesŏk (b. 1940) has held a leading position in Korea's avant-garde theater from the late 1960s until the present day. He is the author of more than thirty highly original dramas whose styles range from raucous comedy to historical tragedy, from evocations of the Korean War to bitter satires of contemporary Korean society. His plays have received numerous prizes and have begun to receive acclaim in the West. In 1974 *Grass Tomb* (Ch'obun) became the first Korean play produced on the professional English-speaking stage when it was staged at La Mama in New York City. In 1999 an anthology of his plays was the first collection of translations of a Korean dramatist published in the United States. At home the Seoul Arts Center, Korea's most prestigious theater, mounted a four-month festival in 1994 devoted entirely to his works—an unprecedented honor for a Korean dramatist. In 1999 he received the coveted Paeksang Award for *Prisoner for a Thousand Years* (Ch'ŏn nyŏn ŭi suin, 1998), a portrait of three prisoners—a Communist who refuses to renounce his beliefs, a soldier who went mad fighting protestors, and An Tu-hŭi, reviled assassin of patriot Kim Ku. Despite such honors, his plays have generated intense controversy due to their experimental forms and iconoclastic dissections of Korean culture. During various political crises over the past two decades he has been forced to postpone productions or withdraw his plays altogether. An innovative stage director, O founded the Mokhwa Repertory Company in 1987, and this group continues to produce his plays to an increasingly wide and receptive audience.

Inherent in nearly all of his drama is a conscious exploration of both native Korean and contemporary Western motifs and theatrical styles, resulting in unique theater pieces that defy easy categorization. Although his plays are invariably centered in what he calls the "Korean ethos," he investigates that ethos in complex dramatic forms that mingle such traditional Korean theatrical forms as the mask dance-drama, *p'ansori* (a traditional oral narrative that is both sung and spoken), and folk puppet theater with contemporary theater forms inspired by such Western artists as Antonin Artaud, Bertolt Brecht, and Jerzy Grotowski. His goal is neither to bring traditional Korean theater up to date nor to valorize native materials. It is rather to create new theatrical forms that, by juxtaposing old and new sources, Eastern and Western styles, reenact Korea's current social and cultural struggles.

O routinely unifies these diverse elements through theatrical metaphors that convey different but reciprocal meanings when seen from various cultural perspectives. In *Bicycle* (Chajŏngŏ, 1983), for example, a village clerk encounters spirits of the dead, the real-life victims of a fire set by North Korean soldiers thirty years earlier, and a family of lepers whose daughter burns down her parents' house in a desperate act of penitential sacrifice. The conflagration is the same, but kaleidoscopic perspectives of past and present, North and South, force us to reconsider our confidence in its meaning.

Often these contrasting perspectives derive from O's resurrection of long-forgotten rituals of birth and death in order to explore the painful transitions facing modern Korean society. In *Grass Tomb* a woman is thus buried so that a town's water supply will not be polluted. *Lifecord* (T'ae, 1974) questions the ethical basis of ancient rites of patrimony as it traces the fate of six scholars who remain loyal to a young king after he is forced to abdicate in favor of his uncle. The new king executes the six as traitors, but he also executes their families, providing O an opportunity to investigate the implications of communal guilt and loyalty to family, king, and country. In the brutally comic *Ch'unp'ung's Wife* (Ch'unp'ung ŭi ch'ŏ, 1976), derived from a classic tale of a wife's search for her philandering husband, O explores the difficult position of women in modern Korean society through ironic shamanistic rituals of birth and death where the boundaries between humans and animals, women and men, life and death are freely trespassed. The tragedy *Intimacy between Father and Son* (Puja yuch'in, 1987) is inspired by the dilemma of an eighteenth-century king whose heir develops a mysterious disease that manifests itself in sexual promiscuity, murder, and an aversion to clothing. In the end, the king must decide whether to force the prince's death or to risk destruction of the dynasty. The climax occurs when the king directs an elaborate death ritual by obliging his son to suffocate himself "voluntarily" by crawling into a rice chest to die. In such rituals, Confucian ideals of duty to family and country are tested in the light of wildly experimental Western dramatic forms that apparently defer to individual freedom over civic harmony.

O's recent dramas take aim at the materialism and chaos of modern urban life by introducing Korean characters who are nevertheless outsiders in their own society. His most celebrated play, *Why Did Shim Ch'ŏng Plunge into the Sea Twice?* (Shim Ch'ŏng-i nŭn oe Indangsu e tu pŏn man ŭl tŏnjŏnnŭnga? 1991), is a jarring revision of the legend of a filial daughter who volunteers to drown herself in return for the restoration of her blind father's sight. In O's violent retelling, the daughter, Shim Ch'ŏng, is abruptly placed in a seamy modern underworld of thieves, pimps, and prostitutes, where her plunge into the sea no longer offers hope of redemption but serves rather as a moving reminder of the fragility of goodness in contemporary society. The protagonists of *The Tartar Fox* (Yŏu wa sarang ŭl, 1996) are Koreans whose families emigrated to China during Japanese colonial rule and who return to Korea only to find themselves, like Shim Ch'ŏng, strangers in their own country, facing the prejudice and greed that O sees as rampant in modern Korea. Despite his mixing of artistic styles and dramatic genres and his extensive use of Western theater forms, critics see him as the most "Korean" of his country's dramatists, perhaps because he portrays the disparate forces impinging on Korean culture with such honesty and power.

—*Kim Ah-jeong and R. B. Graves*

Bibliography

O T'aesŏk. *The Metacultural Theater of Oh T'ae-sŏk: Five Plays from the Korean Avant-Garde*. Trans. and ed. Kim Ah-jeong and R.B. Graves. Honolulu: University of Hawai'i Press, 1999.

134

YANG KWIJA

Few Korean authors can match the critical and commercial success of novelist Yang Kwija. Born in 1955, Yang made her literary debut in 1978, when she received a Newcomers Award from the literary journal *Munhak sasang* (Literature and Thought). In the 1980s she published a steady stream of short stories, first from the Chŏlla region, where she was born and raised, and then from the Seoul area, where she settled after her marriage in 1980. Since the late 1980s she has concentrated on longer works, including the award-winning novella *Hidden Flower* (Sumŭn kkot, 1992) and the best-selling novels *A Distant and Beautiful Place* (Wŏnmi-dong saram tŭl [literally, The People of Wŏnmi-dong], 1987), *I Long to Possess That Which Is Forbidden Me* (Na nŭn somang handa, na ege kŭmjidoen kŏs ŭl, 1992), *A Thousand-Year Love* (Ch'ŏn nyŏn ŭi sarang, 1995), and *Contradictions* (Mosun, 1998).

Yang grew up amid South Korea's single-minded drive for industrialization and has lived most of her life in and around the nation's large urban centers. Her writing explores the modern urban experience with all its opportunities and disappointments, vividly portraying the lives of ordinary Koreans with straightforward prose, compassion, and humor. The protagonists in her early works are often "salarymen," faceless office workers struggling to overcome the alienation and loneliness of Korea's newly industrializing cities. The story "Rust" (Nok, 1985) chronicles the dismal existence of Yi, a would-be journalist sidetracked in the advertising department of a metropolitan newspaper company. The melancholy Yi spends his days groveling at the feet of potential advertising clients and his evenings cleaning his five-year-old son's bicycle, which remains covered with rust no matter how he scrubs. Like so many of Yang's protagonists, Yi is frustrated and angry at what seems to be the broken promise of industrialization. In the midst of modern Korea's remarkable growth, he is helpless, forever denied physical or spiritual comfort and prosperity. He can no more control his destiny than he can control the rust swallowing his son's bicycle.

From 1985 to 1987, Yang pursued this theme of middle-class alienation in a series of stories documenting the lives of those living on the periphery of Seoul, struggling to find refuge somewhere between the modern metropolis and traditional society. (In 1982 Yang, her husband, and their newborn daughter had moved from Seoul to the satellite city of Puch'ŏn, Kyŏnggi Province, driven from the capital by high housing prices.) The Puch'ŏn stories were published individually in literary journals and as the collection A *Distant and Beautiful Place*.

That collection portrays life in one neighborhood of Puch'ŏn in the early 1980s. It revolves around several themes: alienation in a rapidly changing society; the loss of a sense of community as outsiders move into the neighborhood, hoping for a better life; the deterioration of traditional values; and the search for something to replace those values. Throughout, Yang captures the essence of modern Korea in transition. The stories are linked through their characters and recurring issues in the changing community, a microcosm of the larger Korean society.

The stories also showcase Yang's solid writing style: clear and effective narrative, rich and realistic dialogue, and vivid characterizations. They reflect as well her essential optimism and belief in the enduring power of compassion and the value of community. These stories established Yang as a major writer, respected in the literary community and admired by readers from diverse social backgrounds for her sensitivity to the plight of ordinary Koreans amid their country's breakneck drive for first-world status. The collection was also honored with the Yu Chuhyŏn Literature Award in 1988.

Yang's more recent writing reflects her acute awareness of the contradictions faced by Korea's intelligentsia and newly emerging middle class since the inauguration of a civilian government in 1987 and the collapse of socialism on the world stage. In *Hidden Flower*, honored with the 1992 Yi Sang Literature Prize, an author struggling with writer's block searches for answers in a world where long-accepted absolutes no longer apply. This rare (for Yang) semi-autobiographical work probes the meaning of literature in modern Korea, the role of the writer in a democratic society, and the value of compassion and self-examination.

Yang broke new ground in her writing, and in Korean society, with the wildly popular novel *I Long to Possess That Which Is Forbidden Me*, a psychological and political portrayal of a feminist's revenge against a symbol of male oppression. Although the work may seem anachronistic to Western readers accustomed to similar themes since the 1970s, it was a milestone for Korean readers, probing persistent gender roles and the alienation of the modern woman, beyond the stereotyped depiction of *han*, that mysterious blend of resignation, longing, and resentment so often attributed to Korean women.

In the late 1990s Yang remained one of Korea's most successful authors, commercially and critically, with the publication of the best-selling novels *A Thousand-Year Love* and *Contradictions* and the novella *There Once Was a Bear* (Kom iyagi, 1996), which won the *Hyŏndae Munhak* (Contemporary Literature) Literature Prize. During this period she also branched out into more varied literary genres, including essays and *inmul sosŏl* (character sketches).

In the years since the publication of *A Distant and Beautiful Place* in the mid-1980s, Yang has become a popular cultural figure, frequently featured in women's magazines, newspaper columns, and other mainstream media. Her opening a widely acclaimed restaurant in downtown Seoul in the mid-1990s further enhanced her reputation as a capable and well-rounded author and entrepreneur, respected as much for her character as for her writing.

—*Julie Pickering*

Bibliography

Yang Kwija. *A Distant and Beautiful Place*. Trans. Kim So-Young and Julie Pickering. Honolulu: University of Hawai'i Press, 2002.

——. "Rust." Trans. Ahn Jung-hyo. In *Reunion So Far Away: A Collection of Contemporary Korean Fiction*, 149–178. Seoul: Korean National Commission for UNESCO, 1994.

——. "The Tearoom Woman." Trans. Kim So-Young and Julie Pickering. *Korean Literature Today* (Summer 1999): 110–136.

——. "The Wŏnmi-dong Poet." Trans. Kim So-Young and Julie Pickering. *Manoa* 8, no. 2 (1996): 133–145.

135

CH'OE YUN

Ch'oe Yun (b. 1953) is one of the most talented figures in contemporary Korean literature. In addition to writing award-winning fiction, she teaches French literature at Sogang University in Seoul, having completed a dissertation on Marguerite Duras at the University of Provence, and is an acclaimed translator (she and her husband, Patrick Maurus, have set new standards in the translation of modern Korean fiction into French). Her own works include three story collections, two novels, and a volume of essays.

Ch'oe has read widely in Korean and other literatures, and her fiction shows great variety and sophistication in addition to avoiding the tendentiousness of some of her contemporaries in Korea. She writes convincingly from the point of view of both men and women and approaches the upheavals of contemporary Korean history through the eyes of such unconventional protagonists as a riot policeman and an inarticulate laborer. And in stories set as far afield as Venice and Paris she transcends the historical realities of the post-1945 Korean body politic and comes to grips with the psychological and spiritual state of individual Koreans today.

She debuted as a creative writer (she had previously published literary criticism) in 1988 with the novella *There a Petal Silently Falls* (Chŏgi sori ŏpshi han chŏm kkonnip i chigo). Long interested in the writings of Mikhail Bakhtin, Ch'oe utilizes his notion of polyphonic voices to create a trifold narrative that follows the wanderings of a girl traumatized by the violent death of her mother during the 1980 military massacre of citizens of the southern city of Kwangju. As in much of her work, Ch'oe here uses historical fact as a point of departure, seeing in the violation of the citizenry insights into the psychology of brutality and abusive relationships. This was one of the first works of fiction to touch on the Kwangju Uprising, its publication made possible by the June 1987 democratization of the political process in South Korea.

Subsequent stories also use recent Korean history to explore larger themes. "His Father's Keeper" (Abŏji kamshi, 1990), set in Paris, describes a reunion between a man and his father, a defector to North Korea during the Korean War. The meeting is strained by the false expectations and assumptions each holds regarding the other. The sins-of-the-fathers theme of this story is enhanced by the suggestion that history serves to warp and bias memory.

The background of "The Gray Snowman" (Hoesaek nunsaram, 1992)—underground political activism during the regime of dictator Park Chung Hee in the 1970s—is the stuff of heroic literature. Ch'oe, though, set out in this story to demythologize the political activist and focus instead on the plight of an outsider, a young woman who unwittingly becomes involved with a small group of men who print antigovernment materials. The title resonates powerfully, the snow suggesting not only the Korean masses (traditionally clothed in white) but also the psychological weight and numbness resulting from political oppression, while gray suggests a soiling of the unsullied aspirations of youth as well as the shadowy existence of dissidents and other marginal figures.

Two more recent works, "The Last of Hanak'o" (Hanak'o nŭn ŏpta, 1994) and "The Flower with Thirteen Fragrances" (Yŏlse kaji irŭm ŭi kkot hyanggi, 1995), are among the most incisive Korean stories of the 1990s. In the former Ch'oe employs keen irony to expose hollow male stereotypes of women, the exotic setting of Venice casting the male protagonist's provincialism and narrow-mindedness in stark relief. "The Flower with Thirteen Fragrances" is a wry cautionary tale about the ephemeral nature of fame and wealth and offers a veiled critique of petty academics.

Ch'oe Yun is often thought of as an intellectual, experimental writer. She professes bemusement at such categorization: "The important thing for me is to depict reality through the most appropriate language and form. And because reality is always changing, it's only natural that each of my works should be different in language and form.... One needs a unique language and form to depict a changing world, and in this sense a work's world-view creates its own form. I prefer to describe this process not as an experiment but as the pursuit of a different factuality" (Fulton and Fulton 1996:6). It is thus more accurate to consider her an innovative, imaginative author, and as such a writer for the new millennium.

—*Bruce Fulton*

Bibliography

Ch'oe Yun. "The Flower with Thirteen Fragrances." In Suh Ji-moon, trans. and ed., *The Golden Phoenix: Seven Contemporary Korean Short Stories*, 155–197. Boulder, Colo.: Lynne Rienner, 1998.

————. "The Gray Snowman." Trans. Bruce and Ju-Chan Fulton. *Manoa* 8, no. 2 (1996): 78–98.

————. "His Father's Keeper." In Suh Ji-moon, trans. and ed., *The Rainy Spell and Other Korean Stories*, rev. ed., 248–270. Armonk, N.Y.: M. E. Sharpe, 1998.

————. "The Last of Hanak'o." In Bruce and Ju-Chan Fulton, trans. and eds., *Wayfarer: New Fiction by Korean Women*, 11–41. Seattle: Women in Translation, 1997.

————. *There a Petal Silently Falls*. Trans. Bruce and Ju-Chan Fulton. *Korea Journal* (Winter 1997): 221–239; (Spring 1998): 357–392.

Fulton, Bruce and Ju-Chan. "Infinity through Language: A Conversation with Ch'oe Yun." *Korean Culture* (Winter 1996): 5–7.

TIMELINE

ca. 2000–1600 B.C.	Xia dynasty (China)
ca. 1600–1028	Shang dynasty
?1122–770	Western Zhou dynasty
770–c. 256	Eastern Zhou dynasty
770–403	Spring and Autumn Annals
c. 403–221	Warring States period (China)
c. 221–206	Qin dynasty (China)
206 B.C.–c. A.D. 8	Former, or Western Han, dynasty (China)
?57 B.C.–A.D. 935	Shilla kingdom (Korea)
A.D. 25–220	Later, or Eastern Han dynasty (China)
c. 220–c. 280	Three Kingdoms (China)
c. 222–589	Six Dynasties (China)
265–420	Jin dynasty (China)
420–589	Southern and Northern dynasties (China)
552–645	Asuka period (Japan)
c. 581–618	Sui dynasty (China)
618–c. 907	Tang dynasty (China)
646–794	Nara period (Japan)
794–1185	Heian period (Japan)
918–1392	Koryŏ kingdom (Korea)
960–1126	Northern Song dynasty (China)
c. 1127–1279	Southern Song dynasty (China)
1185–1333	Kamakura period (Japan)
c. 1280–1368	Yuan (Mongol) dynasty (China)
1333–1558	Ashikaga or Muromachi period (Japan)
1368–c. 1644	Ming dynasty (China)
1392–1910	Chosŏn kingdom (Korea)
1558–1600	Warring States period (Japan)
1600–1868	Tokugawa or Edo period (Japan)
c. 1644–1912	Qing (Manchu) dynasty (China)
1839–42	Opium War (China); Hong Kong ceded to Britain
1850–64	Taiping Rebellion (China)
1853	Commodore Matthew Perry first arrives in Japan
1868	Meiji Restoration (Japan)
1868–1911	Meiji Period (Japan)
1894–95	Sino-Japanese War; Taiwan ceded to Japan
1900	Boxer Rebellion (China)
1904–5	Russo-Japanese War
1910–45	Colonization of Korea by Japan
1912	Fall of the Qing dynasty; Republic of China established
1912–25	Taishô period (Japan)

1916–25	Warlord Period (China)
1919	May Fourth Incident (China)
	March 1 Independence Movement (Korea)
1923	Great Kantō Earthquake (Japan)
1925–27	Northern Expedition (China)
1925–89	Shōwa period (Japan)
1926	February 26 Incident (Japan)
1931	Japanese Imperial forces occupy northeastern China
1937–45	Chinese "War of Resistance against Japan"
1941	Japan declares war against Allies
1945	Atomic bombings of Hiroshima and Nagasaki; World War II ends; Korean and Chinese liberation from Japan
1945–52	Allied occupation of Japan
1946–48	Civil war between the Nationalists and Communists (China)
1948	February 28 Incident (China)
	Establishment of Republic of Korea (South Korea) and Democratic People's Republic of Korea (North Korea)
1949	Founding of the People's Republic of China
1950–53	Korean War
1956–57	Hundred Flowers Movement (China)
1957–58	Anti-Rightist Campaign (China)
1958–59	Great Leap Forward (China)
1960	April 19 Student Revolution (South Korea)
1961–79	Military coup by Park Chung Hee;
	dictatorship established (South Korea)
1964	Tokyo Olympic Games
1966–76	Cultural Revolution (China)
1968	Kawabata Yasunari awarded Nobel Prize in literature
1972	U.S. President Richard Nixon visits China
1975	Chiang Kai-shek dies (China)
1976	Mao Zedong dies (China)
1978–79	Democracy Wall Movement (China)
1978	Deng Xiaoping initiates economic reform and cultural liberalization (China)
1980	Kwangju Massacre (South Korea)
1986	Lifting of martial law in Taiwan
1987	Democratization Movement (South Korea)
1988	Seoul Olympic Games
1989	Tiananmen Incident: prodemocracy demonstrations (China)
1989–	Heisei period (Japan)
1992	Deng makes his "tour of the south," deepening support for reform (China)
1994	Ōe Kenzaburō awarded Nobel Prize in literature
1997	Hong Kong returned to China
2000	Gao Xingjian awarded Nobel Prize in literature

CONTRIBUTORS

General Editor

JOSHUA MOSTOW
University of British Columbia

Associate Editors

KIRK DENTON
Ohio State University

BRUCE FULTON
University of British Columbia

SHARALYN ORBAUGH
University of British Columbia

Contributors

DI BAI
Drew University

JAN BARDSLEY
University of North Carolina—Chapel Hill

MARILYN BOLLES
Montana State University

CHRISTOPHER BOLTON
University of California, Riverside

YOMI BRAESTER
University of Washington

BROTHER ANTHONY OF TAIZÉ
Sogang University

JANICE BROWN
University of Alberta

JIANHUA CHEN
Oberlin College

LINGCHEI LETTY CHEN
Washington University

XIAOMEI CHEN
Ohio State University

ESTHER M. K. CHEUNG
University of Hong Kong

AMY CHRISTIANSEN
Wittenberg University

HILARY CHUNG
University of Auckland

REBECCA L. COPELAND
Washington University

JOHN A. CRESPI
Swarthmore College

ALEXANDER DES FORGES
University of Massachusetts—Boston

AMY D. DOOLING
Connecticut College

JOAN ERICSON
Colorado College

CHARLES FOX
Ritsumeikan University

PHILIP GABRIEL
University of Arizona

JOHN K. GILLESPIE
Independent scholar

JOHN CHRISTOPHER HAMM
University of Washington

DIANA HINDS
Harvard University

MICHEL HOCKX
School of Oriental and African Studies

JOHN HOLSTEIN
Sungkyunkwan University

NICOLE HUANG
University of Wisconsin, Madison

ANN HUSS
Wellesley College

KEN K. ITO
University of Michigan

SUH JI-MOON
Korea University

BRETT JOHNSON
University of Michigan

ANDREW F. JONES
University of California, Berkeley

GRETCHEN JONES
University of Maryland

NICHOLAS A. KALDIS
State University of New York at Binghamton

AH-JEONG KIM
California State University, Northridge

RICHARD KING
University of Victoria

JEFFREY KINKLEY
St. John's University

DANIEL KISTER
Sogang University

DEIRDRE SABINA KNIGHT
Smith College

MARY KNIGHTON
Osaka University

HELEN H. KOH
Columbia University

SHUYU KONG
University of Alberta

MIRIAM LANG
Monash University

CHARLES LAUGHLIN
Yale University

JENNIFER M. LEE
University of California, Los Angeles

MABEL LEE
University of Sydney

MARK LEENHOUTS
Leiden University

WALTER K. LEW
University of California, Los Angeles

SEIJI LIPPIT
University of California, Los Angeles

CHRISTOPHER LUPKE
Washington State University

MARVIN MARCUS
Washington University

DAVID MCCANN
Harvard University

ANNE MCKNIGHT
McGill University

MICHAEL MOLASKY
University of Minnesota

THOMAS MORAN
Middlebury College

DAISY S.Y. NG
National University of Singapore

JONATHAN NOBLE
Independent scholar

KEVIN O'ROURKE
Kyung Hee University

SAYURI OYAMA
Mount Holyoke College

JULIE PICKERING
Independent scholar

STEVEN L. RIEP
University of California, Davis

DAVID ROSENFELD
University of Michigan

RICHI SAKAKIBARA
Shinshu University

HIROAKI SATO
Independent scholar and translator

ANN SHERIF
Oberlin College

STEPHEN SNYDER
University of Colorado

ANNE SOKOLSKY
University of California, Berkeley

CAROL FISHER SORGENFREI
University of California, Los Angeles

ALWYN SPIES
University of British Columbia

JOEL STEVENSON
Independent scholar

MATTHEW STRECHER
Toyo University

AGNITA TENNANT
University of Sheffield

JOHN TREAT
Yale University

ATSUKO UEDA
University of Illinois, Urbana-Champaign

TIMOTHY J. VAN COMPERNOLLE
Oberlin College

ROBIN VISSER
Valparaiso University

BAN WANG
Rutgers University

LINGZHEN WANG
Brown University

BURTON WATSON
Columbia University

MARK WILLIAMS
University of Leeds

MICHELLE YEH
University of California, Davis

HU YING
University of California, Irvine

JINGYUAN ZHANG
Georgetown University

YINGJIN ZHANG
University of California, San Diego

INDEX

Page numbers in bold refer to complete chapters.

Index compiled by Fred Leise